THE CHALLENGE

of

DELINQUENCY

CAUSATION, TREATMENT, AND PREVENTION
OF JUVENILE DELINQUENCY

by

NEGLEY K. TEETERS
Professor of Sociology
Temple University

and

JOHN OTTO REINEMANN
Director of Probation
Municipal Court of Philadelphia

NEW YORK · PRENTICE-HALL, INC.

PRENTICE-HALL SOCIOLOGY SERIES

Herbert Blumer, Editor

To the Memory of

JOHN STEWART BURGESS
Sociologist and Humanitarian

PREFACE

THIS BOOK is primarily for use in colleges and universities. But it is not meant to be an exclusively academic presentation. It attempts to combine a critical appraisal of theories, particularly regarding causation of delinquency, with a description and an evaluation of the machinery that society has set up to deal with the delinquency problem. It is hoped, therefore, that the book may also serve as a source of information and stimulation to practitioners in the field of youth welfare as well as to those members of the community who feel a real responsibility toward young people and their needs.

The term "delinquency"—as used in this book—refers to children and older youth only, even though today some penologists also apply the term to the criminal behavior of adults.

Geographically, the discussion of juvenile delinquency in this book is confined to the United States, although occasional references are made to other countries. The authors have tried to present the delinquency picture not from a sectional point of view, but rather as a national problem. Special emphasis, therefore, has been placed on the evaluation of the prevailing attitudes and mores of our adult society in which the child grows up and in which his character and behavior are formed. Examples of practical efforts toward the control of the delinquency problem, through governmental machinery and through citizens' actions, have been selected from many parts of the country.

Although the material has been integrated jointly, and most chapters include contributions by both writers, each author assumes responsibility for his chapters. Chapters I–VII and XII–XV were written by Dr. Teeters; Dr. Reinemann wrote Chapters VIII, IX–XI, and XVI–XVII, and assembled the Appendix.

N.K.T.
J.O.R.

TABLE OF CONTENTS

PART I—SCOPE OF THE PROBLEM OF DELINQUENCY

v

LIST OF ILLUSTRATIONS

Part 1

SCOPE OF THE PROBLEM OF DELINQUENCY

Chapter I

DELINQUENCY AS A NATIONAL PROBLEM

1. INTRODUCTORY STATEMENT

CERTAINLY one of the most critical and challenging problems confronting the American people in this generation is the maladjustment of so many thousands of our children and adolescent youth. Whether there are more problem children in proportion to the population now than at any other period is debatable. True, we know more about them today because our law-enforcement agencies, social agencies, and public bureaus dealing with youth are better organized than ever before. And since we know very little about the over-all picture of maladjustment among children during earlier eras, it is difficult to state arbitrarily that delinquency is an ever-increasing problem, except in terms of population increase.

Our modern society is perennially concerned with both the younger group of delinquents up to the age of sixteen and also with that adolescent group extending from sixteen to twenty-one or older. It is fairly well agreed that much of the serious delinquency committed by the older group stems from the frustration and insecurity they experienced during their earlier years when parents and school officials failed to diagnose or treat certain behavior patterns as predelinquent manifestations.

Those who are most familiar with dissident youth are unanimous in stating that it is imperative to "save the youth of today from becoming the criminals of tomorrow." Although it is true that many persons do not commit crimes until they are adults, records of penal establishments clearly show that most of their inmates found themselves in difficulty with the police or guidance clinics either in adolescence or prior to the onset of that explosive age. The Wickersham Commission, in a study of the prison population of adult penal institutions in 1930, found that 54.8 per cent had been less than twenty-one years of age when committed. This commission, known officially as the National Commission on Law Observance and Enforcement, is without doubt the most ambitious official study of the problem of delinquency and crime ever made in this country. Although its statistics as well as its findings are twenty years old, much of its work still stands and carries weight among students of the problem. Authorities are constantly referring to the fact that youth seem to predominate in the courtrooms of the nation, in the jails and lockups, in our reformatories, and even in our adult penitentiaries. The same story comes from Great Britain. Dr. John Bowlby of the Tavistock Clinic of London points out that youthful offenders are conspicuous in the courtroom, and adds significantly that nine criminal cases out of ten deal with theft. Excluding the offenses of drunkenness and violation of traffic ordinances, he states that 72 per cent of all other offenses deal with larceny. And of all the larceny cases, fully half are committed by youth under twenty-one years of age, and 20 per cent are committed by children under fourteen years of age.[1]

These data from England merely substantiate the thesis that the crime problem is closely associated with children and older youth. However, it was perhaps the publication of a revealing book written in 1938 by Leonard V. Harrison and Pryor M. Grant, *Youth In the Toils*,[2] that focused sharp attention on the seriousness of the crime problem as it involves American youth.

A discussion of the problem of juvenile delinquency must be many-sided. First, we are deeply concerned with maladjusted youngsters, less than sixteen, both boys and girls. We see many of these young people in schools, guidance centers, and child clinics. Second, we feel impelled to deal in a large way with overt delinquency— that is, violations of penal codes—of youngsters as well as older youth. (Indeed, it is this phase of the problem that dominates the headlines of our newspapers and thus focuses the attention of the public on the dilemmas of prevention and treatment.) And third, we must discuss the problem of so-called incorrigibility of children as

---

[1] *Forty-Four Juvenile Thieves: Their Characters and Home Life*, Baillière, Tindall & Cox, London, 1947, p. 1. For recent figures for the United States, see Chapter XIV of this book, p. 514.

[2] Macmillan, New York. We shall have more to say about the implications of this book in Chapter X.

well as of the young adult who becomes a nuisance in the school-room and on the streets. Obviously, little can be done with the older youth unless we attempt to learn something about the problems of childhood and, to a lesser extent, those problems occurring in actual infancy.

Because the legal definition of delinquency is so vague, the average citizen thinks of the delinquent child only as one who has violated a law. The legal definition of a delinquent child in the Commonwealth of Massachusetts may be taken as typical: "A child between seven and seventeen years who violates any city ordinance or town by-law or commits an offense not punishable by death or by imprisonment for life." But the term "delinquency" is much broader in its implications. The National Probation and Parole Association [3] defines a delinquent child as (a) one who has violated any law of the state or any ordinance or regulation of a subdivision of any state; (b) one who by reason of being wayward or habitually disobedient is uncontrolled by his parents, guardian, or custodian; (c) one who is habitually truant from school or home; (d) one who habitually deports himself so as to impair or endanger the morals or health of himself. [4]

The White House Conference of 1930 defined delinquency as any juvenile misconduct that might be dealt with under the law. It is obvious, however, from this last definition that the emotionally maladjusted child is not delinquent until his behavior seems serious enough to enlist the police power of the court. The eminent British psychologist, Dr. Cyril Burt, defines delinquency as occurring in a child "when his anti-social tendencies appear so grave that he becomes or ought to become the subject of official action." [5] This definition covers not only those who are apprehended but also those who ought to be for various reasons. The late Dr. James S. Plant, an authority on problem children, thought of juvenile delinquents as young people who "habitually respond to serious and prolonged frustration in aggressive ways." [6]

---

[3] Since we cite and quote from so many publications of this organization, we shall abbreviate its title in the footnotes by the letters N.P.P.A.

[4] *Proceedings*, 1925, p. 198.

[5] *The Young Delinquent*, Appleton, New York, 1925 edition, p. 15.

[6] Quoted in *The Forty-seventh Yearbook, National Society for the Study of Education*, Part I, University of Chicago Press, 1948, p. 9.

In a stimulating and provocative work, Professor William H. Sheldon and colleagues, after making 200 biographical sketches of delinquent youth, paying particular attention to their constitutional make-up, come to the conclusion that delinquency is "behavior disappointing beyond reasonable expectation." [7]

We feel impelled to discuss in this book the problems of those who are legally labeled delinquent and, in addition, the difficulties of that vast army of children whose emotional lives make them potential or incipient delinquents. We shall not quarrel with the legal definition, but our society must consider those children and adolescents who may, if not handled intelligently, become overt delinquents.[8]

Many persons and groups have a tendency to propagandize the public through every known medium on the alleged value of their particular program in the control of delinquency. To cite a few examples: A principal of a small school system in a rural township in eastern Pennsylvania complained bitterly that the voters had turned down a bond issue to provide a new school to relieve the overcrowded conditions. In his remarks he stated that only through the provision of a new school would juvenile delinquency be reduced. It is doubtful that this particular township experiences more than its share of delinquency, yet the school man felt it was necessary to upbraid his constituents by reminding them that delinquency, rather than overcrowding, was the issue. When funds are requested on radio or elsewhere for police athletic clubs, community chests, and the like, juvenile delinquency is always mentioned. Mme. Olga Samaroff Stokowski, in advancing the cause of music, stated she found that out of 30,000 youngsters who studied at the New York Settlement Schools over the preceding quarter of a century, not one had ever been brought before a juvenile court for delinquent behavior.[9] Furthermore, the governor of Pennsylvania once urged the clean-up of the state's rivers and streams as an aid in curbing delinquency. There seems to be a childlike faith in the assumption that delinquency can be checked merely by asking the public for money to support causes, movements, agencies, and programs that only incidentally deal with delinquent children.

---

[7] William H. Sheldon, Emil M. Hartl, and Eugene McDermott, *Varieties of Delinquent Youth*, Harper, New York, 1949, p. 822.

[8] See Sol Rubin, "The Legal Character of Juvenile Delinquency," *The Annals*, January 1949, pp. 1–8.

[9] *The Layman's Music Book*, Norton, New York, 1935, pp. 62–63.

Reformers, pulpiteers, moralists, and civic leaders have all advanced their favorite reasons for delinquent behavior. One could easily collect a hundred alleged causes, each with its adherents today, and an equally large number advanced in the past but now abandoned. For example, the dime novel and the cigarette were both denounced at the turn of the century as leading the youth to crime. Today it is likely to be the comics, the radio, or the taproom that become the whipping boy for the prevalence of delinquent behavior.

We still find a number of "crackpot" theories of delinquency causation that are accepted by large numbers of superficially informed, though well-meaning, people. In addition, many suggestions are offered that have some merit but that do not answer the question of delinquency with any degree of finality.

News articles reporting speeches of people, some of whom are distinguished in their own fields, give such causes of delinquency as the following: (1) youth has forgotten God, or has strayed from the church, or no longer goes to Sunday School; (2) the family is breaking down and children no longer respect parental authority; (3) the radio, movies, television, dance halls, taprooms, and poolrooms exercise harmful effects; (4) a lack of moral discipline, brought about in large measure by new ideas in education, has developed.

It is of some interest to know what the proverbial "man on the street" thinks are the causes of delinquency. A poll conducted in the state of New Jersey in 1948 gives the following results: [10]

	Per cent
Lack of home training, parental neglect, etc.	70
Lack of recreational facilities	12
Crime and gangster pictures	6
Children don't have enough to do	6
The aftermath of the war	3
Too many mothers working	3
Children on streets too much	2
Comic books	2
Radio programs, especially crime programs	2
Lack of discipline in the schools	2
Wrong ideas children have today	1
Various other reasons	12
Don't know	4

[10] Taken from Trenton (New Jersey) *Evening Times*, November 18, 1948. Figures add to more than 100 per cent since many people named more than one reason.

An interesting study was made by James S. Wallerstein, of the Randen Foundation, of opinions regarding the causes of delinquency and crime. He submitted a questionnaire to 223 business and professional men and to 258 men who had a criminal record. The conventional causes of crime all had a wide sprinkling in the responses. So far as the cultural media as causes were concerned, he found the following:

	Businessmen Per cent	Ex-offenders Per cent
Movies	61	38
Radio	65	46
Press	71	58

Professional men were more critical of all these media than were the ex-offenders. Their chief complaint was that all were guilty of "playing up" crime and delinquency.

Let us see what the same groups thought of some of the social factors as causes of crime:

	Businessmen Per cent	Ex-offenders Per cent
Bad housing	49	90
Lack of recreation	48	89
Lack of jobs	44	81

From these attitudes, it might be concluded that the professional group feels fairly certain that the socio-economic order is not so bad as many authorities on crime and delinquency maintain. In another question, dealing with money and excitement as contributing factors to crime, both groups rated in the upper seventy percentiles.[11]

As much as the writers of this book would like to present answers to the many questions resulting from the problem of delinquency, it must be frankly stated at the outset that this is impossible. The more we study the many facets of delinquency, including prevention and control, the less certain we are of the tailor-made answers that emanate from hundreds of well-meaning persons who labor in this field or who are deeply distressed concerning delinquency and crime.

---

[11] "Testing Opinions on Causes of Crime," *Focus*, N.P.P.A., July 1949, pp. 103 *ff.*

The amount of written material on the subject of juvenile delinquency is prodigious. Aside from news stories relating to the exploits of delinquents, thousands of articles and dozens of volumes are published each year on the subject. Then, in addition, there are hundreds of studies of small or large groups of various kinds of delinquents, all of which arrive at various conclusions. It has been stated that next to treatises on the Bible and Shakespeare more has been written on this subject than on any other matter.

The very task of being selective in citing authorities and conclusions on delinquency is a formidable one. There is danger of overlooking some excellent material as well as of being repetitious. If the reader is not satisfied with authorities quoted in this book, he is referred to various bibliographies of delinquency.[12]

The social agencies, crime prevention bureaus, police departments, and state and Federal agencies also have in their files much valuable material. Much of this has particular bearing on local conditions, whether it be a large metropolitan center or regional area. Even some small cities and towns have agencies that collect material or statistics and make studies of delinquent children.

It has been suggested more than once that *now* is the time to act, to do something about delinquency. As the well-known penologist, Austin H. MacCormick, states in his foreword to a book on the subject, delinquency has not gone up and up because of the lack of ideas on what to do about it, but rather because of the failure to act.[13]

But what to do! Much action can be recorded, some effective and some, perhaps much, totally ineffective. There are as many answers to the question as there are people asking pertinent questions. In a moving article published a few years ago, it was pointed out that President Truman had stated that the roots of delinquency lie in the homes, the schools, the neighborhoods, and the churches of our nation. The writer, one who has been working in the delinquency field for many years, contended that this is not the total picture, since the roots "lie in business interests which exploit youth for

---

[12] See Philippe Sidney de Q. Cabot, *Juvenile Delinquency: A Critical Annotated Bibliography*, Wilson, New York, 1946; see also an earlier work by Walter A. Lunden, *Systematic Source Book in Juvenile Delinquency*, University of Pittsburgh Press, 1938.

[13] See Ben Solomon, *Juvenile Delinquency—Practical Prevention*, Youth Service, Inc., Peekskill, New York, 1947.

profit, and in every city, state, and national law-enforcing department which fails to enforce protective laws," and that "today, children from good homes, schools, and churches, as well as those deprived of *all* children most need, are confused by the discrepancies
between what they are taught and what they find exist in our city
life and government. They have lost respect for integrity and government." [14] We shall comment on this attitude later in this chapter.

Many governmental agencies have done much in the preventive
field. The Federal government has acted through various departments, such as agriculture, labor, and justice, to mention only a few.
The creation of the Children's Bureau in the Department of Labor
in 1912 was a laudable step in dealing with thwarted childhood. Also,
there were the various White House Conferences [15]—held in 1909,
1919, 1930, 1940, and 1950 [16]—which were dedicated to the essential
needs of childhood.

Even more to the point was the National Conference on the Prevention and Control of Delinquency, held in Washington in November, 1946.[17] Called by former Attorney General Tom Clark, it was
attended by hundreds of persons working in the delinquency field.
This conference, like those preceding it, was a brave attempt to cope
with the various perplexing problems of childhood. Many informative speeches and constructive discussions took place. Out of the
Conference came the publication of eighteen pamphlets (reports)
covering practically all phases of the problem of delinquency. In
addition, a continuing committee published a handbook entitled
"First Steps in Organizing State and Local Conferences" on the
prevention and control of delinquency. The committee also issued
periodically a small magazine called *Accent on Youth*. The Conference prided itself that it was an *action* conference and labeled its
various recommendations "Tools of Action." [18]

[14] Jessie F. Binford, "Postwar Problems of Youth," *Federal Probation*,
October–December 1947, pp. 7–11. See also Lawrence K. Frank, *Society as the
Patient*, Rutgers University Press, 1948.

[15] For an analysis, see Homer Folks, "Four Milestones of Progress," *The
Annals*, November 1940, pp. 12–17. Also James H. S. Bossard, *The Sociology
of Child Development*, Harper, New York, 1948, Chapter XXVII.

[16] See *infra*, Chapter XVI.

[17] We shall refer to this throughout this book as the National Conference.

[18] This material may be secured by writing to the United States Government
Printing Office, Washington, D.C.

It is perhaps too early to appraise the results of the National Conference. The first published results of a large-scale community follow-up describe what has been done in Philadelphia thus far. Several panels have been set up by police, churches, community coordinating councils, and other organizations to make a thorough study of the over-all problem.[19] But it is obvious that the heroic effort focused on this problem, even nationally, will have little appreciable immediate effect in stemming the tide of delinquency. Social problems are not solved through efforts of this type alone.

Turning to the field of education, we find an excellent monograph, "Juvenile Delinquency and the Schools," which compares favorably with the work of the National Conference, mentioned above.[20] This work considers the traditional phases of the problem but places the emphasis on the need for adult understanding of the causes of delinquent behavior. The role of the school in detecting incipient delinquency is, of course, appropriately handled, but little is said about the importance of providing efficient and well-balanced curricula for all children. We shall allude to this study as well as to many of the Reports issued by the National Conference in a later treatment of the various aspects of the problem of delinquency.[21]

Americans are justly proud of the forthright way they can "lick" some material problem. All-out production to win a war is possible, albeit many drones do not participate. It makes little difference that in solving the war problem a huge debt of 250 billions is amassed. In the material world many bottlenecks are split wide open through Yankee ingenuity. But there are exceptions even here—housing, or flood control, for instance. Selfish interests are so deeply intrenched that many material problems remain unsolved.

But our social problems are of a different hue. Cultural lag is present at all times. Juvenile delinquency is not the only serious

[19] See J. Francis Finnegan, "The Philadelphia Conference on the Prevention and Control of Delinquency," *Yearbook,* N.P.P.A., 1948, pp. 263–273; see also *infra,* Chapter XVI, p. 662.

[20] *The Forty-seventh Yearbook of the National Society for the Study of Education,* Part I, edited by Nelson B. Henry, University of Chicago Press, 1948.

[21] See also Vol. 261 (January 1949) of *The Annals,* edited by Thorsten Sellin, which is devoted to "Juvenile Delinquency." *The Nebraska Law Review* dedicated its entire issue of May 1950 (Vol. 29, No. 4) to the problem of juvenile delinquency.

social problem arising in each generation. The whole field of crime can be cited. Prostitution, mental disease, drug addiction, alcoholism, suicide, poverty, unemployment, to cite only a few, are typical of what each generation must face. All these, together with juvenile delinquency, flow from our culture. They are all deeply rooted in the eternal problem of living. So we need not get impatient if the solution to any one of them is not just around the corner. Thousands of well-trained people are giving their best to prevent these problems from becoming more serious. Here and there and from time to time, these people produce some heartening results. And that is about as much as we can expect. One generation can do so much and no more.

Our social institutions evolve to interpret our culture and to control the individual. An efficient institution in our Western civilization that places great emphasis on the democratic way of life must take cognizance of the dignity of the personality. Hence controls must not be too severe. Regimentation is repugnant to our philosophy of life. The question is, then, how far can society control the individual and still respect his personality or elicit from him loyalty and enthusiasm?

The old techniques used in manipulating and controlling children did not recognize personality. Regimentation and a hollow discipline may have broken the will of the child, but they failed miserably in developing him into a socially well-integrated person free from the bitterness of frustration and insecurity. All attacks on delinquency must safeguard the person.

2. THE EXTENT OF DELINQUENCY

The over-all picture of delinquency or maladjustment varies with various national cataclysms. It is this phenomenon in the life of American youth that complicates any appraisal of the extent of delinquency. For example, if we start with the Great Depression, the alarming problem was the large number of idle youth who were simply unable to find employment. Many took to the road to avoid becoming a burden to their harassed parents. Many simply loafed about the corner drugstore or became frequenters of poolrooms. As early as 1934, social investigators were writing poignant stories of young migrants who had broken loose from their moorings.[22] Thou-

---

[22] See Thomas Minehan, *Boy and Girl Tramps in America*, Farrar & Rinehart, New York, 1934.

sands of these young hoboes were familiar sights in the "jungles" of all our large cities, and in the agricultural areas and manufacturing centers. Not too many years earlier, we were reading of the wild children of Russia who were preying on society because they had been set adrift as an aftermath of World War I. Some people in this country boasted that such a tragedy "could not happen here." Yet it did. Not until the Federal government inaugurated the National Youth Administration and the Civilian Conservation Corps was it possible to cope with this serious problem.

Next, the era of World War II brought about an entirely different mass maladjustment that affected both adolescent youth and young children. Scare headlines throughout the country painted pictures of a moral disintegration of adolescent boys and girls, as well as of "trailer camp" children whose parents worked in mushroom war plants. It was reported that venereal diseases were spreading at an alarming rate and that thousands of girls were giving themselves as a patriotic gesture. Every metropolitan center as well as every camp city mobilized forces to combat this alarming condition. Delinquency was prevalent everywhere.[23] In addition, many young girls, and boys unable to join the armed forces, were making big money in war plants and were spending it on riotous living. The "swing shift" came into existence, something new to our Victorian mores. Thousands of persons, youth as well as adults, were frequenting nightclubs, tap-rooms, dance halls and other places of entertainment *after* they finished their late-hour shift. Such a practice broke sharply with the tradition that late-at-night entertainment was immoral. The writers know of one Philadelphia magistrate who was very much alarmed at the "antics of swing shift workers carousing around at ungodly hours of the night."

And again, long before the "boys came home" from the war, it was frequently predicted that a wave of not only ordinary delinquency, but unprecedented violence would sweep the country. Such predictions have not been realized. Our soldiers went back to work or continued their college or trade-school education and, on the whole, made an amazingly good adjustment to postwar life. Adequate governmental preparation for demobilized youth through the

---

[23] *Cf.* Whitcomb H. Allen, "Young Camp Followers," *Yearbook*, N.P.P.A., 1943, pp. 66–75; see also Goodwin Watson, *Youth After Conflict*, Association Press, New York, 1947.

GI Bill of Rights may have had much to do with the orderly transition into civilian life that eliminated a so-called "lost generation" similar to that which is alleged to have followed World War I.

Legally, the lowest age limit for considering a child as delinquent (subject to official action) is seven years. This follows the Roman as well as the common law, which did not consider the child less than seven as responsible for his acts. It is obvious that such an age limit is arbitrary and is at best only a convenient figure. The upper age limit varies from sixteen to twenty-one, depending on the state.[24]

Formal research indicates that the largest percentage of delinquency (but not maladjustment) begins at puberty. Sheldon and Eleanor Glueck report after an intensive study of 510 prisoners in the Massachusetts Reformatory that 420 were between the ages of 11 and 18 at the time of their first known delinquency.[25] Another student of the problem, Maude A. Merrill, states that ". . . nine times out of ten, he is an adolescent between the ages of thirteen and twenty-one." [26] Healy and Bronner state: "From juvenile court statistics it would seem that the prime age for the onset of delinquency is in early adolescence, at 13 to 15 years." [27]

The National Education Association report further indicates that "more than five times as many boys as girls are arrested for delinquent conduct." [28] This is borne out by the sample figures of delinquency submitted by the juvenile courts of seventy-six cities for the past several years. The ratio of girls' cases to boys' cases runs from 1 to 4 to as high as 1 to 19.[29]

Just how prevalent, then, is delinquency at any given time? This question cannot be arbitrarily answered. We must rely on opinions and guesses. And these can be made only after we have agreed on just what we mean by delinquent behavior.

---

[24] For details regarding juvenile court age, see Chapter IX, pp. 310–313.

[25] *Later Criminal Careers,* The Commonwealth Fund, New York, 1937, p. 270.

[26] *Problems of Child Delinquency,* Houghton Mifflin, Boston, 1947, p. 111.

[27] William Healy and Augusta Bronner, "What Makes a Child Delinquent?," *Forty-seventh Yearbook, op. cit.,* p. 39.

[28] National Education Association, Research Division, Co-ordination of Youth Services To Prevent Juvenile Delinquency, Washington, D.C., 1947, p. 25.

[29] Cf. Edward E. Schwartz, "Statistics of Juvenile Delinquency in the United States," *The Annals,* January 1949, pp. 9–20. For data concerning Federal juvenile offenders, see *Federal Prisons 1948,* Department of Justice, 1949, pp. 83–92.

So far as *criminal* behavior is concerned, we are on reasonably safe ground. We have penal codes in each state, and any violation of the codes represents criminal conduct. But even in this area we have difficulty in tabulating the extent of crime, since our statistics are so inadequate. Since 1930, the Federal Bureau of Investigation has been collecting criminal statistics, but no one can claim that they are complete. The *Uniform Crime Reports*, issued semi-annually by the Federal Bureau of Investigation, record crimes known to the police, offenses cleared by arrest, persons held for prosecution, and persons released or found guilty. The Bureau must rely on police chiefs throughout the country to supply such data and even today many of these officials do not cooperate.

But when we come to juvenile delinquency, we find even greater difficulty and confusion. A large proportion of those children who may be labeled delinquent have not violated any section of the penal code. Many have not committed an overt act considered unsocial. Incorrigibility, for instance, is delinquent but not criminal. Truancy is considered delinquent, but, again, not criminal. On the other hand, children may on occasion violate the law, but such an overt act may not be recorded by police or juvenile court.

A study made some years ago by members of the staff of the Cambridge-Somerville project (Boston) showed that of some 6,416 infractions of the law by boys over a five year period, only 95 became a matter of official complaint. In other words, officials took action in less than 1.5 per cent of the infractions. Approximately 1,400 were merely violations of city ordinances, none of which became a matter of official complaint; 4,400 were considered minor offenses, and only 27 of them were prosecuted by the authorities; and of the 616 labeled serious, only 68 were prosecuted. Yet it is quite obvious that the vast majority of these offenses represented certain types of juvenile maladjustment and would be delinquent if they were finally and officially recorded.[30]

The number of officially recorded delinquencies in a particular city may be estimated from the local juvenile or criminal courts.[31]

---

[30] Fred J. Murphy, Mary M. Shirley, and Helen L. Witmer, "The Incidence of Hidden Delinquency," *American Journal of Orthopsychiatry*, Vol. 16, No. 4, 1946, pp. 686–696.

[31] For reference, see Paul W. Tappan, "Unofficial Delinquency," *Nebraska Law Review*, May 1950, pp. 547–558.

But, as stated above, many children's unsocial acts are not recorded. For instance, the third White House Conference on Child Health and Protection (1930) cryptically remarks:

1. There exists no accurate statement as to the amount of delinquency in this country, nor whether it is increasing or decreasing.
2. There is no accurate conception as to what actually constitutes delinquency.
3. The approach has been so individual to different communities and to different leaders that there exists no general philosophy, no unified working hypothesis concerning the problem.[32]

The United States Children's Bureau has, since 1926, maintained statistics on delinquency which include reports on cases disposed of by about 500 juvenile courts. But there are approximately 3,000 courts scattered throughout the country which handle juvenile cases, and in the past quarter-century only about one-sixth of these made reports. About one-half of the 500 courts reporting are located in the east-north-central geographic division of the country. In fact, according to Sophia M. Robison, an astute student of the problem, almost one-fourth of these reporting courts are located in one state —Connecticut. Miss Robison asks, "How can it then be claimed that such figures are a reliable basis for estimating either the extent or the character of juvenile delinquency in the United States?" [33]

Let us look at the reasons advanced by Miss Robison on why juvenile court statistics have not in the past been a reliable measure of delinquency:

1. The juvenile court plays a different role in different communities. In some, it is an administrative social agency; in others, it operates according to the rules of evidence, mitigated to be sure by mercy and understanding.
2. The jurisdictions of juvenile courts differ considerably as to the age of the young people referred to them and the area of coverage in a community. The machinery of informal and formal hearings, dismissals, referrals, and so forth, vary with the court personnel as well as with the fashions in the local community.
3. The types of behavior brought to the attention of the court vary widely.

---

[32] *The Delinquent Child*, Century, New York, 1932, p. 23.
[33] See her article, "Wanted—An Index of Crime and Delinquency," *Proceedings*, American Prison Association, 1945, pp. 203–212.

4. Communities differ in their provision of alternate methods of care: *i.e.*, in New York City, in the Borough of Richmond, the court is the only agency that records delinquent behavior, while in Manhattan the court competes for its customers with many agencies in which offenders can be and often are referred.

5. The mores in the various communities vary tremendously regarding delinquent behavior. For example, community attitudes toward offending girls vary. Generally five or six times as many boys are referred to courts than are girls. Boys are seldom referred to court for sex offenses other than homosexual acts; and girls are seldom referred for anything but sexual misconduct.

Thus we see that juvenile court statistics are a poor index to the extent of delinquency, so far as national coverage is concerned. Since 1946, the Children's Bureau has been attempting to deal with national coverage of delinquency on a more adequate basis. The direct collection of statistics from the individual courts has been abandoned. As a substitute, state summaries are being accepted. Those summaries are now compiled by state departments of welfare, probation departments, and other state-wide agencies interested in the work of juvenile or other courts dealing with dependent, neglected, and delinquent children. The summaries include those cases of children that are disposed of unofficially. The revised reports cover not only delinquency cases but all other cases disposed of by juvenile courts, unofficially as well as officially. Although this new method may be more accurate than the older, it still will not be able to give us more than a sketchy picture of the extent of delinquency.[34]

One other source from which a very inadequate appraisal of the extent of delinquency may be obtained is from the fingerprint records sent to the Federal Bureau of Investigation by various chiefs of police throughout the country. These records indicate age, among other data, so it is possible to know just how many fingerprint records of children under eighteen years of age are sent to the F.B.I. annually. For instance, 32,922 children's records were listed for the

---

[34] For an excellent article on this new trend, see Edward E. Schwartz, "Community Experiment in the Measurement of Juvenile Delinquency," *Yearbook*, N.P.P.A.*, 1945, pp. 157–181. Also, by the same author, "Statistics of Juvenile Delinquency in the United States," *The Annals*, January 1949, pp. 9–20. See also *Report No. 18*, National Conference, Government Printing Office, 1947; also, *infra*, Chapter IX, p. 337, and Chapter XVI, p. 624.

year 1949. These figures are particularly misleading, however, since many jurisdictions maintain a strict policy of never fingerprinting children. And again, many police chiefs who fingerprint juveniles do not send such records to the F.B.I. files.

The writers have no clear-cut answer to the question of just how much delinquency there is or whether the rate is rising or falling. It would be satisfying to say that it was falling, but so many factors are involved that no such answer can arbitrarily be given. Here is what one student of the problem has said:

> Nation-wide data on the extent of juvenile delinquency are not available. The juvenile court statistics and the police arrest rate now being collected by federal agencies do furnish a crude indication of national trends in the number of children getting into difficulty with the law and as such give some insight into the delinquency trends.
>
> Based on these data the number of children getting into trouble with law-enforcement and judicial agencies seem to have increased sharply during the war to a peak in 1945. . . . From the peak of 1945, children brought into court or arrested decreased sharply in 1946 and continued downward in 1947, following the end of wartime conditions. The decrease may reflect also the strengthening of existing services to children and efforts by local, state, and federal agencies to prevent conditions that lead to juvenile delinquency.[35]

During the year 1948, 94,236 children's cases were disposed of by 399 juvenile courts reporting from 17 states. Two-thirds of these cases were delinquencies; one-third what we may call "care and protection" cases. About one-half of the cases (51 per cent) were disposed of unofficially—that is, without formal judicial action. The United States Children's Bureau estimates that if the volume of delinquency continues at the 1948 level, 275,000 children may be expected each year to come before the juvenile courts of the nation.

The foregoing data, together with estimates by persons who are professionally interested in the juvenile field, indicate that about six in every one thousand children under eighteen years of age in the country are involved in juvenile court delinquency cases.[36] This figure naturally does not include thousands of children who come to

---

[35] I. R. Perlman, "The Meaning of Juvenile Delinquency Statistics," *Federal Probation*, September 1949, p. 67.

[36] Edward E. Schwartz, "Statistics of Juvenile Delinquency in the United States," *loc. cit.*, p. 12.

the attention of social agencies, crime-prevention bureaus, or child-guidance clinics.

Another difficult problem confronting students of delinquency is how to estimate the number of children who are repeaters or recidivists. Few if any records are available that would give any reliable answer to this question. The Department of Welfare for the state of Ohio publishes statistics which have some bearing on this matter. Of 101,043 children dealt with by the juvenile courts in that state during the five-year period 1943–1947 inclusive, 57.3 per cent came before the court for the first time.[37] Just how this figure would apply in other jurisdictions is not known.

It is obvious, then, that only a nation-wide picture of juvenile maladjustment can be satisfactory in appraising the extent of delinquency. We have seen that definitions are inadequate and that statistics are woefully weak. Perhaps it is too much to expect the development of some central registration bureau, but until we have some such service we shall never know with any degree of certainty just how much delinquency there is in this country.

3. TYPES OF DELINQUENTS

Classifying human beings is always dangerous, since, in the last analysis, every person is unique—biologically, socially, and economically. But we live in a world that prides itself on being practical, so we too must be practical so far as delinquency is concerned. Let us remember, however, that every delinquent or maladjusted child or young adult is unique.

In our later chapters we shall discuss some of the various approaches to the problem of delinquency: the biological, the socio-economic, the cultural, and the orthopsychiatric. What we shall attempt in this section is to point out a few of the more prevalent types of maladjusted children, although we shall see that these cut across the various approaches we shall later appraise.

One classification, suggested by Harriet Goldberg, includes: mentally retarded, emotionally unstable and those with neurotic patterns, neurotics and psychoneurotics, psychopathic personalities

---

[37] Figures quoted by C. H. Growden, "A Group Study of Juvenile Homicide," State Bureau of Juvenile Research, Department of Welfare, Columbus, Ohio, October 1949 (pages unnumbered).

and the mentally ill, and the physically ill and the socially handi-capped.[38]

Another interesting and fruitful classification is that proposed by Robert Lindner. The first, the "situational," would cover about two-thirds of our delinquent youth. These have crime thrust upon them. They are not delinquent no matter how many laws they break nor how serious their offenses. Their behavior is the result of the socio-economic-moral atmosphere in which they have grown up. In con-trast to this type he lists the "adventitious" or basic delinquent whose wrong-doings are "symptoms of inner stresses and strains in the same way as pain is the symptom of organic disease." He finds basic delinquency to be caused "biologically or through mistakes and errors in child rearing." [39]

Still another classification is that advanced by three British students of the problem. They list three types: the mentally disordered, the mentally defective, and the "normal." The normal is characterized by the person who approves of criminality—who has no guilt feel-ings and whose ideal of himself as a criminal is assured.[40]

Other classifications emphasizing the psychiatric or medico-psy-chological approach may be found in the works by English and Pearson.[41]

From these and similar classifications we may note several common factors that deserve restatement so far as the medico-psychological approach is concerned: (a) mental deficiency, (b) organic disease or trauma, (c) functional psychoses, (d) psychopathic personality, (e) "normal" with some immaturity in personality development. It is not our purpose in this work to discuss delinquency from the medical or neurological points of view. However, as stated above, we shall appraise the various approaches in our later chapters.

---

[38] *Child Offenders*, Grune & Stratton, New York, 1948. See also Karl Birn-baum, "A Court Psychiatrist's View of Juvenile Delinquents," *The Annals*, January 1949, pp. 55–63.

[39] "Crime and the Child," *Focus*, N.P.P.A., September 1948, pp. 143–146.

[40] E. Bunbury, G. de M. Rudolf, and T. M. Ling, *Mental Hygiene*, London, Vol. IV, 1938, p. 78; abstracted in *Journal of Criminal Psychopathology*, Vol. I, 1939, p. 73.

[41] O. Spurgeon English and Gerald H. J. Pearson, *Common Neuroses of Children and Adults*, Norton, New York, 1937, pp. 146–147, and *Emotional Problems of Living*, Norton, New York, 1945, p. 265. See also Melitta Schmide-berg, "Psychological Factors Underlying Criminal Behavior," *Journal of Criminal Law and Criminology*, March–April 1947, p. 458.

As an example of our confusion regarding delinquent children, we may cite the case of the child who is a truant because he is mentally retarded or because of some emotional difficulty, or, perhaps rare in these days—because he has no shoes to wear to school.

Let us approach the problem of classification in terms of the acts of children rather than in terms of their mental or emotional condition. As we stated earlier, many children are delinquent because they have violated a statute. The first type, then, is the child who has committed an overt act that is regarded as a violation of the penal code or of some city ordinance. (See Appendix, Case 15, pp. 735–738.) Many juvenile court judges prefer to have this type before them, since the behavior *seems* to be so obvious. The child *stole* some object, *destroyed* some property, *created* a disturbance, and so forth. Most of the jurist's attention is focused on the specific act rather than on the reasons *why* the child committed the act. It would be difficult to state with any degree of accuracy just what percentage of delinquent youth actually commit overt acts. Since most of these acts are merely slight transgressions of the penal code, we shall refer later to the more serious offenders as a special type.

A second type of delinquency is referred to as incorrigibility. This is frankly a blanket term and could be variously defined. Many truants are incorrigible, but we prefer to list under the heading of incorrigibility the problem or emotionally maladjusted child, rather than the chronic truant and the child who commits an overt act. The incorrigible child is a nonconformist. He is the youngster who causes the teacher considerable trouble. He finds it difficult to adjust to the conventional routine of the classroom. He is often a "trouble-maker" or, more accurately, an uncomfortable child to have around more amenable and docile children. Many incorrigible children, of course, do commit overt acts of delinquency. (See Appendix, Case 11, pp. 728–729.)

Although there are many incorrigible children of tender age, it is in the period of adolescence that we find their numbers increasing; and understandably so, since this age period presents many serious difficulties to the boy or girl. Dr. William Healy has this to say about the adolescent:

> It is the age of physical changes with all their concomitant needs and urges that develop between the early years of adolescence and young manhood. Psychologically considered, it is often a time of confused ideas, desires, and impulses. We may occasionally note a case in which

the confused mental states suggest a mild psychosis. It is the period of vocational adjustments which unfortunately are frequently so difficult to make. These older adolescents often find themselves at sea in making their social contacts; they have not the stabilized situations that have been experienced earlier or will normally be found later.[42]

One of the most perplexing problems confronting educators today is that of adolescent boys and girls who are regarded by teachers as problem cases. They cannot leave school until they reach the age set

Dr. *William Healy*   Dr. *Augusta Bronner*
                                        (*Mrs. William Healy*)

PIONEERS IN DELINQUENCY RESEARCH

by law; they are socially maladjusted and cannot fit into the traditional curriculum. They harass the school authorities and often become a menace to the community because of their frustrations.

The only recourse many school administrators have is to fall back on the flogging technique or "busy work" after school in the prin-

---

[42] "A New Program for Treatment of Youthful Offenders," *American Sociological Review*, August 1940, pp. 610–617. For an interesting article on the problem confronting the school, see Arthur C. Johnson, "Our Schools Make Criminals," *Journal of Criminal Law and Criminology*, November–December 1942, pp. 310–315.

cipal's office. State laws usually permit corporal punishment, so what we see is incipient rebellion in the classroom. Often the juvenile judge will do nothing because such a boy's behavior does not come within the generally accepted notion of delinquency. In a later connection, we shall discuss the methods by which the progressive school attempts to deal with such children. But the community must share in the responsibility of meeting this serious problem by supporting programs and agencies that focus their attention on developing wholesome young people. Too often even the school boards do not support their teachers and administrators in dealing intelligently with the problem of the incorrigible or emotionally maladjusted. Certainly flogging and other sterile punishments have no place in the understanding and treatment of this type of delinquent.

A third type of delinquent is the truant. (See Appendix, Case 5, pp. 716–717.) Most authorities agree that truancy is symptomatic of some maladjustment that is more serious than the mere disinclination to attend school. But the history of truancy shows that the oldfashioned truant officer possessed little insight in coercing children into attending the school they hated. His more modern counterpart, the attendance officer, is better trained, especially in the larger cities, and frequently calls upon the counseling service of the school system to cope with the problem. The extent of truancy is debatable. Reckless and Smith contend that it is more widespread than any other form of delinquency.[43] These authors devote an entire chapter to the problem of truancy. To the United States Children's Bureau, truancy is the "kindergarten of crime." Other authorities, such as Healy and Bronner, the Gluecks, and Sullenger, speak of the dissatisfaction delinquents manifest regarding school when they are brought before court or clinic. All these delinquents, however, are not actually truants. It goes without saying that most truants are boys. For example, Reckless and Smith refer to a study of 7,354 cases of truancy in Chicago. Of this number, only 769 were girls.[44]

Another type of delinquency is linked with the sex problem. This problem is primarily associated with adolescent girls. (See Appendix, Case 9, pp. 723–725.) Although there are obviously numerous cases of emotional maladjustment among young boys and girls wherein the

---

[43] *Juvenile Delinquency*, McGraw-Hill, New York, 1932, p. 161.

[44] *Ibid.*, p. 161; see also Mark Roser, "The Importance of Understanding the Treatment Needs of Truants," *Federal Probation*, December 1948, pp. 29–34.

sex aspect is the crux of the situation, the highest incidence of sexual looseness is to be found among adolescent girls. Most of the girls sent to reform schools are there for sexual reasons. Naturally some male is an accessory in practically every case, but it is most frequently the older male who is involved rather than the boy of approximately the same age as the girl. With the awakening of the sex urge at the onset of adolescence, many girls who find school boring or beyond their mental capacity seek excitement elsewhere. They have little trouble in meeting older boys and men who are all too eager to take advantage of them. It is from this group of intellectually dull adolescent girls that most of our sex cases are drawn. Many are sex-starved as a result of the lack of appreciation of their problem at home; others who are apprehended have used their wiles merely to gain attention or favors from men. A puritanical morality has little meaning for most adolescents today. Even in these modern times most of our boys and girls must pick up their sex knowledge from the street corner or schoolyard. It is not surprising that thousands of young girls go astray in our prudish and apathetic culture. We are concerned here only with the fact that most girls who are labeled delinquent are also labeled sex problems.

Although the young male commits few sex offenses compared with other types of overt delinquency, some sexual maladjustment is often the basis of the other types. We shall deal with the sex-offender in a later chapter.[45] The more spectacular sex crimes make the headlines; many of them are serious and distressing and many end in brutal murder. In recent years much attention has been paid to the young "killer," whether it be boy or girl. Victor Cohn, in the Minneapolis *Tribune*, states that in 1946, 808 boys and girls under 21 years of age were arrested for homicide—that figure represented 12 out of every 100 murderers. Of these, 256 were under 18 and 69 were 15 and under. The trend continued in 1947: 415 boys and girls under 21 were arrested for homicide. Many of these killings involved sexual motivation.[46]

Still another type of delinquent, which often cuts across one or more of the others previously mentioned, is the highly processed young criminal or thug. (See Appendix, Case 4, pp. 714–716.) He

---

[45] Chapter XIV.
[46] In a series of articles, December 1947.

may be no more than twelve years of age, but he is more likely to be older. Here, again, he may be suffering from deep-seated emotional maladjustment, or he may be normal in his responses but abnormal in his sense of civic responsibility. As a rule, he is a dangerous person, and all the resources of law-enforcing agencies must be unloosed to cope with his bravado and criminal skill. The only reason we consider him delinquent is because he is a minor. In his earlier years he may have been placed in one of the other categories mentioned earlier. But now he is a potentially dangerous young thug who preys on society without compunction. Doshay describes this type, comprising about 10 per cent of those coming before the juvenile court, as the "vicious, hardened and aggressive habitually delinquent type who espouse antisocial behavior as a career and the gang as a medium of protection, comfort and training for effective operation." [47]

Thus, it is difficult to group delinquents into distinct categories or types. As Lowrey explains in his analysis of delinquent personalities, what we are actually dealing with is behavior of an individual—the external and observable responses or activities of the individual. He further maintains that there are no such entities as delinquent and criminal personalities.[48] Yet in any work on juvenile delinquency some practical analysis must be attempted so that the reader may distinguish between types. However, as we shall point out on numerous occasions, each delinquent is a person and every person is a distinct entity so far as his heredity and his environment are concerned.

It is important at this point to set down just what is meant by "environment." The average layman thinks of the environment as merely the more apparent factors in the life of an individual, such as his neighborhood, the house he lives in, his family life, the church, school, primary or secondary groups, and the like. These factors are, of course, part of environment. But the sociologist thinks of environment as every stimulus that impinges on the individual's structure from the moment of conception—the moment the new life begins. The environment is represented by every possible interaction

[47] Lewis J. Doshay, "The Challenge and Solution of Juvenile Delinquency," *Journal of Clinical Psychopathology and Psychotherapy*, Vol. 6, 1944, pp. 335–354.

[48] L. G. Lowrey, "Delinquent and Criminal Personalities," Chapter 26, Vol. 2, of *Personality and Behavior Disorders*, J. McV. Hunt, ed., Ronald Press, New York, 1944.

between the individual and every other individual with whom he comes in contact—not only physically but through every cultural medium. Thus what the individual absorbs from his reading, from the motion picture, the radio, television, all are a potent part of his environment. Each interaction, regardless of intensity, has its effect in forming character. The innuendo, the nuances, the whisperings, the off-the-record remarks one hears, the adult repartee, the gossip, all must be accepted as environment. Walt Whitman cogently expresses this situation in his poem *A Child Went Forth:*

There was a child went forth every day,
And the first object he look'd upon, that object he became,
And that object became part of him for the day . . .
Or for many years or stretching cycles of years.
The early lilacs became part of this child . . .
And the old drunkard staggering home from the tavern . . .
And all the changes of city and country wherever he went.
And the friendly boys that pass'd, and the quarrelsome boys . . .
The mother at home quietly placing the dishes on the supper-table . . .
The father, strong, self-sufficient, manly, mean, anger'd, unjust,
The blow, the quick loud word, the tight bargain, the crafty lure,
The family usages, the language, the company, the furniture, the yearn-
    ing and swelling heart . . .
The doubts of day-time and the doubts of night-time . . .
Men and women crowding fast in the streets . . .
The streets themselves and the facades of houses, and goods in the
    windows . . .
The light falling on roofs and gables of white or brown . . .
These became part of that child who went forth every day, and who
    now goes, and will always go forth every day.

In turn, the individual helps create the environment for every other person with whom he comes in contact. In short, developing the environment is a reciprocal process. Measurement of an environmental stimulus is difficult. Repetition of a stimulus has its effect, but the intensity of a specific stimulus upon a structure that is just ripe for that stimulus determines the magnitude of the response. Thus a whisper or a chance remark may have far more importance in determining behavior or forming character than a more apparently profound remark repeated over and over.

4. THE DELINQUENT PERSONALITY

It is difficult to place delinquents in categories, but it is almost presumptuous to establish a delinquent "profile." Many behavior patterns or mechanisms that appear early in many children and that may be considered diagnostic tend to disappear under the most informal and even witless day-by-day interaction with others—for example, aggressiveness. How aggressive should the young child be and how much time should elapse before this behavior is considered a danger signal? Or excessive shyness, or the resort to temper tantrums? The young child feeling his way in an adult-centered world is forced to rebel when he is frustrated in his desires.

Many questions are posed in attempting to lay down a convenient formula for incipient delinquency. Yet from the thousands of studies of delinquent and maladjusted boys and girls patterns of behavior emerge that clearly describe the emotional strain under which they live. These patterns apparently have not been resolved during the early years of these children. Only when they run afoul of the law, the attendance officer, the school counselor, and others working in the field of maladjusted childhood are we able actually to label them as precipitating toward delinquency or maladjustment.

With the above warning in mind, we might mention the four goals toward which the maladjusted child, according to Dr. Rudolf Dreikurs, directs his disturbing behavior: (1) to gain attention; (2) to demonstrate his power or superiority; (3) to punish or get even; and (4) to give up in complete discouragement.[49] How valid are these goals? Can we generalize so easily? Professor Mervin A. Durea, who has studied thousands of delinquent children, thinks he has found a "delinquency index" based on the duration, frequency, and numerical weighting of offenses.[50] He and his colleagues found in their studies, through the application of various tests, that delinquent children are quite different from nondelinquents in emotional ma-

---

[49] "The Four Goals of the Maladjusted Child," *The Nervous Child*, Vol. 6, No. 3, 1947, pp. 321–328. See also Dreikurs' book, *The Challenge of Parenthood*, Duell, Sloan, and Pearce, New York, 1948.

[50] "A Quantitative Method of Diagnosing the Seriousness of Asocial Behavior of Juvenile Delinquents," *Journal of General Psychology*, Vol. 14, 1936, pp. 412–431.

turity; [51] that by means of responses to certain tests possible tendencies toward delinquent behavior may be discovered.[52]

Emotionally immature delinquents may be detected by such traits as egocentrism or infantilism, seclusiveness or boastfulness, or a certain amorality with little regard for others. As Dr. Ralph S. Banay points out, they care little for people who cooperate or are considerate, and they are attracted by good looks, fine clothes, and money.[53] But then, so are many children who do not become delinquent.

We are skeptical of laying down a personality pattern for the delinquent. We agree that many behavior mechanisms are present in almost all children at an early age that need checking by wise parents and teachers before they become so fixed that maladjustment or delinquency results. Delinquency cuts across so many phases of antisocial and atypical persistent behavior that it seems unlikely that we shall ever be able to draw the profile of the delinquent type before he is available for study by the psychologists.[54]

5. DELINQUENCY AS A BREAKDOWN OF CULTURAL CONTROLS

In later chapters we shall discuss the various conventional causes of delinquency, all of which have a certain bearing on the problem. In this chapter we wish to call attention to several aspects of our peculiar social structure which present difficulties to all American youth during the growing-up process. We see in some areas of our culture certain glaring anomalies, paradoxes, and inconsistencies that not only confuse but even frustrate many children and adolescents. In fact, they disturb many adults as well. But such it undoubtedly

---

[51] Mervin A. Durea and M. H. Fertman, "Personality Characteristics of Juvenile Offenders," *Journal of Criminal Law and Criminology*, Vol. 32, 1941, pp. 433–438. See also Elio D. Monachesi, "Some Personality Characteristics of Delinquents and Nondelinquents," *Journal of Criminal Law and Criminology*, January–February 1948, pp. 487–500.

[52] Mervin A. Durea and J. C. Heston, "Differential Diagnosis of Potential Delinquency: Additional Suggestions," *American Journal of Orthopsychiatry*, Vol. 11, 1941, pp. 338–341.

[53] *Youth in Despair*, Coward-McCann, New York, 1947, pp. 135–136.

[54] If the reader is further interested in delinquent traits, he is referred to the index of Cabot's bibliography, *op. cit., supra*. The constant and meticulous work of the investigators is conveniently catalogued.

was in every generation. Here is what Socrates said of the children of his day:

> The children now love luxury. They have bad manners, contempt for authority, they show disrespect for elders and love chatter in place of exercise. They no longer rise when their elders enter the room. They contradict their parents, chatter before company, gobble up dainties at the table, cross their legs and tyrannize over their teachers.

First we may examine our economic philosophy. Despite the apostles of thrift, we are geared in the United States to spending and waste. On all sides we are bombarded with clever advertising urging us to buy a hundred different gadgets so that we may enjoy the "better life." It matters little whether the victim of slick-paper magazine advertisements or radio soothing-syrup dispensers have the ready cash. On the next page of the magazine or on the next radio soap opera other enticing advertisements tell us where we can obtain the money at only a slight interest rate. The victim is urged to use charge accounts, or to take advantage of installment buying, deferred payments, or some other cleverly devised "come on" so that the purchase may seem less painful financially. The "easy-money" complex is an integral part of our culture. That is the way we keep up the production of our factories. This situation is all to the good from many points of view. But the philosophy does get its victims. Millions of families take the easy way to live beyond their means, little realizing that a day of reckoning will confront them.

The small wage-earner and his children are constantly confronted by needs that only a few years earlier were considered luxuries. This was true of the automobile a generation ago. Today it is true of radio and television sets and all the electric contraptions found in the modern kitchen and laundry to relieve the drudgery of housework. The movie habit might also be added to this category. Courses in advertising are prevalent in all our colleges. It is doubtful if there has ever been a course offered in sales resistance. According to capitalistic philosophy, it just isn't cricket to talk about sales resistance as a virtue.

When there isn't enough money to go around, many older boys go out and look for opportunities of obtaining money the easiest way. Hard work is unattractive, especially if it does not include the wearing of a white collar. The easy-money complex, so prevalent in the days of the "robber barons"—about whose exploits all children learn in school—and also prevalent in the lush nineteen twenties as well as during the last war, have discouraged millions of adolescents from learning a trade or working a full day for a small wage. What they want is a "connection" with short hours and a degree of status, such as that of a salesman or a front man for some shady operator. The route to delinquency is short and bedecked with primroses. We shall have more to say about this in our discussion of the delinquency of the older boy.

The theory of the leisure class, exposed so devastatingly by the great economist, Thorstein Veblen, has unmistakably encouraged the thinking, shallow though it is, of millions of young people who want "something for nothing." These adolescents and young adults can point to the activities of high-salaried businessmen who are engaged in shady pursuits, many of which are within the law but somewhat immoral nevertheless. A very fine line exists between what the law lays down and the transactions that are actually made. "White-collar" activities, many of which were illegal and most of which were immoral, described so expertly by Professor E. H. Sutherland, need not be reviewed here. The financial activities of Samuel Insull, Ivar Kreuger, Stavisky, Whitney, the Van Sweringens, Sinclair, and others, all of which were front-page news prior to the late war, have been supplanted by the connivance of "white-collar" war criminals like General Bennett Myers, the Garssons, Congressman Andrew May, the "Five Percenters," and many others who capitalized on all-out war production.[55]

In 1943, for example, the Anaconda Wire and Cable Company and five of its top-flight executives were convicted of faking tests and thus actually delivering defective cable to the armed forces overseas. Aside from callously exposing our soldiers to possible death, the activities of these morally defective big-business executives defrauded the government of some five million dollars. For this reprehensible crime a Federal judge fined the men $31,000 with suspended sentences. John R. Ellingston, in his book, *Protecting Our Children from Criminal Careers*, cites this incident and then adds that in the same year "a washer in a tank factory in Pennsylvania was found

---

[55] See the revealing work by Bruce Catton, *The War Lords of Washington*, Harcourt, Brace, New York, 1948, a story of greed, ineptness, and arrogance during World War II.

guilty of damaging an army tank by injecting water into its exhaust pipe. He caused the damage 'so he could go to lunch on time.' " This non-white-collar worker got three years in prison for disrupting the war effort.[56]

Differential treatment of this sort does little to stabilize the nation's moral fiber. Thus it is not surprising to find that an occasional delinquent justifies his act by pointing to such glaring inconsistencies in our legal dispensation of justice. Gabriel Tarde, the great French sociologist, declared that social imitation spreads from the top downward. This concept might help to explain why many youths attempt to emulate the socially *élite* in manipulating people and productive goods for their own selfish gain regardless of laws or morality. In other words, the shrewd and shady practices engaged in by the moguls of big business in any era have permeated the lower middle class. Conspicuous spending and what Veblen called "pecuniary emulation" have become the goals of millions who simply cannot realize such extravagance without breaking the law.

Nor can this cynical philosophy be blamed on the war morality. "He gets his and I'm going to get mine" is an all too prevalent attitude in our acquisitive society. Ellingston calls our attention to a series of articles in the *Reader's Digest* (July–September 1941) which describe the results of a nationwide investigation of the business ethics of garages, radio repair shops, and watch repair shops. Two investigators, a man and a woman, spent three months getting service at a large number of repair shops. They found that 63 per cent of the garage men took them for suckers and charged them for unnecessary work; 195 radio repair men took advantage of them by "fixing" their radio even though there was nothing defective; and 49 per cent of the watch repair men also fleeced them.[57] Professor Sutherland has made a penetrating analysis of white-collar crime and has set down a number of arrogant remarks made by businessmen through the years, including the period of the last war, which demonstrate that a large element of our manufacturers definitely and persistently do business illegally.[58] Nor should we overlook the arro-

---

[56] Prentice-Hall, 1948, p. 8.
[57] See Ellingston, *op. cit.*, pp. 20–21.
[58] See his *White Collar Crime*, Dryden Press, New York, 1949, for his findings.

gance and fraud of Congressman J. Parnell Thomas of New Jersey, who was convicted and sent to prison for forcing salary "kickbacks" from his office help. It is this nonchalance and arrogance with which so many businessmen and elected officials carry out their illegal acts that is disturbing to the bulk of the American people.

The black-market operations during the war turned to gray-market traffic in scarce commodities immediately after the cessation of hostilities. In addition, we were confronted by the callous practices of many automobile salesmen and dealers in hi-jacking buyers into purchasing unwanted accessories as well as in demanding large fees for making sales, and by rent-gouging by landlords and realtors' agents. Such reprehensible practices do much to condition young-sters to become parasites and disciples of the "something for nothing" philosophy. Any fine moral fiber they may have started life with soon becomes undermined so that immorality and "within the law" activity easily shades into illegal behavior.

A second point that should be made in this section deals with the breakdown of controls aside from our economic life. We have alluded to this subject above. In spite of the moral platitudes emanating from church, school, character-building agency, and the home itself, the child grows up in a culture which, in its confusion of values, winks at the double standards of morality. Children in the growing stages become confused when they find one set of standards employed by their parents and friends and another suggested in school and church. For example, children must learn to develop a pattern of falsehoods to be used under certain conditions and a philosophy of truth-telling to be used in other connections. This confused set of standards carries over into the field of honesty and dishonesty. The child is told to be scrupulously honest but hears his parents tell hilariously of a shady deal.[59]

In short, the American child lives in a world of double standards of morality in which distinctions between right and wrong are seldom made, or, if they are made, they are made with a sinister inconsistency. Social definitions of what is permitted and what is prohibited are poorly drawn and thus confuse and even frustrate many children.

---

[59] See Lester D. and Alice Crow, *Our Teen Age Boys and Girls*, McGraw-Hill, New York, 1945, Chapter IX, "Teen Age Problems in Social Life."

A third consideration concerns the corruption in politics, especially in local areas. The alliances between the lawless elements and the police are an integral part of the American pattern and need little comment. The metropolitan political organization cannot carry on without corruption and graft or, to varying degrees, without the criminal element. It is a familiar pattern to all who can read. From the days of Lincoln Steffens, with his pioneer work, *The Shame of the Cities* (1904), down to Robert S. Allen, with his *Our Fair City*,[60] the sordid story is the same.

To anyone familiar with urban life, the terms *machine* and *organization* mean the hierarchy of the political party in power at the moment. The machine dominates not only city politics but state politics as well, often even exerting a powerful and deplorable influence over national politics. No machine can function smoothly and last for long without the constant recruiting of young, potential voters in the neighborhoods, wards, and districts. Manipulating the residents of all sections of a large city by dispensing jobs, handing out charity, extending favors and certain types of immunity from embarrassment or arrest, and by using common psychological devices of the party system such as party names, catchwords, and slogans, enables politicians to acquire control of the city government. They maintain that power by building up powerful voting machinery and by encouraging youthful gangs and clubs to take an active part in politics—of their own brand. Thus the delinquency structure is linked with the organized political life of the neighborhood. Nationwide criminal elements who control gambling machines, the numbers rackets, and the dispensation of licenses for operating taprooms and houses of prostitution are closely linked with the politicians on this lower level. Young voters as well as those who will soon vote are initiated into this sordid combination; they are solicited to see that the voters get out on election day and to pass out literature. In short, young gangs are given status by the politicians and by the questionable characters who feed at the trough of the political machine. Thus have the big organizations of Chicago, New York, Philadelphia, Atlantic City, and Kansas City been built up and maintained.[61]

[60] Vanguard Press, New York, 1947. See also, *The Tax Dodgers,* by Elmer L. Irey and William J. Slocum, Greenberg, New York, 1948; also Robert S. Allen, *Our Sovereign State*, Vanguard Press, New York, 1949.

[61] For further details on the tie-up between politicians and the criminal ele-

A fourth point that should at least be stated is the restlessness of youth as a reflection of the frontier philosophy that has dominated the country from pioneer days. How strong this urge is to move about seeking thrills is uncertain. The late Courtney Ryley Cooper made much of this adolescent drive for excitement in his book, *Designs in Scarlet*,[62] but much of what he described grew out of the depression era of the early thirties. But youth, especially the older boy and girl, still yearns for the open road—witness the large number of hitch-hikers and movie-mad recruits to Hollywood. Many of these youth find themselves in trouble with the Federal laws that prosecute offenses in automobile theft (over state lines), trafficking in narcotics, including marihuana, and violation of the Mann Act ("white slave" crime). About 700 youngsters in the Federal reformatories (Englewood Correctional Reformatory near Denver and the National Training School, Washington, D.C., as examples) are there for violations of these and other Federal laws.

The frontier philosophy and its emphasis on individualism and the uncontrolled way of life fostered a blatant bravado and a toughness of character that often nurtured a defiance of law and order. This defiance condoned illegal and anti-social adventure. How much of this kind of philosophy still persists is debatable, but there is some justification for believing that much of our delinquent youth are still imbued with it. Certainly it cannot be avoided entirely in any appraisal of delinquency among older adolescents.

Still another point that cannot be overlooked is that the commission of *some* types of delinquency is widespread in all cultural and social groups. The onus of delinquency is not so much in the commission of the act but in getting caught. Just as in adult crime, since the *infamy* is generally attached to the punishment rather than to the actual commission of the offense, the commitment of a child

---

ment, see Barnes and Teeters, *New Horizons in Criminology*, Prentice-Hall, New York, 1943, pp. 65–76. See also William Foote Whyte, *Street Corner Society*, University of Chicago Press, 1943; also "The Chicago Rackets," *Life Magazine*, November 29, 1948, pp. 95–103.

[62] Little, Brown, Boston, 1939. A book called *Jailbait*, by a writer with the pseudonym William Bernard (Greenberg Press, 1949) follows in the Cooper tradition. This book graphically paints a sordid picture of delinquency, among pre-adolescents particularly. Although the book is not documented, the facts, in general, can be attested to by those working in the field of delinquency.

to a reform school carries more social stigma than does the commission of an offense. Thus we find certain delinquent acts engaged in by children in some of the upper levels of society without fear of admonition or punishment. This is particularly true of sexual laxity among girls of high-school or college age. It is even true of girls in the lower social groups. Some of those who are detained on "non-arrest" or arrest charges involving sex, and who receive some sort of subsequent discipline by public officials, are likely to be stigmatized in their neighborhoods, but many lose no caste whatsoever among their friends.

The widespread incidence of certain occasional offenses is shown by A. L. Porterfield in a comparative study of representative college students and juvenile court cases.[63] College students were given a list of 55 offenses and were asked to check those offenses they had committed prior to and after matriculation. The results are interesting but not surprising. Of the 417 students who did the checking, all were guilty of committing at least one of the offenses; the average number of offenses committed by men prior to entering college was 17.6; after entering college, 11.2; and by the girls in pre-college days, 4.7. Porterfield believes that minor delinquencies are much more widespread than they are usually thought to be. He feels that whether or not a child becomes a confirmed delinquent depends on a variety of social factors.

Here, of course, we are confronted by a number of factors. Many minor violations of the penal code are committed by a large segment of the population, regardless of economic or social status, when and if they can "get away with it." Traffic violations are in this category. Again, certain types of offenses are "smart" to commit, providing the individual has a certain status or is relatively immune to discipline. Then, too, differential treatment by police officers or detention officials must be admitted. So far as college students are concerned, they belong to the *in-group*, relatively free from any drastic action by the public authorities. Fraternity brawls during football season, property damage during class conflicts, and the like, seldom move beyond the realm of the dean's office. On the other hand, the police are quite likely to crack down and arrest any delinquencies occurring in a labor-management dispute.

[63] "Delinquency and Its Outcome in Court and College," *American Journal of Sociology*, Vol. 49, 1943, pp. 199–204.

We shall have more to say about differential treatment in our chapter on race and nationality, but we want to mention here the figures compiled by Warner and Lunt in their study of the number of arrests in Newburyport, Massachusetts. Seven years of arrests in that city are analyzed according to six classes into which the community was broken down according to economic and social status. The following results are revealing:

Class of the Community	Percentage of Population	Percentage of Arrests
Upper Upper	1.44	0.43
Lower Upper	1.56	0.28
Upper Middle	10.22	1.84
Lower Middle	28.12	7.80
Upper Lower	32.60	24.96
Lower Lower	25.22	64.69

In the seven years under consideration, the percentage of the Lower Lower class with records of arrest was 10.77; of the Upper Lower, 3.22; and of no other class over 1.25. And in the Lower Lower class, which was nine parts foreign (ethnic) and seven parts Yankee (native), the arrests were ten foreign to six Yankee. The total population was made up of 54 per cent Yankee and 46 per cent foreign, and the total arrests were 40 per cent Yankee and 60 per cent foreign.[64] It is obvious from these figures that there is a differential treatment of the lower social and economic classes who lack the ability or influence to avoid arrest. This fact is, of course, well attested to by all who are familiar with police attitudes and methods.

It has been the purpose in the last section to draw in some of the ideas and suggestions made by persons who have observed certain tangential or segmental aspects of the problem of delinquency. We have discussed them briefly in this connection because they cannot be ignored and also because they are not generally handled in any conventional list of causes. Yet they must be adequately appraised in any work on juvenile delinquency.

Here we find, first, the confusion among large numbers of our population regarding our economic philosophy and structure which, through the glittering advertising of the makers of material gadgets,

---

[64] W. Lloyd Warner and Paul S. Lunt, *The Social Life of a Modern Community*, Vol. I of the Yankee City Series, Yale University Press, New Haven, 1941, p. 376.

and of small loan companies and banks, give the impression that money can be borrowed easily and that the "good life" can be attained painlessly. Second, we have the cynical morality and ethics of many businessmen and officials which seep down to the masses, developing a "something for nothing" concept of life, including the shopworn remark that "he got his, I'll get mine." This philosophy encourages a breakdown in controls, a breakdown in values and in concepts of what is right and wrong, moral or immoral, and a confusion in social definitions of what is permitted, what is prohibited, and what is winked at or even encouraged. We see much of this frustration in family, neighborhood, and community authority, with a subsequent weakening of respect for such institutions as the school, the church, and the family. Third, we see the alliances exposed to public view between police, politicians, and the criminal elements, especially in heavily populated areas of our large cities. Resulting from this situation, we see, just as in areas of white-collar criminality, such features as dishonesty, taking advantage of out-group people, sharp practices, reliance on influence and pull, and conniving to beat the law. All these acts constitute a type of functioning ethic that easily becomes a central core of the social philosophy of young recruits to the political machine. Fourth, we have a typically American restlessness among large elements of our youth, characterized by a floating migratory life, hitch-hiking, vagabondage, and loose sexual morality. All too frequently this restlessness ends up in the commission of crimes such as automobile theft and traffic in narcotics and in white slavery. And fifth, we have the realization that many delinquent acts are widespread and are committed by young people in communities and social classes where ordinarily they are not presumed to take place.

All these points are vital to the understanding of the over-all picture of delinquency and crime. There are doubtless others. We shall allot considerable space to the more fundamental and conventional causes of crime in later chapters. But it must be emphasized that the total picture must be appraised in realistic perspective if we are fully to understand this complex problem.

6. CONCLUDING REMARKS

In succeeding chapters we shall demonstrate that the plague of delinquency is not new to our culture, even though the term may be of recent origin. Other terms, which are considered quaint today and which were applied to dissident or maladjusted youth, were: depraved, perverse, wayward, headstrong, stubborn. It was alleged that these tragic and misunderstood children came from the "perishing" or "dangerous" classes, the degraded, poverty-stricken masses who lived in slums and rookeries of the large cities. Legal terminology, unintelligible to the layman, together with the medieval concepts of the law, tended to debase childhood. Thurston reports a case of a boy sent to a reform school by a Chicago criminal court around the turn of the century. On his commitment papers it was recorded that he had "burglariously, feloniously, and maliciously broken into his stepmother's pantry and had stolen a jar of jam." [65]

Another equally quaint notion that has become widespread among parents, especially, is that the child—their child—would be good and would walk in the moral path of rectitude were it not for "bad companions" with whom he plays or associates. It is always the child's company that has made him delinquent, not the child himself who is at fault. "Shun evil companions" has been the adage down through the years.

Although poverty and misery were the stock reasons advanced for most delinquency up to quite recently, it was generally agreed throughout the pre-scientific era, and even today in some circles, that perverse behavior is due to lack of will power. This ephemeral and nebulous entity, it is further alleged, can be developed, since man is a free moral agent and can carve out his own destiny along lines of his own choosing. All the child needs, then, is the *will* to be good.

As we shall point out in a later chapter, the first challenge to the popular doctrine of free will emerged from the conviction that many children were retarded intellectually and thus were unable to distinguish between right and wrong. Early psychologists became enthusiastic in their desire to demonstrate that true delinquency was closely associated with the feebleminded. But later investigations showed that many of the mentally deficient never became delinquent and that many delinquent children were normal or superior in intelligence. The works of Goddard and Tredgold, to mention two of the

---

[65] Henry W. Thurston, *Concerning Juvenile Delinquency*, Columbia University Press, New York, 1942, p. 69.

early pioneers, were quoted as proof of the thesis that there was a high correlation between feeblemindedness and delinquency.[66]

With the establishment of the first child-guidance clinic by Dr. William Healy in Chicago in 1909, the emphasis was placed upon psychiatry or mental hygiene, and it has remained there ever since. However, the socio-economic causes were not overlooked. These causes were given status several years later by the works of Clifford Shaw, Henry McKay, Frederic M. Thrasher, and others who developed the popular delinquency area concept.

Many child-guidance clinics were organized throughout the country. The findings of these clinics tended to crystallize into what may be called an eclectic approach. This approach views the whole child, taking into account all the social, economic, biological, and emotional forces which impinge upon the structure of the child from the day he is born and which bend him toward his general behavior. Although Dr. Healy pioneered the way for the guidance clinic, one of the first case studies of juvenile delinquents, if not the first, was made by Mabel Carter Rhoades at the University of Chicago in 1907, two years before Healy opened his clinic.[67]

In the meantime, the clinical psychologists have done yeoman service in devising tests to measure not only intelligence, but personality, emotional tone, attitudes, and other capabilities and potentialities of children.

In the nineteen twenties and early thirties great emphasis was placed upon the ecological approach to the problem of delinquency. For many years thereafter the concept of the delinquency area—which contended that it was the blighted areas of the large city that were the foci of infection—swept the country and has remained not only popular but authoritative. Only recently has there been a slight swing away from this common-sense view of the problem. This shift has been due largely to the more critical interpretation of what constitutes delinquent behavior. It has also been due to the ascendency of the psychiatrist in interpreting the behavior we do not like as being determined largely through frustration at an early age and emerging primarily from familial relationships.

---

[66] See Chapter III, pp. 88–91.

[67] Mentioned by E. H. Shideler, "Family Disintegration and the Delinquent Boy in the United States," *Journal of Criminal Law and Criminology*, January 1918, pp. 709–732.

In the following chapters dealing with the numerous causes advanced for delinquent behavior, we shall note that students of the problem do not repudiate wholesale any phase or aspect of etiology that is carefully advanced and substantiated by scientific techniques. But we shall persistently caution the reader against taking any one-sided thesis enunciated by over-zealous reformers who have the tendency of going all-out for some pet hobby to the exclusion of other and, perhaps, more carefully constructed theories.

We shall also discuss the steps taken in coping with the delinquent: apprehension, detention, the hearing, and finally the disposition of the case. We shall critically appraise the conventional methods of dealing with the young boy or girl who is regarded as a problem in our adult-centered culture.

The evolution of attitudes concerning the treatment of the delinquent will also be discussed. The rise of child-saving agencies and institutions, culminating in the reform school and the reformatory for the older boy, will be discussed and appropriate criticism will be suggested.

In our last section we shall review and appraise the work of prevention, including the police, crime prevention units, recreation agencies, the community, school, child-guidance clinics and governmental agencies.

Chapter II

EARLY METHODS OF CARING FOR DELINQUENT AND DEPENDENT CHILDREN

1. ANCIENT AND MEDIEVAL CONCEPTS OF THE DELINQUENT CHILD

The term "delinquency" is relatively new in our culture. Just when it began to appear is uncertain; probably no more than a century ago. But the equivalent of the term and of the state of delinquency has been known since ancient days. Wild children, wayward youth, and headstrong progeny are terms we meet in medieval literature. The problem of lawless youth is not new.

But when we review the past in order to ascertain just what was done to cope with delinquent children, we find no lines of demarcation drawn between delinquent, neglected, depraved, or abandoned children. Instead of focusing attention on the delinquent child, ancient and medieval people developed "child saving" asylums to care for all types of underprivileged children. Our American customs stem from those on the Continent and in Great Britain. In short, the history of the delinquent child is synonomous with that of the abandoned and neglected child. This relationship is of importance in understanding what follows in this chapter. We have attempted here to interpret the roots of treatment of the delinquent, especially before the era of the modern reform school and probation. These are but the modern counterparts of the colonial techniques of dealing with underprivileged children.

It has been the tradition since the days of the Romans to view the child under the age of seven as not being culpable for his delinquent acts. It is interesting that in the Catholic Church a child under that same age cannot take Communion. Both Church and State have regarded the child under seven as irresponsible and helpless.

41

Roman law divided children into three categories, so far as responsibility was concerned: under seven, no responsibility; seven to the age of puberty, punishable if it could be ascertained that some insight or discernment was present; from puberty to twenty-five, chronological age was considered in determining punishment.

Later, the *Code Napoléon* conceived of limited responsibility for children under the age of sixteen, which was later raised to eighteen. The English common law accepted the age of seven as the age below which no responsibility could be ascribed but, according to the great Blackstone, at eight the child could be guilty of a felony.[1]

It seems strange that even today we accept the chronological age in determining responsibility rather than mental or psychological capacity to differentiate between right and wrong. The so-called age of discernment still haunts our courts and legal procedures.

Little is known of the treatment of the delinquent child among the ancients. We do know that abandoned, destitute, and neglected children were given succor among the Romans as well as among early Christians. The practices of infanticide and exposure as well as the selling of infants were widespread among the Roman provinces, especially if the victims were physically or mentally defective or unwanted by their parents. Judged by modern standards of child care, the disposition of children by such methods represents a callous philosophy, yet it was a part of the mores of that day. Charles Loring Brace, a pioneer in child care, describes these practices in his work, *The Dangerous Classes of New York*. He cites many Roman and Greek authorities as evidence:

> How . . . common was the dreadful exposure of children who were physically imperfect or for any causes disagreeable to their parents, so that crowds of these little unfortunates were to be seen exposed around a column near the Velebrum at Rome—some being taken to be raised as slaves, others as prostitutes, others carried off by beggars to be maimed for exhibition, or captured by witches to be murdered, and their bodies to be used in their magical preparations.[2]

Despite such repugnant practices, the Romans did make provision for destitute and dependent children by establishing orphanages,

---

[1] See *infra*, Chapter IX, p. 281. See also Frederick J. Ludwig, "Rationale of Responsibility for Young Offenders," *Nebraska Law Review*, May 1950, pp. 521–546.

[2] Wynkoop & Hallenbeck, New York, 1880, p. 14.

schools, and asylums. The Emperor Trajan, for example, as early as A.D. 110, supported some 5,000 orphans at public expense.[3] We usually think of modern charity as stemming exclusively from the early Christians, but pagan people had their charitable methods also. Brace pays tribute to the Visigoths for their denunciation of the practices of infanticide, exposure, and abortion, and for their making such offenses punishable by death or blindness.[4]

But it was definitely the early Christian movement that gave impetus to the salvaging of helpless and poverty-stricken persons. This development was due in large part to the thesis that every individual was acceptable to God. Foundling homes and asylums for abandoned children were established as early as the sixth century at Trêves, and at Angers in the seventh, although parish orphanages were in existence even earlier. During the twelfth century the first Children's Aid Society was founded at Montpellier "for the protection, shelter, and education of destitute children, a fraternity which subsequently spread over Europe." [5]

Slavery and feudalism during ancient times were scarcely distinguishable. Both systems handled the problems of the adult poor and the dependent child. The slave-owner was responsible for the welfare of his human property, as was also the lord of the manor under feudalism. The wealthy landowner was required to care for his serfs. Thus we find little institutional care aside from the foundling homes and monasteries that were established by the early Christian church.

With the breakdown of feudalism and the confiscation of the monasteries, radical measures had to be employed to cope with the social debtor classes. It took centuries for feudalism to disappear completely, but from the time of the Black Death in 1348 down to the reign of Queen Elizabeth new concepts of local responsibility were being forged. The Poor Laws, culminating in 1601, were the result. By this date, quite definite techniques for dealing with unfortunate children may be seen. In fact, the American colonies began with the Poor Laws, so far as their local government was concerned. (We shall discuss this relationship later.)

---

[3] *Ibid.*, p. 18.
[4] *Ibid.*, p. 20.
[5] *Ibid.*, p. 21.

2. EARLY PENAL ESTABLISHMENTS FOR CHILDREN

The first establishment of which we have any record that was specifically created for the corrective treatment of delinquent youth was opened by Pope Clement XI in Rome in 1703. It was called the Hospice of San Michele and was designed along monastic lines by the architect Carlo Fontano. The good Pope, disturbed by the behavior of wayward boys of the city, established his famous institution to teach them discipline as well as a trade. Over the door he placed this inscription: "It is insufficient to restrain the wicked by punishment unless you render them virtuous by corrective discipline." He explained his scheme in his *Motu proprio* of November 14, 1703. He provided for two types of delinquents: first, youth under twenty sentenced by the court for the commission of crimes; and second, incorrigible boys who could be placed under his control by parents. Despite the fact that education was stressed, the establishment was quite severe. The juvenile offenders worked together at spinning and knitting in a central hall. Chained by one foot and under a strict rule of silence, they listened to the reading of religious tracts. The incorrigible boys were constantly kept separated, day and night, in their little cubicles or cells. Large signs, hung throughout the establishment, admonished *Silence*. Floggings were resorted to as penalties for "past mistakes" as well as for infractions of rules.[6]

It is quite possible that Pope Clement received his inspiration from a home for vagrant boys operated in Florence by one Filippo Franci, a Catholic priest. The set of rules this priest drew up anticipated many ideas that became an integral part of the penitentiary system a hundred years later. For example, the boys were obliged to wear hoods drawn down over their faces in order to avoid recognition. The hood, or mask, became an important factor in later penitentiary discipline.

It is interesting that John Howard (1726–1790), the great British prison reformer, felt kindly disposed toward the program of treatment in San Michele—to such a degree that he built his penitentiary concept around its features. Like so many austere and deeply religious fanatics, Howard thought solitude and religious instruction

---

[6] See Max Grünhut, *Penal Reform*, Oxford University Press, London, 1948, p. 21.

held within them the seeds of reformation. (This concept became widespread, as may be more particularly seen in the penitentiary movement for adult criminals.) Charles Lamb, in one of the papers of *Elia,* describes Christ's Hospital in London and reviews the cruelty imposed on children there. For petty offenses they were confined to poorly lighted, solitary cells. Their confinement was broken only twice a week, for floggings. He makes this contemptuous statement regarding Howard: "This fancy of dungeons for children was a sprout of Howard's brain: for which . . . methinks I could spit willingly upon his statue." Here is one of the roots of imprisonment which spread all over the world during the nineteenth century and which we still follow down to the present day.

Another root of imprisonment which cannot be overlooked, even so far as the incarceration of youthful delinquents is concerned, was the House of Correction, which had its beginnings in the latter part of the sixteenth century. The first institution of this type was started in the city of London in 1557, and was known as the Bridewell. It had for its purpose the imprisonment and discipline of beggars, vagrants, and dissolute women.

These institutions were rapidly organized and put in operation all over the Continent, after the London example. The philosophy of the House of Correction, or workhouse, was that offenders would be deterred from leading a life of wantonness and idleness by being forced to work hard at disagreeable tasks. Mr. L. Owen Pike colorfully describes the inmates of such an establishment:

> There were the practicers of unlawful games—the forerunners of our modern skittle-sharpers, welshers, and gaming-house keepers. There were persons who "used physiognomy, palmistry, or other abused sciences, tellers of destinies, deaths or fortunes." There were "minstrels not belonging to any honorable person of great degree," unlicensed buyers of rabbit-skins, sellers of aqua vitae, petty chapmen, tinkers, pedlers, jugglers, bear wards, fencers, unlicensed players in interludes. There were begging sailors pretending losses at sea, and unable to show a license from two justices living near the place where they landed. There were Irish men and Irish women "of the sorts aforesaid," who lived by begging. There were hedge-breakers and petty pilferers of wood. There, too, were scholars of Oxford and Cambridge that went about begging "not being licensed by the chancellor or commissary." [7]

---

[7] *History of Crime in England,* Smith, Elder & Co., London, 1873–1876.

Serving Dinner at the Boys' Prison, Tothill Fields, England (Mid-nineteenth Century).

Many vagrant children, as well as depraved and delinquent children, were sent to these Houses of Correction. So were unruly and runaway apprentices. The great novelist, Charles Dickens, has given us many pictures of these houses of despair as they were operated during the nineteenth century.

3. THE CHILD-SAVING MOVEMENT IN ENGLAND

As early as 1618 a scheme was devised to send wandering and depraved children collected from the streets of London to the colony of Virginia. These children were described as "running wild in the streets, sleeping under stalls at night and begging during the day." [8] They were taken to the House of Correction in preparation for their banishment, which was eventually effected in February 1619, when, it is recorded, seventy-five boys and twenty-five girls set out for their new home and scene of labor. The scheme was considered so successful that another boatload was prepared in 1621.

As happened so frequently, the authorities seem to have had the welfare of the children in mind, rather than that of the colonists, since the children were to receive "a grant of lands and houses, cattle and corn," when they came of age. Many of these fledglings, however, perished on the voyage or in the new wild country of Virginia. As O'Donoghue gravely speculates, in writing of this episode in child-saving: "I wonder what became of two of these little Bridewell birds—Prudence Nation and Barbara Dowse!" He further surmises: "Possibly a few of these Bridewell boys or girls, if they escaped massacre and plague, were the ancestors of some of the 'first families of Virginia.' " [9]

The pioneer group to work with unfortunate juveniles in Britain was the Philanthropic Society of London, which was founded as early as 1788. It is just possible that the great John Howard's personal solicitation for wayward youth led to the establishment of this society. Howard had said: "Boys confined for correction should always be separated from other prisoners, and indeed from one another. A kind and tender monitor should often see them, and,

---

[8] Edward Goeffrey O'Donoghue, *Bridewell Hospital, Palace, Prison, Schools, from the Death of Elizabeth to Modern Times*, John Lane, Ltd., London, 1929, Vol. II, p. 21.

[9] *Ibid.*, p. 12.

without tiring their attention, converse with them as a friend and parent." [10] We noted earlier how the work done by Pope Clement XI in the Hospice of San Michele for boys in Rome had pleased Howard. Separation, one from the other, and kind ministrations by the Brothers, had sounded a new note in the care of delinquent boys.

This first philanthropic organization is not to be confused with the one started in 1815 as the outgrowth of interest in children incarcerated in Newgate Jail. We shall discuss that organization a little later.

The members of the Philanthropic Society were appalled at the large number of vicious and vagrant children in the London metropolitan area who were actually trained to live by begging and pilfering—the type later portrayed in Dickens' *Oliver Twist*. Starting with one child, the Society increased its activities by acquiring three small cottages to house the youngsters picked up from the city's streets. At this early date (1788), the Society thought in terms of the *family* system of child care and used agriculture as the principal means of rehabilitation. As Enoch Wines writes of its work:

> It distributed the children into families of twelve in its modest dwellings, placing at the head of the whole group a general superintendent, and in the three families severally a gardener, a tailor, and a shoemaker, with their wives. It sought in this way to realize to the youthful objects of its charity the happiness and benefits of a home. . . . One rubs his eyes in astonishment as he reads the reports of the Society—those for example, issued in 1788 and 1789.[11]

These reports envisaged agriculture as "the grand source to which the Society looks for employment for its wards. Agriculture means natural life, and is the primary spring of health and happiness." In 1806, the Society organized an asylum. There can be no doubt that this movement represented the first organized effort to do something for delinquent children aside from throwing them into jails or workhouses.

A few years later, in 1813, Elizabeth Fry, the great Quaker visitor, was making her first trips to Newgate Jail in London. There she found, in addition to debauched females, many small children who

---

[10] Quoted by Enoch C. Wines, *State of Prisons*, Cambridge, Massachusetts, 1880, p. 75.
[11] *Ibid.*, p. 76.

had been obliged to accompany their mothers.[12] But it was not until 1817 that she began her work of jail reform in earnest. In the meantime she had enlisted the cooperation of her influential brothers-in-law, Sir Thomas Fowell Buxton and Sir Samuel Hoare, who were interested in penal reform in an academic sort of way. Both these men loom large in prison reform from this time forward.

The first task that demanded Elizabeth Fry's energies was the establishment of a school for the children of the female prisoners at Newgate. This she accomplished with one of the prisoners as teacher. Aside from religious and some academic instruction, she supervised lessons in hygiene and cleanliness. Although Elizabeth Fry is primarily associated with adult females, we must not forget her concern for the children obliged to spend time in jail only because their mothers were delinquent.

Growing out of these ministrations, the Society for the Improvement of Prison Discipline and for the Reformation of Juvenile Offenders was formed in 1817. (This was later known as the London Philanthropic Society, but it is not to be confused with the earlier one founded in 1788.) This organization had behind it the strength and influence of the two brothers-in-law of Elizabeth Fry, mentioned above, and of her brother, Joseph John Gurney. In addition, many of her personal friends joined and took a vital interest in the objectives of the organization, which were especially aimed at child welfare. Early in its career, it conducted what we would now call research into the causes of delinquency. Its list of causes sounds much like comparable lists today: homelessness; parental neglect; abnormal family relations; want of mental, moral, and religious education; want of employment; dislike of work; destitution; the corrupting influence of prisons, "flash-houses" of drink, debauchery, and all manner of wickedness; and the fairs in and about London, "where temptation seduced young lads into thefts, for which their subsequent commitment to prison sealed their ruin." [13]

The Society was especially impressed with the responsibility of taking abandoned and depraved children off the streets and giving them a new lease on childhood. Sir Thomas Fowell Buxton, in his

---

[12] For the work of Elizabeth Fry, see, for example, Janet Whitney, *Elizabeth Fry, Quaker Heroine*, Little, Brown, Boston, 1936.

[13] Quoted by Wines, *op. cit.*, p. 77.

work *An Inquiry whether Crime and Misery Were Produced or Prevented by the Present System of Prison Discipline in England*, relates case histories of depraved boys who were debauched primarily because they had not been prevented from committing crime by the agencies of society, but who, on the contrary, had learned most of their wickedness in the prisons.

Several buildings secured by the Society were devoted to a program of different mechanical trades. Separate dormitories were provided for boys and girls, and all the buildings were enclosed by a wall. After learning trades, the boys were farmed out as apprentices, although some were sent to America. The girls learned the conventional tasks of mending, washing, and needlework. At a "suitable" age they too were indentured. In 1849, this institution was removed to a farm at Red Hill, Surrey, away from the noise and confusion of the city.

From these early experiments, England, and especially London, experienced a great impetus in child-care efforts. For instance, in 1817 the magistrates of Warwickshire established at Stratton-on-Dunsmore, near Birmingham, an asylum or reformatory for juvenile offenders; in 1830, Captain Edward Pelham Brenton, with the aid of an association known as the Children's Friend Society, opened a small retreat for boy vagrants at Hackneywicke, London; shortly thereafter, a girls' reformatory school was opened by a Miss Murray, maid of honor to Queen Victoria, at Cheswick, a London suburb.

It was the practice of Brenton's school to apprentice the boys to farmers, either in Canada or the Cape of Good Hope. Perhaps as many as 2,000 children were housed, clothed, and assisted by this school, but despite its excellent reputation for doing good, its management was attacked by some editors for "carrying on a virtual slave trade under the mask of benevolence." The unjust criticism crushed Brenton. Eventually the rugged sea captain died of a broken heart. The criticism also killed the Children's Friend Society.[14]

In commenting on Captain Brenton's rugged program, it should be noted that there is a school of thought even today, among virile men and some women, that what boys, especially, need is a Spartan-like program so that they may learn discipline, a sense of duty and

---

[14] *The Prison Chaplain: A Memoir of the Rev. John Clay*, by his son, Walter L. Clay, Macmillan, London, 1861, p. 372.

responsibility, a respect for authority (especially toward their elders), and a fortitude of stern proportions. It might further be added that the Borstal system in Britain today accepts the thesis that *certain* boys not only need this type of regimen but can thrive on it.[15]

Girls' School at Tothill Fields Prison, England.

It should be mentioned at this point that almost a hundred years earlier, in 1756, the wealthy and philanthropic merchant, Jonas Hanway (1712–1786), had founded the Marine Society to train boys taken off the streets for the naval service. Taking their cue from this man's idea, the authorities of Bridewell, in 1774, drafted young vagrants into the fleet.[16]

Thus, by the year 1838, when Parliament authorized institutional care for depraved and vagrant boys and girls in the Parkhurst Act, several establishments were already functioning. But even with the

---

[15] See section on Borstals, Chapter XIV.
[16] Edward Geoffrey O'Donoghue, *op. cit.*, Vol. II, pp. 212–213.

authority of this act, Hepworth Dixon could write ten years later of the vicious conditions to which children were being subjected in adult prisons:

For the most part, they are ignorant beyond the power of belief. We have met children in the London prisons who could not tell their own names, beyond Bill, Sam, or the slang word by which they were known in their own circle, such as Lanky, Snip, and so on. It is very common to meet such as do not know their ages, where they were born, or their parents' names. Sometimes you meet a child who had no distinct notion of what the words "father" or "mother" mean . . . in Preston gaol, including adults, more than sixty per cent of all persons committed are unable to name the months of the year. The same average could not tell the name of the reigning sovereign of the country. . . .

Thousands of children, between seven and fourteen, crowd the streets of London—samples of them turn up in plenty at all ragged schools—who are either orphans, foundlings, or the children of criminal parents who have deserted them or been removed from the country by force. They live on the *pavé*, and sleep in the gutters—a doorway is a luxury which is denied them by the vigilant police. As to employment, they sell matches, fusees, tapes, fruits, in the streets, or hold horses and sweep the steps of omnibuses. Take a single illustration: "M., eleven years of age; parents unknown; a casual pauper; died of cholera; sick nine hours. September 9th, 1849. Taken in from Orange street, half-starved—stomach full of blackberries." What a history in a sentence! [17]

Up to the year 1838, all such institutional treatment, aside from the common gaol and workhouse, was private. Children were not sent to these places from the court, but rather were picked up from the streets. This was the situation when the friends of children in the United States were casting about for some remedial treatment for depraved, abandoned, and dependent waifs who swarmed the larger cities. We shall discuss the genesis of this movement in another chapter.[18] In order not to lose the continuity of child-care in Britain, we shall briefly sketch what occurred following the passage of the Parkhurst Act in 1838.

The preamble of this act observed that it might "be of great public advantage that a prison be provided in which young offenders may be detained and corrected, and receive such Instructions and be sub-

---

[17] *The London Prisons*, 1850, pp. 176–177.
[18] Chapter XII.

ject to such Discipline as shall appear most conducive to their Refor-mation and to the Repression of Crime," and further, "the buildings of Parkhurst [near Newport] in the isle of Wight, lately used as a Military Hospital and as a Medical Asylum for the Children of Soldiers," might "conveniently be used for such a Prison." [19]

This prison, for that is definitely what it was, was in reality brought into existence to serve as a substitute for the transportation of youthful offenders to the penal camps of Australasia. But it is dubious that this substitute was any less severe than a life in the Antipodes. It is reported that the régime was hard and repressive, consisting of the "penal correction of the offender, by confinement, spare diet, rigorous enforcement of rules, hard work, so as to deter from future crimes." [20]

The next step in the official program to handle delinquent children was the Industrial School Act of 1857, which made it possible for private industrial schools to take children showing delinquent tend-encies or to place them in their own homes, if they could be profit-ably employed there. With the growth of these private reforma-tories, Parkhurst was finally abandoned as a prison for juveniles in 1864. Since that year it has been used as an adult prison. One of the writers of this book visited the Parkhurst prison in the summer of 1949. Today it is used for hardened recidivist adult criminals. The buildings are bleak, grim, and severe. It is hard to realize in retrospect that this establishment was once used for juvenile delinquents.

By mid-century, Britain had a large number of private agencies in child-saving work in addition to many semiofficial institutions and so-called reformatories. An interesting example of this latter type of school for unfortunate children was the reformatory established by the eminent Thomas Barwick Baker on his private estate, Hardwicke Court, Gloucester, in 1852. This school, the first of its kind in Britain, was maintained for many years at Baker's own expense. It caught the attention of one American penologist, at least, in the person of General Roeliff Brinkerhoff, of Ohio, who visited Mr. Baker and his school in his later years. Part of the success of this school can be credited to its first superintendent, George Bengough, an Oxford

---

[19] Edmund F. Du Cane, *The Punishment and Prevention of Crime*, Mac-millan, London, 1885, pp. 202–203.

[20] Dixon, *op. cit.*, p. 175.

graduate with a strong desire to do something for the young repro-
bates who were sent to his school. He "devoted himself bodily to his
task, living, working, and even sleeping among" his boys. Both he
and Baker were disciples of Captain Brenton.

During the same year, 1852, a second reformatory was opened at
Birmingham by a Mr. Adderly and Joseph Sturge, who picked as
their superintendent a shoemaker from London named John Ellis.
This school was later moved to Saltley. Ellis was apparently a remarkable man. His earlier life had been devoted, as a Ragged School
teacher, to reclaiming young criminals in the streets of London.
Tendered a large gift of money for his work, he gathered around
him several of the most desperate boy-thieves of the city and literally
lived with them. His success was so significant that the magistrates
of the city suggested that a reformatory be opened with Ellis as
superintendent.

Another interesting movement that was distinctly British was the
Ragged Schools, which took their name originally from the
"wretched ragged little heathens" who came to the first Sunday
Schools started in 1781 by Robert Raikes in Gloucester. The idea of
caring for the poor children by giving them instruction spread
rapidly. By 1844, a distinct movement was launched for the purpose.
Prior even to that early date, however, a shoemaker, John Pounds
of Portsmouth, established a small group in his community not only
for "book learning" but for trade training. Miss Mary Carpenter,
long one of Britain's outstanding penal reformers, and superintendent
of the Red Lodge Reformatory for Women, gave Raikes and Pound
credit for starting the Ragged School movement.[21]

In these Ragged Schools impoverished youth, orphans, and abandoned children were cared for in the traditional and conventional
severity of the times. Trades were taught and discipline was severe.
The school to which the child was sent was selected by the local
magistrate, but the school authorities had the option of refusing any
whom they thought not adaptable to the program.

Another child-saving movement that cannot be overlooked was
that begun single-handed by Dr. Thomas John Barnardo (1845–
1905). When he was a young interne in medical school, Barnardo

---

[21] *Reformatory Schools for the Children of the Perishing and Dangerous
Classes*, C. Gilpin, London, 1851. See Chapter II, "Evening Ragged Schools."

became interested in a boy of the streets—ten-year-old Jim Jarvis— whose plight shocked this sensitive young man. The result was that Barnardo, in 1865, began to work with the street urchins of London's East End and, two years later, opened his first home in Stepney Causeway. His career is remarkable. During his lifetime he opened 112 district homes for underprivileged youth. He began caring for girls in 1872, when he opened his first home for their reception.

Trade training and schooling in general were the bases of his program of rehabilitation, and religion played an important role. But perhaps the most remarkable aspect of his program was the emigration of thousands of his boys to Canada, South Africa, and Australia. Barnardo had great faith in his convictions. He maintained during his later years that less than two per cent of his boys who emigrated from London were failures. He was especially proud that many of them became men of distinction in the Dominions. He contended that if street boys were snatched from their haunts early enough and given good training, poor heredity would have little bearing on their future. To him environment meant everything. His institutions cared for over 60,000 children up to his death in 1905. The work he began is still being carried on by his successors.[22] A counterpart of Barnardo's practice of sending boys away from the big city was that of Charles Loring Brace, superintendent of the New York Children's Aid Society, which we shall discuss later.[23]

In concluding this section dealing with the long historical development of child-saving agencies and institutions, it should be stated that Britain today depends on privately operated "approved schools" rather than on public reform schools to care for the younger delinquents in her population. There are no public institutions throughout the entire realm comparable to those in this country, which we shall describe in Chapter XII. The British Approved Schools are so named because they have the stamp of approval of the Home Secretary. Each is under private managers but is partially subsidized by the Home Office. Many of the schools we have mentioned or described above are still receiving "care and protection" cases as well

---

[22] See J. H. Batt, *Dr. Barnardo, the Foster Father of Nobody's Children,* Partridge and Co., London, 1904; J. Wesley Bready, *Dr. Barnardo,* George Allen & Unwin, London, 1930; and A. E. Williams, *Barnardo of Stepney,* Allen & Unwin, 1943.

[23] Chapter XII.

as delinquents from the juvenile courts. We shall discuss these approved schools in more detail in our chapter on commitment.[24]

In another connection we shall discuss the famous Borstal movement, which was begun by Sir Evelyn Ruggles-Brise, director of British prisons, during the latter part of the nineteenth century, and which has been brought to its fruition during the past fifty years. The Borstals were specifically designed for older delinquent youth who were convicted by the courts. There is some connection between these establishments and the Reformatory, which appeared in the United States following 1876.[25]

4. CHILD-SAVING ON THE CONTINENT

The earliest movement dealing with delinquent, destitute, neglected, and exposed children in the German states was made in 1695 by August Hermann Francke (1663–1727) in the city of Halle. This pietist preacher and scholar started his modest haven with the "goodly capital" of three and one-half dollars, on which he stated "I must do a great work." With a most insignificant beginning, his benefactions eventually enabled him to "pile up the largest, highest and most imposing series of buildings in Halle," a school known for over two centuries as the *Francke'sche Stiftung* (Francke Foundation).[26]

More than a century later, in 1813, Johann Daniel Falk (1768–1826), German author and philanthropist, and a friend of Goethe, opened a children's institution in Weimar. Although Falk was a native of Danzig, it was at Weimar that he made his greatest contribution to child welfare. He began his philanthropy for children following the death of his own four "promising and dearly beloved children" within a few days of one another. He dedicated his life to unfortunate children "who were in the path of crime and destruction." He also founded a Society of Friends in Need for children of criminals, one of the first of its kind in the world. He adopted a fitting symbol for his school—a picture of children converting their chains into useful tools on an anvil. After Falk's untimely death, his

---

[24] For an analysis of the British system, see *Penal Reform In England*, edited by Leon Radzinowicz and J. W. C. Turner, Macmillan, London, 1946, Chapter VIII.

[25] See Chapter XIV, pp. 521–526.

[26] Enoch C. Wines, *op. cit.*, p. 73.

schools were taken over by the state in 1829. Up to World War II, they still existed as the *Falksches Institut*.

Several other children's establishments were those founded by Count Adalbert von der Recks-Vollmarstein, Friedrich Wadzeck, and Johann Heinrich Wichern—all famous institutions for child-saving.

The first of these three schools was created in 1819 at Overdyck, near Bochum, in Prussia. A few years later, in 1822, Count Adalbert expanded this school and removed it to an old monastery at Düssel-thal, near Düsseldorf, where the children were given a program of common trades and simple farming. The second school, that operated by Wadzeck, was a "beggar school" in Berlin. By the time of his death in 1823 it was caring for 150 poor boys, 190 poor girls, and a number of infants whose parents worked during the day—a sort of pioneer day nursery. The program of this school also offered training for nurses who were expected to serve in homes for dependent children. Another Berlin movement at about this time was the Society for the Education of Morally Neglected Children, which opened a House of Refuge in 1824.

But perhaps the most famous of these early German institutions for delinquent, abandoned, neglected, and unfortunate children was the Rauhe Haus at Horn, near Hamburg, founded in 1833 by Dr. Johann Heinrich Wichern, aided by his mother. It was under the supervision of a home-missionary society founded in 1832 and known as the "Inner Mission." The founders maintained that "if the Kingdom of Christ is again to be established in our city [Hamburg] it is necessary among other things to found a house for the sole object of rescuing children from sin and disbelief." [27]

Dr. Wichern and his mother sought out twelve of the worst boys they could find from the "lowest haunts of vice and misery" of Hamburg and took them to a "very rough farm" which they had secured for the purpose. It is stated that the name of the school came from the roughness of the farm and house.[28] The founder said of his experiment:

---

[27] B. K. Peirce, *A Half Century with Juvenile Delinquents*, Appleton, New York, 1869, p. 133.

[28] Liefde, in his *The Charities of Europe*, gives another derivation for the term. He stated that the house used by the Wicherns for their school was built a century earlier by a Mr. Ruge, and that a corruption of his name may have evolved the word *Rauhe*. See Peirce, *op. cit.*, p. 134.

The children's institution was not to be a work-house, nor an orphanage, nor a place of punishment, nor a house of correction; but an institution that allied itself to the family, to the gospel, to the forgiveness of sins, to the first and last thought—that is, to the essential nature and work of Christianity.[29]

Johann Heinrich Wichern.

We have no way of knowing how ideal a place Rauhe Haus was —whether it was a prison or a repressive school. We do note in studying institutional treatment for delinquent and dependent children, however, that there is a universal tendency for those who hold the destiny of thousands of children in their hands to make platitudinous, though sincere, remarks concerning their work.

The children at Rauhe Haus were taught "wholesome learning, the truths of the Gospel, and honest labor," by Dr. Wichern himself. Here we see, perhaps for the first time on a practical scale, the family type of "institution." But we must not overlook the earlier work of

---

[29] Quoted by Wines, *op. cit.*, p. 74.

The Original "Rauhe Haus," Near Hamburg, Germany.

59

the Philanthropic Society of London, which, as we pointed out before, thought in terms of the family unit in 1788. At Rauhe Haus, however, we find the "house father" and the "house mother," who are to be found in many children's reform schools today. In fact, Dr. Enoch Wines, one of our early authorities on child welfare, says of this institution: "The fundamental idea of the Rauhe Haus is that of the family; and it is the mother of all those child-saving institutions, of which the number is constantly increasing, that have since been organized on the family plan." [30]

As more children entered Wichern's school, other cheap houses were constructed. Later a church was built, then a school building, and still later some factories. In time, a sizable community had grown up. The Brothers of the Inner Mission who were drawn to the leader also made a distinct contribution to the school. Aside from teaching the children, they mingled among the poor of Hamburg, preached the Gospel, and, perhaps more important, supervised the children who had left the school and were serving as apprentices to artisans. Dr. Wichern stated in his reports that the attempt was made to visit each boy in his master's house once every two weeks, or once each week, if thought necessary. Thus we see a follow-up or crude parole supervision.

Three principles were combined to make Rauhe Haus noteworthy as a child-saving institution. The first was the genuine spirit of religion that animated every member of the staff; the second was the spell of the home in which each child felt complete security and possessed a deep sense of belonging; and third was the industry of the place, whereby the dignity and value of labor well done were inculcated at every turn.

Although the success of the school has been conceded everywhere, it was not altogether unmitigated. Dr. Wichern had his problem children who caused him and his staff no little concern. As one writer states: "Sometimes, under the influence of some two or three ringleaders incurably wicked, the evil passions of the half-tamed savages would wake up into defiance and rebellion." [31] He adds that on one occasion the evil spirit grew so virulent that a plot was laid to burn down all the buildings.

---

[30] *Op. cit.*, p. 74.
[31] Clay, *op. cit.*, p. 373.

Perhaps the most important thing to remember about Rauhe Haus and its philosophy is that it served as a model for the later and better-known agricultural colony at Mettray, near Tours, in France, started by the judge Frédéric Auguste Demetz in 1839. Just as some of the earlier experiments in Britain and on the Continent were responsible for the development of the Houses of Refuge in America, so the Mettray colony became the pattern for later children's reform schools throughout many of the states after 1840. On the other hand, Demetz was to no little degree inspired by the work of the three Houses of Refuge which were operating in Boston, New York, and Philadelphia during the eighteen twenties. He and the architect,

Frédéric Auguste Demetz, 1796–1873.

Guillaume Blouet, had been commissioned by the French government in 1837 to visit America to inspect the penitentiary systems in operation. While on this mission, Demetz visited the Houses of Refuge; upon his return to France, he inoculated the Société de Patronage (a discharged prisoners' aid society) with his views on child care. At the suggestion of the society, Demetz toured Europe visiting children's colonies and reformatories. It is said that what he saw at the time in Belgium and Holland "furnished him excellent examples of what to avoid." He then proceeded to Horn and was highly impressed with Rauhe Haus.

Looking at the problem of delinquency through the eyes of a judge, Demetz was shocked that minors were thrown into jails, and he determined to set up some dignified establishment where children could be reclaimed for the state without being demoralized and degraded. Upon returning from his tour of inspection, he founded a small Société Paternelle for the purpose of enlisting support for his movement. He was immediately aided by a former school friend and wealthy landowner, Vicomte de Bretignières de Courteilles of Touraine, who gave him the land for his institution. This friend also took a warm personal interest in the school and proved to be a loyal supporter of Demetz in his efforts.

The school's progress was rapid under the enthusiastic leadership of the humanitarian Demetz aided by the financial generosity of his companion the Vicomte. By 1840 the first house was ready for the reception of the youthful offenders, and capable teachers were employed. Nine children, carefully selected from the prison at Frontrevault, made up the nucleus of the school. By May, 1841, six houses were completed and a chapel was practically finished. Believing in agriculture as reformative treatment, Demetz adopted as a motto for his school, "The moralization of youth by the cultivation of the soil."

The program of the school was arduous. Demetz believed in hard work on the farm. He and his staff aimed to send their charges to bed completely tired out, without so much as an evening's romp in the dormitories. As the school was based on the family unit, the boys were grouped according to their disposition and character in separate cottages under special masters. Each family was distinct and had no connection with the others except at work, recreation, and divine services. The cottages were three-storied. On the ground floor was the workshop; on the first, the dining room, school, and some of the dormitories; on the second floor were more dormitories.

There was also a form of self-government. The boys selected two monitors or frères aînés (older brothers) monthly, who worked out the system of rewards and disciplines with the père (father) or house monitor. The régime was military in nature, and no doubt paved the way for the adoption of this type of discipline by many schools both in France and the United States. Although the Mettray experiment met with almost universal favor, it did have its critics. For instance, Prince Peter Kropotkin, the Russian humanitarian, described the system as most cruelly severe, and the French reformatories generally as most demoralizing to children.[32]

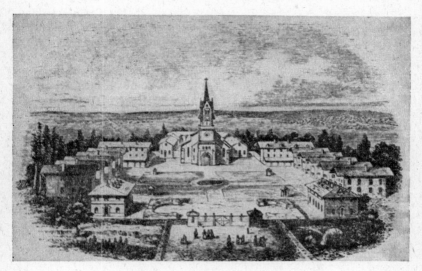

Agricultural Colony at Mettray, France.

The Mettray colony was called in France a "glorified copy" of Rauhe Haus. The same dignity was assigned to labor, the same family system was adopted, and the same genuine spirit of religion permeated the whole establishment. One enthusiastic writer who visited the place pointed out the subtle differences of the two schools as follows:

But there was still a difference throughout. The German homeliness of the *Rauhe Haus* brightened into French sentiment at Mettray; the quiet domesticity of Wichern's little households reappeared in the *esprit-de-corps* in Demetz's *familles;* emulation, not to say vanity, was systematically stimulated; the worship of *l'honneur* was carefully culti-

<hr />

[32] Quoted by Major Arthur Griffiths, *Secrets of the Prison House,* Chapman and Hall, London, 1894, Vol. II, p. 416, from Kropotkin, *Russian and French Prisons.*

vated by means of badges of distinction, tablets of merit, and little dignities of all kinds. The young *colons* were encouraged to establish a perfect tyranny of public opinion, and to shame each other into submission to its dictates; and of course the discipline was military throughout. In short, Mettray is truly said to be "glorified." *La gloire*, of a wholesome kind it is true, but still *la gloire*, in spite of all attempts to sober down to *l'honneur*, is the life of the system.[33]

Another criticism of Mettray was that the boys were intimidated by the constant threat of being sent back to the penitentiary if they did not behave. In the *Journal of Prison Discipline and Philanthropy*, the official publication of the Philadelphia Society for Alleviating the Miseries of Public Prisons (now the Pennsylvania Prison Society), an American critic had this to say about Mettray in 1861:

> The famous reform school at Mettray is often referred to as a successful experiment with young delinquents, but it is not always borne in mind that it is not alone the "domestic or family spirit" which prevails there that makes it successful. It is one of the distinguishing features of their system that pupils, *before coming to them*, undergo a vigorous penitentiary discipline, to which they must dread to return. Without this, the fatigue and moral restraints imposed at Mettray would make them desire to return to their idle and comparatively comfortable life. Expulsion from Mettray is sure to be followed by a return to the prison as the greatest punishment they can inflict.[34]

The Mettray was also attacked on account of its great cost. To this criticism Demetz said simply: "Reform as cheaply as you can, but—reform."

One other group of experiments, dealing more with educational methods rather than child-saving, was that of the renowned Johann Heinrich Pestalozzi and his disciple von Fellenberg, in Switzerland. Later we shall notice their influence on the movement in the United States which brought into existence the Houses of Refuge during the first part of the nineteenth century. Although Pestalozzi was associated with child-saving, he is best remembered for developing a progressive philosophy of education. His work made a deep impression on many early American educators.

---

[33] Clay, *op. cit.*, p. 375.
[34] July, 1861, p. 124.

5. THE DELINQUENT CHILD IN COLONIAL AMERICA

We know very little about colonial children. We have the impression that their lot was somewhat drab, with few pleasures. The following statement about the dearth of material on children of that period was written by Alice Morse Earle in 1899:

> When we regard the large share which child study has in the interest of the reader and thinker of today, it is indeed curious to see how little is told of child life in history. The ancients made no record of the life of young children; classic Rome furnishes no data for child study; the Greeks left no child forms in art. The student of original sources of history learns little about children in his searches; few in number and comparatively meagre in quality are the literary remains that even refer to them.
>
> We know little of the childhood days of our forbears, and have scant opportunity to make comparisons or note progress. The child of colonial days was emphatically "to be seen and not heard,"—nor was he even to be much in evidence to the eye. He was of as little importance in domestic, social, or ethical relations as his childish successor is of great importance today; it was deemed neither courteous, decorous, nor wise to make him appear of value or note in his own eyes or in the eyes of his seniors. Hence there was none of that exhaustive study of his motives, thoughts, and acts of a child which is now rife.[35]

Mrs. Earle collected a great deal of information regarding the day-by-day activities of colonial children. So far as discipline is concerned, she points out that parents, ministers, and schoolmasters all seemed to conspire against childhood, their thesis being "Foolishness is bound up in the heart of a child." Their only cure for this "foolishness" was a program of repression and "sharp correction." Liberal use of the rod was condoned by all. Ingenious punishments were devised and liberally used by schoolmasters, and even parents

---

[35] In the Foreword of her book, *Child Life in Colonial Days*, Macmillan, 1899, p. vii. See also a revealing book by Marion L. Starkey, *The Devil In Massachusetts*, Knopf, New York, 1949. The author has recreated the witchcraft frenzy of 1692 and shows that it all started when two little girls, the daughter and niece of the village pastor, Rev. Samuel Parris, became bored with the austere lives they were doomed to live and fraternized with a female Negro slave, a cook in the household, who was given to black magic. The author points out that these children became gravely ill, as a result of the strain of coping with an adult world.

tended to discipline their offspring without any compunction what-soever.

It is strange, however, to note that Mrs. Earle collected nothing that tells us how children were treated for violations of the law. In another of her works, *Curious Punishments of Bygone Days*, she describes the brutality of the colonial penal practices, but in none of her pages do we find any account of brutality against children. Yet we know colonial youth were subject to the same penal codes as were their elders.

There seems to have been no provision in early colonial America for what we refer to as delinquent children except incarceration in county jails. Children were simply not supposed to be delinquent. Destitute, neglected, and dependent children were indentured or sent to almshouses, following the British Poor Laws practices. The system of indenture and the almshouse, together with the county jail, were well-developed institutions in England prior to coloniza-tion in America, and it was but natural that they should be estab-lished here. The workhouse also came to the colonies, but it was usually only an adjunct of the county jail until the early part of the nineteenth century.

Indenture as a system, which was legalized as early as 1660 in Massachusetts, was widely practiced not only for homeless young-sters but also for the children of the poor. Since the privileges of an education—even the rudiments thereof—were not for the poor, the only avenue left open for the child was to learn a trade at the hands of a master. The youth of early America had very definite obliga-tions, especially if they came from the lower economic classes. If they failed to measure up to the terms of the contracts entered into by their parents, their lot was likely to be far from pleasant. Such children were expected to assume obligations far beyond anything modern children would or could accept. If they failed to fulfill any of the terms of their contracts, they were usually jailed. Many of them ran away rather than yield to a harsh master or a jail term. The larger communities of Massachusetts, Pennsylvania, Maryland, and New York were full of runaway apprentices. The colonial watch-men, progenitors of our modern police, were kept busy apprehend-ing and jailing these headstrong youth or more pathetic urchins.

Early reports of prison societies and other early welfare organiza-tions are full of complaints that children were mingling with adults in unwholesome receptacles known as jails. Little or no segregation was provided; women, children, and adult men were thrown together into "night rooms." There they slept on the floor without any bedding except a little straw they could purchase from the jailer or procure from those interested in their welfare. The notorious "fee" system was in practice in all the colonies, and later in the states; food, clothing, and firewood for keeping warm had to be purchased by the inmates of the jails. Thus, those children in the jails—and there were often very many—fared no better than did the adults. Here is an example of what it was like in the Walnut Street Jail in Philadelphia in 1789; this passage is from a report of a committee from the Philadelphia Society for Alleviating the Miseries of Public Prisons, organized two years earlier in 1787. Denouncing the ease with which the inmates could procure liquor from the bar operated by the jailer within the walls of the establishment, it continued:

> Under this head it may be proper to remark that children both in the gaol and workhouse are frequently suffered to remain with their parents whereby they are initiated in early life to scenes of debauchery, dishonesty, and wickedness of every kind—the female convicts are at present kept in the workhouse where for want of proper apartments they are asked to associate with girls and young women confined there by their masters and mistresses for sale or temporary punishment, by which dangerous intercourse many unhappy creatures who are perhaps only confined by the caprice of their owners, are gradually seduced from their original innocence.[36]

This same reform society was still protesting the unsegregated treatment of "lads of tender years" in 1821 and up to the organization of the House of Refuge, which was effected in Philadelphia in 1828. And even the opening of this institution did not stop the practice. In 1854, William J. Mullen, agent for the prison society, wrote: "A very great injustice is done little boys by putting them in cells with old convicts who corrupt their morals. If boys who are imprisoned by their parents or masters could be kept in separate cells it would be much better."[37]

The same situation was to be found in New York. A report of

---

[36] Negley K. Teeters, *They Were in Prison*, Winston, Philadelphia, 1937, p. 450.
[37] *Ibid.*, p. 299.

the Society for the Prevention of Pauperism for 1819 complained of the large number of children mingling with adults in the Bellevue Prison, which occupied the same grounds as the city almshouse. As was pointed out above, juveniles were governed by the penal codes of the day just as were adults. However, as we shall see below, efforts were made by the judges both in Britain and in the colonies and states here to mitigate the most severe penalties so that relatively few, if any, children of tender years convicted of a capital offense were hanged.

Protests such as were mentioned above could have been made against conditions of juveniles who ran afoul of the law in most of our large cities in early days. They were perforce thrown into jails and workhouses.

Aside from the apprentice system, colonial America resorted to the county almshouse, or poorhouse, to which, by law, it was easy to send homeless, abandoned, neglected, or indigent children, most of whom were not delinquent. As stated above, the English Poor Laws were the heritage of colonial days, and even these were considered an enlightened step when they were promulgated in the last half of the sixteenth century. They represented the break with feudalism and introduced the philosophy of community responsibility for the social debtor classes, which, up to that time, had been succored either through private charity or through the manor house.

Thus we find runaway apprentices, impoverished, neglected, depraved, or abandoned children, and others who today we would call problem children, turned over to the magistrates or overseers of the poor (1) for a term in the county jail; (2) to be apprenticed out; or (3) to be sent to the almshouse.

Although the harsh codes of England applied to children as well as to adults, there is little tangible evidence that the children were actually subjected to the brutal penalties described in the law. Many children were transported to the American colonies and hundreds of unruly apprentices were sent to the workhouses or Bridewells, where it is quite possible they were given a good flogging.

Professor Wiley B. Sanders of the University of North Carolina, who has done some valuable research in this area, points out that, although there is considerable evidence that child offenders were found guilty of many crimes, they were actually shown great leniency.[38] As early as 1675, children under fourteen were considered unable to commit felonies, yet the penal code did not excuse minors of their acts, except for very young children under the age of seven. It would seem that the treatment of children was governed more by public opinion than by codes of jurists. Professor Sanders states that in looking over the records of Old Bailey in London, he failed to find a single instance of a child-hanging during the period from 1680– 1731. Cases were recorded in which children "were sentenced to be burnt" or whipped, but we have no way of knowing whether the sentences were actually carried out.[39] Contrary evidence, however, shows that in 1801—many years later—a child of thirteen was hanged at Tyburn for stealing a spoon.[40]

There is little concrete evidence to prove that children were actually punished according to the penal codes of colonial America. They were tried in criminal courts and many were declared guilty. But apparently the jurists felt constrained to sidestep the penalties. Professor Robert G. Caldwell, who has familiarized himself with colonial penal practices in Delaware, found no evidence of the public flogging of young children at that state's whipping-post.[41]

An occasional citation alleges that young boys have been hanged in this country, but it is difficult to get authentic evidence. It is *alleged* that a boy of thirteen was hanged in New Jersey in 1828 for an offense he had committed when he was twelve.[42] Henry W. Thurston mentions a law that was passed in the colony of East Jersey in 1688 calling for the hanging of any child convicted of stubbornness or of cursing his parents.[43] But there is no evidence that any stubborn child was ever hanged. Apparently we need more research

---

[38] "Some Early Beginnings of the Children's Court Movement in England," *Yearbook*, N.P.P.A., 1945, pp. 58–70.

[39] *Ibid.*, p. 62.

[40] Cited by Judge Atwill Westwick in *Yearbook*, N.P.P.A., 1939, p. 188.

[41] In a letter to the authors. Professor Caldwell is author of *Red Hannah*, the story of the whipping-post in Delaware, University of Pennsylvania Press, 1947. He found that in 1873 two children, aged "about thirteen," were flogged (p. 22). Undoubtedly others over 12 years of age were subjected to that penalty.

[42] See Westwick, *loc. cit.*

[43] *Concerning Juvenile Delinquency*, Columbia University Press, New York, 1942, p. 69.

in this field before we slander our ancestors for wanton brutality toward children of tender years.

Young children were, however, sent to state penitentiaries after the introduction of these institutions during the first quarter of the nineteenth century. Such cases occur today. A thirteen-year-old girl, Sarah Garber, was sent to the Eastern Penitentiary at Philadelphia in 1852 for killing a baby she was caring for (an early baby-

A Little Convict in the 1880's.

sitter) by forcing it to swallow pins. She received a four-year sentence.[44] A few years ago a thirteen-year-old boy was sentenced to life imprisonment in Colorado for the murder of his sister. This case

---

[44] From the warden's journal in the records of the Eastern Penitentiary.

attracted considerable interest, since the warden permitted him to live in his own quarters. Later he was sent to Boys Town, but he ran away and was returned to the Colorado state prison.[45] A still younger boy, aged 10, was sent to the state prison of South Carolina in 1949 for holding up a filling station, because he was "too young" to be sent to the state reform school.[46]

Isolated instances of brutality toward children have been recorded but they have not been a part of the sentence. Rather, they have been disciplinary punishments in institutions. Whippings and severe floggings have always occurred in boys' reform schools. One instance of utter sterility of treatment is herewith recorded. It occurred in a chain gang in Florida during the latter part of the nineteenth century. A "mere child" had been sentenced for horse stealing.

> Warden Martin . . . placed two bricks at each end of the prison yard, and giving the black baby two more, ordered him to carry them to one of the piles, lay them down, pick up the other two, which in turn he carried to the further end, exchanged again, and so on back and forth all day long, always carrying two bricks. He was warned that he would be whipped if he failed to pile the bricks neatly or broke any of them. He grew up at the task, and the constant abrasion of merely picking up and laying down wore out four sets of bricks before he was put to other labor. He served in all seventeen years and some months.[47]

We shall now discuss the historical development and the role of some of the methods used to cope with underprivileged children, aside from the House of Refuge, in the nineteenth century. This discussion will be helpful because many of the same methods are employed today. The orphanage, or children's home, is still with us, as is the placing-out system, which manifests itself in the foster home. We shall also trace the development of some of the child-saving movements that we take for granted today. We cannot understand the treatment of delinquency without familiarizing ourselves with these social movements. We have deferred our discussion of the rise and development of reform schools, stemming from the original Houses of Refuge, to Chapter XII.

---

[45] For this story, see *Life Magazine*, April 12, 1946, and October 17, 1949.
[46] AP news story, August 7, 1949.
[47] J. C. Powell, *The American Siberia*, H. J. Smith & Co., Chicago, 1891, p. 16.

6. THE ORPHANAGE AND CHILD CARE

During the early nineteenth century, exponents of child care gradually turned to the orphanage. The term, orphanage, however, is a misnomer. Few institutions bearing that name are, in reality, places for full-orphans. Most of the inmates have either both parents living or are half-orphans. The orphanage was considered a step forward in treating underprivileged children, whether they were neglected, dependent, or delinquent. Indenture persisted down to quite modern times, but as a system of child care it has been frowned on by most persons who know anything about the welfare of children. And the asylum or poorhouse also gave way gradually to enlightened public opinion. However, child care in the United States has not been marked by sharply delineated stages, with one type yielding completely to another.

We shall present here only a brief sketch concerning the development of orphanages, since they were primarily developed for dependent and neglected children. The first orphanage, called the Ursuline Orphanage, was established in New Orleans in 1729. Later, in 1790, the Charleston Orphan Home, of Charleston, South Carolina, was opened at public expense, the first of its kind in America.[48]

Most of the children sent to orphanages were "problem children" in the sense that they were potential social liabilities and consequently the stuff from which delinquents are often made. The first orphanages were created during the early part of the nineteenth century, and, after a century, there were hundreds of them in the country. They were organized by churches, lodges, patriotic organizations, labor unions, and through endowments left by wealthy people. Many of these institutions took children from the courts in the hope that they could thwart delinquent careers. Thousands of young girls were sent to them in an attempt to save them from a life of sexual irregularity or prostitution.

Orphanages were, and still are, unsatisfactory places to incarcerate children. At best, they are abnormal so far as homelife is concerned. Regardless of the many scientific services, the introduction of trained

---

[48] For an interesting historical treatment of child-saving institutions, see Emma O. Lundberg, *Unto the Least of These*, Appleton-Century, New York, 1947, Chapter IV.

personnel, more modern buildings, and other features incorporated in recent years, they are still unsatisfactory places for the healthy nurturing of young children. A vast literature deals with the children's home, or orphanage, most of which reviews its background, development, and program. The reader is referred to such books and reports for a better knowledge of its place in American life.

The eminent authority on child care, the late Hastings H. Hart, said this about institutional care for dependent children:

> The writer . . . believes that there is a legitimate field for a certain amount of temporary institutional work for some dependent children; but no intelligent student of dependent childhood can overlook the fact that the trend of public opinion and the tendency in practice is away from the plan of bringing up children in institutions and in favor of the largest possible use of the family home as the natural and divinely established institution for the homeless child.[49]

He further pointed out that at the famous first White House Conference of 1909 the cardinal principle was laid down that no child should be taken from his home because of poverty alone.

The children's institution smacks too much of the Lady Bountiful type of charity. Many homes still being maintained have such titles as "Home for Little Wanderers," "Children's Orphanage," "Sheltering Arms," or "Home for Worthy Indigent Children." In Britain we found the Church of England "Home for Waifs and Strays." These phrases very definitely stigmatize the child. Although some great ball player or politician may have spent part of his early life in one of these institutions, they are at their very best poor places for children.

The growth of children's homes was so rapid that many of them were forced to use questionable methods of keeping up their intake. They begged state legislatures for subsidies for each inmate sent to them and were often guilty of shameless "log-rolling" tactics to insure the receipt of a subsidy. Parents were frequently not only encouraged to send their children to them but often were warned that their children were likely to become delinquent if they were not enrolled. Since it was to the interest of administrators of these homes to have a large population in order to keep down the per capita cost,

---

[49] *Preventive Treatment of Neglected Children*, Charities Publication, Russell Sage Foundation, New York, 1910, p. 69.

children were frequently kept much longer than necessary, with little conscientious effort made to adjust the child to the free community.

7. THE DEVELOPMENT OF FREE FOSTER HOME PLACEMENT

During the middle of the nineteenth century several new concepts of child care emerged. Most of them very definitely repudiated the institution idea, although it was the almshouse rather than the orphanage that came in for most of the indictment.

The idea of placing children in what we refer to as foster homes was not new to the United States, nor did it have to wait until the middle of the nineteenth century to show its influence. Certainly part of the idea came from the older system of indenture, although this practice was rapidly waning, especially after the concept of compulsory education had spread throughout the states. In Philadelphia, as early as 1800, the Magdalen Society was organized to care for young girls who "in an unguarded hour have been robbed of their innocence and sunk into wretchedness and guilt." The noble-minded men—not women—who founded this rescue society envisaged placing these "little Magdalens" in foster homes. The first such child was placed in "a respectable and religious family" where she "would be suitably employed in order to inure her mind to habits of industry." It is reported that after a period of time she returned to the "path of virtue and taught school and did needlework." The second little Magdalen was also successful and married a "religious man." [50]

In 1853, the Children's Aid Society of New York began to take children out of almshouses and place them in foster homes, in which the worst abuses of indenture were avoided. The Massachusetts Board of Charities in 1868 introduced the practice of boarding out children at public expense. The first Society for the Prevention of Cruelty to Children was begun in 1875 in New York City; here again, children from homes where cruelty and abuse were present were farmed out in foster homes.

The founding of this latter organization is of interest. In 1874, the officials of the New York Society for the Prevention of Cruelty to

---

[50] From the records of the Society, quoted by Teeters, *op. cit.*, p. 267.

Animals were confronted with a case of cruelty to a child. A little girl named Mary Ellen had been daily beaten by a foster mother and had been tormented in other cruel ways. Interested persons found to their dismay that there was no redress covering such a flagrant case of abuse except through establishing the guilt of the foster mother under existing legal forms.

Several persons, already interested in the protection of animals, began agitation for a society that would deal with abuses against children. Thus the next year, 1875, saw the establishment of the new organization, with E. Fellows Jenkins as its first superintendent. The movement spread rapidly. Some cities dealt exclusively with children, while others worked with both animals and children.

The combination of these two classes of work is frowned on by some persons, but it was regarded as necessary in some places where funds were limited. The Colorado Bureau of Child and Animal Protection states that "the protection of children and animals are combined because of their helplessness; because all life is the same, differing only in degree of development and expression." [51]

The concept of the foster home spread rapidly; today it is generally agreed that it meets the needs of dependent children more readily than any type of institutional care. We shall have more to say on this point later.[52]

Placing out without formal indenture contracts became extremely popular during the 1850s. Perhaps the best-known exponent of this type of placement was Charles Loring Brace (1826–1890), founder of the Children's Aid Society of New York City. Shortly after graduating from Yale, he became interested in prisoners on Blackwell's Island. A devout man, he was greatly depressed at the misery he saw in the great city of New York. He journeyed to England in 1850 and visited the Ragged Schools, institutions for neglected children. Upon his return, he plunged into missionary work, focusing his attention on the "sin and misery" he witnessed around old Five Points and the other great slum districts of New York. As Henry W. Thurston writes:

> Every day he saw schoolless, churchless, homeless children throng the streets, alleys and wharves of the great city, engaged in paper sell-

---

[51] Hastings Hart, *op. cit.*, article by Roswell C. McCrea, Chapter 11, p. 195.
[52] See Chapter XIII.

ing, begging, rag- and bone-picking, and thieving. Every day these children fought and jostled with each other, with criminal men and women in prison, and with diseased men and women of the almshouse, for the dominant place in the heart of this young man. Contesting for his life's service were also congregations of well-dressed folk sitting quietly in church waiting to listen to his voice as a preacher.[53]

Brace had little difficulty in deciding where his life work lay; he gave it to children.

In 1852, over 300,000 immigrants landed at the port of New York. Brace wrote: "Our poorest streets began to be filled up with a thriftless, beggared, dissolute population. The poor and the idle of a street grew worse for having poor and idle neighbors." [54] The police announced that over 10,000 vagrant children were running loose in the streets, and, even worse, almost 3,000 known thieves, two-thirds of whom were girls between the ages of eight and sixteen. In 1853, it was reported that of 12,000 children in the eleventh ward of the city between five and sixteen years of age, only 7,000 attended public schools and only 2,500 attended Sabbath schools, leaving the vast majority of them without schooling or religious instruction.

The Children's Aid Society was organized by Mr. Brace to cope with these wretched conditions. His program for vagrant children included: (1) boys' religious meetings; (2) industrial schools; (3) workshops; (4) finding places for children to work outside New York; and (5) placing children in family homes in New York. In 1853, the society opened the Newsboys' Lodging House.[55]

Perhaps the most dramatic phase of the work of this society—which really reflected the convictions of Brace—was the migration of thousands of New York's underprivileged children to farms and small towns of the Middle West. Brace appealed to "the farmers and mechanics and manufacturers in the country" to cooperate with him in placing boys. Worthy as the program was, it was merely a variation of the old indenture system, but without the evils of the formal contract. Another criticism of his plan was that it took children from their homes, thus breaking the family ties without attempting to aid or rehabilitate the family unit.

---

[53] *The Dependent Child,* Columbia University Press, New York, 1930, p. 95.
[54] *Ibid.,* p. 97.
[55] See Brace's work, *The Dangerous Classes of New York,* 1880.

In 1854, Brace and his organization began their mass migration of children. A trainload of 138 children, 66 boys and 72 girls, was conveyed to families in Pennsylvania. Each year thereafter the children of New York who had been picked up from the streets were transported out of the city by the hundreds to be placed out in private homes. It is estimated that between 1853 and 1879 the Society sent over 48,000 children to western and southern states.[56] The following letter gives some idea of the hegira to Peoria, Illinois, of 27 children under the direction of the agent, W. C. Van Meter:

Dear Brother Brace: Our journey, though slow, seven days from New York to Peoria, was successful. Twenty-four out of the twenty-seven homeless ones are in good homes. A "mother in Israel," in F—, Indiana, looked at all the children, and fixing her eyes on Elizabeth (the poor girl that nobody would have, because she was so disfigured) said, "This little one needs sympathy more than either of the others. I will take her." I could not ask her to pay for her transportation, and therefore paid it out of my own purse.

John is with Deacon Simms, Tremont, Taswell Co., Ill. Mr. S. is a farmer and a member of the Baptist Church. He is one of the best men in the land. I have long known him. John is happy, and the Deacon delighted. He has one daughter, and now he has a son. He is well off. John has a bright future in prospect.

Charlotte Lord is with Mr. S. S. Stiers, Elgin, Ill., and they are well pleased. Katherine and James Lord were placed in a good home, eight miles from here, in the family of an Episcopal minister. On last Saturday, Katherine became dissatisfied, *without cause*, took James and ran away. [*Italics ours*]

About six o'clock they came to my house, where they will remain until I procure them another place. He paid their expenses out ($32). I refund.

But the best is yet to be told. You remember Nancy T—, whose mother came to your office the day I was there. O, what a dear little one she is. How I love her. She looked so sad as she sat between her father and mother the day I left. How solemn the trust, when those weeping parents gave me their daughter. I promised to be a father to her. None seemed so sad after starting, as she. I wrapped her in my shawl, took her in my arms, talked kindly to her, wiped away her tears, and she slept sweetly. . . . But we had to lose our treasure. Judge

---

[56] Herbert D. Williams, "Foster Homes for Delinquent Children," *Federal Probation*, September 1949, pp. 46–51.

N. R. of this city is one of the noblemen of America. He has one of the finest families I ever knew. . . . The Judge saw Nancy. His heart melted. He took her on his knee. Soon he pressed her to his bosom. The tear was in his eye. He kissed her and asked if she would be his daughter. She answered "Yes." We all cried for joy . . . She is beautifully dressed. She is addressed as "Daughter, sister." [57]

The New York Children's Society sent thousands of children out of the city. Many of them were well treated but hundreds of them were exploited by harsh foster parents. There was little, if any, check-up or follow-up investigation. Brace, in his zeal, was concerned only with getting the children off the crowded metropolitan streets to more sparsely populated areas. His work represents a landmark in child-saving that is worthy of the times in which it was enthusiastically pursued.

Migration of Underprivileged Children to the West.

Nor was Brace's organization the only one that experimented with this method of dealing with underprivileged children. As early as 1828 the manager of the New York House of Refuge made the following entry in his journal: "We saw the eight boys for Ohio start

[57] Thurston, *op. cit.*, pp. 104–105.

in good spirits. . . . It excited considerable warm good feeling to see so many little fellows bound for such a good and suitable place from the house of refuge, among the passengers on board the steamboat." [58] The New England Home for Little Wanderers of Boston also sent trainloads of youngsters to western places. Many years later the eminent Hastings Hart made a study of the children who had been sent to Minnesota by these societies. Henry W. Thurston, formerly of the New York School of Social Work, has written his book around early experiments in child-saving, with much of its emphasis on the work of Brace. He has secured many letters from these children, grown-ups at the time, relating their experiences of an earlier year. This experiment has become an American saga and well worth study by those who are now interested in child care.[59]

There were many critics of Brace's methods. He was accused of sending "criminally minded" youth to the hinterland, but he insisted that this accusation was not justified. Nevertheless, many persons interested in better methods of child care, especially in the care of problem children and outright delinquent youth, saw weaknesses in child-placing methods. For example, in 1863 The Society for the Protection of Destitute Roman Catholic Children was established in New York City. Idle, truant, vicious, or homeless children between seven and fourteen could be committed to this Society by any magistrate or by parents who were concerned with their children's behavior. But here, again, the indenture system reared its ugly head. In the third annual report of this Society, we read that children "were not prepared by previous discipline and education to ensure contentment, obedience and fidelity" to their responsibilities, and "avarice of persons to whom the children were apprenticed caused most of them to be overworked, their education neglected, and the necessary supplies of food and clothing withheld." The report added that three-fourths of those apprenticed out, up to that time, had "become perfectly worthless." [60]

Regardless of what we may think of Charles Loring Brace's methods today, he deserves great credit for dramatizing the problems

---

[58] Homer Folks, *The Care of Destitute, Neglected and Delinquent Children*, Macmillan, New York, 1902, p. 203.

[59] See Thurston's work, *op. cit.*, for Hart's report and these letters.

[60] *Ibid.*, pp. 124–126.

of children during his own day. It must be remembered that there were no child labor laws; that many poor parents were tempted to exploit their children in order to augment their own meager income; that the public school system was none too strong; and that few scientific methods had been established in the field of human behavior. The twentieth century has been labeled the "century of the child," but we cannot be too critical of the inept experimentation that characterized the last century.

A few words at this point are in order regarding the establishment of newsboys' retreats, since they had as their objective the sheltering of thousands of street urchins in our big cities. The latter part of the nineteenth century saw the heyday of these havens. Child labor laws were so undeveloped or unenforceable that vast armies of impoverished youth literally lived in the streets and subways of New York and other large cities. We are all familiar with the stories of Horatio Alger. Alger (1834–1899), a graduate of Harvard and a Unitarian minister, took up his lodgings in the Newsboys' Home established by Brace in 1854. The shy, somewhat frustrated Alger was distressed at the exploitation of New York City's youth by hardhearted and ignorant *padrones*. The *padrone* system was a form of semi-slavery whereby immigrant boys were enticed to America by older, already established immigrants, who saw in the practice a means of getting rich by working their boys in shoe-shine parlors, fruit stands, and other places of business. Since the *padrones* kept their charges in ignorance by shielding them from customers, the children were unable to learn the English language or even that they were being exploited.

The Newsboys' Lodging House became a mecca for boys of the streets, and, as victims of the *padrone* system began to see the light, they too flocked to this haven. It was run by Charles O'Connor, a man of keen insight. He insisted that his boys go to night school, take a weekly bath, and conduct themselves in a respectable manner. Looking about for literature in which his boys might be interested, he ran across a book by one Horatio Alger—its title, *Ragged Dick*—then running serially in *Student and Schoolmate*. The story appealed to him as the type of literature that might inspire his boys to better things. He looked up the author and asked him to come to the Lodging House to live. Alger accepted, and for years he remained there grinding out his famous stories of New York City's street urchins. He wrote over three hundred stories, most of them taking the same pattern of "poor boy makes good." Although Alger was zealously concerned with the plight of the poor boy, the boy whose home was the city's streets, or the boy who was victimized by a *padrone* or some other unscrupulous employer, the truth is that his books are blamed by many child welfare authorities for causing more boys to run away from home than for the good he thought he was doing.[61] There is no doubt that Horatio Alger had good intentions.

A Newsboys' Lodging House.

He was both admired and ridiculed by the boys he helped. He was very naive and was rarely able to detect an imposition. He lent the boys money and was seldom repaid. The story of his life is of historic interest, and the lesson that may be drawn from his life is that well-meaning philanthropists need insight in order to deal with neglected or delinquent youth.

8. THE DEVELOPMENT OF OTHER FACILITIES FOR SALVAGING CHILDREN

Today, as we survey the many societies and agencies dealing with the neglected, destitute, and delinquent child, we are likely to be-

---

[61] See Herbert R. Mayes, *Alger, A Biography Without a Hero*, Macy-Masius, New York, 1928, p. 103.

come bewildered. Both publicly and privately, millions of dollars are spent annually in coping with the forces of neglect and greed that give little thought to the citizens of tomorrow. Although many of these organizations are not specifically concerned with delinquency, they are all dedicated to the task of dealing with the problems of childhood—thwarted childhood. Aside from those already mentioned, we shall enumerate some of the other *firsts*, the successors of which we find operating in the field today:

1854—First Lodging House for Newsboys opened in New York City by Charles Loring Brace.

1868—Establishment of the first directed public playground by the Old South Church at Boston (the Playground Association of America was not founded until 1906).

1869—Establishment of a system of visitation of delinquent children in family homes, by the state of Massachusetts; this called for the appointment of a visitation committee for the oversight of indentured children, who, at the time, numbered over one thousand in that state.

1869—Organization of the "Salem Fraternity" at Salem, Massachusetts, the first boys' club in America.

1870—Establishment of separate courts for children in Massachusetts—the seed of the later juvenile court.

1872—Organization of the National Conference on Charities and Correction.

1873—Enactment of Michigan law excluding children from almshouses, the first effective law of its kind.

1883—Establishment of the National Florence Crittenden Mission for unmarried mothers and their infants.

1887—Establishment of the Neighborhood Guild in New York City, the first settlement house in this country.

1890—Organization of Child Study Association.

1895—Founding of the George Junior Republic at Freeville, New York.

1898—Establishment of the New York School of Philanthropy for training of workers in social work.

1898—Organization of the Catholic Home Bureau in New York City, first Roman Catholic society for placing children in family homes.

1899—Establishment of first juvenile court in Illinois.

1901—Enactment in Colorado of a law directed against parents or other persons contributing to the delinquency of a child.

1904—Organization of the National Child Labor Committee for the reformation of abuses connected with the employment of children.

1912—Establishment of the United States Children's Bureau.

1915—Organization of the Child Welfare League of America in Baltimore (it was incorporated in 1928); its function was to develop standards of care and protection of children in agencies and institutions.

9. AN EVALUATION OF CHILD-SAVING AGENCIES

In evaluating the older techniques and methods of dealing with any social problem, we must be careful to appraise them in terms of the social philosophy of their times. Those interested in coping with thwarted childhood were sincere and forthright. In addition, they were essentially religious. Their concepts of human behavior were colored by the doctrine of free will, which, up to more recently, has been almost universally accepted by churchmen and laymen alike. These early reformers had only a superficial knowledge of causation. The obvious factors were blamed for delinquency. Children went astray either through their parents' neglect, the grog shop, bad companions, or sheer perversity.

The dependent or delinquent child was to be "saved from the burning." He was to be treated sympathetically, but he was also to be handled with firmness. Inculcation of the homely virtues was of supreme importance, and it was assumed that any child, if he wished, could become a model young citizen. It mattered very little that he lacked the capacities to make an abrupt adjustment to some new discipline. If he made a false slip from grace, he was punished; if he persisted in his nonconformist tendencies, he was punished more severely. The existence of free will in the child was excuse enough to exact punishment. An example of this attitude was the stated purpose of the New York House of Refuge, to house children of tender years "under a course of discipline *severe* and *unchanging* but alike calculated to *subdue* and *conciliate*."

The child-saving institutions and agencies gradually became intrenched. Accepted as they were by public opinion, they proceeded on their way unchallenged. A child handled by one of them was considered by the public as "bad" or "wicked" and, of course, a negative influence on other children. It meant little that such a youngster became immediately stigmatized, that he received a scar he would never be able to eradicate from his memory and that would affect his total personality. On the contrary, he was constantly reminded that he was quite fortunate in being "saved" from a life of shame or of crime. He was lectured on the homely virtues; he was immersed in religious instruction; he was coerced into a severe, monotonous routine of physical labor; his rising and retiring hours were excessively early; his recreation was routinized and often very dull; in short, his life was apparently planned to subdue his spirit.

Another very obvious trend that marked the child-saving agencies and institutions was that their administrative officers became suspicious of the public. They were quite sure of their programs and refused to tolerate any criticism. They withdrew from the public gaze, colored their annual reports with enthusiastic and maudlin phrases, and, in many particulars, became a law unto themselves.

Take, for example, the attitude of the management of the New York Society for the Prevention of Cruelty to Children, organized in 1875. This organization was a private, non-profit corporation and held a sort of semi-official status. The state Department of Welfare had the power of visitation, yet its recommendations were not mandatory. In 1936, testimony showed that the Society's agents were incompetent, that the affairs of the organization were improperly administered, and that its methods were antiquated. The commissioner of accounts of New York City stated that its law enforcement work was "unsatisfactory and of poor calibre." [62]

Yet these agencies must be given much of the credit for pressing for legislation that clipped the wings of those who would exploit children in sweat shops and other forms of arduous and meaningless labor, that penalized landlords for excessive rentals or for refusing to renovate their old rookeries where the poor were forced to dwell, and that looked after the welfare of children generally.

---

[62] See Edwin J. Lukas, "Fashions in Crime Prevention," *Yearbook*, N.P.P.A., 1946, pp. 19–39.

Chapter III

THE BIOLOGICAL APPROACH
TO DELINQUENT BEHAVIOR

1. FEEBLEMINDEDNESS AND DELINQUENCY

THE POPULAR AND WIDESPREAD NOTION that a high correlation exists between feeblemindedness and delinquency bears close examination in any work dealing with juvenile delinquency. In fact, on this phase of the subject many oldwives' tales are current that will not down, even among intelligent people. Even college graduates who have actually taken courses in sociology and psychology often go forth to add to the confusion by enunciating half-truths and pure fictions concerning mental intelligence and delinquency. It seems, therefore, highly important that we explore our knowledge concerning this relationship.

The fact that persons differ in mental capacity is so obvious and is demonstrated in so many ways that it would seem that observers must have been aware of it for centuries. But such was not the case. Until comparatively recent times, much confusion has existed in distinguishing between insanity or mental disease and feeblemindedness or mental deficiency. In fact, a great deal of uncertainty exists even today, since, in many cases, there is no clear-cut distinction.

As a matter of record, it was the famous French alienist, Jean Esquirol (1772–1840), who made this differentiation for the first time, in 1838. On this side of the Atlantic, the lesser-known Isaac Ray, a contemporary of Esquirol, followed in his footsteps. Ray first posed the question of whether we can impute crime to one who knows nothing regarding intent or consequence of injury. The problem of moral responsibility of the feebleminded is still unsettled in legal circles, but it is definitely closed in medical science and psychology. Not until 1848 were the mentally retarded patients segregated or placed in a separate wing apart from the mentally diseased at the Perkins Institute in Massachusetts.

Not until the latter part of the nineteenth century and the first two decades of the twentieth was much attention focused on the problem of the feebleminded. In time, more refined and scientific analyses emerged from fundamental postulates enunciated in pioneer days. Many mistaken ideas about the relationship between the mentally deficient and delinquency and crime came either from erroneous statements made by the earlier students of the problem or from misinterpretations of their sounder findings by subsequent scholars. Carl Murchison, pondering on the origin of the notion that criminals are feebleminded, came to the conclusion that it had its origin in religious tradition, literary and dramatic license and speculative hypotheses.[1] He finds no justification for the thesis whatsoever.

It is important that we touch briefly on the deluge of studies of alleged feebleminded families, many members of which were supposed to be criminal. These studies were the stock in trade of the psychologists and sociologists up to comparatively recent times. In fact, their baneful influences may still be seen in the muddy thinking of thousands of social workers, jurists, and educators when they discuss the problem of delinquency.

The first study of a degenerate family has become a classic. It is *The Jukes* by Richard Dugdale (1841–1883), published in 1877. While making an investigation of county jails in central New York State for the New York Prison Association, Dugdale found several persons belonging to the same family stock, although having different names, who were being held for trial for various offenses. Fascinated with the possibilities of a study of this socially bankrupt family, he devoted considerable time to its unraveling. Immediately on publication, the book was accepted as an important document.

Few persons who have ever gone through high school are ignorant of the story of Max Juke, reputed to have been a good-natured, hard-drinking hunter and trapper of the Finger Lake region of New York State. Everyone knows that he was responsible for siring hundreds of criminals, paupers, prostitutes, feebleminded, and insane, whose

[1] "American White Criminal Intelligence," *Journal of Criminal Law and Criminology*, August 1924, pp. 254–257.

incarceration in jails, prisons, and almshouses cost the taxpayers hundreds of thousands of dollars.

It is needless to describe any of the details of the work, but this much is perhaps of importance: Two of Max Juke's sons married two of six sisters, one of whom Dugdale called Ada but who was known locally as Margaret, "mother of criminals." In 1874, Max's entire progeny amounted to 709 individuals. Of this number, 540 were of Juke blood and 169 were of other strains connected by marriage or illegitimate cohabitation. Of the total: 180, or more than one-quarter, had received pauper care amounting to more than 800 years; 140 were guilty of criminal offenses; 60 were thieves; 7 were murderers; 50 were prostitutes; 40 were infected with venereal disease and had infected 440 known persons; and 30 had been prosecuted on bastardy charges.

The importance of this book is that it set off a long list of similar studies, which, in their aggregate, influenced the thinking of the academic and lay public in such a manner that error and half-truth have been the rule rather than the exception. Dugdale's work was variously interpreted. Professor Arthur Fink has this to say about the reception of the work:

> Unread, misread, or wilfully distorted, it has been used by hereditarians and environmentalists alike to assert and supposedly to prove their respective positions. . . . At the beginning of his study, Dugdale admitted that heredity and environment were the two limits within which the whole question of crime, its origin, its nature, and its treatment, was contained. His ideal objective, he maintained, was to determine how much crime resulted from heredity and how much from environment.[2]

We now know that neither Richard Dugdale nor any of the other investigators who followed in his footsteps solved that riddle. In 1888, the Rev. Oscar McCullough produced *The Tribe of Ishmael*, a study in "social degradation," and in 1897 F. W. Blackmar wrote *The Smoky Pilgrims*. These two works were avowedly concerned with the deteriorating effects of an unfavorable environment and only incidentally concerned with crime or the inheritance of criminal tendencies. Many of these studies were more or less moral in tone

---

[2] Arthur E. Fink, *Causes of Crime*, University of Pennsylvania Press, Philadelphia, 1938, pp. 179–182.

and gave the impression that feeblemindedness in a family strain would produce all types of human misery, such as delinquency, crime, alcoholism, prostitution, insanity, and shiftlessness.

After the turn of the century, a number of other studies were produced which either hinted at the relationship between feeblemindedness and crime or delinquency, or suggested measures to eliminate undesirable stocks before they exacted such a financial toll upon society.[3]

Perhaps the most significant of all these studies was *The Kallikaks*, by the distinguished psychologist, Henry H. Goddard. At the training school at Vineland, New Jersey, Dr. Goddard noted the frequency with which a certain name appeared in his clinical records. Curious, he began to work out the genealogy of this particular name, which, at the moment, was borne by a woman in the state institution for the feebleminded. Goddard called this family Kallikak. The word is derived from two Greek adjectives, *kalos* meaning "beautiful" or "fine," and *kakos* meaning "bad."

The field worker who did the investigating in this study "traced" the family strain back to a Revolutionary War soldier named Martin. He presumably had had sexual relations with a "feebleminded" and nameless barmaid. The son of this illicit union left a long line— mostly socially and mentally deficient. Of the group of 480, Goddard opined that 143 were feebleminded and only 46 were mentally normal. Of the others, 36 were illegitimate; 33 were immoral, mostly prostitutes; 24 were confirmed alcoholics; and others, in small numbers, were definite social liabilities. For the most part, this degenerate breed married into other families of their own type. Out of 1,146 individuals resulting from these unions, 262 were considered by Dr. Goddard as feebleminded. It is significant to note, however, that of the 480 members studied by the investigators, only 3 were ever classified as criminal.

But there is a bright side to this amazing story. The Revolutionary soldier, after doing his duty for his country, returned home and married a presumably normal girl, a member of a biologically good

---

[3] Among these studies were: Henry H. Goddard, *The Kallikaks*, 1912; Charles B. Davenport and Florence H. Danielson, *The Hill Folk*, 1912; Arthur H. Estabrook and Charles B. Davenport, *The Nam Family*, 1912; Elizabeth S. Kite, *The Pineys*, 1913; and Mary S. Kostir, *The Family of Sam Sixty*, 1916.

family, and together they raised several children. The descendants of this happy union were strong, healthy individuals who all married into good families and made real contributions to the state as lawyers, jurists, educators, physicians, and other conventionally reputable, good, and respectable citizens.

Probably the real importance of this study was that its author questioned the hereditary nature of crime (and delinquency, for that is what interests us here) and specifically stated that criminals were *made*, not born. This assertion in itself is significant. He went further, however, and contended that the best material out of which criminals are made is the feebleminded. He even suggested that the "born criminal" of the great Italian anthropologist-physician, Cesare Lombroso, might have been feebleminded. We cannot discuss Lombroso's work here, but it is worthy of mention. While the Italian physician was particularly interested in adult criminals, his thesis of a specific criminal type—one bearing certain anatomical stigmata by which he could be identified as *the* "born criminal"—certainly applied to children as well. Such persons were doomed to lead a life of crime, since nature had cruelly marked them with these stigmata. There have been rumblings of this thesis for almost a century, and even today Lombroso's followers, most of whom are in South America and Continental Europe and follow the "constitutional school" of criminality, are much more concerned with heredity as a cause of crime than with environmental influences.

In Professor Goddard's later work, *Feeblemindedness: Its Causes and Consequences* (1914), he suggested that the criminal type is really a species of feebleminded, misunderstood to such a degree that he is driven into crime, for which he is "fitted by nature." [4]

In recent years, considerable criticism has emerged of the methods employed in the gathering of data for the studies mentioned above. Merely because these studies are still being discussed in some colleges without any qualifications whatsoever, we append here two citations of criticism which are not unusual. The reader is referred to Dr. Abraham Myerson's *The Inheritance of Mental Diseases* [5] for an analysis of the work done by the field workers in the *Kallikak* study,

---

[4] One should read Goddard's *Criminal Imbecile*, Macmillan, New York, 1915, for an analysis of the legal dilemma posed by the feebleminded delinquent.

[5] Williams & Wilkins, Baltimore, 1925, pp. 78–79.

and to Dr. Samuel J. Holmes' *The Trend of the Race* [6] for a criticsim of the work done in the study of *The Hill Folk*. Most of this criticism revolves around the apparent glibness with which the investigator assumes, often without a question of doubt, that the case is feebleminded. In many instances, the person being investigated had been dead for a long time, yet he is labeled feebleminded simply because someone who remembered him thought he was mentally deficient.

However important this criticism is, it is even more significant to our particular interest that a certain assumption grew out of these studies—namely, that a high correlation exists between feeblemindedness and delinquency. As early as 1890, Isaac N. Kerlin, superintendent of the training school for the mentally defective at Elwyn, Pennsylvania, contended that the "moral imbecile" was one who "seemed to act without relation to the accepted moral values because of mental weakness." [7] Kerlin also insisted that it was from such "degenerate stock"—the feebleminded—that the delinquent, or criminal, was drawn. In 1908, Dr. Walter E. Fernald stated that the high-grade imbecile (Goddard's *moron*, for it was he who coined the now shopworn word to designate the high-grade imbecile) was a potential criminal, needing only the proper environment to develop his delinquent tendencies. [8]

By 1912, Goddard had pointed out in his work that 25 per cent of the adult criminals were feebleminded, and two years later he was sure that the percentage was as high as 50. He quotes from a study made by Dr. Olga Bridgman that in the institution for delinquent girls at Geneva, Illinois, the percentage of feebleminded was as high as 89. Other high percentages were found at the Bedford Reformatory in New York state; the Lancaster, Massachusetts, school for delinquent girls; the New Jersey State Home for girls at Trenton; and at three reformatories in Virginia—all over 70 per cent. [9]

Nor were Americans the only ones to arrive at such conclusions. From England, Dr. Charles Goring, in his *The English Convict* (1913), called the feebleminded, "unteachable, unemployable, a

---

[6] Harcourt, Brace, New York, 1921, pp. 33–34.

[7] Arthur E. Fink, *op. cit.*, p. 213.

[8] *Ibid.*, p. 215.

[9] Goddard, *Feeblemindedness: Its Causes and Consequences*, Macmillan, New York, 1914, p. 9.

nuisance to themselves and everyone else. The feebleminded," he continued, "could hardly fail, in the long run . . . to swell disproportionately the criminal ranks." [10] Others from abroad had much the same to say. Tredgold, prominent British authority on amentia, placed mental defect high in the causes of delinquency and crime. He quotes from a study by H. W. Gruhle of 105 youths in the reformatory at Fleningen, in Baden, that unwholesome environment was the chief factor in only 18 per cent of the cases, whereas in 82 per cent an inborn disposition was solely or chiefly responsible for the delinquency. In 46 per cent, both factors operated in molding the individual's behavior.[11]

Since the pioneering days of Goddard, Tredgold, and others, critical investigation has almost completely upset their views. It has been shown, for example, that perhaps not more than one-fourth to one-half of feeblemindedness is hereditary. The remainder is due to physical disease, bodily injuries, malnutrition, and other unfortunate early circumstances to which the child has been subjected. This evidence demonstrates that if every living feebleminded person were prevented from breeding through segregation or sterilization, the mentally defective could not possibly be eliminated. We shall defer the question of sterilization until later.

In a more recent article, Dr. Lloyd Yepsen makes this statement about the hereditability of feeblemindedness:

We no longer believe that almost all mentally deficient persons are so because of heredity or neuropathic ancestry. We are aware that physical modifications may account for almost one-half of the subnormal individuals. These, generally, are offspring of perfectly normal parents and may be characterized as the "seconds" of the human race.

He then lists the occupations of fathers of 81 children under the ages of five awaiting admission to a unit for babies in an institution for the mentally deficient. His list is as follows: [12]

---

[10] Stationery Office, London, see p. 262. See also, Maurice Parmelee, *Criminology*, Macmillan, New York, 1918, Chapter XI, "The Criminal Ament," for a discussion of the relationship between criminality and feeblemindedness.

[11] Quoted by A. F. Tredgold, *Mental Deficiency*, William Wood & Co., New York, 2nd ed., 1914, p. 320.

[12] "Where We Stand at Present in Care of Mentally Deficient," *Welfare Reporter*, New Jersey Department of Institutions and Agencies, August 1949, p. 5.

	Number	Percentage
Professional	16	20
Business (employed)	23	29
Business (self-employed)	3	4
Skilled labor	17	21
Semi-skilled labor	6	7
Unskilled	7	5
Undetermined	9	11

Scientific authority maintains that the feebleminded are not inherently or necessarily vicious or delinquent. But since the feebleminded are unusually susceptible to suggestion, they are naturally more easily influenced than normal types by either good or evil surroundings. If they are properly protected and directed, it is actually easier to keep them law-abiding and moral than it is to produce and maintain such behavior in normal types. On the other hand, if they are exposed to conditions making for crime or vice, they are more likely than the normal to fall into evil ways.

The term feebleminded is an unfortunate one, but since it has such general usage it is difficult to assay the subject of the mentally defective without using it. The reader should therefore understand that it is employed only as a general term and not in a scientific sense. The idiots and imbeciles do not concern us in this connection, since few delinquents come from these lower types. If we cannot recommend euthanasia—painless extermination—for these groups, certainly segregation is the only panacea so far as society is concerned.

Many delinquents, when they run afoul of the law, seem to show signs of mental defect when they are tested. But on closer examination they reveal symptoms of mental confusion, and, consequently, are subjects of a psychiatric examination. Such individuals come under a category other than that of mental defectives, and we shall discuss them in another connection.[13]

The press, and reports of crime prevention agencies, courts, and other official bodies have publicized the idea that most delinquents are retarded mentally, that feeblemindedness is the major problem in their antisocial behavior. Without minimizing this serious allegation whatsoever, it is only fair to state that a very large percentage of delinquent youth is not feebleminded at all, that a very large portion is normal mentally or, as hinted above, emotionally confused

---

[13] See Chapters VII and XIV.

or unstable. A look at some of the more recognized studies will help us understand this point.

The pioneer, Dr. William Healy, made a study of 4,000 cases of habitual juvenile delinquents in Chicago and Boston. He discovered that 72.5 per cent were mentally normal and that only 13.5 per cent were feebleminded. Although we cannot overlook the statement Healy made that "the feebleminded appear among serious delinquents from five to ten times more frequently than in the general population," [14] we must take cognizance of the fact that the feebleminded are greatly outnumbered by the mentally normal. The common notion, once so prevalent even in psychological circles—as we pointed out above—that the feebleminded are "naturally" delinquent, is absurd. Now let us examine Dr. Healy's and Dr. Bronner's later study, *Treatment and What Happened Afterward*, a revealing and authoritative work.[15]

Of one set of 400 cases studied by the Healy clinic, 207 were classed as "personality and behavior problems." None of these particular children was sent to the clinic by the court, but all represented problems of delinquency, or, at least, were problems either in the home or in the school, or to social agencies that came into contact with them. These children, of course, are not true delinquents as we have defined the term earlier, but they do represent the stuff out of which overt delinquency stems. Here is a table of the intelligence rating of all the 400 cases, showing, also, the category in which they were placed:

INTELLIGENCE LEVELS

Intelligence Quotients	Behavior and Personality Problems [a]	Noncourt Delinquents	Court Delinquents	Total
70–79	3 (1.5%)	7 (5%)	5 (9%)	15 (3.75%)
80–89	21	15	7	43
90–109	92	72	35	199
110 plus	91 (44%)	43 (31%)	9 (16%)	143 (35.75%)
Total	207	137	56	

[a] For analysis of the "Behavior and Personality Problem" cases, see pp. 602–603.

Let us look at the noncourt cases. They had committed a wide variety of offenses or had at one time or another been guilty of anti-

---

[14] *Delinquents and Criminals*, Macmillan, New York, 1928, p. 151.
[15] Judge Baker Guidance Center, Boston, 1939.

social conduct. The more serious of these delinquencies, and their frequency, were as follows: "long record of stealing," 36; larceny, 9; breaking and entering and larceny, 4; auto stealing, 3; serious truancy, 8; excessive truancy, 3; malicious fire-setting, 7; forgery, 1; serious sexual misconduct, heterosexual, homosexual, exhibitionism, 12; blackmail, 1; and "extreme waywardness," 1. The court cases, numbering 56, had committed delinquencies similar to those of the noncourt cases.

Assuming that the mental tests were valid, and there is no reason to believe otherwise, we can see from the table above that few of the 400 cases were seriously retarded. Healy himself states that only two of the cases were morons.

A study by Weiss and Sampliner of 189 adolescents (16 to 21) who were first offenders reveals that the distribution of intelligence follows the distribution in the population.[16] As L. G. Lowrey puts it: "Feeblemindedness is not the universal factor in delinquency it was once thought to be. Even inferior intelligence, broadly conceived, cannot be considered to be an outstanding feature of the personality of delinquents." [17]

Many studies in the past that dealt with adult criminals, who were usually tested in prisons, show conclusively that the intelligence of these criminals compares favorably with the intelligence of the general population.[18] And these are the actual convicts—the ones who were caught and convicted and, therefore, the ones who were not too adept. Many believe that the more intelligent criminals are seldom brought to book. Such persons would argue that our criminal population is probably above the average in intelligence.

Now, so far as the mental astuteness of juvenile delinquents is concerned, it would seem that many of the brighter children are

---

[16] H. R. Weiss and R. Sampliner, "A Study of Adolescent Felony Offenders," *Journal of Criminal Law and Criminology*, March–April 1944, pp. 377–391.

[17] *Delinquent and Criminal Personalities in Personality and the Behavior Disorders*, ed. J. McV. Hunt, Ronald Press, New York, 1944, Vol. II, p. 808.

[18] Carl Murchison, "American White Criminal Intelligence," *Journal of Criminal Law and Criminology*, August–November 1924, pp. 239–317, 435–494; E. A. Doll, "The Comparative Intelligence of Prisoners," *ibid.*, August 1920, pp. 191–197; L. D. Zelany, "Feeblemindedness and Criminal Conduct," *American Journal of Sociology*, Vol. 38, 1932–1933, pp. 564–576; and Simon H. Tulchin, *Intelligence and Crime*, University of Chicago Press, 1939.

saved from an institutional experience and so are not included in studies of reform school populations. Thus, when it is maintained that delinquents are below average in intelligence simply because of the scores made by inmates of the schools, we can readily see that these groups are a selected percentage of the total number of children apprehended for delinquent acts. The brighter children are saved from incarceration and, quite frequently, from detention, arraignment, and formal apprehension.

We shall close this section with a few words regarding sterilization, since it is so frequently recommended as a panacea for almost everything, notably delinquency and crime. As a result of the early alarm, mentioned above, regarding the alleged role of the feeble-minded in committing delinquencies and crimes, a wave of near hysteria broke out for both sterilization and emasculation as a check in cutting down the number of criminals and the potentially dangerous.[19]

Sterilization, known as vasectomy in males and salpingectomy in females, was first performed in this country by Dr. Harry C. Sharp as early as 1899 among inmates of the old Jeffersonville, Indiana, Reformatory. Sharp performed the operation many years before it was considered legal. The first eugenic sterilization law was introduced in the state of Michigan in 1897, but it failed to pass. Pennsylvania passed a law, but it was vetoed by the governor. The first actual law to get on the statute books was passed by Indiana in 1907. Altogether, some thirty states have passed such laws. They have run the gantlet of the courts, which have declared invalid some of the acts that have been introduced and passed. The issue was carried to the United States Supreme Court back in 1927 in order to test the constitutionality of the Virginia law. The Court upheld the statute, with Justice Oliver Wendell Holmes making his famous laconic statement: "Three generations of imbeciles are enough." Despite this ruling of the high court of the land, states have been very conservative in enforcing their sterilization laws or in passing new ones. This reluctance is probably due to widespread repugnance to practices that seem to violate human rights. Of course, what is needed most is a sensible and scientific program of education regarding both sterilization and castration of defective individuals.

---

[19] See Fink, *op. cit.*, Chapter IX, for a historical treatment of this subject.

However, as we hinted above, it is not possible to eliminate the feebleminded by sterilization, regardless of how much we may wish to do so. Professor H. S. Jennings, eminent biologist, states that, since only half of the feebleminded are thus by heredity, preventing all propagation among the hereditary feebleminded in a given generation would reduce the number of the total who are mentally defective by only about 11 per cent, and further prevention of propagation would have little further effect in keeping the number down to that already reached.[20] Professor Samuel J. Holmes calculates that to get rid of the larger part of our hereditary defectives it would be necessary to sterilize the lowest 10 per cent of the total population, that is, about 15,000,000.[21]

Furthermore, sterilization as applied to the criminal population has no practical significance as a punitive device or as a means of reducing the number of delinquents, since the thirty states now having sterilization laws on their statute books have not had the courage of their convictions. In all the years that these laws have been applicable, less than 50,000 defectives have been subjected to sterilization, and most of these have been in California. In appraising sterilization as a form of over-all social policy, one is tempted to ask the knotty question: "Who will sterilize whom?"

Emasculation, or castration, need not concern us, since no one has yet seriously suggested this drastic procedure for any persons under the age of full physical maturity. But the practice is carried out in Denmark and Holland, for example, on adult sex offenders and has met with considerable approval. Dr. G. K. Stürup, superintendent of the prison-hospital at Herstedvester in Denmark, is an enthusiastic advocate of castration, and maintains that it is the most effective way of eliminating the dangerous sex offender. It will be a long time, we feel sure, before this method will find enthusiastic endorsement in the United States, despite any of the points in its favor.

Few persons interested in the future of our society will object to a carefully thought-out program of eugenics. Such a long-range

---

[20] In his article on "Eugenics" in the *Encyclopedia of the Social Sciences*, Vol. V, p. 619.

[21] *The Eugenics Predicament*, Harcourt, Brace, New York, 1933, p. 161. For an analysis of the dilemma of the eugenist, the reader is referred to Leslie C. Dunn and Theodosius Dobzhansky, *Heredity, Race and Society*, Mentor Books, New York, 1946.

program should be as much concerned with encouraging the higher intellectual types to propagate—perhaps through subsidies—as with the prevention of the unfit to bring children into the world. The problem is one of social engineering that calls for courage and a strict adherence to democratic principles. Sterilization should never be introduced as a punitive device, but as a policy that has for its ultimate goal the elimination of those who are intellectually incapable of education for citizenship.[22]

2. THE ENDOCRINE GLANDS AND BODY-BUILD

In an analysis of the biological approach to delinquent behavior, the claims of some endocrinologists must be cited and appraised. We say "some," since a fringe of the endocrine cult has been most zealous in emphasizing this field in explaining delinquent behavior. And this emphasis is not peculiar to North America; in fact, one of the most important causes of delinquency and criminal behavior in South America is supposed to be the malfunctioning of the ductless glands.

The impressive literature and the overzealous claims of the endocrinologists make the layman feel that much has been accomplished in reducing behavior problems to the malfunctioning of glands. First, let us present an example or two of the exaggerated claims of one or two writers who espouse this cause. M. G. Schlapp, writing in the *Journal of Heredity* some years ago, states: "It would not surprise the writer if investigations were to reveal that a third of all present convicts were sufferers from emotional instability, which is to say gland or toxic disturbance. This does not include feeble-minded or insane people." [23] The same Schlapp, together with his collaborator, E. H. Smith, in their amazing work, *The New Criminology*, describe the thief and the murderer in glandular terms. For example, the "man capable of murder is disturbed in his glands, cells and nerve centers" and "not until he has consummated his crime does the emotional strain and excitement abate." [24]

There can be no doubt that the glands secrete at a lively rate when a person is on the verge of committing a crime, especially if

---

[22] See a positive plea for a careful policy of sterilization by Dr. Justin Fuller, "Diagnosis and Treatment of Mentally Abnormal Offenders," *California Youth Authority Quarterly*, Vol. 2, No. 2, Summer 1949.

[23] "Behavior and Gland Disease," Vol. XV, 1924, p. 11.

[24] Liveright, New York, 1928, p. 230.

he is not a professional criminal. But then it is quite possible that anyone under an unusual strain of any sort, such as participating in an athletic match or even watching one from the sidelines, or suddenly being precipitated into a crisis where heroism is called for, will undergo certain glandular reactions similar to those described by the authors mentioned. There is reason to believe that delinquents and criminals suffer no more from glandular dysfunctioning than does the general population.

Dr. William Healy has the following to say on this subject: "Conservative scientific endocrinologists who have undertaken very careful and prolonged special examinations of offenders for us, account in their reports for very little indeed of the antisocial behavior, and in spite of the much-advertised and much-used extracts of glands, offer very few suggestions for treatment." [25]

Professor M. F. Ashley-Montagu, eminent anthropologist and anatomist, has this to say about the subject of endocrinology and delinquency:

> I should venture the opinion that not one of the reports on the alleged relation between glandular dysfunctioning and criminality has been carried out in a scientific manner, and that all such reports are glaring examples of the fallacy of *false cause*. . . . The fact is that as far as the endocrine system and its relation to personality behavior are concerned, we are still completely in a world of the unknown.[26]

In fact, Professor R. G. Hoskins, long a leader in the field of endocrinology, states that "before psychology, sociology, and criminology can be convincingly rewritten as merely special aspects of endocrinology, many more facts than are now available will have to be collected and integrated." [27]

It is not the purpose here to discount the excellent and even startling work that has been done in relieving certain tensions and discomforts of persons suffering from a glandular imbalance. The alert schoolteacher or parent may be suspicious of such imbalance in their

[25] *Human Biology and Racial Welfare,* Edmund B. Cowley, ed., P. B. Hoeber, New York, 1930, Chapter XVI, pp. 399–400.

[26] "The Biologist Looks at Crime," *The Annals,* September 1941, p. 55.

[27] Quoted by Ashley-Montagu, *idem.* One of the best nontechnical books on modern endocrinology is by Dr. Hoskins, *The Tides of Life,* Norton, New York, 1933.

children and may call on their school or private physician for advice. Glandular treatment often clears up such atypical behavior problems. Our point in this discussion is that the delinquent suffers no more from such dysfunctioning than do members of the general population, and that such anomalous physical tendencies need not necessarily lead to overt delinquency or, for that matter, incipient incorrigibility.

Going far beyond the realm of "the glands of destiny" or "the chemistry of the soul," dramatic terms sometimes applied to endocrinology, is the so-called "body-build" concept as it is applied to the behavior of the individual. Following the earlier work of Ernest Kretschmer, Professor William H. Sheldon and his associates at Harvard University, in laying the basis for the field of constitutional physiology, contend that all persons may be roughly grouped into three categories, by which their personalities as well as their potentialities can be predicted. These groups are: (1) endomorphic—involving a soft roundness throughout the various reaches of the body; short, tapering limbs; small bones; soft, smooth velvety skin; (2) mesomorphic—with a relative predominance of muscle, bone, and connective tissue; large and well-muscled trunk; heavy chest, wrists, and hands; and (3) ectomorphic—characterized by linearity; fragility and delicacy of body; small, delicate bones; droopy shoulders and prominent ribs; small face; sharp nose; fine hair.

These three types have their accompanying component temperaments, according to Professor Sheldon: (1) viscerotonic, characterized by general relaxation and appearance of comfort; (2) somotonic, marking the active, dynamic person given to talking noisily and asserting himself; and (3) cerebrotonic, marking the "introvert," whose life history usually shows allergies, skin troubles, insomnia, and who usually shrinks from crowds.[28]

Although these authors are, at least in this earlier work, quite cautious in stating that "body build" is an important factor in delinquent behavior, they do state "that the physique as a whole consists of a patterned organization of elemental components which all together produce the observed aspects of the individual personality." [29]

---

[28] W. H. Sheldon, S. S. Stevens, and W. B. Tucker, *The Varieties of Human Physique*, Harper, New York, 1940.

[29] *Ibid.*, p. 232. See also their later work, *The Varieties of Temperament*, Harper, New York, 1942.

A more recent work by Sheldon and some of his associates has attempted to correlate physical types with delinquent behavior and thus brings out into the open the conflict between the environmentalists and the followers of the constitutional school. The thesis of this 800-page book may be summed up in the following words: "Where essential inadequacy is present the inadequacy is well reflected in the observable structure of the organism." [30] The study follows the lives and adventures of 200 young adults who had been referred to the Hayden Goodwill Inn, a South Boston social center, by several Boston agencies. The period covered the years between 1939 and 1946. The authors' thesis is that behavior is a function of structure and, with careful measurement and interpretation, fairly accurate predictions concerning the individual's behavior may be made. This latest work by Professor Sheldon, aside from being provocative, is written in a fascinating and witty manner. The writers make some telling thrusts in the direction of psychiatrists.

Although studies such as those by Professor Sheldon and his associates have a real classificatory value in the establishment of types or trait-categories of either a biological or behavioral nature, limitations do exist in the assumption of a causal relationship between the different levels of classification involved—namely, the biological constitution and the personality or behavioral constitution. The existence of such a relationship depends in great part upon statistical correlations between the constructed biological types and the constructed personality types. Personality is a social phenomenon derived from and constructed through the interaction of the individual with others in his social world; thus attitudes and modes of behavior grow out of the cultural medium, in time or place.

Admittedly, the individual interacts socially as a biological organism and it may well be that his unique organic structure is directly related causally with the manner in which he plays his role within his social group. Yet no social group revises its complex of attitudes completely to fit each generational change or each new set of members; in fact, the reverse seems to be true. It is therefore possible that, rather than the constitution of any single member of

---

[30] William H. Sheldon, Emil M. Hartl, and Eugene McDermott, *Varieties of Delinquent Behavior*, Harper, New York, 1949, p. 752.

the group determining his attitudes toward that group, the attitudes of the group, already in existence and solidified, predispose certain types of behavior toward, and consequently from, individuals of that constitution.

If correlations could be shown to exist in a cross-cultural level, irrespective of the attitude-system of any particular society, it then would be quite apparent—even to the sociologist—that a causal relationship does exist between biological constitution and personality. With the evidence as it exists, however, the constitutional approach to social behavior—particularly as it applies to criminality and delinquency—is a rather sterile approach to a dynamic problem. It implies the impossibility of remedies aside from some drastic eugenical program through which the species could be purged of its anti-social biological types. Such a program, while nowhere explicit in the works of the constitutionalists, would seem to be a rather pessimistic one—and, in view of the evidence, a dangerous one.

3. PHYSICAL HANDICAPS AND DELINQUENCY

Many personality problems of children and adolescents are precipitated by physical handicaps. (See Appendix, Cases 1, 12, and 13, pp. 707–709, 729–731, 731–732.) Unusually short stature, skin blemishes, crippled legs and arms, poor eyesight, abnormal obesity, encephalitis, to mention only a few, are likely to cause serious handicaps in children at a period in their lives when status within the group plays an important role. Compensatory behavior often develops in such a manner that forms of delinquency result. But, here again, thousands of children have serious physical handicaps and manage to make an adequate adjustment.

Just how many physically defective delinquent children there actually are is unknown. Authorities disagree on the results of their findings. Professor Mihanovich has gone through the current literature and has found the following:

> On the one hand, Reckless and Smith indicate a comparatively higher prevalence among delinquents than among non-delinquents. Slawson concluded from his studies that among delinquents there was a higher incidence of visual and auditory defects than among non-delinquents; and although 70 per cent of Cyril Burt's delinquents had physical defects, he concluded that the majority of them were normal rather than diseased.

The other side is represented by the Gluecks and by Healy and Bronner. In the Judge Baker Foundation clinic study by the Gluecks, about one-eighth of the delinquents were in poor physical condition. Drawing a conclusion from their own controlled studies, Healy and Bronner found more delinquents in good physical condition than average school children.

It may be safely concluded, in spite of the differences of opinion, that physical shortcomings are primarily accessory and aggravating influences in delinquency.[31]

Apparently no direct correlation seems to exist between defective physique and delinquent behavior. Other factors must be weighted in diagnosing each case under consideration.

Certainly one of the factors involved is the rejection of physically or mentally handicapped children by their parents. Feelings of guilt develop in some parents regarding their children's handicaps; these feelings, in turn, have a bearing on the behavior of such children. If parents were emotionally stable, they could assist their handicapped children in making adequate social adjustments, and delinquency and other forms of frustration would not develop.[32]

The school can do much in dealing with children who are physically handicapped or rejected at home. Medical, dental, and eye clinics established by school boards can begin their work with children at the time of enrollment. Medical and counseling advice can be furnished to parents concerning their children's weaknesses. In cases where the handicap will be a definite part of the child through life, counseling services can be extremely helpful in aiding both child and parent to make the necessary social adjustment.[33]

Physical disfigurement is cited by Banay as a factor in delinquency and crime. He describes the present-day criminal whose career is determined by his appearance as "a shy youngster with a slight physi-

---

[31] Clement S. Mihanovich, "Who Is the Juvenile Delinquent?," *Social Science,* Vol. 22, No. 2, April 1947, p. 146.

[32] See Norman Westlund and Adelaide Z. Palumbo, "Parental Rejection of Crippled Children," *American Journal of Orthopsychiatry,* Vol. 16, 1946, pp. 271–281.

[33] See Harry J. Baker and Virginia Traphagen, *The Diagnosis and Treatment of Behavior-Problem Children,* Macmillan, New York, 1935, for further material on this subject; also E. W. Wallace, "Physical Defects and Juvenile Delinquency," *New York State Journal of Medicine,* Vol. 40, 1940, pp. 1586–1590.

cal defect; a nose that's too big, eyes of two different colors, crossed eyes, acne, a disfiguring birthmark, or a club foot." Such disfigurement often produces a complex in the individual that the world will not accept him. Others, who are equally disfigured, may develop their energies into becoming powerful tycoons. Others may rationalize the situation and renounce all desires for material success. And still others may try to escape the problem by retreating into a psychosis or may develop an antisocial attitude and commit crime.[34]

4. IDENTICAL TWINS AND BEHAVIOR

It has long been popular in certain academic circles to cite the various studies of identical twins to prove that socially approved behavior on the one hand and delinquent behavior on the other are inherited. Although the evidence accumulated both in this country and abroad shows conclusively that in a vast majority of cases identical, or one-egg, twins, are both either delinquent or nondelinquent, this evidence still does not rule out the influences of the social environment.

Twins are of two types: *dizygotic*, where the individuals are developed from different fertilized ova and are usually known as fraternal; and *monozygotic*, where the individuals are developed from the same ovum and are generally known as identical. In fraternal twins, the heredity of each is dissimilar, just as that of ordinary brothers and sisters; in identical twins, the heredities are exactly alike. Thus it is that identical twins make excellent material with which to study the effects of hereditary influences on behavior.

If both twins manifest the same type of behavior—for example, delinquency—their behavior is labeled "concordant." If the twins do not manifest the same type of behavior, it is labeled "discordant." The following table was prepared by Professor Ashley-Montagu; following the table is a discussion of his criticism of the hereditary concept of identical twins and delinquency. The table shows the results of five studies made in this field by students both here and abroad.

---

[34] Ralph S. Banay, "Physical Disfigurement as a Factor in Delinquency and Crime," *Federal Probation*, January–March 1943, pp. 20–24. See also, Hans von Hentig, *The Criminal and His Victim*, Yale University Press, New Haven, 1948, Chapter III, "Physical Traits and Peculiarities."

CRIMINAL BEHAVIOR OF TWINS [35]

Author	One-Egg Twins		Two-Egg Twins	
	Concordant	Discordant	Concordant	Discordant
Lange (1929)	10	3	2	15
Legras (1932)	4	0	0	5
Kranz (1936)	20	12	23	20
Stumpfl (1936)	11	7	7	12
Rosanoff (1934)	25	12	5	23
Total	70	34	37	75
Per cent	67.3	32.7	33.0	67.0

Now, to paraphrase Professor Ashley-Montagu, if the hereditary theory is to be upheld, the proportion of two-egg twins affected should be higher than the proportion of one-egg twins in which only one member is affected. The figures above show, however, that the proportions are almost identical: 33 per cent for two-egg *concordance* and 32.7 per cent for one-egg *discordance*. Ashley-Montagu then quotes from Professor Reckless: "If biological determination of destiny is correct, a discordant monozygotic [one-egg] twin set should be impossible, whereas discordant dizygotic [two-egg] sets should be frequent." The actual findings, however, reveal that one-third of the one-egg pairs of twins investigated were discordant.[36] Ashley-Montagu goes on to say: "The factor of environment has been virtually omitted from these studies of criminal behavior in twins." [37]

No environmentalist would deny that the close association of twins, especially one-egg twins, is due in great degree to their iden-

[35] Ashley-Montagu, in *The Annals, op. cit.*, from J. Lange, *Verbrechen und Schicksal: Studien an kriminellen Zwillingen*, Leipzig, 1929; A. M. Legras, *Psychose en Criminaliteit bij Tweelingen*, Utrecht, 1932 ("Psychose und Kriminalität bei Zwillingen," *Zeitschrift für die gesamte Neurologie und Psychiatrie*, Bd. 144, 1933); H. Kranz, *Lebensschicksal krimineller Zwillinge*, Berlin, 1936; F. Stumpfl, *Die Ursprünge des Verbrechens*, Leipzig, 1936; A. J. Rosanoff, *et al.*, "Criminality and Delinquency in Twins," *Journal of Criminal Law and Criminology*, January–February 1934, pp. 923–924.

[36] *Loc. cit.*, p. 54, The quotation from Reckless is from his *Criminal Behavior*, McGraw-Hill, New York, 1940, p. 186.

[37] *Idem.*

tical heredity. Hence, a vast amount of their social behavior is, for most practical purposes, almost identical. Yet the figures above show many cases of discordant behavior.

There is an impressive literature on twinning; much of it attempts to prove that a delinquency or criminal taint is inherited, or at least that such a tendency is hidden somewhere in the germ plasm. The reader may be interested in examining some of the clinical work in this field.[38]

Quoting Ashley-Montagu further, we see that "there is not the slightest evidence to believe that anyone ever inherits a tendency to commit criminal acts. Crime is a social condition, not a biological condition." [39]

The age-old controversy regarding the respective roles of heredity and environment in precipitating human behavior has not been settled by the investigations of identical twins. Delinquent and criminal behavior is obviously a social phenomenon—that is, crime, and most delinquency, are socially determined. The delinquent finds it difficult to subscribe to the social dicta laid down by conventional and traditional sanctions. True, in many cases this difficulty is due to his constitutional inability to develop inhibitions or to recognize "right" from "wrong," and in these cases society must search for these weaknesses.

This question is dealt with in a statement from Dr. Nathaniel Cantor, who examined the work of the crimino-biologists in Germany some years ago:

The least that may be said of the crimino-biological movement is that it represents an attempt to investigate the criminal personality as a whole; that it focuses attention upon the reciprocal influence and interplay of organic constitution and environment. It recognizes . . . that a causal-statistical analysis of crime will in itself prove unfruitful; that a dynamic cross-section of the offender's personality at the time of the commission of the criminal act must be understood. . . . The

[38] Aside from that included in previous footnotes, see H. H. Newman, *Multiple Human Births: Twins, Triplets, Quadruplets and Quintuplets*, Doubleday, Doran, New York, 1940; H. H. Newman, Frank N. Freeman, and Karl J. Holzinger, *Twins: A Study of Heredity and Environment*, University of Chicago Press, 1937; William B. Tucker, "Is There Evidence of a Physical Basis for Criminal Behavior?," *Journal of Criminal Law and Criminology*, November–December 1940, pp. 427–437.

[39] *Loc. cit.*, p. 35.

crimino-biologists assume that while no one is born predetermined to a life of crime, heredity plays the more important role in determining the *manner* in which one's social experience will be undergone and assimilated. The crimino-biological investigations to date will not stand up under careful scrutiny. Their central assumption has not been scientifically established. Whether it may be validated remains to be seen.[40]

Dr. Ben Karpman, after reviewing the most significant studies on delinquent behavior, is quite dubious concerning the contributions of those who emphasize the constitutional or hereditary aspects of the individual. He contends that the best that can be said of this approach is that we do not know. He continues by stating that certain types of constitutional defect are found in both the delinquent and nondelinquent types, and implies that we must look elsewhere for the real causes of delinquency. Karpman, of course, emphasizes throughout his extensive works that the psychiatric approach offers the most fruitful results in appraising maladjustment and delinquent behavior.[41]

We have reviewed in this chapter some of the biological factors related to delinquent behavior. There is no gainsaying that the complex phases of this approach are important. Yet all must agree that other factors play their part in precipitating children into delinquency. Obviously a synthesis of causes must be constructed in each case if we are to solve this eternal riddle. We in this country have espoused the environmental approach, whereas the Continental and Latin-American countries have almost slavishly followed the biological and anthropological schools. The answer may lie somewhere in between.

[40] "Recent Tendencies in Criminological Research in Germany," *American Sociological Review*, June 1936, p. 415.

[41] *Orthopsychiatry: Retrospect and Prospect, 1923–1948*, American Orthopsychiatric Association, Inc., New York, 1948, p. 169.

Chapter IV

NATIONALITY, RACE, AND DELINQUENCY

1. THE EUROPEAN IMMIGRANT AND HIS CHILDREN

FOR THE FIRST HUNDRED YEARS after the establishment of this country, the Old-American or Anglo-Saxon stock dominated the thinking of politicians, educators, and reformers. This was a land of North European virility and, as such, was destined to be not only great but moral and religious as well.

But, with the impetus given to the immigration of South Europeans after the eighteen-eighties and up to World War I, this country changed from its Anglo-Saxon complexion to an amalgam of many ethnic or national groups. There can be no mistaking this fact—the United States is no longer dominated by the so-called Old-American stock, whether this is for good or bad. Of course, the die-hards who bemoan this development maintain that the newer elements are either directly or indirectly responsible for the social ills of the country. They further contend that a homogeneous population, like that of the Scandinavian countries or Australia and New Zealand, is much more healthful than is a heterogeneous population. This assumption would be difficult to prove and we do not intend to discuss it here. Our thesis is that since ours is a country made up of immigrants from more than a dozen European countries, with a fair number of people from Asia, Latin America, and Africa as well, we can no longer make valid distinctions between the Old-American stock and the immigrant.

Aside from the relatively few immigrants who have come to this country under the quota law, most non-native Americans are well past middle age and their children are practically all native-born. Most of the fears that were expressed during the period between 1880 and 1920 concerning the criminality of the immigrant and his native-born children are no longer of any consequence, even though

107

some justification for such apprehension may have existed at that time. The latest immigrants have become reasonably well assimilated and their children have assumed most, if not all, of the conventional traits usually assigned to Americanism.

This brief introductory statement is made because some day, not in the too distant future, we are going to find that we are, in truth, an amalgam people, that the Old-American stock has vanished, that we have very few immigrants in our midst, and that even second-generation immigrants are disappearing. When that time comes, all the studies of the relationship between immigration and delinquency will have only historical interest. We shall still have studies dealing with race and crime embracing Negroes, Chinese, Japanese and Indians, but Europeans and other segments of the white race will have been merged with the total white population in such a manner that they no longer will be identifiable.

At the outset, it is our purpose in this section to differentiate between nationality and race. Thus we shall first discuss the alleged relationship between delinquency and nationality or ethnic groups; then we shall discuss race and delinquency. In the first part of our discussion, we shall appraise the European immigrant and his children and the Mexican-American group, which represents a large minority in the Southwest and Pacific Coast area; then we shall take up the studies of the Negro and delinquency, primarily, and include a few words about the Chinese, Japanese, and Indian.

Race is a biological concept. The term is used to differentiate mankind on the basis of common hereditary traits possessed on a relatively large scale. Since all large groups possess more or less all of the traits common to mankind, theoretically there are no *pure* races. All peoples have some mixed ancestries.

But aside from this biological concept, we are constantly confronted by a sociological or cultural confusion of the terms *race* and *nationality*. People speak of the Italian or German races, of the Jewish or English races. All these, including the Jews (since the establishment of Israel) are nationality groups. The Jews maintain their identity primarily through their cultural and religious background. So, when we hear that Italian boys commit more delinquencies than others, we cannot say that it is a racial trait, but rather that it results from their culture.

As was pointed out in our introductory statement, the tradition in this country has been to regard immigrant stocks as more delinquent than the older stock which preëmpted this country prior to and immediately following the Revolutionary War. Arguments against the allegedly criminal tendencies of the immigrant stocks were enunciated as early as 1835, certainly along the Eastern Seaboard. Of course we now know that many of these charges were prompted by economic fear, since those already established saw in these impoverished groups a threat to their jobs.

Most of the studies that were made dealt largely with the adult immigrant and crime. They seemed to indicate that a high correlation existed between such immigrants and antisocial behavior. More recent studies seem to dispute this conclusion. It is now apparent that the earlier studies failed to consider certain variable cultural factors, such as language difficulties, culture traits peculiar to specific groups, and lack of understanding of the mores of the United States. In addition, police were prone to arrest immigrants on slight provocation, so naturally their criminal and delinquent rate was increased. But as patrolmen became more accustomed to immigrant types and their habits, formerly considered strange and bad, their behavior was overlooked as a part of the community setting.

Although we are tempted to cite the many studies that have been made of the crime situation as related to the adult immigrant, these groups do not really concern us here. It is their children, most of them born in this country, in whom we are interested.[1]

The problems of social and cultural maladjustment for the second-generation immigrant were and are serious indeed. The customs and folkways of the parent culture have a less potent influence over this group and are less effective in restraining them from delinquent and criminal conduct. Yet, at the same time, the children of immigrants have not been sufficiently assimilated into the traditional American culture to permit American folkways to exert a normal disciplinary influence. Not finding themselves culturally adjusted to the old or the new, they seek an adjustment of their own, too often in gangs which may turn their energy into criminal activities. As Professor Frederic M. Thrasher sums it up:

---

[1] According to the United States Census of 1940, less than 9 per cent of the total population was foreign-born, and very few of them were in the juvenile age group. But almost one-fifth of the entire population has foreign or mixed parentage; naturally there is a large number of juveniles in this group.

The facts recounted . . . can lead us to but one explanation of the excessive delinquency of the children of foreign-born parentage. They are the unknowing victims of disorganized social conditions and a superficial Americanization that goes little beyond contacts with the vice, crime and political corruption which are characteristic of the blighted areas in which they live. The solution of the problem, then, is clear. It lies, on the one hand, in curtailing the evil influences which play upon the children of these areas, and on the other, in opening up to them more adequate opportunities to participate in the cultural heritage which we like to think of as being most truly representative of American life.[2]

However, since some groups have more difficulty in making the necessary adjustment to American life than do others, we must not make the mistake of lumping all second-generation immigrants into one large mass of maladjusted individuals. A study made by Professor Donald R. Taft, in which he examined some data submitted by the United States Census Bureau in 1933, throws some light on this matter. The report showed that in 16 states and the District of Columbia the second-generation immigrants had a commitment rate lower than the sons of native citizens, whereas in nine states the rate was somewhat higher.[3]

Commitment rates to penal institutions may not be the best indicators of trends in antisocial or delinquent behavior, but these data have some significance. Taft, after careful analysis, concludes that those states where second-generation immigrants show the lower commitment rate have the so-called "old" immigrant type preponderant in the population (Scandinavian, German, Scotch-Irish,

---

[2] Quoted by F. J. Brown and J. S. Roucek, *Our Racial and National Minorities,* Prentice-Hall, New York, 1937, p. 710. See also Eleanor T. Glueck, "Culture Conflict and Delinquency," *Mental Hygiene,* Vol. 21, January 1937, pp. 44–66; Thorsten Sellin, *Crime and the Second Generation of Immigrant Stock,* Foreign Language Information Service release, Series C, No. 7, May 23, 1936.

[3] Donald R. Taft, "Nationality and Crime," *American Sociological Review,* October 1936, pp. 724–736. The 16 states in which the ratio of native parentage was greater than that of foreign parentage were: Indiana, Michigan, Minnesota, West Virginia, Arkansas, Louisiana, Oklahoma, Texas, Wyoming, Nevada, Wisconsin, Iowa, South Dakota, Nebraska, Washington, Oregon. The nine states showing the reverse conditions were: Massachusetts, Connecticut, New York, New Jersey, Pennsylvania, Ohio, Vermont, Rhode Island, Illinois.

English); and those states where the children of immigrants show a higher commitment rate than the native stock have more of the "new" immigration, from South Europe primarily.

But these findings can be qualified by two factors: first, the children of the "new" immigration find it much more difficult to adjust to the American culture patterns because of the great contrast between the mores of the countries from which their parents came; and second, differential treatment is given to such children by the authorities who either do not care to understand their "strange" ways or who are deeply prejudiced against them as persons or against their unpronounceable names.

One other study deserves comment because it takes into consideration the effects of the quota laws. E. H. Stofflet, writing in 1941, states that the amount of crime committed by immigrants and their descendants now and in the future will depend largely upon the effects of the quota laws. Because of the reductions in such immigrant quotas during the past quarter-century, the number of immigrants who are at the ages when criminal behavior is more prevalent will eventually become smaller. The present foreign-born will soon be identified as Old-American stock, and third-generation children will have absorbed the traditional American culture. Thus the patterns of criminality followed by second-generation children will then become the standard of comparison.[4]

2. MEXICAN-AMERICANS AND DELINQUENCY

Readers of this book who live in parts of the country other than the Pacific Coast area and the Southwest are more familiar with tensions existing between descendants of Old-American stock and European immigrants and their children. But along the Pacific Coast and in the states of the Southwest, the stresses flowing from nationality conflict derive in large measure from the large number of Mexicans, a great percentage of whom, like the European immigrants and their children, are American citizens. Whenever a minority group is large enough to threaten the Old-American stock, friction is bound to develop. And this threat will elicit from the dominant

---

[4] "The European Immigrant and His Children," *The Annals*, January 1941, pp. 84–92.

group all the bugaboos of the social inferiority of the challenging minority.

The Mexicans are a proud ethnic group of mixed Spanish and Indian descent, the relative proportion of these bloods depending upon the particular area of their origin. Nine-tenths of the Mexican population of this country live in five states—Texas, California, Arizona, New Mexico, and Colorado. Because of their aloofness, it has been easy for the dominant Old-American stock to segregate them, especially in areas where they have settled in large numbers. However, it should be mentioned that in many areas the Mexicans have been settled for a much longer period than have their dominant-group neighbors. The population of Mexicans in the United States numbered only some 700,000 in 1920; in 1930, this number had increased to 1,422,000; in 1940, there were 1,525,000; and in 1950 it was estimated that there were altogether about 3,500,000 Spanish-speaking people in the country, the majority of whom are of Mexican extraction. Since Mexicans do not come under the quota laws their entry into this country is illegal except under drastic regulations. Thus the peon workers, eager to better their economic condition, trickle over the border by the thousands. This illegal entry of these "wetbacks," as they are known along the border, presents a serious problem to immigration authorities and to county enforcement officers and sheriffs as well.[5]

Most of those who emigrate to this country are of the peasant group. Hence they are in large measure ignorant and superstitious and can be easily segregated. Many of them are quite artistic and prone to look upon life in an easygoing manner. They are dominantly agricultural; few of them are interested in learning a mechanical trade. They are poorly equipped to adjust to our culture because of language difficulties, superstitious religious views, and a low standard of living. Since they are ignorant of our customs and are confused concerning our laws, they tend to irritate our law-enforcement officers.

But those who know Mexicans well regard them as worthy neighbors. In our own Southwest, there are sharp contrasts so far as real

_____

[5] For an interesting and revealing discussion of this problem, see Bera Casey, "County Jails Along the Mexican Border," *Prison World*, September–October 1949, pp. 10 ff.

understanding is concerned. To the credit of the state of New Mexico, let it be stated that the Hispano and the Old-American stocks have worked out an amicable way of life. On the other hand, stories of discrimination and intolerance come largely from Texas and California. The tolerance found in New Mexico is, according to Carey McWilliams, the key to the development of mutual and permanent understanding.[6]

In an early study of Mexicans and their alleged propensities to delinquent behavior, Paul S. Taylor found in discussing the problem with law-enforcement officers that Mexicans are regarded as a "bad lot," and as "natural thieves," who have "no idea of private property." Taylor found that the Mexicans had an unfavorable crime record generally, but in some sections he found that it showed up favorably.[7]

Another study of Mexicans, by Professor Max Handman, concluded that the nomadic life of these peasants tends to demoralize them. He found that in one county in Texas, where 75 per cent of the population was Mexican, they contributed 71 per cent of the delinquency. Yet one of the justices in that county contended that most of them who appeared in his court were not residents but transients. Handman states: "There is no evidence to show that the Mexican runs afoul of the law anymore than anyone else, and if the complete facts were known they would most likely show that he is less delinquent in Texas than the non-Mexican population of the same community." [8]

Studies of delinquents in areas where Mexican youth abound show them to be more delinquent than the native Anglo-Saxon youth. There are more Mexican children than others in reform schools in proportion to their numbers in the general population. But as we point out in a later section dealing with the Negro versus the white child, such data merely show differential treatment and discrimination. No evidence demonstrates that the Mexican child is actually more delinquent than the children of any other group.

---

[6] Cf. Carey McWilliams, *Brothers Under the Skin*, Little, Brown, Boston, 1948 edition, p. 144.

[7] "Crime and the Foreign-Born: The Problem of the Mexican," National Commission on Law Observance and Enforcement, No. 10, 1931, pp. 199–243.

[8] "Preliminary Report on Nationality and Delinquency: The Mexican in Texas," *ibid.*, pp. 245–264.

In southern California, especially in the larger cities, the Mexican delinquent boy is considered quite apart from the other young white malefactors. Aside from the differential treatment he may receive from the authorities, many allege that he and his gang represent a real problem. The problem was certainly acute prior to World War II and up to the history-making "zoot-suit" riots of 1943 in downtown Los Angeles. The trouble resulted from the zeal of servicemen and others who questioned the patriotism of Mexican youth. At that time psychiatrists, as well as newspapers in and around Los Angeles, made much of the eccentric characteristics of the adolescent Mexican boys' gangs. The newspapers whipped up the latent prejudice by calling attention to the peculiar garb worn by the Mexican youth and to his *pachuco* hair-do and "high-rise" trousers; the psychiatrists explained such dress as symbolic of the disorganization of an oppressed group.[9]

The serious riots that took place in June of 1943 can be explained in terms of the discrimination and misunderstanding of the authorities and, to a degree, in terms of fascist groups that made an appeal to the nationalism of the Mexicans. Less than half of the Mexican boys arrested wore "zoot suits" and many who were beaten up by the police or by servicemen were not guilty of any misconduct.

There are not and never have been "zoot-suit" gangs, but there were what was known as *pachuco* gangs. These are described by Ruth Tuck as "disoriented, tough, drifting boys and their admirers."[10] At the time of the riots these boys had a penchant for wearing their hair long in the back and curled around their heads, and their trousers high on their hips. The girls had a flair for tight sweaters or Basque shirts with broad and sometimes gaudy stripes. A sort of free-masonry exists among these gangs just as it does among all adolescent gangs in other sections of the country. Dress quite

---

[9] The word *pachuco* is colloquial. The "zoot suit" is no longer the style among Mexican youth, but rather an outfit that resembles the army sun tan, with cuffs turned up, paratrooper boots, and tee shirts. The hair-do is often referred to today as "duck tail." There are also *pachuco* marks or symbols tattooed on the face, usually between the eyes, or on the heavy flesh between the thumb and forefinger. These symbols take the form of a blue cross or perhaps only a blue dot.

[10] *Not With the Fist: Mexican-Americans in a Southwest City*, Harcourt, Brace, New York, 1946, p. 130.

frequently plays a major role in developing a solidarity among youth of this age. For example, Baltimore adolescent gangs ushered in 1950 with "drapes" with narrow cuffs, and with hair "seaweed" long.[11]

The second-generation Mexican boy and girl are distinct social problems, as are their counterparts elsewhere. However, as mentioned above, some Western and Southwestern states and communities are proud of their Mexican population. Only where members of this group find discrimination do they tend to strike back.

In the reform schools and Youth Authority camps of California, the Mexican boys naturally tend to clannishness. Many of them persist in wearing their distinctive hair-do and bizarre tattooing, which represent badges of solidarity. Some camp counselors good-naturedly permit the unique hair-do but others insist that the hair be cut in the conventional manner.

3. RACE AND DELINQUENCY

a. The Negro

Members of the white race have a traditional belief that members of other races are prone to commit more crimes and delinquent acts than seem justified by their numbers. This belief results in part from a deep-seated prejudice and discrimination against such groups, and is given seeming support by available statistics, which are based on the differential treatment accorded to minorities. Negroes in the South and in the northern cities, and the Japanese, especially in some far-western states, are presumed to be much more delinquent than the whites of these areas.

Most authorities who have given serious thought to this problem are in agreement that basically Negroes and other racial groups are no more delinquent or criminal than are whites. An array of evidence can be adduced to support this thesis, and we shall cite some of it as we proceed in our discussion. We shall deal first with the Negro and his problem of adjustment in a white-dominated world and then make a few remarks concerning other races found in lesser numbers in specific geographic areas of the country. Let us first look at a few figures dealing with the extent of crime and delinquent be-

---

[11] *Time Magazine*, January 30, 1950.

havior among whites and Negroes. For further data, the reader is referred to the latest *Uniform Crime Reports*, published by the Federal Bureau of Investigation.

A total of 792,029 fingerprint arrests were received at the Federal Bureau of Investigation in 1949. Members of the white race made up 582,447 of this total; 198,596 were Negroes; 6,881 were Indians; 743 were Chinese; 302 were Japanese; and 3,060 were representatives of other races.[12]

Concerning juvenile delinquency cases, the figures compiled by the United States Children's Bureau for 1947 show that there were 21 per cent non-white (preponderantly Negro) juvenile court cases and 32 per cent non-white children in institutions. These percentages are significantly higher than the 13 per cent of non-white children in the child population of the country. Edward E. Schwartz, analyzing these figures, adds that the high proportion of non-white children in institutions is partly due to the great inadequacy or total absence of alternative facilities and services for Negro and other non-white children in some parts of the country.[13]

Figures from most large cities where big Negro populations exist point to the fact that, in proportion to their numbers, they do get into more trouble with the police, commit more crimes, and are sent to prisons more frequently than the whites. But, as we shall point out in the pages to follow, members of the Negro race are discriminated against by many law-enforcing units, and the public at large is prone to believe the many myths and half-truths that have evolved in a white-dominated culture that show the Negro in a bad light.

For example, it simply is not true that Negroes are "by nature" addicted to sexual crimes. This myth has been carefully built up and nurtured, as all such myths are, in order to rationalize the economic fear of a large minority in the midst of an area of white supremacy. The Negro has also been accused of shiftlessness and "family irresponsibility," but these are indictments that are actually more apparent than real.

Although the South is accused of wanton discrimination against

---

[12] *Uniform Crime Reports*, Vol. XX, No. 2, 1949, p. 117.

[13] "Statistics of Juvenile Delinquency in the United States," *The Annals*, January 1949, p. 17.

the Negro, such a practice is not unknown in the North, especially in the larger cities. Differential treatment of the Negro, not only by the police but by juries and even judges, plays a very important part in presenting the Negro to the general public as a potential delinquent. Newspapers habitually play up the delinquencies of Negroes and similarly play down those of the whites, especially where both may be involved in the same acts. It is not unusual to find the names and addresses of Negro boys who have been arrested, conspicuously spread out in the news story, but seldom is the identity of white youngsters revealed. The identity of any juvenile delinquent, whether he be Negro or white, should not be publicized.

Because of the tragic poverty of thousands of Negro families, their home life is often broken; mothers must work, leaving their children to roam the streets. In large Negro areas, it is a familiar sight to see hundreds of Negro children idling along the sidewalks, playing boisterous games, and appearing "suspicious" generally. Such behavior is certainly not delinquent, but the "cops" have their eyes on them ready to pounce on any overzealous youth who may go "too far" in his seemingly carefree activity.

Myrdal, in his *An American Dilemma*, states that if Negroes seem to commit more crimes than whites—judged by statistical data—it is because of: (1) discrimination; (2) poverty, ignorance of the law, and lack of influential connections; and (3) the existence of the slavery tradition and the caste situation.[14]

Robert L. Cooper, former executive director of the Wiltwyck School, New York, ascribes the high incidence rate of delinquency among Negro boys to the "frustrations that plague the Negro as a result of the majority concept that the Negro people are inferior; that always they remain infantile or childlike; that their smiling, happy faces are but conclusive evidence that they are not capable of seriousness of purpose or of sustained intellectual participation." After describing his experiment at Wiltwyck School, an interracial institution near Hyde Park, New York, where the famous motion picture, *The Quiet One*, was filmed, he continues: "When one talks about the comparatively large number of Negro children appearing before courts as delinquents, our comment is simply this: we are

---

[14] Gunnar Myrdal, *An American Dilemma*, Harper, New York, 1944, pp. 974–975.

not at all amazed that there are large numbers before the court; what amazes us is that all of us are not before the court. Minority status and all that it implies, superimposed on everything else that poor working class families have to meet, seems to us to be asking the Negro child to shoulder and carry an impossible load." [15]

It is generally conceded that the Negro child has fewer wholesome resources than has the white child. We have already mentioned poverty. It is a truism that in periods of economic crisis the Negro male adult is first to be laid off and the last to be rehired. He is the marginal man in industry, and naturally his family suffers. Policies of segregation force Negro families to seek out the best possible neighborhood in which the whites will permit them to dwell. Here also marginal white families may often be found, many of whom nurse deep resentment against the Negro and blame him, instead of the real causes, for their plight. So conflict grows up between the two groups. Brawls among children and older boys are the rule. In some instances, the white participants are discharged and their Negro foes are held for court action. Serious riots, like that many years ago in Chicago, are often precipitated by arguments among children.

As an illustration of the differential treatment of Negroes and whites, Arthur P. Miles, of Tulane University, in making a study of the population of a correctional school in New Orleans, states that although the most numerous offenses, like petty larceny and grand larceny, were evenly distributed between whites and Negroes, only the Negroes were charged with assault and battery, cutting and wounding, entering with intent to steal, attempted rape, stabbing and wounding, and wounding with intent to steal. It may be a crime for a Negro to stab a Negro, but it is obvious to even a casual observer that, from the point of view of southern mores and customs, it is not quite the same offense as if a Negro stabbed a white person. In respect to recidivism, Miles found that 41 per cent of the white boys in the correctional school had been committed two or more times before, whereas 60 per cent of the Negro boys were in this category.[16]

---

[15] "Racial Antagonism as a Factor in Delinquency," *Yearbook*, N.P.P.A., 1946, pp. 77–85; see also, Donald W. Wyatt, "Racial Handicaps in the Negro Delinquent," *Probation*, April 1943, pp. 112–115.

[16] "Double Liability for Negro Boys," *Probation*, October 1942, pp. 19–21.

If play space, settlement houses, and clubs do aid in prevention of delinquency, it is notoriously true that few of these exist for Negro children. In many metropolitan areas, playgrounds in mixed neighborhoods are often restricted to white children. Even if there is no discrimination regarding actual play space, there is certainly restriction in swimming and wading pools. Equal facilities are rarely provided. Such discrimination breeds hostility and frustration in the Negro boy or girl. The result is too frequently some overt anti-social act. A revealing article on this question was written by Mary Huff Diggs, of Hunter College, in which she states:

> The significant thing to be noted here is that the Negro child fre-quently participates in antisocial behavior simply because his com-munity provides him with nothing better to do. He drifts into it out of sheer boredom, out of the need for vigorous childhood energy to expend himself. That this discharge of energy is in the direction of social misadventuring is due to the fact that society has provided no direction at all.[17]

Negro boys and girls in our metropolitan areas have a practice of carrying knives, perhaps much more so than white children. Police women have told the authors that adolescent Negro girls of the lower economic groups are adamant in hanging on to these weapons. The girls say frankly that their only protection is that others know they are armed. When these knife-carriers are convinced that "nice" girls just don't go about their work carrying concealed weapons, they are usually willing to give them up. Thus it is that when Negro boys are arrested by the police they must face the more serious charge of being armed. Myrdal, in an interview with a member of the New York grand jury, learned that the law defines the Negro's method of fighting as a crime, but the white man's more subtle method of provoking a quarrel is not so regarded.[18]

The Negro's group solidarity also plays a part in his war on the society of the white man. Hedged in as he is by restrictions of various kinds, he soon learns as a child to hate and fear his socially more fortunate white fellow. As Professor Reuter pointed out some years

---

[17] "The Negro Child and the Law," *Focus*, N.P.P.A., January 1948, pp. 7–12.
[18] *Op. cit.*, p. 969.

ago, many Negroes become "romantic figures warring against the white man's society." [19]

The development of stereotypes of Negro habits and actions also cannot be overlooked. The dominant race has attitude patterns that it habitually associates with the Negro. These are inculcated early into the white child's thinking, and the Negro, in order to adjust himself, often plays the role he is supposed to assume.

The Wickersham Commission, years ago, summed up the situation most adequately as follows:

> Thus, when one views the congestion in poor dwellings in crowded neighborhoods; the lack of recreational facilities and the presence of unwholesome, artificial devices where Negroes may spend their leisure; the prevalent system of segregation and discrimination whereby Negroes are denied the privileges and conditions of citizens compatible with the greatest good; the element of prejudice that enters into the administration and execution of the law, either subtly or overtly; the unique distribution of occupational opportunities making Negroes the marginal workers . . . the total lack of a scientific formula for guidance and training in vocations; a disfranchised working class which Dr. W. E. B. DuBois has called "a menace not simply to itself, but to every group in the community," that will be diseased, criminal, ignorant, the plaything of mobs, and insulted by caste restrictions; in short, "a system of color caste having to do with separation in travel, in schools, in public accomodations, in residence, and in family relations, in the kind and amount of public school education and in civil rights of various sorts and in courts, jails, fines, lynching, and mob violence"; [20] such a one is forced to conclude that the experience so far gained indicates that the volume of crimes among Negroes is susceptible to vast improvement by effecting changes in the factors underlying this crime.[21]

Relatively little crime or delinquency exists in rural areas or communities where Negroes are the dominant group in terms of popula-

---

[19] Edward B. Reuter, *The American Race Problem*, Crowell, New York, 1938, p. 355.

[20] Quotation from Charles S. Johnson, *The Negro in American Civilization*, Henry Holt, New York, 1930, p. 471.

[21] National Commission on Law Observance and Enforcement, *Causes of Crime*, Vol. I, pp. 252–253. The reader is also referred to E. Franklin Frazier's book, *The Negro in the United States*, Macmillan, New York, 1949, Chapter XXV, "Crime and Delinquency," for more material on this subject.

tion. In such situations, the Negro is relatively law-abiding. For example, in Mound Bayou, Mississippi, a community of 8,000 Negroes living on 30,000 acres, there is no jail, and no major crime has been reported there for many years.[22] Boley, Oklahoma, is another all-Negro real-estate development with a fine record of freedom from crime. A very different kind of community is St. Helena, one of the Sea Islands off the coast of South Carolina, where a Negro community has long been established under less modern conditions. For 20 years the average number of convictions per year in the local magistrate's court was only 28. Most disputes are settled here in a church court.[23]

An interesting survey of delinquency areas is reported from Houston, Texas. There, Negroes had a higher rate of delinquency than whites for the city as a whole. However, when broken down according to census tracts, the rates varied in accordance with the density of the Negro population. When rates of Negro delinquency were computed for the various census tracts, it was found that the higher the proportion of Negro population, the lower was the rate of delinquency. For instance, 30 tracts with a Negro population below 10 per cent had more than twice the rate of delinquency as four tracts with 90 to 100 per cent Negro inhabitants.[24]

In short, if the Negro's criminality is high, it is due largely to his socio-economic handicaps and to the conditions flowing from his conflict with the white man.

It is encouraging to find organizations composed of both white and Negro leaders dealing with the objectives of securing more equitable social, political, and economic rights for this minority group. The movement for Fair Employment Practices legislation on the Federal, state, and municipal levels, has gone far in bringing about fair play and justice in business. The trend to employ Negro police officers throughout the South as well as in Northern cities is a healthy sign of cooperation between the races. As of September

---

[22] Waldron Webb, "All Black, a Unique Negro Settlement," *Survey Graphic*, January 1938, pp. 34–36.

[23] Clyde Vernon Kiser, *Sea Island to City*, Columbia University Press, New York, 1932, pp. 78–81.

[24] From "Social Statistics: The Houston Delinquent in His Community," Bureau of Research, Council of Social Agencies, Houston, Texas, Vol. II, No. 1, June 1945.

1, 1948, Negro police were employed in 54 cities in 11 Southern states.[25] Certainly the famous phrase coined by the great Negro leader, Booker T. Washington, "You cannot keep a man down in a ditch unless you remain down there with him," might be taken to heart by the white man.

As Negroes become better educated by being afforded equal advantages; as discrimination is lessened in the sphere of economics; as housing covenants are outlawed so that Negroes who can afford better homes can rent and buy them; as schools, settlements, and recreational facilities eliminate discrimination against Negro children; and as white families begin to recognize that children must be accepted for their worth and not by the color of their skin, the delinquency rate of Negro youth will decrease. As Professor Thorsten Sellin states: "The responsibility lies where power, authority, and discrimination has its source, the dominant white group. To that group the existence of a high crime rate and delinquency among Negroes is a challenge which cannot be brushed aside by platitudes about 'race inferiority,' 'inherited depravity,' or similar generalizations." [26]

Some of the results of an exhaustive study made by G. Gordon Brown in the city of Philadelphia are pertinent in this discussion:

> Reviewing all the information obtained regarding the relationship between the police and the Negro population, a summary statement might be made as follows. An appreciable proportion, which is possibly at least 40 per cent, and may be over 60 per cent, of the Negro population, believe that they are given differential treatment by the police. Of informed Negroes, a much larger proportion believe they are objects of discrimination. This may be because they are in a better position to know the facts, or it may be partly conditioned by the position of the informed Negro. In his dealings with whites, he often feels himself called upon to be a representative of his race, and he tends, perhaps, to attach great importance to every act which can be labeled discrimination. It is, however, a serious enough fact that so many informed Negroes, and that so many of the Negro general public, do believe themselves discriminated against.

---

[25] "Negro Police in Southern Cities," *New South*, Vol. 2, October 1947, pp. 1–5; Vol. 3, September 1948, pp. 7–8.

[26] *The Annals*, November 1928, p. 64. See also Marshall B. Clinard, "Secondary Community Influences and Juvenile Delinquency," *ibid.*, January 1949, p. 53.

The actual fact of discrimination is hard to establish, and the acts which are interpreted as being discriminatory may merely be incidents which would occur in connection with any economically depressed group. However, a review of the evidence does suggest that individual members of the police force at times do act in a discriminatory fashion —by making arrests on inadequate grounds, in lack of concern for disputes between Negro and Negro, in resort to excessive violence, and, possibly, in lack of concern for Negro neighborhoods. This discrimination is not official police policy, but occurs because of the attitudes of members of the force, which attitudes reflect those of a large portion of the general public.[27]

And again:

Legally the Negro has a position of complete equality . . . and in terms of objective fact, there is no officially sanctioned or systematic discrimination. Isolated acts of discrimination do occur.

The police force has a right to feel a degree of satisfaction from the fact that acts of discrimination against Negroes are not so numerous as they are reported to be in some other cities. However, there is no ground for complacency. Incidents which can most easily be interpreted as discriminatory against Negroes are sufficient in number to give at least some justification to the feelings and beliefs of many Negroes.[28]

Concerning juveniles, the report adds:

The disposition of juvenile cases by the court is to some extent conditioned by available institutional care, and by the belief in the differences of ability on the part of the parents to care for their children. Thus, differential treatment, while kindly meant, sometimes assumes an appearance of discrimination.[29]

Thus we see that the tradition held tenaciously by Negroes that discrimination and differential treatment are widespread among law-enforcement officers and courts yields very slowly, and each new instance of such practices sustains them in their belief. We also see, so far as this Philadelphia study is concerned, that discrimination is not officially sanctioned, but isolated police officers and judges occa-

---

[27] *Law Administration and Negro-White Relations in Philadelphia*, Bureau of Municipal Research, Philadelphia, 1947, pp. 134–135.
[28] *Ibid.*, p. 153.
[29] *Ibid.*, p. 154.

sionally yield to their prejudice against the Negro. In committing juveniles to institutions, the judge often has no other recourse, since the home life of these Negro youngsters manifests few assets for rehabilitation. So some instances of differential treatment may be explained, not in terms of prejudice, but in terms of expediency.

In several communities, special efforts have been made in recent years to instruct law-enforcement officers in the skillful handling of interracial problems. To disseminate objective information on the background and conditions of minority groups has been one of the important features of these endeavors. An excellent example of such work is the preparation of a manual for the use of the Chicago Park District Police Training School. The crime-prevention units of police departments, which will be described later, have in many instances done a pioneering job in the field of interracial understanding.[30]

Obviously, as the studies show, the total setting in which the Negro group finds itself in a white-dominated society must be meticulously analyzed. The emotional difficulties of both white and Negro investigators militate against accuracy. Objectivity is the only insurance against biased conclusions.[31]

b. Other Racial Groups

Much as the Oriental has been shunned in the United States, neither he nor his children can be charged with a high criminal or delinquent rate. The Japanese immigrant, especially, was discriminated against prior to and during World War II, but the war merely aggravated a deepseated antagonism that has its roots in economic competition. The familiar "red herring" of race has been used to rationalize the fear that the whites, especially in agriculture, have felt when they have been confronted by the Japanese worker. Differential treatment of aliens must always be considered in the appraisal of charges against such groups.

In evaluating the Japanese in terms of delinquency and crime, we find that they are essentially a law-abiding group. *The Uniform*

[30] *The Police and Minority Groups,* prepared by Joseph D. Lohman, Chicago Park District Police Training School, Chicago, 1946. See also Davis McEntire and Robert B. Powers, "A Guide to Race Relations for Police Officers," California Department of Justice, Sacramento, 1946.
[31] See Walter R. Chivers, "The Negro Delinquent," *Yearbook,* N.P.P.A., 1942, pp. 46–59.

Crime Report of the Federal Bureau of Investigation notes that of 792,029 fingerprint arrest records for 1949, only 302 were of Japanese.[32] It is alleged that the reason for their low crime rate is their strong family life. This fact was borne out some years ago by Professor William Carlson Smith in his work *Americans in the Making.*[33] Discussing delinquency among Japanese boys, Professors Norman S. Hayner and Charles N. Reynolds show that wherever the boys are closely controlled by the racial community, they get into little trouble.[34] This fact is also substantiated by Andrew W. Lind in his study of delinquency in Honolulu.[35] He states that where the Japanese population is concentrated, no delinquency exists among the children; but where it is mixed with the rest of the population, the children tend to get into some trouble.

Only a word need be said about the delinquency among Chinese and the American Indians. Referring again to the F.B.I. report, we see that there were 6,881 Indian fingerprint arrests in 1949 and only 743 Chinese. Over half of the Indians were slated for drunkenness. Both groups are essentially law-abiding. In China, peasants have always been controlled by group customs, particularly the patriarchy system which looked upon a disgression from the traditions of the family as a disgrace.[36] Aside from the banditry indigenous to China prior to the Japanese invasion, the Chinese boy grew up knowing little about delinquent behavior. Those Chinese who emigrated to the United States brought with them many of their family traditions and patriarchial customs, and much of their clannishness. Most of their behavior is regulated by self-appointed control groups having a sort of quasi-official court character.

Most American Indians live on government reservations and their problems are handled by agents from the Department of Indian Affairs. Indians constitute such a small percentage of the population that nothing need be said concerning their participation in delinquency.

---

[32] Vol. XX, No. 2, 1949, p. 117.

[33] Appleton-Century, New York, 1939, pp. 84, 97.

[34] "Delinquency Areas in the Puget Sound Region," *American Journal of Sociology*, Vol. 39, 1933, p. 319.

[35] "The Ghetto and the Slum," *Social Forces*, December 1930, pp. 206–215.

[36] For an analysis of crime in China, see Ching-Yueh Yen, "Crime in Relation to Social Change in China," *American Journal of Sociology*, November 1934, pp. 298–304.

The statistics of crimes committed by this group show that they are more often guilty of larceny-theft than of any other type of offense. Of the lesser offenses, we find drunkenness leading the list. No data are available on youth delinquency among Indians, although in some of the towns and areas where they are most prevalent they get into trouble about as consistently as the white children, in proportion to their number. In short, there is nothing significant in their proneness to delinquency or crime.

4. CONCLUDING REMARKS

Gradually racial barriers are being lowered in more and more communities. This trend is doubtless due to education in both public schools and colleges, to forum discussion on the radio, to some excellent motion pictures that deal with racial tension and overt conflict and that point out their futility in a democratic state, and to organizations such as coordinating councils and interracial groups. All these leavening processes and institutions play their part in resolving the difficulty and reducing the prejudices. It is a slow process but not a hopeless one. A fair deal for minorities is emerging in all parts of the country and, in time, many of the tragic conflicts that have marred the American scene will disappear.

Chapter V

SOCIO-ECONOMIC CONDITIONS

1. POVERTY AS A CAUSE OF DELINQUENCY

FOR HUNDREDS OF YEARS economic misery, lack of material goods, hunger, and cold—in short, poverty—have been emphasized by students of the problem of delinquency as the main cause of anti-social behavior. No treatise on juvenile delinquency can ignore this thesis. And in reviewing it in all of its ramifications, the writers feel obliged to comment on a few of the classic studies that have been made throughout the years. It would be a formidable task merely to mention all the studies in this field, and a discussion of them all is certainly out of the question in a book of this type.

First, however, let us make our position clear on the question. Poverty *per se* is not a cause of delinquency or criminal behavior; this statement is evidenced by the courage, fortitude, honesty, and moral stamina of thousands of parents who would rather starve than steal and who inculcate this attitude in their children. Even in the blighted neighborhoods of poverty and wretched housing conditions, crime and delinquency are simply nonexistent among most of the residents. True, since much lawlessness is conspicuous, some of these neighborhoods come to be known as "delinquency areas." But the fact remains that the majority of the children living in these areas do grow up to be tolerably good citizens. And occasionally outstanding citizens do emerge from such neighborhoods.

Many delinquencies, crimes of violence, and offenses against private property can be traced to economic causes, but most of the people who commit such offenses are driven to them by causes other than sheer hunger or economic misery. The economic basis, then, resolves itself to the offenders' dissatisfaction with their meager income from legal pursuits.

Eminent scholars have discussed the extent and causes of poverty, but we can not attempt a discussion of such an important subject here. Suffice it to say that no person with any degree of social insight can or does condone poverty in this land of affluence and vast natural resources. Every effort should be made by the government and by private initiative alike to eliminate this curse from our national life. Many causes contribute to poverty, but the most important cause is political and economic conditions. And this cause could be largely eliminated if we could somehow abolish the inordinate greed, indifference, and selfishness of our captains of industry and our city and county political bosses. But these individuals themselves are socially conditioned by our social and economic philosophies of "get-rich-quick" and "something-for-nothing," which we mentioned in our first chapter. A thorough education in social responsibility is perhaps the only answer to this problem, slow though such a process undoubtedly would be.

To go through life forced to submit to a substandard living is monotonous and even ghastly. Yet millions of people in this country know nothing better. Most of the time, even during the years of maximum employment—not to mention depression years—millions of families attempt to live on incomes far below what experts insist is necessary to support a normal home with just the barest necessary items to maintain decent health and comfort status. At this moment, ten million families have an income of less than $2,000 per year and, even worse, eight million individuals and families have a yearly income of less than $1,000.[1] John L. Thurston of the Federal Security Administration, appearing before a Congressional committee in December 1949, stated that five million persons were unable to earn any wages whatsoever. He painted a distressing picture of the plight of millions of American citizens in this land "with the highest standard of living in the world," a phrase so often enunciated by smug individualists.

One must not think for a moment that poverty is found in big cities alone. Although we talk a great deal about the blighted areas of our metropolitan centers, we must not overlook the amount of squalor and economic misery of the small towns and rural sections of this vast country. The perennial articulate demand of the nation's coal miners for a decent annual income is evidence of the misery

---

[1] Bureau of Census figures released February 1949.

these men and their families have experienced for so many years in this sick industry. Sharecroppers are even now marginal so far as a decent income is concerned, and they have no powerful union to fight their battles. Even the unskilled workers in factories of small towns as well as of the larger cities find it exceedingly difficult to maintain families on their precarious incomes. A fact frequently overlooked is that large numbers of white-collar workers have an insufficient income to maintain their families adequately.

Regardless of where they may live, children from poverty-stricken families constantly hover between delinquency and a life of moral rectitude. Every day, the poor contrast their economic lot with the good fortune of those who enjoy good food, comfortable clothes, an occasional movie, perhaps a car, and a "date" with a girl. When children constantly have few or none of the things that are usually taken for granted by many people as the "good way of life," their thoughts invariably turn to self-pity or envy. (See Appendix, Case 14, pp. 732–735.) And such feelings are likely to result in frustration and bitterness, which, in turn, may lead to delinquency unless the children are lucky enough to be subjected to wholesome influences. Such influences do actually offset the potential delinquency of thousands of children subjected to poverty. It is the home of courage and of high moral standards that thwarts much delinquency.

We shall now proceed to the studies that attempt to establish a correlation between poverty and crime or delinquency. One of the pioneers in this field was the Italian, Fornasari di Verce, who pointed out that the poorer classes of Italy, amounting to about 60 per cent of the total population, furnished 85 to 90 per cent of the convicted criminals.[2] Bonger, the Dutch criminologist, argues that poverty disposes to crime, because the present structure of society brings about innumerable conflicts. He further comments on the excessive use of alcohol by the poor, which indirectly causes a great amount of crime.[3]

The relation of juvenile delinquency to poverty was studied by the eminent British authority on delinquency, Dr. Cyril Burt, author of the definitive study, *The Young Delinquent*. His studies showed

---

[2] *La Criminalità e le Vicende economiche d'Italia*, 1894, pp. 3–4.

[3] W. A. Bonger, *Criminality and Economic Conditions*, Little, Brown, Boston, 1916, p. 643.

that 19 per cent of the delinquents of London came from the homes of the *very poor*, whereas only 8 per cent of the city's total population came from such a group; 37 per cent of the delinquents came from the next two classes, labeled *moderately poor*, though the total population percentage in these two classes was only 22. In short, over half of the total amount of juvenile delinquency was from poor and very poor families.[4]

But here Burt hastens to add a factor that should always be recognized, but that seldom is, in evaluating this alleged correlation between poverty and delinquency—that most of the delinquents from the comfortable groups succeed in avoiding "official inquiry and action." His final conclusion is that poverty alone does not produce crime. As he so succinctly puts it: "If the majority of the delinquent are needy, the majority of the needy do not become delinquent." [5]

Before proceeding to other contemporary studies of this age-old problem, let us digress to see what one authority on the subject had to say a century ago. She is Miss Mary Carpenter, long the superintendent of the famous Red Lodge Reformatory for Women at Bristol, England. In her stimulating books, she described conditions in her time, and students today may well go to her reports for sound advice in dealing with children as well as with adult female offenders.

In the opening chapter of her work, *Juvenile Delinquents*,[6] she describes five classes of delinquents. The first group consists of "daring young offenders, who are already outlaws from society, caring for no law divine or human." They live by plunder, "their hand against every man." She further states that this group has had "an undisciplined childhood." The second group is even more dangerous, because "more systematic is their life of fraud." They are trained in a life of crime by their parents or by others of professed dishonesty, usually as pickpockets or "coiners." An example of this class shows that "since he was ten years old he was employed to watch when his father was at work, and he was then promoted to the higher office of uttering the base money his father had coined."

In her third class, Miss Carpenter includes children who are not

---

[4] *The Young Delinquent*, University of London Press, 1938, pp. 68–69.
[5] *Ibid.*, p. 92.
[6] W. & F. G. Cash, London, 1853.

hardened or daring at first but who, from "culpable neglect" of their parents and a "want of all religious and moral influence at home," gradually acquire habits of petty thieving. Apparently, she feels, there is some hope for this group, provided they are stopped in time. Before presenting her other two classes of delinquents, Miss Carpenter states that the first three groups are not incited to crime because of destitution, adding that "if these children are poor, it is a poverty caused directly by vice."

Members of the fourth group, however, consist of those "who have been actually driven into crime by their utter destitution . . . while their claims on support from the National Poor Laws have been either passed by unnoticed, or rejected by the administrators." She adds: "The *Ragged School Magazine* furnishes numerous and touching examples of this class . . . who will and *must* lapse from poverty to vice, unless cared for, not only by public charity which often slumbers and gladly escapes from its charge, but by the watchful guardianship of Christian love."

The fifth class of delinquents live, both parents and children, in a condition of squalid poverty, yet with a profession of honest living, for they are "hawkers, merchants of small wares, and indignantly repel any who would interfere with them, in the exercise of their lawful calling."

Here, then, are Miss Carpenter's five classes of juvenile delinquents of the 1850s. It may be seen that Miss Carpenter dismisses poverty as a cause of most delinquency, although she admits that certain youngsters are definitely driven to a life of crime because of a hard economic life. In her over-all picture of the five groups briefly described above, she states: "It is generally imagined that poverty and destitution are the great causes of juvenile crime. But the facts carefully considered will lead to a very different result,—at any rate with respect to that crime which is indicated by conviction and punishment." [7] For example, she cites some statistics of 1844 from the Parkhurst Prison. These show that of 957 children, only 30 had never been to school, 732 had attended day schools longer than a year, and 163 had attended five or more years. Studies made at the reformatory of Stretton-on-Dunsmore indicate that by far the greatest majority of the boys sent there had had considerable school-

---

[7] *Ibid.*, p. 33. The material preceding may be found on pages 23–32.

ing for those days, had been employed when they had stepped into trouble, and had been living at home with both parents. "Only fourteen of forty-nine were orphans," states Miss Carpenter, although to us living a hundred years later, that seems like a fairly high percentage. Except in cases where the parents of these children had been "transported" to Australian penal camps, their fathers were mechanics, one a jeweler, one a grocer and one a druggist. In her concluding remarks in this section, Miss Carpenter says: "It cannot be said then that it was destitution which caused the necessity of establishing this asylum." [8]

Now let us look at two early and authoritative studies from this country. The first, by Dr. William Healy, shows that in only 0.5 per cent of his cases was poverty a major cause, and that in 7.1 per cent it was a minor one. [9] The second, by Breckinridge and Abbott, alleges, according to Dr. Burt's comments, "that 'in round numbers, nine tenths of the delinquent girls and three fourths of the delinquent boys come from the homes of the poor.' " [10] Burt, commenting on the discrepancies between these two pioneer studies, states: "English readers are astonished to find how small an emphasis is placed upon poverty by Healy . . . in a volume of over eight hundred pages the short paragraph devoted to poverty occupies no more than seventeen lines." [11] One might also register amazement at Breckinridge and Abbott's figures, which place such a high poverty rate among delinquents.

In a later study by Dr. Healy and his co-worker, Dr. Bronner, a scale of standards similar to that used by Dr. Burt was employed: (a) *destitution*, (b) *poverty*, a constant struggle to "make ends meet," (c) *normal*, (d) *comfort*, and (e) *luxury*. Of 675 juvenile delinquents whom they studied, they found 5 per cent in the *destitute* class, 22 per cent in *poverty*, 35 per cent in *normal*, 34 per cent in *comfort*, and 4 per cent in *luxury*. In other words, 27 per cent of the cases came from poverty-stricken homes. Summarizing their work, Dr. Healy says:

---

[8] *Ibid.*, p. 35.

[9] *The Individual Delinquent*, Little, Brown, Boston, 1915.

[10] Sophonisba Breckinridge and Edith Abbott, *The Delinquent Child and the Home*, Russell Sage Foundation, New York, 1912. Above quotation is from Burt, *op. cit.*, p. 69.

[11] *Idem.*

Thus it is clear from the figures (73 per cent coming from normal, or better, homes) that great importance cannot be attached . . . to the effects of economic status on cure of delinquent trends.[12]

These same two writers, in their 1936 study, *New Light on Delinquency and Its Treatment,* formulated a statement that minimizes poverty *per se* but correctly emphasizes the unsatisfactory human relationships that usually flow from destitute and poverty-stricken homes and neighborhoods.[13]

Studies attempting to show that delinquency rises or falls during periods of prosperity or depression are conflicting. A study of Michigan rural and urban areas by Paul Wiers shows that the manner in which income is spent develops either security or frustration in the children. Although Wiers does not minimize poverty and its attendant evils, he points out that juvenile delinquency cannot be eliminated merely by raising the average income of a community.[14] A British study of delinquency also cautiously appraises economic income as a cause of maladjustment by arriving at substantially the same conclusion.[15]

A study of delinquency in Philadelphia from 1923 to 1945, a period that witnessed high prosperity, depression, and a war boom, indicated the following:

(a) 1923-29—Reasonably high prosperity, average proportions of delinquency.
(b) 1930-35—Period of depression, high delinquency rate.
(c) 1936-40—"Normal" economic development, neither prosperity nor depression, delinquency rate low.
(d) 1941-45—War prosperity, delinquency rate very high.[16]

A study by David Bogen of delinquency in Los Angeles showed that the rate decreased during the depression and began to rise during

[12] William Healy and Augusta F. Bronner, *Delinquents and Criminals,* Macmillan, New York, 1926, p. 121. By permission of The Macmillan Company, publishers.

[13] Yale University Press, New Haven, p. 301.

[14] *Economic Factors in Michigan Delinquency,* Columbia University Press, New York, 1944, p. 8.

[15] *Young Offenders,* A. M. Carr-Saunders, Hermann Mannheim, and E. C. Rhodes, Macmillan, New York, 1944, p. 95.

[16] John Otto Reinemann, "Juvenile Delinquency in Philadelphia and Economic Trends," *Temple University Law Quarterly,* Vol. XX, No. 4, April 1947, pp. 576-583.

the later years of prosperity. He based his findings on the possible fact that many families become disorganized during periods of high wages.[17]

The following studies also have bearing on the relationship between economic status and delinquency: Maud A. Merrill found marked differences in the economic status between a group of delinquent children and a controlled group of non-delinquents in spite of the fact that they lived in the same neighborhood. Two-thirds of the delinquents came from the economically marginal group, as against half of the non-delinquents.[18] Kvaraceus, in his study of delinquency in Passaic, New Jersey, reports that out of 453 families from which boys and girls were referred on delinquency charges, 110 were classified as falling into the comfortable income group, 181 into the marginal, and 162 into the dependent group. Broken down as to sex, girls tended to come from families of even lower economic status than did the boys. The same study reveals that slightly over 25 per cent of the delinquents had mothers who were employed at the time of their referral. The Negro group reported 44 per cent of the mothers as employed, while only 25 per cent of the mothers of white children worked.[19]

Another study, in Philadelphia, of 220 truants revealed that in 30 per cent of the cases the family income was so low that the mothers were compelled to secure part-time or full employment.[20] However, this study is probably less pertinent, for truancy can hardly be classed as one of the more serious types of delinquency, except in persistent cases. According to the Annual Report of the Juvenile Court of Allegheny County (Pittsburgh), Pennsylvania, for 1947, the delinquency ratio per 10,000 children between 10 and 17 years of age was 371.5 in the lowest economic third of the population and 114.9 in the highest economic third.[21]

---

[17] "Juvenile Delinquency and Economic Trend," *American Sociological Review*, Vol. IX, 1940, pp. 178–184.

[18] *Problems of Child Delinquency*, Houghton Mifflin, Boston, 1947, pp. 77–78.

[19] William C. Kvaraceus, *Juvenile Delinquency and the School*, World Book Company, New York, 1945, pp. 87 and 90.

[20] John Otto Reinemann, "The Truant Before the Court," *Federal Probation*, September 1948, pp. 8–12.

[21] "Focus the Child," published by the Juvenile Court of Allegheny County, 1947, p. 12.

Inadequacy, frustration, and various forms of insecurity often flow from poverty, and, in so far as they do, poverty cannot be minimized as a potent cause of delinquency. Poverty-stricken homes are very drab places in which to inspire socially acceptable behavior. And so are the surrounding neighborhoods, with their poor, frustrated residents who resent any display of wealth or influence. For example, the ostentatious display of wealth, as portrayed in the movies, builds up a resentment within certain individuals who feel they can never hope to obtain such comfort except by illegal means. It may be argued, then, that poverty alone does not force a person into delinquency, but it does produce the conditions most conducive to resentful, antisocial behavior.

Envy and ambition, as well as hunger and cold, stimulate much delinquency in the same manner that greed and ruthless ambition urge on the big-time racketeers. Not merely the lack of enough clothing to cover the body, but the inability to own and wear expensive frocks tempts hundreds of girls, for example, to sell themselves to men with big bankrolls and thus eventually to swell the ranks of prostitution. And so with the 16-to-21-year-old group of boys who are arrested mainly for stealing automobiles and holding up stores and filling stations. Obviously economic conditions often lie at the basis of such acts. But may it not be argued that many of these offenses are due to sex? In most cases these young hoodlums want money and cars to make an impression on their girl friends.

In the following section we shall discuss the "delinquency area" concept; here, again, the influence of poverty and drabness is admitted as a cause of much delinquency. We note from students of this concept (notably Shaw, McKay, and Thrasher) that the congestion of poverty-stricken neighborhoods and the lack of adequate recreational facilities have fostered a quasi-delinquent attitude on the part of many youngsters. These children are proud of their "toughness" and tend to simulate the "big shots" who frequent such neighborhoods. Since these disorganized neighborhoods attract the criminal type, there are more persons to arrest there. So we see that recorded arrests are out of proportion to the inherent delinquency and criminality of such neighborhoods.

Perhaps the most that we can admit, in concluding this preliminary section, is that a close relationship exists between poverty and delinquency, but that poverty cannot be classed as a direct cause. Most competent students will bear out that conclusion by their own studies.[22]

2. THE ECOLOGICAL APPROACH—DELINQUENCY AREAS

The ecological approach to the problem of delinquency has long held the field as one of the most popular methods of calling public attention to the seriousness of the high rate of juvenile delinquency. The number of studies that have followed the initial pioneer work of Professors Robert E. Park and Ernest W. Burgess in 1926 is indeed impressive. Many of the earlier studies have become classics, and are frequently quoted by those who appraise the problems of social disorganization as strictly community problems. It is not our purpose to clutter the student's mind with an encyclopedic enumeration of the endless studies emphasizing the ecology of delinquency, despite the excellence of most of these works. We shall merely attempt to set down a few statements of clarification and then cite a few of the more significant studies as typical of this school.

The pioneers in this field, Breckinridge and Abbott, made a study of cases from the juvenile court in Chicago. They showed on a spot map that certain areas in that city housed more delinquents than others. This study was made as early as 1899–1909. In 1925–1926, Professor Manuel C. Elmer found that the highest delinquency rates were in the down-town disorganized areas of Minneapolis and St. Paul.[23]

The names most frequently associated with this approach are those of Clifford R. Shaw and Frederic M. Thrasher, pioneers whose work gave impetus to many studies of delinquency in various metropolitan centers. But back of their work stand their mentors, Professors Park and Burgess.

---

[22] For further evidence, see Sophia M. Robison, *Can Delinquency Be Measured?*, Columbia University Press, New York, 1936, pp. 27–36. See also Edward G. Posniak, "Does the Slum Breed Crime?," *Federal Probation*, April–June 1941; and John Kobler, "The Case That Rocked New Jersey," *Saturday Evening Post*, August 7, 1948, the story of a group of young boys from good substantial homes who embarked on a disastrous criminal career.

[23] "Maladjustment of Youth in Relation to Density of Population," *Publications of the American Sociological Society*, Vol. 20, July 1926, pp. 138–140; and "The Juvenile Delinquent in St. Paul, Minnesota," *The Community Chest*, St. Paul, 1926. These studies are cited by Reckless and Smith, *Juvenile Delinquency*, McGraw-Hill, New York, 1932, p. 134.

The outstanding feature of the ecological approach is the emphasis on "delinquency areas" in our larger communities—neighborhoods where delinquent behavior breeds as a result, primarily, of the blighted nature of the area. Usually these areas are near the center of the city's business district or adjacent to it; they are often in the warehouse districts. Housing is exceedingly run-down; few or no playgrounds, community centers, or cultural agencies exist; and streets and alleys are permitted to deteriorate. Often railroad yards and sidings abound and small factories have taken over portions of the area. Such neighborhoods are inhabited by marginal families who attempt to eke out a precarious existence on sub-standard wages. Since these families are often quite large, their economic lot becomes more difficult. As one proceeds from such crowded and run-down neighborhoods and passes into more substantial areas, delinquency rates tend to diminish; the rates become progressively less as the neighborhoods become more pretentious and roomy.

Most delinquents in such deteriorated areas are not basically inferior to children in other more privileged neighborhoods. Their delinquency stems from their bitter economic and social experience, their day-by-day deprivation of the good things of life and—of great importance—the traditions that eventually flow from a harassed economic battle for a place in the sun.

The people who move into these tumble-down areas are, or have been in the past, immigrants, or Negroes up from the agricultural South, attempting to "break in" to the precarious economic life of a great city. They gravitate to these areas because of the low rentals. But even the low rentals are an illusion, since the rent per room is often higher than that in more comfortable neighborhoods. Thus two or more families must double-up to save on the monthly layout for housing.

The various groups that move into these blighted areas differ tremendously in their cultural backgrounds and tend to clash with each other. Few, if any, stabilizing community forces remain, such as settlements, playgrounds, and clubs; if any do remain, they find it difficult to finance an inclusive program that will be of any constructive assistance to their clients.

Perhaps the most significant contribution of the "delinquency area" concept is its emphasis on the deterioration of the fundamentals and characteristics of social control in such neighborhoods. In other words, instead of thinking in terms of the significance of poor housing, overcrowding, low standards of living, low educational standards, and other such conditions, this approach looks upon these conditions as merely symptomatic of more degenerative processes.

Federal Public Housing Authority

Slums in the Nation's Capital.

The early students of the delinquency area concept make it quite plain that a definite relationship exists between these areas and juvenile delinquency. In fact, in later studies Shaw and his associates have expanded their research to several cities where conditions were similar to those reported and described in the pioneer study, *Delinquency Areas*. The conclusions reached by these investigators are that group delinquency, which characterizes much of our modern crime, is deeply imbedded in the roots of modern community life; that attitudes prevailing in metropolitan centers seem to sanction delinquency through the conduct, speech, and gestures of adults with whom city juveniles come in contact; that the competing values of modern life confuse the growing boy and encourage him to seek a life of excitement in which he can gain a satisfying status among his kind; and that year after year this situation grows more serious. Any solution, these writers feel, must come from community agencies' focusing their attention on the setting or neighborhood life from which these young delinquents emerge.[24]

Other studies conducted by sociologists interested in this phase of ecology are worthy of brief mention. However, since so many have been made during the past two decades, it will be impossible in this brief section to include them all.

For example, R. Clyde White studied a bad central area of Indianapolis. He charted the city in concentric circles at one-mile intervals, making five zones. In the first zone, more than a third of the land was used for business; in the fifth, less than one-thirtieth. In the first, the general mobility rate was 15.1, while in the fifth it was only 8.7. In the first, the rate for family welfare cases was 30; in the fifth, only 3.2. Delinquency and crime rates decreased markedly in the concentric zones between the first and fifth.[25]

For Long Beach, California, a satellite city of Los Angeles and hence very different from the larger cities mentioned previously, Elsa S. Longmoor and Erle F. Young, published a map in 1936 with contour lines for levels, or altitudes, of delinquency. The different method showed the same general pattern.[26]

One exception to this pattern of centralized delinquency is presented in a study of New Haven, Connecticut, and Cleveland by Maurice R. Davie.[27]

---

[24] The earlier work to be consulted is Clifford R. Shaw, *Delinquency Areas*, University of Chicago Press, 1929; the later, Shaw and McKay, *et al.*, *Juvenile Delinquency and Urban Areas*, University of Chicago Press, 1942. Cities studied include Philadelphia, Richmond, Cleveland, Birmingham, Denver, and Seattle. For a more recent discussion of the role of the neighborhood in delinquency, see Henry D. McKay, "The Neighborhood and Child Conduct," *The Annals*, January 1949, pp. 32–41.

[25] "The Relation of Felonies to Environmental Factors in Indianapolis," *Social Forces*, Vol. X, May 1932, pp. 498–513.

[26] "Ecological Interpretations of Juvenile Delinquency, Dependency and Population Mobility, A Cartographic Analysis of Data from Long Beach, California," *American Journal of Sociology*, Vol. 41, 1936, pp. 598–610.

[27] In George Peter Murdock's *Studies in the Science of Society*, Yale University Press, New Haven, 1937, pp. 133–161.

In 1928, the New York State Crime Commission published an analysis [28] of District 1 of the Manhattan Children's Court, an area south of Third Street and east of the Bowery, containing 21 per cent of the borough's population and 32 per cent of the borough's delinquency. The population of this district was rapidly decreasing. Its housing was bad; 16 out of 17 tenements were of old-law construction, built before 1901. The district's 97,000 children of school age, the *Study* pointed out, would have had just enough room to stand pressed together tightly—as in a crowded subway—if they had all been brought together at one time into the scanty school and park playgrounds in the district.

A part of Harlem (New York City), with an arrest rate of 72.3 per 1,000 (against 28.1 for nonslum areas), and with the typical bad housing, poor recreational equipment, and low income levels of delinquency areas, was intensively studied by Halpern, Stanislaus, and Botein in their book *The Slum and Crime* (1934). Harlem in Manhattan and Red Hook in Brooklyn, according to J. B. Maller, had a delinquency rate twice what would have been expected had delinquency for the whole city been proportioned to population. Maller contrasted a delinquency rate of 25 in Harlem with a rate of under 1 in outlying, nonslum regions. [29]

T. Earl Sullenger analyzed five areas in the much smaller and less composite city of Omaha. [30] These areas, "definite foci of infection," furnished a large proportion of the city's delinquents (a total of 1,000 from these areas in six years). Since these areas exemplify diverse cultural forces and different characteristics of delinquency areas, they are worth listing here. The first area, 50 blocks in all, south and east of the packing plants, includes 16 nationality groups; some of these groups were notorious for their conflict with civil laws, since the parents were opposed to compulsory school attendance. The second area, 96 blocks, a former aristocratic residence section, now houses Syrians, Bohemians, and Negroes. The third, 60 blocks, near unprotected railroad tracks and yards, has many children working at street trades—and playing on railroad tracks.

---

[28] *A Study of Environmental Factors in Juvenile Delinquency in a District of Manhattan Borough*, Albany.

[29] *The New York Times*, April 15, 1934.

[30] *Social Determinants in Juvenile Delinquency*, Wiley, New York, 1936.

The fourth, a 40-block ghetto, has a younger Jewish generation out-growing the controls of orthodoxy, and an influx of Negroes. The fifth area, a "Harlem" 350 blocks in area, houses many Negroes new to city life and supported largely by public relief.

Another study, by Professor Sutherland, showed the concentration of delinquency in the business and congested districts of Chicago. He showed that, in 1931–32, stores of a certain large chain were robbed twice as frequently inside the city of Chicago as they were in a 25-mile zone around the city (59.6 to 29.8), and that the in-city rate was more than nine times the rate in the 100-to-125 mile zone (59.6 to 6.2).[31] In Detroit, Stuart Lottier observed a similar relationship for chain-store robberies inside and outside the city limits.[32]

In the counties of Kansas, to take a comparatively rural state, juvenile delinquency rates were found to bear a relation to the size of the largest community in each county, being higher near the larger communities and declining "as tier distances from a focal county increase," according to statistical studies by Mapheus Smith.[33]

A report from Birmingham, Alabama, states that a study of the city's 52 census tracts in 1940 revealed that "if high population density, low economic value of houses, physical deterioration and lack of necessary equipment, and high rate of tenancy can be evaluated as indicators of poor housing, the findings of this investigation present objective confirmation of the general principle that poor metropolitan housing tends to be associated with high rates of delinquency, and *vice versa*." [34]

A study covering all children referred to the Municipal Court of Philadelphia as delinquents during the year 1944 (except those who were runaways and lived outside Philadelphia) revealed that about one-third (32 per cent) of Philadelphia's delinquent children live in neighborhoods that have relatively high delinquency ratios, *i.e.*, upwards from twice the average for the city as a whole. They live

---

[31] E. H. Sutherland, *Principles of Criminology*, Lippincott, Philadelphia, 1947, pp. 135–136.

[32] "Distribution of Offenses in Metropolitan Regions," *Journal of Criminal Law and Criminology*, Vol. 29, 1938–1939, pp. 39–43.

[33] "Tier Counties and Delinquency in Kansas," *Rural Sociology*, Vol. II, September 1937, pp. 310–322.

[34] Quoted in *Focus*, N.P.P.A., March 1949, p. 59.

in 10 per cent of the census tracts of the city that have a child population amounting to 11 per cent of the total city-wide child population. The area of highest delinquency extends about 2¾ miles north
from the center of the city, 1⅛ miles to the south, 1¼ miles to the
east, and from 1 to 2 miles to the west (following the Schuylkill
River). Although this area covers only one-twelfth of the city's

Slum Conditions Breed Delinquency. (*Courtesy Philadelphia Housing
Association. Photo by Curtis George*)

territory, it contains almost one-fourth of its population and almost one-half of all the city's delinquent children. The delinquency ratio of this area is 40 per 1,000—almost twice as high as the city-wide average (21 per 1,000). More than half of all census tracts with highest population density (121 to 150 persons per acre) and exactly one-half of all census tracts falling into the second highest category of population density (91 to 120 persons per acre) are to be found in this area.

In this area are located almost two-thirds of all census tracts in the city which show less than 20 per cent owner-occupied dwelling units; in other words, tracts in which 80 per cent or more of the dwelling units are rented homes, apartment houses, or rooming houses. The percentage of sub-standard housing ("sub-standard housing" means, according to the United States Census report, a dwelling unit that is in need of major repair or has no private bath) in this area was more than twice the average for the whole city— 39.7 as compared with 17.8 per cent. Almost three-quarters of all the geographical units (census tracts or combinations of census tracts) in this area show above-average figures for both sub-standard housing and juvenile delinquency.[35]

Reports from several urban communities describe the wholesome low-rental housing projects that replace slum areas. Americans will watch with deep interest the results of the long-range housing bill passed by Congress in 1949.[36] As one of the results of such public housing projects (Federal or municipal), the lower delinquency rate is often mentioned. For instance, one area in New Haven produced a juvenile delinquency rate of 3.18 per hundred children annually during the years from 1924 to 1940. After its conversion into a new housing project area, an annual average of only 1.64 per hundred children was reported from 1940 to 1944.[37]

Studies conducted in Chicago during 1948 pointed out some of

---

[35] For further details, see J. O. Reinemann, "Where Do Philadelphia's Delinquent Children Live?," *Thirty-Second Annual Report of the Municipal Court of Philadelphia*, 1945, p. 379–388.

[36] See Senator Paul Douglas' article in *Collier's Magazine*, July 9, 1949, "Democracy Can't Live in These Houses."

[37] Reported in *Journal of Housing*, January 1946, p. 27. This study and other surveys are mentioned in "Housing and Juvenile Delinquency," by Sydney Maslen, *Federal Probation*, June 1948, pp. 40–44.

the results of public housing, such as the improvement of the school attendance of children in the housing projects as compared with the attendance of children in the surrounding slum areas. This study covered 4,400 children in the housing projects and a total of 13,300 children in the surrounding neighborhoods. It was found that although 33 per cent of the children in all the schools studied came from the housing projects, only 27 per cent of all unexcused ab-

Blighted Area. *(Courtesy Philadelphia Housing Association. Photo by Edward E. Gallob)*

sences, particularly truancy, were caused by these children. In some of the projects, the difference was even more marked. For example, in one of the schools studied, 43 per cent of the children lived in a housing project, but they were responsible for only 28 per cent of the unexcused absences.[38]

It is not always fair to compare delinquency rates in housing projects with the city average; rather, a comparison should be made of these rates with the figures obtained for the surrounding slum areas. Thus in Cleveland, out of a total of 4,018 children living in six low-rent housing projects, the rate of delinquency in 1947 averaged 1.57 per cent. The rate for the city as a whole was 1.8, and in the slum areas adjacent to the housing projects the average rate was 2.26 per cent.[39]

The Philadelphia Housing Authority reported that in 1948 the rate of arrests of boys living in public housing projects was 2.27 per cent. This rate compared favorably with the delinquency rates of the areas surrounding these housing projects. The arrest rate in the largest project (Richard Allen Homes) was 4.11 per cent, whereas the rate of arrests of boys for the surrounding area was 11.34 per cent.

Another type of pioneer work, especially in the larger metropolitan areas, was the study of gang life among adolescent boys. The name of Frederic M. Thrasher stands out in this field, although studies of the gang had been made prior to his definitive work, *The Gang*, published in 1927.[40] As early as 1900, Jacob Riis demonstrated in his *Ten Years' War* the potency of the gang in stimulating delinquency by giving its members a false sense of belonging and self-esteem. Puffer, as early as 1912, indicated the importance of gangs in an understanding of delinquency.[41]

But it was Thrasher who, with his background of sociological methodology, focused attention on the powerful role of the gang in indoctrinating its members with the delinquency mores of the blighted and congested areas of the great cities. His findings were based on a study of some 1,313 gangs in the Loop district of Chicago. He showed that "gangland," in this area, represents a geographically and socially interstitial area between the business district and the

---

[38] Digested from an article by James S. First, "Public Housing Measured," *The American City*, February 1949, pp. 97–98.

[39] *Journal of Housing*, October 1948, p. 265.

[40] University of Chicago Press; revised in 1936.

[41] J. A. Puffer, *The Boy and His Gang*, Badger, Boston, 1921.

residential districts. He made it plain that the village and small-town gangs do not usually become a social problem, and that all city gangs are not necessarily delinquent, although many serve as training schools for crime. So his research, though it was not primarily concerned with delinquency, made important contributions to the natural history of urban regions that are the habitat and nursery of delinquency. He pointed out and described the location and characteristics of these spots. He further stressed that delinquency and crime originate on the edges of respectability and in communities imperfectly adjusted to normal conditions.

One other feature of this and other similar studies is that the gang appeals to a socially nurtured longing for adventurous recreation, to the gang's importance as a social group, to its cultivation of an intense spirit of loyalty, and to other qualities that have social values. Thrasher's study shows some of the requisites that must be built up into activities to remedy the antisocial effects of the gang—in a sense, these requisites are socially approved adaptations of gang traits. But the outstanding and immediate ecological contribution of his book was the mapping and description of gangland.[42]

A more recent study, by William Foote Whyte, describes the corner gang in an Italian community. Whyte shows how the boys, during adolescence, are used by the politicians to aid in the spread of racketeering. Capitalizing on group loyalties, but at the same time scrupulously respecting the social structure of the group, the overlords secure the services of many young adults in "cornervilles" all over the country.[43]

3. A CRITICAL NOTE ON THE DELINQUENCY AREA CONCEPT

As we have seen, the nineteen-twenties and thirties witnessed a plethora of ecological studies of delinquency by competent sociolo-

---

[42] Another writer, Winifred Richmond, lays great stress on the gang as a potential influence for both good and bad during puberty. See *The Delinquent Boy*, Farrar & Rinehart, New York, 1933.

[43] *Street Corner Society*, University of Chicago Press, 1943. See also, for a revealing story of the gang with its feuds, loyalties, and so forth, "The Boy Gangs of Mousetown," by Bradford Chambers, *Reader's Digest*, August 1948; also James R. Dumpson, "An Approach to Antisocial Street Gangs," *Federal Probation*, December 1949, pp. 22 ff.

gists. Many of these studies were accompanied by charts and maps of cities and areas of cities which lent dignity to the accompanying scholarship. In more recent years, the emphasis seems to be away from the ecological approach. This trend is due to two factors, at least.

The first of these, pointed out by Sophia Robison in her provocative work, mentioned earlier, *Can Delinquency Be Measured?*, is that the term "delinquency" is so variously defined and considered, and so subjectively interpreted, that it cannot be used as a unit of measurement. As she states:

> Although the *delinquency area* technique of study, developed in Chicago and later extended to an examination of the locus of delinquency in other cities, has received official recognition, the suspicion persists that this method is not only essentially invalid to indicate the extent of juvenile delinquent behavior but that it does not furnish any very useful approach to the problem of understanding or preventing delinquent behavior.[44]

Her analysis of delinquency in New York City failed to validate an index of delinquency said to be established by the Chicago study, as well as by studies in other cities.[45] Miss Robison furthermore cannot accept the thesis so prevalent in most ecological studies that delinquency decreases from the general business district outward.[46]

A more recent critical note concerning the delinquency area concept was prepared by Professor Christen T. Jonassen.[47] He points out that many factors may influence delinquency rates but not influence delinquent behavior directly. Among these he lists the differences in laws; in police policies of enforcement; in the administrative policies of courts; and in the cultural orientation of specific areas within the community.

The second factor that tends to militate against the area concept is the psychiatric approach to the problems of maladjustment and delinquent behavior. Although no one can deny that the great bulk of what is popularly known as delinquency comes from the blighted

---

[44] *Op. cit.*, p. 4.
[45] *Ibid.*, p. 210.
[46] *Ibid.*, p. 16.
[47] "A Re-Evaluation and Critique of the Logic and Some Methods of Shaw and McKay," *American Sociological Review*, October 1949, pp. 608–617.

areas of our large cities, this fact cannot obscure the existence of much delinquency in the homes of the economically favored. Delinquency in such homes just isn't officially recorded as frequently as is delinquency in the blighted areas. The psychiatrists are not much impressed with the ecological or statistical studies, made in most cases by sociologists.

For example, Alexander and Healy in their work, *Roots of Crime*, maintain that such studies do nothing more than call attention to a phenomenon that every policeman knows and that needs no further explanation.[48] To Karpman, psychiatrist at St. Elizabeth's Hospital in Washington, D. C., the entire approach means nothing more than the elaboration of the obvious, a criticism often hurled at the sociologist.[49]

Although the above criticisms are not serious, they are worthy of record. Another qualification of the delinquency area concept would arise, if studies in any quantity were available, that would show just how many children grow up in such blighted neighborhoods and do not become delinquent. One such study of a Chicago slum area was made by Boorman some years ago. Staff members of a boys' club rated 26 out of 103 members as of high character, 46 as somewhat neutral but still promising, 27 as problems due to maladjustments of one or another type, and 4 definitely criminal.[50]

Still another criticism of the area concept may be mentioned. Although the work done and the approach itself are valuable, attention has been diverted from the individual delinquent's maladjustment, which must be considered in any diagnosis or treatment. The concept also permits various people and reform organizations to offer the popular bromides of poverty, broken homes, poor housing, and so forth, as *the* basic causes of delinquency.

Nevertheless the sociologist, through such studies, has made a distinct contribution to the analysis of delinquency, despite some psychiatrists' criticisms who now feel that they alone possess the key to

[48] Franz Alexander and William Healy, *The Roots of Crime*, Knopf, New York, 1935, p. 274.

[49] Benjamin Karpman, "Milestones in the Advancement of Knowledge of the Psychopathology of Delinquency and Crime," *Orthopsychiatry: 1923–1948*, American Orthopsychiatric Association, Inc., 1948, pp. 100–189.

[50] William R. Boorman, "Delinquency Area: Another Viewpoint," *Religious Education*, Vol. 26, 1931, pp. 858–863.

an understanding of the problem. An ecological study of delinquency in an urban area can be of practical, as well as of research, value. A few samples of the practical use of such studies may be cited. They may be of help to city departments in charge of public safety, public welfare, and public health; to private and public agencies engaged in developing low-cost housing projects; to boards of education, recreation bureaus, and family welfare and other social agencies. Neighborhood and community councils and other civic organizations devoted to improvement of specific areas need factual information along these lines. State and city planning commissions preparing blueprints for improved living conditions will find such studies of inestimable value in determining needs.

Thus there is no doubt that the delinquency area concept has served a useful purpose in assisting in the fight against delinquency and crime. But the danger exists that it will continue to be used, as it has been all too frequently in the past, as an oversimplification of the problem of delinquency.

4. THE BROKEN HOME AND DELINQUENCY

Persons working in the field of delinquency, as well as many who have conducted studies in the etiology of delinquent behavior, have placed great emphasis on the broken home as a predisposing cause. (See Appendix for several cases in which physically and psychologically broken homes contributed to delinquency; those in which these factors are evident are Cases 2, 6, 8, 9, 10, and 11.) As we did in our discussion of poverty as a cause, we must clarify this approach after we have reviewed some of the literature in the field.

The significance of the well-integrated and socially mature home cannot be denied. But the ideal home is very rare in these confused days when the stresses and strains of modern life make it extremely difficult to attain "peace of mind." Of course, all confused homes do not produce delinquents, but neither are they especially healthful places in which to rear children. But what constitutes a "normal" home? Several years ago, Dr. Miriam Van Waters set down what she thought the home should furnish the child:

> The home has primary tasks to fulfill for its young: to shelter and nourish infancy in comfort, without inflicting damage of premature anxiety, enable the child to win health, virility and social esteem; to educate it to meet behavior codes of the community; to respond effec-

tively to human situations which produce the great emotions, love, fear and anger; to furnish practice in the art of living together on a small scale where human relationships are kindly and simple; finally the home has as its supreme task the weaning of youth, this time not from the breast of the mother, but from dependence, from relying too much on that kindliness and simplicity of home, so that youth may not fail to become imbued with joy of struggle, work and service among sterner human relationships outside.[51]

What Miss Van Waters wrote in 1925 cannot be improved on today. Juvenile maladjustment and, to some degree, delinquency, may be found in homes not usually labeled broken. Rather they should be referred to as homes in which there is lack of insight into the emotional needs of the child. (This kind of home will be discussed later in Chapter VII.) Here we are concerned with the broken home, whether it is a *psychologically* broken home, or a *physically* broken home. The former is often described by psychiatrists as a "tyranny ruled over by its meanest member." [52] It is the home where both parents, and, perhaps, several children, reside physically, but where constant bickering occurs, where little respect is shown the rights of each individual, and where the child is "pushed around" or ridiculed. It is the authoritarian home in which the father assumes the old-fashioned patriarchal role; the wife and children are relegated to a passive status; and the old bromide "children should be seen and not heard" is the rule. In such homes the child is too often rejected, never having the genuine experience of "belonging." As a result, he becomes desolate, anxious, restless, or often hostile. Our child-guidance clinics are full of such cases, and there is plenty of evidence that thousands of others unfortunately never get to the clinics. They are supposed to "outgrow" their peculiarities.[53]

The second type of broken home is the one that is physically broken, the one in which one or both parents are missing, dead, divorced, or deserted. Is there a high correlation between the physi-

---

[51] *Youth in Conflict*, The New Republic, 1925, p. 64.

[52] *Ibid.*, p. 48.

[53] See Irene Kawin, "Family Dissension as a Factor in Delinquency," *Yearbook*, N.P.P.A., 1946, pp. 66–76; also Harry M. Shulman, "The Family and Juvenile Delinquency," *The Annals*, January 1949, pp. 21–31; and Charles W. Coulter, "Family Disorganization as a Causal Factor in Delinquency and Crime," *Federal Probation*, September 1948, pp. 13–17.

cally broken home and delinquency? Many studies have been made of this aspect of the problem, but as in other phases of the subject, there is not complete agreement. We shall cite some of the traditional studies to show this lack of agreement.

The early study of Breckinridge and Abbott, *The Delinquent Child and the Home*, based on an analysis of 13,000 cases of delinquent children, shows that 34 per cent came from broken homes.[54] Nathaniel Cantor cites studies made by the Catholic Charities Probation Bureau of the Court of General Sessions in New York City. These studies showed that over 47 per cent of some 3,000 delinquent children came from broken homes. Cantor also cites a study of 11,176 cases appearing before the Children's Court in New York; of these children, 56 per cent came from physically broken homes.[55]

Figures compiled by the Municipal Court of Philadelphia regarding home conditions of delinquent children over several years show that 47 per cent of these children came from broken homes. In 1949, 46 per cent of the boys came from broken homes, while the much stronger influence of the lack of normal home life on the girl is manifest in the 65 per cent of girls' cases thus classified. Regarding racial composition, 40 per cent of white boys and 56 per cent of Negro boys came from broken homes; the corresponding figures were 54 per cent of white girls and 72 per cent of Negro girls.[56] A four-year study by the California Youth Authority showed "that 62 per cent of the state's juvenile delinquents were the result of broken homes." [57] One could continue indefinitely to pile up studies showing the significance of broken homes in delinquency causation.

On the other hand, the famous Wickersham Commission made a study of 40,503 children appearing in 93 different courts during the year 1919. It showed that 64 per cent of the children lived with both parents, whereas only 36 per cent came from broken homes.[58] The same report includes other significant figures: "The statistics for the year 1927, from the Children's Bureau, U. S. Department of Labor,

[54] *Op. cit.*, pp. 91–92.

[55] *Crime and Society*, Henry Holt, New York, 1939, p. 51.

[56] *Thirty-sixth Annual Report of the Municipal Court of Philadelphia*, 1949, p. 42.

[57] Quoted in *Federal Probation*, December 1948, p. 59.

[58] *National Commission on Law Observance and Enforcement*, Vol. I, "Report on the Causes of Crime," 1931, p. 67.

showed that 67 per cent of 16,258 delinquent boys and 48 per cent of 3,040 delinquent girls were living with both parents. Thus 33 per cent of the boys and 52 per cent of the girls came from broken homes." [59] Students of this problem generally agree that the percentage of female delinquents from broken homes is higher than that of males, but, as H. Ashley Weeks contends, this difference is more apparent than real.[60] Nevertheless, Weeks finds a positive relationship between delinquency and the broken home.

Healy and Bronner have also contributed to this question. After studying some 4,000 cases, both in Chicago and Boston, they found that "normal parental conditions (both parents alive and living at home) existed in only a little over half of the cases in each city." [61] They state: "Certainly broken home conditions exist more often in the background of delinquency than is average for the general population." [62]

Sheldon and Eleanor Glueck, in their evaluation of 1,000 cases of juvenile delinquency, found that the broken home or "poorly supervised home" looms large. They say: "Our delinquents come largely from homes which were for one reason or another broken or distorted. There can be no doubt that these boys had an unwholesome home life. Even the possibility of nondelinquents having so high an incidence of inadequate homes would not make it less necessary to take into account the home background in developing any treatment program for delinquency." [63] This study, of course, takes both types of broken homes into consideration.

The White House Conference study of the delinquent child states: "Estimates as to the prevalence of this condition [broken home] in the histories of juvenile delinquents range from about 20 to nearly 50 per cent." [64] Professor Lowell Carr, in his penetrating work,

---

[59] Quoted from reports of Children's Bureau, Table 4, Juvenile Court Statistics for 1929, 3rd annual report, in Wickersham Commission Report, p. 67 n.

[60] "Male and Female Broken Home Rates by Types of Delinquency," *American Sociological Review*, August 1940, pp. 601–609.

[61] *Delinquents and Criminals*, Macmillan, New York, 1926, p. 122. By permission of The Macmillan Company, publishers.

[62] *Ibid.*, p. 208.

[63] *One Thousand Juvenile Delinquents*, Harvard University Press, 1934, p. 76. Reprinted by permission of the President and Fellows of Harvard College.

[64] *The Delinquent Child*, Report of the Committee on Socially Handicapped— Delinquency, Century, New York, 1932, p. 351.

Delinquency Control, minimizes the role of the physically broken home in producing delinquency. He points out that perhaps one-eighth of the homes in America are physically broken and that their contribution to delinquency is slight indeed. He further states that most actual delinquents continue to come from homes that are not so broken.[65]

Studies dealing with the family status of children incarcerated in institutions show that most of the inmates, especially the girls, come from broken homes. This phenomenon is not unusual, since juvenile court judges are traditionally obsessed with the "broken-home-causes-delinquency" thesis and despair of any other disposition of such cases. Thus they feel constrained to send their charges to institutions. Of course, hundreds of children from broken homes are also placed in foster homes, whether they are delinquent, neglected, or dependent.

For the student to wend his way through such a welter of conflicting opinion, coming as it does from experts, is indeed a confusing task. What he wants to know is: "Is there a positive relationship between the broken home and delinquency?" Apparently no definite answer can be made to this question. An answer might be attempted if we knew how many homes in the nation are broken or what percentage of broken homes manage to rear non-delinquent children.

But very few studies provide us with this kind of information. Shideler, on the basis of the census of 1910, estimated that approximately 25 per cent of *all* children in the United States lived in homes that might be called "broken." [66] Slawson found that 45 per cent of the delinquent boys sentenced to New York state correctional schools, but only 19 per cent of a group of 3,198 boys from three public schools in New York City, came from broken homes.[67] The White House Conference mentioned above, in evaluating a thorough-going study of this subject by Shaw and McKay, felt that the "rate of broken homes in the general population had probably been underestimated." These authors, studying 7,278 cases of delinquent

[65] Harper, New York, 1940, p. 140.

[66] E. H. Shideler, "Family Disintegration and the Delinquent Boy in the United States," *Journal of Criminal Law and Criminology,* January 1918, pp. 709–732.

[67] John Slawson, *The Delinquent Boy,* Badger, Boston, 1926, p. 359.

boys in the city of Chicago, had sought to establish the incidence of broken homes: (1) among boys living in areas with different rates of delinquency; (2) among boys of different nationalities; and (3) among boys of different age groups. They found: (1) that 42.5 per cent of the delinquent boys and 36.1 of the non-delinquent (school) boys studied came from broken homes; (2) that the incidence of broken homes varied in different national and racial groupings, from 16.3 per cent for Jewish children to 46 per cent for Negro children; and (3) that the older the child, the greater the percentage of broken homes—26.2 at age ten to 38.9 at age sixteen. The same authors made another study of an area, with a predominantly Italian population, on the "Near West Side" of Chicago. Here they found that of 93 delinquent boys studied, 25.8 per cent came from broken homes, and that of 1,167 non-delinquent school boys 26.4 per cent were from broken homes. The Shaw and McKay studies indicate that there is "no consistent relationship between rates of broken homes and rates of delinquency." [68]

We can leave this phase of the subject by stating that the phenomenon of the physically broken home as a cause of delinquent behavior is, in itself, not so important as was once believed. In essence, it is not that the home is broken, but rather that the home is inadequate, that really matters.

Many mothers, and some fathers, who have lost their mates through separation, divorce, or death, are doing a splendid job of rearing their children. It is not so much the physically broken home as the home that is confused or inadequate because of ignorance, indifference, or faulty conception of the child's place in the general scheme of things that contributes to the high delinquency rates. (See Chapter VII for further discussion of this important phase of the subject.)

5. DELINQUENCY IN SMALL TOWNS AND RURAL AREAS

Much of the discussion thus far has dealt with delinquency and antisocial behavior in the larger metropolitan areas. In terms of delinquency and incorrigibility, the urban community apparently outdistances the smaller towns and open country. However, in pro-

---

[68] Quotation from National Commission on Law Observance and Enforcement, *Report on Causes of Crime*, Vol. II, 1931, p. 67.

portion to population, this comparison is doubtful. Precise and comparable statistics are difficult, if not impossible, to secure. Categories and methods of reporting figures differ widely. Inefficiency and indifference on the part of the officials in many rural and thinly populated towns and villages also make comparisons difficult.[69]

Several regional studies have been made of rural communities, but no categorical statements on the rarity of delinquency in sparsely settled areas are possible. For example, M. G. Caldwell shows that, in Wisconsin, counties in which there are cities tend to have a high rate of delinquency—but so do isolated logging counties on the northern tier of the state in which there are no cities of any size.[70] Paul Wiers made a study of delinquency in rural areas of Michigan. He found that the rate for sparsely settled northern counties was higher than the rate for the southern agricultural counties, although it was lower than the rate for urban Wayne County, which embraces the city of Detroit.[71] In a study cited earlier in this chapter, Wiers points out that low delinquency rates are highly correlated with "favorable conditions of population density and urbanization," rather than with merely rural or urban conditions alone.[72]

There are several obvious reasons why delinquency seems to be an urban rather than a rural problem. Cities are characterized by an anonymity that makes it easier for persons prone to delinquent and criminal acts to hide against arrest; organized vice abounds on a larger scale, since a much larger clientele is interested in such exciting diversions; cities have a greater proportion of unmarried persons who crave recreation, even of an illegal nature; the tense, nervous life of the city favors indulgence in artificial and extreme forms of entertainment, much of which is lacking in small towns and rural areas; family life is less normal and living conditions are less wholesome in the row-house and apartment-house dwellings of cities.

Moreover, operators of vice and gambling establishments in the

---

[69] For a discussion of the rural officers, see Barnes and Teeters, *New Horizons in Criminology*, Prentice-Hall, New York, 1943, pp. 147–149.

[70] "The Extent of Juvenile Delinquency in Wisconsin," *Journal of Criminal Law and Criminology*, Vol. 32, 1941, pp. 148–157.

[71] "Juvenile Delinquency in Rural Michigan," *ibid.*, Vol. 30, 1939, pp. 211–222.

[72] *Op. cit.*, p. 47. See also, Arthur L. Wood, "Social Organization and Crime in Small Wisconsin Communities," *American Sociological Review*, Vol. 7, 1942, pp. 40–46.

city have a far greater prospect of remunerative returns than they do in the village or crossroads community. Taprooms, nightclubs, and marginal illegal emporia are a constant reminder to the city's youth that "easy money" is to be found in such types of business. Children of the streets see vice and sexual looseness all about them. The numbers racket and other forms of petty crime are an integral part of the urban mores, especially in the congested areas. In other words, the temptation to delinquency and petty crime is rampant in the large metropolitan areas, but is almost totally lacking in the smaller communities.

Professor George Vold explains the scarcity of rural lawlessness—including juvenile delinquency—in another way. He contends that the traditional American culture serves as an insulation against crime:

> Rural culture also has its effects on the individual. The value and respectability of work, of family stability and continuity, of land as insurance against want and as an indicator of status, and a general scorn for pleasure-seeking and "soft" life, are all part of the traditional rural pattern. Its effect on the individual is, among other things, to provide a pattern of conformity, an acceptance of the regulations and controls of the settled community.[73]

Of course, play gangs exist in small towns and open-country hamlets, but, as Thrasher pointed out, they do not present the same social problem as their urban counterparts do. The advantages of life in the outdoors tend to temper the behavior of the country gangs. True, a maladjusted boy or girl occasionally comes to grief and is either disciplined by the county juvenile judge or is sent away to a reform school. But such cases are less frequent than in the urban community.

However, the ease with which rural boys and girls can get away from village controls by means of automobiles often leads them to participate in the fast life of the county seat or larger cities. Sexual offenses are just as prevalent in the small town, in proportion to the population, as in the city. The natural sex drive is no respecter of adolescents, whether they grow up in cities or in small towns. Professor Kinsey finds that there are few significant differences between the sex histories of boys raised in cities and those raised on farms, or

---

[73] "Crime in City and Rural Areas," *The Annals*, September 1941, p. 45.

between adult males in urban and rural areas.[74] But since village controls are more personalized, irregular behavior is not openly indulged in as it is in the cities. It is true, however, that the ranks of prostitution are recruited from girls who have become bored with the humdrum existences of their rural or small-town homes. Since very few studies have been made of these matters, we can only speculate on what seems to be obvious.[75]

One other phase of this urban-rural contrast is detection by peace officers. Many minor delinquencies and other forms of boisterous behavior are unrecorded in rural areas either because they are undetected or because the perpetrators are known personally to the officers and dealt with in sympathetic, home-spun fashion. The impersonal relationship of city police to small-time offenders, especially older boys who commit pranks, prompts them to record such offenses on the police blotter. Thus a higher delinquency rate is built up for the city.

But social and economic maladjustment is certainly plentiful in our small towns. A great deal has been written about the ugliness and monotony of the small community. Poverty, malnourishment (among grown-ups and children alike), frustrating social cleavages, poor housing, and similar conditions exact their toll in the village and the small town. Many children growing up under such conditions gravitate to the city and become lost in the anonymous rooming-house districts or slum areas. There they present a constant source of delinquency and criminal behavior.

In the over-all attack on delinquency as a national issue, the National Conference (1946) did not overlook the "rural aspects" of the problem. An excellent special pamphlet set forth the nature of rural populations, their special interests, their institutions, and their child-care assets. Such statements remind us that the problem of delinquency in sparsely populated areas is very real and calls for the concerted attack of all existing agencies, just as it does in urban communities.[76]

---

[74] For statistics, see Alfred C. Kinsey, et al., Sexual Behavior in the Human Male, Saunders, Philadelphia, 1948, pp. 448–464.

[75] See James West, Plainville, U.S.A., Columbia University Press, New York, 1944, pp. 91–107.

[76] Report No. 17, "Rural Aspects of Juvenile Delinquency," Government Printing Office, Washington, D.C., 1947.

Chapter VI

CULTURAL FACTORS AND DELINQUENCY

1. INTRODUCTORY STATEMENT

IT IS OUR PURPOSE in this chapter to review and appraise what we choose to call the cultural influences at work on each individual for good or ill. Professor Marshall B. Clinard refers to these as "secondary community influences" which are "administered or controlled by forces outside the immediate local community or neighborhood." [1] Technically, two of the community services described in this chapter—religion and recreation—may not fall under such a heading, since both are definitely operated through the neighborhood. However, they are more impersonal than is the home itself. But we shall also discuss the press, movies, radio programs, and the comics, and we shall review the deleterious effects of certain vices, such as drug addiction, gambling, and other "snares" of youth. All these influences fall within the framework labeled "secondary" by Clinard.

2. RELIGION AND DELINQUENCY

Frequently, some outstanding civic or educational leader maintains that the delinquency rate could be lowered if only the church would play its part in guiding youth along the paths of moral rectitude. One of the *clichés* often noted in the press and in the pulpit is that the youth of our day has strayed from the straight and narrow path, or has "forgotten God." Sunday morning radio sermons are monotonous in their dire imprecations to the younger generation regarding the wages of sin. In fact, religion is almost universally assumed to be the most important influence in checking delinquency and crime. Certainly it is important that both religion and morality be appraised

---

[1] Marshall B. Clinard, "Secondary Community Influences and Juvenile Delinquency," *The Annals,* January 1949, pp. 42–54.

in any discussion of cultural influences affecting the age-old problem of delinquency.

In a later chapter (Chapter XV) we shall discuss the important work of the church in combatting delinquency. It would be a dereliction of duty if we failed to recognize the importance of church activity in the fight against delinquency. But here, we feel constrained to make a few remarks about the efficacy of instruction in church and Sunday School and about the moral instruction of various character-building agencies. We intend these remarks to serve as a buffer against the enthusiastic claims made for these agencies as deterrents of delinquent behavior.

One could collect many examples similar to the following, which reflect the thinking of a large segment of the population regarding the place of religion in character formation. The pioneer probation officer, E. J. Cooley, in his excellent book *Probation and Delinquency* (1927), says, on page 14: "The most vital force in the upbuilding of the character of youth is the influence of religion and the church." Now this is an opinion only, even though it comes from a successful probation officer with many years' experience. It seems almost unkind to question such a statement, yet there are many other successful men and women working in the field of delinquency and other types of maladjustment whose opinions are just the reverse.

We may refer to a study made some years ago by Dr. George Rex Mursell, at one time psychologist of the Ohio Department of Welfare, who found that the inmates of a reform school had received fully as much religious training as had the children outside. His conclusion was that in general no significant relationship existed between religious training and delinquent or non-delinquent behavior. Further, he stated that religious training, knowledge, attitudes, or background, as measured by the tests he used, cannot be regarded as causes of delinquency or of non-delinquency.[2] Professor P. R. Hightower, after testing some 3,000 children for lying, cheating, and deception, concludes that "there appears to be no relationship of any consequence between Biblical information and the different phases of conduct studied. . . . It indicates very definitely that mere knowl-

---

[2] *A Study of Religious Training as a Psychological Factor in Delinquency,* Ph.D. dissertation, Ohio State University, 1930.

edge of the Bible is not in itself sufficient to insure proper character growth." [3]

More recently, W. C. Kvaraceus made a study of 761 delinquent children in Passaic, New Jersey. Practically all these children were connected with some church, and two-thirds were members of the Roman or Eastern Orthodox churches. Not only were they members, but 54.2 per cent of them attended church *regularly* and 20.4 per cent attended occasionally. Only 6.8 per cent admitted non-membership in any church and only 25.4 per cent stated they rarely visited any church. [4]

A study by Middleton and Fay of 83 delinquent and 100 non-delinquent girls ranging from the eighth to tenth grade levels showed that the delinquent girls measured (on three Thurstone Scales measuring social attitudes) more favorable attitudes toward Sunday observance and the Bible than did the non-delinquent girls. [5]

If Sunday School attendance and training are to count in inculcating morality and obedience to law and order in our youth, as well as in teaching them Biblical culture, the churches must give a great deal more thought to physical facilities and the training of acceptable teachers. A survey of the country's Sunday Schools made by the magazine *Pageant* affords some revealing information. First, the attendance of children at Sunday School was reported to have gone down during the past decade (in 1906, it was 14,685,997; in 1916, it was 19,935,890; in 1926, it was 21,038,526; and in 1936, the last official census year, it had dropped to 18,389,001). In view of the phenomenal increase in population, this decrease should give religious leaders concern. It is estimated, however, that present figures would show a slight trend toward the 1926 figure. Second, the physical setting was found to be shoddy, and the teaching, in most cases, was found to be colorless and poorly conducted by untrained teachers. Third, the children were found to be woefully ignorant of Biblical information. Although it is difficult to poll the moral values children receive in Sunday Schools, it is possible to learn what information they have gleaned from their instruction. The poll showed that in

---

[3] *Biblical Information in Relation to Character and Conduct*, The State University of Iowa, Department of Publications, 1930.

[4] *Juvenile Delinquency and the School*, World Book Company, New York, 1945, pp. 101–103.

[5] Warren Candler Middleton and Paul J. Fay, *Journal of Educational Psychology*, Vol. 32, 1941, pp. 555–558.

a simple test of Biblical knowledge, Protestant children who attended Sunday Schools failed with an average mark of 35 per cent; Catholic children did slightly better with an average of 46 per cent; and the children who did not go to Sunday School made an average score of 30.4 per cent. The author of the article, Roland Gammon, commenting on the above findings, adds that "in the more intangible but probably more important factor of religious *feeling* our youth shows dismaying lack of interest." To possible critics of this poll, it should be stated that the International Council of Religious Education in Chicago gave its cooperation and advice, and that the test was compiled by Professor S. R. Laycock, of the University of Saskatchewan, Canada.[6]

Again, let it be emphasized that what is needed is more studies rather than mere opinions. Here is what C. V. Dunn has to say in the conclusion of a study he made of the religious affiliations in adult prisons and in some reform schools over twenty years ago:

> In a group of 27 penitentiaries and 19 reform schools a total of 71.8 per cent of the population were affiliated with some religion (22.5 per cent Roman Catholic and 49.3 per cent Protestant) while only 46.6 per cent of the United States population are members of any religious body. . . . In any event [and this is what we are concerned with at this point in the discussion] there is no reliable evidence indicating whether religious affiliation, training, or conviction does or does not aid in crime deterrence. Indeed, we should first have to define carefully what was meant by the terms religion and crime.[7]

In any survey dealing with the religious affiliations of delinquents or criminals, many false statements are likely to be made to the investigator. Those who run afoul of the law, especially those who are incarcerated in an institution, are prone to make false statements in the hope of making a favorable impression. But, of course, it is probably true that many youngsters—perhaps most of them—have been exposed to some religious instruction, especially in their earlier years. It is also probably true that most of these children, as well as our older criminals, have been brought up in orthodox surroundings rather than in homes of free-thinkers.

---

[6] Roland Gammon, "The Plight of Our Sunday Schools," *Pageant Magazine*, December 1949, pp. 20–23.

[7] "The Church and Crime in the United States," *The Annals*, 1926, pp. 246–247.

Still another study has bearing on this subject. Dr. John R. Miner, in an article written some years ago in *Human Biology*,[8] revealed an apparent correlation between certain types of religion and homicide. He pointed out that states with a high percentage of Roman Catholics have a low homicide rate, whereas states with a high percentage of Methodists and Baptists have a high rate. He concluded by stating that there is little evidence to show that churches play any major role in crime prevention. But Dr. Miner's findings are at variance with those of the distinguished European criminologists W. H. Bonger and Gustav Aschaffenburg, who contend that Catholics tend to be more criminal than Protestants, and that Jews are the least criminal of the three groups.[9]

These latter conclusions are borne out by Kvaraceus in his Passaic, New Jersey, study, to which we referred above. Only 2 per cent of the delinquents were Jewish and only one-fifth were Protestant. In New York City, where the population is rather evenly divided among Catholics, Protestants, and Jews, Sophia Robison found that in the court count there were seven Catholic children to each white Protestant child; the ratio between Catholic and Jewish children was three to one.[10]

Findings such as those quoted above must be regarded cautiously, since other factors influence any evaluation of the criminality or delinquency of large numbers of individuals. Economic conditions, which play a role in criminality, must be appraised when we try to arrive at the etiology of crime. It has been frequently stated that if there is a low rate of crime and delinquency among Jews, it may be because of the closer control of the home and the Jewish neighborhood on individual members.

No study of this subject would be complete without discussing the classic analysis by Professors Hartshorne and May entitled *Studies in the Nature of Character*.[11] These authors attempted to

---

[8] "Church Membership and Commitment to Prisons," Vol. 3, September 1931, pp. 429–436.

[9] See John L. Gillin, *Criminology and Penology*, Century, New York, 1926, pp. 246–247.

[10] *Can Delinquency Be Measured?*, Columbia University Press, New York, 1936, p. 207.

[11] Hugh Hartshorne and Mark A. May, Macmillan, New York, 3 vols., 1928–1930; see especially the volume, "Studies in Deceit."

make a scientific analysis of moral and religious instruction as an element in character education. One of the questions they hoped to answer was whether children who go to Sunday School regularly are more honest than those who do not. The investigators came to the conclusion that there was no great difference between the two groups.[12]

Another study made by these scholars involved children who were deliberately exposed to a "moral" system of education designed to make honesty a definite part of the children's lives. Each day the children kept a record of their good deeds, including truth-telling. At the end of the experiment, the investigators found a startling situation: the members of this truth-telling and highly moral group cheated more on each test given them than did the non-members. The only exception was in athletic events, in which there were no differences between the groups. They also found that the higher the rank achieved in the system of morality, the greater the deception.

The obvious comment to make on this and other studies of the same type is that we have not yet devised any mechanical character-building program for young people to substitute for the day-by-day relationship between parents and their children. Home training is still of vital importance. A few hours each day spent in school and one or two hours per week spent in Sunday School, with perhaps an evening spent in some character-building agency, cannot offset the influence of a home where the moral tone is on a low level. Where home influences are good, the child will profit little in morality by participation in these organizations.

Hartshorne and May maintain that parents are the most potent source of personality influence and formation, especially so far as moral judgments are concerned. For instance, correlations of such judgments were: between child and parents, .55; between child and friends, .35; between child and club leaders, .14; between child and school teachers, .03; and between child and Sunday School teachers .002.[13]

---

[12] See Vol. I, p. 359.
[13] "Testing the Knowledge of Right and Wrong," *Religious Education*, Vol. 21, pp. 539–554, quoted by Herbert H. Stroup, "What Does Generic Case Work Really Mean?," *American Journal of Orthopsychiatry*, Vol. 16, pp. 329–332 (see p. 331).

Obviously the child may acquire other values away from home, such as nature lore from the Boy Scouts, or Biblical knowledge from Sunday School, but *morality* and *honesty* develop at a much slower tempo than that at which these organizations and groups can function. Rewards for honest conduct, morality, good turns daily, and other character traits frequently become so socially compulsive that the pursuit of them often develops behavior in children at the opposite extreme from that intended. In other words, a child who must be rewarded for being honest and truthful is under such emotional strain that he tends to be such only by stealth and fraud.

It is interesting and encouraging that the study made by Professors Hartshorne and May was sponsored by the Institute of Social and Religious Research. In evaluating religious and moral ideas in young people, we must recognize that most persons are likely to keep their religion quite separate from their moral code. A fair question to ask is: What do we want, orthodoxy with its sterility, or moral integrity? This question must be faced by religious leaders and answered with honesty and conviction before religion can cope with crime.

The material cited above shows that any particularistic cause of delinquency and crime is inadequate and is usually presented by those who either are uninformed regarding the true nature of delinquent behavior or who have predilections in a certain direction. It is popular to say publicly that delinquent children are not religious or to condemn parents of children who get into trouble for ignoring their religious instruction. But it is not necessarily accurate. A narrow view of any problem is certainly not broadened by having a wealthy, respectable, and popular organization back of it—or by the enthusiasm of the organization's sponsors, even though such sponsors may be judges in juvenile courts or ministers of the Gospel.

The writers are convinced that the oft-repeated exhortations claiming that the rate of delinquency would be lowered if only parents would send their children to Sunday School and church are oversimplified attempts to answer this serious question. As Eduard C. Lindeman writes: "I reject the notion that an increase in the number of persons receiving the type of religious education now prevalent will automatically result in a diminution of crime." [14]

---

[14] "Underlying Social Causes of Crime," *Yearbook*, N.P.P.A., 1941, p. 111.

3. LACK OF RECREATION AS A CAUSE OF DELINQUENCY

Adequate play space properly supervised is still lacking in hundreds of American cities and rural communities. Thousands of congested neighborhoods in our crowded metropolitan areas have none. No person with the slightest concern for our children and youth can seriously be opposed to a supervised playground. However, playgrounds cost money, so indifference and penurious policies deprive millions of children of adequate space and facilities for play and recreation in all too many communities.

Closely akin to playgrounds are the boys' and girls' clubs, settlement houses, neighborhood centers, and various character-building agencies, such as the Scouts—all of which are wholesome influences in the child's life. It is our purpose in this section to discuss the importance of these influences in the prevention of delinquency.

No child should be forced to play in the street merely because he has no safer place to play. The traffic risk alone is too hazardous. Yet we must recognize the fact that primary group contacts are in the neighborhood. If play facilities are too far from the child's home, intimacy of contacts may encourage him to play in the neighborhood streets in front of or near his home. Children often prefer free play rather than more formalized recreation among secondary contacts a mile or so from home. The South Park Commission of Chicago boasts that a playground is provided for every child within one mile of his home. But a mile is a long walk for many children; so they play at home in the street. And we can hardly expect communities to set up supervised playgrounds much closer, since they are expensive to operate.

As early as 1868 the first public directed playground was established. This was at Old South Church in Boston. The following year, "Salem Fraternity," the first boys' club in America, was opened. The settlement movement began in 1887, with the establishment in New York City of Neighborhood Guild—later known as the University Settlement—by Stanton Coit. In 1889, Jane Addams and Ellen Starr founded Hull House in Chicago. These three pioneers had visited Toynbee Hall in London a few years earlier and had been greatly influenced by the work of Samuel Barnett, who had opened his famous settlement in 1884. The settlement movement spread rapidly in this country. Although its original objective was

the "democratization of culture," recreation and clubs were organized for both adults and children of the congested neighborhoods.
During the first decade of the twentieth century, hundreds of playgrounds were opened, many of them privately sponsored and financed by local organizations, such as women's clubs and churches; dozens of settlements and neighborhood centers were organized and various boys' clubs were sponsored. The Playground Association of America, launched in 1909, had for its objective the development

Unmet Recreational Needs. *(Courtesy Big Brother Movement)*

of municipally owned and supported playground systems. The Boy Scout organization began in 1912, and the Girl Scout movement started shortly thereafter. Today we find many other children's organizations whose programs are partly recreational in nature—for example, the 4-H clubs, which cater to the needs of rural youth.
All these organizations are doing a fine job in providing wholesome facilities for the growth and character-building of our children

and adolescent youth. More and more of them should be provided. But we are concerned here with their role in preventing delinquency rather than in merely providing supervised recreational advantages. It is sad, indeed, to walk through the congested areas of our large cities and to find hundreds of children frustrated because they have no facilities for play. Equally distressing is the fact that millions of rural children have no resources, either, simply because it is thought that the open country provides them with enough play space. We may indict the leaders of small communities for their neglect of children as easily as we do those responsible for the neglect of children in our large cities. Children's needs are the same everywhere, and the hazards of childhood are present in rural centers only to a lesser degree than in metropolitan cities.

The old saw that the devil finds mischief for idle hands is undoubtedly true in many cases. But, on the other hand, relatively few children are entirely devoid of "something" to do. A group of students who were sent out to investigate what older children no longer in schools were actually doing with their time were told not to put down that the older children "were doing nothing," since it is very difficult to engage in "nothing." This was during the Great Depression when there was little work for adolescent boys and girls who had left school for various reasons. Many of these children had little to challenge them, except for odd jobs about the house. They did find much idle time on their hands and were subsequently bored. Some took to the road and became hoboes. Others walked the streets trying to find employment. And—some got into trouble. But they might have got into trouble even though they had been working or going to school. The cultural setting of each boy or girl must be carefully examined before we can blame delinquent acts or idleness on the lack of playgrounds alone. Many youngsters who frequent recreational centers manifest behavior that might be termed delinquent off the playground. Many supervisors of boys' clubs and play centers handle overt socially disapproved conduct themselves rather than turn such children over to the police for booking. We must constantly remember that the delinquency rate goes up only when the behavior is counted—that is, when the child is booked by a police officer.

The frequent references to the lack of playgrounds as a cause of delinquency represent one more oversimplification of the problem.

We have become so inured to the claims of playground officials and others interested in wholesome recreation that we find it difficult even to appraise their statements. The following quotation is an example of a critical view of the situation:

> Organizations organizing financial campaigns have told the public of the extensive programs for the prevention of delinquency conducted by recreational agencies, and have in no uncertain terms portrayed future devastating results in community life should the recreation programs be impaired. Statistics have been misinterpreted, thus seeming to prove that participation in recreational programs by those with delinquent tendencies has resulted in the development of socially accepted behavior and in the eradication of the anti-social results of juvenile delinquency.
>
> With complete disregard of other factors involved in a program of community betterment such as churches, schools, probation departments, modern police departments, and efficient juvenile courts, it has not been uncommon for recreational agencies in the past to claim the full responsibility for the curtailment of crime and the prevention of juvenile delinquency.[15]

Few recreational organizations and character-building agencies have ever permitted an objective study to be made of their work. The public is asked to contribute to such organizations and to take at face value and without criticism the reports submitted by the staff members themselves. They naturally play up the good they do and rarely even mention their failures; in fact, they are often actually unaware of their mistakes or ineffectiveness. There are, in addition, a gross waste of money and a serious duplication of effort, especially in the larger cities where many such organizations represent the vested interests in the charity field.

The Boy Scouts, for example, is an excellent organization but its enthusiasts tend to make exaggerated claims for its activities and influence on the youth of the nation, especially so far as prevention of delinquency is concerned. Many years ago, W. I. and Dorothy S. Thomas in their evaluation of public and private agencies dealing especially with child welfare had occasion to question the Scouts. Their contention was that while the organization exercised a good influence, its program was characterized by "bizarre" features. They

---

[15] Robert Heininger, "Group Work as an Aid to the Treatment of Juvenile Delinquency," *Proceedings,* American Prison Association, 1937, p. 101.

furthermore contended that the Scouts fail to reach the under-privileged boy or the boy who has serious problems, and that it does not touch the mass of gang life so characteristic of large metropolitan areas.[16]

Wholesome recreation is without doubt important, as we have already pointed out, but a broad program of activity is vastly more vital in directing the child's tendencies toward good citizenship. School, church, and municipal programs are all necessary, and they should be developed toward a goal of well-rounded living and not merely one of crime prevention.

In some of our larger cities, Crime Prevention Bureaus or Police Athletic Leagues sponsor recreational activities for older boys for the expressed purpose of nipping antisocial behavior in the bud or of preventing further delinquencies. The cities of Philadelphia and New York, for example, are doing work along these lines. The police often refer to such agencies boys between the ages of 16 and 21 who have been apprehended for minor infractions of the law. Funds are usually secured from citizens who are interested in "crime prevention" rather than in boys' clubs or playgrounds as such. The practice of enticing adolescent boys into an athletic program operated by police merely because such boys are potentially delinquent is open to question. It is debatable whether the police should be promoting recreational activities at all. We shall discuss this later in Chapter XV.

We must face the fact that in many of our congested areas thousands of youngsters who have few opportunities for wholesome recreation do not become delinquent. They come from impoverished homes and experience very few advantages as they go through the process of growing to maturity—yet they manage to develop into reasonably good citizens. The lack of recreation *per se* causes little juvenile delinquency directly.

Professor Frederic Thrasher, in his study of the effectiveness of boys' clubs in New York City, brings some pertinent questions to the welfare worker for consideration. Although this study covers only one boys' club, in a crime-breeding area, it emphasizes typical difficulties that constantly face those who are attempting to use this sort of agency and program in the drive to prevent delinquency.

---

[16] *The Child in America*, Knopf, New York, 1928, p. 174.

Thrasher found that: (1) "the Club was not an important factor in the prevention of juvenile delinquency during the four initial years of its existence"; (2) "the Club did not reach the originally estimated membership of 6,000 boys. Furthermore, large numbers of boys in its immediate area were not enrolled by the Club. Obviously, the general conclusion is that the Club did not succeed in reaching a large number of boys whom it was designed to serve"—this, despite the fact that facilities were considered adequate enough to attract boys of the age group desired; and (3) "no more than 13 per cent of the Club's membership went to camp, so the program was decidedly curtailed and the Club did not affect many boys during the summer months."

It is only fair to state, however, that Professor Thrasher contended, despite his study, that "the Boys' Club is one of the most important and essential elements in any crime prevention program." He is convinced that a club of this sort performs many functions for underprivileged boys, especially in congested neighborhoods, such as "recreation, health service, vocational placement, etc., and that *crime prevention might well be regarded as a function incidental to this service.*" [17]

In a careful and objective study of five selected communities in the Chicago area comprising the out-of-home and school activities of some 15,000 boys and 8,000 girls, the Chicago Recreation Commission, in 1938–39, found some data pertinent to this discussion. The study was "*not* undertaken to prove that recreation is a preventive of or a cure for juvenile delinquency" but "rather to discover what the relationship is between the two." [18]

The children were divided into three groups: delinquents with court records, non-delinquents, and "unofficial" delinquents. A summary of this study showed that:

(1) More provision was made for the supervised recreation of boys than for girls.

(2) Boys over fourteen do not attend recreational agencies in as large numbers as do those under fourteen.

---

[17] Frederic M. Thrasher, "The Boys' Clubs and Juvenile Delinquency," *American Journal of Sociology*, July 1936, pp. 66–80 (*Italics ours.*)

[18] From the Foreword of the study, *Recreation and Delinquency*, made by Ethel Shanas and Catherine E. Dunning, Chicago Recreation Commission, 1942.

(3) Delinquents do not take part in supervised recreation in as large proportions as non-delinquents, and when they do they prefer competitive sports and nonsupervised activities like the game rooms.

(4) Delinquents attend the movies more often than the non-delinquents, but all boys and girls spend twice as much time at the movies as in supervised recreation.

(5) In the four neighborhoods with higher delinquency rates all children were particularly fond of radio crime and mystery stories, while in the neighborhood with the lower delinquency rate both boys and girls preferred comedies and variety hours.

(6) Participation in supervised recreation reduces juvenile delinquency. Delinquents who did not take part in supervised recreation during the year became repeaters 30 per cent more often than those who did take part. The proportion of non-delinquents who did not participate in recreation but who became delinquent during the year was three times as high as the similar rate for non-delinquents in the recreational program.

The chief recommendations made in this study were that more supervised recreation for both boys and girls seems necessary; that efforts should be made to reach and hold boys of fourteen years and older; that agencies should adapt their programs to appeal to and influence known delinquents and all high-spirited adolescents; that "unofficial" delinquents should be given individualized treatment; that records of attendance should be kept by the agencies; and that all community resources as well as the home should be mobilized in combating delinquency.

In the excellent report, "Recreation for Youth," compiled by the National Conference of 1946, the importance of leisure-time activity as a right of every child is emphasized. Nothing in the report smacks of the exaggerated claims of many agencies, but all that is set down points to the value of recreational pursuits for everyone.   Under the heading *Recreation—a major necessity and safeguard*, it states, "Recreation is a living process; one of a family of social services. It is recommended that it be presented to youth positively, with emphasis on his choice in free time and on his dignity as an individual, *rather than as a cure-all for his delinquencies.*" [19]

---

[19] Government Printing Office, Washington, D.C., 1947, p. 3. (*Italics ours.*) For a concrete analysis of what recreational programs can do for children, see

An interesting study from Detroit calls attention to the importance of family recreation as an aid in preventing delinquency. From a positive point of view, it might well be stated that few delinquent boys or girls will emerge from those families in which all the members participate to some degree in each other's leisure-time activities. Especially is this true of boys whose fathers participate in their play to some extent. The Detroit study, one of the few of its kind, attempted to ascertain to what degree the parents of boys brought into juvenile court participated in their recreation. Analysis of the frequency of parental participation in the recreation of 2,137 boys is worked out in the following table:

Degree of Participation	Number	Per Cent
Regular	176	8.2
Occasional	667	31.2
Seldom	1218	57.0
Never	19	0.9
Not Stated	57	2.7

We see, then, that less than one in twelve boys is fortunate enough to have parents who regularly take part in his play. The kinds of participation are ball games, fishing trips, picnics, and the like, in which either the father or the entire family join in the fun.[20] How much this obvious preventive to delinquent behavior may be attributed to recreation and how much to the warm, wholesome atmosphere of a socially well-integrated family that appreciates each individual member as a person would be an interesting problem for discussion. Participation by various members of the family in the joys and interests of each member is perhaps of more value than mere participation in recreational activities.

4. THE PRESS AND DELINQUENCY

One of the perennial questions debated wherever delinquency or crime is discussed concerns the influence of the metropolitan newspaper on aiding or preventing antisocial behavior. Journalists have

---

Ben Solomon, *Juvenile Delinquency: Practical Prevention*, Youth Service, Inc., Peekskill, New York, 1947, Chapter VII; also by the same author, "Recreation and Delinquency," *Journal of Educational Sociology*, January 1948, pp. 284–290. This entire issue is devoted to recreation and children.

[20] William W. Wattenberg, "Family Recreation and Delinquency," *Focus*, January 1950, pp. 6–9.

taken the position that the newspaper, by printing crime news, has done society a service in reducing crime and delinquency. Reformers, as well as most astute students of the problem, all contend that the press uses methods to glamorize crime and thus it fails in its responsibility to the public.

Two interesting facts stand out: First, the amount of space devoted to crime news has greatly increased during the past quarter century. It may well be that this situation has, through the power of suggestion, served to stimulate the commission of crime and delinquent acts. The modern machinery of news distribution—gigantic presses, leased wires, specialty writers—all have made it possible for millions of people to follow every detail of a crime and its perpetrator's progress through apprehension, trial, and commitment. Second, crack reporters are employed who are ambitious to get ahead in their profession and who know that skill in writing news stories is the criterion for advancement. Part of their job is to "blow up" an insignificant story to absurd proportions so that the public will clamor for more.

As stated above, most journalists and editors take the position that news reflecting human interest is the stock in trade of the newspaper; that this sort of human interest material is of vital concern to the public; and that any restriction placed on the press is an encroachment on its freedom. It follows, then, that such material should have adequate coverage in conspicuous places. One successful journalist describes this position in the following words:

> I will say, simply and frankly . . . that in my judgment the newspapers will go on printing all the crime news that is available, in the future as in the past, and that furthermore they should continue to do so as a matter of good newspaper making and sound public policy. Only publicity will awaken our people to the prevalence, constancy, and importance of crime. Only publicity will arouse public opinion. Publicity, more than anything else, will stir laggard public officials to courageous action. This publicity, copious and unpleasant, frequently hated by every conservative element in the community, disliked and deplored by the newspapers themselves, offers the surest and most sweeping approach to the clean-up.[21]

---

[21] *Proceedings*, Attorney General's Crime Conference, Washington, D.C., 1934, p. 84; remarks made by Grove Patterson, at that time editor of the Toledo *Blade*.

Arguments concerning the amount of crime news published by the press are somewhat futile. It is not necessarily the *amount* of the news that is significant, but rather the emphasis that is given to it—whether it is splashed across the front page or tucked away on the inside pages—as well as the way in which it is "dished up" by the reporters. Editor Paul Deland of the *Christian Science Monitor* takes the position that crime news *does* encourage delinquency.[22] The American public knows the policy of the *Monitor*, which, since its founding, "consistently refuses to sensationalize crime, to exploit admitted reader interest in crime, or to build circulation on any appeal to morbidity."[23]

In addition to condemning the amount of space given to crime news, Mr. Deland deplores the manner in which the reporter's skill is distorted to make a story "appeal" to the public, and which, in many instances, builds up the delinquent or criminal rather than brands him for what he is. He cites, for example, the reporters' penchant for conjuring up a catchy name for the criminal or his victim. He uses as examples: "Lone Wolf Shouts in Court" spread across the front page in type one and one-half inches high; and the "Black Dahlia" case in California, in which "newspapers seized upon such a name to build up a sensation."[24]

Juveniles in particular, and adults, too, who find it difficult to distinguish between the glamorous and the antisocial are influenced adversely by the cynical and blatant news stories dealing with crime. As Deland continues:

> The wrong perspective of conditions given by selection, proportion and relative size of stories is obvious. But the writing up or glamorizing of a story is a mystery not so readily comprehended outside the newspaper office. "Dressing up" the story for circulation purposes is the trick that does most of the damage. What figures can be made to misrepresent by a clever manipulator is scarcely comparable to the damage a clever rewrite wordsmith can do in making a dull, drab, sordid crime story deceitfully glamorous, thrilling and important by a misuse of words and correlation of ideas.[25]

---

[22] See his article, "Crime News Encourages Delinquency and Crime," *Federal Probation*, April–June 1947, pp. 3 *ff*.
[23] *Ibid.*, p. 5.
[24] *Ibid.*, p. 3.
[25] *Ibid.*, p. 4.

There is no statistical method of arriving at the number of persons who become delinquent as a result of what they read in the newspapers. And the influence of the press is the same as that of the motion picture, radio, and comics. Nevertheless, it seems quite likely that many people absorb the ideas they read or hear and later put them into antisocial practice. The constant repetition of crime stories can affect readers in two different and dangerous ways: it may affect some highly suggestible persons, among whom are many young people, to commit similar crimes; or it may create an indifference to law and order. Stable people, juveniles and adults alike, will be little affected by what they read concerning crime, since this is only one phase of their cultural intake. But the unstable and socially maladjusted may be affected, and it is from this suggestible and abnormal group that most of our delinquents come.

Public censorship is definitely not the answer. A free press is one of this country's most cherished possessions. But the press has a sacred responsibility to discipline itself for the common good. Some newspapers do exercise restraint, but they are in the minority, despite the fact that the American Society of Newspaper Editors, in their "Code of Ethics," adopted the following principle: "A newspaper cannot escape conviction of insincerity, if while professing high moral purpose, it supplies incentive to base conduct such as are to be found in details of crime and vice, publication of which is not demonstrably for the general good." [26] There seems to be no solution to this problem except through the action of the profession itself.

To carry this discussion a few steps further, let us point out the harm that is done by the press in trying a case "by city desk," as Raymond Moley puts it.[27] Some newspapers, besides trying the case in the paper, publish information that defeats efforts to round up the criminal. Some years ago the criminal court of Baltimore, Maryland, ordered that any of the following acts on the part of a newspaper could be grounds for contempt charges: (1) making photographs of the accused without his consent; (2) the issuance, by the police or any other person connected with the case, of any statement relative to the conduct of the accused or any statement or admissions made by the accused; (3) the issuance of any forecast as to the future

---

[26] *Idem.*
[27] *Our Criminal Courts*, Putnam's, New York, 1930, p. 93.

course of action of either the prosecuting attorney or the defense relative to the conduct of the trial; (4) the publication of any matter which may prevent a fair trial; and (5) the publication of any matter obtained as a result of the violation of this rule.[28] Unfortunately, this action by the court was challenged, and eventually, in 1949, the United States Supreme Court sustained a Maryland court decision that such a policy was unconstitutional.

A policy generally followed by the newspapers in children's cases is not to publish the child's name in the story and not to use his picture. Of course, if the offense is serious, such as a homicide, all bars are down and just the reverse is true. Every large city has experienced such unfortunate publicity in the course of the years, and the damage done, particularly among youngsters of the same age group as the delinquent himself, can hardly be overestimated.

An editorial in the *Journal of Criminal Law and Criminology* points up the newspapers' dilemma in handling violent crimes committed by juveniles. Assuming that each year approximately 800 'teen-agers will commit murder, "about 50 of whom will be 15 or less," the editorial states:

> The suggestion is frequently received, "If you have to print it, at least you could put it inside the papers somewhere and not on the front page." Editors point out that such reasoning begs the question, that it amounts to the old argument that what you don't know won't hurt you, and suggest that the indignation of the reader ought really to be directed not at the story but at the situation the story describes.

The editorial probes to the heart of this question:

> If we are correct in saying that readers ought to be angry about the crime itself, rather than at the story about the crime, maybe the fault is partly ours. Ought we to be digging more deeply, getting below the surface facts of the story and giving readers more insight into what kind of children, and what kinds of homes, schools, churches and corrective methods produce such shocking news? [29]

In an attempt to find an answer to this question, the Minneapolis *Tribune* assigned a crack reporter, Victor Cohn, to write a series of

---

[28] See "Trial by Newspaper," *Journal of Criminal Law and Criminology*, November–December 1941, p. 13.
[29] Vol. 39, No. 2, July–August 1948, pp. 216–217.

articles about children who kill. He studied reports of psychiatrists and talked with experts in every field of human behavior. His findings confirm what most students of delinquency have maintained for years: delinquency is a form of maladjustment brought about by frustration and insecurity.[30]

It is obvious that the press can do more than it has done in the past in informing the public about the tragedy of delinquency, especially in pointing out the needs of children.[31]

5. THE ROLE OF THE MOVIES AND THE RADIO IN DELINQUENCY

Theories denouncing the movies and the radio are just as short-sighted and limited as other "single-track" theories concerning our cultural media that are advanced to account for delinquency. It is easy for superficially informed citizens to blame the movies and the juvenile radio scripts for much of the behavior they deplore in children. And these good citizens, moved by a sort of righteous morality, include many teachers, ministers, and jurists who deal with children. Quite understandably, a court judge finds himself exasperated when confronted by a young offender whose foray into criminal behavior seems to parallel the exploits of a screen bad-man. Indeed, the youth may actually tell the judge that he was encouraged to run amuck because of what he witnessed at a neighborhood movie or what he heard on the radio.

As much as we may deplore the shortcomings of both the radio and the movies as media of art and education, we cannot help feeling that many critics who have indicted them and who have eagerly set them up as scapegoats have acted without sober reflection.[32] No one can deny that the movie and the radio have great influence on both children and adults. But it is imperative that mere opinion or common-sense appraisal be taken for only what they are worth rather than as scientific fact. Let us first make an evaluation of the

---

[30] We shall refer to these articles by Mr. Cohn later. They appeared in the Minneapolis *Tribune* through December 1948.

[31] For further discussion of this problem, see Chapter XVII.

[32] See Ralph S. Banay, *Youth in Despair*, Coward-McCann, New York, 1948, pp. 62–63. For an opposite opinion, see Ben Solomon, *Juvenile Delinquency: Practical Prevention*, Youth Service, Inc., Peekskill, New York, 1947, p. 4.

screen as a delinquency precipitant, then add a few words concerning the radio.

Alarmists often describe the movies as not being true to life and contend that this situation is deplorable. Pictures dealing with crime often show that it is easy to live without working legitimately and that crime is bold and exciting, even though it does not pay in the long run—according, of course, to the movies. These alarmists also point out that the movies depict proper ways of carrying guns; of snuffing out the lives of those who stand in one's way; of evading the law; and of enjoying many of the good things of life, such as snappy cars, cleverly dressed women, luxurious hotels and nightclubs, rich food, hurry-up transcontinental trips by fast planes, and other glamorous materialistic proofs of the easy life. They outline the danger of such training to the young boys who see the movies.

By the same token, young girls often take home from the movies the thought that illicit love can be thrilling and even pleasingly dangerous, that fine clothes make the woman, that men seek girls with easy virtue, that *finesse* in using make-up and wearing clothes aids in "getting their men," and that, if a girl is astute, she can have all the good times and pretty things she craves. Indeed, many girls appearing before juvenile court jurists tell just such a story to explain their sexual escapades.

Although these complaints are quite valid, one must, in all fairness, point out also that the screen often depicts much of what is conventionally good, such as tales of heroism and virtue and homely stories of simple folk. The cinema quite obviously reflects human experiences, in addition to many sojourns into the realm of fantasy. Many of these experiences cannot be attained by most people in reality, but, like athletic events, they do make it possible for the average person to enjoy vicariously the fantastic or unattainable. In fact, this is one of the greatest contributions of the moving picture. It must depict life as it is or as we would like to have it, since both attitudes are essential in a humdrum world.

We cannot count too much on outside censorship of the movies, since there is so little agreement on what should be portrayed on the screen. Some of the best literature is filled with powerful suggestion to "evil," glamour, and delinquent behavior. A few years ago on a Town Meeting program this topic of the movie as a delinquent precipitant was discussed. One expert on the panel pointed out that a boy had seen a crime picture in a New York City movie house and had immediately gone out and held up a filling station. On the strength of this alleged cause of the boy's delinquency, the speaker pleaded for the removal of this particular film from circulation. However, an equally well-informed expert, an anthropologist, stressed the point, in rebuttal, that perhaps millions of boys through-out the country had seen this same picture and had shown no overt or tangible ill-effect. The picture in question was the much-discussed *Dillinger*, which portrayed the life of the swashbuckling bad man of the 1930's.

It must be recognized that an idea transmitted to one person, if it is acted upon, might have a detrimental effect on society; the same idea, transmitted to another person, might ultimately benefit the community. Upon millions of Americans who attend the movies, youngsters and adults alike, the worst possible films exert little ap-preciable influence, because they represent only one element in a person's total culture. If other activity patterns are wholesome, they tend to leaven the possible deleterious effect of certain motion pictures.

The well-known juvenile court judge, Camille Kelley of Memphis, Tennessee, stated in this connection that of "the 45,000 to 50,000 cases which had come before her," in less than six could the trouble have been laid to the motion pictures.[33]

Many experts agree that we must accept the moving picture within the framework of our total culture. It represents merely a part of the conditioning process and must be regarded as only one contributing factor in the development of the personality of the child. In similar manner, the church, the home, the school, the place of employment, the character-building agency, the neighborhood, and all the rest of the institutions whose influences impinge upon the structure of the individual play their part in determining the behavior of the person. This fundamental and quite obvious truth was emphasized in the ambitious study made some years ago and referred to as the Payne Fund studies. Because of the importance of these studies, we shall discuss them at some length.[34]

---

[33] *The New York Times*, May 4, 1947.
[34] The Payne Fund Studies, Macmillan, New York, 1933. See particularly, *Movies, Delinquency and Crime*, by Herbert S. Blumer and Philip M. Hauser.

The Payne Fund Studies represent just the sort of investigation that is needed to explore the influences of the movies on the delinquency rate. However, no study of this magnitude has been made since the results were published. The series, composed of twelve studies of the influence of motion pictures upon children and youth, was made at the request of the National Committee for the Study of Social Values in Motion Pictures, later known as the Motion Picture Council.

By using various techniques, notably the questionnaire method and personal histories, the authors attempted to ascertain from several hundred inmates of juvenile reform schools, and from other, non-delinquent groups, information on these subjects: (1) the role of motion pictures in the lives of delinquents of both sexes; (2) the effects on the inmates of movies shown at the reform schools; and (3) the effects of crime pictures on non-delinquent boys and girls.

They found that only 10 per cent of the 368 male delinquents interviewed believed that their criminal careers could be directly traced to the movies they attended, although the boys did think that the plots of the movies had made a noteworthy impression on them. Professors Blumer and Hauser have this to say: "Many impulses and ideas of crime are aroused in the mind of the individual by motion pictures, without coming to immediate expression in criminal behavior. Ideas and impulses are checked, they are held within the mind for the given time, being confined, so to speak, to mere incipient activity. In the course of time they may pass away, without leaving any trace; but they may also work in subtle ways into a pattern of life." [35]

The investigators further report that 49 per cent of the male delinquents questioned indicated that the movies gave them a desire to carry a gun; 28 per cent, that the movies taught them methods of stealing; 21 per cent that they learned ways to "fool the police"; 12 per cent that they were encouraged to pull an adventuresome job because they saw a similar crime depicted in the movies; 45 per cent that they got notions of "easy money" from the shows they saw; 26 per cent that the movies encouraged them "to get tough"; and 20

---

[35] *Ibid.*, p. 37. By permission of The Macmillan Company, Publishers.

per cent that they were led to daydreaming concerning bandits and gangsters.[36]

Of the 252 girls between the ages of 14 and 18 who were questioned, 25 per cent stated that their sexual relations with men were the direct result of being aroused by passionate scenes they had witnessed in the movies; 41 per cent admitted they went to wild parties and "hot spots" because girls do that in the movies; 38 per cent claimed they began to stay away from school because they wished a gay life similar to that depicted by the shows they saw; 33 per cent maintained they were encouraged to run away from home because of the movies; and 23 per cent claimed they were led into the sexual delinquencies for which they were serving time.[37]

Before the actual results of the Payne Fund studies were made available to the public, a popularly written book was released summarizing the studies' findings. This book was received with great alarm by parents and educators, since it played up the dire effects of certain movies on the behavior of young children and adolescents.[38]

Both this book and, later, the Payne Fund studies themselves, aroused much criticism of the movie industry. For a time, it looked as though censorship might result. But a few years later, Professor Mortimer Adler, in his book *Art and Prudence*,[39] criticized the methods and techniques used by some of the academicians in the various studies. He also attacked some of the conclusions.[40]

Anyone dealing with delinquents knows that what they say about their escapades, especially about how or why they were led into them, must be taken with the proverbial grain of salt. Since most of these children are highly susceptible, suggestible, and imaginative, their accounts are likely to be greatly garbled and confused. Those who are psychopathic, constitutionally weak, or unadjusted emotionally are quite likely to be affected adversely by certain scenes in

---

[36] *Ibid.,* p. 71.

[37] *Ibid.,* p. 111.

[38] Henry James Forman, *Our Movie Made Children,* Macmillan, New York, 1933.

[39] Longmans, Green, New York, 1937. See especially Chapters X and XI.

[40] See also Raymond Moley, *Are We Movie Made?,* Macy-Masius, New York, 1938, for a digest of Adler's contentions.

movies that are judged excellent by cultural standards. Even a movie of *Little Red Riding Hood* could cause children of this type to react improperly. It would certainly be desirable for high-strung children to be barred from movies, but it would be impossible to do so.

It is undoubtedly true that delinquents attend the movies more frequently than do non-delinquents. This situation may be due to lack of other interests or to the pulling power of certain themes. Preferences for particular kinds of pictures divide along sex lines rather than along lines of delinquency and non-delinquency. The boys' top choice is adventure, and the girls' is the romantic love theme, although adventure is a close second for delinquent girls. Non-delinquent girls prefer the romantic love *motif* just as do their delinquent sisters, but they show little interest in adventure.[41]

Perhaps the main criticism of the movies' effect on children is that stuffy, crowded theaters represent a threat to the children's health; too frequent attendance may lead to eyestrain. Psychological health, too, is affected by the overstimulation during exciting scenes.

But there is no universal formula to protect our constitutionally weak children from overstimulation. Many European countries permit children to attend programs only *for* children, and this rule is actually enforced. In some countries of South America it is the custom for theater managers to advertise their shows as acceptable for all, *para todos*, or for adults only, *censura para mayores*. But this practice is not compulsory. Parents who are interested in the type of movies their children see, or have knowledge of the possible ill effects of a particular movie, should forbid their children to attend questionable productions.

Sensible restrictions set up in the home are probably the best cure. Censorship from without is no cure.[42] Common sense persuades us that few normal Americans—men, women, or children—are vitally affected by what they see or hear in the movies unless other media, such as the literature they read, the type of friends or contacts they have, and their total institutional interactions, support or reinforce their impressions.

---

[41] Maud A. Merrill, *Problems of Child Delinquency*, Houghton Mifflin, Boston, 1947, pp. 257–258.

[42] See Morris L. Ernst and Alexander Lindey, *The Censor Marches On*, Doubleday, Doran, New York, 1939.

In March 1930, the motion picture industry formulated and adopted a code to govern the making of moving and talking pictures. According to this code, "No picture shall be produced which will lower the moral standards of those who see it." Specific reference is made to the way crimes are to be shown on the screen. "Crimes against the law," the code stipulates, "shall never be presented in such a way as to throw sympathy with the crime against the law and justice, or to inspire others with a desire for imitation." [43]

Spokesmen of the motion picture and radio industries often allege that they are most sensitive to criticism by pressure groups or even by the letters of protest sent in by dissatisfied persons. Occasionally the Catholic Legion of Decency takes a stand against a picture which in its judgment is not fit for children to see. A year or two ago, in Philadelphia, Cardinal Dougherty issued an edict to his constituents forbidding them to witness *Forever Amber* and the western picture, *The Outlaw*. The Cardinal went even further; he told the managers of the theaters showing these pictures that if they were not withdrawn he would not permit his flock to attend *any* picture in these theaters for a period of one year. One manager withdrew the supposedly offensive picture his theater was showing. It is obvious that the Catholic church is potent enough to exercise control over the habits of millions of its communicants and, to a large degree, over the media of entertainment.

In the smaller communities, pressure groups that do not have the vast influence of the Catholic church can exercise some control over the local movies. Parent-teacher groups and women's clubs can do much to raise the standards of the movies shown in their towns if they are positive in their criticism. The larger cities present a more serious problem. Nevertheless, interested persons have access to the Parents' Film Council and to the Children's Film Library of the Motion Picture Association of America if they ask for advice or service. But certainly governmental censorship is no answer to this problem, since most of us resent such types of control.

To those persons really concerned over the potential ill effect of movies on children, we advise a reading course in the books we have

---

[43] The text of the Motion Picture Production Code is found in the *International Motion Picture Almanac*, 1948–49, Quigley Publications, New York, pp. 725–733; see also Geoffrey Shurlock, "The Motion Picture Production Code," *The Annals*, November 1947, p. 142.

cited in this presentation. Throughout the 1930s, this problem was universally aired in the press, on the radio, and in the popular journals. Much time and serious thought were spent in investigating the problem, as witness the ambitious Payne Fund studies. Those who damn the movies as a vehicle on which our children are going off to hell should first become familiar with what has been done along this line before making absurd charges against the movies. It is important, however, to point out again that no one familiar with the history of the cinema can endorse completely what is being produced. Many of the productions represent a low cultural level; yet it is possible that this is the kind of production most desired by our people.

The National Probation and Parole Association has published some articles on the effect of movies and radio programs on the behavior and attitudes of children. Although there may be a few points of difference to be found in these articles from what we have stated in our presentation, they are substantially the same. We suggest that the reader review these articles.[44]

Our remarks on the effects of movies on children apply to the effects of radio as well. Again, it depends upon what type of boy or girl is listening to a specific program of crime, love, or adventure. Just as some delinquents say they started on their career of lawlessness from reading Sherlock Holmes, we might find some who got the same idea from listening to the current Sherlock Holmes series on the air. Probably millions of children listen to exciting crime scripts, but it would be absurd to state that most of them are adversely affected by what they hear. Educators may well deplore the drab and lurid radio scripts—with such highly suggestive names as "Gang Busters," "The Shadow," "The Green Hornet," and the like —but it is doubtful whether any socially well-adjusted child will be

---

[44] See *Yearbook*, N.P.P.A., 1947: Harold E. Jones, Director, Institute of Child Welfare, University of California, "Motion Pictures and Radio as Factors in Child Behavior," pp. 66–77; Franklin Fearing, Professor of Psychology, University of California at Los Angeles, "The Effects of Radio and Motion Pictures on Children's Behavior," pp. 78–92; and Ruth B. Hedges, State Chairman, Committee on Motion Pictures, California Parents and Teachers, Los Angeles, "The Community's Responsibility for Children's Motion Picture Entertainment," pp. 92–101.

led into delinquency by the details of crimes presented in these programs.

On the other hand, no doubt hundreds, perhaps thousands, of adolescent boys and girls are to a greater or lesser degree adversely affected by these thrillers on the air, just as they are by sensational movies. Many may actually commit delinquent acts as a result, but they are the maladjusted children who are always on the borderline of antisocial behavior. Our chief criticism of the thrillers on the radio is that they are cheap and tawdry, and that they reflect the low tastes and cultural levels of many American homes.

The National Council of Juvenile Court Judges, at its annual conference in Atlantic City, April 1948, which was attended by 155 judges, adopted the following resolution: "There are many radio broadcasts harmful to the youth of America in that they place too much emphasis on crime and violence, story serials and court episodes conveying to the minds of children lasting and harmful ideas and impressions not conducive to proper development of the youth of the Nation." [45]

Some time ago the National Association of Broadcasters adopted a code of standards that contains general statements of policy regarding ethics and good taste. The purpose of this code was to suggest the types of programs that should be presented by individual members of the chains as well as by the networks themselves. Concerning children's programs, it was suggested that scripts should be based on sound social concepts and should be presented with a high degree of craftsmanship. The homely virtues of honesty, respect for law and order, clean living, fair play, and respect for parents should be consistently emphasized. Conversely, programs should not contain sequences involving horror or torture, nor should they make use of the supernatural, the superstitious, or any other such material that might overstimulate the young listener. [46]

In 1947 the radio stations affiliated with the National Broadcasting

---

[45] News report, Associated Press, April 14, 1948.

[46] Ernst and Lindey, *op. cit.*, p. 313. For references on radio, see Hadley Cantril and Gordon W. Allport, *The Psychology of Radio*, Harper, New York, 1935; for an analysis of the radio and its effect on the cultural life of the nation, see "New Horizons in Radio," *The Annals*, January 1941, edited by Herman S. Hettinger.

Company voted unanimously to refuse to broadcast "crime or mystery shows" before 9:30 P.M.[47]

This action and, more especially, the broadcasters' code are at least attempts to regulate this medium of cultural art *from within.* Much pressure from outside sources, such as the parent-teacher and other groups, has also played a definite role in raising the standards of radio, especially those of children's programs.[48]

An example of parent disapproval occurred when one radio network revived the athletic exploits of the old-time Frank Merriwell. This redoubtable hero, after winning an athletic game, was sometimes sent on the trail of criminals. So many protests came from parents—who probably knew the six-letter Yale fictional character in their youth—that the broadcasting officials agreed to drop the G-man ambitions of their revived immortal. This example illustrates what can be done when parents pay attention to the scripts that are offered to their children. One should mention here the efforts of Edgar Dale and I. Keith Tyler, of Ohio State University, who edit *News Letter,* which is dedicated to bringing information to the teacher about the radio, the press, and the motion picture.

There is much room for improvement in radio programs—those for adults as well as those for children. Many people would like more artistic radio programs as well as better movies. The same can be said for television programs. But, in this brief discussion, we would hesitate to pass judgment on what should be excluded from the air. We live in a culture dominated to a great extent by the motion picture, the radio, and television. Self-imposed censorship by parents seems, at the moment, the most fruitful means of guiding children in their selection of entertainment.[49]

6. COMIC BOOKS AND COMIC STRIPS

One other medium by means of which children receive many of their ideas and which has recently been violently criticized, is the comic strip in the daily paper and the "comic books," which are being published and distributed by the millions. The sale of these

---

[47] *The New York Times,* September 14, 1947, p. 1.

[48] See A. L. Eisenberg, *Children and Radio Programs,* Columbia University Press, New York, 1936, particularly Chapter I.

[49] The reader is referred further to Paul F. Lazarsfeld and Patricia L. Kendall, *Radio Listening In America,* a report conducted by The National Opinion Research Center of the University of Chicago, Prentice-Hall, New York, 1948.

comics to children, and to adults, has become big business; many millions of dollars are spent on them annually. A whole new group of artists and cartoonists has grown up to satisfy the demand. It is alleged that four out of five children over six years of age read regularly what is somewhat erroneously called "the comics." These materials appear in some fifty million copies of daily papers and in forty-four million copies of Sunday supplements. It is further estimated that some forty million comic books are sold each month. The influence of this material, especially on children, is of significant importance and should be appraised along the same lines as the motion picture, radio, and television.

Comics and their influence on children were discussed on a radio session of the popular Town Meeting of the Air (March 2, 1948). During the discussion, comics were both defended and violently attacked.[50] The high light of the meeting was their defense by Al Capp, creator of *Li'l Abner*.

Periodically, raids are made on the newsstands of various cities in order to confiscate those strips and books that are deemed harmful by capricious police officials and moral defenders of youth. A news story from Detroit, dated April 29, 1948, stated that "thirty-six comic books, which censors termed corrupting to youth, were banned today from city news stands." [51]

There are many types of comic magazines. Some, by all standards of culture and decency, are unwholesome and pernicious; others are tolerably respectable and educational. The Child Study Association of America has made a study of the various comics and finds them no better or worse than other media of expression.[52]

As was stated in relation to movies and radio, we may condemn the comics, or at least some of them, as being on a low cultural level, but it is doubtful whether they are directly responsible for much delinquency. The incipient delinquent child may read the comics

---

[50] For serious condemnation of the comics, see Judith Crist, "Horror in the Nursery," *Collier's Magazine*, March 27, 1948; also Frederic Wertham, "The Comics—Very Funny," *Saturday Review of Literature*, May 29, 1948. Wertham condemns comics by calling them "a systematic poisoning of the well of childhood spontaneity." A book purporting to rationalize the comics is Coulton Waugh, *The Comics*, Macmillan, New York, 1947.

[51] Philadelphia *Evening Bulletin*, April 29, 1948.

[52] See in particular two pamphlets, "The Comics as a Social Force," by Sidonie M. Gruenberg, and "Looking at the Comics," by Josette Frank, both published by the Child Study Association, 132 East 74th St., New York City.

more avidly and more exclusively than the healthy and socially well-adjusted child, and the effects may stay with him longer, but that alone is not sufficient grounds for some overzealous police officer or self-appointed censor to bar the comics from sale. In a sense, comics are in the same category as the earlier dime novel of a generation ago. We must look at their plots and their pictures, gaudy and suggestive though they may be, through the eyes of the child before we ban them.

Dr. Paula Elkisch, in a paper "The Child's Conflict About Comic Books," [53] stresses that children tend to identify themselves with the aggressor, since imitation and identification are among the most primitive of impulses. As Dr. Elkisch points out, "appeal to primitiveness is the effect that is at the basis of the influence comic books have on children. The child's primitive impulses, instead of being gradually transformed into socially desirable behavior and attitudes, are constantly being stirred up." Emphasizing that comic books are written basically in picture language, she further states that "it is well known that children indulge in 'bad' language and yet are repelled by it, particularly during latency. The same must be true of the children's reactions to the utterly crude, violent, and, frequently, sexually stimulating 'picture language' of the comics. Again and again the child is exposed to conflict. Different methods aim at the same goal, the goal of primitiveness, enhancing, *vice versa*, their fascination over the child."

As stated above, some comics are wholesome from the standpoint of education. What, for example, should be done with the comic strip or book that allegedly stimulated two twelve-year-old Oklahoma boys a year or so ago to steal an airplane, fly it 120 miles, and bring it down without mishap? The boys maintained that they learned to fly by observing how a plane is operated in a comic book they read. Obviously the comics should not be held accountable for the theft or the joyride; the boys might well have learned this skill from some popular technical magazine. Since the exciting episode terminated without mishap, the father of one of the boys admitted he wasn't sure whether he was proud of his son or not. The young adventurers were given a juvenile court hearing but were let off with only a lecture.

---

[53] *American Journal of Psychotherapy*, July 1948, pp. 483–487.

It is significant that the publishers of comics have banded together to appraise their products and to attempt to eliminate much that has been so vulnerable over the years. Here is the code adopted by the Association of Comics Magazine Publishers, Mr. Phil Keenan, president, in August 1948:

> The Association, realizing its responsibility to the millions of readers of comic magazines and to the public generally, urges its members and others to publish magazines containing only good, wholesome entertainment or education, and in no event to include in any magazine comics that may in any way lower the moral standards of those who read them. In particular:
>
> (1) Sexy, wanton comics should not be published. No drawing should show a female indecently or unduly exposed, and in no event more nude than in a bathing suit commonly worn in the U.S.A.
>
> (2) Crime should not be presented in such a way as to throw sympathy against law and justice or to inspire others with the desire for imitation. No comic shall show the details and methods of a crime committed by a youth. Policemen, judges, government officials, and respected institutions should not be portrayed as stupid or ineffective, or represented in such a way as to weaken respect for established authority.
>
> (3) No scenes of sadistic torture should be shown.
>
> (4) Vulgar and obscene language should never be used. Slang should be kept to a minimum and used only when essential to the story.
>
> (5) Divorce should not be treated humorously nor represented as glamorous or alluring.
>
> (6) Ridicule of or attack on any religious or racial group is never permissible.

Moreover, certain cities, acting through citizens' groups, are bringing pressure to bear on the distributors of certain comic magazines. One of the first to take positive action was San Diego, California, acting through its Coordinating Council. Fortunately, this group readily gained the cooperation of the two largest distributors of such literature, both of whom agreed to "remove from circulation comic books violating the national code." The attitudes of the San Diego group toward the comics and their effect upon children are of interest. The group takes the position that children, as well as adults, who have weak characters or who lead drab lives "are often stimulated by collections of pictures and stories of criminal deeds, bloodshed and lust" and "do in fact commit acts of delinquency and crime, stimulated at least partly by such publications." It agrees that while this belief "is not capable of statistical demonstration, it is supported by experience as well as by the opinions of specialists qualified to express [themselves] regarding criminal psychology." The group says further "while more stable children may not commit acts of delinquency, frequent reading of crime comics gives them a distorted attitude toward life." Its conclusion is that "it is far more desirable to control the circulation of unwholesome publications through voluntary action of the publishers and local distributors than by legislation." [54]

Seattle has mobilized parent-teacher forces to develop wholesome substitutes and self-censorship of those comics considered harmful. This action was an outgrowth of the report of a committee appointed by the city's mayor, William F. Devin.[55] With the aid of high-school students working with representatives of parent groups and churches, St. Paul, Minnesota, has also codified comic books on sale in that city. It is of further interest that the French National Assembly has passed a law regulating what may be sold under the label of "comic." [56]

One of the most violent critics of the comics, Dr. Frederic Wertham, is skeptical of the code of ethics announced by the comic book publishers. He sees relief from this type of questionable literature only through the mass disapproval of parents, teachers, and others concerned with child welfare. He lists seven specific objections to most comics: "They often suggest criminal or sexually abnormal ideas; create a mental preparedness or readiness for temptation; suggest the forms a delinquent impulse may take; may act as the precipitating factor of delinquency or emotional disorder; may supply rationalization for a contemplated act which is often more important than the impulse itself; set off chains of undesirable and harmful thinking in children; and create for young readers a mental atmosphere of deceit, trickery and cruelty." [57]

Here we see the dilemma. All comics are not unwholesome or vicious. Just as with other books, some type of control is necessary

---

[54] Quotes are from the resolution adopted in San Diego, California, August 12, 1948.

[55] *The New York Times*, May 1, 1949.

[56] See *Federal Probation*, March 1949, p. 60.

[57] Quoted from a digest of Dr. Wertham's remarks before a meeting of N.P.P.A., *Focus*, November 1948, p. 178.

so that young children—especially emotionally maladjusted children —will not be debauched. We must rely on community action in stamping out those comics that by all standards are salacious and dangerous.

It is of interest to recall here that the popular late Fiorello La Guardia endeared himself to his young New York radio listeners by reading comics to them every Sunday during a newspaper strike. Moreover, John R. Cavanagh makes this bold assertion: "No one has conclusively demonstrated that the comic books are detrimental in any way and campaigns to eliminate them are useless." [58]

Criticism against the comic books is definitely on the wane. *The New York Times Magazine* reports (March 5, 1950) that children are tiring of comics because of the appeal of television. But, of course, this would only apply to those comfortable families who can afford this new amusement device. The article continues by stating that the only effective means of dealing with the bad effects of the comic magazine is parental supervision.

7. SNARES FOR THE OLDER YOUTH

What we have discussed above applies primarily to the younger child. The next few pages will be devoted to certain activities and vices that tempt the adolescent boy and girl into delinquent behavior.

During the Great Depression, a great deal of alarm was registered by writers concerned with the well-being of youth. Many studies were made and several somewhat sensational books were written which tended to show that the youth of those days were a "lost generation." Perhaps one of the most startling of the books was *Designs in Scarlet*, by the late Courtney Ryley Cooper.[59] Cooper vividly described many of the conventional snares that precipitate delinquent and criminal behavior. We shall discuss a few of these, since they are still with the youth of today.

First, there is salacious literature. Police officials, reformers, and others concerned with youth have long been disturbed by the pornographic literature and pictures that periodically deluge the places where adolescent youths congregate. Not infrequently, such ma-

---

[58] "The Comics War," *Journal of Criminal Law and Criminology*, May–June 1949, pp. 28–35.
[59] Little, Brown, Boston, 1939.

terial is peddled outside schools and motion picture theaters, as well as on newsstands, small corner stores, filling-stations, and the like. Such literature is highly suggestive; the pictures leave nothing to the imagination.

Police women in our larger cities, who are constantly on the alert for such "contraband," report that it seems to be available in waves, appearing and disappearing as publicity against it is turned on and off. Much of this literature—if it can be called such—attempts to be "art," but it is frankly lewd and sexually stimulating to adolescents. Nudity is the rule and variant forms of sexual behavior are graphically presented in realistic poses. Beautiful girls are pictured in compromising positions and nothing is left undone to titillate the sexual cravings of those who purchase the pictures. There can be no doubt that most of the purchasers of these pornographic exhibits are maladjusted individuals, and, as such, presumably need community protection, just as they do in respect to movies and other such pastimes. The only recommendation suggested in combatting such material is the alert control of specially trained police, either male or female, who see to it that city ordinances against salacious literature and pictures are enforced. We are not naive enough to overlook the fact that such supervision is difficult. Overzealous, untrained police officers do not make good censors, since, under the cloak of delinquency control, they confiscate such books as *Raintree County* and the works of James T. Farrell, to mention only a few.

A decision by Judge Curtis Bok of the Philadelphia Common Pleas Court, in a case dealing with police confiscation of books in that city, was hailed by the New York *Herald Tribune* as a "resounding contribution to the law of obscenity in literature" when he cleared books by Erskine Caldwell, James T. Farrell, William Faulkner, and others.[60]

There are many borderline books, magazines, and pictures that cause a great deal of trouble, including an occasional court action. The people who produce these items are both shrewd and amoral. Their control and prosecution call for equally shrewd public officials who can count upon community cooperation from public-spirited organizations.

---

[60] This interesting and detailed decision may be found in full in *Legal Intelligencer*, Philadelphia, March 23, 1949.

Other snares that serve as a tempting diversion and that are fraught with dangers for modern youth are the taprooms and suburban or roadside "dine and dance" joints. Although these cheap emporia are not in themselves outwardly offensive, they are hanging-out places for disreputable characters who often entice adolescents into various forms of petty crime and sordid vices. Cooper, in his *Designs in Scarlet*, mentioned above, makes much of these "joints," or "dumps," or "hamburg dance joints." Many of them are located just outside the limits of our metropolitan centers, safe from city police control, and cater to many youngsters who have not yet reached their majority. Cooper contends that these places are headquarters for contraceptives, salacious literature, and other contraband materials that appeal to the excitement-craving minors.[61] Cooper has been accused of sensationalism and exaggeration, but it is interesting to note that he had the endorsement of J. Edgar Hoover when he was making his investigations.

Another tempting snare for the young, especially for the adolescent, is gambling.[62] The most accessible forms of gambling are the numbers, or policies, game and the pin-ball and slot machines. Both forms of gambling are deeply intrenched in our larger cities and are tightly controlled by racketeers of the underworld. In 1949, the California Crime Study Commission estimated that the slot machine and pin-ball racket alone does a twenty-billion-dollar business annually. In an article entitled "The Big Slot Machine Swindle," Norman and Madelyn Carlisle place the total "take" at thirty billions.[63]

The policies, or numbers, game is simply a lottery that pays the successful guesser of certain types of numbers, such as the total volume of daily bank clearings, the statement of the United States Treasury balance, the runs scored in baseball games, or the pari-mutuel figures given out at selected race tracks. The results are thoroughly "fixed" and the "sucker" rarely wins.

The pin-ball or slot machine seems to have the strongest appeal to

---

[61] *Op. cit.*, Chapter IV.

[62] See Virgil W. Peterson, "Gambling—Should It Be Legalized?," Chicago Crime Commission, 1945; also Carey McWilliams, "Machines, Political and Slot," *The Nation*, May 28, 1949, pp. 608 ff.

[63] *Collier's*, February 19, 1949, p. 26. See also the California Crime Study Commission, 1949, p. 37.

the casual adolescent. He is likely to become so ensnared that he begs, borrows, or steals to get more money to play it.

Many types of slot or pin-ball machines are used by organized gamblers. These harmless little bagatelle "toys" have a fascinating appeal to the childlike nature of many people. The machines may be found in poolrooms, taprooms, cigar or drug stores, or in any place where people are likely to loaf. They are pretty little devices, with colored lights and with pins that make pleasant musical sounds. The participant in the pin-ball game has no chance of winning cash. He just stands about and loses his money. In the slot machines, or "one-armed bandits," the percentage of winnings is fixed in advance by the racketeer. The sum is believed to be the minimum bait necessary to keep a sufficiently large number of suckers permanently interested.

Estimates place the total number of pin-ball games in operation in this country between 250,000 and 300,000; the average cost of each machine is estimated at $250. Fifty per cent of the gross earnings of each machine is usually paid to the establishment in which the game is placed, thus making it a valuable source of revenue.

Acting on the principles, "Variety is the spice of life" and "Play the sucker for all he is worth," the gamblers controlling these gadgets have succeeded in fleecing the youth and the intellectually dull adults in this country of hundreds of millions of dollars. These apparently "harmless" games of chance generate the gambling fever in thousands of adolescents, boys and girls alike, who then pass on to other forms of gambling. Lack of municipal control, and tie-ups between politicians and the criminal element are largely responsible for rackets of this kind.

In a revealing brochure, Ernest E. Blanche points out the reasons why it is impossible to win at various gambling games: every system of betting breaks down or fails sooner or later; the mathematical probabilities are always against the bettor; so-called games of skill are really games of chance that even skilled players cannot win. In addition, he states that there is only one chance in 2,000 of receiving any money in chain-letter systems or from "pyramid clubs." [64]

Persistence in gambling focuses attention on the fact that most small-time gamblers are doubtless neurotic, just as heavy drinkers are.

---

[64] *You Can't Win: Facts and Fallacies About Gambling*, Public Affairs Press, Washington, D.C., 1949.

It does little good to warn them that the odds are all against them. They will still gamble. A New York *World-Telegram* dispatch, dated November 14, 1949, states that Federal employees by the thousands are victims of gambling professionals who siphon off some $20,000 each week in baseball and football pools. It is estimated that the total "take" in petty gambling around governmental buildings in Washington is five million dollars annually.

Many authorities are of the opinion that the most sinister crime problem of the day is the control of gambling concessions of the country by powerful crime syndicates, closely allied with political machines. These large-scale operators capitalize on the gambling mania of millions of people and arrogantly cater to them with lavish profits to themselves. Aside from the fact that one or two states have legalized gambling, it is quite unlikely that controls will ever be developed to cope with this national menace. The moral indignation expressed by Governor Thomas E. Dewey at the proposal of Mayor William O'Dwyer of New York City that certain types of gambling be legalized is diagnostic. It is obvious that so long as the situation remains as it is today gambling under the control of racketeers and national criminal combines will remain a menace to adolescent youth.

The use of marihuana among teen-age boys and girls has probably been exaggerated by many alarmists, but it does have its devotees among American youth. Marihuana is a substitute for hashish, one of the most insidious drugs known to man. Its effect is achieved through smoking. The plant from which it is derived is technically known as *cannabis sativa* and is referred to by its smokers as "fu," "mezz," "moocah," and other such terms. Unfortunately, marihuana grows wild throughout most of the United States; it is most prevalent in the Southwest.

According to most authorities, marihuana is more potent than any other drug in common use. It destroys all sense of restraint and self-control and incites its users to behavior that often ends in tragedy. Cooper shows no restraint in damning this insidious drug, and he claims to have got his facts from the Federal Bureau of Narcotics.[65] A man in position to know the facts regarding this weed and the

---

[65] *Op. cit.*, pp. 333–341. See also Robert P. Walton, *Marihuana, America's New Drug Problem*, Lippincott, Philadelphia, 1938.

extent of its use by youthful devotees is H. J. Anslinger, United States Commissioner of Narcotics. He minimizes its use as follows:

> Fortunately, the abuse of marihuana by our youth is not as prevalent as numerous accounts would indicate. The peculiar susceptibility of adolescents to the cigarette-smoking practice, however, and the fact that the price . . . is not prohibitive, like other drugs, makes it a definite menace to the younger element of the population.[66]

In 1934, Mr. Anslinger, deplored that Federal laws did not cover the abuses growing out of the use of marihuana. But now we do have such laws, and the fad has tapered off in recent years, perhaps for that reason. The smoking of "reefers," which was at its height during the years of the depression, was often referred to as a serious cause of crime among youth. Although the practice has not disappeared completely, it has not been cited recently as a cause of delinquency.

A few years ago it was reported that many adolescents used benzedrine as a kind of drug. Since it was impossible to purchase this ingredient without a doctor's prescription, they frequently diluted the contents of the inhalers in water or in a soft drink. Then they drank the mixture or poured the liquid on a cloth and sniffed it until they became dizzy and exhilarated. It could not, however, be established that any appreciable number of juveniles referred to the courts were indulging in these practices. According to latest reports, the habit has died down among adolescents, probably partly as a result of the action of organized retail druggists, who, in order to stamp out this unwholesome practice, refused to sell benzedrine inhalers to minors. On the other hand, Congressman George Grant of Alabama, after being informed of the shocking use of benzedrine inhalers by prison inmates in his home state, conducted a survey of this habit, which supposedly started in military disciplinary barracks during World War II. A number of wardens of state prisons and penitentiaries, in answer to a letter from Congressman Grant, stated that this practice had been going on in their institutions and that they were combatting it with more or less success. As newspaper columnist Drew Pearson reported on February 21, 1949, Congressman Grant, in order to check this dope craze, was drafting a bill to restrict the sale of benzedrine inhalers to those persons who could produce a doctor's prescription.

---

[66] Quoted by S. R. Winters, "Marihuana," *Hygeia*, October 1940, p. 886.

Chapter VII

THE ORTHOPSYCHIATRIC APPROACH
TO DELINQUENCY

ONE APPROACH to the etiology of maladjustment, including, of course, delinquency, is the psychiatric. A vast amount of literature has emphasized this approach. Many persons working in the field of prevention as well as of treatment feel that it is perhaps the most fruitful of all. However, in this chapter we prefer to use the term orthopsychiatric rather than the older and more encompassing term, psychiatric, which is more familiar to the layman.

Just what is meant by the orthopsychiatric approach? Orthopsychiatry might be referred to as mental hygiene. It is a subdivision of psychiatry which concerns itself with the diagnosis and treatment of borderline mental deviations of personality rather than with the deepseated psychoses. It is especially identified and concerned with conduct disorders and incipient maladjustment in children and adolescents. The American Orthopsychiatric Association, organized some years ago, publishes the American Journal of Orthopsychiatry. Members of the Association, unlike members of the American Psychiatric Association, are drawn not only from the field of psychiatry but from social work and psychology as well.[1]

Although we may be enthusiastic about the activities of those who are dedicated to this approach, we must emphasize once again that there is no magic formula for the prevention or cure of maladjusted individuals. But with the wider acceptance of psychiatry and social case work, the frontiers have been explored and extended to such a degree that it is possible to prevent an ever-increasing amount of

---

[1] See "The Birth of Orthopsychiatry," by Lawson G. Lowrey, in *Orthopsychiatry: Retrospect and Prospect 1923–1948*, American Orthopsychiatric Association, 1948, pp. 190–208.

maladjustment, especially among children, provided it is detected and treated in time.

Most American parents have taken their cue from the poets and romanticists who picture childhood as a period of unmitigated bliss. Few fathers and mothers look upon the growing-up process as one fraught with many moments of unhappiness and even personal misery. Paraphrasing Madeleine L. Rambert in her intriguing book, *Children In Conflict,* thoughtful parents become perplexed concerning what goes on inside their child—who can be so adorable at times and at others behave like a little demon.[2] But most parents take the child as he comes, hoping that he will outgrow his poutings, stubbornness, meanness, and temper tantrums. They then take on a second child, "to keep the first one company," without so much as a thought of "sibling rivalry," a term they have never heard of. Our culture is full of bewildered parents and bruised children, whether or not we are honest enough to admit it.

Many persons were startled some time ago when John L. Thurston of the Federal Security Administration made a chance remark before a congressional committee that in the average schoolroom of thirty children, three would spend some of their lives in a mental hospital.[3] This statement was attacked by some articulate persons but it was attested to by more than one psychiatrist. It points up the need for more instruction in mental hygiene.

Regardless of what we say in this chapter regarding the shortcomings of parents, we do not wish to give the impression that we blame parents for the delinquency or emotional maladjustment of their children. They, too, are products of a culture that poorly equips them for the responsibilities of parenthood. It is the task of the educator to experiment in child care and then to use every resource to transmit his findings to those who are or plan to be parents. We cannot make a scapegoat of parents.

The very process of being born is a devastating experience. Much has been made of the "birth trauma" by followers of Otto Rank, the Austrian analyst. The harrowing experience of being catapulted into the big, buzzing, and confusing world from the comfortable, warm prenatal medium is catastrophic to the human organism. Yet this is

---

[2] International Universities Press, New York, 1949, p. ix.
[3] In a press release, December 12, 1949.

life and the amazing thing is that the vast majority of babies make the necessary adjustment in a reasonably satisfactory manner.

But let us not overlook the basic fact that babies and young children do have serious problems. It is the responsibility of parents to understand this reality and to ease their children over the rougher parts of the road of life wisely and judiciously, yet without sheltering them to such a degree that they become "hot house" plants.

The right to be well born physically and mentally is being recognized more and more as our knowledge of the elements of prenatal care expands. Yet there are still millions of babies born each year throughout the world who start life with the most serious of handicaps. Mental defect is all too prevalent, and congenital ills that leave a scar on the child are common.

The process of growing up in an adult-centered world is a serious problem for the child, even though he is adequate mentally and physically. His world experiences begin at birth; even the treatment he receives in the hospital prior to the time he is taken to his home may have an effect on his personality. The unintentional neglect he may experience here at the hands of overworked or improperly trained nurses may have significant results. It is true, however, that such early neglect may be offset by the cuddling he receives after he is comfortably enthroned at home. More babies are being left at the mother's side during the period of hospitalization, so that the baby's needs for food and reassurance are more adequately met.

Experts in the care of infants enumerate the many types of neglect that the average baby suffers in the average home. We are only beginning to understand the basic needs of the baby and young child, aside from the need for proper foods. Certainly the child has the right to be wanted. Millions of them are not wanted—at least, not at the time they are born; they are merely tolerated by their mothers. Then, as they become an integral part of their parents' lives, they are accepted, outwardly at least. But the harm done to their personalities prior to that moment of acceptance may never be completely eradicated. And, of course, there are many definitely rejected children whose childhood is extremely harsh. For example: (1) there is the parent who superficially accepts the child but who inwardly rejects him; (2) there is the parent who overindulges the child as a compensation for the latent hate she may have for him; (3) there is the parent who rejects the child because he is not as talented or as good-looking as another child in the family, or because he cannot win traditional rewards in a competitive society.

It would be difficult to estimate just how many children suffer from various forms of rejection, insecurity, or frustration arising only from their parents' apathy. Blithely conceiving and bringing a second child into the world before the first is emotionally prepared to accept the sibling is a universal, shortsighted practice. A revealing study which points up this rejection is that by Dr. John Bowlby of the Tavistock Clinic of London entitled *Forty-Four Thieves*. A large proportion of his cases showed definite signs of instability resulting from the denial of mother love.[4]

Ignorance of the fundamental needs of the child during the early years is, then, widespread. As a rule, prospective parents know very little about the physiological needs of their children and practically nothing about their psychological or emotional hungers. And, parenthetically, few reliable and standardized sources of information are accessible. Too often, young parents resort to a faulty memory of what they experienced as children, or they fall back on inadequate, if not completely false, ideas received from friends, neighbors, mothers, or in-laws. They may not choose their pediatrician wisely either. It is not difficult, then, to understand why so many babies and young children fail to mature in an emotionally healthy manner.

The psychiatric, or rather, the orthopsychiatric, approach to the causes of crime and delinquency and to the causes of other forms of maladjustment has become somewhat the fashion. However, this approach is based on solid postulates; it is not just a fad. We may see much of this emphasis in the early classic work of Dr. William Healy, *The Individual Delinquent*,[5] which is considered a milestone in the delinquency field. Healy's later work, *Mental Conflicts and Misconduct*,[6] describes cases in which mental conflict causes antisocial behavior. The psychoanalytic approach, which has been developed through the years, is apparent in August Aichhorn's work, *Wayward Youth*,[7] and later in Alexander and Healy's *Roots of Crime*.[8] Aichhorn, in his correctional school in Austria, used indi-

---

[4] Baillière, Tindall & Cox, London, 1947, p. 1.

[5] Little, Brown, Boston, 1915.

[6] Little, Brown, Boston, 1917.

[7] Viking, New York, 1925.

[8] Franz Alexander and William Healy, Knopf, New York, 1935.

vidual therapy in effecting cures. He insisted that it is important to know what the child is thinking and to divert his overt acts into corrective channels rather than to repress them. He viewed delinquency as symptomatic of a neurosis. Admirers of the great Austrian psychoanalyst have dedicated a book of collected papers to him in honor of his contributions in the field of delinquency.[9] Samuel W. Hartwell's *Fifty-Five "Bad Boys"* also stresses the use of applied psychoanalysis.[10] His "unloved and unwanted" boys would today be referred to as "rejected" and "insecure."

Regardless of the apparent reasons why the child has gone astray, whether they be socio-economic or biological, no complete picture can be gained until the less obvious phases of the problem are assayed by the psychiatrist working in conjunction with the psychologist and the psychiatric social worker.

However, mastery of the technical jargon of the psychiatrist or the psychoanalyst is not essential to an understanding of the orthopsychiatric approach.[11] Many of the works dealing with this thesis seem utterly confusing to the average reader. This confusion is partially due to the fact that we in the United States have become cultists in our adherence to the systems of a variety of pioneers such as Freud, Adler, Jung, Kempf, and Rank, to mention some of the most outstanding names. The psychiatrist or the orthopsychiatrist may use the language of the analyst, but we are more interested in psychiatry here than in the deeper therapy of the analyst.

In nontechnical language, we see the human individual in the light of his original nature as mainly aggressive and assertive. He starts at birth to want things, many of which he is denied either at the moment he craves them or later. He naturally makes a vehement protest. The young baby cries until he is either exhausted or satisfied. As the

---

[9] *Searchlights on Delinquency*, edited by K. R. Eissler, International Universities Press, New York, 1949.

[10] Knopf, New York, 1931.

[11] O. Spurgeon English and Gerald H. J. Pearson have two standard works in this field: *Common Neuroses of Children and Adults* (1937), somewhat technical in its approach, and *Emotional Problems of Living* (1945), written especially for the informed layman. Both are published by Norton, New York. See also *The Psycho-Analytical Approach to Juvenile Delinquency* by Kate Friedlander, International Universities Press, New York, 1947, and Nandor Fodor, *The Search for the Beloved*, Hermitage House, New York, 1949.

child grows older, many of his basic desires come into sharp conflict with adult norms and other realities of life. That is, under the normal conditions of life, society obstructs much of the direct and spontaneous expression of human nature.

The child is socially compelled to live as a member of several groups, of which the family is the first he encounters. Through long experience, the specific culture in which the child is placed by birth has worked out gradually, often irrationally and despotically, a code of beliefs and practices with respect to social behavior. These are imposed, consciously as well as unconsciously, upon the child from the moment of birth, a few at a time, until he conforms. He learns by bitter experience that other individuals have the same desires and that there does not seem to be enough satisfaction to go around. In other words, a constant struggle exists between the latent or innate drives of human nature and the discipline that is supplied by the customs and folkways of the social group. The socializing process is functioning bit by bit and the child must adjust or be penalized.

The wise mother—and father—will attempt to understand this conflict and reduce it to a minimum. For example, there are many situations in the home in which the growing child may be permitted to express himself without being disciplined or penalized. Many of these situations *seem* to make a great deal of difference but, in reality, they do not. Modern experts in child care are pointing out that during the various periods of development certain elements of growth manifest themselves and are thus considered normal. Should these be ignored, accepted, or penalized? Too many children are penalized or admonished for doing just what they are expected to do at the specific period of growth. For instance, their hundreds of little exploratory forays, which are but natural, are sometimes made at the expense of furniture, living-room rugs, bric-a-brac, potted plants, or garden flowers. And that often means trouble for the child.

Or, conversely, they often fail to do what is hopefully expected of them. For example, too early toilet training has caused many children to grow up with manifestations of maladjustment. Rebellion, or aggression as it is most frequently called, either overt or latent, often begins during this period. Through rebellion, the child becomes master; it is one of his strongest weapons, and one that causes great parental concern. The mother must not only yield to the child's whims, but she must convey to the child, by her nonchalance, that his apparent eccentricity makes no difference to her. A child left free to adjust to social good taste in toilet habits in his own time is not likely to show signs of rebellion during the early years of his life—assuming, of course, that his parents are consistent in other important matters, such as, for example, the feeding routine.

Strict scheduling of the baby is no longer the fashion. As Mowrer and Kluckhohn point out, "Responsively gratifying the infant's needs during these early months does not mean that a child is 'spoiled.' The 'spoiled' child shows just those traits we have predicted from scheduling care, and he is either one who has never met any conditions for being rewarded or who has been inconsistently rewarded. . . . If the rewards which the child receives bear no consistent relation to his behavior, education will not proceed efficiently in its substantive aspects and an apathetic and anxious or hostile individual is likely to result." [12]

The question of premature weaning is another area of parental uncertainty. Should the baby be forced away from the bottle or permitted to give it up when he desires? There is practically universal agreement that too early weaning is detrimental to the child, and that it may give rise to emotional problems.

We are all familiar with the term *sublimation*, which implies a struggle between our desires and social inhibitions. This struggle often produces conflict within the individual. Only if guidance has been rational and understanding on the part of parents, teachers, and others who have had close contact with the child, can an adequate and satisfying adjustment be made. If a successful sublimation takes place, the individual's conflict may be an asset to him as well as to society. But the opportunities for a healthy sublimation may be limited, or the demands for sublimation may be carried to an impossible extreme. In such cases, the child's personality development may be subjected to real danger. Often a flight from reality results that is intense and persistent enough to produce symptoms that can be diagnosed by a psychiatrist. A definite regression to infantile types of thinking and emotional expression may occur; the individual may retreat psychologically and retrieve from his unconscious infantile

---

[12] O. H. Mowrer and Clyde Kluckhohn, "Dynamic Theory of Personality," Vol. I of *Personality and the Behavior Disorders,* edited by J. McV. Hunt, Ronald Press, New York, 1944, pp. 89–90.

memory types of responses which at one time gave some degree of gratification. Certain forms of phantasy may make their appearance. Imagination of great power or of unusual status may result. Daydreaming in itself is natural to all of us, but when it becomes the only realm the child knows it becomes dangerous. Often, the child may show signs of sadism or even masochism.

The mechanism of *overcompensation* also plays a great role. This mechanism manifests itself frequently in everyday life, as when an unusually small or insignificant person assumes an attitude of exaggerated self-assertiveness and inflated importance to compensate for his lack of physical impressiveness. This behavior can be quite normal, but it may become pathological. Exaggerated *defense mechanisms* may grow into fears and phobias. These usually arise as defenses against desires that are socially taboo. What is known as *ambivalence*, or the love-hate complex, is frequently found among the mental attitudes of the psychopathic. A person may be rejected by someone for whom he or she has a deep affection. This frustration might be intolerable were it not for the possibility of substituting extreme hatred for equally intense affection. The pathological antipathy makes more endurable the real disappointment. In fact, it may completely obliterate the disappointment.

Young children exhibit feelings of ambivalence, especially toward their parents, who are not only the love objects but also the withholding agents of society. Parents should recognize and understand the roles they must play in dealing with their offspring. This understanding is especially difficult in a home where two or more children are competing for the affection of their parents.

Another frequent mechanism known to the psychiatrist is *projection*. If a person's own acts or conduct are reprehensible and bring about an uncomfortable sense of guilt, he can rid himself of this guilt by imagining that others, not he, are guilty of these deplorable acts. That is, by throwing the responsibility for our own shortcomings and failures upon others, we make it easier to bear with ourselves.

Still another well-known mechanism is *symbolization*. Any object may come to stand for some other object or experience because of similarity between them or because of mental association. This tendency to find symbols appears to be quite general among us all. Not only does one object stand for another, but the symbol comes to be invested with the emotional content of the object symbolized. Many of our symbols are unconscious and may be quite infantile. Even though they may be forgotten, they remain potent in our actions.

Although these and many other mechanisms are present in mental and nervous disorders and in many instances present deep-seated personal difficulties, it must be pointed out that all individuals make some use of them at various times in their lives. It is only in the extreme development of such mechanisms that we become aware of emotional difficulty and call in the psychiatrist. The child, in his conflict with adult-made standards of behavior, is likely to resort to one or more mechanisms that reflect his frustration or rebellion.

Much of this conflict can be avoided by parents who try hard to understand their children. In other words, prevention of emotional misery and abnormal aggression in the child is all-important.[13] Cuddling and other manifestations of affection are extremely potent in convincing the child that he is wanted and loved. The older behavioristic philosophy of child rearing ignored this fundamental fact. To those critics of cuddling who contend that there is danger of the child's becoming spoiled, one may well answer that it is the spoiled child who really lacks what he wants most—parental affection. In such cases, the parents may lavish material gifts on the child and "get him everything he wants," but either withhold entirely or give grudgingly, their affection.

Obviously, the child must learn the lessons of life and be taught a sense of responsibility. But the secure child will penetrate and explore the new and the unknown in his own good time if he knows he has a sympathetic haven to which to retreat when he feels it necessary. As stated above, the child is ambivalent by nature. He wants security but he also wants to assert himself and be independent.

In many situations the child may select his course without interference from parents, but it is the practice of the wise parent to guide him in making his choices. Innumerable frustrations will be experienced, but the child will learn life's limitations through doing, under skillful parental guidance. If the child has a parent who is there when emotionally needed, he will have little difficulty in growing into a socially mature adult. Of course, the parent, especially the

---

[13] An incisive book dealing with aggression is *Hostility in Young Children*, by Anneliese Friedsam Korner, Grune & Stratton, New York, 1949. See also Edmund Ziman, *Jealousy in Young Children*, Wyn, New York, 1949.

mother, must not be emotionally dependent upon the child. She must accept the maturation process as it unfolds. Many traditional but outmoded attitudes concerning child care conspire to thwart discerning parents. These attitudes must be appraised by those parents who are determined to do a good job in rearing their children.

The gradual social weaning of the child is a life task for both parents, and it should be accepted courageously as an integral part of the life process. First experiences with sexual differentiation, meeting new playmates, sharing playthings, the first day at school (a very serious venture), the first day at camp, or the first few days in a new neighborhood—all of these must be met by the growing child. The parent can make or break a child's emotional life by the way in which he aids him in these experiences. Public ridicule, to save the mother's face, is a cruel technique, but it is quite prevalent. The teacher also has a responsibility in this process, as does the camp counselor and others working with young children.

There is a wealth of literature on this approach to child care. As stated above, the works written in scientific jargon need not bewilder anyone, since many writers are adapting the findings of the psychiatric profession to everyday reading. In fact, the orthopsychiatrist and pediatrician are doing just that themselves.[14]

Few children grow up without manifesting signs that are symptomatic of stress or emotional strain. When these signs begin to appear, they should be noted with calm objectivity. If they persist, the parents should seek professional guidance from a psychiatrist, a child-guidance clinic, or a progressive pediatrician, or by perusing some reputable work on child care. Certain of these mechanisms may emerge from some conflict in the home, such as bickering between parents, or the child's jealousy of one of the parents or of a brother or sister.

Child-guidance clinics find many of these manifestations in their clinical experience. A partial list includes:

---

[14] See Charles A. Aldrich, *Babies Are Human Beings: An Interpretation of Growth,* Macmillan, New York, 1938; Margaretha A. Ribble, *The Rights of Infants,* Columbia University Press, New York, 1943; and Benjamin M. Spock, *The Common Sense Book of Baby and Child Care,* Duell, Sloan & Pearce, New York, 1946.

aggression

apparent inability to talk or to learn to read

banging of head in crib

bashfulness or withdrawing from reality

biting parts of body, usually knuckles or fingers

biting or scratching others

boastfulness

boisterousness

boldness

bullying

cruelty

crying or whining

daydreaming

defiance

dependence

destructiveness

disobedience

eating problem

effeminate behavior

enuresis

excessive masturbation

exhibitionism

gritting of teeth

holding of breath

hostility

jealousy

nail biting

negativism

selfishness

sexual deviations

silliness

stubbornness

sulkiness

tantrums

tattling

tenseness

thumb-sucking

Many of these mechanisms are quite normal among children; it is their persistence that is symptomatic of emotional difficulty.[15] We may go even further and mention some of the manifestations of sexual aberrations such as the oedipus conflict, father-hatred, the castration complex, and others falling into these categories which are familiar to the psychiatrist.[16]

In our treatment of the child-guidance clinic, we incorporated some of the results of studies made by Healy and Bronner in the Judge Baker Guidance Center of Boston, as well as those of the Institute for the Scientific Treatment of Delinquency of London, which have bearing on the emotional approach. We noticed in the Healy and Bronner studies that 207 of the 400 cases studied were labeled "personality and behavior" problems.[17] The mechanisms listed are not harmful in themselves if they appear only occasionally. Skillful guidance by parents will be extremely helpful in negotiating

---

[15] See Lauretta Bender, "Genesis of Hostility in Children," *American Journal of Psychiatry*, Vol. 105, No. 4, October 1948, pp. 241–245.

[16] See Friedlander, *op. cit.*, Part II.

[17] See p. 93.

such passing phases. Only if they persist will professional help be needed. But inept handling of children who show these tendencies makes future trouble for child, parent, and society.

It should also be stated that emotionally disturbed children do not necessarily become delinquent. Their constant frustration often does result in behavior that may be labeled delinquent, but frequently it may result in neurotic behavior. In any case, the child is obviously unhappy. He may misbehave in order to win attention or recognition, or he may withdraw from members of his groups and compensate by leading an isolated existence.

The work of the Child Study Association is pertinent to a discussion of the orthopsychiatric approach. Organized in 1890 as the Society for the Study of Child Nature, it changed its name in 1910 to the Federation for Child Study. In 1924, it adopted its present name. According to the Association's own reports, its objectives are to act as a family guidance center, to secure and distribute information concerning development and practical application of methods of child study, to undertake original research, to furnish means of cooperation between organizations having similar aims, and to conduct discussion groups, conferences, and lectures. In its New York office (132 East 74th Street), it maintains a library of some 5,000 technical volumes dealing with family guidance, parent education, and child study. The organization also publishes a valuable quarterly entitled *Child Study*, containing the latest philosophy of child care.

Another organization whose objectives and literature are significant in the orthopsychiatric approach is the National Committee for Mental Hygiene (1790 Broadway, New York City). We have mentioned this organization in connection with the development of the child-guidance and counseling service movements. It was organized in 1909 through the heroic efforts of Clifford Beers. Today, the organization works directly through its associated state societies and local committees for the conservation of mental health. As part of its program of disseminating reliable information, it publishes two magazines, *Mental Hygiene* and *Understanding the Child*, both quarterlies. It also prints and distributes pamphlets dealing with subjects pertinent to mental health for both professional and popular use. For example, in 1947 it published a series of pamphlets called "Some Special Problems of Children," which discussed especially children of the ages two to five. The titles of the pamphlets are: "When a Child Hurts Other Children," "When a Child Is Destructive," "When a Child Uses Bad Language," "When a Child Won't Share," "When a Child Still Sucks His Thumb," "When a Child Still Wets," "When a Child Masturbates," and "When a Child Has Fears." [18]

Another pamphlet, entitled "Avoiding Behavior Problems," written by Dr. Benjamin Spock and published by the Bureau of Mental Hygiene of the New York Department of Health, lists the following as traditional parental difficulties with children: (a) early feeding problems; (b) weaning conflicts and thumb-sucking; (c) bowel training; (d) urine training; (e) anxieties in the early years; (f) jealousy of the new baby.

The Harriet Johnson Nursery School, known as "69 Bank Street," publishes pamphlets that deal with other problems of early childhood. For example: "Learning To Be Socially Acceptable" by Irma Simonton Black; "How Does It Feel To Be Bad?" and "What Do Children Need Most: From Parent, From Teacher?," both by Barbara Biber. Dr. Biber is research psychologist in the Bank Street School.

Also, several professional journals emphasize the point of view reviewed in this section. One of these, *The Nervous Child*, dedicates one issue (Vol. VI, No. 4, 1947) to "correcting basic concepts of juvenile delinquency." This journal, together with *The Journal of Child Psychiatry*, is published by Child Care Publications, 30 West 58th Street, New York City. *The Nervous Child*, an independent journal, "belongs to no one organization and represents no one group or school. Its aim is to further progress in any type of study and care of nervous and mentally diseased children." [19] *The Journal of Child Psychiatry*, according to the editorial board, "is created to serve all the workers in the fields of child psychiatry, neurology, clinical psychology as applied to children and in the field of institutional care of children."

The Child Welfare League of America, Inc. (130 East 22nd Street, New York City) is still another organization working in the field of

---

[18] See also Lili E. Peller, "Character Development in Nursery School," *Mental Hygiene*, April 1948, pp. 177–216.

[19] Thus stated on the back cover of the publication. See also *Handbook of Child Guidance*, edited by Ernest Harms, and published in 1947 by Child Care Publications.

child care and protection. Organized in Baltimore in 1915, it was incorporated under the laws of New York State in 1928. Its objective is to develop standards of service for child care in children's agencies and institutions. It is also interested in developing community programs in behalf of children. The League publishes pamphlets from time to time dealing with problems of childhood, especially on the community level.

The Caroline Zachry Institute of Human Development, Inc. (17 East 96th Street, New York City) is another organization dedicated to the work of mental health and child development. It was organized in 1939 as the Institute of Personality Development, with Dr. Zachry, well-known expert on child care, as its director. Following her death in 1945, the name of the organization was changed as a memorial to her driving energy and leadership in the field of mental health.[20]

An organization especially identified with the family is the Family Service Association of America (122 East 22nd Street, New York City), which is national in scope. Founded in 1911, it has for its purpose the promotion and extension of family social work as well as the development of sound, healthful, and normal family life. There are 239 member agencies in the United States and Canada. The Association publishes *The Journal of Social Case Work* and *Highlights*. Membership is based on standards of administration and personnel. It assists member agencies in improving services through consultation, information, and publications.

The National Association for Nursery Education is a source of material to guide parents in selecting good nursery schools. Only seven states have laws regulating the establishment and operation of nursery schools. The nursery school, properly administered and with a progressive philosophy, can do much in assisting parents in the work of social and emotional weaning of young children.

Various progressive pre-schools that use the orthopsychiatric approach to behavior problems are doing important work that merits the attention of school boards everywhere. A happy, socially mature youngster who has learned from very early childhood to solve his

---

[20] See Dr. Zachry's incisive article on adolescence in *Encyclopedia of Criminology*, Philosophical Library, New York, 1949, pp. 2–10.

problems is not likely to become delinquent, regardless of the serious crises he is bound to meet as he goes through life. Writing of parent-teacher cooperation in one of these progressive schools, Dr. Barbara Biber states:

> The parents . . . look upon the rearing of their children as a job they want to do well beyond all else. They have long since forsaken the hit-or-miss attitude toward the young, and have passed the stage of expecting to reduce an intricate human relation to an outlived rule-of-thumb procedure. When these parents and teachers meet to talk and learn together, they are trying to carve out a genuinely happy way of living with children, happy for children and grown-ups alike.[21]

It may be argued that most parents have neither the time nor the social background to devote so much attention to their children's growth. This is, indeed, a just comment. But, somehow, a new orientation concerning the parent-child relationship must be developed. As a generalization, we might state, as does Alice V. Keliher, that delinquency is a "family affair." [22]

The spade work must be done in the schools. Teacher-training institutions must scrap their old-fashioned philosophy and adapt their programs to this new emphasis. Parents can learn about the implications of this approach by reading well-chosen syndicated articles in the daily newspapers and magazines and by participating in parent-teacher groups. Nursery schools and kindergartens can be expanded in even the smallest school systems, and parental guidance can become an integral part of their programs. The radio and motion picture can be utilized in disseminating information to parents. Obstetricians and pediatricians, as well as hospital administrators, can advance this new approach to prospective mothers.[23]

---

[21] In the *Foreword* to her pamphlet "What Do Children Need Most: From Parent, From Teacher?," publication of 69 Bank Street, New York City.

[22] See "Juvenile Delinquency: A Family Affair," *Federal Probation*, December 1948, pp. 26 ff.

[23] See Gordon Hamilton, *Psychotherapy in Child Guidance*, Columbia University Press, New York, 1948; and Leon J. Saul, *Emotional Maturity*, Lippincott, Philadelphia, 1948. The former work states the role of the social worker in psychotherapy, while the latter discusses emotional development and is slanted toward the lay public.

A CONCLUDING STATEMENT ON CAUSATION

If the reader is confused after reading the various chapters dealing with causes of delinquency, he need not fret too much; as we have seen, the experts in the field are also confused. Our analysis was not so much an attempt to arrive at conclusions as to warn the reader against dogmatism on the subject. The ill-informed or partially informed person always has a comfortable, tailor-made reason to advance for delinquency, but those who have studied the problem assiduously are much more cautious.

No physical abnormality, no degree of insanity or emotional instability, no extent of feeblemindedness, no glandular imbalance, no extremity of poor health or physical handicap, no degree of physical deprivation, no extreme of poverty or misery, no filth of slum life, no lack of recreation, no stimulation of the press, movie, radio, or comic magazine, no hysteria or crime wave will certainly, without exception, cause a delinquent act. A delinquency or crime is committed only when just the correct combination of personal and social factors come into existence to create a specified delinquent situation. And—viewed in a merely external fashion—the same *apparent* combination of factors might not produce a delinquent act the next time they are brought together. In the particular situation in which the act is committed, the act is the inevitable outcome of all the elements in the picture—as inevitable an outcome as any physical occurrence could possibly be. But external and apparent similarities and repetitions in social situations may not be actual and complete repetitions.

Thus, we can never be sure that a given set of factors will produce a delinquent act. As a result of this observation, we cannot accept the thesis held by some writers that it is futile to discuss the causes of delinquency. But, on the other hand, we cannot accept without skepticism the glib statements made by many persons that certain influences or factors are the exclusive causes of delinquent behavior. We have seen that every human being is different—biologically, intellectually, socially, and culturally. No two individuals have identical environments—not even children in the same family, even though they may be twins, fraternal or identical.

The perennial question asked by the curious is: Why do children in the same family differ in delinquent and nondelinquent behavior? The answer is easy: No two children in the same family have the same heredity or environment. Perhaps all they have in common are the same parents and the fact that they put their feet under the same table when they eat their meals. A ten-year-old boy has his primary group contacts and his eight-year-old brother has his. The former stands in one relationship with his mother and father and the latter in another. We have elaborated on the real nature of the environment in our first chapter.

We shall never learn very much about delinquency and delinquent children through generalized studies and abstract dogmatism. We must build up our knowledge by studying particular cases, although such study will have little permanent value unless we discover from it the particular personal and social situations most likely to produce the delinquent act. Unless we discover what these conditions are, we can do little to reduce the unhappiness and frustration among children from which most antisocial acts arise.

Furthermore, it is important that we avoid the pitfalls of dogmatism as well as of intellectual snobbery. Without for a minute contending that they will inevitably lead to delinquency, it is apparent that certain conditions are more favorable to delinquency than others.

What can we conclude, then? Simply that bad heredity, physical defect, mental imbalance, mental retardation, emotional insecurity, a slum environment, poor education, bad companions, poverty, a psychologically broken home are obviously more favorable to delinquency than are good heredity, physical normality or superiority, a sound mind, normal or superior intelligence, social maturity, healthy economic conditions, adequate education, normal and law-abiding companions, material security, and a set of understanding parents. Of course, even all these favorable conditions do not constitute a gilt-edge insurance against delinquency. Certain imponderables enter the picture which cannot be predicted beforehand. A child may well commit an indiscretion accidentally.

Certainly we may dismiss completely the old notion that some children are just perverse and mean by reason of birth. Perversity has no meaning except as a symptom of certain unfortunate factors in the life of the individual. It is important that these factors be ferreted out through skillful investigation before we make a diagnosis.

One central theme, however, stands out in any analysis of the delinquent child. This is *conflict* or *disorganization*, either cultural or emotional. The psychiatrist speaks of the "rejected personality," and the sociologist refers to "social maladjustment." Thorsten Sellin, in his *Culture Conflict and Crime*, points out the need for determining and cataloguing conduct norms so that society can definitely understand their full meaning when they are applied to the behavior of the individual.[24]

As the distinguished British authority on delinquency, Dr. Cyril Burt, has stated: "Crime is assignable to no single universal source, nor yet to two or three; it springs from a wide variety, and usually from a multiplicity, of alternative and converging influences." [25] Burt further points out that at least four sets of factors are present in any specific case of delinquency, and that these factors may be gauged in importance in terms of their intensity in the specific case. They are: (1) the principal or most conspicuous influence (if any); (2) the chief cooperating factor or factors; (3) minor predisposing or aggravating conditions; (4) conditions present but apparently inoperative.

Here we have what is often termed the "multiple causation" theory of delinquency or crime. This is the thesis held by most students of these problems. Only by careful study can we begin to solve the riddle of delinquency. There is no short cut.

---

[24] *Social Science Research Council Report, 1938,* p. 107. See also Robert E. L. Faris, *Social Disorganization,* Ronald Press, New York, 1948, Chapter 6, "Crime and Social Disorganization."

[25] *The Young Delinquent,* University of London Press, 1938, pp. 599–600.

Part II

CONTROL AND TREATMENT OF
JUVENILE DELINQUENCY

Chapter VIII

APPREHENSION, DETENTION, AND INVESTIGATION

1. APPREHENSION

As THE SUBSEQUENT CHAPTERS WILL SHOW, the treatment of juvenile offenders is founded upon the principle of their need for guidance toward rehabilitation. The procedure, therefore, is essentially non-criminal.

The initial stages of the proceedings—*i.e.* apprehension, detention, and pre-hearing investigation—apply this concept in varying degrees.

a. Initiation of Proceedings

Most juvenile court laws prescribe the filing of a petition as the formal way of instituting proceedings. This right is often given to any citizen who has knowledge of a situation (an offense committed by a juvenile, the waywardness or truancy of a child, and so forth) that comes within the purview of the juvenile court's jurisdiction. In some states certain additional requirements are attached,[1] such as verification of the petition, or the swearing out of affidavits, or the provision that an investigation be made [2] prior to the filing of a petition in order to determine whether formal jurisdiction of the case should be taken. Commitment to the juvenile court by a magistrate or justice of the peace of a child arrested for a violation of the law is mentioned in the Pennsylvania Juvenile Court act as an alternate form of starting proceedings. It is used primarily in rural counties.

---

[1] See Gilbert Cosulich, *Juvenile Court Laws of the United States*, N.P.P.A., 1939, pp. 47–48.

[2] The Standard Juvenile Court Act, a model law prepared by a committee under the auspices of the N.P.P.A. (for details, see Chapter IX), includes such a provision (Section 11 of the revised edition, 1949).

In some states informal complaints are considered sufficient. This method has been used increasingly in recent years in accordance with the tendency of juvenile court procedure to become less formal and legalistic.

Actually, arrest by law-enforcement agents—*i.e.* local and state police, railroad and street railway police, and in rare instances the Federal Bureau of Investigation—is by far the most prevalent form of instituting procedure in a juvenile delinquency case.

Other sources of referral are school authorities, social agencies, other courts and probation officers, parents, relatives, or neighbors.

The United States Children's Bureau's compilation of juvenile court statistics for 1945, covering 374 juvenile courts and 37 per cent of the population of the United States, showed that 71 per cent of all cases for which the source of reference was reported originated with the police,[3] *i.e.* 75 per cent of the boys' cases and 52 per cent of the girls' cases.

b. Arrests by Police

The following discussion centers primarily around the apprehension by police of those juvenile offenders who are considered "children" according to the juvenile court laws of the various states.[4] Youthful offenders above juvenile court age are (with the exceptions noted in Chapter X, pp. 344–354) treated like adult offenders; their apprehension by the police and the initiation of proceedings against them are identical with the handling of adult persons arrested for crime.[5]

The arresting power of the police represents the most spectacular expression of the principle of protection of society. It is only natural that the men who have been entrusted with the exercise of this power should be guided in their thinking and their actions by this principle, sometimes to the exclusion of any other conception. They might feel

---

[3] See "Social Statistics," Supplement to Volume 11 of *The Child* (November 1946 Supplement), Juvenile Court Statistics, 1944 and 1945, Federal Security Agency, United States Children's Bureau, Washington, D.C.

[4] See Chapter IX, pp. 310–313, for the age limits of juvenile court jurisdiction in the different states.

[5] The Standard Juvenile Court Act (Section 15) states that the taking into custody of a child shall not be termed an arrest; in practice, however, the term "arrest" is often used even in cases of children.

that the treatment of juvenile offenders, founded upon the idea of
rehabilitation, is in contrast with the exigencies of public safety. It
is in the initial stages of juvenile delinquency proceedings, when the
police as law-enforcement agents are conspicuously active, that the
two points of view—protection of society, and welfare and guidance
of the individual delinquent child—appear to clash most vigorously.

Police officials seem to feel that "there are cropping up indications
of a tendency to restrict the arresting power" [6] as regards delinquent
children. Such indications are found "in instances where the police
must first get the authority of some judge or other court officer
before an arrest is made." [7] Actually, the majority of juvenile court
laws are silent concerning the apprehension of children and direct
their specific provisions toward the subsequent stage of development,
that of detention.

In recent years there has been a growing realization among responsible police administrators that the manner in which the police handle
child offenders is apt to determine to a large degree the juvenile's
attitude toward the authority of the law. The administrators became
convinced that police officers should be specially trained in the
understanding of the problems presented by children. A "Manual
for the Guidance of Enforcement Officers in Dealing with Juvenile
Offenders" [8] was compiled by the National Advisory Police Committee to the Federal Security Administrator in consultation with
the United States Children's Bureau and approved by the International Association of Chiefs of Police (the representative organization of police administrators in this country) and the National
Sheriffs' Association. It mentions the following procedures as having
"been found by practical experience to be the most conducive to
the juvenile's welfare, as well as in the best interests of the police
department's aims and purposes": [9]

Do This:
(1) *Treat the juvenile with consideration.*
    Remember that what he thinks of you and your conduct may

---

[6] *National Conference Report No. 7*, "Role of Police," Government Printing
Office, Washington, D.C., 1947, pp. 3–4.

[7] *Ibid.*, p. 16.

[8] "Techniques of Law Enforcement in the Treatment of Juveniles and the
Prevention of Juvenile Delinquency," Government Printing Office, Washington, D. C., 1944.   [9] *Ibid.*, p. 11.

influence his future attitude to be in favor of, or opposed to, social and legal requirements.

(2) *Be friendly.*

Many juveniles feel that the world is against them. Do not let your conduct further the development of an anti-social attitude in the child. Many juveniles are discouraged. They believe they are failures, though they haven't had time to be. You wouldn't expect a half-completed airplane to fly. You can't expect an undeveloped child to function as an adult.

(3) *Be firm.*

Appeal to his intelligence, his reason, his sense of fairness.

(4) *Discover the child's problems, if you can.*

His problems are as important to him as yours are to you. If you know his problems, you may be able to help him.

(5) *Try to gain his confidence and respect.*

In attempting to determine the child's guilt or innocence with respect to any overt act, your chances are far better if he believes in you.

(6) *Remember that the child of today is the man of tomorrow.*

A boy who hates a police officer because of the officer's abusive attitude will, as a man, have little respect for him.

(7) *Be positive in your attitude.*

Show the benefits that come from an attitude of conformity with lawful requirements rather than dwelling on the harmful effects of anti-social behavior.

Don't Do This:

(1) *Don't resort to vulgarity, profanity or obscenity.*

The use of such language by a police officer is especially reprehensible and should not be tolerated under any circumstances.

(2) *Don't "brand" the juvenile.*

Epithets such as "thief," "liar," "burglar," "forger," etc., should never be used towards juveniles whether in custody or not; nor should such terms be used in reference to juveniles in their presence or in the presence of their parents or relatives, or of any other person not a member of the police department—nothing is to be gained by it, and there is definite indication that it is very injurious to the child. Such epithets give rise to justified complaints. They are rightfully resented by the parents. The use of such epithets towards juveniles is a reflection upon the character and intelligence of the officer using them.

(3) *Don't lose your temper.*
  To do so is an admission of mental inferiority to the person being interrogated.[10]

In order to carry out these principles, a number of communities have established special juvenile bureaus in their police departments (sometimes called Juvenile Aid Bureau, Crime Prevention Bureau, or Youth Bureau) to which all police cases involving children are referred. Usually such a bureau consists of a specialized group of plain-clothes officers selected for their understanding of young people. Although any police officer may pick up a child, only the members of the juvenile bureau may question or reprimand him, confer with his parents, or decide to detain him.

These bureaus are primarily devoted to crime preventive work, as will be described in a later chapter.[11] But in many instances they are also empowered to dispose of minor cases and thus to avoid formal arrests and referrals to the juvenile court. In 1948, the Juvenile Aid Bureau of the Police Department of New York City adjusted 11,950 cases out of a total of 20,854 cases referred to them.[12]

A unique procedure with similar aims has been in operation for a number of years in Jersey City, New Jersey. There a Bureau of Special Service of the Board of Education was established in 1931, coordinating for this purpose, the school, the police, the medical services, and all other facilities dedicated to the welfare of youth. This bureau consists of a staff of visiting teachers who act as social case workers, the police unit, representatives of the recreation field, the school attendance department, and other health and child welfare agencies. The fact that the police are included in this bureau as an integral part of the coordinated group has proved most helpful. The plain-clothes officers, who operate under an inspector of police, have been carefully selected for their demonstrated ability in understanding and handling youth problems. No child in Jersey City may be taken into a police station or transported in a patrol wagon. Whenever a child is detected as having committed some offense of sufficient importance to demand police attention, he is escorted to his home by a police officer, and a complete report is forwarded to

---

[10] *Ibid.,* pp. 11–13.
[11] See Chapter XV, pp. 580–582.
[12] Annual Report, Police Department of the City of New York, 1948.

the police unit of the Bureau of Special Service, giving vital information on the child together with the description of his offense. The parents are then notified to present themselves at the Bureau, accompanied by the child. After a complete discussion of the case, the parents are counseled in regard to the proper regulations of the child's environment and habits, reminded of their responsibility for his guidance and control, and warned of the consequences of their disregarding their duties. If necessary, plain-clothes officers make follow-up visits to the home, the school, and the neighborhood in order to effect adjustment. Through this method it has been possible in many cases to desist from formal procedure involving arrest, detention and court hearing.[13]

The success of juvenile aid bureaus depends in large measure upon the availability of qualified personnel. A program of specialized training for police officers who are assigned to deal regularly with juveniles has therefore been recognized as a necessity, but only sporadic attempts have been made to translate the idea into practice.

The "Delinquency Control Institute" of the University of Southern California under its able director Dan G. Pursuit has made a singular contribution in this respect. In 1943 a committee of police practitioners of the Los Angeles area met with educators of that university with the view of organizing training courses for police officers to help them understand the causes, treatment, control, and prevention of juvenile delinquency. The outcome of their deliberations was the establishment of the "Delinquency Control Institute," which started to operate in October 1946 and which is housed on the university campus in its own small building. The official sponsoring groups who joined with the University of Southern California in establishing the Institute were the California Peace Officers Association, California Sheriffs' Association, California Youth Authority, California Youth Committee, Department of Justice of the State of California, and District Attorneys' Association of California.

Each group of students attends the "Delinquency Control Institute" full-time during a period of twelve weeks beginning in Sep-

---

[13] For further details, see Vincent J. O'Shea, "Jersey City Prevents Delinquency," reprinted from *The Welfare Reporter*, official publication of the New Jersey State Department of Institutions and Agencies, September 1947.

tember, January, and March respectively. Each class is limited to a maximum enrollment of twenty students at a time. Sixteen places are reserved for peace officers employed in police departments or sheriffs' departments. The remaining four students may be probation or parole officers, school attendance officers, social workers, or members of district attorneys' staffs. All students are recommended by the chief administrative officer of their department and approved by an Institute committee on scholarships.

Full tuition scholarships are granted to all students. Students in attendance at the Institute continue to have their regular salaries paid by the department or agency that employs them. In addition, a travel and subsistence allowance of $250 for the session may be granted to students coming from outside the Los Angeles area, since many of the students are married and have expenses that continue while they are away from home.

There is no rigid requirement for admission regarding previous education or rank and function within the law-enforcement agency from which the student comes. Students have ranged from newly appointed patrolmen to captains in charge of juvenile bureaus. Both men and women are admitted and there is no age limit. Since the inception of the program in 1946 to June 1949, 97 students were graduated.

The basic courses are on the university level and deal with the following topics: Social Treatment Aspects of Delinquency Control, Special Police Techniques, Conditioning Factors in Juvenile Delinquency, Delinquency Prevention Techniques, Administrative Aspects of Delinquency Control, Techniques of Learning and Teaching, Legal Aspects of Delinquency Prevention, Clinics in Delinquency Control, and Field Work. In addition to the lecture courses, visits are made to a number of agencies active in the field of juvenile delinquency control and prevention in the Los Angeles area.[14]

The employment of policewomen in many cities is valid proof of the advanced thinking of police administrators. The first unit was organized in Portland (Oregon), in 1905, at the time of the Lewis

---

[14] For further details on this project, see "Progress Report of the Delinquency Control Institute," University of Southern California Press, 1949; see also Lt. Donald Imler, "Training Peace Officers To Understand and To Work with Youth," *Federal Probation*, March 1949, pp. 42–44.

and Clark Exhibition, as a protective service for girls. It is reported that in 1949 more than 1,000 policewomen were employed in about 140 cities and in several state police departments. This represented a 60 per cent increase over 1940.[15] The policewoman movement has been closely identified with the crime-preventive activities of the police,[16] but women officers also play an increasingly important part in the arrest and detention of female offenders. As the previously cited Manual points out:

> Some departments have an iron-clad rule regarding the use of police-women in cases where females are detained or are to be interviewed. As soon as the girl or woman is taken into custody, the Policewomen's Division is notified. A policewoman is immediately dispatched to the scene. No male officer is permitted to be alone with the female prisoner except for the brief period of time required for the policewoman to arrive at the scene of arrest or detention. This is sound policing. It removes the possibility of a "frame-up" of the arresting male officer.[17]

c. *Fingerprinting of Juveniles*

A brisk controversy has been raging around the fingerprinting of arrested juveniles. Proponents, mostly police officials, of fingerprinting of juveniles point out that it is an accurate method of identification, that it protects the innocent, that it completes the records, and that it would enable the Federal Bureau of Investigation to include nationwide juvenile delinquency statistics in their Uniform Crime Reports. They also maintain that fingerprinting may act as a deterrent to future offenses. They deny that it constitutes a stigma *per se*. If there is any stigma, so they argue, it emanates just as much from being in a detention home, before a court, under supervision of a probation officer, or in an institution. They also point to a certain trend toward universal fingerprinting which has gained impetus as a result of the great number of fingerprints taken during World War II from civilians and members of the Armed Forces; also, the growing number of footprints of babies born in hospitals is cited. Con-

---

[15] Figures quoted from *The Outlook for Women in Police Work*, Bulletin No. 231, Women's Bureau, United States Department of Labor, Government Printing Office, Washington, D.C., 1949, p. 7.

[16] Details on the history and development of policewomen's units will be found in Chapter XV.

[17] P. 19.

sequently, a lessening of the stigma associated with fingerprinting in the public mind is claimed by this group.[18]

Opposition to the fingerprinting of arrested juveniles centers largely around this question of stigma. It is held that so long as universal fingerprinting is not used for purposes of identification, fingerprinting is still connected in the public mind with criminal procedure. Introduction of the fingerprinting of juveniles would constitute a complete reversal of juvenile court procedure which in its methods and aims is noncriminal. Even if juvenile court laws do not specifically forbid fingerprinting of juveniles (and general crime reporting or criminal identification laws and ordinances usually do not mention any minimum age limits), the practice of fingerprinting juveniles would violate the spirit of juvenile court legislation. The opponents, largely composed of child welfare specialists, also state that, since sufficient identification is obtainable in the very complete juvenile court records, in cases of subsequent offenses no difficulty in the identification of the delinquent can arise. Psychologically the effect of fingerprinting today must still be considered harmful, primarily because of the popular association of fingerprinting with criminal procedure. At the onset, an attitude of hostility would be created in the child, or in his parents, especially if they were sensitive, while a "tougher" youth would feel important as a result of this experience and would boast to his fellow gang members of having been treated "like a real criminal." [19]

An interesting contribution to this discussion was made by Inspector James McKnight, liaison officer between the Police Department and the Juvenile Court of Allegheny County, Pittsburgh, Pennsylvania. He stated that he did not use or believe in fingerprinting children because it was unnecessary and militated against the child's future. When identification of children of juvenile court age is absolutely necessary, as a result of fingerprints' being found at the

---

[18] According to a report in *The New York Times* of May 30, 1948, the civilian file of the Federal Bureau of Investigation now consists of 65 million fingerprint cards, while the criminal file includes the fingerprint cards of about 7.5 million individuals.

[19] For the "pro" and "con" of this question, see Warden L. Clark Schilder, "Juvenile Offenders Should Be Fingerprinted," and Judge Victor B. Wylegala, "Juvenile Offenders Should Not Be Fingerprinted," *Federal Probation*, January–March 1947, pp. 44–48.

scene of crime, the fingerprinting of the suspected juvenile must be requested from and approved by the juvenile court judge. Such prints are retained by the juvenile court and may be destroyed on judicial order. They are not kept in the police files.[20]

The police seem to show much less desire to request the right to photograph the arrested child (corresponding to the "mugging" of arrested adults).[21]

d. Slating

An adult is taken to the police station to be "slated" or "docketed" for a specific offense or number of offenses, but the juvenile offender (as will be discussed later in this chapter) should be brought to a specified place of detention for juveniles. Although most of the laws are very clear about this provision, there is a variety of thought as well as practice regarding the charging of juveniles with the commission of a specific offense. Since the general idea of juvenile court procedure is that the child is not tried for a crime, it would, of course, be logical to charge him only with "juvenile delinquency." The Federal Juvenile Delinquency Act of 1938 emphatically states that "such person shall be prosecuted . . . on the charge of juvenile delinquency, and no prosecution shall be instituted for the specific offense alleged to have been committed by him." Many juvenile courts, whether state laws so prescribe or not, follow the same rule and enter the following caption in their records: "In the matter of John Doe, alleged to be a delinquent child" (instead of "The People of the State . . . versus John Doe").[22] Other courts hold that, if only for interpretative purposes, the listing of specific offenses has its value. A much clearer picture of the degree of seriousness of delinquency can be drawn if detailed statistical break-downs are available indicating the types of offenses committed by juveniles.

---

[20] Excerpt from a talk by Inspector Knight before the Pennsylvania Committee on Penal Affairs, Philadelphia, on March 15, 1948.

[21] The Standard Juvenile Court Act (Section 15) provides that "neither the fingerprints nor a photograph shall be taken of any child taken into custody for any purpose, without the consent of the judge."

[22] See decision of the Pennsylvania State Superior Court of 1923, quoted in "A Juvenile Court Is a Court of Equity," by Judge Gustav L. Schramm, in *Federal Probation*, January–March 1947, p. 36. Section 11 of the Standard Juvenile Court Act suggests the caption: "In the interest of . . . , a child under eighteen years of age."

2. DETENTION

a. Reasons for Detention

The term "detention" refers to the temporary holding of a child away from his own home pending investigation and decision by the juvenile court.

The most apparent purpose of detention is to assure the presence of the child for the investigation and study of his case and its disposition through court hearing. Other reasons, to be outlined later, may also call for detention. Whatever the reasons are, the impact of detention upon children is usually bound to produce a severe emotional shock. Good juvenile court laws and practices, therefore, tend to prevent unnecessary detention of children. This goal can be achieved in the following manner: In cases that do not originate through arrest, the juvenile court customarily issues a *summons*, a *citation*, or any other less formal type of notice to the parents or custodians of the child requesting the appearance of the child at the court at a stated time. In the overwhelming majority of instances this practice has proved sufficient and successful. Of course, the juvenile court is empowered to issue warrants if the attendance of the child in court cannot otherwise be secured.

In cases of apprehension by the police the immediate disposition of the case varies greatly in the different local communities. It depends upon the nature of the offense, the time of arrest, the age of the youngster, the special instructions issued to the police officers for the handling of juvenile offenders and the degree of cooperation between police and juvenile court. It can take any of the following forms: The police officer may give the child a good lecture and send or escort him home; this procedure may technically not be called an arrest, and has become a frequent practice in cases of first-time violation of curfew regulations. He may take the child to the police station for a limited period or directly to the office of the juvenile court (if arrest occurs during office hours). He may take the child to the detention home or other facility provided for the detention of children, either directly or after he has first been temporarily held at the police station.

In order to bring any arrest to the attention of the juvenile court as speedily as possible and also to avoid unnecessary detention, "many juvenile court laws require that the court, a probation officer, or under the Federal Juvenile Delinquency Act, the Attorney General, be notified immediately upon such an arrest or that the arrested child be taken directly to the court or to the place of detention designated by the court." [23]

The aim of reducing the detention of children to a minimum is further apparent in the provision contained in many existing laws and formulated in the Standard Juvenile Court Act (Section 15), as follows: "When a child is so taken into custody, such officer shall notify the parent, guardian or custodian of the child as soon as possible. Whenever possible, unless otherwise ordered by the court, such child shall be released to the custody of his parent or other responsible adult upon the written promise, signed by such person, to bring the child to the court at a stated time or at such time as the court may direct."

The setting of bail—the usual procedure, in cases of adult offenders, of assuring the presence of the accused person—though not excluded by juvenile court laws, is not customary in child delinquency cases and should not be used, since it is a typical feature of criminal court practice. [24]

Who determines the need for detention of a child arrested for delinquency? Here, too, great variations are to be found. In some instances, the police officer or officers decide the need and length of detention of children. This must be considered an unwholesome practice. The role of the police as law-enforcing agent should be confined to the apprehension of the juvenile offender and his delivery to the court office or designated place of detention. In other communities, the superintendent of the detention home, who is independent of the juvenile court, is entrusted with the decision. This system is likely to produce conflicts between the superintendent of the detention home and the juvenile court authorities. The most desirable practice is that the juvenile court control intake and release and that no child be detained except by the authority of the juvenile court judge or his representative, who might be a probation officer, or the superintendent of the detention home, or a specially designated referee or examiner. Not infrequently the chief probation

---

[23] Cosulich, *op. cit.*, p. 57; see also Standard Juvenile Court Act, Section 15.
[24] See Standard Juvenile Court Act, Section 15.

officer of the juvenile court functions also in the capacity of superintendent of the detention home. Rules governing intake should be worked out in cooperation between police and juvenile court.

As is characteristic of juvenile court procedure in general, the decision concerning detention must be based on the individual attributes of the case. Age, type of offense, recidivism, home background, physical and mental condition of the child, and the requirement of public safety are some of the factors to be considered. More than one reason might warrant detention in certain cases. In others, grounds calling for detention must be weighed against those favoring release into parental custody.

The National Conference's *Report on Juvenile Detention* mentions the following three major groups of children who must be placed in detention:

(1) Children so beyond control that parents or guardians may not be able to prevent a repetition of behavior which is menacing to themselves or the community, such as repeated offenses, armed robbery, serious assault, and certain sex cases.

(2) Children who are in physical or moral danger in their own homes and for whom no other immediate care (such as with friends, relatives, or neighbors) is possible.

(3) Children whose presence in court, return to another jurisdiction or community, longer time placement or uninfluenced testimony, can only be assured by detention.[25]

This list takes into account only the custodial aspects of detention for juveniles, namely the assurance of the child's presence before and at the court hearing, the protection of the child against improper influences, and the protection of society against particularly aggressive offenders. In these respects the reasons for detention of juveniles and adults are quite alike.

However, detention of juveniles has developed additional features which so far have been only rarely extended to adult prisoners awaiting trial. Detention of children is considered an important part of the whole treatment process through which juvenile delinquency cases are handled. Helen D. Pigeon, in *Probation and Parole in Theory and Practice*, a study manual published by the N.P.P.A. in 1942, speaks of the "laboratory use of detention," indicating the use

---

[25] *Report No. 5*, pp. 18–19.

of the detention facility as a social and psychological clinic. This plan includes the study [26] and classification of the child as well as services to him, such as the clearing up of physical infections and defects if short treatment suffices. "Or a child may need a thorough physical cleaning up to make him more attractive and improve his personal habits and manners." [27]

In a slightly different enumeration, Sherwood and Helen Norman, in their study, *Detention for the Juvenile Court*, mention three responsibilities of detention:

(1) Physical care and custody under safe and healthful conditions.

(2) Meeting non-physical needs, particularly supervision of disturbed children.

(3) Observation and clinical study of the child's capacities and needs as revealed during detention, and information of these findings to the court.[28]

The frequency with which detention of delinquent children is used varies greatly throughout the country. The previously quoted statistical report of the United States Children's Bureau for 1945 points out that "in some localities children brought to court in delinquency cases are detained for almost all types of offenses, whereas in others only certain types of delinquency are considered serious enough to warrant detention care." This report covers a total of 122,851 delinquency cases, but only in 76,002 cases was the inquiry regarding the use of detention care answered. In 32,902 cases (or 43 per cent of those supplying data on this item) detention care overnight or longer was used, namely in 41 per cent of the boys' cases and in 54 per cent of the girls' cases. The higher percentage of detention care among girls results from the fairly large proportion of sex offenses and such other acts of delinquency as incorrigibility, disorderly conduct, and running away, which might indicate possible sex offenses, necessitating physical examination and, therefore, detention care. Although accurate statistics for each county in the

---

[26] Some progressive administrators now use the name "Youth Study Center" rather than the term "detention home."

[27] Pigeon, *op. cit.*, p. 37.

[28] Sherwood and Helen Norman, *Detention for the Juvenile Court*, N.P.P.A., March 1946, pp. 2–3. Details of this study will be presented later.

United States are lacking, it is estimated that the number of children detained each year may run as high as 300,000.[29]

b. Prohibition of Jail Detention

Even before the enactment of specific juvenile court legislation, laws were passed in several states prohibiting the placement of children in prisons or other places of confinement or in vehicles of transportation in company with adults charged with or convicted of crime. This fundamental postulate of keeping children separate from adults during the various stages of procedure won further recognition in the provision in practically all juvenile court laws [30] prohibiting the detention of children under a specified age in jails, lock-ups, police stations, or other places in which adults are confined. Contamination through close contact with adults awaiting trial has been considered one of the greatest obstacles to rehabilitative treatment of juvenile delinquents. As the National Conference's *Report on Juvenile Detention* puts it: "We have come to know that jailing a child will never frighten or shame him into reforming. We now see that when society jails youthful offenders instead of protecting itself from them it makes them the more determined, the more distrustful, the more cunning and resourceful in their enmity toward society. When we talk about keeping children out of jails we are talking not about the kind and humane thing but about the practical thing to do to save society from the waste and destruction of further criminality." [31]

In spite of the general recognition of this principle, statutes restricting or prohibiting jail detention vary widely in different states.[32] This variation is particularly great regarding the age of children below which jail detention is prohibited.[33] Some laws contain op-

---

[29] See Katherine F. Lenroot, "The Juvenile Court Today," *Federal Probation*, September 1949, p. 10.

[30] See Florence M. Warner, *Juvenile Detention in the United States*, University of Chicago Press, 1933, p. 169.

[31] *Report No. 5*, p. 4.

[32] See Marjorie Bell, *Children Under Lock and Key*, N.P.P.A., 1944, p. 6.

[33] According to Cosulich, *op. cit.*, p. 59, and additional later information obtained from the N.P.P.A., jail detention of children under twelve years of age is prohibited in three states, under fourteen years of age in nine states, under fifteen years of age in one state, under sixteen years of age in thirteen states, under seventeen years of age in three states, and under eighteen years of age

tional provisions making the application of the rule dependent upon the existence of special detention homes in the counties. Others— the Federal Juvenile Delinquency Act, for instance—make allowance for jail detention in exceptional cases. Some state laws require a specific order by the juvenile court judge if jail detention has to be resorted to. Several statutes, though permitting the holding of children in jail detention, require their placement in specially designated quarters, their strict separation from adults, and a limitation regarding the length of time of such detention.[34] There is, obviously, very little uniformity in the legislative picture.

Another weakness pointed out by Cosulich is that "few juvenile court laws contain any specific directions for the punishment of persons who violate the provisions forbidding jail detention of children." [35] As Cosulich further states, "The enforcement of these provisions is also made difficult in some states by inaccurate or incomplete statements on the prohibition of jail detention. Under the terms of these clauses in several states, apparently only the juvenile court judge is prohibited from placing children in jail, though doubtless the intent was to give the clauses a broader application."

The actual picture is even more disconcerting than the legislative confusion. According to a survey in 1948, only two states, Connecticut and New Hampshire, claimed never to use jails for children. According to the previously cited statistics of the United States Children's Bureau for 1945, 25 per cent of the children for whom detention care overnight or longer was required, were held in jails or police stations. This figure includes children cared for part of the time in jails or police stations, and part of the time elsewhere. In 1948 more than 1400 federal offenders under 18 years of age spent some part of the period awaiting court action in local jails.[36]

According to Sherwood Norman,[37] over 7000 children were held

---

in twelve states and the District of Columbia. However, the prohibition of jail detention is very often not an absolute prohibition, but one that may be disregarded by the judge or probation officer.

[34] See Standard Juvenile Court Act, Section 15.

[35] *Op. cit.*, p. 60.

[36] *Federal Prisons 1948* (Report of the Work of the Federal Bureau of Prisons), p. 15.

[37] Sherwood Norman, "Detention Facilities for Children," *Yearbook, N.P.P.A.*, 1946, p. 87.

in jail in 1944 in 29 localities which he and his wife visited during their survey. And these were communities with the best juvenile detention facilities in the country.

The National Conference's *Report on Juvenile Detention* estimates that 40,000 children were detained in jails in the United States in 1946.[38] Austin H. MacCormick, executive director of the Osborne Association, speaks of 50,000 to 100,000 children a year held in jails, "most of which are unfit even for adults." [39]

Merrill Conover, of the Social Service Division of the United States Children's Bureau, gathered on-the-spot information on the use of jails for detention of children in three southern states in 1941–42. According to his survey, "Georgia reported 830 cases of children under 16 years of age held in county jails in 1941, and North Carolina reported 500 cases of children under 16 years of age so held in the fiscal year 1941–42. Many of the children were quite young. In 84 (17 per cent) of the 500 North Carolina cases, the children were 12 years of age or even younger; in 23 cases they were not yet 11 years old. Of a group of 35 children reported as being in North Carolina jails in June 1942, nine were 12 years of age or younger. The ages of the 62 children detained in a South Carolina county jail ranged from 10 to 17 years; 13 were 12 years of age or younger. Information regarding ages was not given for Georgia." [40]

Richard W. Wickes, a Maryland probation officer, in an article "There Are Children in Our Jails," describes experiences in his former capacity as jail inspector for the Federal Bureau of Prisons:

. . . One of the last official visits I made was to a large city jail with a population averaging about 900 inmates. As I stood in the center a sheriff's deputy brought in two prisoners—one a handcuffed man and the other a small boy who was not handcuffed. There is a routine in this jail. All prisoners were booked and searched when they were received. Then they are sent to the shower where they bathe. After the bath they are given back their clothing if it is clean, a clean blanket, mattress cover, towel and a bar of soap. Later I again saw the boy and

---

[38] *Report No. 5*, p. 2.
[39] "The Community and the Correctional Process," *Focus*, May 1948, p. 67; see also Austin H. MacCormick and James H. Dooling, "Keeping Children Out of Jails: It Can Be Done," *Federal Probation*, September 1949, pp. 40–45.
[40] "Children in Jail," *The Child*, April 1943, pp. 143–147.

the adult prisoner. They had gone through the routine together and
had been assigned to the same cell. Certainly the jail was cleaner than
others, and certainly the food was better. But this boy would associate
with hardened criminals of that great city. Every hour of the day he
would hear stories of their exploits. He would be trained in their way
of life. In a city of almost a million people the city authorities had not
and have not provided a proper place for holding children. In that jail
that day there were seventy-two children sixteen years of age and
under. They sleep in the same cells with adults, they eat in the same
dining room, they associate with them during the long dragging hours
of the day . . .[41]

Other Federal Prison inspectors describe similar experiences:

Today I found a 10 year-old boy in a cell one door removed from
two older prisoners. The youngster told me he had been picked up for
refusing to go to school and had been committed to jail by the juvenile court judge. . . . I was deeply touched by the plight of this little
boy who cried and begged to be released . . . promising me that he
wanted to go back to school. . . .

There were in the county jail yesterday morning 53 juveniles 17
years of age and under . . . there is no wonder that murder, violence,
perversion, cruelty and torture go on. . . . Twenty, twenty-five and
sometimes thirty boys are locked in a dark cell block together. They
are left to forge for themselves, their medical needs are taken care of
by a trusty in jail on an habitual drunk charge. Their keepers pay them
no attention except when their rioting becomes an annoyance to them.
. . . The citizens of the city and county need not be surprised if, after
being treated like animals, they behave like animals of the jungle. . . .
God alone knows what is going on there—the sheriff and jailers don't.

This is probably the worst jail in the state and it ranks among the
worst in the country. A very active and authoritative kangaroo court
is permitted to operate. No provisions have been made for either boys
or girls despite the fact that about 25 percent of the commitments to
the jail are children, some as young as 11 and 12 years. Boys have to
be put into men's quarters and girls into women's . . . the jail is never
free of vermin. Trash, litter, junk and filth is everywhere, and a thorough housecleaning seems never to be done.[42]

---

[41] *Probation*, December 1943, pp. 43–47. (This passage appears on p. 46.)
[42] Quoted by Roberts J. Wright, executive secretary, National Jail Association, in his article, "What! The County Jail Again?," *Federal Probation*, July–
September 1944, pp. 17–20.

Summing up this shameful situation, the *Handbook of Correctional Institution Design and Construction* states:

> Here, in dismal, cheerless surroundings, in constant association with drunks, perverts, and hardened offenders, and usually in complete idleness and under perfunctory supervision, they are given their first extensive education in the ways of crime. The experience is one that is seldom forgotten, and all too frequently it leaves emotional wounds and scars from which the victim never fully recovers.[43]

Why are children held in jails?

Inadequate or ambiguous legislation and the absence of enforcement clauses have been mentioned before. Even though many state laws contain provisions that counties must furnish detention facilities for children apart from jails, this does not guarantee their establishment. So-called "economy" has frequently prevented county officials from carrying out the mandate of state legislatures. Efforts directed at the pooling of resources of several adjacent counties for the establishment of regional detention homes have been frustrated by a false conception of home rule.

A particularly regrettable situation exists in respect to the older age groups of juvenile offenders, primarily those between 16 and 18 years. Some juvenile court laws permit placing children 16 years of age and over in a jail or other place of detention for adults. The legislative intent was to make it possible for certain offenders within that age group who require maximum security detention to be detained in places providing such custody. But in a number of communities this provision in the law, which was intended to apply only to exceptional cases, has been used as a pretext not to provide any special detention quarters for this older group and thus to compel the juvenile court authorities to hold all offenders of these age ranges who require detention in the only available custodial facility—the jail.

There are other reasons, all equally deplorable, why children are held in jails. The National Conference's *Report on Juvenile Detention* enumerates a few:

> (1) In many communities the jailing of children continues because it is believed in; the myth that to jail is to reform still has a firm grip on some authorities and on large segments of the population.

---

[43] Issued by Federal Bureau of Prisons, Washington, D.C., 1949, p. 164.

(2) Hundreds of children who have been committed to overcrowded state training schools are held in jail awaiting a vacancy; when a training school finally gets one of these boys, it is severely handicapped by what his waiting in jail has done to him.

(3) The fee system whereby payment is made at a daily rate for the care and feeding of each jail inmate has resulted in much unnecessary jail detention; it is to the obvious advantage of the sheriff to keep the jail as nearly full as possible and to have children who are arrested during the evening held for release the next morning.[44]

The full significance of this shameful detention of children in jails is brought home by the reports of the Federal Bureau of Prisons, which inspects jails regularly to determine their fitness for the confinement of Federal prisoners held for trial or committed for short sentences. The Federal rating is a composite score on sixteen items that cover every phase of jail administration and operation. Of 3,120 jails and workhouses inspected from 1930, when this inspection program was started, to 1948, 83 per cent rated under 50 and 97 per cent under 60 on the scale which would rate the hypothetically "perfect" jail at 100. In 1947, 539 jails were inspected. Of these a considerable number seemed no better and no worse than when last inspected, but fully as many had become worse as had improved.[45]

But there is also a brighter side to the picture. Not only does the Federal Bureau of Prisons report that more and more local officials are seeking the Bureau's advice and assistance to help them construct, organize, and maintain their jails; real progress has been made in establishing better standards of cleanliness and sanitation, and more attention is being given to the selection of jail personnel.[46] Also on the state level, the power to inspect jails, which in a number of states is placed in the hands of state departments of welfare or correction, is more conscientiously used than before. A good example is North Carolina where the commissioner of the State Board of Public Welfare, Dr. Ellen Winston, reduced to a near minimum the number of children held in jails within a relatively short period after she took office in 1944. A similarly efficient program was carried out in New

---

[44] *Report No. 5*, pp. 2–3.
[45] See *Federal Prisons 1947*, p. 46, and *Federal Prisons 1948*, p. 49.
[46] See *Federal Prisons 1947*, p. 46.

Jersey by the State Department of Institutions and Agencies under the leadership of its commissioner, Sanford Bates.[47]

The prohibition of jail detention in the various state laws usually includes police stations or lock-ups. In practice, children in numerous communities are held in police stations from a few minutes to several hours or overnight, until the parents have been called to the station house and further decision has been made regarding detention or release of the child. Even if the time of detention in police stations is comparatively short and even if the children are held in a separate room, like the matron's room, or the guard or signal room, the detention is still undesirable, though not always avoidable. It usually results from lack of adequate and accessible special detention facilities for children, or from lack of cooperation between police and juvenile court authorities. Florence M. Warner, in *Juvenile Detention in the United States*, rightly stresses that "when it becomes a practical necessity to question children at a station or to hold them briefly pending transfer to the detention home, this should be done privately in an inner office or some place where the child is not under observation himself, nor in contact with adult offenders and all the objectionable features of the place." [48]

The prohibition of transporting children in vehicles together with adult offenders is contained in several state laws, but in practice it is disregarded as frequently as the prohibition of jail detention is.

c. The Detention Home and Its Program

Several state laws, implementing the prohibition of jail detention, require the provision by local authorities of suitable accommodations exclusively for the temporary detention of children. This provision is mandatory in some states and in others discretionary; in several states it applies only to the larger counties.[49] Rarely does the law specifically prescribe the type of detention quarters to be established. Some state laws forbid the mingling of dependent and neg-

---

[47] For further details, see Austin H. MacCormick, "Children in Our Jails," *The Annals*, January 1949, p. 156. For a description of the improvements in North Carolina, see Kathryn Close, "Jail Is No Place for a Child," *Survey*, March 1950, pp. 138–143.

[48] University of Chicago Press, 1933, pp. 157–158.

[49] For details, see Florence M. Warner, *op. cit.*, pp. 171–172.

lected children with delinquent children in the same detention facility. This is in accordance with the standards set up by the United States Children's Bureau.[50]

Larger cities frequently have the congregate or central house of detention. In less populated communities the small institution type, with a capacity of about 15 children, is most often used. The following discussion centers around these two types of detention facilities. It draws to a certain extent on a survey undertaken by the National Probation and Parole Association in 1945, in response to a great number of requests from many communities asking for assistance and advice in providing detention care facilities. Such requests are a good sign. They are symptomatic of the growing realization on the part of the authorities and interested citizens' groups that many of the existing facilities are inadequate. They are probably an outcome of the widespread publicity, in professional and popular magazines,[51] on the disgraceful use of jails for detention of children.

The study was undertaken "with a view to discovering the best in all types of detention care wherever they may exist." [52] It did not confine itself to an evaluation of the physical facilities, but paid particular attention to the "social climate of each home." The survey covered 68 facilities, located in 22 states including the Northeast, the South, the Midwest, and the Far West. These were some of the findings of the investigation: [53]

> We found no uniformity in the administration of detention homes. Two-thirds of the detention homes studied were overcrowded. We found great variations in the length of stay. The survey showed that

---

[50] *Ibid.*, p. 41; see also Marjorie W. Lenz, "A Yardstick for Measuring Detention Homes," *Federal Probation*, April–June 1942, pp. 20–23.

[51] See, for instance, Leon T. Stern, "In the Shadow of the Jails," *The Proceedings of the National Conference of Juvenile Agencies*, March 1946; Vera Connolly, "Get the Children Out of Jails," *Woman's Home Companion*, November 1944; Albert Q. Maisel, "America's Forgotten Children," *Woman's Home Companion*, January 1947.

[52] Sherwood and Helen Norman, *Detention for the Juvenile Court* (A Discussion of Principles and Practices), N.P.P.A., March 1946, p. iii.

[53] Quoted from Sherwood Norman, "Detention Facilities for Children," *Yearbook*, N.P.P.A., 1946, pp. 86–99, which contains a summary of the findings of that study. See also by the same author, "New Goals for Juvenile Detention," *Federal Probation*, December 1949, pp. 29–35, and "Building the Detention Home," *Federal Probation*, March 1950, pp. 29–36.

the better detention homes did provide reasonably good physical care but the kind of life for children conducive to mental health was frequently lacking. Delinquent children requiring security detention were often found cared for in the same institution as dependent and neglected children. Nowhere did we find realistic provision for the 16 and 17-year-old delinquent youngster although juvenile court jurisdiction in over half of our states now includes this group. Underpaid, untrained and unqualified staffs are the rule rather than the exception. Finally, in most detention homes we found the very conditions which out in the community are pointed to as causes of delinquency: lack of understanding relationship between children and adults; the presence of companions who act as delinquency seducers; lack of a full recreational program; lack of a meaningful school program; lack of professional child guidance service, etc.

On the positive side, the probers secured at least some valuable information from each detention home visited. The outcome of their survey was a compilation of principles and practices that might serve as a manual for developing detention facilities in the various communities. It pointed up the shortcomings of existing accommodations and made suggestions for desirable plans. Their report covers such items as the physical plant, location, administration, personnel, services to the child, information to the court, length of detention, and planning for detention facilities.

The *building design and construction* [54] must be adapted to the special demands of detention care, as distinguished from long-term institutional care. The structure should meet the requirements of custody and also make provision for active and constructive living. This is not an easy task. Until recently little thought has been given to this type of architecture, but in a number of communities new detention facilities have either just been completed or are in the process of construction, or are at least in the blueprint stage. In many instances, the plans for these buildings were drawn with the expert advice of national and state agencies which have devoted a

---

[54] A very detailed treatment, "The Planning and Construction of Juvenile Detention Homes," including many practical suggestions for design and layout, is found in the *Handbook of Correctional Institution Design and Construction*, issued by the Federal Bureau of Prisons, 1949, Chapter X. For detailed technical information, see also Sherwood Norman, *The Design and Construction of Detention Homes for the Juvenile Court*, N.P.P.A., 1947.

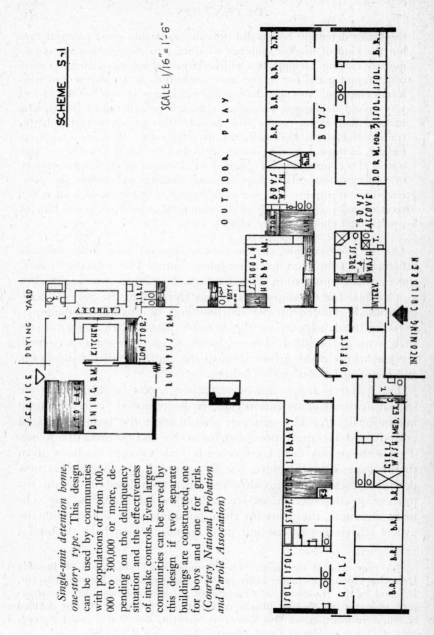

Single-unit detention home, one-story type. This design can be used by communities with populations of from 100,000 to 300,000 or more, depending on the delinquency situation and the effectiveness of intake controls. Even larger communities can be served by this design if two separate buildings are constructed, one for boys and one for girls. (Courtesy National Probation and Parole Association)

SCHEME S-1

SCALE 1/16" = 1'-6"

OUTDOOR PLAY

INCOMING CHILDREN

SERVICE   DRYING YARD

GIRLS

LAUNDRY

DINING RM.   KITCHEN   LOW STOR.

STORAGE

RUMPUS RM.

GIRLS

B.R.   B.R.   B.R.   BOYS WASH   SCHOOL & HOBBY RM.   BOYS

DRESS & WASH   DORM. FOR 3   ISOL.   ISOL.   B.R.

BOYS ALCOVE   T.

INTERV. WASH

OFFICE

STAFF   LIBRARY

ISOL.   ISOL.   B.R.   B.R.   MED. EX.   GIRLS WASH   T.

GIRLS   B.R.   B.R.

great deal of time to the study of the problem involved, such as the National Probation and Parole Association and the California Youth Authority. The construction of detention places should be simple and durable and, in order to provide the external framework for a healthy emotional climate, there should be emphasis on cheerfulness, livability, and ease of maintenance. Single sleeping rooms are preferable for older children, especially those needing security detention. Dormitories are more useful for younger children, for whom the solitude of a single room, away from their own home, is a frightening experience. In larger institutions, complete living areas should be provided for each group unit. These units should not exceed 15 or 20 children, so that a family-like atmosphere can be provided. Living and activities rooms should be so located and arranged with reference to each other that they permit a variety of individual and small-group pursuits to go on at one time within view of the supervisor. Ample room should be provided for indoor and outdoor play and game activities. Much is to be said for separate buildings [55] or the spread-out single-story plan.

The choice of *location of the building* must be carefully considered. If the court and probation offices are not housed under the same roof, or at least in adjacent structures, it is advisable to erect the detention facility at a convenient distance from these offices as well as from other social agencies and clinical services. It is best to locate the detention home away from so-called "delinquency areas" and by all means away from the local jail.

The *administration of detention care* is far from uniform both in current practice and in the plans for the future. So much depends on local conditions that it is hard to single out one type of administration as most desirable. (1) The detention facility might be operated by the county commissioners or the county board of supervisors. This type of administration has the advantage that those responsible for

---

[55] Juvenile Hall in Los Angeles is so constructed; it comprises six buildings on seven acres of ground, including playground space and lawns, surrounded by a stucco wall. The buildings consist of a hospital unit, a school building, dormitories for boys and girls, and a separate building for non-delinquent children, with its own outdoor play space. For further details on Juvenile Hall, see David Bogen (its superintendent), "Large Scale Detention," *Probation*, February 1945, pp. 65–68, 86–90; also Rosalind Lee, "Children at the Crossroads," *Hygeia*, December 1947 (illustrated).

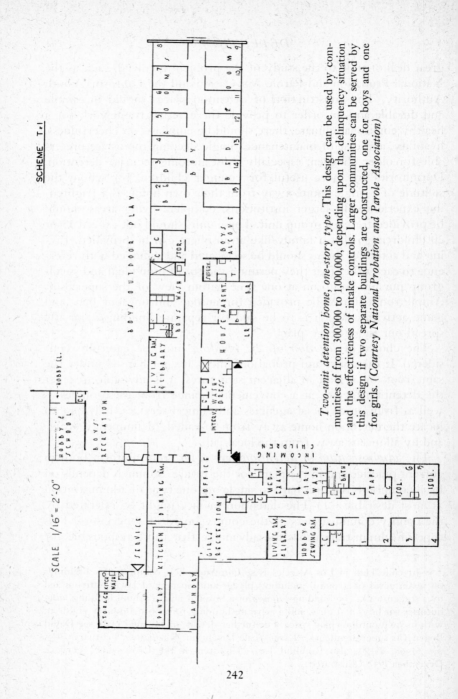

SCHEME T-1

SCALE 1/16" = 2'-0"

Two-unit detention home, one-story type. This design can be used by communities of from 300,000 to 1,000,000, depending upon the delinquency situation and the effectiveness of intake controls. Larger communities can be served by this design if two separate buildings are constructed, one for boys and one for girls. (*Courtesy National Probation and Parole Association*)

242

the detention home are also directly responsible to the taxpayers for the expenditure of funds. Otherwise, however, this form of administration must be considered as the least desirable one. Members of such county boards who have many other duties to perform are rarely qualified to understand the objectives of detention beyond the concept of custody and are probably not favorably inclined toward the securing of necessary funds for good detention service. Consequently, in small communities and rural areas, wherever this system of administration prevails, one seldom finds any provision made outside the jail. Where personnel is not selected under civil service, as is still the case in many counties, the danger of political appointments for positions in detention facilities is quite obvious. (2) The juvenile court would appear to be the logical agency to assume responsibility for the operation of detention care. Actually, there are quite a number of good examples for this type of administration. As Florence M. Warner points out in her book *Juvenile Detention in the United States*, "The relationship between the juvenile court and the detention home ranges from a merely cooperative one to full jurisdiction of the court over the home. In some areas the court appoints the staff, but has no control over the budget; while in others the court does not make appointments but has control of the budget." [56] There are several advantages in a system that places the full responsibility for the detention home in the juvenile court (and preferably its probation department). The court personnel is acquainted with the problems of children and is therefore in an excellent position to understand the prerequisites and needs of adequate detention care. The court, which ideally controls in-take and release,[57] could guide the policies of detention and maintain a close relationship with the staff in the detention facility. One of the drawbacks that the survey of the National Probation and Parole Association mentions is that juvenile courts are often understaffed and therefore unable to give sufficient attention to the problems of detention administration. (3) Private child-welfare agencies have frequently offered their shelter facilities for the detention of children. However, it is quite generally agreed that this is a public function, and its assumption by a private agency can only be accepted as a temporary measure or for a limited

---

[56] *Op. cit.*, p. 72.
[57] See Chapter VIII, p. 228.

period to demonstrate what can be accomplished. (4) A well-functioning and properly staffed local department of public welfare that has jurisdiction over foster-home placement, the licensing of institutions, and the temporary shelter care for dependent and neglected children might also be in a position to establish and administer the proper detention facilities for children awaiting juvenile court hearing for delinquent behavior. (5) The authors of the N.P.P.A. study see in a state agency (either a state-administered juvenile court or a state department of welfare) the most desirable agency for the administration of detention care, because it is capable of insuring uniformity throughout the state, and because, through the promotion of regional detention homes for several counties, it is efficiently able to prevent the detention use of jails for children. The authors of the study admit that such thinking may be ahead of current practice, but emphasize the increasing trend toward widening the state's responsibility in the child welfare field. At present, state control is mostly limited to visitation, inspection, and the correction of objectionable conditions, but even this service is seriously hampered by lack of funds and personnel in many state welfare departments. (6) Advisory boards, comprised of citizens' representatives, can be of real value, particularly for detention institutions administered by the county commissioners, the county board of supervisors, or the juvenile courts. Their greatest advantage lies in their position of liaison between the public as taxpayer, and the detention home and the juvenile court.

Personnel in a detention home should consist of individuals who have had varied and successful experiences with children. They should have warmhearted personalities of unquestionable character and should possess "a strong constitution, abundant good humor and intellectual curiosity." [58] The superintendent of a detention home must be particularly capable of understanding the problems of emotionally disturbed children and of organizing a constructive and active program that evokes the interest of each age group. Work assignments should be so organized as to leave the supervisors (this term is used in preference to "guards," "attendants," or "matrons," which suggest only custodial care), teachers, and group workers

---

[58] Sherwood Norman, "The Detention Home," *The Annals*, January 1949, pp. 158–165, especially p. 161.

free from maintenance jobs that would curtail their time with the children. Teachers must be exceptionally qualified in view of the special problems created by the impact of the detention experience upon the individual child and the continuous change of the pupil population. The ratio of staff to children should be considerably higher than in an institution for long-time care; fifteen children to one supervisor during all waking hours should not be exceeded.

The *services to the child* in a detention home that realizes its important function within the whole treatment process are manifold. They include good physical and custodial care, professional services —such as medical examinations—psychological and psychiatric tests, child guidance and case work, and an activities program of schooling (including remedial instruction for children with speech defects, reading difficulties, and other special problems), recreation, and religious teaching. The importance of meeting the non-physical needs of a child in a detention facility has in recent years been more and more recognized. (See Appendix Cases 5 and 6.) However, in still too many instances a look into the so-called recreation room reveals a group of youngsters sitting on the floor, the table, or slouched on chairs—"occupied" for hours with nothing but half-torn, soiled comic books. The entire social atmosphere of a detention home determines whether the experience of the child in custody is to be a positive or negative one. Richard Allaman, superintendent of the Juvenile Court Detention Home in Dayton, Ohio, in a challenging paper, "True or False? Some Questions About Your Detention Home," [59] mentions as most essential criteria of a good detention facility, "a welcoming and cheerful emotional climate created and maintained by the staff, and the constructive use of youthful group spirit instead of fear and repression of it."

The *information to the court*, based on observation of the child in detention, will include physical health data, the results of mental tests, and the reports of case workers, group workers, and teachers. Such information can convey to the probation officer and the judge a better picture of the youngster than is possible to glean from short or even detailed interviews, which are necessarily influenced by the artificiality of the occasion. In the detention home, "The child lives

---

[59] *Focus*, May 1948, pp. 69–75. The Dayton, Ohio, Detention Home is mentioned later in this chapter as an example of good detention facilities.

and plays with a group under supervision. His ability to adjust to other children and to adjust in the classroom, to participate in group play, to give and take in activities, his ability to work, his sociability or lack of sociability, his dependability when on a trusted errand, all can be observed in a detention home, and all give an unusual opportunity for increasing our knowledge of a child's personality." [60]

d. Length of Time of Detention

Realizing that detention, even in the most adequate facility available, is almost always a traumatic experience for the child, it is essential to make detention as short as is consistent with the purpose to be achieved.

Florence M. Warner, in her *Juvenile Detention in the United States*, reports that in 1929–30, out of 16,757 children in 141 areas in 38 states and the District of Columbia, 12.4 per cent of the boys and 8.1 per cent of the girls were detained less than one day; 51.9 per cent of the boys and 40.8 per cent of the girls stayed in detention from one day to one week; 13.6 per cent of the boys and 14.5 per cent of the girls from one to two weeks; and the remainder for more than two weeks, with 1.1 per cent of the boys and 2.0 per cent of the girls one year and over. These data included all types of detention quarters, from the private boarding home to the jail. [61]

The report of the Federal Bureau of Prisons for 1948 gives the average length of detention for Federal prisoners under 18 years of age as 20 days. [62]

In 1948, at the Child Study Institute (the detention facility of the Lucas County Juvenile Court, Toledo, Ohio), 43.7 per cent of the children were in custody less than 10 days; 37.5 per cent from 10 days to one month; 15.4 per cent from one month to two months; 2.6 per cent from two to three months; and the remainder of 0.8 per cent three months and more. [63]

A number of factors determine the length of detention; some of them are justified, others are born from a lack of facilities or from

---

[60] John Chornyak, M.D., "The Child in Detention as Seen by the Psychiatrist," *Yearbook*, N.P.P.A., 1939, pp. 151–156.

[61] *Op. cit.*, p. 139.

[62] *Federal Prisons 1948*, p. 15.

[63] *Your Juvenile Court Is Different*, Annual Report of the Lucas County Juvenile Court, Toledo, Ohio, 1948, p. 22.

ignorance. A boy or girl in need of immediate and prolonged physical care, or a child whose emotional disturbance requires continuous observation and study, will justifiably remain in detention for a longer period. So will a youngster whose detention is dictated by his need of protection against the brutality or indifference of a parent, the exploitation by an adult, or the attempts to influence his testimony when an adult offender is involved.

There is no excuse, however, for unduly long detention because of the heavy case load of probation officers who have not sufficient time for a speedy investigation of all cases of detained children. Infrequent court hearings are equally invalid as a reason for prolonged detention. As Sherwood Norman states, "Many long-time residents of the penitentiary have pointed to the bitter resentment towards society which grew into reality during the days when they were awaiting hearing in juvenile court—the days when they were 'kept on ice' until the court decided what to do with them." [64] To extend the detention period as a means of punishment is doubly unwholesome, since it not only mistakes the purpose of detention but also negates the principles of rehabilitative treatment. One of the most frequent causes for protracted detention was found by the authors of the N.P.P.A. study in the lack of adequate institutional and foster-home placement facilities. In many of the communities that they surveyed, "The juvenile court is placed in the incongruous position of making plans for children whose homes are unfit for their return, yet for whom no other immediate placement is possible. Many groups of children suffer from this lack of placement opportunities and may be kept in the detention home for periods of months waiting for 'something to happen.'" [65]

On the other hand, if detention is necessary, it should not be too short. Overcrowded and inadequate detention facilities or misguided sentimentalism have prompted too early releases of children, before medical examinations and social investigations could be completed.

---

[64] Sherwood Norman, "The Detention Home," *The Annals*, January 1949, p. 159.

[65] Sherwood and Helen Norman, *op. cit.*, p. 7. The Standard Juvenile Court Act provides that "no child shall be held in detention longer than two days, excluding Sundays and holidays, unless an order for such detention is signed by the judge" (or the chief probation officer or other person to whom he has delegated that power) (Section 15).

The sole criteria for ordering detention and determining its duration should be the needs of the child and any other purpose that detention aims to serve, such as the protection of society.

e. The Public Attitude to the Problem of Detention

One of the greatest obstacles to the development of adequate detention care for children awaiting court action is the lack of public understanding. True, it is not easy to interpret the objectives of detention to the tax-paying public. But this community education is the key to successful planning and developing of detention care.

A widespread notion is that children stay in detention quarters only for a comparatively short time and that, therefore, less elaborate facilities and services will not harm the child. A good answer to this penny-pinching attitude was given by a superintendent of a detention home, as quoted in the N.P.P.A. study: "They stay only a few days, but 4000 children pass through our home each year. Each child is on edge and in an impressionable state. We cannot afford to have 4000 children a year in this community taste a kind of care that will shake their confidence in the court and in authority." This statement applies also to smaller communities where the yearly figure of children in detention might be counted only in hundreds or dozens.

In a community that has poor or no detention facilities at all, an active citizens' committee, so the N.P.P.A. report advises in its final chapter, "is usually instrumental in effecting changes; such a committee should thoroughly familiarize itself with the problem, call in professional help where needed and enlist the aid of both professional and civic groups." [66]

It is gratifying to note that the law-enforcement agencies, too, realize the importance of constructive use of detention care. The National Sheriffs' Association, at its meeting in December 1943, passed a resolution "to inform the nation's sheriffs about better methods of juvenile detention and to urge every sheriff to advocate the use of separate detention facilities for juvenile delinquents." [67] As the manual of the National Advisory Police Committee, mentioned before,[68] emphatically states:

---

[66] *Ibid.*, p. 35.

[67] Quoted in *The Child,* monthly publication of the United States Children's Bureau, August 1944, p. 25.

[68] See Chapter VIII, p. 219.

A successful juvenile program must be based upon the desire to help, rather than punish, the young person. Except in rare instances, when the misdeed is serious or the child needs protection, detention should be the last resort. There is probably no longer night in the lifetime of any child than the first one spent in official custody. Such an experience will create a lasting impression on him. It is extremely important, therefore, that the proper type of juvenile detention facilities be provided.

The New York State Department of Welfare's appointment of a detention consultant represents the first time that a specialized consultant in this field has been added to the staff of a state welfare department.

f. Some Examples of Good Detention Homes

As Marjorie Bell reports in the previously mentioned N.P.P.A. booklet, "Children Under Lock and Key," "A number of cities have detention homes where children receive not only the best of care but scientific examination and treatment as well."

Youth House, the detention home for boys in New York City, functions as a completely non-punitive institution; its program is based on the needs of the boys. It shelters annually several thousand boys from 7 to 16 years of age.[69] It houses up to 120 boys at a time. It has a staff of 92, including a psychiatrist, a physician, and six social workers. In 1949, a new program was launched offering clinical in-service training at Youth House to eleven fellowship students of New York University. These students spent four months at Youth House working with and learning from the regular staff.[70]

When a boy comes to Youth House he is at once greeted by a qualified social worker who tells him about the House, what is expected of him, and what he can expect. The boy then undergoes a physical examination. Every boy who will stay at least five days is seen by the psychologist within 24 hours of admission; he is also assigned to a case worker, to whom he can always turn, who maintains continuity of interest and is ready to discuss troubled situations.

---

[69] In the five-year period 1944–1949, it cared for 15,704 boys.

[70] *Focus,* July 1949, p. 122, and *Fifth Annual Report* of Youth House, 1948–1949, p. 32.

Every dormitory floor consists of single and double bedrooms opening into a central hall or clubroom. No room is ever locked. It is up to each boy whether he prefers to have a bedroom to himself or whether he wants to share it with a roommate. There is a "house council," consisting of sixteen boys, elected by the other boys, which assists the staff in maintaining order, settling disputes between boys, encouraging neatness, and welcoming newcomers. Teaching at Youth House is not restricted to elementary instruction; it includes classes in art and music.

Serious behavior deviations and nonconforming behavior are met not by administrative action but by the social workers; a boy is confronted with his behavior as part of his total problem and every effort is made to give him an understanding of his difficulties.[71]

This approach is described in some detail in the Third Annual Report of Youth House for 1946–1947:

> We still have our problems. Hardly a day goes by when some difficulty does not arise. These problems however are being met by a staff whose experience and training at Youth House have given them an awareness of the deeper significance of the symptomatic behavior characterizing a boy's disturbance. Meeting the challenge is therefore carried on calmly and deliberately, which in and of itself has a quieting effect on the greater number of inhabitants of Youth House. Particular consideration is given to the individual in his adjustment to the group and to the House. He soon finds that there are adults around him who want to help. By this kind of an approach we reduce to a minimum climatic situations which usually result in serious disturbance.
>
> What is perhaps most amazing in comparison to our early experience is the decrease in sex assaults. This was a preponderant problem in the early days, but has now reduced itself to minor proportions. The change can be accounted for by a number of factors. We took many steps to improve the physical structure of the House so as to facilitate more adequate supervision. Of greater significance, however, is the

---

[71] For further details, see Frank J. Cohen (executive director, Youth House, New York City), "The Child in the Detention Home Program," *Federal Probation,* January–March 1946, pp. 36–41. For a popular description of Youth House, see Vera Connolly, "No Straps, No Paddles," *Woman's Home Companion,* December 1947. Harriet L. Goldberg, in her book *Child Offenders,* Grune & Stratton, 1948, calls Youth House "one of the most progressive" detention homes (pp. 190–191).

direct application of understanding treatment to the boys' disturbances, which has resulted in reducing their tensions. In addition, they have been given a sense of acceptance. This, together with their opportunity to participate in the formulation and carrying out of the rules which affect their conduct has helped to bring about the exercise of greater self control. We have gone through week-ends without a single report of behavior difficulties. We always have some fighting, but even this is kept within fairly good controllable bounds. We feel that this has been accomplished by the tone set in the House and by discussions individually and in groups as to what is involved in living together in harmony. The boys' participation in this control is constantly solicited.[72]

Since 1946, Youth House has also administered a temporary shelter for delinquent girls, called Girls' Camp, located on Welfare Island. It consists of an administration building and eight cottages on twelve acres of ground. Originally built by the Department of Hospitals for convalescent care, the place proved admirably designed to meet the health needs of children, in terms of space, light, and modern buildings. It certainly is not in the pattern of the traditional detention facility. The average daily population in 1948 was 55 girls. The spirit and atmosphere characteristic of Youth House also determine the program at Girls' Camp. Here, too, a camp council, consisting of two representatives elected from each cottage and meeting every week with the camp director, assumes the responsibility for welcoming new girls, introducing them to their social worker, and accompanying them to the camp clinic. (See Appendix Cases 5 and 6.)

Concerning the "art of living together" at Girls' Camp, the following is reported:

Our group work program, as Girls' Camp conceives it, doesn't start after school at 3:15. It is an around-the-clock exercise in getting on with other people with direction from our children's supervisors whose chief qualifications for group leadership lie in a sustained and intimate tie with the girls. We believe that cleaning a cottage *together*, making a garden, or shoveling snow, requires just as much skill in leadership and has just as much value to the girls as playing a game of volley ball. It is an exercise in group action—if the girls decide *together* who shall do *what* in Saturday morning cleaning. We think of our super-

---

[72] Pp. 8–9.

visors as group leaders, who utilize their knowledge of girls to reduce conflict and to work toward healthy inter-dependence.[73]

Similar features of a progressive detention home program are found at the Montgomery County Detention Home, Dayton, Ohio, which rates among the best in the country. This detention facility serves delinquent as well as dependent and neglected children. During 1948, the average daily population was 46. Special emphasis is laid upon a diversified activities program, which includes work details, school classes, craft classes, play, and diversional pastimes. Evening events include family visits, Red Cross classes, religious services, movies, and a weekly party and amateur hour. Activities outside the institution include training and recreation for all boys two afternoons a week at the Salvation Army gymnasium, weekly swims for both boys and girls at the Y's, weekly basketball squad practice at a boys' club, and league games during the basketball season. In summer there are frequent visits to parks and playgrounds, regularly scheduled hikes, and an occasional picnic.

The superintendent of this home, Richard Allaman, reports on one aspect of detention work that has been the topic of many controversial discussions—namely, the degree of segregation according to sex.

Co-ed activities and natural daily contacts between boys and girls should be mentioned. Boys' and girls' dormitories and day rooms are on separate floors of the same building. Boys' and girls' groups rotate separately during the day between work, school, craft and recreation periods. Some boys eat in the girls' dining room but girls will not eat in the boys' dining room. In the playground and in evening activities generally boys and girls are together, and indeed some activities such as the weekly party and amateur hour and dancing class are directly designed to be co-ed activities. We realize that these practices run counter to generally accepted practices in detention care and might in some quarters stir up all kinds of adult anxieties about sex. We not only have found far fewer troubles in such management than in a

---

[73] Quoted from the *Fourth Annual Report* of Youth House, 1947–1948. This report contains an excellent statement by the executive director of Youth House, Frank J. Cohen, on the purpose and scope of detention, detention practices and the various types of boys in custody, especially the repeater. It also includes a detailed report on Girls' Camp by Alice Overton, camp director.

regime of strict segregation by sex, but we have seen unhealthy attitudes and excitement about sex relieved and changed in our program.[74]

Limited self-government is also encouraged at this detention home. It centers in a weekly assembly of all children with the superintendent for the purpose of electing committees, airing and talking over grievances, and making constructive suggestions. Interested citizen groups have over the years assisted materially by donating additional furnishings, equipment, and craft supplies.[75]

Another Ohio county has for many years provided an excellent detention care program. The Child Study Institute of the Lucas County Juvenile Court in Toledo was organized in 1937 as a successor to the old detention home. As the name implies, emphasis is on study and observation. The professional staff consists of three psychologists, a part-time psychiatrist, a pediatrician, a nurse, several teachers for academic and trade training, and probation counselors (as the probation officers are called in that court), all of whom are trained workers. The staff members are responsible for supervision on the respective floors of the Institute to which they are assigned, and for the execution of the daily program. They are called "leaders," rather than supervisors, matrons, and so forth.

The activity program includes weaving, knitting, various handicrafts such as plaster molding and decorative painting, airplane modeling, group singing under competent leadership, games of various types, boxing, and wrestling. A special visual-education program with motion pictures includes films on good manners, race relations, and sex hygiene. The sex-hygiene instruction is available to any child on the request and written consent of the parent. It is given by the psychologist for the boys and by the nurse for the girls. The film "Human Growth" is used and a question period always follows.

All children who are detained at the Institute following their preliminary hearing in court are under the immediate guidance of one of the psychologists, who is responsible for the child's orientation and adjustment to the Institute as well as for all mental tests administered and the final psychological report submitted for the court hearing.

---

[74] From a paper entitled "A Detention Home Activities Program," read before the Annual Congress of Correction in Milwaukee in September 1949.

[75] For further details, see *Annual Report of the Domestic Relations and Juvenile Court of Montgomery County, Ohio, 1948.*

Model of a Juvenile Detention Home. (*Courtesy of Wernert, Taylor, Sanzenbacher and Morris, architects, Toledo, Ohio. Photo by Toledo Photographic Service.*)

The psychologist works in close cooperation with the probation counselor, who is required to make a personal visit to the child every third day during the period of detention. Serious disciplinary matters arising during the period of detention are referred to the psychologist.

A unique feature of this detention program is the "privilege system," which extends to children at the Child Study Institute certain privileges, depending upon their ability to accept the responsibility placed upon them. In most instances, the child leaves the building without supervision to attend the zoo, the art museum, baseball games, movies, and so forth, although certain types of privileges

Corrective Reading as Part of a Good Detention Program. (*Courtesy of Gazette and Daily, York, Pennsylvania*)

require nominal supervision. During 1948, 469 children of a total of 901 detained were granted the privilege of leaving the building. Violations of this trust were less than one per cent.[76]

---

[76] The authors are indebted to L. Wallace Hoffman, director of the probation department, Domestic Relations and Juvenile Court, Lucas County, Toledo, Ohio, for the information on the Child Study Institute; see also *Your Juvenile Court Is Different*, annual report of the same court for 1948.

Excellent detention services are provided at the Receiving Home in York, Pennsylvania, a former residential home which accommodates between 10 and 15 children. A foster-father and foster-mother are in charge. Each child has his own room. The spirit of this home is expressed in the report of Henry Lenz, chief probation officer: "We have discovered that when these detained youngsters are given time for reflection they become very impressionable and sensitive, and that they require firm, understanding and sympathetic but not sentimental supervision." [77] Special emphasis is laid upon a school program directed chiefly toward helping children to relate the subject matter to the concrete problems of everyday life, helping them to acquire at least the beginnings of an education in "living." Lessons in corrective reading are included in the educational curriculum.

Another example of a good detention facility, in a less populated and chiefly rural county, is Juvenile Hall in San Mateo County, California.[78] It is a charming one-story building erected on a hill outside the limits of the county seat, Redwood City. It consists of dormitories for the younger children and single rooms for the older ones. It has ample play facilities for indoor and outdoor activities. There are dining rooms, school rooms, and offices for physical and mental examinations. In special rooms set aside for children who must be temporarily removed from the group for disciplinary reasons, a blackboard is attached to the wall and chalk is put beneath it. It was found that children who had to be placed in such solitary rooms used the blackboard to write, scribble, or draw the expressions of their feelings and thus had a needed outlet for their pent-up emotions. Administrators of detention homes in other communities have followed this example.

---

[77] Annual Report of the Juvenile Court of York County, Pennsylvania, 1946, p. 14; see also "The York Story," *The Quarterly* (publication of the Pennsylvania Association on Probation and Parole), January 1948, pp. 16–36.

[78] Juvenile detention facilities in California are called "juvenile halls"; they are often part of a larger building which also houses the court rooms and probation departments. Several of them have special wings serving as shelters for dependent and neglected children. For more information on the Juvenile Halls in California, see Harold B. Kehoe, "The Juvenile Hall as an Observation and Study Facility," and Arden Houser, "The Juvenile Hall as a Treatment Facility," *California's Challenge in Corrections*, published by the California Probation and Parole Association, Los Angeles (ed. Nort Sanders), 1949, pp. 23–29.

g. *Other Types of Detention Facilities*

In addition to the congregate form of detention facility, either of the large or small institutional kind, other types have been used in several communities.

There is, first, the so-called residence-type detention home. It has the appearance of an ordinary home, although it is operated by the juvenile court or by a city or county department which has leased or purchased a roomy residential house for this purpose. It is administered as a small-sized house of detention, described before. Such a residence-type detention home is primarily suitable for smaller communities. In larger communities, probably more than one home of this kind would be required.

Mealtime Is Training Time in a Good Detention Home. (*Courtesy of* Gazette and Daily, *York, Pennsylvania*)

The *Report on Juvenile Detention* of the National Conference describes the set-up of such a home in a Massachusetts city as an example:

> A residence was secured by the supervising agency to accommodate a maximum of nine delinquent boys, most of whom were between 12 and 17 years of age. The home was staffed with a married couple both of whom gave full time to the job. Some additional help was provided to relieve them. In this home there was a very solid structure of rules and routines of the kind that is easily understood as the fair and square thing. There was a hearty give and take between boarding parents and boys. Nothing was under-cover; there was no subject that could not be discussed freely. Although space for boys' activities was extremely limited, there was always something to do. The boys had a well organized share in the work of the house which was kept with a military neatness. In free time, play was not limited to cards, checkers and funny books. The program was given vigor and variety enough to let off steam and challenge interest by the liberal use of trips. Ball games, hikes, and exploring of museums, supervised by the boarding father, were part of every day. The supervising agency kept in closest touch, with ever ready guidance and help to the couple in charge.[79]

Second, in accordance with the general trend in the child welfare field to provide foster-home care, wherever feasible, rather than institutional placement, some communities have instituted boarding-home care in foster families for the detention of delinquent children. Appraising the potentialities of this type of detention care, Florence Warner, in her *Juvenile Detention in the United States,*[80] and Sherwood and Helen Norman in their N.P.P.A. survey [81] on detention care emphasize that subsidized boarding homes should be used only where there is a carefully worked-out plan for their selection and where intensive supervision is provided. Advantages of using foster homes are found in the family home-like atmosphere, and in the more individualized attention given to the child. Further, as the *Report on Juvenile Detention* of the National Conference states, "It insures the minimum of delinquency glamor, the minimum of delin-

---

[79] *Report No. 5,* pp. 11–12.

[80] *Op. cit.,* p. 94.

[81] *Op. cit.,* p. 11. See also Herbert D. Williams, "Foster Homes for Juvenile Delinquents," *Federal Probation,* September 1949, pp. 46–51, especially pp. 47–48.

quency contagion and the minimum of group aggression." [82] There are, however, a number of difficulties to be faced. Foster-home detention care does not seem feasible, as a rule, for juveniles over 16 years of age. Other difficulties lie, as the N.P.P.A. study points out, "in maintaining high standards in selecting the home, training boarding parents for the specialized job of detention care, keeping the interest of boarding parents who have proved satisfactory. Some of these difficulties may be caused by the meager allotments allowed boarding parents who are called upon to make use of their own homes and to do a skilled, time-demanding and often nerve-racking job.[83]

According to Katherine F. Lenroot, Chief of the United States Children's Bureau, seven states have made application to the Bureau for the granting of moneys from its general child care funds to subsidize foster homes for detention and other temporary care. This shows a growing awareness in the various state agencies of the value of boarding homes for the detention care of children.[84]

Erie County, New York, has used such boarding-home care for detention on a large scale since 1932. Eight boarding homes are now in use; five for boys, three for girls. One boys' home and one girls' home are somewhat specialized and serve as receiving homes where children are admitted at any hour of the day or night. They may be transferred later to another home. The most difficult boys are detained at the boys' receiving home, which has been remodeled for security and ease of supervision. Both boarding parents give full time to this home, which has a capacity of eight boys. The other homes have capacities ranging from two to six.

Henry Lenz, formerly chief probation officer of the Children's Court of Erie County, Buffalo, New York, later chief probation officer in York, Pennsylvania, and his wife, Marjorie Wallace Lenz, formerly director of the Children's Division, Erie County Probation Department, who had been spearheading this program, report on it as follows: [85]

---

[82] *Report No. 5*, p. 11.

[83] *Op. cit.*, p. 11.

[84] See Katherine F. Lenroot, "The Government and Child Welfare," *Yearbook*, N.P.P.A., 1948, pp. 80–95, especially p. 91.

[85] Marjorie Wallace Lenz, "The Use of Boarding Homes for Detention," *Yearbook*, N.P.P.A., 1939, pp. 130–150; Henry Lenz, "Juvenile Detention: Ten Years' Use of Boarding Homes," *ibid.*, 1942, pp. 133–148.

The building up of a group of foster homes adequate for the work of detention in association with a busy children's court is a slow and gradual process. Years of experience in homefinding by the workers who made the selections helped to define the basis for selection and to shape the character of the homes themselves to ways better adapted to this purpose. Selection is the task of the homefinder who, with the minimum of definite requirements, must depend largely on her experience. We require our homes to be within a reasonable distance of the court building and also of the children's hospital of Buffalo where the medical work is done. The foster parents must own the house in which they live or secure the express permission of the owner to do the type of work required, a permission not always easy to secure.

The children do not go out to school. Instead, the teacher who is supplied to us through the Board of Education visits the foster homes. Each home has a fully equipped textbook library as well as other facilities for home study supplied by the school department. The educational program is coordinated with the school system. Each child is given individual attention. It is the teacher's responsibility not only to classify the child correctly in terms of his academic standing, but also to point out and interpret in the written report lags in the child's achievement. Whenever needed, special tutoring is given so that children are better equipped on their return to school.

Although we do not like to emphasize the custodial aspect of our work, especially to the point of making it our chief concern, we do have a real obligation to see that we hold on to the child who is placed with us. During 1941 we had 19 abscondings out of 621 referrals. All but one of the children were returned. We try to keep the children involved in different kinds of delinquency separated, and whenever possible, the older children are held apart from the younger ones.

Third, several suggestions have been made for a combination of some of the described types. The N.P.P.A. study, for instance, considers a combination of boarding homes and a small institution (or several small institutions) as "the best answer to the detention problem in most communities. Such a plan provides for flexibility and meets the demand for the various types of temporary care needed. All children who can respond to a family type of care (younger children and those who need less rigorous control) should be given the advantages of boarding homes. The small institution could be reserved to meet the needs of older children who require specialized group care and maximum supervision." [86]

---

[86] *Op. cit.*, pp. 13–14.

The detention-study home combination is mentioned as a possibility in the *Report on Juvenile Detention* of the National Conference. This obviously is a set-up primarily designed for the study of the child's problems and needs, and only incidentally serves as a detention facility. However, this solution seems impractical as well as

Music Hour in a Good Detention Facility. (*Courtesy of* Gazette and Daily, *York, Pennsylvania*)

wasteful, as the *Report* itself points out, because "children will be held in detention for the sake of the clinical study when they do not need to be removed from their own homes for the usual reasons; also children may be given intensive study unnecessarily." [87]

A much more logical pooling of detention facilities, especially in less densely populated areas, would consist of well-supervised local boarding homes in combination with a small regional detention home, operated and financed jointly by adjacent counties. A great advantage in such a set-up would be the benefit of professional services which are usually not available to local facilities. It should be realized, however, that any proposal of a joint bi-county or multi-

---

[87] *Report No. 5*, p. 15.

county administration—as has been suggested for prison farms,[88] for instance—is bound to encounter opposition from individuals and groups who hide their personal or political vested interests behind the slogan of home rule. The promotion of regional detention projects seems to be more hopeful in those states where detention is controlled by a state agency (department of public welfare, and so forth).

In some instances, training schools or other long-term care facilities have been used for detention purposes. This practice is not desirable, since detention care presents adjustment problems different from those encountered in long-time commitment. Also, segregation of children in special detention units within such institutions is bound to complicate administration and to confuse the functions of both detention and long-term care.

3. CASE INVESTIGATION

Regardless of whether the child is held in detention or is permitted to remain in the custody of his parents pending the juvenile court hearing, this period of time must be utilized for the study of the case preparatory to its disposition by the judge. The case investigation is one of the most important phases of juvenile court procedure. It is indispensable if the idea of treatment and guidance of the juvenile offender is to be translated into practice. It provides the necessary information regarding the development of the child, his environment, and his physical and mental condition. From these data, an analysis of the reasons for the child's misconduct should be gleaned and clues for the appropriate treatment should be found.

The investigation of a juvenile delinquency case prior to its disposition is concentrated on the child's personality rather than on the nature of the offense. The recognition of the need for such an investigation, and its scope and contents, represent one of the many features which distinguish juvenile court procedure from proceedings in cases of adult offenders. In adult cases, conviction is based upon evidence, related exclusively to the alleged crime; social in-

---

[88] See Louis N. Robinson, *Jails (Care and Treatment of Misdemeanant Prisoners in the United States)*, Winston, 1944, p. 156; see also Barnes and Teeters, *New Horizons in Criminology*, Prentice-Hall, 1943, pp. 862–872.

formation about the personality of the defendant cannot be introduced into the trial procedure. It is true that in some cases the judge orders pre-sentence investigations regarding the antecedents and the social and environmental history of the adult defendant; [89] but the resultant findings of the probation officer or any other designated person or agency can be used by the judge only as guidance in pronouncing sentence after conviction or plea of guilty.

In juvenile court cases, these pre-hearing investigations are a preponderant rule, and their findings should govern the proceedings from beginning to the end. However, they are seldom mentioned as mandatory in the various state laws. In some jurisdictions—for instance, New York—the child must first be given a hearing and adjudged delinquent before an investigation is made.

a. Collection of facts

The first step in the process of a case investigation is the collection of facts. Although the reason for referral to the court, through arrest or complaint, might be of secondary importance in the final diagnosis of the case, it is most likely the starting point of the investigation. Time and place of the offense, number of companions—juveniles and adults—involved, the methods used, the damage done, the disposal of the goods, and the circumstances of detention and arrest are essential parts of the statements of the arresting officer or the complainant. The reasons for the admission to the detention home can be gleaned from the records kept there.

Previous delinquent acts committed by the juvenile offender and his siblings resulting in court dispositions are found in the juvenile court records. In juvenile courts that also have jurisdiction over child dependency and neglect, or that are connected with courts of domestic relations, the additional information referring to these situations is presented in the court records and can be used in the preparation of the history of the current case. If the child had been committed before, institutional records should also be consulted.

Much of the family history and the child's history will be learned from interviews. The interview, according to Webster, is a "visit for the purpose of obtaining particulars respecting a person or his opin-

---

[89] See Chapter X, pp. 371–375.

ion." Due largely to the influence of the principles of social case work in which interviewing is one of the most important tools,[90] the interview in cases of juvenile delinquency is considered not only as a means to elicit information but, at least so far as the child and his parents are concerned, as a part of the treatment process.

A good probation officer in charge of the pre-hearing investigation should be familiar, therefore, with such interviewing techniques as properly introducing himself, selecting a place conducive to the interview, explaining the situation, listening creatively, meeting people on their own terms, controlling the interview, and closing the interview. The skillful use of these techniques plays a great part in establishing relationship between the probation officer and the child and his family. The success or failure of the initial interview can often determine the whole trend of the ensuing treatment process.[91]

Regarding family history, the investigator is advised by a "Guide for Recording Initial Social Study," prepared by the N.P.P.A., to assemble the following data:

> State the family background including racial, religious, social and economic facts, with delinquency records of family members, if any. Give in detail early history, education and employment data for both parents, also circumstances preceding marriage, the success or failure of the marriage, and reasons therefor. Describe present living conditions. Note moral and ethical standards of the home. Give personality data for each member of the family, mental and physical health, education, employment experiences, attitude of parents toward each child and of children toward parents and each other, attitude of family toward child's situation.

It is obvious that in order to secure this information, an office interview is not sufficient. A visit to the home is an indispensable part of every investigation. Not only does such a field visit convey an impression of the physical housing and neighborhood conditions; it is

---

[90] A great number of books and articles on interviewing have been published in the social case-work field. Pauline Young's *Interviewing in Social Work*, McGraw-Hill, 1935, has a bibliography of 242 items dealing, for the most part, with interviewing. See also G. I. Giardini, "Interviewing—A Two Way Process," *Yearbook*, N.P.P.A., 1948, pp. 174–189.

[91] For the psychiatrist's view on the meaning of the first interview, see Carl A. Whitaker, "The Delinquent's First Interview," *Probation*, October 1944, pp. 15–20.

the only way to observe at close range the child's place within the family orbit.

For the child's case history, we again follow the guide published by the N.P.P.A.; it appears that this outline contains what is considered a minimum of information required for an adequate juvenile court record. The list enumerates these items:

> Attitude of parents toward birth of child, developmental history, age of weaning, teething, walking, talking, pre-school life, status in the family; discipline in the home and child's reaction; neighborhood and its effect on child's personality; periods of separation from family and reaction of the child; physical history, illnesses, and their effect, physical and emotional; personality traits and behavior trends; significance of previous court or institutional experience, and of other delinquent experiences; practical meaning of religion to the child, application of religious principles to everyday experience; school experience, grade attained, attendance, reasons for truancy, and other misconduct, attitude toward teachers and classmates and vice versa, reasons for leaving school; work records, jobs held, how secured, wages, reasons for leaving, vocational interests, results of tests given, attitude toward job or employers; recreational outlets, group activities (including organized and supervised); status in group, type of movies, hobbies, type of reading matter, recreation with family, kind of companions; child's attitude toward present situation, his explanation of conduct; plans for the future.

Special significance is attributed by various writers [92] to the offender's "own story." Beyond supplying vital statistics and other objective data, the "own story"—even if it is not accurate in all details—is of great value in that it reveals attitudes, habits, and behavior patterns. Pauline Young, in her book *Social Treatment in Probation and Delinquency*,[93] summarizes what Clifford Shaw in his book *The Jack-Roller* considers as the three main characteristics of "the own story":

> (1) It reveals the interviewee's point of view—that is, personal attitudes, feelings, interests, the role the person conceives himself to play

---

[92] See Clifford R. Shaw, *The Jack-Roller*, University of Chicago Press, 1930, pp. 1–23; also William Healy and Augusta Bronner, *Judge Baker Foundation Case Studies*, Series #1.

[93] 1st ed., pp. 55–56 (quoted by courtesy of McGraw-Hill Book Co.) (rev. ed. on press).

in relation to others and the interpretation he places on the social situations in which he lives.

(2) It reveals the social and cultural world in which the person lives. Human behavior can best be explained in relation to the social and cultural context in which it occurs.

(3) It reveals the sequence of events. Early experiences and influences shape and direct the course and behavior trend of a person. The interviewer seeks to visualize the process involved in the fixation of a particular behavior trend, as the successive events of life.

From the previously quoted list of items to be included in the child's history, it is apparent that important information must be secured outside the home of the child's family. The school ranks first among these other sources of information. In smaller localities the teacher or the principal is consulted. In larger communities the school attendance officer, and in a growing number of cities, the school counselor and the school psychologist should be able to throw light upon the child's misconduct. It is not sufficient to know the scholarship rating or the number of school absences. The child's adjustment in school, his outward appearance, his relationship with schoolmates, and his participation in extracurricular activities are important clues for the appraisal of the child's personality. In addition, the counselor and the attendance officer have frequently been in contact with the child's parents and are therefore able to supply the investigating probation officer with valuable information on parent-child relationship, attitude of parents toward the school, truancy, or other school behavior problems of the child's siblings.[94]

More and more, public and private agencies concerned with health, family welfare, child guidance, recreation, public assistance, and social security are offering their services in all parts of our country. Many of the families of delinquent children have been known to agencies of this kind, and their experiences often contain valuable knowledge of the child and his home. Pauline Young, in her previously cited book, *Social Treatment in Probation and Delinquency*, lists three major items which the investigating probation officer should be able to learn through the reading of the records of these agencies or through the summarizing reports which those agencies are willing to furnish upon request:

---

[94] For a discussion of the school's role in the prevention and control of juvenile delinquency, see Chapter XV, pp. 586–596.

(1) What is already known about the family?
(2) What has already been attempted in working with the family?
(3) What degree of success or failure has the given plan had? [95]

How does the investigating probation officer know of the existence of previous contacts of other agencies with the child's family? Every case referred to the juvenile court should immediately be reported to the local or regional Social Service Exchange, sometimes known as the "Social Service Index," "Confidential Exchange," or "Central Clearing Office." The Social Service Exchange is

> . . . a central clearing bureau in which the case records of social and health agencies are registered. It reports to a qualified agency, upon inquiry, the names of all other agencies which have previously registered a particular family or individual. The purpose of the Exchange is to facilitate exchange of information between agencies, thus enabling them to coordinate their work, avoid duplication of relief and other services, and plan more constructively with the families and individuals who come to them for help. It records on its index cards identifying data only, such as names and addresses, plus the names of the agencies that have registered the case, and the dates of registration. . . . The Social Service Exchange directory for 1948, "Social Service Exchanges in the United States and Canada," lists 291 exchanges. Of these, 134 are operated under the auspices of a community welfare council, 57 under a public welfare department, 53 under a community chest, 17 under a private direct service agency and 30 under an independent board.[96]

Through the use of the Social Service Exchange, the probation officer is in a position to secure information from the agencies that have had contact with the family of the child whose case he is investigating. Wherever possible, he works closely with these agencies in preparing a treatment plan for the child. The exchange of information between *bona fide* health and welfare agencies is predicated upon the observance of confidential treatment, to which the cooperating agencies are pledged.

---

[95] *Op. cit.*, p. 59 (quoted by courtesy of McGraw-Hill Book Co.)
[96] Sarah E. Marshall, "Social Service Exchanges," *Social Work Yearbook*, Russell Sage Foundation, 1945, pp. 441–445; Beatrice R. Simcox, "Social Service Exchanges," *Social Work Yearbook*, 1949, pp. 494–497. See also John W. Joyce, "The Social Service Exchange and Probation," *Federal Probation*, January–March 1943, pp. 34–37.

Special caution is required in approaching other possible sources of information, particularly individuals who are neither legally nor ethically bound to confidential treatment of imparted information. Relatives and neighbors, therefore, should be interviewed only in those cases in which they can be expected to possess pertinent information that can otherwise not be gained, or if they participate in the preparation of a plan for the child, as for instance, placement in a relative's or neighbor's home. Often the clergyman proves to be not only a genuinely interested observer of the child's development and his home background, but also a willing helper in formulating a treatment plan for the child. The family physician might play a similarly important part.

b. The Use of Tests and Examinations

The probation officer, by nature of his training and type of assignment, is confined to the assembling of the social history and to the preparing of a social diagnosis of the case. The completeness of the picture of a child's personality, however, can only be assured by physical and mental examinations. Although it might be desirable for all children referred to the court for delinquency to receive such examinations, such a procedure is often not practicable. The availability of community resources on the local level will determine the extent of this service.

Report No. 4 on "Juvenile Court Administration" of the National Conference advises:

> Physical examinations should be made at least of all children given temporary care in boarding homes or detention homes, all children to be placed in family homes and institutions, and in all other cases in which the social investigation indicates the need. For this purpose all community facilities for diagnosis and treatment should be used, women making the physical examinations of girls. The larger court may have its own medical examiner or can easily arrange for medical service through local hospitals and clinics. The smaller court may be able to arrange for service through the local health department, may use the facilities of a hospital or may be able to obtain the services of a socially minded private physician. (P. 14.)

Mental tests are given by psychologists who measure the mental age of the child and probe into his abilities and handicaps, and by psychiatrists who determine the presence of mental diseases or abnormalities. Since fewer facilities are available on the local level for these tests than for physical examinations, it might be advisable to let the findings of the social study be the determining factor for the need of psychological and psychiatric diagnoses in the individual case. There is a growing awareness among juvenile court judges and probation officers of the desirability of mental examinations for the largest possible group of delinquent children.

On the other hand, the late Dr. James Plant, director of the Essex County Juvenile Clinic, Newark, New Jersey, pointed out long ago "how unreasonable it is to give a child a mental test at the time he is brought into court, upset and distraught, and expect the results to picture his true ability.[97] True though that may be, the court has to reach a decision relatively quickly and therefore needs to have the results of mental examinations furnished speedily. So the tests often have to be given in the detention quarters or probation department offices. Qualified psychologists and psychiatrists should be able to make proper allowance in evaluating tests conducted in an environment that is likely to cause excitement and uncertainty in the child.

Many courts in larger cities have either their own medical departments, staffed not only with general practitioners but also with psychologists and psychiatrists; or they have agreements with child-guidance clinics in the community or with psychological examiners in the public school system, staff members of psychology departments in universities and colleges, and psychiatrists in hospitals. The smaller court, particularly in rural areas, may be able to arrange for these services through state-administered, centrally located or traveling clinics or regional child-guidance centers.

A steadily growing number of different psychological tests have proved of great value in the examination of juveniles referred to the court for delinquent behavior.

The authors are indebted to Carlton W. Orchinik, psychologist, Municipal Court of Philadelphia, for the following résumé of these tests:

Psychological tests on juvenile delinquents are of value for several reasons. They measure quantitatively how well an individual performs. They offer a standardized situation under which he can be observed

---

[97] Clinton W. Areson, "Casework in the Training School," *Probation*, October 1947, pp. 10–14.

and his reactions recorded. They point up areas of maladjustment. They are a means whereby the effectiveness of a particular form of therapy can be measured and are a basis on which to begin therapy. Finally, they are an aid in predicting future behavior and adjustment.

Individual tests are those which require a trained clinician to administer each to a single subject at a time, while group tests are administered to more than one subject at the same time.

Psychological clinics working with delinquents rely heavily on the individual tests for measuring intelligence and personality. These tests permit the psychologist to determine whether the subject's performance is on an optimal level. Emotional state, degree of motivation, interest, orderliness of work habits and many other conditions will seriously affect test results. Observation of performance under a standardized set of conditions contributes toward making an accurate appraisal of personality. Only a few of the most commonly used tests will be considered here. Those cited will be individual tests unless otherwise noted.

The New Revised Stanford-Binet Tests of Intelligence (1937) are the most widely used for measuring the mental ability of apprehended, younger child offenders. There are two fairly equivalent forms of these tests, Form L and Form M. Each consists of 122 subtests and 7 alternate subtests. The range of the tests is from the two-year level through four adult levels—Average Adult and Superior Adult I, II, III. A mental age is obtained from which an Intelligence Quotient (I.Q.) may be derived.[98]

Although the 1937 Binet (New Revised Stanford-Binet) contains tests up to the superior adult levels, there is a great reliance on verbal test material. Hence, high school students and graduates tend to get test scores which are too high, while others who did not receive equivalent education are penalized.

Other performance tests are frequently administered as a supplement to the 1937 Binet. The Porteus Maze, in addition to measuring nonverbal factors, helps the examiner to judge certain personality characteristics such as planfulness, impulsiveness, indecision. This test consists of a series of progressively more difficult labyrinths—each presented on a separate paper. The subject is required to trace directly on the paper the correct path to the exit. The maze range is from 3 years to adult level. (A revision and extension of the Manual, *Maze Tests and Mental Diagnosis*, by Stanley D. Porteus, was published in 1950 by Pacific Books, Palo Alto, California.)

---

[98] For more information on the Stanford-Binet Test, see L. M. Terman and M. A. Merrill, *Measuring Intelligence*, Houghton Mifflin, Boston, 1937.

The Pintner-Patterson Scales, the Arthur Scales and the Cornell-Coxe Performance Ability Scale are also useful intelligence tests which minimize language ability. They are standardized for use from ages 4–5 years to 15–15½ years.

The Wechsler-Bellevue Intelligence Scale, which was published in 1939, is applicable for use on ages 10 to 60 and is probably the most extensively used individual test of adolescents and adults.[99] It overcomes some of the handicaps of the 1937 Binet as applied to this group. There are two main parts: the verbal, containing five subtests—Information, Comprehension, Arithmetical Reasoning, Digit Memory Span, Similarities, plus an alternate test of vocabulary; the performance part also contains five subtests—Picture Arrangement, Picture Completion, Block Design, Object Assembly, and Digit Symbol. No Mental Age is obtained, but an I.Q. is derived for the Verbal part, the Performance part, and the Full Score.

The Vineland Social Maturity Scale [100] is a useful complement to standardized tests of intelligence. It consists of 117 items related to social competence and arranged to indicate progressively increasing capacity for social independence. These include some aspects of self-help, self-direction, locomotion, occupational activities, communication, and social relations. This information is usually obtained from someone who is very familiar with the person being scored. A social age equivalent and a social quotient are derived.

By comparing the degree of social competence with attainment on an intelligence test, it is often possible to differentiate between feeblemindedness, mental retardation with social incompetence, and mental retardation without social incompetence which cannot be considered feeblemindedness. In some cases, on the basis of the Vineland Social Maturity Scale, particular areas of insufficiency can be noted and appropriate measures may then be recommended for their development.

Questionnaire-type personality tests do not appear to be very commonly used in the clinical studies on delinquents. In most of these questionnaires the subject is presented with a series of printed statements to which he is required to indicate *Yes* or *No* or *True* or *False*. One personality questionnaire, the Minnesota Multiphasic Personality Inventory, has received considerable attention. It consists of 550 cards,

---

[99] See David Wechsler, *The Measurement of Adult Intelligence*, Williams & Williams, Baltimore, 1939; see also Geraldine Seiler, "Testing Adults and Older Boys and Girls with the Wechsler-Bellevue Adult Intelligence Test," Annual Report of the Municipal Court of Philadelphia, 1943, pp. 381–382.

[100] For further information see E. A. Doll, *The Vineland Social Maturity Scale*, The Training School at Vineland, N. J., 1936.

each of which contains a statement which the subject is to classify as true, false, or cannot say. The subject is evaluated in terms of tendencies toward certain entities such as depression, hysteria, or psychopathic deviation.[101]

Other tests have been developed which appear to measure such qualities as annoyance, aspiration, conflict, consistency, euphoria, happiness, reaction to frustration, maturity, punctuality, sociability, and social adjustment. Unfortunately, their application in the study of the delinquent has not been widespread.

There are some things about himself that the delinquent will not tell, even though such information would have therapeutic value, because he is actually not conscious of them. In this area are many of the desires, aspirations, frustrations, defense mechanisms, and attitudes toward others which are especially significant in understanding the dynamics of the individual and are valuable in planning treatment.

New techniques known as Projective Methods are attempting to get at these rather inaccessible aspects of the personality. The test procedure is generally as follows: The subject is presented with an ambiguous situation. Only limited indications are given of the inferences that the subject is expected to make, and the psychological meaning is not apparent. The subject must, therefore, rely on his own "inner forces" to organize the situation. In doing so, he provides the examiner with the information he is seeking.

One of the most extensively used projective methods is the Rorschach Test.[102] The subject is presented with a series of relatively unstructured inkblots. He is required to indicate what the blots "could be" or "look like." The test is intended to reveal the basic personality picture. It does not pretend to reveal behavior but rather points out the structure on which behavior is based. Included are such aspects of personality as: the relationship between spontaneity and control; the *Erlebnistypus,* or experience balance, which expresses the degree of dominance of promptings from within (introversion) and promptings from without (extratension). Some intellectual aspects of the personality which indicate the degree of intelligence as well as the kind of intelligence, such as originality and organization, are evaluated. Increased study and standardization of this test are making it one of the

---

[101] See S. R. Hathaway, and J. C. McKinley, *Minnesota Multiphasic Personality Inventory,* University of Minnesota, Minneapolis, 1943.

[102] See Fritz Schmidl, "Use of the Rorschach Personality Test," *Focus,* September 1948, pp. 133–136, and "The Rorschach Test in Juvenile Delinquency Research," *American Journal of Orthopsychiatry,* January 1947, pp. 151–161.

most important techniques yet devised for use in the diagnosis, prognosis, and treatment of personality and behavior disorders.[103]

The Thematic Apperception Test is another of the more significant projective personality tests. It differs from the Rorschach in that it presents an actual social situation in the form of pictures. The subject is required to respond by telling a story of the situation as it is at the moment, the events that led up to it, the feelings of the characters, and the final outcome. Interpretation of this ambiguous situation requires the subject to call again on the "inner forces" that structure the story and may reveal motives and attitudes. There is considerable flexibility in scoring, and the analysis of the story by the examiner will vary depending on the specific purpose for which the test was given. Thorough training and skill are required for the administration, scoring, and interpretation of these projective techniques.[104]

c. The Case Record

The face sheet of every record serves as a kind of table of contents. It includes all the pertinent identifying information, vital statistics, and certain social data. In order to assist local courts in pre-

---

[103] For full information see: B. Klopfer, and D. M. Kelley, *The Rorschach Technique*, World, New York, 1942; S. J. Beck, *Rorschach's Test*, Volume I, "Basic Processes," 1944; Volume II, "A Variety of Personality Pictures," 1945, Grune & Stratton, New York; P. L. Boynton, and B. M. Wadsworth, "Emotionality Test Scores of Delinquent and Non-delinquent Girls," *Journal of Abnormal and Social Psychology*, 1943, pp. 87–92; J. L. Endacott, "The Results of 100 Male Juvenile Delinquents on the Rorschach Ink-blot Test," *Journal of Criminal Psychopathology*, 1941, pp. 41–50; G. A. Geil, "The Similarity in Rorschach Patterns of Adult Criminal Psychopaths and Pre-adolescent Boys," *Rorschach Research Exchange*, 1945, pp. 201–206; D. M. Kelley, "Preliminary Studies of Rorschach Records of Nazi War Criminals," *Rorschach Research Exchange*, 1946, pp. 45–48; R. M. Lindner, "The Rorschach Test and the Diagnosis of the Psychopathic Delinquent," *Journal of Criminal Psychopathology*, 1943, pp. 69–94.

[104] For further information, see H. A. Murray, *Thematic Apperception Test Manual*, Harvard University Press, 1943; S. B. Kutash, "Performance of Psychopathic Defective Criminals on the Thematic Apperception Test," *Journal of Criminal Psychopathology*, 1943, pp. 319–340; for detailed information on psychological tests in general, consult the excellent and comprehensive work *The Third Mental Measurements Yearbook*, edited by Oscar K. Buros, Rutgers University Press, 1949; for a discussion of personality tests see J. B. Maller, "Personality Tests," pp. 170–213, and R. W. White, "Interpretation of Imaginative Productions," pp. 214–251, in J. McV. Hunt (ed.), *Personality and the Behavior Disorders*, Vol. 1, Ronald, New York, 1944.

paring these forms and also to achieve a much needed uniformity of record keeping throughout the country, the N.P.P.A. has devised a sample face sheet, which is reproduced on the opposite page.

The investigative part of the contents of the case record consists of two main items: the interviews with the various persons involved, and the data recorded under such topical headings as family relationships, home and neighborhood (home conditions, economic status, neighborhood), findings of physical and mental examinations, school report, church affiliation, recreational interests and activities, impression of personality, causative factors, and sources of information.

As Agnes C. Sullivan, in "Principles and Values in Case Recording," [105] advises:

> The preliminary investigation should be recorded with a view to its practical use, and with consideration for the weight which it carries, both in determining disposition and as a guide in initiating treatment. Accuracy, honesty, objectivity and clarity characterize the well-recorded preliminary investigation.

A complete history is not achieved merely by an accumulation of data. It requires a synthesis that relates the assembled facts and impressions logically and interprets them in terms of the child's personality, the causation of his misconduct, and his needs.

An investigative report, therefore, should always close with a summary containing the social and, whenever possible, the medical diagnosis. The process and value of such summarizing and interpreting have been formulated by Dr. Samuel W. Hartwell as including the following ways of thinking:

(1) A thinking *about* the individual, in which all the facts collected from investigation, tests and interviews are considered and systematized to gain full understanding of the situation.

(2) A thinking *with* the individual, understanding and entering into his situation and into his emotional life, knowing how he feels about things and what he will accept into his life.

(3) A thinking *for* the individual, constructively planning for him, either by an improvement of his environment or a change of his emotional responses and attitudes; thinking out clearly the kind of helpfulness which the worker can offer. This does not mean trying to

---

[105] *Yearbook*, N.P.P.A., 1936, pp. 240–252.

Form 1		Juvenile **FACE SHEET**			Family record no.	

Probation department   Court   3

Name	Address	Tel.	Color	Sex

Lives with

Parents	Address	Birth date, place	Ver.	Death	Religion	U. S. citizen	Marriage date, place	Occupation School grade
F.								
Maiden name.								
M.								
S.F.								
S.M.								
Children (chronological, including subject)								
Others in home	Relationship							

Agencies and others interested	Address	Date latest contact	Relationship or interest

Major Court Hearings

Date	Reason for referral	Docket no.	Disposition	Probation officer

National Probation Association, 1790 Broadway, New York City

Sample Face Sheet of a Juvenile Court Case Record. *(Prepared by the National Probation and Parole Association)*

superimpose on him a plan which he must follow blindly, but rather formulating the kind of help he needs and planning how to give it to him.[106]

Not only does a summarizing diagnosis serve as a test for the investigator's full understanding of the case, it also has a practical value. It enables the judge, who often has not the time to peruse a lengthy case report, to read at a glance the highlights of the investigation and their interpretation.[107] Whether the probation officer is requested to include in his investigative report a recommendation regarding the disposition of the case depends on the attitude of the individual judge. Such requests are customary in many juvenile courts but are less common in pre-sentence investigations of adult defendants.

Apprehension of the child offender, his detention and examination, and investigation of his social history all lead up to the disposition of his case through a juvenile court hearing. The philosophy, the legal basis, and the procedure of the juvenile court will be presented in the following chapter.

---

[106] *Fifty-Five "Bad" Boys,* Knopf, New York, 1931, p. 9, and quoted in condensed form by Helen D. Pigeon, *op. cit.,* p. 268.

[107] See also Franklin C. Hochreiter, "Streamlining Case Recording," *Federal Probation,* October–December 1943, pp. 16–18.

Chapter IX

THE JUVENILE COURT

1. PHILOSOPHY AND HISTORY OF THE JUVENILE COURT

a. *The Concept of Social Jurisprudence*

COURTS OF LAW were established to dispense justice between two or more individuals or groups of individuals in litigation, and, in cases of a criminal nature, between the state and the individual. Consideration of individual natural rights—their preservation or their restraint—governed legal thinking through several hundred years and reached its culmination in the nineteenth century.

The person who was the subject of the court's attention, either in civil or criminal matters, was regarded as a mere abstraction, and not in terms of his relationship to any group or in his position within a social setting. The only social interest that was recognized as a controlling factor during that period was the social interest in the general security. In nineteenth-century legal thought, general security meant security of acquisitions and security of transactions.[1]

The approach of the twentieth century brought a change in this conception of law. The rapid industrial development of the Western world, the growth of the cities, the movement of populations, the organization of labor, the rise and fall of the economic curve—all these phenomena left their imprint upon the law.

It is true that law is conservative and essentially resistive to change, but as a living expression of the social order it can never be static. The discoveries and teachings of a new discipline—social science—began to penetrate legal theory and practice. In the criminal law, in particular, the maxim of "making the punishment fit the crime"

---

[1] For a detailed elaboration of this point, see Roscoe Pound, "The Rise of Socialized Criminal Justice," *Yearbook*, N.P.P.A. 1942, pp. 1–22.

was the target of these influences. In it were manifest the two oldest goals of criminal justice: retribution and deterrence. The idea of rehabilitation as the modern aim of penal treatment came to the fore as a result of the influence of social science, and the concept of "making punishment fit the *offender*" began to replace the older premise.

Two basic concepts are inherent in this modern idea: The first of these is the realization that an abstract offender, an abstract thief, an abstract arsonist, an abstract murderer, has no existence. Nor does a person who can unqualifiably be assigned to the category of burglar or sex-offender or forger. The offender is a concrete human being who differs in every respect from all other individuals, whether they are law-abiding citizens or law-breakers or even co-defendants convicted of the same crime. The differences that distinguish his personality must be taken into consideration if the principle of adjusting the sentence, or (in modern terms) the penal treatment, to the needs of the individual offender is to be applied in earnest. Thus we speak of "individualization of justice." [2]

There is no discrepancy between this idea and our basic philosophy of democratic justice as expressed in the constitutional axiom of "Equal justice under law." That maxim, emblazoned in huge letters upon the facade of the Supreme Court building in Washington, means that nobody may claim special privileges before the courts of justice. Judicial decisions must be rendered without regard to the race, religion, national origin, political affiliation, or social and economic status of the individual who stands before the bar of the court. But this principle of "Equal justice under law" does not deny individual differences, nor does it forbid taking into consideration the physical and mental conditions of a defendant, and the environmental influences that have formed his personality.

The second basic concept is that, in order to implement the idea of "individualization of justice," sociological as well as psychological tools are required. These consist of inquiries into the social, economic, cultural, and emotional factors that have shaped the life history of the individual, the interpretation of data regarding his

---

[2] For a historical treatment of this idea, see Paul W. Alexander, "Of Juvenile Court Justice and Judges," *Yearbook*, N.P.P.A., 1947, pp. 187–205, especially pp. 188–189.

family, his school career, his employment record, his recreational outlets—briefly, the social and psychological diagnosis of his personality. Thus is introduced into the criminal procedure a host of data which—from the strictly legal point of view—have nothing to do with the subject matter under consideration, *viz.*, the commission of the specific crime. But from a social and psychological vantage point, these data explain the behavior of the individual offender and serve as guideposts in the determination of the proper penal treatment. "Socialization of procedure," therefore, becomes a necessary complement of "individualization of justice."

The foremost protagonist of the school of "social (or sociological) jurisprudence," Roscoe Pound, dean emeritus of Harvard Law School, summarizes its historic development and its basic tenets as follows:

> The history of law shows a continually widening area of recognized and secured interests. But the history of juristic thought shows also attempts to reduce the recognized and secured interests to some one type, with resulting exclusion of those which are not readily adjustable thereto. Today jurists are in reaction from one of these attempts, and the stage of legal development which this reaction reflects may be called the socialization of law in order to bring out the contrast to the abstract individualism of what may be called the maturity of law in the nineteenth century. What has been called socialized criminal justice is a phase of this general movement to expand the circle of legally secured interests by increased insistence upon the social interest in the individual life.[3]

The application of the principles of sociological jurisprudence is still far from general. In the orbit of criminal procedure against adult offenders, it has produced probation and parole, the indeterminate sentence, pre-sentence investigation, and classification of offender before sentence. But these devices are mostly discretionary in the hands of judges; their implementation is often sporadic and the needed machinery on the local or state level is frequently lacking.

The juvenile court has been the first and so far the only institution in which the idea of sociological jurisprudence has found full realization. It is not surprising that it was legislation creating *children's* courts which made the modern concept of sociological jurisprudence

---

[3] Roscoe Pound, *op. cit.*, pp. 1–2.

a reality. In many fields of public policies the concern for children and their welfare has preceded—sometimes by long periods—the interest in adults. Curtailment of working hours and protection against hazards to health and morals in certain occupations are examples in the field of labor legislation. The Mothers' Assistance pensions, benefiting children deprived of their fathers, were the first social insurance measures adopted in the United States. It is a truism in penology that what seems good and sound for children in one generation is likely to be adopted for adults in the next. Thus probation for juveniles antedated probation for adults, and the introduction of individualized treatment for adolescents in reformatories was later followed by the application of the same ideas in prisons for adult offenders. Parole as a full-fledged working system was first instituted in Elmira Reformatory for adolescent offenders. In the mental hygiene field, guidance clinics were first established for children; years later, many of them were expanded to include adult patients.[4]

b. Common Law Basis of the Juvenile Court

Although socially and administratively the juvenile court was a new invention, it had its legal and historical roots in the English common law.

The first common law basis of the juvenile court is found in the principle of equity or chancery. This principle, which goes far back into feudal law, is founded upon the idea that there should be a recourse to the king against the strict application of the rigidities of the law so that a more equitable decision can be reached. Its essential idea is "welfare or balancing of interests; it stands for flexibility, guardianship and protection rather than rigidity and punishment." [5] The king entrusted his chancellor, as head of the judicial system, with this special kind of jurisdiction, and thus the term "chancery" and "equity" were and still are used interchangeably.

One particular aspect of this principle was the doctrine that the king was "the ultimate parent of all such minors as require his care

---

[4] For more details on mental hygiene clinics, see *Social Work Yearbook*, 1949, Russell Sage Foundation, New York, p. 320.

[5] For an analysis of this principle, see Herbert H. Lou, *Juvenile Courts in the United States*, University of North Carolina Press, 1927, pp. 3–4 (above quotation on p. 4); also, Henry W. Thurston, *Concerning Juvenile Delinquency*, Columbia University Press, 1942, pp. 88–89.

and protection," [6] and that he acted as *parens patriae*, i.e., as "parent of the whole fatherland" or as "father of his country." In individual cases, he acted in *loco parentis*, in lieu of the (natural) parent.[7] This prerogative of the king was delegated to his court of chancery; in our country, following the Revolution, the state has exercised this right through its existing courts, whether they are separate courts of equity, as in some states, or courts having both law and equity jurisdiction.

The juvenile court's origin in chancery procedure is today accepted by many authors and has been confirmed by the decisions of a number of high courts.[8] Although the chancery court principle of *parens patriae* originally applied only to children who were, in modern terms, "dependent" and "neglected," it was the concern for children who committed crimes that gave the juvenile court movement its main impetus.

This particular jurisdiction in child delinquency cases points up the second common law basis of the juvenile court, namely the rule that children under seven years of age are incapable of committing a crime.[9] Between the ages of seven and fourteen, according to common law, the capacity of the child to distinguish between good and evil was to be determined through examination of each individual case. Later, the age limit below which there was no criminal responsibility was further modified. It is a moot question whether the juvenile court's jurisdiction in delinquency cases is the result of such gradual raising of the age of criminal responsibility or whether children of the age span which the juvenile court's jurisdiction covers today should be accorded a *limited* criminal responsibility, as in various continental laws. As Lou states:

> There may be some historical reason for ascribing the basis of delinquency jurisdiction to the legal fiction of the age of criminal respon-

---

[6] Lou, *op. cit.*, p. 3.

[7] See Gustav L. Schramm, "The Judge Meets the Boy and His Family," *Yearbook*, N.P.P.A., 1945, pp. 182–194, especially p. 183, and "A Juvenile Court Is a Court of Equity," *Federal Probation*, January–March 1947, pp. 35–37, and "Philosophy of the Juvenile Court," *The Annals*, January 1949, pp. 101–108.

[8] See Lou, *op. cit.*, pp. 4–5.

[9] Common law held that a child under seven years of age was *doli incapax*, *i.e.* incapable of felonious intent. For a historical development of this principle see Chapter II, pp. 41–42.

sibility, yet its logical justification seems to lie in the recognition of the failure of the older criminal courts to prevent crime and the experimentation in judicial methods and procedure. It is an attempt to relieve juvenile offenders under certain circumstances from the rigidity of the law prevailing in courts of more general jurisdiction.[10]

This statement points up still another theory, namely, that the original chancery jurisdiction of the juvenile court over dependent and neglected children was extended, under the influence of the modern concept of sociological jurisprudence, to include delinquent children. In this connection, the following is quoted from the report of the committee of the Chicago Bar Association which drafted the first juvenile court bill enacted into law:

> The fundamental idea of the (juvenile court) law is that the state must step in and exercise guardianship over a child found under such adverse social or individual conditions as develop crime. . . . It proposes a plan whereby he may be treated, not as a criminal, or legally charged with crime, but as a ward of the state, to receive practically the care, custody, and discipline that are accorded the neglected and dependent child, and which, as the act states, "shall approximate as nearly as may be that which should be given by its parents." [11]

c. The Origin of the Juvenile Court Movement

During the nineteenth century there were sporadic signs of a growing conviction that juvenile offenders should be accorded a different treatment from that used toward adult offenders; that their lack of maturity and, consequently, their limited criminal responsibility should be taken into consideration; and that measures of reform and moral encouragement, rather than punishment, should be applied to wayward children in their formative period of life. This slowly but steadily developing attitude was reflected in critical reports in newspapers and other publications, in the adoption of specific laws, and in the efforts of individuals.

A few interesting illustrations of these endeavors may be cited here. Henry Thurston, in his book *Concerning Juvenile Delinquency*, quotes from a report in the New York *Evening Post* of

---

[10] Lou, *op. cit.*, p. 7.

[11] Quoted by Roscoe Pound, "The Juvenile Court and the Law," *Yearbook*, N.P.P.A., 1944, pp. 13–14.

1815. The report was concerned with a little girl of six who was frozen to death while sitting at a door on a city street:

> We have lamented until we are tired, for the want of a society to authorize and provide for the prevention of so many children being bred up to ignorance, vice and destruction by street begging, an evil which increases among us to the shame of every institution for religious, moral or charitable purposes in the city. Humane societies rescue persons from drowning—no society arrests the little troops of mendicants from moral and intellectual perdition. In summer pilfering and in winter begging, are trades to which great numbers of depraved parents devote their children, who ought to be in schools, manufactories and houses of industry. The streets are infested with the little vagabonds, and we drive them from our doors and take no more thought of them until we hear of them in Bridewell or the State Prison.[12]

The early Houses of Refuge, opened in New York, Boston, and Philadelphia in the 1820s, had as their avowed purposes the reformation of young delinquents and their separation from old and more experienced offenders.[13]

The laws of Illinois in 1831 provided that for certain offenses the penalties for minors might differ from those of adults. In 1861 the legislature of Illinois authorized the mayor of Chicago to appoint a commissioner before whom boys between the ages of six and seventeen could be taken on charges of petty offenses; this commissioner had authority to place the boys on probation, to send them to reform schools, and to use other methds of treatment. In 1867 this work was transferred to the regular judges of the courts.[14]

In the years 1841 to 1859, a shoemaker in Boston, John Augustus, who became known as the "first probation officer," [15] did a pioneering one-man job in caring for adults and children haled before the criminal courts. From his own report, the following account of his work for young persons is quoted:

> In 1847, I bailed nineteen boys, from seven to fifteen years of age, and in bailing them it was understood, and agreed by the court, that their cases should be continued from term to term for several months,

---

[12] *Op. cit.*, pp. 69–70.

[13] For more details on this development see Chapter XII, pp. 431–435.

[14] For more information on this early period see Lou, *op. cit.*, pp. 13–19.

[15] A more detailed reference to the life and work of John Augustus will be found in Chapter XI.

as a season of probation; thus each month at the calling of the docket, I would appear in court, make my report, and thus the cases would pass on for five or six months. At the expiration of this term, twelve of the boys were brought into court at one time, and the scene formed a striking and highly pleasing contrast with their appearance when first arraigned. The judge expressed much pleasure as well as surprise, at their appearance, and remarked, that the object of the law had been accomplished, and expressed his cordial approval of my plan to save and reform. Seven of the number were too poor to pay a fine, although the court fixed the amount at ten cents each, and of course I paid it for them; the parents of the other boys were able to pay the cost, and thus the penalty of the law was answered. The sequel thus far shows, that not one of this number has proved false to the promises of reform they made while on probation. This incident proved conclusively, that this class of boys could be saved from crime and punishment, by the plan which I had marked out, and this was admitted by the judges in both courts.[16]

Another Boston pioneer in this field was Rufus R. Cook. Of his work, the Massachusetts State Board of Charities reported in 1868:

> He watches for the little ones as they are brought in the Police Court of Boston by the officers; and whenever it seems advisable, he interposes the shield of mercy between the sword of justice and its victim. He becomes bondsman for the offender, and takes him tenderly in charge, until some fitting place is found for him. Out of nearly four hundred children whom he has so bailed, eighty percent are now doing well.[17]

In 1869, as Barnes and Teeters report, "A law was enacted in Massachusetts calling for the appointment of a visiting agent. Before any child under sixteen could be committed to a jail or an institution, the agent had to be informed. He was expected to attend all hearings regarding the case and even to make recommendations to the judge. In 1870 separate hearings were required for juveniles in Massachusetts. Various other states, notably Rhode Island and New York, soon followed the example set by Massachusetts and provided the same court procedure." [18]

---

[16] *John Augustus, First Probation Officer*, published by N.P.P.A. (with an introduction by Sheldon Glueck), 1939, p. 34.

[17] Quoted from Thurston, *op. cit.*, p. 79.

[18] Harry Elmer Barnes and Negley K. Teeters, *New Horizons in Criminology*, Prentice-Hall, New York, 1943, p. 925, quoting in part from T. Earl

The most spectacular landmark on this road toward a constructive approach to the wayward child was the establishment of the first juvenile court in this country in Chicago on July 1, 1899.[19] Here for the first time the idea of treating the child offender in a way entirely different from the procedure used in adult cases found its legal expression. This development was not merely a modification of the application of criminal laws in cases of children, or the appointment of a special agent to sift out children from the machinery of otherwise unmitigated criminal procedure, or the establishment of specific institutions for children apart from adult prisons. The adoption of the law by the Illinois Legislature on April 14, 1899, entitled "An Act To Regulate the Treatment and Control of Dependent, Neglected and Delinquent Children," gave circuit and county courts jurisdiction over these cases and created the first juvenile court in Cook County, Chicago. This was an event of first magnitude, because it applied the principle of rehabilitation of juvenile offenders not only to parts of the process but to the entire procedure—i.e., prior to, during, and after the court hearing and the judicial disposition of the case.

The story of the spade-work that prepared the creation of the first juvenile court in Chicago is told by Grace Abbott in Volume II of her documentary work, *The Child and the State:*

> Lucy L. Flower, Julia C. Lathrop and Jane Addams were the moving spirits in formulating the new and basically different conception of the treatment of juvenile delinquents which it represented. They first became interested in the more than five hundred children in the Chicago House of Correction, and under their leadership the Chicago Woman's Club induced the Board of Education to establish a "school" for the boys in this institution. But this obviously did not meet the need, and they began a more fundamental attack on the problem. After the usual preliminary discussion a committee was appointed by the Illinois State Conference of Charities at its meeting in 1898. In addition to Miss

---

Sullenger, *Social Determinants in Juvenile Delinquency*, 1936, p. 225 (reprinted by permission of John Wiley & Sons, Inc.).

[19] Outside the United States, in two English-speaking countries, similar efforts had been made: in 1890, children's courts were introduced in South Australia by ministerial order and were subsequently legalized under a state act in 1895; at about that time legislation looking to the same end was also passed in the Province of Ontario, Canada, but practically nothing was done under it.

Lathrop and Mrs. Flower, Miss Mary M. Bartelme, later a judge of the Cook County Juvenile Court, Dr. F. H. Wines, secretary of the Illinois State Board of Charities, and Hastings H. Hart, director of the Illinois Children's Home and Aid Society, urged that the conference undertake to get a law drafted. The problem was to find how to make a fundamental change in criminal law and criminal procedure which would be upheld by the courts as constitutional. In co-operation with a committee of the Chicago Bar Association, a bill was finally worked out and agreed upon by the interested groups.[20]

d. The First Juvenile Courts

Denver, Colorado, was the next city in which a juvenile court was created. This court was the result of the efforts of another great pioneer in the juvenile court movement, Judge Benjamin Lindsey, then in Denver, later of Los Angeles. Sitting as judge of the County Court of Denver, he interpreted a school attendance law which the Colorado legislature had passed in May 1899, and which contained certain juvenile court features, as all-inclusively applicable to children under sixteen years of age charged with any offense. In 1903, a juvenile court law proper was passed in Colorado. Judge Lindsey later won international acclaim through his thought-provoking book,

---

[20] University of Chicago Press, 1938, pp. 330–331. A very interesting account of the various steps leading up to the establishment of the juvenile court in Chicago in 1899 and its subsequent history is found in the *Fiftieth Anniversary Report,* Juvenile Court of Cook County, Chicago, 1949, pp. 13–25. Julia C. Lathrop, mentioned above, later became the first chief of the newly formed United States Children's Bureau in the Department of Labor; Jane Addams acquired international fame through many of her activities, particularly her leadership in Hull House, Chicago, one of the first settlement houses in the United States; the Committee of the Chicago Bar Association referred to above was headed by Judge Harvey B. Hurd. For additional information on the origin of the first juvenile court law, see Thorsten Sellin, "Foreword" to the Juvenile Delinquency issue, *The Annals,* January 1949, pp. vii–viii; Thurston, *op. cit.,* pp. 80–87; and Emma Octavia Lundberg, *Unto the Least of These,* Appleton-Century, New York, 1947, pp. 114–123 (for biographical notes on Hastings H. Hart, *ibid.,* pp. 217–220; Julia C. Lathrop, pp. 224–229; Dr. William Healy, pp. 267–269; Homer Folks, pp. 277–280). A valuable historical source is *The Child, the Clinic and the Court,* New Republic, Inc., New York, 1927, a group of papers by Jane Addams, William Healy, Augusta F. Bronner, Frederick P. Cabot, Grace Abbott, Benjamin B. Lindsey, Julia C. Lathrop, Julian W. Mack, Timothy D. Hurley, and others. See also Charles L. Chute, "The Juvenile Court in Retrospect," *Federal Probation,* September 1949, pp. 3–8.

Revolt of Modern Youth,[21] in which he set down his ideas on the treatment of children.

Other protagonists in the movement were Julian W. Mack (from 1905 to 1907, judge of the Chicago Juvenile Court), George W. Stubbs, Harvey H. Baker (first judge of the Boston Juvenile Court), Bernard Flexner, Timothy D. Hurley (first chief probation officer of the Chicago Juvenile Court), Henry W. Thurston (later succeeding Mr. Hurley in his position), and Homer Folks.

Judge Benjamin Lindsey Conducting a Juvenile Court Hearing in Denver, 1921.
(Courtesy of National Probation and Parole Association)

In the five years after 1899, juvenile court laws were passed in the following states: Pennsylvania, Wisconsin, New York, Maryland, California, Missouri, New Jersey, Indiana, Iowa, and Ohio. Passage of laws, however, did not necessarily mean that all counties of these states set up juvenile courts. Some laws were state-wide, others applied only to the larger cities; even if the law was state-wide in scope,

---

[21] Benjamin Lindsey and Wainwright Evans, Boni and Liveright, New York, 1925.

often only one or two cities actually created juvenile courts. As will be discussed later, these early juvenile courts were not independent courts, but special branches or special sessions of existing courts.

Herbert H. Lou characterizes this pioneer era of the juvenile court movement as "largely a period of experimentation, sentiment and of missionary work by individuals." [22] Soon this newly created tribunal had to meet the rigid test of constitutionality. As has been emphasized in the description of its origin, and as will be outlined in more detail later, the juvenile court—in theory and practice—is established as a non-criminal court, because its purpose is the re-education or rehabilitation of the child and *not* his punishment. The juvenile court, consequently, is devoid of many attributes of the criminal court which serve to implement the constitutional rights of the defendant. So it was only natural that the question of its constitutionality should arise in many states. Lou mentions fifteen leading cases concerning thirteen different state laws in which the constitutionality of juvenile court acts was upheld by higher courts.[23]

One of the most frequently cited decisions was rendered by the Pennsylvania Supreme Court in 1905 in the Commonwealth vs. Fisher case,[24] in which the constitutionality of the Pennsylvania Juvenile Court act of 1903 was questioned, particularly in respect to the "due process of law" principle.

The decision first deals with the objection that "the act offends against a constitutional provision in creating, by its terms, different punishments for the same offense by a classification of individuals." It points out that the Juvenile Court act is not concerned with the punishment of offenders, but with "the salvation of children, not particularly children of a special class, but all children under a certain age, whose salvation may become the duty of the state in the absence of proper parental care or disregard of it by wayward children." The decision further explains that the act simply provides a procedure so that children who ought to be saved may reach the court to be saved, and that such legal provisions can "never be regarded as undue processes for depriving a child of its liberty or prop-

---

[22] *Op. cit.,* p. 22.

[23] *Op. cit.,* p. 10, footnote 1.

[24] The major portion of this decision is reproduced in Grace Abbott, *op. cit.,* pp. 401–404.

erty as a penalty for crime committed." Finally, the decision disposes of the objection that the act denies the appellant his constitutional right of a trial by jury. To this objection the answer is that "there is no trial for any crime here, and the act is operative only when there is to be no trial; the very purpose of the act is to prevent a trial."

The same principles that governed this judgment found expression in the court decisions of other states.

e. The Spreading of the Idea

The idea of creating juvenile courts spread to all states of the union. Within ten years after the adoption of the Illinois Juvenile Court act, more than twenty states and the District of Columbia had passed laws providing for some kind of a juvenile court. That period also saw the beginning of one of the most outstanding contributions of the juvenile court movement—the establishment of clinics for the scientific study and treatment of personality problems of children. These clinics were originally organized as adjuncts to the juvenile court and became the forerunners of the modern child-guidance movement.[25]

Another example of the direct impact of the juvenile court movement in its early phases upon community welfare in general was the mothers' pensions or mothers' assistance fund program. Prompted by many cases of dependent children which they were called upon to decide, juvenile court judges advocated this new social service of public assistance. For some time juvenile courts in several states were charged with the administration of such programs. Thus the way was prepared for the later enactment of the national Aid-to-Dependent-Children program as part of the Social Security legislation of 1935.[26]

By 1920, all but three states had enacted juvenile court laws. Wyo-

---

[25] The history, development, and present program of child-guidance clinics are presented in Chapter XV. See also Lou, *op. cit.*, pp. 199–203; Pauline Young, *op. cit.*, pp. 598–608; Frank J. Bruno, *Trends in Social Work* (as reflected in the Proceedings of the National Conference of Social Work, 1874–1946), Columbia University Press, 1948, pp. 172, 295.

[26] For more information on the mothers' pensions program as an adjunct to the juvenile court, see Grace Abbott, *op. cit.*, p. 229, and Lou, *op. cit.*, p. 63.

ming at last joined the ranks in 1945. Today all states, the Federal system, the District of Columbia, Alaska, Hawaii, and Puerto Rico have juvenile court legislation on their statute books.[27]

Following the American example, and often based upon studies of the American prototype, other countries introduced juvenile court or children's court legislation adapted to their own judicial and administrative systems and to their special social and educational needs. Great Britain passed such an act as early as 1908; Canada followed in the same year. At present, legislation providing for juvenile courts, or at least for some form of special procedure in children's cases, is in force in all European countries (except in Albania and Iceland), in all British dominions, in some British and French colonies and possessions, and in other parts of Africa and Asia, as well as in Australia and New Zealand. In Latin America, Argentina was the first republic to introduce a special procedure for dealing with young offenders, by means of a law of 1919 which applied to Buenos Aires and to the National Territories. Since then, juvenile court laws have been enacted in some of Argentina's provinces and in at least eleven of the other twenty American republics.[28]

2. JUVENILE COURT LAWS

a. Type of Laws

In accordance with the principle of the Federal structure of our government, the judiciary is centered within the sovereign states,

---

[27] For the years of first enactment of juvenile court laws in the various states, see Cosulich, *op. cit.*, p. 9.

[28] For details, see Anna Kalet Smith, *Juvenile Court Laws in Foreign Countries*, United States Children's Bureau, Publication No. 328, Government Printing Office, 1949; see also Lou, *op. cit.*, p. 23, footnote 1; N. K. Teeters, *World Penal Systems*, published by the Pennsylvania Prison Society, Philadelphia, 1944; N. K. Teeters, *Penology from Panama to Cape Horn*, University of Pennsylvania Press, 1946. On British juvenile courts, see L. Radzinowicz and J. W. C. Turner (ed.), *Penal Reform in England*, Macmillan, London, 1946, and Abbott, *op. cit.*, pp. 445–460, which includes the text of the Children's and Young Persons' Act of 1933. On juvenile courts in Germany, see W. Friedlander and Earl D. Myers, *Child Welfare in Germany Before and After Nazism*, University of Chicago Press, 1940, pp. 143–165. The League of Nations in 1935 published "L'organization des tribunaux pour enfants et les expériences faites jusqu' à ce jour" (Société des Nations, Comité de la protection de l'enfance).

except in matters of Federal judicial power. Consequently, juvenile court laws are state laws passed by the legislatures of the 48 states. Because they were enacted at different times within a span of almost half a century (the first one in 1899, the latest one in 1945), it is natural that there are many variations in these statutes. In some states, original juvenile court acts were later amended due to the progress of social and medical sciences. In other states, few changes were made, so their juvenile court laws still contain many remnants of traditional criminal procedure and antiquated terminology.

Juvenile court legislation has been called still unstandardized, inconsistent, and "in many states incomplete and defective." [29] The lack of uniformity regarding age limits, the type of court having jurisdiction, the scope of jurisdiction, the nature of proceedings, and the administration of probation bear out this statement. On the other hand, it can be said that the fundamental ideas which originally prompted special legislation for the handling of cases of children are reflected in practically all state laws. It is also significant that more than 30 laws specify that they are to be liberally construed.

Federal laws prescribing procedure in juvenile delinquency cases came much later than most of the state legislation in this field. In 1932, Congress provided for transfer of individuals under 21 years who violated Federal laws to state authorities willing to receive them. The Federal Juvenile Delinquency Act was passed in 1938. Applicable to youths under 18 years of age, charged with violation of Federal law (exclusive of offenses punishable by death or life imprisonment), the Act embodies some of the principles and authorizes some of the procedures of state juvenile court laws. The cases may be heard before a United States District Court, using a procedure similar to that prescribed by the state juvenile court laws. However, the Act of 1938 did not supersede the provision of the Act of 1932 permitting the diversion of such cases to the State authorities. Actually, where well-functioning juvenile courts are established, the Federal authorities frequently transfer Federal offenders of juvenile court age to the local juvenile courts.

In order to promote greater uniformity in the state legislation on

---

[29] Will C. Turnbladh, in *Foreword to the Standard Juvenile Court Act*, Revised Draft, 1949, p. 5.

juvenile courts and to encourage the passage of laws based on recognized modern principles of child care, a model law was drafted entitled a "Standard Juvenile Court Act."

The impetus for the drafting of such a standard act came from a conference on juvenile court standards held in 1921 under the auspices of the N.P.P.A. and the United States Children's Bureau. This conference instructed a committee to prepare a statement on juvenile court standards. The statement was adopted at a similar conference in 1923.[30] Subsequently, another committee was appointed to draft a model act that would translate these standards into the form of a law. The outcome was the Standard Juvenile Court Act, first adopted at the annual meeting of the N.P.P.A. in 1925 and later revised several times in order to keep up with developments in the child welfare field.[31]

This Standard Juvenile Court Act has been drawn upon quite extensively by legislative bodies, children's code commissions, and others, in the preparation and amendment of juvenile court laws. Arizona, the District of Columbia, Indiana, Michigan, Mississippi, Montana, New Jersey, Ohio, Pennsylvania, Rhode Island, Utah, and Wisconsin have incorporated nearly all sections of the model act into their statutes. Other states (California, Connecticut, Minnesota, New Hampshire, New York, Oregon, and Virginia) have included certain parts of it in their laws. Reference will be made later to several provisions of the Standard Act.

b. The Court Having Jurisdiction

In most states, the geographical and political area in which the juvenile court has jurisdiction is the county. In some states it is the town, the city, the borough, or the judicial district.

Until recently, the county system was considered to be the most desirable, primarily because it is in conformity with our established governmental structure. Not only is the general judicial administration of the states founded upon the county unit, but other public and private agencies with which the juvenile court necessarily cooperates are also organized within county limits. Moreover, the county-unit

---

[30] "Juvenile Court Standards," United States Children's Bureau Publication No. 121, reprinted 1947.

[31] *A Standard Juvenile Court Act*, Revised Draft, N.P.P.A., New York, 1949.

system has been regarded as providing the best guarantee that rural as well as urban areas will be served by juvenile courts.

However, the same disadvantage of the county system that we mentioned in connection with the detention situation [32] also affects the juvenile court set-up: most counties cannot afford specially selected judges or trained juvenile court personnel. As Lou correctly points out, "A court having jurisdiction over a district, which may be composed of several counties, sufficiently large to permit specialization, has a great advantage over one or more courts serving small areas." [33]

Utah, Connecticut, and Rhode Island have abandoned the county-unit system and have set up state-administered and state-financed juvenile court systems which operate in larger jurisdictional areas within the states. This system makes it possible, administratively and economically, to assign specially appointed judges to juvenile court hearings that can be held according to a circuit system, and to select qualified court personnel. [34] The experiences of these three states prompted the N.P.P.A. to adopt the following resolution at its annual meeting in Atlantic City in April 1948:

> WHEREAS, although the law of every state in the Union provides for juvenile courts, large areas of most states are still without effective juvenile courts, and even when the need for an adequate separate juvenile court and its service to the community is recognized and the desire for its establishment prevails, it is impractical to set up such courts in rural or less densely populated areas on a county basis because there is not sufficient population or sufficient volume of work to justify a full time qualified juvenile court judge, probation staff, clerical employees and detention facilities for a separate juvenile court in every county with the attendant financial cost; and
>
> WHEREAS, certain states, notably, Utah, Connecticut and Rhode

---

[32] See Chapter VIII, pp. 261–262.

[33] *Op. cit.*, p. 36. For a constructive discussion of juvenile court standards in small towns and rural areas, see Lowell Juilliard Carr, "Most Courts Have To Be Substandard," *Federal Probation*, September 1949, pp. 29–33.

[34] For a description of the Utah system, see John Farr Larson, "Utah's State-Wide Juvenile Court Plan," *Federal Probation*, June 1949, pp. 15–17. For an excellent presentation of the advantages of state juvenile courts, especially regarding the selection of qualified judges, the improvement of detention systems and probation services, and the increased use of psychiatric and other community facilities, see Sol Rubin, "State Juvenile Court—A New Standard," N.P.P.A., 1949 (mimeographed).

Island, have established and found effective the system of area or district courts to serve a combination of counties, towns and smaller cities within the borders of such area or district having a sufficient population and volume of work to justify an adequately staffed court and its attendant expense;

BE IT RESOLVED: that the plan of such area or district courts is commended and recommended.[35]

But the previously mentioned resistance to the establishment of governmental agencies on a district—*i.e.* a two-county or multicounty—basis is likely to prevent the setting up of regional or state-administered juvenile courts. It seems more realistic, therefore, to strive for implementation of modern juvenile court principles on the local level, within the framework of the existing county court system.

It is estimated that there are approximately 3,000 juvenile courts in the United States. Of course, in many instances the juvenile court is established only on paper—*viz.* the paper on which the state law is written. Special efforts are often necessary to assure the carrying out of the legislative intent. In such situations local citizens' committees, concerned with a modern approach to the problem of juvenile delinquency, have been able to stimulate public support for the creation and development of a real juvenile court and to arouse the interest of judges and other county officials in this project.[36] Such groups might also function as permanent advisory councils to the courts or to probation departments and assist them in achieving and maintaining high standards of work performance. In various localities these committees have been instrumental in interpreting to the community the philosophy, methods, and policies of the juvenile court.[37]

Another way of achieving the implementation of juvenile court laws would originate at the state level. Many state departments, com-

---

[35] See Standard Juvenile Court Act, Alternate Section 1, pp. 6–7.

[36] For more details on citizenship participation, see Chapter XVI, p. 648.

[37] A good example is the Advisory Council of the Juvenile Court of Indianapolis, which consists of forty-two community leaders, representing business, the professions, the schools, the police, labor, and minority groups. According to the report of the Court's chief probation officer, C. H. Boswell, as quoted in *Focus*, July 1949, pp. 119–120, "The council acts in many matters as a gadfly, pressing the county commissioners and other officials into action. It prepared the budgets for the juvenile court and the Juvenile Center and then worked for the approval of both budgets."

missions, and boards of welfare possess advisory or consultative functions in regard to local juvenile court administration and practice, and should, therefore, be in a position to promote the establishment and development of good court and probation services.[38]

One should not assume that all juvenile courts are necessarily separate and independent courts. As a matter of fact, in most instances, the existing county, probate, municipal, district, superior, common pleas, quarter sessions, circuit, and other courts exercise jurisdiction in juvenile cases; while functioning in this capacity, they are called juvenile courts. Lou describes them as "designated courts, that is, courts appended to other court systems, consisting legally of special sessions or divisions or departments of some existing court, served by one or more judges, assigned from that court or chosen specially to hear children's cases." [39]

Also in operation are a number of separate juvenile courts entirely divorced administratively from other courts. Such separate and independent juvenile courts exist in 28 states of the Union (including the District of Columbia) and in two of the possessions, but only in a small number of counties within these states.[40]

Because many of the separate juvenile courts are presided over by the judge of the ordinary county, probate, or other court, the difference between the two systems is hardly distinguishable.[41]

Legally, it is important to remember that in the early period, in order to uphold the constitutionality of state laws creating juvenile courts, appellate court decisions ruled that they were not new courts but that additional jurisdiction had been conferred upon existing tribunals.[42]

Similarly, Roscoe Pound, primarily for legal reasons, proposed to

---

[38] For details on state participation, see Chapter IX, pp. 336–338, and Chapter XVI, p. 632.

[39] *Op. cit.*, p. 34; see also Sutherland, *Principles of Criminology*, Lippincott, 1947, p. 306.

[40] Figures based on *Directory of Probation and Parole Officers*, N.P.P.A., 1947.

[41] See Cosulich, *op. cit.*, p. 13.

[42] The previously quoted decision of the Pennsylvania Supreme Court in Commonwealth vs. Fisher held that "it is a mere convenient designation of the court of quarter sessions to call it when caring for children a juvenile court, but no such court, as an independent tribunal, is created. . . ."

make the juvenile court "not a separate court but a branch of the court of general jurisdiction of first instance."

It prevents failure of proceedings, in whole or in part, because of statutory jurisdictional difficulties. There are cases in the recent reports where children have been released from custody because the wrong judge acted or acted in a wrong court. This could not happen where all judges of first instance are judges of one court, with all the powers of a judge of that court and what is done in any branch is done by the court. With a proper administrative head given power of assigning the work of the court and responsibility for so doing, transfer of a case or of a judge from one branch of the same court to another obviates such unnecessary difficulties. Yet the separate branch can have its own special facilities and special methods, and still be able, under an appropriate administrative system and organization of the whole court, to secure the advantage of the facilities and methods of the other branches, whenever important to use them in a particular case.[43]

In addition to the two types described thus far (the juvenile court as an especially designated session or division of the existing local court, and the separate and independent juvenile court), there is a third type. It is the juvenile court that is co-ordinated with another special court created to handle cases that present social problems. This is the Domestic Relations Court, sometimes called Family Court. Thus the juvenile court might be a subdivision of the Domestic Relations Court (as for instance in New York City) or a co-ordinated branch with the Domestic Relations branch of a "Juvenile and Domestic Relations Court" (as for example in seven Ohio counties and throughout Virginia).

Because of the large number of cases referred from the schools to the Children's Court of New York City, a special division was created in 1944, called the "School Part." It has jurisdiction over cases of truancy, unlawful detention of children from school by parents or guardians, and misconduct within schools.[44] In 1945–1946 it handled 1,078 cases.

---

[43] Roscoe Pound, "The Juvenile Court and the Law," *Yearbook*, N.P.P.A., 1942, pp. 10, 11.

[44] For details on the procedure and methods of the "School Part," see Herbert A. Landry, *The Prosecution of School Non-Attendants* (published under the auspices of the Board of Education, New York City), 1949; *Children Absent from School*, a report by the Citizens' Committee on Children of New York

In view of the vastness of this country, the variety of historical traditions, and the differences in state and local administrations and in urban or rural developments, it is impossible to give preference to any of the three systems or to try to achieve administrative uniformity throughout the nation. There should, however, be uniform recognition of the legal status of the juvenile court. It is not to be considered a part of the minor judiciary (magistrates, justices of the peace, and so forth), but as "a court of superior jurisdiction and a court of record." [45]

Although, in general, the term "juvenile court" is preponderantly used both in practice and in literature, names like "Children's Court," or "Juvenile Division," "Juvenile Department," and "Juvenile Sessions" (of the existing local court) are also in usage.

c. Scope of Jurisdiction

The juvenile courts in all states have jurisdiction in cases of delinquency, and it has been estimated that approximately 275,000 children come before the juvenile courts each year because of delinquency. The definition of a "delinquent child," however, varies from state to state. The violation of a criminal statute, or, in other words, the act which in the case of an adult person would constitute the commitment of a crime, is mentioned in most laws as the principal category of delinquency. But in all states delinquency goes beyond the violation of a state law or municipal ordinance.

Incorrigibility, waywardness, habitual disobedience, being beyond control of parents, guardians, or custodians, habitual truancy from school or home, endangering the morals of self or others, association with immoral persons, and similar forms of misconduct are often added in the juvenile court laws as constituting delinquent behavior. [46]

The comprehensiveness of these terms is indicative of the non-

---

City, Inc., 1949, pp. 65–71. See also Harriet L. Goldberg, *Child Offenders,* Grune & Stratton, New York, 1948, pp. 6–10.

[45] See *Juvenile Court Standards,* p. 1, and *Standard Juvenile Court Act,* Section 1.

[46] For a discussion of the definition of "delinquent child," see Chapter I, pp. 19–25; for a complete enumeration of items mentioned in all juvenile court laws of the United States as constituting delinquency, see Sol Rubin, "The Legal Character of Juvenile Delinquency," *The Annals,* January 1949, p. 2.

criminal, non-legalistic character of the juvenile court. Whereas the application of the criminal law in cases of adult offenders is governed by the narrow interpretation of the exact text of the statute, the intent of the juvenile court laws and the practice of juvenile courts call for inclusiveness of all possible situations that might warrant the action of the state, represented by the juvenile court, in behalf of the child.

This comprehensiveness (or vagueness, as the legally trained mind calls it) has found its extreme expression in the *Standard Juvenile Court Act* (Section 7) and in the laws of some states which, instead of defining a *delinquent child*, enumerate certain *acts and conditions* that may bring a child under the jurisdiction of the juvenile court. The California law, for example, provides that children found to come within this description may be adjudged "wards of the court." Similar provisions are found in the laws of five other states and the District of Columbia. The purpose of phrasing the law in this manner is to avoid tagging a child a delinquent and thus to underscore the basic philosophy "that in the juvenile court a child is being protected and helped and not categorized as anti-social." [47] Practically, the difference is hardly apparent, since even if a child is classified as a delinquent, the effect of such adjudication is likewise non-criminal.

Contrary to widespread public opinion, delinquency is by no means the only type of case that falls within the jurisdiction of most juvenile courts. In almost all states, cases of dependent and neglected children are included in the jurisdiction. According to the United States Children's Bureau's statistics, based on reports from 399 juvenile courts throughout the country for 1948, non-delinquency cases amounted to one third of their total case load.[48] A "neglect" situation exists when a parent (or other person legally responsible for the child) neglects or refuses, though able to do so, to provide proper or necessary support, education as required by law, and medical, psychiatric, or other care necessary for the child's well-being. Abandonment is also considered neglect. "Dependency" exists when a child is without proper care, custody, or support as a result of no one's fault but rather as a result of an unfortunate situation, such as

---

[47] Sol Rubin, *loc. cit.*, p. 5.
[48] See *Preliminary Statement, Juvenile Court Statistics, 1948,* published by United States Children's Bureau, December 1949.

the death or physical or mental incapacity of the child's parents or guardians.

In addition to dependent and neglected children, a number of states, through either their juvenile court acts or special laws, have conferred jurisdiction over cases of feeble-minded children upon the juvenile court. In other states, juvenile courts, even without specific legislation, are handling cases of mentally defective children by classifying them as cases of child dependency. Also included under the general jurisdiction of the juvenile court, according to the laws of various states, are cases of guardianship, custody, adoption, illegitimacy, physically handicapped children, consent of marriage of minors, and annulments of marriages of minors.[49]

Although this discussion deals with juvenile delinquency only, the significance of the wider scope of the juvenile court, as just described, deserves proper consideration here. The inclusion of non-delinquency cases under the juvenile court's jurisdiction serves to emphasize the court's non-criminal character. Further, in the daily practice of investigation, diagnosis, and disposition of juvenile cases it is often very difficult, if not arbitrary, to differentiate between manifestations of delinquency and situations of dependency or neglect. Even if such distinction can be made fairly accurately, the factors causing delinquency, dependency, or neglect in a given case are frequently identical.

In another respect, the juvenile court's jurisdiction transcends the category of the delinquent child. In most states the juvenile court has certain jurisdiction over adults[50] in cases in which children are involved. According to many state laws, the juvenile court may order the parents or other legally responsible persons to contribute toward the support of a child within the court's jurisdiction. The juvenile court is also given jurisdiction to try adults charged with contributing to, or causing or tending to cause, the delinquency, neglect, or dependency of a child. In specifying "the adult" in this connection, most statutes refer directly to the parent or guardian,

---

[49] For details of jurisdiction of juvenile courts in the different states over non-delinquency cases, see Cosulich, *op. cit.*, pp. 42–46; see also *Standard Juvenile Court Act*, Section 7. In this connection the reader is referred to a discussion of the family court, Chapter X, pp. 376–382.

[50] An adult in this context means a person above juvenile court age; juvenile court age limits are described later in this chapter.

while other laws mention "any person," "any adult," or "whoever" causes a child to require the care and protection of the court.[51]

Because of the increase of juvenile delinquency during World War II, which was attributed by the United States Children's Bureau and others [52] to the lack of supervision by parents, it has become almost a fad to ascribe juvenile delinquency primarily to parental neglect or indifference and to call for punishment of the parents by invoking the statute regarding adults' contributing to the delinquency of children. However, the application of this legal provision, which makes contributing to the delinquency, dependency, and neglect a crime (*i.e.*, in most statutes, a misdemeanor) and which prescribes fine or imprisonment or both as punishment, has been most sporadic. Judges are reluctant to use this legal weapon except in flagrant cases. In most delinquency cases the economic conditions of the parents are bad and the payment of a fine is often impossible, while imprisonment of the bread-winner would punish the rest of the family more than the parent himself and thus might, *per se*, be a contributing factor to continued delinquency of the child.

Still, the public clamor for disciplining parents for the delinquent acts of their children has not subsided in the postwar period. It is suggested that the parents rather than their children be sent to prison. Here and there a jurist or a magistrate makes news by going through with such a procedure. A New York magistrate a few years ago brought down on his head a great deal of public censure—and from certain persons a word of commendation—when he ordered a young mother to the House of Correction for contributing to her child's delinquency. It is difficult to evaluate such an attitude, since it is just possible that some parents might conceivably improve by a jail sentence. Yet this practice nullifies careful analysis of the specific causes in the child's delinquency; it definitely fails to get at the root of the problem. Further, it seems the easiest way out of a dilemma and obviously often not the correct method.

---

[51] See Sections 18 and 21 of the *Standard Juvenile Court Act*. For the list of states having such jurisdiction, see Cosulich, *op. cit.*, pp. 69, 70.

[52] See *Controlling Juvenile Delinquency*, United States Children's Bureau Publication No. 301, 1943, p. 10; see also Frieda Romalis, "The Impact of the War on Family Life," *Yearbook*, N.P.P.A., 1943, pp. 111–117, especially p. 114; Charles L. Chute, "Juvenile Delinquency in Wartime," *Probation*, June 1943, pp. 129–134, 149–153.

Fortunately, we have some documentary evidence to bring to this question. Judge Paul W. Alexander of the Domestic Relations and Juvenile Court of Toledo, Ohio, submits his findings relative to the practice of punishing parents. What he has to say is worthy of quotation. Stating that his court has been punishing parents in some cases for over ten years (1937–1946), he makes the following conclusions:

> Our total sampling consists of 1,027 cases; approximately 500 of these were against parents. Mothers arrested outnumbered fathers by a ratio of four to three. Seventy-six per cent of these parents either pleaded or were found guilty; 17 per cent were dismissed or acquitted; 7 per cent of the cases were pending. Of the guilty, 83 per cent were given suspended sentences and 17 per cent were sentenced to prison. . . . Altogether we actually have punished 91 parents with prison terms totaling over 80 years. The number of parents arrested for contributing has increased steadily from 7 in 1937 to 118 in 1946. . . . During the first 3 of our ten year study, our delinquency rate was comparatively stationary. With the increase of war industry and the beginning of the war, it zoomed, reaching a peak in 1943. Since then it has constantly declined.[53]

Judge Alexander describes five categories of delinquent parents:

> (1) *Runaway Parents* who leave their children with inadequate or no supervision; (a) working mothers; (b) those who go on drinking sprees; (c) those who wholly abandon their children. (2) *Vicious Parents* who expose their children to vice (a) in public places such as night clubs; (b) in their own homes, *e.g.*, a parent having a paramour in the presence or with knowledge of the children. (3) *Aiders and Abettors* who directly encourage delinquency in their children; (a) who encourage or permit them to be truant from school; (b) who, in various ways, defy or refuse to co-operate with constituted authority (school, police, court, agency); (c) who harbour or conceal children who have run away or escaped from institutions; (d) who instigate or sanction engaging in vice, *e.g.*, sexual delinquency; (e) who condone their engaging in crime by receiving or concealing property stolen by the children. (4) *Triangular Parents* involved in extra-marital love affairs to the general detriment of the children. (5) *Inadequate Parents* (more important than all others combined) who have failed to give their children adequate moral and ethical teaching, training, supervision, etc.

---

[53] "What's This About Punishing Parents?," *Federal Probation*, March 1948, pp. 23–29 (quotation, p. 24).

What are the results of punishing these types of neglectful parents as shown by the Toledo juvenile court? Stating that "punishing parents is no panacea," Judge Alexander concludes from his experience:

> In fine, we might say our study seems to show that to punish parents . . . accomplishes very few, if any, of the things claimed for it except revenge; that in some cases where the parent is refractory and resists the case work approach, a certain amount of actual punishment may bring about co-operation; that in selected cases, where other methods have failed, prosecution and the threat of punishment, without actual punishment, are rather effective.[54]

Judge George W. Smyth, of the Westchester County Children's Court, New York, arrives at similar conclusions. Appraising the powers which the juvenile court judge possesses in dealing with neglectful parents, he states that "these powers should not be used principally for the purpose of vindication or as a deterrent to others, but as an aid in securing compliance on the part of obdurate parents, with the broad objectives of the juvenile courts." [55] He considers guidance through the court's probation officers for "the purpose of alleviating harmful conditions and strengthening the moral and ethical concepts and conduct of both children and parents" as the most constructive method of dealing with offending parents. He calls threats, instilling of fear, or actual imprisonment neither effective nor desirable. But he admits that there are cases of recalcitrant parents with whom the court must use authoritative measures. Exclusion of the offending parent from the home may be necessary in some instances (he mentions cases in which the father was guilty of incest), and fines or imprisonment for reasonable periods may be necessary in others, in order "to check misconduct and to bring about reformation and permanent improvement." In these situations, he emphasizes, probation service should continue—*i.e.*, during the period of exclusion from the home and after termination of the prison sentence.

Another jurist, Judge Gustavus Loevinger of the District Court of St. Paul, Minnesota, expresses his opinion that a juvenile court

---

[54] *Ibid.*, p. 29; see also Judge Alexander's earlier article, "Punishing Parents," *Probation*, June 1944, pp. 154–156.

[55] "The Juvenile Court and Delinquent Parents," *Federal Probation*, March 1949, pp. 12–17 (quotation on p. 17); see also "Parents in Court," by the same author, *Focus*, September 1949, pp. 135–140.

hearing should not be used for a trial of parents and others who have contributed to the delinquency of a minor. "The hearing, instead of remaining an investigation, would frequently become an inquisition; instead of an impartial inquiry into the condition of a juvenile it might become a contested court trial with the judge as the accuser; instead of frankly admitting misconduct the child, probably cautioned or coached, would admit nothing and involve no one; instead of getting confidence and co-operation from parents, relatives and friends, one would be likely to find them on guard against being incriminated or incriminating anyone." [56] That is the reason, too, why some juvenile court judges, when hearing cases of adults charged with contributing to the delinquency of a minor, do not try them in juvenile court but—acting as committing magistrates—hold them for the ordinary criminal court. Moreover, extreme cases of child neglect, including contributing to delinquency, are usually covered by the general criminal statute of the state and, therefore, are triable in the ordinary criminal courts.

But even at trials in the courts of general criminal jurisdiction, certain difficulties are encountered in obtaining convictions of those who by acts of omission, rather than by the much more obvious acts of commission, contribute to the delinquency of their children. In this connection mention should be made of a statute adopted in Minnesota to the effect that there is a presumption of the parent's guilt when more than one adjudication of delinquency of a child has been made.[57] In California, in 1945, a section was added to the juvenile court law requiring the court to inquire into the question of whether or not a complaint should be issued charging the parent or guardian with contributing to the delinquency of a juvenile. This mandatory requirement, however, was modified in 1949 to make such inquiry permissive with the court.

---

[56] "The Court and the Child," *Focus*, May 1949, p. 65.

[57] For an interesting inquiry into the legal side of this problem and a compilation of numerous comments from judges and probation administrators on this matter, see Daniel J. Vaughan, "Should Parents Be Punished for the Delinquency of Their Children?," *Intramural Law Review of New York University*, School of Law, May 1949, pp. 230–245, and *The Juvenile Court Judges Journal*, January 1950, pp. 11–14, 31–36. See also Judge Dudley F. Sicher, "Debate Punishing Parents," *ibid.*, April 1950, pp. 26–29. For the legal problems involved, see Lou, *op. cit.*, pp. 55–60.

To educate—by compulsion if need be—rather than punish parents who are neglecting their children has also been widely suggested. In San Francisco such a project has been in existence for several years. There parents are placed on probation on condition that they attend adult education classes on child care.[58]

There are a number of other types of adult cases over which juvenile courts are given jurisdiction in certain states or only in some counties of other states—viz., offenses committed by adults upon children, violation of child labor laws by adults, non-compliance by parents or guardians with school attendance laws. A recent amendment to the law governing the Children's Court of New York City gives the judge the power to remand a parent to a psychiatric hospital for observation.

One of the fundamental principles of the juvenile court idea is the exclusiveness of jurisdiction, that is, the assurance that the all-inclusive function and scope of this court, established to deal with children in need of aid, protection, and guidance, should not be curtailed or abridged.[59] In reality, however, a considerable number of states exempt certain offenses—e.g., murder, manslaughter, rape, and other felonies—from the jurisdiction of juvenile courts; such exception might apply merely to children above a specified age or only to certain counties within the state.[60]

Exclusiveness of juvenile court jurisdiction also means that no other court shall have power to hear cases over which jurisdiction has been conferred upon the juvenile court. In reality, the juvenile court in at least forty states has concurrent jurisdiction with other courts, so that cases of delinquent children may be handled by either the juvenile court or the criminal court. The decision as to which

---

[58] For an evaluation of the "Parental School" of San Francisco see Chapter XVI, pp. 640–642. For a further discussion of this whole problem, see Samuel Whitman, "Stop Sniping at Parents," *The Child*, May 1947, pp. 184–189; Howard Whitman, "Let's Stop Blaming the Parents," *Woman's Home Companion*, September 1949, pp. 4, 159–160; "Are Parents or Society Responsible for Juvenile Crime?," *Town Meeting of the Air Bulletin*, February 21, 1946.

[59] See *Juvenile Court Standards*, p. 1.

[60] Tables showing these exceptions according to offenses and states can be found in Cosulich, *op. cit.*, p. 3; and Paul W. Tappan, "Children and Youth in the Criminal Court," *The Annals*, January 1949, pp. 129–130.

court should hear the case may be in the hands of the magistrate, the district attorney, the judge, or may be even left to the child himself. In several states the criminal court may take jurisdiction over juveniles only when the offense is a felony or an indictable crime. Concurrent jurisdiction is often limited by state law to the cases of children above a specified age, or to certain types of offenses, or to specific counties within the state.[61]

These provisions limiting the exclusiveness of the juvenile court, either through total exemption of certain offenses or through the overlapping of authority between juvenile court and criminal court, are inconsistent with the basic principle on which the juvenile court is founded, namely, that a child is incapable of crime. They indicate clearly that the remnants of criminal court attitudes and procedures have not yet entirely been eliminated in our dealing with lawbreaking children. They are a compromise with the public demand that serious offenses, even of children, be tried in full public view before the ordinary criminal court.

However, the current trend is to limit more and more the jurisdiction of the criminal court over children. In 1948 a law was passed in New York state which gave to the children's court exclusive jurisdiction in homicide cases committed by children up to 15 years of age. With regard to children between 15 and 16 years committing offenses which in cases of adults are punishable by death or life imprisonment, a transfer to the children's court [62] at the discretion of the criminal court judge is provided for. Formerly, these offenses were altogether excluded from children's court jurisdiction. In

---

[61] A table showing exclusive and concurrent jurisdiction in delinquency cases, according to states, will be found in Cosulich, *op. cit.*, pp. 37–39, and Tappan, *loc. cit.*, pp. 129–130. For further details, especially the legal implications, see Lou, *op. cit.*, pp. 37–42. See also the chart, "Juvenile Court Jurisdiction in the United States," on p. 312 of this chapter. An intelligent provision is found in the Ohio law. There the juvenile court may not release its jurisdiction over offenders under eighteen years of age to the criminal court, even in a felony case, until a physical and mental examination has been made by the Bureau of Juvenile Research, or by other qualified persons. Such study and observation become an important factor in the decision of the juvenile court judge on whether or not to release his jurisdiction.

[62] Sixteen years is the upper age limit of juvenile court jurisdiction in New York state.

Massachusetts, offenses punishable by life imprisonment have, since 1948, been included in the definition of delinquency and now fall within the jurisdiction of the juvenile court.

Whereas these changes of juvenile court laws were concerned with bringing crimes of the most serious nature under the exclusive jurisdiction of the juvenile court, a challenging and largely unsolved problem remains on the other end of the scale of law violations. We are referring to the offenses against traffic regulations. Douglas H. MacNeil, Director of the Division of Community Services for Delinquency Prevention, New Jersey Department of Institutions and Agencies, who has made a thorough and objective study of the matter, poses this question: "Is the public safety and the welfare of the youthful driver better safe-guarded by assigning jurisdiction in such cases to the juvenile court? Or should they be dealt with by the courts which ordinarily hear traffic cases?" [63]

The age at which most states may grant motor vehicle operator licenses is 16 years. In 41 states and the District of Columbia, the age of eligibility for obtaining driver licenses is below the maximum age of juvenile court jurisdiction. In most of these states the law confers jurisdiction in these cases upon the juvenile court. However, even where juvenile courts have exclusive jurisdiction, they seldom hear traffic cases. Sometimes the juvenile court judge designates the traffic court judge as a referee to act for him in such cases; sometimes the traffic court judge assumes jurisdiction with the tacit approval of the juvenile court judge without formal authorization. According to a study on traffic courts by George Warren,[64] the police and traffic court judges are sometimes unaware or even deliberately ignorant of exclusive juvenile court jurisdiction in these cases.

MacNeil lists the arguments advanced by both sides—*i.e.* handling of these cases by the juvenile court or by the traffic court. One of the reasons in favor of juvenile court hearings is that the juvenile court deals not primarily with offenses but rather with individuals and with the causes of underlying maladjustments. Further, the juvenile court is not limited to the imposing of stereotyped sentences like fines or short jail terms. It can work out plans for the treatment

---

[63] Douglas H. MacNeil, "Judicial Treatment of the Juvenile Traffic Offender," *Focus*, November 1948, pp. 166–170, 182–184.

[64] *Traffic Courts*, Little, Brown, Boston, 1942, p. 157.

of the situation based on full knowledge of the causes for juvenile behavior. A juvenile court judge can advise or order the parents to restrict the use of the family car by the youngster. He might impose a fine upon the parents but insist that the son or daughter pay the fine out of their own earnings. He can order a course in safety education. Another advantage of juvenile court procedure is that violations of traffic laws might sometimes bring out more deep-seated maladjustment, and the probation and clinical services which are available to the juvenile court judge can be utilized for the treatment of such a situation.

One of the main arguments for assigning these cases to traffic courts is that an individual who is sufficiently mature to be eligible for a driver's license should be old enough to assume full responsibility for any misuse of the privileges which the license confers on him. This point is particularly stressed by law enforcement agencies. They want to see traffic cases handled by responsible judges and magistrates who have a thorough knowledge of traffic laws and regulations, in other words, by courts whose primary business is in the traffic field. On the practical side, it is emphasized that many arrests of young traffic violators are made during evening hours or on week-ends and frequently in places which are a long distance from the home of the youngster. The juvenile court is closed at that time. If the case has to go before the juvenile court, it involves detention and social investigation before the case is heard. Also, every juvenile court has its own routine, which varies from county to county, whereas magistrates usually follow standardized routines developed by traffic safety agencies in the law enforcement field. In such cases, therefore, where traffic courts have jurisdiction, the arresting officer can take the youngster to the nearest magistrate and obtain an immediate hearing and disposition.

Traffic safety people make another criticism against juvenile court hearings of these cases. Motor vehicle departments often are empowered by law to suspend or revoke licenses of habitual violators and for this purpose they like to maintain a central record of traffic violations. If cases are heard before the juvenile court as a non-criminal court, information will not be made available to this central record because it would be contrary to the principles of juvenile court procedure.

On the strength of nearly two years' experience with the handling of traffic violations of juveniles in the juvenile courts, New Jersey recently amended its law to the effect that juvenile traffic violations charged against licensed drivers are excluded from the jurisdiction of the juvenile court. The juvenile court retains jurisdiction over cases involving unlicensed drivers, including those who never had a license and those whose license has been canceled.

In Rhode Island a law has been considered that would allow magistrates to transfer cases of juvenile traffic violators to juvenile courts when behavior problems appear to underlie motor vehicle violations. This provision would include habitual speeders and reckless drivers as well as others whose erratic behavior on the highway seems to be the result of basic antisocial or irresponsible attitudes.

Alan Canty of the Psychopathic Clinic of Recorders Court, Detroit, stated that among the young traffic violators who are referred to the traffic division of this clinic are many boys who are "reacting to deeply ingrained feelings of inferiority for which they attempt to compensate by aggressive or exhibitionistic driving behavior." [65] The traffic clinic of the Detroit court has been established by the judges for the examination of traffic violators subsequent to conviction and prior to sentence. Most of the youthful offenders referred to this clinic are above juvenile court age, but a number of them are under 17 years, and are thus juveniles according to the Michigan Juvenile Court Act. Canty stated that in many cases probation is being recommended, which might or might not be accompanied by the suspension of the driver's license. An interesting experiment is reported from Muskegon, Michigan, where a "juvenile jury," consisting of high school students, hears and disposes of cases of traffic offenses involving drivers under seventeen years of age. [66]

The Special Crime Study Commission on Juvenile Justice appointed by California's Governor Earl Warren, in its final report of June 30, 1949, recommended that provision be made for appointing referees for handling minor traffic offenses under the supervision of the judge of the juvenile court. It is the practice in Los Angeles to let local law enforcement officers handle all juvenile offenders against

---

[65] Alan Canty, "The Youthful Problem Driver," *Yearbook*, N.P.P.A., 1942, pp. 210–223.
[66] See Ralph W. Daniel, "A Juvenile Jury for Young Traffic Offenders," *Focus*, January 1950, pp. 23–26.

traffic laws without reference to any court. Petitions are filed in juvenile court concerning only those offenders whose repeated violations have indicated a lack of amenability to unofficial control. All juvenile traffic offenses are registered with the central juvenile index of Los Angeles, which gathers statistical information of all problems presented by individual youths throughout the county.[67] The juvenile court of San Francisco has its own traffic division. Its aim is to develop in the mind of the young driver an awareness of the significance of careful and considerate driving. Chief probation officer George W. Ososke, in the court's annual report for 1948, reports that, in contrast with the somewhat perfunctory procedure of the average traffic court, understanding and cooperation are factors generally stressed in the initial contact of the probation officer with young violators. The first offender is made to understand that repetitions of driving misconduct may result in curtailment of driving privileges. It was necessary to suspend or revoke licenses from approximately 12 per cent of the youths coming to the court's attention. This court maintains a traffic school for those youngsters whose violations show a lack of knowledge of the fundamentals of traffic safety. In 1948, 172 boys were referred to this school as a condition of driving probation. Mr. Ososke reports an 8 per cent decrease in traffic violations in 1948 as compared with 1947. He further reports that none of the 88 traffic fatalities that occurred in San Francisco during 1948 was chargeable to a youth whose age was within juvenile court range.

Throughout the nation many high schools have organized courses in automobile driving as a result of reports on the high proportion of accident cases caused by youthful drivers. A recent survey in New York, for instance, showed that, though only 14.4 per cent of the licensed operators are under 25 years of age, they had 28.5 per cent of the fatal accidents and 23.8 per cent of the non-fatal mishaps. As a result of this investigation, New York State restricted youths under eighteen years of age to operate automobiles after dark only when on the way to and from school.

The National Training School at Washington, D.C., a well-known institution for Federal youthful offenders, started driver training

---

[67] See John M. Zuck, "The Probation Officer Participates in Delinquency Prevention," *Yearbook*, N.P.P.A., 1948, pp. 286–287.

courses in 1948. The boys are assigned to this class during the month immediately preceding their parole hearings.

d. Age Limits

One of the most conspicuous variations in the state laws concerns the age limitation. The definition of the word "child" is always found in the juvenile court law. Since the jurisdiction of most juvenile courts includes cases of dependency and neglect, usually no minimum age is mentioned in the law. Where a specific reference in the statute is made to a minimum age in cases of delinquency, it most frequently is seven years. The practice in those states where the law is silent usually considers seven years as the minimum age limit in delinquency cases. This usage is based upon the common law concept that a child under seven years is "incapable of felonious intent." [68]

Most jurisdictions (twenty-seven states, Alaska, Hawaii, and the District of Columbia) set eighteen years as the age limit; six states set seventeen years; seven states, Puerto Rico, and the Virgin Islands set sixteen years; and two states set twenty-one years. (In six of these states a different age limit is set for a particular city or for a few counties in the state.) The remaining six states prescribe different age limits for different classes of cases and for the two sexes; whenever a distinction according to sex is made, the age limit for girls is usually higher than that for boys. The Federal Juvenile Delinquency Act applies to juveniles under 18 years of age. The Standard Juvenile Act also provides for the 18-year age limit (Section 2). [69]

The chart on page 312 shows the age limits of juvenile court jurisdiction in all states and territories. [70]

The general tendency in recent years has been to raise the juvenile court age to 18 years. However, any such changes in the law are bound to encounter some opposition, especially whenever a particularly shocking crime is committed by a 16- or 17-year-old youth

---

[68] See Chapter II, pp. 41–42, and Chapter IX, p. 281; see also Sol Rubin, *loc. cit.*, p. 6.

[69] Regarding age limits of juvenile courts in Europe, see Sol Rubin, *loc. cit.*, p. 7.

[70] Reproduced from *Probation*, June 1946, pp. 144–145; see also Cosulich, *op. cit.*, pp. 20–28; and Tappan, *loc. cit.*, pp. 129–130. Some changes have taken place since the drafting of the chart.

whose external appearance at least is that of a full-grown person. In order to offset such criticism, the following provision has been proposed by the *Standard Juvenile Court Act* (Section 10):

> If a child sixteen years of age or older is charged with an offense which would be a felony if committed by an adult, and if the juvenile court after full investigation deems it contrary to the best interest of such child or of the public to retain jurisdiction, the juvenile court may in its discretion certify such child for proper criminal proceedings to any court which would have trial jurisdiction of such offense if committed by an adult; but no child under sixteen years of age shall be so certified.

Many states have adopted similar provisions, using either the 16-year or a lower age level.[71] This provision, however, should not be construed as constituting a retreat from the principle of the 18-year age limit as the most desirable one.

In order to insure adherence to the provisions regarding juvenile court age and the exclusiveness of juvenile court jurisdiction as incorporated in various legislations, the following complementary provision, as formulated by the *Standard Juvenile Court Act* (Section 8), is needed:

> If during the pendency of a criminal or quasi-criminal charge against any minor in any other court, it shall be ascertained that the minor was under the age of eighteen years at the time of committing the alleged offense, it shall be the duty of such court forthwith to transfer the case, together with all the papers, documents and testimony connected therewith, to the juvenile court. The court making such transfer shall order the minor to be taken forthwith to the place of detention designated by the juvenile court or to that court itself, or release such minor to the custody of some suitable person to be brought before the court at a time designated.

Similar provisions are already part of many state laws.

Although jurisdiction in individual cases must be acquired before the child has reached the upper age limit as defined by law, the juvenile court's authority does not automatically cease once the child has reached this age limit. In many states and in the Federal Judiciary System the juvenile courts retain jurisdiction over a child,

---

[71] For details, see Cosulich, *op. cit.*, p. 40.

JURISDICTION OF JUVENILE COURTS IN THE UNITED STATES

Age

////// Exclusive juvenile court jurisdiction of dependent, neglected & delinquent children.
∷∷∷ Jurisdiction concurrent with criminal court.

especially if he is placed on probation, until his twenty-first birthday. Such retention of jurisdiction, however, is usually terminated
by the commitment of a new offense. Many laws also provide that
commitment to agencies and institutions must be made for the minority of a child, thus frequently lasting beyond the upper juvenile
court age limit.[72]

An interesting legal and psychological problem arises when a girl
marries within the age limit during which juvenile court jurisdiction
obtains. Although it is generally held that marriage should not terminate juvenile court jurisdiction, some court decisions have stated
that a female minor, if married, cannot be a delinquent child.[73] The
Juvenile Court Standards recommends that "marriage of the child
should not terminate jurisdiction."

e. The Juvenile Court Judge

The matter of selection of juvenile court judges is closely related
to the previously discussed question of whether the juvenile court is
a separate court or a special branch or session of the ordinary local
court. In the former situation, selection of the judge according to
special qualification for his assignment is more likely.

Judges in general are either elected by the people or appointed,

---

Explanatory notes concerning the chart on the opposite page:
Alabama: Jefferson and Montgomery counties, exclusive jurisdiction girls to 18.
   Mobile county to 16 only, boys and girls.
Colorado: 16 to 18, capital and life cases included.
Delaware: New Castle County, to 18, boys and girls.
Florida: Rape, murder, manslaughter, robbery, arson, burglary excluded.
Kansas: 16 to 18, incorrigible girls, probate court.
Louisiana: Orleans Parish, capital crimes and assault with intent to rape ex-
   cluded.
New York: Youthful offender procedure in criminal courts. Wayward minor
   cases all courts, 16 to 21.
North Carolina: 14 to 16, crimes punishable by ten years' imprisonment or over
   excluded.
Pennsylvania: Philadelphia Municipal Court, wayward youth 18 to 20, inclusive.
South Carolina: Greenville County, concurrent jurisdiction to 16.
Tennessee: Colored girls, concurrent jurisdiction to 18.
Texas: Delinquency jurisdiction to 17, boys; to 18, girls.

---

[72] For details, see Cosulich, *op. cit.*, pp. 28–29; see also *Standard Juvenile
Court Act,* Section 9.
[73] For details, see Lou, *op. cit.*, p. 49.

as, for instance, in the Federal judiciary.[74] In both systems, political influences may play a harmful role. Civic-minded citizens and bar associations have recently considered ways and means to insure the selection of the best-qualified persons for judgeships. The so-called "Missouri Plan," in force in that state since 1941, has been hailed as the most desirable method. It is endorsed by the American Bar Association. Under this system, the judge is appointed by the governor from a list of three names submitted to him by a selective commission, to serve for one year "on trial"; he then runs for election for a full term, to be either confirmed or defeated by popular vote.

Reform of the methods used in the selection of judges in the various states would be of great benefit to the juvenile court, since in most cases the judge, sitting as juvenile court judge, is not elected for this special assignment but rather as judge of the ordinary local court. Less populated counties often have only one judge for all types of cases. In larger courts with more than one judge, the president judge or the board of judges may designate one of their number to sit as juvenile court judge. This appointment may be made according to seniority or in rotation at regular intervals. The system of rotation, however, has been censured because constant changes of assignment are not bound to increase the interest of the judge in juvenile cases and because they obviate the necessary specialization in this field.[75]

In those relatively few jurisdictions where, either by law or by practice, the judge sitting in juvenile cases is especially chosen for this function, the following methods for selection have been employed: popular election, appointment by governor, appointment by the city or county government, appointment by the mayor, appointment by judges of other courts, appointment by a local juvenile court committee, appointment by a state commission, and mixed systems that include more than one of the enumerated features.[76]

---

[74] For a thorough survey of the various forms of selection of judges in all states, see *Minimum Standards of Judicial Administration*, published by the National Conference of Judicial Councils, 1949.

[75] See Sutherland, *op. cit.*, pp. 309–310; Lou, *op. cit.*, p. 71.

[76] For further details, see Cosulich, *op. cit.*, pp. 79–84; and *Standard Juvenile Court Act*, Section 3, and comment, pp. 11–13.

Because of the great variations in the judicial system of the different states, especially among the types of juvenile courts in urban and rural areas, it is impossible to designate one single method as the most desirable one for the whole country. The *Standard Juvenile Court Act* proposes that in each county having a population of 100,000 or more, a judge of the juvenile court shall be appointed by the governor from a list of three persons submitted by a panel of seven persons; these seven are the presiding judge of the court of general jurisdiction, two members designated by the county welfare department, two by the organized bar of the county, and two by the board of education of the county. Where state juvenile courts are in existence, the panel shall consist of nine members chosen by the respective state agencies and departments, including the state department of health or mental hygiene (Section 3). In smaller counties, the Act recommends decision by majority vote of the population as to whether the judge shall be selected in the same manner. In 1949, the California Crime Study Commission on Juvenile Justice proposed that the juvenile court judge should be selected by a panel consisting of the presiding judge of the superior court and four other members appointed by the Board of Supervisors, and that three of the panel members should be representatives of public education, public welfare, and the legal profession.

Although no uniformity is possible in the method of selection of juvenile court judges, the soundness of the principle that juvenile court judges should be chosen because of their special qualifications for juvenile court work cannot be questioned.

Are such qualifications mentioned in the law? In most of the courts of general jurisdiction dealing with children's cases, the judges must be trained in the law. In those states where separate juvenile courts are established, some laws make no mention of any qualifications for the judge; others require him to be a lawyer, or do not even contain this requisite. In a few jurisdictions, special qualifications are mentioned; for instance, in Jefferson County, Alabama, either a man or a woman [77] is eligible for the judgeship provided that the appointee is "of high moral character, of clean life, and shall be selected for his or her special fitness by training, education and experience to deal

---

[77] There are several women juvenile court judges throughout the country.

with the problems of dependent, neglected and delinquent children and of the home and family life." The judge of the Juvenile Court of the District of Columbia must "have a knowledge of social problems and procedure and an understanding of child psychology." Georgia specifies that the juvenile court judge should be an attorney of at least three years' practice and should have an interest in children as well as a knowledge of the problems of social service, philanthropy, and child life.[78] According to the 1945 act creating a Family Court for New Castle County, Wilmington, Delaware, "The judge shall be a person duly admitted to the practice of law in the state of Delaware who, in the opinion of the governor, shall be qualified to be a judge of the court by his acquaintance with social problems and understanding of child psychology." The *Standard Juvenile Court Act* proposes that juvenile court judges "shall have been admitted to the practice of law in the state, and shall be selected with reference to their experience in and understanding of problems of family and child welfare, juvenile delinquency and community organization" (Section 3).[79]

Unfortunately, neither the law schools nor the judiciary system itself provides possibilities for adequate training of jurists for juvenile rehabilitation work.[80] A challenging opportunity presents itself here for our universities to include in the curriculum of their law courses instruction in social problems that require judicial handling, such as juvenile delinquency and dependency, domestic relations matters, custody of children, adoption, and illegitimacy. Field trips to juvenile courts, training schools, reformatories, and penal and mental institutions should also be part of such courses.

A problem closely related to the selection of qualified judges is the matter of tenure. Here the *Juvenile Court Standards* suggest that "the tenure of office should be sufficiently long to warrant special

---

[78] For further details, see Cosulich, *op. cit.*, pp. 85–86.

[79] The same idea is expressed by Sutherland, *op. cit.*, p. 310.

[80] See Marshall B. Clinard, "Secondary Community Influences and Juvenile Delinquency," *The Annals*, January 1949, p. 43. In order to spread information on juvenile problems, the New York County Lawyers' Association started in 1948 to hold annual conferences for members of the Bar and representatives of social agencies on "Law, Children and Unstable Families." The New York Academy of Medicine later joined in the sponsorship of such conferences. (For details, see *Survey*, April 1950, p. 202.)

preparatory studies and the development of special interest in juvenile work, preferably not less than six years." [81]

In his article, "A Yardstick for Measuring Juvenile Courts," Judge Donald E. Long of the Court of Domestic Relations and the Juvenile Court, Portland, Oregon, states:

> A juvenile court cannot be successful if it has a good judge and a poor staff of probation officers, nor a poor judge and a good staff. The effectiveness of the one may be offset by the incompetence of the other. A judge of any juvenile court should be socially minded, have knowledge of the law, and possess an understanding of social problems and child psychology. He should not be rigid in his attitudes, nor should he possess in his make-up any prejudices, whims or aversions to certain types of cases (for instance sex cases of children). The judge should recognize and accept all available community resources and facilities, such as child guidance clinics, psychiatry, psychology, psychoanalysis, medical therapy, etc. In addition to these special qualifications the judge should be willing and anxious to explore new fields cautiously and objectively. He should be a person of strong character and one who merits public approval and confidence. The term of office of a judge should be not less than 6 years, preferably 10 years; and when he seeks re-election, he should run against his record—not another candidate. And too, the judiciary should be nonpartisan.[82]

Many juvenile court judges throughout the country have joined together in the National Council of Juvenile Court Judges for the purpose of improving standards of juvenile court work. There also are several state associations or councils of juvenile court judges.

In about one-third of the states, the law authorizes the judges to appoint referees and to delegate certain functions to them, including the disposition of cases, subject to the judge's subsequent approval. Even if no mention is made in the statute, judges of courts having

---

[81] *Loc. cit.*, p. 2; a six-year term is also contained in the *Standard Juvenile Court Act*, Section 3.

[82] *Federal Probation*, October–December 1942, pp. 34–36. Similar thoughts were expressed by Judges George Smyth, of Westchester County (N. Y.) Children's Court ("Our Juvenile Courts," *Probation*, June 1946, pp. 142–143); Paul W. Alexander of the Domestic Relations and Juvenile Court, Toledo, Ohio ("Of Juvenile Court Justice and Judges," *Yearbook*, N.P.P.A., 1947, pp. 187–205); Nochem S. Winnet of the Municipal Court of Philadelphia ("Is a Juvenile Court a Court?," *The Shingle*, published by the Philadelphia Bar Association, June 1947, pp. 131–133).

equity jurisdiction exercise this power anyway. This procedure makes it possible, *inter alia*, to extend the power of the court to rural districts which are far removed from the county seat where the juvenile court hearings usually are held. Particularly in girls' cases, it enables the judge, if he so wishes, to assign cases of sex delinquency to a properly qualified woman referee.[83]

The principle that juvenile courts must be presided over by professional judges trained in the law, though hardly ever questioned in this country, is not accepted in all other countries. In England, for instance, juvenile court hearings are conducted by lay magistrates. The justices of the peace [84]—lay judges—who constitute the English criminal courts of first instance (called "courts of summary jurisdiction" or "petty sessional courts") elect from among their own number men and women who are especially qualified to deal with cases of juvenile offenders. These then form the juvenile court panel. As a rule, the juvenile court which is a court of summary jurisdiction consists of three justices and, as the law prescribes, includes at least one member of each sex. In the County of London and in some other large urban centers there are also professional or stipendiary magistrates, who may sit in juvenile courts together with two lay justices of the peace. Some other differences exist between the Metropolitan Police Court District (*i.e.*, the County of London) and the rest of the country; for example, the justices who form the juvenile court panel in London are appointed by the Home Office. Thus one of the main characteristics of English juvenile court practice is the emphasis on lay participation in the most decisive phase of the proceedings, namely the hearing and the disposition of the case.[85]

A somewhat more limited lay participation in the conducting of juvenile court hearings and the formulation of court decisions is

---

[83] For details, see Cosulich, *op. cit.*, p. 87; see also Frederick W. Killian, "The Juvenile Court as an Institution," *The Annals*, January 1949, pp. 96–97; *The Standard Juvenile Court Act*, Section 4, provides for the use of qualified persons, selected through merit-system examinations, as referees.

[84] The words "magistrate" and "justice of the peace" are used interchangeably in England as in this country.

[85] For further details regarding English juvenile courts, see L. Radzinowicz and J. W. C. Turner (ed.), *Penal Reform in England*, Macmillan, London, 1946, pp. 98–105; see also A. E. Jones, *Juvenile Delinquency and the Law*, Penguin Books, 1945, pp. 59–71.

found in the German Juvenile Court Law (of the Weimar Republic era), which was revived after World War II. This law of 1923 created juvenile courts as special divisions of the county criminal courts. It stipulated that the judge—a professional judge trained in the law and appointed as a lifelong civil servant—who would be assigned to hold juvenile court hearings should be versed in matters of education and child psychology. The law further prescribed that the judge presiding over juvenile court hearings must be assisted by two lay jurors who may both be male or one of each sex, who are familiar with child welfare work, and who are chosen from a panel compiled upon recommendations of the local department of child welfare. Originally, the presence of these lay jurors was required at all juvenile court sessions, but a later change in the law restricted their attendance to the more serious cases.[86]

These two examples of strong lay participation in juvenile court hearings in countries known for their high standards of juvenile court work are worth pondering in this country where, so far, the layman's part in the operation and administration of juvenile courts has been confined to purely advisory functions in a comparatively small number of communities.

3. PROCEDURE BEFORE THE JUVENILE COURT

a. *Informal Adjustments*

A growing tendency in recent years has been to dispose of certain cases informally, that is, without formal petitions being filed, without an official court record being prepared, and without a court hearing being held. To bring about such informal adjustments might be the function of the probation officer assigned to the case, or of a specially designated referee who is authorized by the judge to hear cases informally and to adjust them if feasible. In some cities the crime prevention divisions or juvenile bureaus of the local police department have engaged in this form of handling children's cases.[87] There is,

---

[86] For more details on German juvenile court legislation, see J. O. Reinemann, "The Youth Criminal Law in Germany," *The Prison Journal*, January–April 1935, pp. 150–152. See also W. Friedlander and Earl D. Myers, *Child Welfare in Germany Before and After Nazism*, University of Chicago Press, 1940, pp. 143–165.

[87] See Chapter VIII, p. 221.

unfortunately, a great amount of variation throughout the country regarding this practice; lack of uniformity exists even within the confines of some cities. According to the United States Children's Bureau Statistics for 1948, 58 per cent of delinquency cases reported from 399 courts in 17 states were disposed of informally or unofficially.[88] But in the individual courts the percentage of cases disposed of in this manner varies greatly, *i.e.*, from zero to 91 per cent.

Arguments in favor of and in opposition to the practice of informal handling of juvenile delinquency cases have been advanced for a long time, without producing a clear-cut solution.[89] The report on juvenile court administration of the National Conference contributed the following to the discussion:

> Many juvenile courts handle some cases informally. The types of cases so handled and the nature of the informal treatment varies greatly. Some of the cases involve situations in which is needed nothing other than a conference to bring about an adjustment; others require investigation. Some are cases which could be handled effectively by social agencies other than the court, others are definitely potential court cases. A well-organized intake service is needed to determine whether cases referred can best be dealt with formally or informally, or when other agencies are better equipped to deal with them, or whether they can best be referred directly to such other agencies for treatment.[90]

The *Juvenile Court Standards* suggests:

> The judge, or a probation officer designated by him, should examine all complaints and after adequate investigation determine whether a petition should be filed or other formal action should be taken. It should be the duty of the court to bring about adjustment of all cases without such formal action whenever feasible.[91]

Wherever the answer to this problem lies, it seems necessary that uniformity of procedure, at least on the local and state level, be assured, and that the decision of whether a case should be heard informally or officially be placed in the hands of competent per-

---

[88] See *Preliminary Statement, Juvenile Court Statistics, 1948,* published by United States Children's Bureau, December 1949.

[89] See Lou, *op. cit.,* pp. 126–127.

[90] *Report No. 4,* p. 17.

[91] *Loc. cit.,* p. 3.

sonnel. This screening should be done within the juvenile court so that the court maintains its position as general clearing house for the handling of all delinquency cases under its jurisdiction.

b. The Hearing

The preceding chapter dealt with the initiation of hearings before the juvenile court through the filing of a petition and the other steps prior to court hearing, *viz.*, social investigation and medical examination.[92]

The hearing itself is the focal point of the whole juvenile court procedure. The investigation of the case is completed prior to the hearing and the treatment process will begin immediately after, and as a consequence of, the hearing. The significance of the hearing lies primarily in its legal and psychological aspects. It is the first and frequently the only time that the judge himself is apparent. For the child and his parents the hearing symbolizes, more than any of the preceding steps, the state's judicious though benevolent interest in the welfare of the young person.

The juvenile court hearing, to be really meaningful, must be much more than a formal or perfunctory adjudication of the case. Its conduct should reflect the principles that originally prompted the establishment of juvenile courts. It should, therefore, be free from the legalistic and often antiquated forms and technicalities which are the attributes of criminal trials of adult offenders. Juvenile court hearings, consequently, are characterized by informality. But informality does not mean lack of dignity; dignity in the proceedings can be utilized as a constructive, therapeutic tool.

The quarters in which juvenile court hearings are held should guarantee the strict separation of children from any contact with adult offenders. They should be accessible to the population served and conveniently located for the judges and the probation staff. Frequently these requirements are not met. As the report on juvenile court administration of the National Conference points out:

> In most cities the courtroom and probation offices are located either in the courthouse or in the detention home. Each has certain advantages. The courthouse is generally conveniently located with reference to car lines and the center of population. Moreover, there is economy

---

[92] See Chapter VIII, pp. 262–273.

of time if the judge serves another court and gives only part of his time to the juvenile court. These advantages are offset if children cannot be protected from the surroundings of the criminal court. When the courtroom and probation offices are in the juvenile detention home or in a building devoted to juvenile court purposes the danger of undesirable contacts is generally removed. Under such an arrangement the question of transportation from the detention home to the place of hearing is solved, although the location of the detention home as to accessibility then becomes a matter of importance.[93]

The juvenile court hearing room itself should be comparatively small. Its external appearance should avoid the depressive drabness and oppressive ornateness which characterize many of our court buildings and courtrooms. There are two schools of thought concerning the arrangement of the equipment in a juvenile courtroom. Some persons engaged in juvenile court work believe it desirable to retain something of the accoutrements of the formal courtroom in the belief that these tend to impress the child and the parents with the dignity of the court. Others prefer a room resembling a small office, where the judge meets informally with the probation officer, the child, and his parents. Several judges hear juvenile cases almost exclusively in chambers.

It seems that no uniform rule can be adopted here. Certainly in the cases of younger children the most informal arrangement is desirable. On the other hand, in view of the many jurisdictions which extend to the upper age limit of eighteen or even higher, there are numerous situations in which the external formality of a courtroom lends emphasis to the dignity of the proceedings and thus has a useful effect upon the mind of the juvenile offender of a more advanced age.

Most state laws [94] contain some provision regarding the exclusion of the general public from juvenile court hearings. Privacy is generally recognized as a fundamental feature of juvenile court procedure but is often not observed. Not only does the presence of spectators tend to create an atmosphere of criminal proceedings, but also from a psychological point of view it must be considered most

---

[93] *Report No. 4*, p. 11.

[94] See Cosulich, *op. cit.*, pp. 49–50; see also *Standard Juvenile Court Act*, Section 17.

unwholesome for a youngster to find himself the center of attraction in a crowded courtroom. Only the child,[95] his parents, witnesses (if necessary), and the probation officer should be present. Representatives of the school authorities and social agencies may also be admitted if necessary. If more than one case is listed, the child and his parents should wait in an anteroom until the case is called and they should leave as soon as the case has been heard.

Judge Paul W. Alexander Conducting a Juvenile Court Hearing in Toledo, Ohio, 1942 (*Courtesy* LIFE. *Copyright* TIME, Inc.)

The report on juvenile court administration of the National Conference summarizes the underlying philosophy of a juvenile court hearing:

As the purpose of the juvenile court is to prevent the child's being tried and treated as a criminal, all means should be taken to prevent the

---

[95] The *Standard Juvenile Court Act* provides that "the presence of the child in court may be waived by the court at any stage of the proceedings" (Section 17).

child and his parents from forming the conception that the child is being tried for a crime. In every case the court should explain to the child and parents the nature of the proceedings and the disposition made of the case. Frequently both parent and child come before the court in fear. The right atmosphere gives them the confidence needed so that they can speak freely to the judge. The parent sees that the court is really interested in and sincerely desirous of helping the child, and the judge has an opportunity to draw the parent into taking part in the solution of the problem. The child gains confidence in the belief that he is to be fairly treated and develops courage to tell his story truthfully and face his difficulties.[96]

Privacy of juvenile court procedure is also predicated upon the strict avoidance of newspaper publicity. The rule not to give names of children who have been arrested and who are given a juvenile court hearing to the newspapers is adopted in principle by most juvenile court administrators, but in practice it is frequently violated. Names are often divulged at the time of apprehension. In general, the press shows little inclination to attend juvenile court hearings. If the purpose of juvenile court procedure is interpreted to newspaper editors and if their cooperation is enlisted by judges and probation officers, experience shows that press reporters not only refrain from attending juvenile court hearings but also that names or other identifying information concerning juvenile offenders are withheld from publication.[97]

The swiftness of a court decision has its value in children's as well as in adult cases. But there should always be sufficient time for a thorough study and investigation. Detention should be as short as the purposes that detention aims to achieve permit. As has been stated before,[98] to prolong detention only because court hearings are held

---

[96] *Report No. 4*, p. 15. See also the very instructive article by Judge Walter H. Beckham (of the Juvenile and Domestic Relations Court, Miami, Florida), "Helpful Practices in Juvenile Court Hearings," *Federal Probation*, June 1949, pp. 10–14.

[97] The draftsmen of the *Standard Juvenile Court Act* deemed it necessary to include the following provision in the model law: "The name or picture of any child under the jurisdiction of the juvenile court shall not be made public by any newspaper, radio or television station except as authorized by order of the court." The violation of this provision is made a misdemeanor, punishable by fine or imprisonment, or both (Section 28).

[98] See Chapter VIII, p. 247.

infrequently is bad practice. Again, no uniform rule regarding the frequency of hearings can be prescribed, because of the great differences of the number of cases in the various counties. In more densely populated areas, regular daily hearings are desirable in order to preclude the accumulation of cases. Large court lists disposed of in rapid succession in an assembly-line fashion, allowing hardly more than an average of two or three minutes for each case, are bound to undermine the impression that a juvenile court hearing should make on the child and his parents.

The conduct of the hearing should reflect the basic concept that juvenile court procedure is non-criminal in nature and that the child is not to be classified as a criminal. About half of the state laws contain such a statement,[99] and in the other states this principle is generally accepted even if not explicitly mentioned in the statutes. Consequently, the juvenile court hearing differs in many respects from the trial in adult cases. This difference is indicated by the following list of features characteristic of juvenile court hearings:

(1) *Privacy of hearing:* (See discussion on pp. 322–324).

(2) *Manner of hearing:* The hearing is held in a summary or informal manner; most laws emphasize that the court is not bound by technical rules of procedure.[100] The strict adherence to the rules of evidence, a principle rigidly enforced in adult cases, would be contrary to the avowed aims of juvenile court procedure. The establishment of the fact that a specific offense has been committed by the defendant (the only issue in adult trials) is much less relevant in juvenile cases. In the juvenile court, the hearing seeks to ascertain *why* the offense was committed, what conditions brought about the delinquency of the child, and what treatment will be best adapted to prevent further delinquency and to guarantee the child's normal and sound development. As Lou states,

> The juvenile court does not protect the child by discharging him merely because there is no technical legal evidence when the weight of evidence is preponderant that the child comes within the provision of the law. Since the object of the juvenile court is to determine the

---

[99] See *Report No. 3* on juvenile court laws, *National Conference*, p. 6.

[100] For details, see Cosulich, *op. cit.*, pp. 51–52; and *Standard Juvenile Court Act*, Section 17.

truth and to understand the child, the strict application of rules of evidence that exclude certain kinds of truth from the ear of the court as improper is certainly out of place in the juvenile court. The judge should not reject as immaterial any fact that throws light on the child's character and condition.[101]

On the other hand, the *Juvenile Court Standards* point out that "in the ascertainment of facts the juvenile court should always bear in mind the rules of evidence; this does not imply, however, that in the application of these rules the court must conduct a formal hearing." [102] The swearing of witnesses is the usual procedure, but an oath is seldom administered to the child or his parents.

(3) *Jury trials:* Jury trials should not be permitted in children's cases. They are held to be inconsistent with the spirit of juvenile court legislation. In reality, most laws are silent regarding the use of juries in children's cases. Some more recent laws exclude jury trials. Other laws provide that a jury trial may be had on demand by the child, the parent, any other interested person, or on the court's own motion.[103] The whole problem is closely tied up with the question of constitutional rights. But, as has been shown before, the constitutionality of statutes which do not provide for a jury trial in children's cases has been almost universally upheld.[104] Constitutional considerations, however, apply to cases of adults over which the juvenile court has jurisdiction. Therefore laws that expressively forbid jury trials for children usually mention that an adult brought before the juvenile court for an offense triable by jury is entitled to have his case transferred to the ordinary criminal court.[105]

(4) *Representation by counsel:* This, too, is a constitutional right. Juvenile court laws are silent on this matter. Attorneys, therefore, are not prohibited from appearing at juvenile court hearings, although it would appear that the non-criminal nature of the proceedings makes the employment of counsel unnecessary. Some juvenile courts have at least discouraged the practice. Actually attorneys appear in behalf of children only in a small number of instances.

---

[101] *Op. cit.,* p. 139.

[102] *Loc. cit.,* pp. 5–6.

[103] For details, see Cosulich, *op. cit.,* p. 53.

[104] Lou, *op. cit.,* p. 137; see also Chapter IX, p. 289, and *Standard Juvenile Court Act,* Section 17, and comment, pp. 24–26.

[105] See *Standard Juvenile Court Act,* Section 21.

If they do appear, the court frequently enlists their cooperation in interpreting to the parents the purpose of court hearing and court decision.

(5) *The prosecuting or district attorney:* The district attorney is present in some jurisdictions; in others he is not represented at all at juvenile court hearings, or only in specific cases or certain types of cases. One of the reasons advanced for the presence of the district attorney or his assistant is that juvenile delinquency hearings might disclose the existence of unlawful conditions or actions in which adults are involved. Investigation and, if necessary, prosecution can thus be immediately initiated. As a general rule, the role of the district attorney in juvenile court hearings is a modest one, since the interrogation of witnesses, because of the informality of the hearing, is usually carried on by the judge.

(6) *Pre-hearing investigation:* As discussed in the previous chapter, an investigation of the child's personality and his environment prior to court hearing is the preponderant rule, though not a mandatory requirement. (In some jurisdictions, however, *e.g.,* New York City and Boston "a finding of delinquency" must precede the investigation by the probation officer.) The results of said inquiries are brought out at the juvenile court hearing and govern the judge's decision. In adult cases, such investigations can only be made prior to sentencing and cannot be used in the trial.[106]

(7) *Court decision:* As will be discussed later, the disposition of the judge in a juvenile court hearing is subject to subsequent rehearings and to modification whenever this is warranted by a change of circumstances either in the physical or mental development of the child or in the family conditions. Such flexibility of court decisions is unthinkable in the criminal procedure against adults.

(8) *Imposition of civil disabilities:* Such imposition ordinarily results from conviction in adult cases, but it is held inconsistent with juvenile court philosophy and practice. It is explicitly prohibited in many state laws and in the *Standard Juvenile Court Act.*[107]

(9) *Terminology:* As a rule, the terminology used in connection with juvenile delinquency cases is another indication of the difference between juvenile court and adult criminal procedure. There

---

[106] Concerning pre-sentence investigations in adult cases, see Chapter X, pp. 371–375.

[107] Section 18.

is no "criminal" in the juvenile court, but a "delinquent" boy or girl; the child is not accused of the commission of a specific "crime," but is alleged to be a "delinquent child"; an arrest is usually called a "delinquent petition"; the word "defendant" is hardly ever used; there is no "trial," but a "hearing," no "sentence," but a "court disposition." There are no arraignments, indictments, or convictions. A child is not "found guilty," but is "adjudged to be delinquent" or in some jurisdictions made a "ward of the court."

(10) *Privacy of information and records:* Many state laws prescribe that juvenile court records shall be considered privileged information and may be disclosed only to persons having a legitimate interest. The purpose of such a provision is "to prevent the humiliation and demoralizing effect which follow upon publicity of children's cases, making it more difficult for the juvenile court to utilize the child's feeling of self-respect in effecting rehabilitation." [108] Since the social records of juvenile courts often contain highly confidential information regarding the attitudes and conduct of members of the family toward one another, the relationship between probation officers and parents and children would be greatly jeopardized if the probation officers could be compelled to produce these records and to testify in proceedings in other courts.

c. The Disposition

On the basis of the findings of the case investigation prior to the hearing and the facts disclosed and the impressions gained at the court hearing, the judge can make the following kinds of disposition: [109]

(1) The judge may place the child under supervision or (more formally) on probation in his own home or in the custody of a suitable person elsewhere, upon such conditions as the court shall determine. (See Appendix Cases No. 1, 3, 7, 15.) The whole subject of probation will be discussed in Chapter XI.

(2) The judge may commit the child to the custody or guardianship of a public or private institution or agency authorized to care

---

[108] See *Standard Juvenile Court Act*, Section 28, and comment, p. 34.

[109] The list of possible dispositions follows, in general, Section 18 of the *Standard Juvenile Court Act;* most of the existing juvenile court laws have similar provisions.

for children or to place them in family homes, or under the guardianship of a suitable person. In committing a child to a private institution or agency, the court shall select one that is approved by the state department or state board of welfare which supervises and

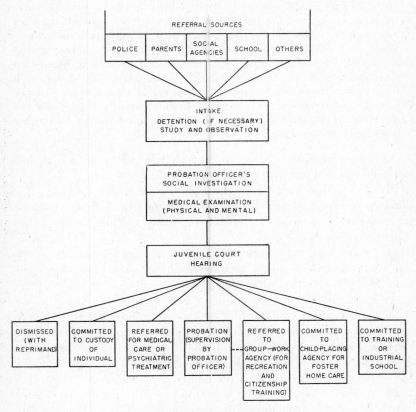

Standard Juvenile Court Procedure.

licenses private institutions and agencies. Mention should be made here of two provisions contained in the *Standard Juvenile Court Act* which are also found in many state laws:

In placing a child under the guardianship or custody of an individual or of a private agency or institution, the court shall whenever practicable select a person or an agency or institution governed by persons of the same religious faith as that of the parents of such child (Section 19).

Whenever a child is committed by the court to custody other than that of his parents, or is given medical, psychological or psychiatric treatment under order of the court, and no provision is otherwise made by law for the support of such child or payment for such treatment, compensation for the care and treatment of such child, when approved by order of the court, shall be a charge upon the county where such child has a legal settlement. The court may, after giving the parent a reasonable opportunity to be heard, order and decree that such parent shall pay in such manner as the court may direct, such sum, within his ability to pay, as will cover in whole or in part the support and treatment of such child. If such parent shall wilfully fail or refuse to pay such sum, the court may proceed against him as for contempt (Section 20).

All commitments shall be for an indeterminate period but shall not continue beyond the twenty-first birthday.[110]

(3) The judge may order the examination and treatment of a child by a physician, psychiatrist, or psychologist. For this purpose he may place the child in a hospital or other suitable facility. (See Appendix Case No. 3.)

(4) The judge may order such other care and treatment as the court may deem to be in the best interest of the child. (See Appendix Case No. 9.) This provision is purposely worded in a general form to give the court wide discretion in dealing with the child in any way that serves his welfare. For instance, the court has the right to continue or postpone a hearing in order to have more time for a thorough study and observation of the child; or, if the child has run away from his home county, the court can order the case to be transferred to the juvenile court of the child's residence. Numerous other kinds of dispositions might be warranted in individual cases.

(5) The judge may dismiss the petition if no further court action is necessary. Such an "adjustment" or "discharge" of a case usually occurs in situations that reveal only a technical violation of a law or municipal ordinance, but no real delinquency. Frequently, a reprimand by the judge is all that is required.

(6) The judge might order restitution or reparation of damages.

---

[110] For details concerning commitment, see Chapters XII and XIII, which are entirely devoted to that topic. See also Appendix Cases No. 2, 8, 10, 11, 15.

Several state laws specifically authorize this practice.[111] In other jurisdictions, where the law is silent on this matter, restitution is imposed as a condition of probation. The *Juvenile Court Standards* recommends that "restitution or reparation should be required only in cases where they seem to have disciplinary value or to instill respect for property rights." Especially when older children are involved, the order to pay restitution can have educational value, and parents should expect their children to earn something toward payment of restitution in a way suitable to their age.[112] Restitution should not be confused with the imposition of a fine. It is generally held that fines, which are a means of punishment, are inconsistent with the idea of juvenile court procedure. The *Juvenile Court Standards* recommends that "fines should never be imposed in children's cases."

The table on page 332 shows the proportion of the major types of dispositions as reported by 374 juvenile courts to the United States Children's Bureau for the year 1945.[113]

Most juvenile court laws recognize as a fundamental principle that adjudication in juvenile court does not constitute a conviction, that a child shall not be classified as a criminal, and that the disposition of a case or any evidence given in a juvenile court proceeding shall not be lawful evidence against the child in any civil, criminal, or other proceeding or court.[114] The *Standard Juvenile Court Act* (Section 18) adds that "the disposition made of a child or any evi-

---

[111] For details, see Lou, *op. cit.*, p. 66.

[112] Concerning the value of restitution in adult cases, see Irving E. Cohen, "The Integration of Restitution in the Probation Services," *Journal of Criminal Law and Criminology*, January–February 1944, pp. 315–321, and *Probation*, June 1944, pp. 147–153. Regarding the legal aspects involved in the matter of restitution in juvenile cases, see William B. Harris, "Struggle To Fix Liability in Juvenile Delinquency Cases," *Temple Law Quarterly*, January 1946, pp. 325–329.

[113] *Juvenile Court Statistics 1944–1945*, published as supplement to the November 1946 issue of *The Child*, monthly publication of the United States Children's Bureau.

[114] See Lou, *op. cit.*, pp. 141–142, who quotes a case decision that upheld the principle of inadmissibility of evidence secured in juvenile court in a trial before a criminal court. See also *Juvenile Court Standards*, p. 1; *Standard Juvenile Court Act*, Section 18; *Report No. 3*, on juvenile court laws, of the National Conference, p. 6.

JUVENILE DELINQUENCY CASES, 1945: DISPOSITIONS OF BOYS' AND GIRLS' CASES, DISPOSED OF BY 374 COURTS

Disposition of Case	Juvenile Delinquency Cases					
	Number			Per cent		
	Total	Boys	Girls	Total	Boys	Girls
	122,851	101,240	21,611			
Disposition reported	114,887	95,027	19,860	100	100	100
Case dismissed, adjusted, or held open without further action	49,040	42,184	6,856	43	45	35
Child supervised by probation officer	34,981	28,829	6,152	30	30	31
Child committed or referred to an institution	10,101	7,748	2,353	9	8	12
State institution for delinquent children	5,789	4,640	1,149	5	5	6
Other institution for delinquent children	3,157	2,346	811	3	2	4
Penal institution	222	206	16		1	
Other institution	933	556	377	1	1	2
Child committed or referred to an agency or individual	5,400	3,546	1,854	5	4	9
Public department	1,751	1,183	568	2	1	3
Other agency or individual	3,649	2,363	1,286	3	3	6
Other disposition of case	15,365	12,720	2,645	13	13	13
Disposition not reported	7,964	6,213	1,751			

332

dence given in the court shall not operate to disqualify the child in any future civil service application or appointment." This is a very good proposal but is still far from realization. It should be included in the state juvenile court laws and—more important—should be implemented in the practices of the state and Federal governments, particularly in the armed services.

d. Modification of Dispositions and the Right To Appeal

In accordance with the general principle of juvenile court procedure, the disposition of a case is not a final decree as is the sentence in adult cases, which, as a rule, can be changed only by a decision of an appellate court. Juvenile court decisions are largely guided by the physical and mental condition of the child and the circumstances of the family and home environment; in other words, by factors subject to more or less frequent changes. Orders of the juvenile court, therefore, must be flexible, and many laws provide for modification of juvenile court dispositions. Such petitions to amend or change a previous court decision may be filed by parents or guardians, by the probation officer or the district attorney, by a child-placing institution or agency, by the court itself, or by any other interested person.

The right to appeal against decisions of the juvenile court is mentioned in several laws. In other states it is assumed to exist just as in all other cases heard by the court exercising juvenile jurisdiction. According to a number of state laws, an appeal against juvenile court decrees is allowed only on questions of law, or only if errors of fact or of law are alleged, or only from judgments removing a child from the custody of his parent or committing him to an institution. In some jurisdictions a rehearing or review by the juvenile court upon demand by parents or guardians within a specified time must precede the filing of an appeal.[115] The court to which an appeal is to be taken is either mentioned in the juvenile court law of the state or, if not specifically mentioned, is that appellate court which, in general, hears appeals against decisions of the court having juvenile jurisdiction.

It might be doubted whether the right of appeal with its strong

---

[115] For details regarding appeals, see Cosulich, *op. cit.*, pp. 76–78; see also *Standard Juvenile Court Act*, Section 29.

emphasis on legal matters fits into the whole picture of non-criminal, non-legalistic, non-formal juvenile court procedure. There is, however, no question that juvenile court decisions often consist of rather severe curtailments of individual prerogatives, particularly parental rights. Lou, in weighing these aspects of the problem, declares himself in favor of the right to appeal, and summarizes his opinion as follows:

> Unquestionably the right of appeal is open to objection, but there is more objection to the arbitrary action of a judge not subject to review by appellate courts. The right of appeal is not only in the interest of the child and the parent, but it makes for greater care and more sympathetic consideration of the case on the part of the judge. It should be permitted in all cases in which the custody of the child is actually disturbed, at least on the question of law. When an appeal is taken, it should not operate to suspend the order of the juvenile court. If the order is affirmed or modified, the child should remain under the jurisdiction of the juvenile court, as if no appeal had been taken.[116]

4. THE PLACE OF THE JUVENILE COURT IN THE TOTAL CHILD AND FAMILY WELFARE FIELD

a. Cooperation with Other Agencies

The juvenile court is dependent, in the proper discharge of its function, upon the existence and activities of a great number of other agencies in the community. They (1) determine the court's intake, (2) help the court in its preparation of cases for the court hearing, and (3) serve the court after the case disposition.

(1) The referrals to the court, as outlined in Chapter VIII, might come from the police, the school (teachers, principals, counselors, attendance officers, school nurses), public and private child welfare agencies, family welfare agencies, health agencies, or other such sources.[117]

(2) The probation officer who prepares the case for the court hearing calls upon all agencies reported to him by the Social Service Exchange [118] as having had contact with the family and the child, in

---

[116] *Op. cit.,* p. 141.

[117] See Chapter VIII, p. 218. Referrals by parents are not mentioned here because the present discussion concerns itself only with community agencies.

[118] See Chapter VIII, p. 267.

order to secure all available information. He might also consult with these agencies concerning the most suitable case disposition to be recommended to the judge.

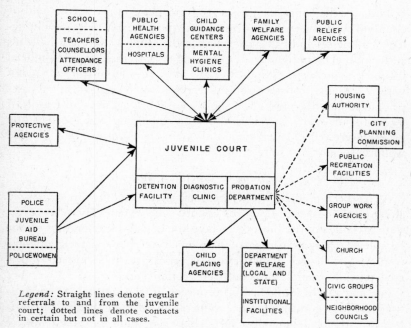

Legend: Straight lines denote regular referrals to and from the juvenile court; dotted lines denote contacts in certain but not in all cases.

The Juvenile Court in Its Relationship with Other Community Agencies.

(3) Probation as well as commitment rely very heavily upon the availability of proper agencies and institutions. Probation, as will be seen in Chapter XI, needs the help of educational, character-building, recreational, and counseling agencies in order to make it more than purely perfunctory supervision and in order to provide constructive guidance. Placement, whether in foster homes or in institutions, presupposes the accessibility of these community resources operated on a local or state, public or private level. (See Appendix Cases No. 1, 2, 3, 7, 8, 9, 10, 11, 15.)

Rightly therefore, does the *Standard Juvenile Court Act* include a special provision, entitled "Co-operation" (Section 30):

It is hereby made the duty of every public official or department to render all assistance and co-operation within his or its jurisdictional

power which may further the objects of this act. The court is authorized to seek the co-operation of all societies or organizations having
for their object the protection or aid of children.

The juvenile court occupies a strategic place in the whole field of
community agencies. From this vantage point it can most clearly detect weaknesses and gaps in services in the child welfare area. It thus
adds another function to its many-sided activities. It is a judicial
tribunal, constituted as such by law; it is an administrative agency
with a staff of probation officers engaged in investigation of cases
prior to court hearing; it is a social case-work agency by reason of
its probation work; and it is also a co-ordinating and social action
group interested in an efficient and comprehensive program of child
welfare, locally and state-wide.[119]

b. State Functions in Juvenile Court Activities

As has been pointed out before, most juvenile courts are organized
along local lines based upon the county-unit system. There are a few
state juvenile courts. But even where the courts are operating on the
local level, the state can participate in several ways in their administration. The degree of participation varies greatly from state-oper-
ated juvenile courts and youth correction authorities [120] to a very
vague and rarely implemented provision in the statutes or administrative codes concerning the cooperation of state welfare departments with local juvenile courts. Between these extremes, diverse
forms of state responsibility for juvenile courts are in use. In some
states, independent state boards or commissions of probation, in
others probation divisions of state welfare or correction departments,
have supervision over all probation officers in the various local courts
for both juvenile and adult cases. Such agencies prescribe the qualifications for, and establish, by competitive examinations, lists of persons
eligible for appointment as probation officers by the local courts. In
some instances, the appointment of probation officers is placed in the
hands of such a state agency. In several states, forms of records and
methods of procedure are prescribed uniformly by the state agency

---

[119] For more details on social action, see Chapter XVI; see also Judge Gustav
Schramm, "Philosophy of the Juvenile Court," *The Annals,* January 1949, p.
104.

[120] See Chapter X, pp. 354–371.

for all local juvenile courts; regular reporting by the probation officer on his case load to the centralized agency is required. Many state departments of welfare are requested by law to provide a service of consultation and assistance to local juvenile courts. This assistance might take the form of promoting good standards and of stimulating the development of the courts and probation services. [121]

In spite of well-intentioned legislation providing for state participation in local juvenile court administration, lack of funds and adequate personnel has often made it impossible for state agencies to carry out their assigned duties and responsibilities. Two developments have given impetus to an increased concern of state agencies for juvenile court problems; both originated on the Federal level.

First, the rural child welfare units that were established pursuant to the Social Security Act of 1935 and that provide services for the "protection and care of homeless, dependent and neglected children, and children in danger of becoming delinquent" are administered through state welfare departments or boards. This program naturally has stimulated the interest of these state agencies in local juvenile court administration.

Second, on January 1, 1946, the United States Children's Bureau discontinued its former policy of collecting juvenile court statistics from the hundreds of individual juvenile courts; it now secures these data on a uniform basis from the state welfare departments or similar state agencies. These state agencies therefore are responsible for the assembling of the statistical material from the local courts. Consequently, a state-wide uniform procedure of compiling and reporting statistical data is required.[122]

In addition to these forms of direct relationship between state administration and local juvenile courts, a broader conception of state responsibility in the field of child welfare is presented in the report on juvenile court administration of the National Conference:

---

[121] For further details, state by state, see Cosulich, *op. cit.*, pp. 101–107; for state participation, see Chapter XI, pp. 395–396.

[122] For details, see Edward Schwartz, "Statistics of Juvenile Delinquency in the United States," *The Annals*, January 1949, p. 18, and "Community Experiment in Delinquency Measurement," *Yearbook*, N.P.P.A., 1945, pp. 158–159. For an example of a state-wide reporting system that has been operative for several years, see David G. French, "Michigan's Juvenile Court Reporting System," *Probation*, April 1946, pp. 111–118.

Juvenile courts and probation services are severely handicapped in meeting children's needs and difficulties if the State fails to maintain adequate training schools for boys and girls whose behavior problems require group care, to provide appropriate care and service for children whose difficulties are due primarily to mental and physical handicaps, and to promote the development in local communities of basic social services for children and their families that help to prevent the development of serious problems of neglect and delinquency. All State agencies, therefore, that have responsibilities with respect to children should unite in a State-wide program to promote the well-being of the children of the State and especially of those with special needs.[123]

c. Attempts To Curtail the Juvenile Court's Functions

Practically all measures of social reform, even after they had been working successfully for many years and had received wide acclaim, have from time to time been subject to attack. But, since the general principle of these reforms usually is too deeply imbedded in the public opinion, the attacks often take the form of attempts to narrow and diminish the scope of the reform measures. The juvenile court movement has been no exception.

Attempts to curtail the functions of the juvenile court have been made by means of legislation or court decisions. Restrictive legislation is usually proposed by persons who consider the progressive methods of juvenile court procedure as a scheme of "coddling" youthful offenders. They try to arouse public support by labeling juvenile delinquents as incipient criminals. Bills have been introduced in some legislatures reducing the maximum juvenile court age, but they have in most instances been defeated. Other bills have tried to make inroads into the juvenile court's exclusive jurisdiction, either from a certain age on or for certain types of offenses. Unfortunately, these "compromises" are not uncommon features of some juvenile court laws, as has been pointed out.[124]

A characteristic example of such assaults was the concerted drive in Chicago, birthplace of the juvenile court, in 1935, to amend the juvenile court act so that all children above ten years of age charged with felonies would be tried in adult criminal courts. As Barnes and Teeters report,

---

[123] *Report No. 4*, pp. 10–11.
[124] See Chapter IX, p. 305.

This was defeated, but in a noteworthy case of a fifteen-year old girl charged with murder, the Supreme Court of that state offered an amazing decision, a part of which stated:

"It was not intended by the legislature that the juvenile court should be made a haven of refuge where a delinquent child of the age recognized by law as capable of committing a crime should be immune from punishment for violation of the criminal laws of the state, committed by such child subsequent to his or her being declared a delinquent child." [125]

Federal Judge William H. Holly characterized this Supreme Court decision as follows:

The Supreme Court of the state in the case of the People v. Susie Lattimore decided that the Juvenile Court of Cook County has no legal status—that it existed merely by license of the Criminal Court of Cook County, and that only the Criminal Court had jurisdiction of children over 10 years of age who were charged with crime. The theory accepted for decades, and made the basis of juvenile court jurisdiction, that the state stands in the relation of parent to every child and that it is the duty of the state to protect its children even against their own evil tendencies, was made a nullity by the stroke of a pen.[126]

Other attacks have been leveled against the juvenile court by newspapers. Such attacks are likely to occur whenever a particularly sensational crime has been committed by a youthful offender or when reports on actual or alleged increases in juvenile delinquency rates have been published.[127] The Chicago *Tribune*, for instance, in a leading editorial in May 1939, said among other things:

The criminal court should assert its constitutional jurisdiction over young offenders. The function of that court is to punish offenses against the law. The juvenile court does not inflict punishment. The present maximum age for juvenile delinquents is too high.[128]

[125] *New Horizons in Criminology*, Prentice-Hall, 1943, p. 929.

[126] Foreword to *Detention and Prosecution of Children*, published by John Howard Association (formerly Central Howard Association), Chicago, 1946, p. vii. See also *Fiftieth Anniversary Report*, Juvenile Court of Cook County, Chicago, 1949, pp. 23–24 and 118–119, where a later decision of the Illinois Supreme Court is cited which seems to modify the earlier decision.

[127] For further details on the role of the press, see Chapter VI, pp. 172–177, and Chapter XVII, pp. 679–682.

[128] Quoted by Judge Atwell Westwick, Juvenile Court of Santa Barbara, California, in "Wider Jurisdiction for the Juvenile Court," *Yearbook*, N.P.P.A., 1939, p. 190.

Definite attempts at curtailment of the juvenile court's function have also been made by practitioners in the field of education and social work. We have previously pointed out that much of the juvenile court work is administrative and not judicial in character. Consequently, as early as 1912, it was proposed to incorporate the juvenile court's functions in the public school system.[129] In more recent years, particularly since the adoption of the Federal Social Security Act, the local or state public welfare agency has been held up as the proper office to take over a considerable share of the juvenile court's function. It is only natural that leading personalities in the United States Children's Bureau, which on the Federal level administers the child welfare program under the Social Security Act, have spearheaded such a proposal.[130]

Apparently the main portion of the juvenile court's jurisdiction that the public welfare agency is supposed to take over lies in the field of child dependency and neglect; such attempts are not of primary interest here, since they do not touch upon the activities of the juvenile court in the delinquency area. However, as has been stated before, dependency and delinquency cases frequently overlap.

Furthermore, it seems that the current attack against the juvenile court is more fundamental in nature, as is evidenced by the following statement of Alice Scott Nutt, Director of Special Services, United States Children's Bureau:

> We see the juvenile court exercising functions primarily judicial and law enforcement in nature. These include making decisions affecting the legal status of a child, as in guardianship, adoption, and granting of custody; decisions in controversies regarding custody, and decisions affecting or intervening in parental rights when the child's behavior, or the conditions or circumstances under which he lives appear to be such that organized society as represented by the court has to step in. . . . We see the public welfare agency exercising functions primarily administrative in nature. This means providing social services for children, who by reason of personality problems or the circumstances under which they live, need help in order to develop into well-adjusted adults. Specifically, it includes making social studies, planning for the

---

129 For details, see Lou, *op. cit.*, pp. 212–213.

130 See Elsa Castendyck, "Juvenile Courts in the Light of the White House Conference," in *Yearbook*, N.P.P.A., 1940, pp. 34–46; Alice Scott Nutt, "Juvenile Court Function," *ibid.*, 1942, pp. 94–101.

care of children, and carrying on treatment; placing children in foster family care and for adoption; developing resources for care and treatment, administering group care facilities, and furnishing leadership in community organization for child welfare.[131]

This division of responsibilities might sound reasonable, but it can easily be used as an entering wedge into other services, especially supervision on probation, that have heretofore been considered an indigenous function of the juvenile court. Miss Nutt continues:

> In the future the court may have caseworkers on its staff to handle intake and to make social investigations, which may be regarded as part of the judicial process prior to court disposition, but may turn over the job of treatment to administrative social agencies. Under such a division of work children needing casework treatment in their own or other family homes would be referred by the court to such agencies just as children needing group care in a controlled environment now are committed by it to institutions.[132]

This thesis was expressed even more bluntly in another publication of the Children's Bureau:

> Gradually the belief is being accepted that the juvenile court should deal only with cases of delinquency in which it is necessary to take the custody of the child temporarily from his parents, to settle a controversy, or to exercise court authority in dealing with the child's behavior.[133]

The attack is clearly directed against the juvenile court for embracing administrative (in addition to judicial) functions and for engaging in social treatment. The aim is to relegate the juvenile court's function to matters of adjudication only, not merely regarding cases of dependency and neglect but also in delinquency situations.[134]

---

[131] "The Responsibility of the Juvenile Court and the Public Welfare Agency," *Yearbook*, N.P.P.A., 1947, pp. 206–223 (quotation on p. 213).

[132] *Ibid.*, p. 219.

[133] "Controlling Juvenile Delinquency," United States Children's Bureau Publication No. 301, 1943, p. 21; see also Warrington Stokes, "Social Worker Plays Part in Court Process," *The Child*, December 1947, pp. 89–92.

[134] For the judicial aspects of this problem, see Roscoe Pound, "The Juvenile Court and the Law," *Yearbook*, N.P.P.A., 1944, pp. 14–15; and Gustav Schramm, "Philosophy of the Juvenile Court," *The Annals*, January 1949, p. 102, and "The Juvenile Court Idea," *Federal Probation*, September 1949, p. 21.

The fact that the juvenile court carries out administrative functions, primarily through its probation officers in the field of social investigation and supervision, cannot be cited as valid reason for criticism. In the United States, the differentiation between judicial and administrative functions is not sharply drawn, and it is by no means uncommon to confer administrative powers upon the courts.[135]

The treatment function of the juvenile court, through the means of probation [136] based on case work principles, requires the authority of the court, and no other agency has that authority. The constructive use of authority in the social treatment process is today more and more recognized by practitioners in the social work and educational field after the pendulum in previous years had swung too far in the direction of damning, without qualification, the use of authoritarian methods.

d. Evaluation of the Juvenile Court

What, then, is the picture of the juvenile court situation in our land today? Can we truthfully claim that the juvenile court, as established and operating throughout the United States, is everywhere doing a perfect job? Unfortunately, it is not. Many juvenile courts are still juvenile courts in name only; they are permeated by the philosophy of criminal law and criminal prosecution; they lack adequate staffs, decent detention quarters, study and classification centers, and diversified placement facilities; they are handicapped by meager financial appropriations, causing excessive case loads and the appointment of unqualified personnel.

Such criticism and evaluation is needed, but it is worthless if it does not lead to improvement. A well-functioning juvenile court system living up to generally recognized but frequently unrealized standards would be the best defense against attacks. The National Probation and Parole Association has summarized the standards for a progressive juvenile court in the following manner:

---

[135] Some courts, for instance, possess the right to appoint members of boards of trustees of institutions or of other governing commissions or administrative bodies; also, the granting of citizenship through naturalization, which in itself is a purely administrative act, falls within the jurisdiction of the Federal courts.

[136] See Chapter XI.

(1) Exclusive jurisdiction over children; jurisdiction over adults in children's cases.

(2) A judge chosen for his sympathetic understanding of children and parents.

(3) Private friendly court hearings; informal non-criminal procedure.

(4) A sufficient number of professionally trained probation workers, both men and women.

(5) Facilities for physical examinations and for psychiatric study of problem children.

(6) A well equipped detention home or selected boarding homes for temporary care of children.

(7) An efficient record and statistical system; adequate clerical help.

(8) Co-operation with other agencies; community support through interpretation to the public.

Has the juvenile court so far been a success? Numerous statistics have been compiled, particularly on recidivism, to prove the success or failure of the juvenile court's work. But the data assembled from local juvenile courts have varied so widely that they must be considered inconclusive. The question is largely one of comparison.[137] The juvenile court has been recognized as a great step forward from the conventional criminal court. As Dr. William Healy writes in an article commemorating the fiftieth anniversary of the juvenile court movement, "The great achievement of the juvenile court so far has been, to my mind, the founding of a social institution which respects the dignity and potentialities of children and adolescents. . . . From the standpoint of progress in civilization, it represents justice for youth." [138]

The best proof that, on the whole, the juvenile court's operation and effect have measured up to the expectations of its original and contemporary protagonists can be found in the spreading of the underlying principle of juvenile court philosophy and practice. Examples of such an extension beyond the original scope of the juvenile court will be discussed in the following chapter.

---

[137] See Sutherland, *op. cit.*, p. 317; see also Emma Octavia Lundberg, *op. cit.*, p. 328.

[138] "Thoughts About Juvenile Courts," *Federal Probation*, September 1949, pp. 16–19 (quotation on p. 19).

Chapter X

EXPANSION OF THE JUVENILE COURT IDEA

EVIDENCE of the extension of the juvenile court idea beyond its original scope has been apparent in four specific developments: (1) the establishment of adolescents' courts; (2) the creation of the Youth Correction Authority and similar agencies; (3) the influence of certain juvenile court methods upon procedure in general criminal courts; (4) the idea and practice of the Family Court.

1. ADOLESCENTS' COURTS

In an earlier context,[1] the following example of extension of juvenile court jurisdiction beyond the maximum age limit as set by state legislation was described: In many states the juvenile court retains jurisdiction over a juvenile on probation or in an institution, even after he has passed the maximum age limit (in most states, the eighteenth birthday), provided that the delinquent act was committed before that date. Such retention of jurisdiction, however, is usually terminated by the commitment of a new offense; otherwise it ceases at the age of majority.

Another example of this kind is found in a few state laws that confer upon the juvenile court concurrent jurisdiction with the ordinary criminal courts, either in all cases or only in cases concerning specified offenses committed by youngsters above juvenile court age but below the age of twenty-one. The decision as to which of the courts having concurrent jurisdiction shall exercise its function in a given case might be left to the district attorney or it might be made by the judges of either court, who often sit in both courts anyway.

In New York State, for instance, minors between sixteen and nineteen years of age, who have committed a crime not punishable by death or life imprisonment, may be adjudged *youthful offenders*

---

[1] See Chapter IX, pp. 311–313.

344

in the court of general criminal jurisdiction following an investigation and examination to which the defendant has given his consent. The determination of a minor as a *youthful offender* carries with it the application of a number of principles of juvenile court practice even though the ordinary criminal court is exercising jurisdiction—*viz.*, the *youthful offender* may be placed on probation; he may be committed to a religious, charitable, or other public or private reformative institution; the records of a youthful offender shall not be open to public inspection; and he shall not suffer any loss of civil rights or be denominated a criminal.[2]

This development, however, was preceded by the establishment of special courts for adolescents in the three largest cities of the country.

The Wayward Minors' Act of New York State of 1923 (later amended several times) provides that a person between the ages of sixteen and twenty-one, who is habitually addicted to the use of liquor or drugs, who habitually associates with undesirable persons, who is found in a house of prostitution, who is wilfully disobedient to the reasonable and lawful commands of parent or guardian, or who is morally depraved or in danger of becoming morally depraved, may be deemed a *wayward minor*. This act was passed for the purpose of helping parents to handle incorrigible children who had passed the upper age limit of juvenile court jurisdiction of that state. However, in order to protect older children against parents

---

[2] See Youthful Offender Law of the State of New York (Laws of 1943, Chapter 549). (Text is reprinted in Paul W. Tappan, *Delinquent Girls in Court,* Columbia University Press, 1947, pp. 235–237). Enactment of this act fell short, however, of recommendations aiming at the creation of a more unified court system for New York City and the larger communities throughout the state. Such proposals were contained in a report by a specially appointed committee to the New York State Legislature. The findings and legislative suggestions of this group are published in "Young People in the Courts of New York State," (Legislative Document No. 55), Albany, 1942. A model act for the establishment of a Youth Court with special personnel and limited jurisdiction was prepared by the American Law Institute in 1940, as a companion piece to the Youth Correction Authority Act. (The latter will be discussed in detail later in this chapter.) Valuable information on the operation of the Youthful Offender Law and statistical data for the years 1943–1947 are found in Elmer R. Reeves, "Youthful Offender Law in New York Shows Positive Results in Operation," *The Welfare Reporter* (New Jersey Department of Institutions and Agencies), June 1949, pp. 16–18.

who might call for the invocation of this law on a slight pretext, it is required that the charge must be "established upon competent evidence at a hearing." Jurisdiction over these cases is conferred upon the children's courts (as the juvenile courts in New York State are called) and all criminal courts.

Under this act, an Adolescents' Court was established in Brooklyn in 1935 as part of the City Magistrates' Court in order to deal with boys between sixteen and nineteen years of age. Its scope of jurisdiction, however, transcends the types of offenses enumerated in the Wayward Minors' Act. The procedure in this court was described in its annual report for 1939 by Patrick J. Shelly, then Chief Probation Officer of the Magistrates' Courts of New York City, as follows: [3]

> All adolescent offenders charged with felonies or serious misdemeanors are brought to the Adolescents' Court instead of to the Felony Court. They, therefore, have no contact with hardened or older offenders arraigned every day in the latter court.
>
> Hearings in the Adolescents' Court are conducted in chambers. They are not open to the public and in this way there is no danger of harmful publicity to those youthful offenders and their families.
>
> The arresting officer, the mother or father of the boy, the liaison (probation) officer, an assistant district attorney, witnesses, if any, and the presiding judge, are the only ones present at the time of the boy's arraignment.
>
> If the boy admits his guilt or the Magistrate believes him guilty after a hearing, the case is discussed with the assistant district attorney and the probation officer who has already interviewed the boy.
>
> If the facts warrant it, a wayward minor offense is substituted for the felony or misdemeanor charge. The stigma of the serious offense is thereby taken from the shoulders of a boy whose future is in the making.
>
> A thorough investigation by the probation department follows, which conforms to the standard method of making a complete preliminary social investigation.

---

[3] "Socio-Legal Treatment of the Youthful Offender, A Statistical and Factual Analysis of the Work of the Adolescents' Court," Brooklyn, 1939 (mimeographed); see also "The Forgotten Adolescent," study by the New York Law Society, 1940; "The Adolescent's Court Problem," Society for the Prevention of Crime, New York, 1941; Jeanette G. Brill and E. George Payne, *The Adolescent Court and Crime Prevention*, Pitman, New York, 1938; Paul Blanshard and Edwin J. Lukas, "Probation and Psychiatric Care for Adolescent Offenders," Society for the Prevention of Crime, New York, 1942.

This investigation includes, when necessary, a psychiatric examination in the Mental Hygiene Clinic of Kings County Hospital.

The boy is then almost invariably paroled to his parents. He is, therefore, saved from the disgrace and the harmful effects of contacts with prisons and prisoners.

A priest representing the Catholic Charities of Brooklyn, visits the court on two days each week. Problems affecting the boy's religious duties or the neglect of them are discussed and followed up. Representatives of the Jewish Board of Guardians, the Protestant Big Brothers, and the Urban League also attend sessions of the court and confer with the probation officers at stated times.

Three judges preside in the Adolescents' Court for periods of two weeks in rotation. This makes for uniformity and the closest co-operation with the probation department.

There is no mass reporting. Each officer follows a schedule which permits him to be in his office for sufficiently long periods each week to receive reports from his charges in private. This individualized approach is utilized to the fullest to give the probationer every opportunity to tell his own story in his own way. Mutual understanding and co-operation generally follows. It gives the officer a much needed opportunity to interpret the boy's situation to him, thus enhancing the probability of a change for the better in his future behavior.

Another Adolescents' Court in New York City was created in 1936 as part of the Felony Court of the Borough of Queens. Although both courts—in Queens and in Brooklyn—serve essentially the same purpose, particularly to prevent the contamination of adolescent delinquents by adult offenders and to eliminate the stigma associated with the term "felon," there are some differences of procedure. For instance, the Queens Court meets only once each week, whereas the Brooklyn Court is in session daily; the Queens Court does not adjudge a boy a *wayward minor* until after a thorough investigation by the probation staff, whereas the Brooklyn Court may do so before the investigation; the Queens Court does not take sworn testimony on the original criminal charge, but the Brooklyn Court does.[4]

More recently, the General Sessions Court of Manhattan has be-

---

[4] In 1948, the Brooklyn Adolescents' Court handled 2,265 cases; the Queens Adolescents' Court handled 663 cases. (See Annual Report of the City Magistrates' Courts, New York City, 1948, p. 9.)

gun to apply the *wayward minor* technique in its own way to boys of the same ages as those in the Brooklyn and Queens courts treated above. Like the Queens Court, it adjudges the boy a wayward minor after the investigation.

The Wayward Minors' Court of New York City, with city-wide jurisdiction over girls sixteen to twenty-one years of age, which was first established as part of the Women's Court, has since 1945 functioned independently. It is officially known as "Girls' Term." Its jurisdiction, in distinction from the practice in boys' cases before the Adolescents' Court, encompasses only those types of offenses that are listed in the previously quoted Wayward Minors' Act. Here, in brief, is the procedure of this court:

> A parent, guardian, next of kin, a peace officer, or the duly authorized representative of an agency, may make a charge against a girl of being a wayward minor. After the complaint has been signed, a summons may be issued and given to the complainant to serve (with the assistance of the officer on post if necessary). When the defendant refuses to answer a summons (or if there is reason to feel that a summons will be ignored) a warrant may be issued. Warrants issued in the Wayward Minors' Court are generally executed by a policewoman attached to the Juvenile Aid Bureau. If possible, the warrant is used as an "instrument of persuasion"; and if the girl willingly accompanies the policewoman to the court or to the Florence Crittenton League, she is not "arrested" and "booked" in the station house. The warrant is subsequently vacated. Upon arraignment, as in any other adult charge, the defendant shall be advised of her rights, informed of the charge against her, and given a choice as to whether she wishes to proceed at once to a hearing, or whether she wishes an adjournment. A defendant cannot plead "guilty" to the charge, but the charge must be established upon competent hearing, i.e., presentation of evidence by credible witnesses. After such a hearing, the defendant may or may not be "adjudged" a wayward minor. Defendants are not "guilty," they are "adjudged"; and there are no "convictions," but rather "adjudications" in the Wayward Minors' Court. Girls so adjudged are not fingerprinted and there is no "record" against them. Upon adjudication a wayward minor may be placed on probation for an indeterminate period of time (not to exceed two years) or may be committed to an institution "duly authorized by law to receive such commitments." [5]

---

[5] Excerpt from "The Wayward Minors' Court," issued by the Probation Bureau, City Magistrates' Courts, New York City, 1939 (mimeographed).

Paul W. Tappan, professor at New York University, has published an analytical study of this court. He particularly praises the court for having developed a flexibility in the direction of individualization. He deplores the failure of the public to provide the court with the needed treatment facilities; for this, he also blames the narrowness of the Wayward Minor statute.[6]

To remedy this situation, the New York City Youth Board has established a permanent psychiatric clinic for youths between the ages of sixteen and twenty-one coming before the Magistrates' Courts. This clinic, which is an integral part of the court, includes in its program diagnosis as well as treatment of those referred by the court, either before judicial disposition or afterwards, during the probation period.[7]

A great step forward was the establishment of the New York State Reception Center, occupying one unit of the Elmira Reformatory, in 1945. It came into being as a result of recommendations of an interdepartmental committee on delinquency appointed by Governor Dewey. All convicted offenders sixteen to twenty-one years of age, including those adjudged *wayward minors* and *youthful offenders*, who in the opinion of the judges should be sent to a state institution must now be committed to this Reception Center. The court, in other words, can no longer commit an offender of this age group directly to a specific institution. It can, however, fix the term of imprisonment or can pronounce sentence of imprisonment for an indefinite term, according to the criminal statute of the state, but the particular institution where the offender will serve this term is determined by the findings of the study at the Reception Center.

This procedure represents—within the framework of the existing penal law—the application of the principle of individualization of justice, as developed in the juvenile court, to the older age group. A short summary of the advantages of this Center, therefore, seems justified in this context. It provides careful study of offenders upon admission by a competent professional staff, resulting in the individual's transfer to the institution that appears best suited. It makes

---

[6] For further details, see Paul W. Tappan, *Delinquent Girls in Court* (a study of the Wayward Minor Court of New York City), Columbia University Press, 1947; especially pp. 177–178.

[7] *Focus*, July 1949, p. 121.

possible treatment of the inmate at the institution to which he is finally sent, based upon the study at the Reception Center, and thus relieves the institution from a considerable amount of initial classification work. It provides a sound orientation program for all inmates designed to facilitate adjustment to institutional life at the earliest and most critical time. Studies undertaken at the Reception Center of hundreds of inmates enable the staff to discover unmet needs in the types of correctional services throughout the state, and to contribute greatly to the development of research concerning the causes and treatment of delinquency.

Since the start of operation of the Reception Center on November 1, 1945, through January 31, 1948, 2,662 young men were intensively studied at the Center and transferred to other institutions.[8] The average time spent at the Center was 75 days.

Chicago, the birthplace of the juvenile court, also pioneered in the setting up of special judicial facilities for the handling of adolescents apart from older offenders. In 1914, the Boys' Court was created as one of the specialized branches of the Municipal Court of Chicago. The Boys' Court deals with misdemeanors and quasi-criminal offenses involving boys from the ages of seventeen to twenty-one, but, unlike other similar courts, it has no power to deal with such matters as waywardness, incorrigibility, or association with undesirable persons. The Boys' Court also conducts preliminary examination in cases of felony committed by boys in this age range, holding them for action by the grand jury and possible trial by the criminal court of Cook County.[9] Case investigations and examinations by the Social Service Department and the Psychiatric Institute,[10] both adjuncts of the Municipal Court of Chicago, are typical features of the socialized procedure employed by the Boys' Court. This court has developed a very close and continuing co-operation with four different agencies: the Holy Name Society, the Chicago

---

[8] For further details, see Glenn M. Kendall (director of the Reception Center), "The New York State Reception Center," *Federal Probation*, September 1948, pp. 42–47; much of the above information has been obtained from this article.

[9] For details, see Grace Abbott, *The Child and the State*, University of Chicago Press, 1938, Vol. II, pp. 424–428.

[10] See "A Dynamic Era of Court Psychiatry 1914–1944," edited by Agnes A. Sharp, The Psychiatric Institute of the Municipal Court of Chicago.

Church Federation,[11] the Jewish Social Service Bureau and the Colored Big Brothers Association. According to Judge J. M. Braude, of the Municipal Court of Chicago, a youthful offender—instead of being officially placed on probation—is often referred to one of these organizations for supervision.

Each of these has developed its own special techniques. All the court asks is that these techniques be used to the best possible advantage with respect to the particular defendants assigned for supervision to their respective care. If after the period of supervision the supervisory agency reports that the defendant has made an apparent adjustment and is ready for ultimate discharge, the defendant is then officially discharged on the court records and to all intents and purposes there is no criminal record against him. This system is its own reward and works at least fairly satisfactorily as attested by the fact that of all first offenders given a chance in this manner, 72 percent do not come back while they are still of Boys' Court age, and, of the 28 percent that do return, a good many come back charged with minor or insignificant offenses.[12]

Shortly after the Chicago Boys' Court was established, a similar step was taken in Philadelphia. In 1915, the Municipal Court, created two years before and invested with broad jurisdiction in civil, criminal, domestic relations, and juvenile matters, was given additional exclusive jurisdiction over minors above juvenile court age. The new branches of this court, which took the names Boys' and Men's Misdemeanants' Division and Girls' and Women's Misdemeanants' Division, assumed jurisdiction in cases of minors between the ages of sixteen (the upper juvenile court age limit at that time) and twenty-one "who shall disobey their parents' command or be found idle in the streets" or are deemed "disorderly." The law defined disorderly children as those "deserting their home without good or sufficient cause, or keeping company with dissolute or vicious persons against their parents' command." Social investigation, similar to the practice employed in the juvenile court, precedes and largely

---

[11] According to the annual report of this organization for 1948 (mimeographed, p. 9) its program "is committed to the concept that the Church and religion have a positive role to play in the community in sponsoring and carrying forward a program focused upon the giving of professional case work services to emotionally disturbed boys between the ages of 17 and 21 years."

[12] Judge J. M. Braude, "Boys' Court: Individualized Justice for the Youthful Offender," *Federal Probation*, June 1948, pp. 9–14 (quotation on p. 12).

guides the disposition of these cases; physical and mental examinations are given before the court hearing; probation is frequently used and medical treatment is prescribed and carried out whenever needed. Community agencies are called upon to assist.[13]

All these adolescents' or youth courts appear to be a rather half-hearted answer to the demand put forward by some reformers to raise the juvenile court age generally to twenty-one. A considerable controversy exists regarding this issue. Proponents of a higher juvenile court age point to the inconsistency of the law, which holds an adolescent who is past the upper juvenile court age of his state fully responsible in criminal matters like an adult, whereas since early days, the civil law has not considered a person under twenty-one as possessing that degree of maturity which enables him to take his place as a member of society fully responsible for all his acts. Nor do the constitutions of our states, with the sole exception of Georgia, grant minors the right to vote. From a psychological viewpoint, it is pointed out that the youngster during the period of adolescence, which often extends to the age of twenty, is faced with at least as many, if not more, bewildering problems as is the so-called "juvenile," [14] and that the emotionally disturbed adolescent who gets into conflict with the law requires the guidance of social worker and psychiatrist at least to the same degree as his younger brothers and sisters who are covered by juvenile court jurisdiction.

---

[13] These misdemeanants' divisions of the Municipal Court of Philadelphia also have exclusive jurisdiction over disorderly streetwalkers, irrespective of age. Owing to the provision of social investigation and medical examination by the court, it has become the practice of the police to refer to the misdemeanants' divisions many defendants whose offenses are more or less closely related to the category of disorderly streetwalking, namely, prostitution, assignation, pandering, disorderly conduct, and vagrancy. Similar specialized courts are organized in a number of cities particularly for the handling of female sex-offenders above juvenile court age and without upper age limitation. These are often known as "Women's Courts," "Morals Courts," or "Misdemeanants' Courts." The reason for their creation is the realization that most offenses of this type defy the orthodox approach of criminal prosecution and procedure, but rather call for social and medical assistance. Certain features of juvenile court philosophy and practice, therefore, are apparent in these special courts for adult offenders.

[14] See Dr. William Healy's statement on the adolescent, quoted in Chapter I, pp. 21–22.

On the other hand, arguments against the raising of the juvenile court age, often heard in the chambers of legislative bodies as well as in public discussion whenever a bill of this nature is introduced, usually center around the well-publicized statistics of the Federal Bureau of Investigation on adolescent crime. Figures are quoted showing that during the year 1949, males and females under twenty-one years of age, arrested and fingerprinted, constituted 14.8 per cent of the total arrests; out of 192,122 persons of all ages arrested for crimes against property—*i.e.*, robbery, burglary, larceny, auto theft, embezzlement, fraud, forgery, counterfeiting, receiving stolen property, and arson—52,670 (or 27.4 per cent) were less than twenty-one years old. The conclusion that is expected to be drawn from these statistics is that an extension of juvenile court procedure to the older age group would encourage the commitment of crimes even more and that only harsher measures would efficiently curb the growing menace of adolescent lawlessness. All this is based upon the mistaken assumption that the juvenile court is a "mollycoddling" agency. The public is not aware of the fact that most juvenile courts, because of their social and psychological findings, often apply far stricter measures than many an adult court operating solely on the basis of legal evidence. The youngsters themselves *do* know the difference, however, and it is not infrequent that a youth who has not quite reached the upper juvenile court age deliberately misrepresents his age as being above that limit in order to get off more "easily" in the ordinary criminal court proceedings than he ever would in juvenile court. Another argument is that frequently boys and girls above the present juvenile court age are physically, and to a large degree psychologically, adults.

Even progressive penal experts express the opinion that an attempt to raise the juvenile court age further would meet with so much objection from the public, that to initiate any such steps might possibly backfire and jeopardize the prevalent upper juvenile court age limit of eighteen, which in many states was achieved only against considerable opposition and after long struggle. It is also pointed out by practitioners as well as theorists that the problems presented by the adolescent are essentially different from those encountered in the handling of younger boys and girls and that, therefore, methods and techniques more adapted to the needs of the older age group should be applied.

Rather than concentrate on largely futile attempts to raise the juvenile court age above the level of eighteen, efforts should be made toward establishing a uniform upper juvenile court age of eighteen in all states. Moreover, the juvenile court's jurisdiction should be made truly comprehensive, *i.e.*, inclusive of serious offenses which—as has been discussed in detail in the preceding chapter [15]— at present are often exempted from juvenile court jurisdiction.

With respect to the youthful offender above eighteen years of age, the adolescents' courts, as described here, do not seem to offer the proper solution. These courts are necessarily hybrids, embodying on the one side various but not all juvenile court aspects, and on the other side certain features of criminal procedure, but without all the legal safeguards that the adult offender enjoys in the general criminal court.

A much more adequate approach to the problem of the adolescent or youthful offender is found in the movement for the establishment of a Youth Correction Authority, which we shall discuss next.

2. THE YOUTH CORRECTION AUTHORITY

In 1777, John Howard wrote his famous work *State of Prisons in England,* which revealed the most hideous conditions of degradation and cruelty. Its publication was largely responsible for the institution of much-needed reforms in Great Britain and other parts of the world. It also was a book that in our times gave impetus to a thorough consideration of the problem of youthful offenders and eventually to a constructive attack upon it in theory as well as in practice.

Youth in the Toils, by Leonard V. Harrison and Pryor McNeill Grant,[16] was the outcome of a year-long study of the handling of young offenders sixteen to twenty-one years of age by the judicial machinery in New York City. The two authors were given this assignment by the Delinquency Committee of the Boys' Bureau, a non-sectarian agency caring for homeless and unattached boys of that age group. The book is unorthodox in every respect; the chapter of its case reports, significantly entitled "Grist for the Mill," is free from any professional jargon, and, for that reason, it is particularly impressive. The analysis of detention (in the "Tombs," Manhattan's now abandoned jail for untried prisoners), of arrest and arraignment,

---

[15] Chapter IX, pp. 304–305.
[16] Macmillan, New York, 1938.

of reformatories and prisons, and of their disastrous impact upon the adolescent, is uninhibited in its sharp criticism. The conclusions reached were sensational at the time of the book's publication and are today still considered radical by many persons inside and outside the correctional field. The authors recommended the setting up of a new court, the Delinquent Minor Court, to be "so organized as to provide for the exercise of two separate functions, (a) a judicial function of determining guilt or innocence of offenses charged and, (b) a dispositional function of determining the form of treatment to be imposed upon those found guilty; that disposition of offenders be based on a diagnostic examination by experts comprising a disposition board; and that delinquent minors be under the control of this board until formally discharged from its supervision, or until an order for indefinite segregation is made by it following a decision that rehabilitation is unattainable." [17]

The findings and recommendations of this study aroused the interest of the American Law Institute, a research body devoted to the clarification and systematization of American law and composed of outstanding lawyers, judges, and professors of law and criminology. Recognizing the human, social, and legal aspects of the problem as presented in *Youth in the Toils*, the American Law Institute undertook the task of preparing the draft of a new pattern for the administration of criminal justice for youthful offenders. The careful deliberation of a group selected by the American Law Institute and consisting of members of the legal profession, psychologists, and social scientists, produced the model *Youth Correction Authority Act*,[18] which was approved by the membership of the Institute and was published in 1940 as its official draft.

It is called "An act creating a Youth Correction Authority, pre-

---

[17] *Op. cit.*, p. 131.

[18] A model law is the draft of a bill usually prepared by a private body, *viz.*, an academic institution or a committee appointed by a professional organization and composed of theorists and practitioners in their respective field. It serves to stimulate state legislation, following the lines of the model act, in those states where no such legislation exists or where existing legislation is lagging behind the times. It often strives to bring about greater uniformity in fields where great diversification of state laws prevails—for instance, in respect to marriage and divorce legislation. A good example of a model law is the *Standard Juvenile Court Act;* see Chapter IX. The quotations in the text from the official draft of the Youth Correction Authority Act are made by permission of the American Law Institute.

scribing its powers and duties and providing for commitments, thereto, of convicted persons under 21 years of age at the time of their apprehension." The purpose of the Act is "to protect society more effectively by substituting for retributive punishment methods of training and treatment directed toward the correction and rehabilitation of young persons found guilty of violation of law."

The Act calls for the creation of a Youth Correction Authority, set up in each state by the legislature, "whose function is to provide and administer corrective and preventive training and treatment for persons committed to it." It shall consist of three full-time members to be appointed by the governor for a term of office of nine years, with a possibility of reappointment after the expiration of the term.

The late Judge Joseph N. Ulman of the Supreme Bench of Baltimore, a noted author on problems of criminal justice and a member of the committee that prepared the draft of the Act, described its main features as follows:

> The act provides that convicted offenders within the age group over the juvenile court age and under twenty-one shall be committed to the Youth Correction Authority for correctional treatment in all cases except those in which the trial court imposes the death penalty or life imprisonment at one end of the scale, or imposes a fine or a short term of imprisonment for minor offenses at the other end. The act provides an extended period of control by the Authority which may in exceptional cases, and subject to judicial review, continue for the life of the offender. The Authority is given wide discretion and the greatest measure of elasticity in dealing with the offender. It may release him under supervision before any period of incarceration whatever, it may limit his freedom slightly in a work camp or a supervised boarding home, or severely in a prison cell; and it may change its method of treatment from time to time and from less to more, and again to less severe forms, as the exigencies of the individual case require. This plan differs from all existing practice in that it subjects the offender to continuous planned control by a single responsible administrative body instead of shifting him from one control to another. Finally, the Authority is given the right to terminate its control over the offender conditionally or unconditionally as soon as it appears that the protection of society and the welfare of the individual will be served by such termination.[19]

---

[19] Joseph N. Ulman, "The Youth Correction Authority Act," *Yearbook, N.P.P.A.,* 1941, pp. 227–240 (quotation on p. 234).

One of the outstanding characteristics of the Act is that the Authority is not only empowered to make use of law enforcement, detention, probation, parole, medical, educational, correctional, segregative, and other existing facilities, institutions, and agencies, whether public or private; it is also empowered, when necessary and when funds are available for such purposes, to create and operate places for the detention, prior to examination and study; places for examination and study; places of confinement, educational institutions, hospitals, and other correctional or segregative facilities, institutions, and agencies for the proper execution of its duties; agencies and facilities for the supervision, training and control of persons who have not been placed in confinement or who have been released from confinement by the Authority upon conditions, and for aiding such persons to find employment and assistance; and agencies and facilities designed to aid persons who have been discharged by the Authority from its control in finding employment and in leading a law-abiding existence.[20]

Although the draftsmen of the model act described it as "neither a radical departure from existing law nor even basically novel," [21] it was bound to create opposition, especially since it proposed to curtail the sentencing power of the local judges.

Judge George W. Smyth, of the Westchester County Children's Court, New York, made the following comment:

Whether our people will approve of taking the sentencing power away from the courts is debatable. There are certain definite advantages which the court possesses, in that the judge has an opportunity to become acquainted with the defendant as a result of his observation during the trial, and before sentencing him has the benefit of a full and complete study and report by the probation department. Then too, I believe our people as a rule have confidence in their locally elected judges and in their courts, and there is much to be said in favor of keeping this responsibility in the hands of men who can be held directly accountable for their actions. It is conceivable that under a board the

---

[20] For a discussion of the Youth Correction Authority Act, see William Draper Lewis, "Treatment of Youth Convicted of Crime," *Federal Probation*, May 1940, pp. 20–23; Thorsten Sellin, "The Youthful Offender," *ibid.*, April–June 1942, pp. 14–17.

[21] See "Introductory Explanation of the Official Draft of the Youth Correction Authority Act," The American Law Institute, Philadelphia, 1940, p. xvii.

responsibility would be so divided and would be so remote that there could not be the same degree of personal accountability.[22]

On the other hand, Judge Joseph N. Ulman, whom we have previously quoted, strongly advocated the Youth Correction Authority. He stated:

> The very best judge assisted by the most enlightened staff of investigators gets at the most a static picture of the criminal as he is on the day of his conviction. From that day forward he is bound to change, for the better or for the worse, as all other men change. The Correction Authority is implemented to deal with him continuously as that process of change goes on. It will get a moving picture of him, not just a photograph. It can vary its treatment, can determine how long treatment shall continue, not on the basis of a courtroom impression and a guess, but on the basis of dynamic experience. We judges ought to be able to accept that difference without loss of face.[23]

In the years since the publication of the Youth Correction Authority model law, the issue has left the purely theoretical stage. Three states have passed legislation incorporating the principles and procedures of the model act. In many other legislatures, similar bills have been introduced but so far have failed of enactment. However, there are numerous indications that in the years to come efforts will be made by leaders in the correctional field and civic groups in many states to have such legislation put on the statute books. In September, 1950, the Federal Youth Corrections Act was passed after it had been recommended for many years by the Judicial Conference of Senior Circuit Judges of the United States.[24]

California, true to its pioneering spirit in many fields, was the first state to enact such legislation. Although the original California law of June 1941 establishing a Youth Correction Authority drew heavily upon the model act of the American Law Institute, there were a number of important differences. One of them was the provision allowing the Authority to accept boys and girls from the

---

[22] George W. Smyth, "Analyzing the Y.C.A. Act," *Yearbook*, N.P.P.A., 1941, pp. 241–246 (quotation on pp. 242–243).

[23] *Ibid.*, pp. 235–236.

[24] For details, see Judge Paul J. McCormick, "A Judge Discusses the Proposed Federal Corrections Act," *Federal Probation*, January–March 1944, pp. 3–13 and *ibid.*, September 1950, p. 60.

juvenile courts (the model act limited the Authority's function to youths above juvenile court age). Another deviation from the model act was the extension of the upper age limit to twenty-three years; this limit, however, was later changed to twenty-one years, with the time of apprehension as the decisive date. Unlike the model act, the California law left the power to grant probation with the courts. The name of the Authority was changed in 1943 to "Youth Authority."

Since the California experiment represents a courageous step forward in the direction of a scientific approach to the problem of the youthful offender, and since, as the first undertaking of its kind, it has aroused nation-wide interest, it seems profitable here to include a more detailed report on its development up to date. The authors follow to some degree the presentations of two writers who possess firsthand knowledge of the functioning of the California Youth Authority. They are Karl Holton, Director of the Youth Authority,[25] and John R. Ellingston, Special Advisor on Criminal Justice for Youth of the American Law Institute. Mr. Ellingston's book, *Protecting Our Children from Criminal Careers*,[26] is a thorough study of the operation of the California Youth Authority, presented against the background of our nation's general crime picture. It includes the aspects of correction at the state level as well as services to all youth on the community level.

The Youth Authority is headed by a board of three members appointed by the Governor. A unique feature is that two of the three members are chosen from a list of nominations prepared for the Governor by a panel consisting of the presidents of interested organizations, such as the state Bar and Medical Associations, the California Conference of Social Work, the California Prison Association, the Probation and Parole Officers' Association, and the Teachers' Association.

The first years of the California Youth Authority are described by John R. Ellingston as follows:

> In its first 15 months the Authority set up a skeleton organization; gathered data from all criminal courts on the number and disposition

---

[25] See Karl Holton, "The California Youth Authority," *Yearbook*, N.P.P.A. 1946, pp. 116–126.
[26] Prentice-Hall, New York, 1948.

of young offenders so as to estimate its probable case load; organized an experimental reception and diagnostic center; carried on an educational campaign throughout the state; and took over the administration of the state's three correctional schools for boys and girls under 21.

With respect to the correctional schools, California's enabling Act originally placed no existing facilities under the administration of the Youth Authority. The Act did empower the Authority to establish necessary new training and treatment facilities (when funds were available) and also to commit its charges after diagnosis to existing correctional schools and prisons. However, one of the periodic scandals that strike reform schools in this country speedily changed the original plan. California had three institutions for delinquents under 21: the Fred C. Nelles School for Boys (16 and under) at Whittier; the Preston School of Industry for Boys (15 to 21); and the Ventura School for Girls (up to 21). Though each school was administratively largely autonomous, for budgetary purposes they came under the Department of Institutions. The suicide of two boys on different dates in 1940 while in the punishment cell at Whittier had brought the school under attack from sections of the press and public. Demoralization of the staff had gradually reached a point where the school had almost ceased to function. In April 1942, the Governor and the Director of Institutions asked the new Youth Authority to take over the administration of all three correctional schools. In 1943, the legislature made the transfer permanent.

In this abrupt and accidental fashion the Authority gained full control of all existing state correctional facilities for juveniles and was stamped as the state agency responsible for the care of all delinquent children under 21 requiring corrective custody. Subsequent amendments have gradually reinforced this position until now juvenile courts, like criminal courts, must commit directly to the Youth Authority rather than to one of the correctional schools. The experience of four years has made it clear that chance intervened to good purpose and speeded up an inevitable development.[27]

In 1943, the Division of Probation also was transferred from the Department of Social Welfare to the Youth Authority and in 1945 made part of the Field Services Division of the Youth Authority. However, the functions of this Division are more of an advisory and generally supervisory nature, and include the collection of statistics.[28]

---

[27] *Op. cit.*, pp. 62–63.

[28] See James N. York, "Evaluating the Everyday Work of a Probation Office," *Federal Probation*, September 1948, pp. 24–29. For a detailed descrip-

Probation is still granted and supervised by the local juvenile courts and criminal courts. The Youth Authority may grant probation to persons under its control—*i.e.*, those who have been committed to it by a court.

No wonder that such a new experiment as the Youth Authority, especially in view of the rapid growth of its functions, exposed itself to certain risks and ran into opposition from various sources. To let Ellingston's book again tell the story:

As the months rolled by, the young agency came in for an increasing volume of criticism, and when the 1943 legislature convened, this criticism exploded in a move to repeal the Youth Authority Act. Fortunately, friends of the Authority numbered a substantial majority. The newly elected Governor, Earl Warren, characterized the Authority as an experiment to be weighed by its future possibilities rather than by its fledgling achievements. He said, "This is one of the greatest social experiments we have ever undertaken in this State." At the same time, in the California Senate, an Interim Committee on Penal and Correctional Institutions which had carefully studied the new Authority and its plans in relation to the state's existing facilities brought in a report that contained the following informed approval:

"The committee feels that the State when it established the Youth Correction Authority made a great forward step in that phase of criminal control and prevention which deals with youth, that perpetual reservoir from which 90 per cent of criminals are recruited. It feels, also, that the powers given the Youth Authority should lead not only to prevention, but will prove a great factor in restoring to useful lives those capable of being rehabilitated. It is true that the Authority is still in the stage of experimentation and that it will require the passage of years to demonstrate its true worth, but the committee feels, nevertheless, that the objects sought are soundly based and offer for the first time in the State's history something tangible as against the long cherished idea that little can be done about those who transgress the laws except to confine them behind bars and brand them with the marks of disgrace which endure throughout their lives."

The careful reappraisal of the Youth Authority by the 1943 legislature did result in strengthening the Act and the Authority. Most important, the legislature recognized the urgent need for new state facilities in order to get the juveniles out of jail, and gave proof of its con-

---

tion of the development and scope of the California Youth Authority, see *California Youth Authority: Report and Progress 1943–1948*, Sacramento, 1949.

fidence in the Authority by appropriating $1,020,000 for the 1943–45 biennium, largely for long overdue capital expenditures. This was nearly $300,000 more than the Authority itself had requested.[29]

In addition to the three previously mentioned schools, the California Youth Authority administers three more institutions (one of which is a ranch school) and four forestry camps. This number includes two institutions which were established by the Youth Authority in recent years—the Paso Robles School, with a capacity of 135 boys from fourteen to sixteen years of age presenting difficult personality problems, and Los Guilucos School, for less seriously delinquent girls from eight to sixteen years of age (capacity 110).

Perhaps one of the most gratifying features of the Youth Authority program is the work done with the older boys in the forestry camps. This work is actually under the state Department of Forestry, with supervision under the Authority. The work in fire-fighting, trail-blazing, cutting of undergrowth, and parasite control is in charge of the forestry personnel. On the job, the boys are directly under their supervision, although Authority counselors go out with the boys. All camps are in the mountains, and the boys live in barracks. The counselors are, by and large, college graduates; many of them hold advanced degrees in guidance, sociology, and other social science subjects. An extremely healthful atmosphere pervades these camps and few escapes are recorded. Visiting privileges are generous, the food is better than average, and the recreational program is satisfying to the type of boys sent to these camps. Trips to near-by cities to attend movies and to ocean beaches are planned on frequent occasions. Little discipline is needed and no cruelty exists.

In addition to the boys directly assigned to the forestry camps by the Youth Authority, there is another group of boys who have been at the Preston School of Industry and the California Vocational Institution. Before being released on parole, they are transferred from these institutions to a forestry camp for an intermediate period of three or four months between the intra-mural commitment and the return to the community. The idea behind this program is that a period of training in a forestry camp, with its less restricted atmosphere of semi-liberty, is a good way of preparing the boy for his final release.

---

[29] *Op. cit.*, pp. 64–65.

The Department of Forestry is enthusiastic about the work done by the boys in these camps. It contends that the training the boys receive makes them veteran fire-fighters who will take discipline in their stride when faced with emergencies. Moreover, the valuable conservation work done by the boys saves the tax-payer money.[30]

A Youth Authority Camp. (*Courtesy California Youth Authority*)

Several county juvenile courts in California operate their own camps and ranch schools for boys and girls—for instance, the LaTuna Boys' Camp and the El Retiro School for Girls of the Los Angeles County probation department, and the Log Cabin Ranch

[30] The idea of forestry camps should be imitated in many other states. It is a valuable addition to any state correctional system as a form of intermediate treatment. For a discussion of the values and potentialities of forestry camps, see J. O. Reinemann, "Wanted in Pennsylvania: Forestry Camps for the Rehabilitation of Delinquents," *Prison Journal*, April 1948, pp. 401–404. So far, only the Federal government (Natural Bridge Camp in Virginia) and the states of Michigan and Idaho have established similar camps. (The Natural Bridge Camp will be described in Chapter XIII, pp. 501–502.) The Michigan Camp is for adult first offenders. In Idaho, a parole camp was developed with the purpose of aiding prisoners in finding the road back to civilian life.

School of the San Francisco Juvenile Court. The Youth Authority subsidizes this camp program by paying one half of the operating cost, not to exceed $80.00 per month per child. Reporting on the five junior forestry camps in Southern California, Patrick L. Palace of the Los Angeles County probation department states, "That the highly personalized program of good food, good work habits, good discipline, good personal habits, plus the awareness of trust instead of clubs and guns, is justified is proved by the fact that 85 per cent of the youths 'graduated' have had no other contact with the law."

Morning Briefing Before Leaving for Forestry Work—California Youth Authority Camp. (*Courtesy California Youth Authority*)

The average camp stay there is thirty-two weeks. Log Cabin Ranch School reports that "approximately 92 percent of the graduates remain well-adjusted members of society."

A really well-functioning program of planned institutional placement is predicated upon the services of a diagnostic center. According to Ellingston,[31] the California Youth Authority's clinic at Preston School of Industry occupies its own building, which accommodates 140 youths from fifteen and one-half to twenty-one years of age. They sleep, eat, study, work, and play in complete separation from the youths who have already gone through the clinic and who have been committed to Preston for training. Within the clinic, boys are grouped according to age, sophistication, and conduct record into three segregated companies.

For the younger boys and the girls committed to it, the California Authority has had to provide diagnosis in the various individual training units. This arrangement, like the establishment of the experimental clinic at Preston, is temporary. The Authority believes that best results can be obtained in a reception and diagnostic center that is physically separate from a treatment unit, especially one that has been a custodial institution. It has plans for two such centers, and the legislature has already appropriated funds for these projects. The Authority expects to break ground for both centers, one to be located in Northern California, the other in Southern California.

Ellingston describes the procedure followed in reaching a decision after the diagnosis of an individual case:

> At the completion of the study, a report is drawn up that seeks to assemble all the information gathered into a complete picture of the case. It concludes with the clinical staff's recommendations for treatment. Copies of the report are prepared for each member of the Authority, for the facility to which the youth may be assigned for training and treatment, and for the parole officer who will have to supervise the boy on his return to the community.
>
> Twice a month for a total of six days, the three members of the California Youth Authority meet at its diagnostic clinic to sit as a classification committee on all boys who have spent a month or more in the center. This committee interviews each boy after studying the clinic's report and decides whether he is to be sent to a forestry camp or work camp, committed to Preston School of Industry, to the intermediate institution at Lancaster, or to the penitentiary at San Quentin, retained for further study in the clinic, or otherwise disposed of. The committee gives each case whatever time is needed to satisfy the members of the soundness of the clinic's analysis and recommendations, with

---

[31] *Op. cit.*, pp. 79–80.

which they sometimes disagree. It does a careful job in assigning a boy
to the particular treatment unit that seems likely to meet his needs,
with due regard for the Authority's responsibility to the public.[32]

The Authority grants paroles and supervises parolees through a
staff of officers attached to branch parole offices. As of May 12, 1949,
4,050 young people were on parole, and 2,200 were in the various
facilities of the Authority.

One of the most outstanding features of the California Youth
Authority is its strong emphasis on prevention, under the administra-
tration of Heman G. Stark and a capable staff. The Authority's activities in this field represent a commendable modification of the
original concept that Youth Correction Authorities should primarily
serve as sentencing boards. As Karl Holton told the Annual Conference of the N.P.P.A. in 1946:

> Anyone who has worked in this field soon comes to realize the im-
> portance of programs for delinquency prevention and crime control.
> As we developed our facilities for the care and treatment of juvenile
> delinquents, we also developed a field staff in the sphere of delin-
> quency prevention. The Division of Field Services, in addition to its
> responsibility for parole work, provides consultation service to proba-
> tion departments, juvenile courts, juvenile police bureaus and other
> community agencies requesting service.
>
> Through the children who come to our observation we have the
> opportunity to evaluate factors contributing to their delinquency. We
> try to give these facts to the local communities so that their programs
> for delinquency prevention can be strengthened. In cooperation with
> the State Departments of Education, Social Welfare, Public Health,
> the Federal Security Agency, the National Probation Association and
> community chests and councils, we are constantly assembling informa-
> tion about community programs in crime control, recreation, proba-
> tion and other youth service fields. This material is made available to
> communities requesting our help.
>
> The Youth Authority began making studies of youth services in
> various counties, when requested to do so by responsible officials. To
> date we have made nineteen countywide studies.
>
> The Youth Authority now subsidizes county-operated twenty-four
> hour schools and camps, providing that such schools and camps are
> operated according to standards which we prescribe. The subsidy

---

[32] *Op. cit.*, p. 73.

amounts to fifty per cent of the operating costs. These camps and schools are regularly inspected. Thirteen are now being subsidized and others will be aided later.

In cooperation with the office of the attorney general, our consultant in juvenile control advises police and sheriffs' departments throughout the state concerning record keeping, the best practice in handling juvenile offenders, the relationship of the police department to child-caring agencies, and facilities available for their use.[33]

An advisory committee to the Youth Authority, called the "California Youth Committee," consists of lay persons appointed by the governor. The membership is such that wide representation from each section of the state is obtained, and thus knowledge of the problems of the communities and counties throughout the state is reflected through the committee to the staff of the Authority.[34]

If any criticism can be made of the California Youth Authority, it would be that it finds itself in a quandary concerning its battle-scarred institutions, Preston School of Industry, the Fred C. Nelles School at Whittier, and the Ventura School for Girls, which used to have an unsavory reputation (Whittier especially), as we shall point out in Chapter XII. A definite effort has been made to install new personnel in the schools, and to indoctrinate the staff with more modern methods of institutional care. However, this process is slow, and newly appointed superintendents cannot work miracles. Yet it is obvious that the proof of the success of the California Youth Authority will depend a great deal on how the training programs at these three schools are humanized and socialized.

One unique and hopeful method developed by the Authority, which will almost demand orderly and progressive change in these institutions, is the provision for supervision of the administration and their policies. Supervision is exercised by trained experts in various state departments aside from the Authority. For example, a member of the state's department of home economics will check on

---

[33] *Loc. cit.*, pp. 123–124.

[34] For more details on this matter and on the functional set-up of the Authority, see "California Youth Authority: Organization of the Youth Authority and Outline of Its Program," summary by Vandyce Hamren, Sacramento, May 1949 (mimeographed). The Authority also publishes most valuable information on its own activities as well as on the general delinquency situation in California, in *California Youth Authority Quarterly*, Sacramento.

food and supplies; a member of the state's department of engineering will periodically check the buildings and fire provisions. The Authority's representatives will counsel with staff members and with the superintendents regarding the treatment program. This is a healthy development, one that should be emulated by other states in their correctional institutions.

Summarizing, let it be said to the everlasting credit of California that it broke fairly definitely with the traditional past and courageously set up a new dispensation of dealing with delinquent youth. Their camps for boys are particularly excellent and the Authority's program of community education on an all-state basis is something new and encouraging in delinquency control.

In Minnesota, a Youth Authority was created in 1947, called "Youth Conservation Commission." The Commission consists of five persons, including the director of the Division of Public Institutions, the chairman of the State Board of Parole, and three others appointed by the governor. The district courts commit to the Commission every person under twenty-one years of age convicted of a felony or a gross misdemeanor who is not sentenced to life imprisonment, imprisonment for ninety days or less, or to a fine only. The courts can also place a probationer under the supervision of the Commission. A juvenile court not having a probation officer may request the Commission to investigate and accept for probation juvenile delinquents. Subsequent laws provide for the transfer of the administration of state training schools for boys and girls to the Youth Conservation Commission. Also, a woman member has been added to the Commission.

In the same year, Wisconsin adopted the idea of a youth authority by creating a "Youth Service Commission," consisting of eleven members appointed by the governor. The Commission has the power of inquiry and the responsibility of making recommendations regarding the welfare of children and youth. Its operating arm is the Youth Service Division within the Department of Public Welfare. Wisconsin was fortunate in that its Department of Public Welfare, even before the passage of the 1947 act, had at its disposal a well-integrated correctional service, including a staff and facilities for diagnosis. The law specifies that juvenile court commitments and commitments of minors where the penalty is less than life imprisonment shall be to the Youth Service Division of the Department of Public Welfare, which may confine, permit liberty under supervision and subsequently grant discharge. Other functions assigned to this department are crime prevention work and the performance of pre-sentence investigations when called upon by local courts.

From these examples in three states it is apparent that the basic idea of the model Youth Correction Authority Act has been considered realistic enough to be translated into legislative acts and administrative practice. The California experiment in particular shows the real contribution that the setting up of diagnostic services through observation and classification centers can render to the handling of delinquents. It further proves that the centralization of control of a number of variegated institutional and other services makes possible the assignment of the youthful offender to the proper facilities and the transfer to another place when necessary. It abolishes the haphazard and planless commitment procedure to which the judges in many states are driven as a result of the lack of study centers and the crazy quilt of institutions, public as well as private, which are not co-ordinated with each other and which are often not supervised at all, or only superficially, by a central state agency. Because of its underlying philosophy of a scientific approach to the youthful offender, the idea of the Youth Correction Authority has been called "the most revolutionary step taken in American penology since the establishment of the Elmira Reformatory, and much more promising than that innovation." [35]

The Federal Youth Corrections Act of 1950 created a Youth Correction Division within the Board of Parole, consisting of eight board members, designated from time to time by the Attorney General. Youth offenders (defined as under 22 years of age at the time of conviction), who are not placed on probation, may, in lieu of the penalty of imprisonment, be committed to the custody of the Attorney General for treatment up to a maximum of six years, or, if the court so provides, to a further period, but not beyond the maximum penalty for the offense. Every committed offender must be first sent to a classification center for a complete study. On completion of the study, he may be released conditionally under supervision or sent to an appropriate institution for treatment.[36]

---

[35] Barnes and Teeters, *op cit.*, p. 944.
[36] For further details, see *Federal Probation*, September 1950, p. 60; *Focus*, January 1951, pp. 21–22.

Two other states have enacted legislation somewhat modeled after the Youth Correction Authority idea but have restricted its application exclusively to offenders of juvenile court age. In Massachusetts, a Youth Service Board was established in 1948, consisting of three full-time members appointed by the governor from a list submitted to him by the Advisory Committee on Service to Youth. In its aim to establish crime-prevention programs, the duties of the Board are preventive. They are administrative in that the Board succeeded to the powers of the trustees of the training schools in administering the schools and took over from the State Department of Public Welfare its duties in caring for delinquent and wayward children and school offenders up to seventeen years of age. Juvenile court commitments are now made to the Board rather than directly to the institutions.[37]

Texas in 1949 established a State Youth Development Council of fourteen members, six appointed by the governor and eight state officers ex officio, to serve as a research and advisory body, and to administer the state facilities for delinquent children. The Council is empowered to receive these children committed by the courts as juvenile delinquents and, after study in a diagnostic center, to decide the best form of institutional treatment. The Council may also provide probation service to juvenile courts in counties without probation officers.

Putting certain features, such as diagnostic and classification centers and centralized control of institutional placement, at the disposal of committing juvenile courts is a very welcome development. However, there is a danger that the initial idea of the draftsmen of the model Youth Correction Authority Act—to revamp the traditional criminal procedure against adolescent offenders—may be diluted by the inclusion, within the same administrative agency, of juvenile court cases. Whatever form is chosen, either that of an authority serving both the juvenile and adolescent offender or two separate but cooperating departments for these two groups, the vitally needed services for the adolescent group should not be neglected. It was for

---

[37] The idea and the operation of the Massachusetts Youth Service Board are described in a popular article, "New Hope for Delinquents," *Parade* (syndicated Sunday newspaper supplement), July 17, 1949.

this group that the original proposals of the American Law Institute were exclusively made.[38]

3. THE INFLUENCE OF THE JUVENILE COURT UPON CRIMINAL JUSTICE ADMINISTRATION IN ADULT CASES

We have seen that basic principles of juvenile court philosophy and practice have decisively influenced the Youth Correction Authority movement, especially in regard to the need for social and medical diagnoses before disposition. Although the scope of jurisdiction of youth authorities, both in theory and in practice, is confined to persons below twenty-one years of age, the influence of the juvenile court idea has in several respects crossed the border of that age limit and has invaded the criminal justice administration in adult cases. The two most outstanding examples of this development are the pre-sentence investigation and the use of probation.

The idea of individualization of justice, which has found a concrete expression in the establishment of the juvenile court, has also prompted the demand for pre-sentence investigations in adult cases, similar to the inquiries which are customarily being made in cases of juvenile delinquency.[39] Although this practice is far from universal, an ever-increasing number of judges today realize the necessity for knowing more about the offender than what the trial, with its strict rules of evidence and its exclusive limitation to the determination of guilt or innocence, is likely to reveal. In order to pronounce a sentence that will serve to rehabilitate the offender, the judge must have knowledge of the personality of the defendant, his social environment, and his physical and mental make-up; he must have insight into the defendant's personal needs and, if possible, into the reason for his antisocial conduct. The pre-sentence investigation supplies him with this information. One of the most important features of juve-

---

[38] In this connection, see Roy L. McLaughlin, "Is Youth Authority a Design for Children?," *The Prison World*, September–December 1948, p. 8. An excellent appraisal of the five state youth authorities in existence (which were described in this chapter), including a chart showing the legal provisions in the model act as compared with the five state laws, is found in Sol Rubin, "Changing Youth Correction Authority Concepts," *Focus*, May 1950, pp. 77–82.

[39] See Chapter VIII, p. 263.

nile court procedure thus finds increasing recognition in the handling of adult offenders.

The safeguards that the law provides for the defendant in criminal trials must, of course, be respected. Therefore, information gathered through pre-sentence investigation should be available exclusively to the judge, since the purpose of the investigation has nothing to do with the establishment of guilt or innocence. This information is to be used only after conviction of the accused person.[40]

In the beginning, judges requested pre-sentence investigations almost exclusively in cases where the granting of probation was contemplated. This practice is also apparent in the not too numerous statutory provisions on pre-sentence investigation in several states. The Attorney General's Survey of Release Procedures enumerated the following legal provisions:

> The most complete statutory consideration of the matter of investigation is that of the California law. There before a defendant can be given probation the court must refer the matter to the probation officer for investigation. In Illinois an investigation is mandatory before probation is granted. Felony offenders in Michigan must be investigated before sentence is imposed. Before suspending sentence in any case Minnesota courts may require an investigation into certain aspects of the defendant's character and life; the statute evidently contemplates an investigation before a decision concerning probation is reached but the requirement is not mandatory. In New York no one may be placed on probation, nor in felony cases may sentence be suspended, until the report of the probation officer concerning the results of the investigation is filed. North Carolina's new probation statute contains some provisions with regard to presentence investigation, in that when the services of a probation officer are available probation may not be granted in felony cases until the report of an investigation has been presented to and considered by the court.[41]

---

[40] For an interesting controversy about whether or not pre-sentence investigation reports should be made available by the court to the attorneys for the parties involved, see Judge Carroll C. Hincks, "In Opposition to Rule 34(c)(2), Proposed Federal Rules of Criminal Procedure," *Federal Probation*, October–December 1944, pp. 3–8; also, F. W. Killian, "Pre-sentence Reports," in *Probation*, October 1945, pp. 25–26.

[41] *Probation*, United States Government Printing Office, Washington, 1939, Vol. II, pp. 127–128.

The later development, though still quite sporadic, indicated that not only in those situations where probation was a likely disposition but also in other more serious cases, pre-sentence investigations became in the opinion of many judges a vital necessity. The Federal judicial system has probably gone farthest toward a universal use of pre-sentence investigation. The Rules of Criminal Procedure for the District Courts of the United States, adopted by the Supreme Court in 1946, specify that "the probation service of the court shall make a pre-sentence investigation and report to the court before the imposition of sentence or the granting of probation, unless the court otherwise directs." [42]

Pre-sentence investigations are carried out by the probation departments of the local courts or, wherever they exist, by state probation departments. The compilation of social data follows quite closely the principles governing the preparation of social case investigations in juvenile cases.[43]

In addition to the social inquiry, examinations of the offender by psychologists and psychiatrists are requested by some courts. These examinations are usually made after the defendant has pleaded guilty or has been found guilty, and they consist of observation and study of behavior, resulting in diagnosis and possible recommendation to the judge.[44]

The needed facilities may be offered to the courts by clinics in hospitals and research institutes, or they may be established by the courts themselves as their own special services. An example of this latter type is the Behavior Clinic of the Quarter Sessions Court of

---

[42] Rule 32c. For further comments, see Judge T. Blake Kennedy, "The Pre-sentence Investigation Report Is Indispensable to the Court," *Federal Probation*, April–June 1941, pp. 3–5; Judge F. Ryan Duffy, "The Value of Pre-sentence Reports to the Court," *ibid.*, July–September 1941, pp. 3–5; Judge Lewis B. Schwellenbach, "Information versus Intuition in the Imposition of Sentence," *ibid.*, January–March 1943, pp. 3–6.

[43] See Chapter VIII, pp. 263–268; see also Milton Weiffenbach, "An Approach to Pre-sentence Investigation," *Yearbook*, N.P.P.A., 1942, pp. 165–176; Edwin B. Zeigler, "Pre-sentence and Pre-parole Investigation," *ibid.*, 1946, pp. 154–162.

[44] These examinations must not be confused with the procedures established for testing the sanity of an offender at the time of the crime. For more information on the matter of insanity and criminal responsibility, see Walter Bromberg, "Alienism and Psychiatry in the Law Courts," *Federal Probation*, July–September 1943, pp. 6–10.

Allegheny County, Pittsburgh, Pennsylvania, created in 1937 by the Board of Judges and maintained through funds supplied by the county commissioners. Since its inception, it has made systematic psychological, psychiatric, physical, and social examinations and investigations of thousands of adult offenders. No case is accepted by this clinic unless ordered by the Quarter Sessions Court. However, the personnel of the clinic sometimes suggest that certain cases be examined. Since the judges have always recognized that they need some scientific aid in passing sentence, complete cooperation has existed between the several jurists and the members of the clinic board. Funds are not available to have all the cases appearing before the court examined, but judges and clinic personnel agree that the ideal situation will be achieved only when all cases appearing before criminal courts are examined prior to sentence.

Many of the resources of the community are enlisted in the process of investigation. The director of the Behavior Clinic says: "The social agencies are invaluable to us as a source of information in regard to the past life of the individual concerned, and the environmental factors which have played a part in his development. In turn, they have from time to time assisted in the rehabilitation of individuals after their release from the jurisdiction of the Court." [45]

A statistical compilation shows that this clinic studied 736 cases during the course of one year.[46] A unique feature of the clinic is that 668 of these cases were referred before court trial—*i.e.*, after arrest and while being held for court; 54 had been found guilty and were awaiting sentence at the time of referral; 13 were serving sentence; and one was a private prosecutor. The psychiatric diagnosis of 499 of the total was normal, but 237 (or 32.2 per cent) of the cases revealed sufficient psychopathology or psychological manifestations to prevent them from being considered normal individuals. They were classified as follows: mentally deficient 23, psychotic 97, psychopathic personality 58, psychoneurosis 57, epilepsy (without psychosis) 2.

Another example of a pre-sentence clinic is the Medical Department of the Municipal Court of Philadelphia. This clinic, an integral

---

[45] *Report of the Behavior Clinic, County of Allegheny, Pittsburgh, 1939–40*, submitted by Dr. James M. Henninger, Director.

[46] *Report of the Behavior Clinic, County of Allegheny, Pittsburgh, 1948–49*, submitted by Dr. Edward E. Mayer, Director.

part of the Court, not only diagnoses children but also adults standing trial before its criminal division and those referred by other local and Federal courts in the area. A number of courts throughout the country utilize similar services. Certain states are particularly well equipped along psychiatric lines, notably Illinois, Massachusetts, Michigan, New York, Ohio, and Pennsylvania.

California has gone even a step further. It has established an Adult Authority, similar to the Youth Authority, which in specific cases is entrusted with the power to fix sentences. The Adult Authority, created by law in 1944, consists of three members appointed by the governor. One of the members must be an attorney; one must have had practical experience in handling adult prisoners; and one must be a sociologist in training and experience. Under this law, all men committed to prison for the first time are sent to a state-administered guidance center. There, according to Ellingston's report,

> The men stay generally from four to eight weeks. At the completion of his diagnosis, each man appears in person before the Adult Authority in a hearing purposely made as informal and friendly as possible. The Authority has studied the report of the Guidance Center and all other information available. On the basis of this study and of the hearing, it fixes a definite sentence for each prisoner. This procedure may appear to implement the old philosophy of punishment-to-fit-the-crime and to contradict treatment for correction. Actually it represents an estimate, based upon all the information available, of which the crime constitutes only one item, as to how long it may take to fit a man for complete freedom. It resembles a doctor's prognosis as to the probable duration of a patient's illness. It is always subject to reduction and the man may earn his parole at any time. Finally, concern for the morale of the individual prisoner forced the Adult Authority to adopt this procedure. The prospect of freedom at a definite date seems to give the adult prisoner a certainty that he has to have for his own peace of mind, regardless of how constructive the period of confinement may be.[47]

Probation, which will be described in the next chapter, has its historical roots in the treatment of adult as well as juvenile offenders. As a tool of modern juvenile court procedure, however, probation has

---

[47] *Op. cit.*, p. 355; see also Kenyon J. Scudder, "Progress in Handling the Adult Offender," *Yearbook*, N.P.P.A., 1947, pp. 13–26.

gained a much wider recognition and has generally shown a more advanced development than it has in the handling of adult cases. This very development in the juvenile field has in recent years increasingly influenced the practice of probation for adult offenders. Supervision of adults on probation, though in some jurisdictions still not more than a routine "roll-call" through the probationer's report to the probation officer in person or by mail, has by now been recognized in many progressive courts as a positive and scientific form of correctional treatment. Here the fruitful experience of employing case work principles in the supervision of children has stimulated the use of advanced methods of guidance and counseling of adult probationers. The constructive use of authority in juvenile cases has pointed the way to a similar approach to the adult offender. The use of community resources in the fields of health, family welfare, recreation, and vocational guidance by the probation officer has proved of equal importance in juvenile and adult cases.

4. THE IDEA OF THE FAMILY COURT

Not only did the juvenile court idea expand vertically, permeating, as we have seen, criminal justice procedure in adult cases; it also transcended its original scope horizontally by influencing, to a certain degree, the handling of cases dealing with all kinds of family matters. These cases, concerning situations of domestic relations, legal custody, adoption, illegitimacy, and similar problems, are either under the jurisdiction of the general courts or, by act of the state legislature, are assigned to courts especially created for their adjudication.

The following characteristics of juvenile court philosophy and practice are singularly applicable to the procedure in these cases: (1) the juvenile court is a social—*i.e.*, a non-legalistic—court; (2) juvenile court procedure is distinguished by its lack of formality, its greater flexibility, the broader discretion of the judge; (3) the juvenile court, in addition to its judicial function, is an administrative agency; (4) the juvenile court makes the most intensive use of sciences other than law in its search for causation of juvenile misconduct, neglect, and dependency, and in its aim of rehabilitating the child, if possible, within the orbit of the family; (5) the juvenile court maintains a continuous close cooperation with other public and private agencies.

As has been mentioned before,[48] the juvenile court in some localities is closely connected with the domestic relations court. According to the laws of various states, the juvenile court may have jurisdiction over guardianship, custody, adoption, illegitimacy, consent to marriage of minors, and annulments of marriage of minors. Then, too, probation officers, especially in smaller probation departments, have to handle not only juvenile court cases but also domestic relations matters, usually called desertion and non-support cases, and cases of establishment of paternity of children born out of wedlock.[49] It is obvious that the principles and methods of juvenile court procedure are influencing the handling of all family cases, especially if they are prepared in the same probation department or in a domestic relations court probation department operating in close proximity to the juvenile court.[50]

In general, however, the development of special domestic relations courts, sometimes called family courts, has been much more sporadic than that of the juvenile court. Neglect to support wife and children, desertion, and non-support are in many jurisdictions considered misdemeanors or summary offenses, and the begetting of a child out of wedlock (often called in the statute "fornication and bastardy") also is a criminal offense in a number of states. These cases are, therefore, usually heard in the criminal courts of general jurisdiction. There is still comparatively little social service offered within the court machinery in the adjudication of these cases, although their very nature obviously would call for it. Most adoption proceedings take place in courts having probate jurisdiction, again with considerable emphasis on the legal phase, although in this field public and private welfare agencies play an increasingly important role and assist the courts in the preparation of these cases with regard to their social and psychological aspects.

The idea of establishing special courts with comprehensive jurisdiction in all matters of family and child welfare requiring judicial

---

[48] See Chapter IX, p. 296.

[49] See Chapter XI, p. 400.

[50] For more details on domestic relations courts, see Alice Scott Nutt, "Juvenile and Domestic Relations Courts," *Social Work Yearbook 1949*, Russell Sage Foundation, pp. 270–276; *The Child, The Family, and The Court*, United States Children's Bureau, Publication No. 193, Government Printing Office, Washington, 1939; also Barnes and Teeters, *op. cit.*, p. 291.

disposition has been advanced for several years by leaders in the field of law and social work,[51] but it has been translated into practice only in a few places. It received impetus through the National Conference on Family Life held in Washington, D.C., in May 1948. In a report drafted by a committee of the American Bar Association for this conference, the establishment of family courts, aptly described as "socialized courts with socialized laws," was recommended. This report was unanimously approved by the House of Delegates of the American Bar Association which met in Seattle in September 1948. Pointing to the modern juvenile court as prototype, this report said:

> We suggest handling our unhappy and delinquent spouses much as we handle our delinquent children. Often their behavior is not unlike that of a delinquent child, and for much the same reasons. We would take them out of the quasi-criminal divorce court and deal with them and their problems in a socialized court. When a marriage gets sick there is a cause. This cause manifests itself in the behavior, or misbehavior, of one or both spouses. Instead of determining whether a spouse has misbehaved and then "punishing" him by rewarding the aggrieved spouse with a divorce decree we would follow the general pattern of the juvenile court and endeavor to diagnose and treat, to discover the fundamental cause, then bring to bear all available resources to remove or rectify it.
>
> The socialized court we envision for marital problems would be similarly staffed as the juvenile court and would avail itself of the same outside resources. Most of the advantages are obvious of having all social-legal matters handled by one socialized court. There is an additional advantage not obvious to the uninitiated. Marriages fail because of the defects of the spouses. Spouses of this sort who have children are apt to have contact with juvenile court. Then, when they wind up in divorce court, the judge has before him the complete family record. One year, in as high as 40% of the divorce cases in one such court, the parties had previously had contact with the juvenile court. The information gleaned from these records enables the judge to make inquiries that bring out the whole truth and to find the best solution for the family as a whole. Conversely, in a recent study of divorce in

---

[51] See, for instance, Judge Atwell Westwick, "Wider Jurisdiction for the Juvenile Court," *Yearbook*, N.P.P.A., 1939, pp. 184–202; Judge Walter H. Beckham, "One Court for Family Problems," *ibid.*, 1942, pp. 80–93; also Lou, *op. cit.*, pp. 202–212; and *Standard Juvenile Court Act*, N.P.P.A., 1949, Foreword, pp. 4–5, and Sections 21, 22, 22A–D.

Illinois, many young wards of the divorce court are destined, because of the broken family, to become wards of the juvenile court.[52]

The report further points out that "the proposal to have all justiciable family matters handled by one court is far from new. It has been tried and has long since passed the experimental stage. For over 30 years Cincinnati has had such a court. From the outset the soundness of the idea became more and more apparent, and soon other Ohio cities fell in line and for years the seven largest (next after Cleveland, which has an independent juvenile court) have had such integrated family courts."

Another example of a functioning family court is the Municipal Court of Philadelphia, created in 1913. It exercises jurisdiction over cases of juvenile delinquency, dependency, and neglect; care for crippled and mentally deficient children; cases of run-away, disobedient, and disorderly minors above the juvenile court age of 18; cases of prostitution (irrespective of age); specially assigned criminal cases; adoption cases; cases of custody of children born within and without wedlock; domestic relations situations growing out of marital difficulties; cases of desertion and non-support of wife and children; cases of support for indigent parents; cases of establishment of paternity of children born out of wedlock; and civil law suits under $2,500 value. The judges of this court are aided by a probation department and a medical department, both operating as integral parts of the court's administrative structure.

A more recent law created the Family Court for New Castle County, Wilmington, Delaware. By act of 1945, this court was given exclusive jurisdiction not only over delinquent, dependent, and neglected children, but also over all violations of child labor laws; of laws relating to the sale or furnishing of cigarettes to a minor under seventeen years of age; the sale of deadly weapons to a minor; permitting minors under eighteen years of age to be present at games of chance; admitting a minor under eighteen years of age to, or per-

---

[52] *Report to the National Conference on Family Life (Action Area: Legal Problems)*, prepared by a committee headed by Reginald Heber Smith, chairman, and Judge Paul W. Alexander, vice-chairman, March 1948 (mimeographed). See also "Design for Family Living," *Survey Mid-monthly*, June 1948, pp. 206–207; and "Marriage and the Court," *Focus*, July 1949, p. 107. For a more complete Report of the National Conference on Family Life see *American Family a Factual Background*, Government Printing Office, 1949.

mitting him to remain in, certain places of amusement where intoxicating liquors are sold; and the unlawful sale or delivery of certain drugs to a minor under sixteen years. This court has exclusive jurisdiction in cases of contributing to the delinquency, neglect, or dependency of children, in cases of custody and guardianship, in cases of the maintenance of illegitimate children, and in desertion and non-support cases. Furthermore, it has jurisdiction over offenses, except felonies and wife-beating, committed by one member of a family against another member of said family, and of criminal cases, except felonies, in which one member of a family is complainant against another member of said family. The court also has jurisdiction, with certain qualifications, in cases of consent to marriage of juveniles. In 1949, 1,758 adults were brought before this court. It was found that 32.7 per cent of these cases involved failure to provide support for wives, children, or both. Assault and battery accounted for 24.9 per cent, and breach of the peace for 16 per cent.[53]

A difference of opinion exists as to whether or not divorce cases should be included in the jurisdiction of a comprehensive family court.[54] The previously mentioned report of the National Conference on Family Life favors the handling of divorce cases in the family court. The objection to this proposition is usually based on the argument that it would be incongruous to confer jurisdiction over divorce proceedings upon a family court, which should be principally devoted to the maintenance and strengthening of family life. Another objection is that divorce cases may take too large a part of the court's time and facilities.

But even when divorce cases are heard by courts of general jurisdiction, as is the present rule, the need for social investigation, especially where children are involved, has been recognized by a number

---

[53] These figures are taken from "A Summons For You," Annual Report of the Family Court for New Castle County, Wilmington, Delaware, for 1949; this report not only describes the work of the court, but also gives credit to the "Family Court Association," formerly the "Juvenile Court Association," an advisory committee composed of interested citizens, which over the years has aided the court in reaching a satisfactory standard of performance and which interprets the purpose and objectives of the court to the general public.

[54] Of thirty-three family and domestic relations courts listed in the *Book of the States, 1945–1946* (Council of State Governments, Chicago, pp. 346–347), only nineteen possess divorce jurisdiction. See also Foreword to *Standard Juvenile Court Act*, N.P.P.A., 1949, pp. 4–5.

of judges in several states sitting in divorce cases. Such an inroad of social aspects into the primarily legal procedure in divorce actions is another example of the expansion of juvenile court techniques into related fields.

In a number of New Jersey counties, especially Hudson and Essex, the county probation bureaus make investigations for the Court of Chancery when ordered by the advisory masters hearing the marital dispute. A special staff of investigators in the Court of Domestic Relations in St. Louis makes preliminary investigations where the interests of minors are involved in divorce, separate maintenance, and custody cases. In Michigan it is the statutory duty of the circuit judge of the county to recommend for appointment by the governor a "Friend of the Court," whose duty it is to investigate and make recommendations in motions in divorce, separate maintenance, and annulment cases. The Friend of the Court may also act as referee. In the smaller counties, the positions of Friend of the Court and that of probation officer are frequently combined. Kentucky has enacted a statute authorizing the appointment of a Friend of the Court in counties containing a city of the second class. This Friend of the Court shall, in any action for divorce where the parties have minor children, and when requested by the trial judge, ascertain the facts and circumstances affecting the rights and interests of the children and report to the judge his recommendations as to care, custody, and maintenance of the children. When requested by both parties to a divorce proceeding where the custody of children is involved, investigation may be made by the juvenile probation department of the Department of Domestic Relations of the Circuit Court of Portland, Oregon. The probation departments of Harris and Dallas counties, Texas, are directed by statute to make investigations for the courts with reference to the custody of children in divorce proceedings. In Indiana, in proceedings for divorce, separation, or annulment where minor children are involved, the judge may request the juvenile court to refer the case to a probation officer for full investigation and report to the court.[55]

In the Juvenile and Domestic Relations Court of Cincinnati, which

---

[55] For further information, see Sol Rubin, "Probation in the Divorce Court," *Probation*, April 1947, pp. 102–104; much of the above information has been obtained from this article.

for all practical purposes can really be called a family court and which possesses jurisdiction in divorce proceedings, social service is rendered through the court's probation staff prior to divorce—*i.e.*, during the time after petition for divorce has been filed and before it is granted, a period of from six to twelve weeks. The court's Family Service Division is primarily concerned with the care the children are receiving and the effect the behavior of the father and mother has on the children. Sometimes a reconciliation between the parents is achieved through the efforts of the court workers. The judge orders a social investigation of the family situation whenever he recognizes the need for such a study. At the time of the divorce hearing, the judge has the social case report before him; it helps him to make a satisfactory decision on the support and the custody of the children and on the right of the spouse who has not been granted custody to visit the children under proper conditions.[56]

In the state of Washington, a law enacted in 1949 created family courts in all counties as part of the existing superior courts. The family court has jurisdiction in all marital proceedings; it has power to implement reconciliation, and to issue orders relating to custody of children, possession of property, and so forth. Hearings are private and informal. If reconciliation fails, the family court retains jurisdiction to hear the proceeding for divorce, annulment, or separate maintenance.

The various examples of the expansion of the juvenile court's philosophy and practice, as presented in this chapter, tend to confirm a prophetic statement of Judge Benjamin Lindsey, who was mentioned earlier as one of the first protagonists of the juvenile court. Many years ago he said: "The chief significance of the juvenile court movement is that in breaking away from the old procedure it is preparing the way for a new procedure for adults as well as for children." [57]

---

[56] For further details, see William L. Fiedler, "Social Services in a Divorce Court," *Yearbook*, N.P.P.A., 1948, pp. 96–106. See also William D. Cochran, "Children of Divorce," *The Child*, September 1947, pp. 38–41. The San Francisco Juvenile Court has for several years made investigations in divorce cases The excellent report of this court for 1949, entitled "Youth Guidance in Action," gives the following figures: in 1945, 135; in 1946, 204; in 1947, 164; in 1948, 133; in 1949, 142 requests for investigations were received and carried out by the probation officers.

[57] Maurice Parmelee, *Criminology*, Macmillan, New York, 1918, p. 407.

As has been mentioned in this chapter, one of the best examples of this development is the use of probation. The next chapter will deal particularly with juvenile probation and will discuss its history, present extent, administration, and value as correctional treatment.

Chapter XI

PROBATION

1. DEVELOPMENT OF PROBATION

a. History of Probation

THE TERM "probation," derived from the Latin *probare* (meaning to test, to try, to prove), has been used in relation to criminal matters only since the middle of the nineteenth century.

But the legal source of probation is much older than that. It can be traced to the necessity for mitigating the rigors of mechanistic criminal law [1] which governed the Middle Ages and continued into the modern era. The common law permitted the court to suspend sentence for an indefinite time. The practice of suspension of sentence, allowing the convicted offender to remain at liberty upon condition of good behavior, was later reinforced by statutory provisions.

Probation in the modern sense was a single-handed "invention" of John Augustus, the Boston shoemaker, to whom previous reference has been made.[2] He added an important element to the practice of probation, namely *supervision* during the probation period. The incident that started John Augustus upon his new venture may well be termed an epochal event in the history of correctional treatment. The term "probation" was used for the first time in this connotation in his own description.

> In the month of August, 1841, I was in court one morning, when the door communicating with the lock-room was opened and an officer entered, followed by a ragged and wretched looking man, who took his seat upon the bench allotted to prisoners. I imagined from the man's

---

[1] For details, see *Survey of Release Procedures*, United States Government Printing Office, Washington, D.C., 1939, Vol. II, *Probation*, pp. 3–10.
[2] See Chapter IX, pp. 283–284.

appearance, that his offence was that of yielding to his appetite for intoxicating drinks, and in a few moments I found that my suspicions were correct, for the clerk read the complaint, in which the man was charged with being a common drunkard. The case was clearly made out, but before sentence had been passed, I conversed with him for a few moments, and found that he was not yet past all hope of reformation, although his appearance and his looks precluded a belief in the minds of others that he would ever become a *man* again. He told me that if he could be saved from the House of Correction, he never again would taste intoxicating liquors; there was such an earnestness in that tone, and a look expressive of firm resolve, that I determined to aid him; I bailed him, by permission of the Court. He was ordered to appear for sentence in three weeks from that time. He signed the pledge and became a sober man; at the expiration of this period of *probation*, I accompanied him into the court room; his whole appearance was changed and no one, not even the scrutinizing officers, could have believed that he was the same person who less than a month before, had stood trembling on the prisoner's stand.—The Judge expressed himself much pleased with the account we gave of the man, and instead of the usual penalty,—imprisonment in the House of Correction,—he fined him one cent and costs, amounting in all to $3.76,

John Augustus—"First Probation Officer," 1784–1859. (*Courtesy of National Probation and Parole Association*)

which was immediately paid. The man continued industrious and sober, and without doubt has been by this treatment, saved from a drunkard's grave.[3]

---

[3] *John Augustus—First Probation Officer*, N.P.P.A., 1939, pp. 4–5.

John Augustus in his activities as "first probation officer" (as he has been retrospectively called) included adult as well as juvenile offenders. Until his death in 1859, he bailed and subsequently super-- vised on probation a total of 2,000 persons. In addition, he was often called upon in cases of child neglect and dependency. Immigrant welfare was another of his interests. Although best known for his probation work, he did not limit his interests to this one phase of correctional problems. One of his main concerns was the treatment of men and women who, in his own words, "so frequently render themselves obnoxious to the laws by the vice of intemperance." His first case, and most of his subsequent probationers, belonged to that group. Clearly recognizing that jail sentences could not bring about the reform of these unfortunate persons, he proposed the establish- ment of a state asylum for them. "We desire something different from a House of Correction or Alms-house, in order to save an honest man from being thrust into a den of thieves and robbers . . . a place where he may be able to earn something for the support of his family." Overcoming serious obstacles, during the course of his welfare work he succeeded in being allowed to visit prisoners in jail. In his report he censured the administration of the County Jail and of the House of Correction for their poor and unreliable record keeping and criticized the lack of correlation and cooperation be- tween these prisons and the Police Court, all of which produced unnecessary hardship for sentenced persons and their families. He suggested a change in the complicated and cumbersome procedure required for the discharge of persons who were confined in jail for nonpayment of fines and costs. Thus John Augustus can rightly be called a penal reformer. And, as has almost every reformer, he met opposition. To critics who considered his humanitarian approach toward offenders an "incentive to crime," he replied with words that in their general application transcend his own time and the scope of his work. They are a strong condemnation of prejudices based on generalizations. "Individuals and communities generally are but too prone to infer evil of a class if they but occasionally observe it in individuals. . . ."

Two other pioneers of this period, Rufus R. Cook [4] and Miss L. P.

---

[4] Brief reference to Mr. Cook's activities has been made earlier; see Chapter IX, p. 284.

Burnham, were primarily concerned with the supervision of children. Both worked devotedly for the Children's Aid Society of Boston, which was founded in 1863 and which from the very beginning recognized probation as a promising form of treatment of young delinquents. Rufus Cook was in daily attendance at the various courts before which juvenile offenders had to appear. His efforts were recognized by the judges who placed boys on probation to him for a specified time of supervision and guidance. Miss Burnham, who has been called the first career woman in this field in which so many of her sex later became active workers, early realized the need for investigation of the personality and the environment of these children prior to court hearing, in order to determine their suitability for probation treatment. Other individuals prompted by humanitarian motives, and religious groups that considered this act a service of mercy, came forward to assume responsibility for wayward children placed on probation by the judiciary.[5]

As has been briefly mentioned in another connection,[6] Massachusetts, probably as a direct outcome of these pioneering activities, passed a law in 1869 providing for the supervision of juvenile delinquents by a state visiting agency. This agency was authorized to recommend to the courts probation in suitable cases, to accept the custody of juvenile offenders for supervision and, if necessary, to place them in private families. Thus a probation system for juveniles was for the first time recognized by state legislation and entrusted into the hands of public officials.

However, the use of probation for children during the following three decades remained sporadic; it received its real impetus and gained more general acceptance only with the advent and growth of the juvenile court movement.

b. Definition and Extent of Probation

The object of probation, according to a Supreme Court decision written by Chief Justice Hughes, is "to provide a period of grace in order to aid the rehabilitation of a penitent offender, to take advan-

---

[5] For further details concerning this pioneering era of probation, see Donald W. Moreland, "John Augustus and his Successors," *Yearbook*, N.P.P.A., 1941, pp. 1–22.

[6] See Chapter IX, p. 284.

tage of an opportunity for reformation which actual service of the suspended sentence might make less probable." [7]

The suspension of a sentence can take either of two forms: the judge may pronounce sentence and suspend its execution; or—and this is the generally preferred practice—he may suspend the imposition of sentence. What is the actual difference between these two types? In both instances the condition of law-abiding behavior is attached to the suspension of sentence, and specific conditions, such as abstention from liquor, removal from an undesirable neighborhood, and support of family, are also frequently imposed. Let us assume that the defendant does not live up to these conditions and that he again violates a law. If the execution of sentence has been suspended, the originally pronounced sentence, most often a term of imprisonment, will now be executed. If, however, the imposition of sentence has been suspended, it is now the duty of the judge to pronounce the sentence for the original offense, which will be immediately carried out.

Suspension of sentence in either form is not necessarily accompanied by probation, but in an ever-growing number of cases the judges make use of it. They feel that the social aim of suspension of sentence, namely the rehabilitation of the offender, is immeasurably helped by supervision of an agent of the court. Appropriately, therefore, the definition of probation in the report of the National Commission on Law Observance and Enforcement stresses the social side of probation more than its legal aspects: "Probation is a process of treatment, prescribed by the court for persons convicted of offenses against the law, during which the individual on probation lives in the community and regulates his own life under conditions imposed by the court (or other constituted authority) and is subject to supervision by a probation officer." [8]

In these definitions the four basic elements of probation are apparent: suspension of sentence, a period of freedom in the community, condition of good behavior, and supervision by an agent of the court.

---

[7] Burns v. U.S.—287 U.S. 216, quoted in *Probation*, April 1941, p. 104.

[8] National Commission on Law Observance and Enforcement, *Report No. 9,* "Penal Institutions, Probation and Parole," Government Printing Office, Washington, D.C., 1931, p. 184.

Since probation is being used in order to avoid the incarceration of the offender, it seems worth while to list the advantages that probation has over imprisonment:

(a) The probationer remains in the free society.

(b) His social status is not impaired.

(c) He can continue to support the members of his family who often would become public charges when the breadwinner was imprisoned.

(d) He can pay restitution to the victim of his unlawful act.

(e) He can be rehabilitated through the efforts of the probation officer.

(f) In order to achieve such rehabilitation, the resources of the community can be utilized.

(g) The community saves money, since it costs at least about ten times as much to keep an offender in prison as it does to supervise him on probation.[9]

Probation applied to children has been defined "as a system of treatment . . . by means of which the child remains in his ordinary environment and to a great extent at liberty, but throughout the probation period subject to the watchful care and personal influence of the agent of the court known as the probation officer." [10]

While in adult cases probation remains to a large degree an adjunct of a sentence to imprisonment and is closely tied up with the suspension of the sentence, probation in the realm of the juvenile court has come into its own right, quite apart from other forms of treatment. Nevertheless, in juvenile cases the comparison between probation and commitment to an institution is not a remote one, especially because intra-mural treatment is usually prescribed when probation fails. An enumeration of the advantages of probation over commitment for children is, therefore, presented:

(a) It is the most individualistic form of treatment.

---

[9] According to the Annual Report for 1948 of the Director of the Administrative Office of the United States Courts (Government Printing Office, Washington, 1948), the cost of supervision on probation is approximately 16 cents a day, compared with a cost of $2.98 for imprisonment in Federal institutions (p. 69).

[10] Charles L. Chute, *Probation in Children's Courts*, United States Children's Bureau, Publication No. 80, p. 7.

(b) It applies the methods of social case work.

(c) It leaves the child in his normal home surroundings.

(d) It enlists the help of community resources.

(e) It is not considered punitive and, therefore, is free from social stigma.

(f) As in the case of probation for adults, it is much less expensive.

The extent to which probation is used cannot be measured with accuracy, because few up-to-date, comprehensive statistics are available. The United States Bureau of the Census reported in 1945, on the basis of judicial statistics from 25 states, that of 70,000 offenders convicted in that year, 31.6 per cent were placed on probation or were given suspended sentence. Rhode Island reported the highest rate (64.6 per cent); next came New Hampshire, with 49.8 per cent.[11] Since the Census Bureau discontinued the collection of criminal statistics in 1945, no newer information of this kind is available. In the Federal judiciary system, 9,821 individuals, or 32 per cent of those convicted in the district courts (including those found guilty of juvenile delinquency) during the year ending June 30, 1948, were placed on probation.[12]

Regarding delinquent children on probation, the juvenile court statistics for 1945, published by the United States Children's Bureau and covering almost 115,000 cases reported from 374 juvenile courts throughout the country, showed that probation was ordered in 30 per cent of the cases. Another publication of the United States Children's Bureau states that the 20 per cent decrease from 1933 to 1945 in the number of children in institutions for delinquent children reflects in part the increased use of probation and parole as methods of supervision of delinquent children in the homes of parents or other relatives or in foster-family homes.[13] Thirty-nine per cent of all cases of Federal juvenile offenders in 1948 resulted in probation.[14]

---

[11] *Judicial Criminal Statistics 1945*, published by United States Bureau of Census, 1947.

[12] *Annual Report of the Director of the Administrative Office of the United States Courts, 1948*, p. 70.

[13] See "Children Served by Public Welfare Agencies and Institutions 1945," United States Children's Bureau Statistical Series #3, Government Printing Office, Washington, D.C.

[14] *Federal Prisons 1948*, p. 18.

c. Probation Legislation

Massachusetts, the first state to pass a law on probation for juveniles, also enacted the first statute providing for probation for adult offenders. This was in 1878. Today, forty-two states and the District of Columbia have such probation laws. In the Federal judiciary system, probation was authorized by Congress in 1925 and has been in more extensive use in the Federal courts since 1930. There are, however, several limitations on the scope of probation. In a number of states, probation may not be granted for the most serious offenses, the definition of which varies from state to state; in others, it may be applied only in cases of first offenders; in still others, the use of probation is limited to courts with specified types of jurisdiction or to courts in counties of a specified size of population.

Probation for juveniles is provided for in all states, the District of Columbia, the territories, and the Federal judiciary system. In most cases, it is incorporated in the juvenile court acts as one of the possible case dispositions available to the juvenile court judge. Most often, the law is quite broad in its statutory provision for probation. Early drafts of the *Standard Juvenile Court Act* simply stated that the court may "place the child on probation or under supervision in his home or in the custody of a suitable person elsewhere, upon such conditions as the court shall determine." But the newest edition of the *Standard Juvenile Court Act* has added the following definition of the purpose and methods of probation:

> Probation shall mean casework services during a continuance of the case. Probation shall not be ordered or administered as a punishment, but as a measure for the protection, guidance and well-being of the child and his family. Probation methods shall be directed to the discovery and correction of the basic causes of maladjustment and to the development of the child's personality and character, with the aid of the social resources of the community (Section 18).

The state laws do not always leave the use of probation entirely to the discretion of the judge; they make it mandatory under certain circumstances. For instance, the Pennsylvania Juvenile Court Law provides that a child under twelve years of age can be committed to an institution for delinquents only after he has previously been placed on probation and after the efforts of such supervisory extramural treatment have failed.

In accordance with the non-criminal procedure of juvenile courts, some laws use the term "supervision" instead of "probation," because the word "probation" is an inadequate indication of the social aspects connected with it and is too strongly reminiscent of criminal court nomenclature. However, the word "probation" is still preponderantly employed both in theory and practice.

In the presentation of the development of probation it was found helpful for a fuller understanding of the subject to include material on adult probation. The remainder of this chapter, however, will be confined to juvenile probation. It will deal with the administration of probation and probation as a treatment process.

2. THE ADMINISTRATION OF PROBATION

a. The Probation Department of the Juvenile Court

As was pointed out in Chapter IX, most juvenile courts are organized on the basis of county units either as separate and independent courts or as special sessions, branches, or divisions of general courts. Probation is administered by the probation department, which consists of one or more probation officers and other administrative technical and clerical personnel.

The efficient and successful functioning of the juvenile court is largely dependent upon a well-organized staff of probation officers. In the juvenile court more than in any other judicial branch, the judge must rely on the work of court aides. The wisdom of using the title "probation officer" in handling juvenile cases has been questioned, and the terms "probation counsellor," "youth counsellor," or simply "counsellor" have been substituted in several places. Such other names as "supervisor" and "court social worker" have also been suggested. However, the general usage of the title "probation officer" is still prevalent.

In most cases, the probation department is the administrative adjunct of the court, and its personnel, budget, policies, and procedures are controlled by the judiciary. But some probation departments are entirely independent of the court and serve it in a manner similar to other autonomous agencies, such as the police or the sheriff's office. A notable example of such a set-up is the Los Angeles County Probation Department, which serves the various local courts in juvenile as well as in adult cases, but which is absolutely separate from the courts

and under the immediate administrative control of the County Board
of Supervisors.[15] A favorite argument *for* placing the probation department under the administrative control of the courts is that political influence upon the employees of the probation department will
in this way be reduced. The main objection *against* this system is
that the functions of the probation department are substantially of
an administrative, not a judicial, character.[16] Finally, in some states
probation administration is organized on the state level, as will be
discussed in a later context.

Thus a rather varied picture presents itself. Local factors that influence the administrative set-up of the probation department are the
size and population density of the county, the scope of jurisdiction
of the court, and the availability of community resources.

Moreover, the fact that the various state juvenile court acts provide for probation does not necessarily imply that all counties
throughout the United States have complete probation service coverage. The National Probation and Parole Association reports that in
1947, out of a total of 3,071 counties, 1,610 counties did not have any
such service for juveniles.[17] In many of these counties the lack might
be attributed to the comparatively small number of children referred
to the court. In other instances, however, it is due to uninformed public opinion, to penny-pinching fiscal authorities, and to judges without social vision. Any one of these factors or all three combined
could prevent the setting up of a probation program even though it
might be vitally needed in a given locality. On January 1, 1947, there
were 3,681 probation officers for juveniles in the continental United
States appointed locally or as state employees.

There are many juvenile courts in less-populated counties with a
one-man probation department. Often this probation officer handles
adult as well as juvenile cases. Not all the 3,681 probation officers
are employed full-time in this capacity. The other duties of part-time

---

[15] For more information on the various activities of the Los Angeles County
Probation Department, see Chapter XI, pp. 402–403.

[16] For a discussion of this problem, see Edwin H. Sutherland, *Principles of
Criminology*, 1947 edition, Lippincott, Philadelphia, p. 400, and Martin H.
Neumeyer, *Juvenile Delinquency in Modern Society*, Van Nostrand, New
York, 1949, p. 260.

[17] See *Directory of Probation and Parole Officers in United States and
Canada*, N.P.P.A., 1947, p. 275.

probation officers might include those of sheriff, bailiff, clerk of the court, welfare worker, school attendance officer, and so forth.

It is felt that the present number of probation officers must be more than tripled if the problems of child delinquency are to be adequately handled.[18]

Wherever there are two or more probation officers, one of them is frequently designated as being in charge—*i.e.*, he is the administrative head of the probation department. His title, as a rule, is "chief probation officer," "director of probation," or "supervisor of probation." As chief administrative officer he usually supervises not only all probation officers but also the clerical staff assigned to his department. As mentioned in Chapter VIII, he might also serve in the capacity of superintendent of the detention home. In the larger probation departments he is often assisted by a deputy chief probation officer and assistant or district supervisors.

The number of officers in any probation department should depend upon the volume of work the department is called upon to handle. The previously quoted *Juvenile Court Standards* recommends that not more than fifty cases should be under the supervision of one probation officer at any one time; officers handling girls' cases should be assigned a smaller number. It must be recognized that this is an ideal figure and that in reality it is very frequently exceeded, mostly because of limited budgets.[19] Excessive case loads naturally tend to lower the quality of the probation officers' work. Such false economy might easily result in higher expenditures in the long run, because of inadequate probation supervision and consequently increased recidivism. Taking a realistic view of this situation, Professor Walter Reckless advises that "probation and parole officers cannot look forward to an era of small loads." They are, therefore, "developing ideas of how to classify a load in terms of kinds of help probationers and parolees need, the degrees and intensive or active supervision they require, and the amount of responsible and mature self-propelling of which they are capable." [20]

---

[18] See statement made by Will C. Turnbladh, executive director, N.P.P.A., quoted in *Focus*, September 1949, pp. 154–155.

[19] The *Annual Report of the Administrative Office of the United States Courts for 1948* indicated the high case load of the Federal probation officers; the load consisted of an average of 114 supervision cases, in addition to an average of 106 pre-sentence investigations (p. 68).

[20] Walter C. Reckless, "Significant Trends in the Treatment of Crime and Delinquency," *Federal Probation*, March 1949, pp. 6–11 (quotation on p. 10);

b. State Participation

One way to stimulate the establishment or the improvement of probation services on the local level is through the active participation of state agencies in juvenile court work. Such state action may take various forms. As has been mentioned before,[21] there are only a few state-administered juvenile courts. In about half of the states, a state probation commission or a division of the state welfare department or department of correction has been given some kind of responsibility for the development and operation of probation services for children. In California the Youth Authority may grant probation to persons under twenty-one years of age committed to it by the local courts. The Youth Conservation Commission in Minnesota and the Youth Service Commission in Wisconsin supervise juveniles and adolescents on probation who have been placed under their control by the local courts. In several states, examinations are given by state boards, commissions, or departments for the purpose of establishing eligibility lists from which probation officers are appointed locally (as in Indiana, Nevada, Virginia); in others, probation officers are appointed by state agencies directly (New Hampshire, Wyoming), or their appointment, though made locally, must be approved by a state agency (North Carolina). In a number of states, county welfare agents appointed by and operating under a state department of welfare or assistance may be called upon by local juvenile court judges to render probation service.[22] In West Virginia, the division of child welfare of the state department of public assistance renders juvenile probation service through eight district offices, each administered by a child welfare supervisor. In Virginia, state aid is provided as a means of stimulating the establishment of probation service in local communities by paying one-half of the salary of probation officers in juvenile and domestic relations courts in cities over 10,000 population; appointments are made from a list approved by the state department of public welfare. In New York, the division of proba-

---

the same article appears in *Yearbook*, N.P.P.A., 1948, pp. 1–14 (quotation on pp. 10–11).

[21] Chapter IX, p. 293.

[22] On the service of child welfare workers, particularly in rural areas, to juvenile courts, see "The Juvenile Court and the Public Welfare Agency in the Child Welfare Program," *Child Welfare at the Crossroads*, United States Children's Bureau, Publication No. 327, 1949, p. 29.

tion of the state department of correction, headed by a director of probation, has general supervision of probation officers, both adult and juvenile, throughout the state. The director makes recommendations regarding administration of probation in children's courts and adopts rules regarding methods and procedures in administration of probation throughout the state, except in New York City. In Vermont, the state commissioner of public welfare is *ex officio* the state probation officer. He has general supervision over all probationers, both juvenile and adult. With the approval of the governor he may appoint and remove at pleasure deputy probation officers. In several states the law authorizes a state agency in general terms to cooperate with the courts, to collect reports from probation officers on their case loads, or to give advisory service.

As a rule, good cooperation exists between probation departments of different cities, whether in the same or in different states. This collaboration comprises the undertaking of investigations upon request of probation departments in other localities and the assuming of supervision over probationers who move from the city or town where their case had been disposed of into another community. Also in operation are interstate compacts signed by forty-five states regarding reciprocity in the supervision of probationers and parolees; in cases of juveniles, usually an informal request by the probation department of the child's previous residence to the probation department of the new residence is sufficient. The National Probation and Parole Association has paved the way for such cooperation, particularly through its publication of a directory of all probation and parole officers in the United States and Canada.

c. Federal Probation Service

In spite of the general policy of the Federal authorities to divert cases of children who have committed Federal offenses to the local juvenile courts whenever possible,[23] a considerable number of juvenile cases still come before Federal courts. According to Richard A. Chappell, Chief of Probation, Administrative Office of the United States Courts, approximately 10 per cent of the offenders appearing before the United States Courts are juveniles.[24] In the fiscal year

---

[23] See Chapter IX, p. 291.
[24] See *Federal Probation*, October–December 1947, p. 33.

ending June 30, 1948, 800 Federal juvenile offenders (753 males, 47 females) were placed on probation.[25]

The Federal probation service functions through probation departments attached to the United States District Courts. In 1948, 285 Federal probation officers throughout the country were supervising adult as well as juvenile offenders.

A unique method of handling cases of Federal juvenile offenders, somewhat akin to probation, is the "deferred prosecution plan for juveniles," which was first put into operation in the eastern district of New York at Brooklyn, in 1938 (therefore called the "Brooklyn Plan"). It was officially endorsed and recommended to all United States Attorneys by Attorney General Tom C. Clark in 1946. The prosecuting attorney, according to this plan, holds in abeyance all legal processes in "worthy cases involving juvenile offenders." [26] The juvenile is placed under the unofficial supervision of a probation officer for a definite period—usually eighteen months—and if he adjusts satisfactorily the case is closed without prosecution and, therefore, without any criminal record. However, if the juvenile does not comply with the terms of supervision or if he commits any further offenses, prosecution of the original case takes place. In the year ending June 30, 1947, 125 cases were handled pursuant to this procedure.[27]

A somewhat similar procedure is in operation in New Jersey, where a probationer convicted between the ages of sixteen and twenty years may apply to have his record destroyed after ten years of good behavior.

d. The Functions of the Probation Officer

The probation officer has, as a rule, two main assignments: investigation of social facts and pertinent data concerning the child's personality before court hearing, as described in Chapter VIII, and

---

[25] *Federal Prisons 1948*, p. 89.

[26] For details, see Conrad P. Printzlien, "Prosecution Deferred for Young Offenders," *Probation*, October 1946, pp. 1–8, and "Deferred Prosecution for Juvenile Offenders," *Federal Probation*, March 1948, pp. 17–22; Richard A. Chappell, "Federal Probation Service: Its Growth and Progress," *Federal Probation*, October–December 1947, p. 33.

[27] *Federal Prisons 1947*, p. 27.

probation, which has given title to his calling and which will be discussed in more detail later in this chapter.

In addition to these two tasks, the probation officer is often called upon to handle a number of other assignments. He may be directed by the court to take charge of children before the court hearing; this assignment may include placement of children in a foster home, in a detention home, or, in some smaller communities, in the probation officer's own home. The probation officer has to be present at the court hearing in order to supplement, if necessary, his written report to the judge and to make recommendations to him regarding the disposition of the case. If placement of the child away from his own family is ordered, the probation officer has to take the child to the place of commitment—a foster home, an institution, a hospital, or any other designated facility. In cases of adult offenders in which children are involved either as private prosecutors, witnesses, or co-defendants, it devolves upon the probation officer to accompany the child to the trial and to represent his interests.

In many courts, the probation officer is also given wide discretion in adjusting situations that might cause the delinquency of a juvenile, without recourse to a court hearing. Such incidents include neighborhood frictions, racial tensions, or other community problems where a probation officer, often in cooperation with the juvenile aid bureaus of the police or other crime-preventive agencies, can be of assistance. Another type of "unofficial" case adjustment, sometimes called "friendly service," is the handling of complaints by parents concerning the incorrigibility of their children. Frequently these situations can be straightened out through the probation officer's efforts and do not require any judicial decision. And, as has been mentioned before,[28] the probation officer is often delegated by the judge to act as referee, either in all cases of delinquency or only in a certain type of case, with the power to make decisions subject to the confirmation of the court or to transmit the case with recommendations to the judge for a court hearing and final disposition.

Still another duty of the probation officer is the collection of money. This duty may involve the restitution for damages, payment of which was imposed upon the juvenile or his parents as a condition of probation; or it may involve the enforcement of a court order

[28] Chapter IX, pp. 317–319.

upon parents to pay for the maintenance of the child in a foster home or institution. In juvenile courts that also have jurisdiction over desertion and non-support cases, the probation officer in many instances is responsible for the collection of moneys from the husband and father and for their disbursement to the wife and mother as beneficiary.

In a considerable number of states the probation officer supervises children on parole from state or local institutions where no special parole officers are employed.

Various state laws and rules of local courts provide for additional duties of probation officers,[29] such as the enforcement of school attendance and child labor laws. In some jurisdictions they are given the powers of sheriff, police, or other peace officer in discharging their duties. In general, however, the trend, so far as the actual performance of the probation officer's work is concerned, is away from the approach of mere law enforcement and in the direction of case work and counseling.

The keeping of case records is an important part of the probation officer's job. Case recording has been discussed in Chapter VIII in reference to investigations prior to court hearing; the same principles mentioned there apply to the keeping of records concerning children supervised on probation and parole, and to the recording of informal complaints or any other assignment of a probation officer.

To prepare statistical reports on the types of cases handled (including data regarding the individual child, the manner of the court dispositions, and the number of contacts and visits) is a necessary administrative chore of the probation officer. Statistics collected by individual probation officers serve as basis for the monthly and annual reports which are required, in several instances by state law, from local probation departments for the use of state commissions, boards, and other supervising authorities.

More and more in recent years have the rank and file of probation officers recognized that one of their important, but heretofore often neglected, tasks is to interpret the functions and activities of the juvenile court and the probation department to the public. The various media of disseminating such information will be presented later.[30]

---

[29] For details, see Cosulich, *op. cit.*, pp. 94–97.
[30] See Chapter XVII.

Having listed the extensive number of duties of the probation officer, let us return to his two main functions and examine the principles governing the assignment of individual cases. Here again a great variety of rules is found in the many local probation departments; policy and practice depend naturally upon the size of the territory covered, the total case load of the probation department, and the scope of jurisdiction of the court.

In many smaller probation departments, the probation officer has to handle juvenile as well as adult cases, including cases of domestic relations, usually called desertion and non-support cases, and cases of establishment of paternity of children born out of wedlock. Since many juvenile courts have jurisdiction not only over delinquent children but also over situations of dependency and neglect, custody of children, and adoption, probation officers often handle all these types of cases.

It is recommended by the *Juvenile Court Standards*,[31] and is today quite generally accepted, that girls' cases should always be assigned to women probation officers; cases of boys under twelve years of age may be handled by women probation officers, but all cases of boys above that age should be assigned to men.

Often national origin, racial grouping, and sometimes religious affiliation are taken into consideration in the assignment of cases to probation officers of a certain nationality, color, or faith, partly because of better understanding of language and mentality, partly because of local custom.[32]

To assign the probation officers according to geographical districts, so that they handle all cases of children living in their desig-

---

[31] P. 8.

[32] A very interesting and valuable inquiry into the employment of Negro probation officers was undertaken by George Gittelson, Deputy Probation Officer, Los Angeles, California, who reports his findings in an article "Racial Factors in Staff Selection," *Focus*, July 1949, pp. 97–102. The study is based on replies to the following four questions, which were directed to 263 chief probation officers throughout the United States: "Do you have Negroes on your casework staff? If so, are white subjects assigned to them? In your opinion, is more effective probation work accomplished by segregation or non-segregation? Do you plan to change your policy pertaining to Negro personnel in the near future?" In his concluding remarks, Mr. Gittelson states that "in no case where the use of Negro personnel was instituted or extended did a failure in probation service result or a protest from the community arise."

nated territories, appears to be the most economical method. This arrangement does not preclude the assignment of special cases, such as sex delinquency, to those probation officers who, because of their training and experience, are particularly qualified for this kind of work.

Is it advisable to separate investigation and probation assignments and to have two groups of probation officers, one for investigative, and the other for supervisory purposes? A difference of opinion on this question has existed for many years. Both systems, separation of cases of investigation from those of probation, and assignment of both types of cases to the same probation officers, are in use. Reasons advanced for separation are that the two types of cases present a different emphasis and require different methods of work. Separation, it is argued, provides for more specialization of services and takes into account that some officers are better qualified for the job of investigators, while others are more efficient probation supervisors. On the other hand, proponents of the system that assigns both types of cases to one set of probation officers stress the saving of time and effort resulting from the fact that the officer who had investigated the case and is later assigned to supervise the child already knows the prevailing circumstances. Contact, or, in the social worker's language, rapport, has been previously established between the probation officer and the youngster and his family; the need for a new adjustment of child and parents to a different probation officer is, therefore, avoided. While the probation officer is investigating the case for the judge, he usually formulates and recommends a treatment plan which he can start to carry out immediately after the court hearing.[33]

The main functions of a probation department lie in the field of investigation prior to court hearing, supervision of probationers, and other duties of probation officers as described in this chapter. However, a number of probation departments have expanded their activities beyond this scope. Foster-home finding and placement is considered part of the function of the probation department in a number of localities. A notable example is the Juvenile Court of Allegheny County, Pittsburgh, Pennsylvania, which has its own foster-home

---

[33] For a discussion of this problem, see Walter C. Reckless, *op. cit.*, *Federal Probation*, March 1949, p. 10, and *Yearbook*, N.P.P.A., 1948, pp. 11–12.

department. It has a number of probation officers assigned to the finding and approving of foster homes and to the placement of children in such homes. The average number of children who were wards of the Juvenile Court of Allegheny County and for whom boarding care was provided in this manner amounted to 907 in 1946 and 862 in 1947.[34] A similar program, including foster-home care for delinquent as well as dependent and neglected children, is reported from Stockton, California. There, chief probation officer Kay Kunkel considers foster-home placement as "one phase of probation work." She states that "we must have an adequate, well-trained staff to do the job thoroughly from investigation, through processing for the court, locating the home and supervision of the child afterwards."[35] The Juvenile Court of Cook County, Chicago, reported that as of August 20, 1949, 262 children were under care in foster homes placed by the Court's Temporary Care and Child Placing Division and supervised by the probation officers of that division.[36]

Several probation departments have included delinquency prevention work in their sphere of interest. Outstanding work of this kind has been performed by the Los Angeles County Probation Department, which has its own delinquency prevention division, to which twenty-seven probation officers and the necessary administrative and clerical staff are assigned. This division undertakes group work with adolescents in highly vulnerable areas, particularly in slum neighborhoods where sporadic outbursts of violence resulting from racial tension have occurred. As John M. Zuck, Chief Probation Officer, Los Angeles County, reports, the children living in these neighborhoods are not much influenced by normal youth activity programs provided through public and private voluntary auspices in most of our larger cities. To reach this group in Los Angeles, the Probation Department assigned a special group of probation officers "selected on the basis of their familiarity with the different racial and cultural backgrounds involved, their skills in establishing rapport with this more aggressive type of youth, and

---

[34] *Focus the Child,* Annual Report of the Juvenile Court of Allegheny County, 1947, p. 27.

[35] For further details, see Kay Kunkel, "Foster Placement as Court Function," *Focus,* 1949, pp. 146–149.

[36] *Fiftieth Anniversary Report,* Juvenile Court of Cook County, 1949, pp. 28–29.

their ability to conduct an activity program attractive to problem youth." [37] Over a period of five years this group has established itself with forty-two different neighborhood groups organized in a federation. In the summer of 1948, for the first time, a summer camp in the mountains near the city was conducted with considerable success for a group of young people who usually are not acceptable to or interested in the regular summer camping programs of private agencies.

Another interesting project of the Los Angeles County Probation Department is the toy-lending program established for the benefit of younger children in underprivileged neighborhoods. These thirty-five centers are stocked with a great variety of toys which the children of the neighborhood may borrow with the written permission of their parents for a short period of time. The youngster is credited upon the return of the toy with so many points that enable him to borrow still better toys in the future. Stress is laid on the formation of habits of punctuality, promptness, care of the property of others, and neatness.

In the field of crime prevention, the Los Angeles County Probation Department has sponsored for many years a county organization program known as the "Co-ordinating Council Movement," whereby every community or neighborhood within the county is encouraged to establish committees of citizens whose civic consciousness is the mainspring of their interest in the prevention of crime and delinquency. Over eighty communities in Los Angeles County have these councils, all united in a county-wide federation under the sponsorship of the Los Angeles County Probation Department.[38]

The San Francisco Juvenile Court Probation Department also has its own prevention and special service division. Most of the children referred to this division are socially immature or emotional deviates who have few wholesome attitudes toward social and community

---

[37] For a detailed description of these activities, see John M. Zuck, "A Probation Department's Role in Delinquency Prevention," *Federal Probation*, December 1948, pp. 16–19, and "The Probation Officer's Participation in Delinquency Prevention," *Yearbook*, N.P.P.A., 1948, pp. 280–295; see also *44th Annual Report of the Los Angeles County Probation Department, 1948* (mimeographed), pp. 42–44.

[38] For more information, see Chapter XVI, pp. 655–662.

responsibilities, but whose overt acts are not sufficiently serious to make them wards of the court.[39] Similarly, the Los Angeles County Probation Department provides case work for so-called "non-court cases." It extends its services to people in the community, particularly juveniles, who require some form of help and counseling. Parents may call upon probation officers on a non-court basis to help their child adjust to the demands of society. This type of "informal probation," independent of the court, is also practiced by the Westchester County, New York, Probation Department, according to Director of Probation William J. Harper. Cases are brought to the attention of this department by police, schools, social agencies, or individuals, and in many instances by parents who are worried about their children. Such cases can be accepted for supervision with the permission of the judge but without being brought before the court.[40]

From New York City it is reported that for several years the probation department of the Court of General Sessions has conducted a camp program for children of adult probationers; 3,130 children, chiefly from underprivileged homes, have benefited from this program.[41] Other summer camp placement projects for children under supervision of probation departments are being undertaken in various places, for instance, in Essex County, New Jersey.

Realizing that many children referred to the court for delinquent behavior or for reasons of dependency and neglect are in poor physical condition, especially regarding mouth hygiene, several probation departments provide dental care for their wards. In Philadelphia, the dental clinic is part of the medical department of the Municipal Court, and probation officers refer children in need of dental care to this facility. In 1949, 14,157 treatments were given. In San Francisco, dental care is provided by the Juvenile Court Probation Department; in 1949, attendance at that clinic amounted to 2,697 children.

A number of probation departments have established facilities for children whose parents are either divorced or legally separated; the spouse who does not have custody of the child retains the right to

---

[39] For further details, see *Youth Guidance in Action*, Annual Report, San Francisco Juvenile Court Department, 1949, pp. 22–24.

[40] Reported in *Focus*, July 1949, p. 112.

[41] *Ibid*.

see the child at regular intervals. Since experience has shown that visits in the home of the other spouse often lead to unwholesome scenes of recrimination or even to fights in front of the children, a facility has been established under court auspices where such visits can take place. Nurseries of this kind are in operation in New York, Philadelphia, and other cities; the frequency of their use shows that they meet a real need.

Some probation departments have engaged in providing vocational guidance and in securing jobs for their probationers. Although this service is offered primarily in cases of adult probationers, adolescent boys and girls who were on probation or who were about to be released from training schools on parole have also been assisted.

e. Qualification, Appointment, and Training of the Probation Officer

The probation officer's job, which encompasses the probing and the diagnosis of human behavior and the guidance of young, impressionable individuals, calls for understanding and skill. Recent developments and new discoveries in the social and psychological sciences have greatly influenced the total child-welfare program, of which the probation service for youthful offenders constitutes a notable part. It is, therefore, more and more recognized that certain qualifications regarding educational background, training, and experience should be met by persons desiring to enter the probation field. A committee of the Professional Council of the National Probation and Parole Association, consisting of leading authorities in the probation and parole field, in 1945 formulated *Standards for Selection of Probation and Parole Officers*, after consultation with many administrators in the correctional field throughout the country. The *Standards* [42] suggests these minimum educational and experience qualifications: a bachelor's degree from a college or university of recognized standing or its educational equivalent, with courses in the social sciences; and one year of paid full-time experience under competent supervision in an approved social agency or related field, such as teaching, personnel work in industry, case work in an institution or correctional agency. Moreover, a probation officer must possess a good character and a balanced personality. The following traits are considered essential: "good health, physical endurance, intellectual

---

[42] N.P.P.A., 1945.

maturity, emotional stability, integrity, tact, dependability, adapta-
bility, resourcefulness, sincerity, humor, ability to work with others,
tolerance, patience, objectivity, capacity to win confidence, respect
for human personality, and genuine affection for people."

The educational qualifications are proposed as an entrance minimum for new appointees, and many probation departments strive to
apply these principles when staff vacancies have to be filled. But the
idea is still far from being universally adopted. Many state laws are
silent regarding qualifications for probation officers; others couch
the qualifications in such general terms that they can be met by any
untrained person as long as he is a "discreet person of reputable
character." Political influences, which, as a rule, have been successfully banned in the teaching profession, are still operating in the
probation field and have prevented many states and local communities from adopting minimum requirements for the appointment of
probation officers.

As the introduction to the *Standards* emphasizes, "There are in
many communities devoted and successful workers, qualified by self-
education and assimilated experience, who have attained professional
competence and who are in fact among our best workers." No
suggestion to replace such competent workers is made; the *Standards* refers only to the training and qualifications of future appointees.

Appointments of probation officers are, as a rule, made by the
judge or judges of the local court, often in consultation with the
chief probation officer, and in various communities upon nomination
by a juvenile court or probation committee. In Los Angeles, California, where the Probation Department is independent of the courts,
the chief probation officer appoints his assistants, while he, himself,
is appointed by the County Board of Supervisors. In Alameda
County, California, and in San Francisco City and County, the chief
probation officer, though himself appointed by the judges, appoints
his staff of probation officers. The *Standard Juvenile Court Act*
provides that the judge shall appoint a chief administrative officer
who, with the approval of the judge, appoints the probation officers
and other employees of the probation department (Section 5). As
has been mentioned before, several states have adopted statutory provisions governing the appointment of probation officers; they are
either appointed as state employees to serve on a state-wide or a

local level, or they are certified by state welfare departments or state civil service agencies to local authorities for appointment.[43]

The method of selection of probation officers is closely related to the matter of qualification. The *Standards* suggests that appointments be made from eligibility lists resulting from competitive merit examinations comprising both written and oral tests and conducted under civil service regulations wherever they exist. These examinations should be open to all who meet the stipulated minimum qualifications, regardless of residence. True, too many appointments are still made for reasons other than qualification for the job; but the trend is toward an increasing awareness by the public, the judges, and other appointing bodies—and naturally the probation officers themselves—that probation service has become a profession. For instance, various progressive courts, even without specific legal requirements, have instituted a voluntary merit system for the appointment of probation personnel.

In order to promote high standards of qualification and selection of juvenile court personnel, special consideration must be given to the training of probation officers, including pre-service and in-service training.

Training prior to entrance into the probation career is determined by the adoption of the previously cited educational and training requirements. The *Standards* states that "the best training for probation and parole work is in a graduate school of social work," realizing, however, that the educational requirement of a bachelor's degree or its equivalent, with courses in the social sciences, is probably as much as can at present be hoped for as a minimum in many parts of the country. A difference of opinion exists as to whether case work training is a good preparation for probation work or not. Walter C. Reckless,[44] for instance, thinks that "the trained probation officer should have a good foundation in criminology and in the field of corrections, both juvenile and adult. He needs to take specially organized courses in probation and parole work which can give him

---

[43] See discussion of state participation in Chapter IX, pp. 336–338, and Chapter XI, pp. 395–396.

[44] "Training Probation and Parole Personnel," *Focus*, March 1948, pp. 44–48; see also "Training Reconsidered" (comments on Reckless' article), *Focus*, November 1948, pp. 180–182; and Walter C. Reckless, "The Controversy about Training," *Focus*, January 1949, pp. 23–25.

a specific preparation rather than a case work preparation." He is of the opinion that "the basic underpinning of probation and parole should not be casework and its allied psychiatric point of view, but rather criminology, corrections and social psychology." Reckless considers the schools of social work and the departments of sociology to be the best places for the training of probation officers, but realizes that on the one hand "our schools of social work have been reticent about including courses in penology and corrections," while on the other hand "many departments of sociology have frowned disdainfully at the prospect of offering practical training." [45]

Regardless of the merits of either side of this controversy, no uniform and generally accepted course of professional preparation for the position of probation officer has as yet been charted. True, a growing number of courses on problems of juvenile delinquency are being offered in the colleges and universities, and schools of social work have included probation, parole, and institutional work in their teaching curricula. In comparatively few places, students of schools of social work are assigned to field training in probation departments.

But in general, as George H. Grosser, formerly connected with the Boston Juvenile Court, states, "Few schools have as yet evolved specialized training programs in the field of juvenile delinquency or criminality." As a valuable contribution to the solution of the problem, the Boston Juvenile Court, through its Citizenship Training Department, has instituted a program of internship for probation officers.[46] The program is designed to give balanced training in work at the court, case work with individual offenders and their families, and group work with juvenile delinquents. It includes field trips to correctional institutions and other agencies. Judges and probation officers have given readily of their time to instruct the students and to help them familiarize themselves with statutes and procedures. A field-work supervisor, available to the students almost daily, supervises the writings of their reports and interprets to them the work

---

[45] See comments on professional education of probation officers in Marian B. Nicholson, "Juvenile Behavior Problems," *Social Work Yearbook, 1949,* pp. 280–281. See also Katherine F. Lenroot, "The Juvenile Court Today," *Federal Probation,* September 1949, p. 15.

[46] See George H. Grosser, "An Internship for Probation Officers," *Focus,* May 1949, pp. 75–77; for more information on the Citizenship Training Department of the Boston Juvenile Court, see Chapter XI, pp. 422–424.

of the probation department. It has been found that advanced students in the second year of social work or graduate students with some training in the social sciences are best prepared to benefit from the training program. Close cooperation between the colleges and the persons responsible for the training program is maintained.

In-service training has in recent years come to the fore in many branches of public administration; in the correctional field, in particular, it has gained widespread recognition and realization. In-service training cannot and should not be a substitute for adequate pre-service training. It will have its greatest value for presently employed probation officers who did not have the benefit of professional schooling and in those probation departments which do not consider professional pre-service training a necessary requirement even for newly appointed staff members. However, in-service training should not be confined to these two groups; the well-trained staff member, too, needs in-service training as a helpful instrument for maintaining high standards of job performance.

The following types of in-service training programs have proved successful in various parts of the country: (1) Many probation departments of juvenile courts have organized their own in-service instruction for staff members by supervisory personnel or specially assigned instructors. (2) In Pennsylvania, the State Department of Public Instruction, helped by Federal funds appropriated on the basis of the George-Deen Act (later superseded by the George-Barden Act of 1946), has conducted in-service training courses for correctional workers on the local and state level since 1940. The probation administrators of the various courts have availed themselves of this opportunity by enrolling their staff members in these courses.[47] (3) A number of in-service training courses or institutes open to probation officers of the local courts have been conducted by universities—e.g., the University of California in Berkeley, the University of Southern California, the College of William and Mary in Virginia, and the Universities of Minnesota, New Hampshire, Ohio, Wisconsin, and so forth.[48]

---

[47] For more details on this program, see J. O. Reinemann, "Pennsylvania Experiments with Public-Service Training," *National Municipal Review*, October 1940, pp. 672–674.

[48] See Helen D. Pigeon, "In-Service Training for Probation and Parole Officers," *Federal Probation*, July–September 1941, pp. 8–14.

An ideal combination of pre-service and in-service training program is offered by the Los Angeles County Probation Department Newly appointed probation officers are given a training course for one year before being employed full-time. While in the training course they receive $150 monthly, and, since most of them are veterans, they also receive an allowance under the GI Bill of Rights. At the end of one year's training, they take the civil service examination for deputy probation officers. An entrance test is required for admission to the training program.

The modern technical device of sound-recording instruments has been used in several probation and parole departments as a valuable medium of in-service training. At the annual conference of the N.P.P.A. in Cleveland in 1949, Chief Probation Officer L. Wallace Hoffmann, of the Toledo, Ohio, Juvenile and Domestic Relations Court, presented the recording of a preliminary hearing in a delinquency case. Chief Probation Officer Samuel B. Haskell of the Cincinnati, Ohio, Common Pleas Court played back a recorded initial interview between a probation officer and a probationer. He pointed out the value of such a recording for the study of the probation officer's approach to his client, including inflection and voice quality and the response of the probationer. This sound-recording technique can be used for teaching purposes as well as for self-evaluation by the individual probation officer.[49]

Full realization of the professional status of probation service is predicated upon the guarantee of an adequate salary, reasonable tenure, and a retirement system. As several surveys undertaken by the National Probation and Parole Association and state associations have indicated, in many communities salaries are vastly below a reasonable standard. At present, little or no national or state-wide uniformity exists in this matter, and often individual courts lack a standardized and fair salary system. The previously quoted *Standards* suggests that "officers meeting the qualifications should be paid a beginning salary of from $2,600 to $3,000 per year, with payment of necessary expenses," and with periodical salary increases, preferably annually.[50]

---

[49] For further details, see Samuel B. Haskell, "Wire Recording for Self-analysis," *Focus*, January 1950, pp. 9–11.

[50] As a result of the rise in living costs after 1946, the above figures must be considered outdated. The N.P.P.A. published salary surveys in 1947 and 1949, based on data obtained by contacting fifty-three state departments and more

Reasonable tenure should be provided. Tenure is of particular importance in view of the preponderant number of probation officers who are appointed by local judges whose office term is usually limited by statute and who often have to engage in political campaigns for re-election. In states having well-organized civil service systems, the probation officers should be in the classified civil service. An adequate retirement or pension system should be established for all probation officers, whether they are protected by civil service provisions or not.

The attainment of professional status for the probation officer has been the particular aim of the National Probation Association, founded in 1921, and known as the National Probation and Parole Association since 1947. The Association is engaged exclusively in the effort to extend and improve probation and parole services and juvenile and other specialized courts for effective dealing with child and family problems. It conducts state, county, and city surveys, provides consultation services, holds conferences, publishes educational literature,[51] and acts as a clearing house of information on all phases of probation and parole service in the United States. It is concerned with the coordination of probation, parole, and institutional work, and is interested in all measures for constructive social treatment and the prevention of crime.

On the state level are many associations of probation and parole officers that have as their aims the advancement of methods and standards in the probation and parole departments and the promotion of progressive legislation in the correctional field.

f. The Volunteer in the Probation Field

Volunteer service in the probation field can take either of the following forms:

---

than 500 local departments in the probation and parole field. Charles L. Chute, vice-president of the N.P.P.A., reports that the average salary of full-time probation officers in 1949 was approximately $3,000, "a minimum under present standards for this work." ("The Juvenile Court in Retrospect," *Federal Probation*, September 1949, p. 6.) See also Leon T. Stern, "Probation Service in Pennsylvania," *The Quarterly* (of the Pennsylvania Association on Probation and Parole), November 1948, pp. 1–27.

[51] Frequent reference has been made in this book to the publications of the N.P.P.A., especially the *Yearbooks*, the bimonthly magazine *Focus*, and its predecessor, *Probation*.

First: In small towns and sparsely populated rural areas an interested lay citizen, as a neighborly sponsor, may take over the supervision of a youngster placed on probation. This volunteer worker should be carefully selected by the probation department of the county juvenile court and should be responsible to it. Such an arrangement makes it possible to give supervision to children living in remote parts of the county who, because of the heavy case load and geographically extensive work area of the regular probation officer, would not receive the benefits of probation service.

However, certain dangers in the practice of using volunteers should be pointed out. Experience has shown that "volunteers who undertake this work from a sentimental or morbid interest soon tire and do more harm to the child than any possible good that can be accomplished." [52] As Barnes and Teeters state, "Many judges have almost a childlike faith in releasing offenders, especially those of tender years, to volunteer agencies or individuals"; some judges "bank on people with 'good intentions' or executives of boys' clubs or settlement houses." [53] There is also the danger that the services of volunteers (and, to a certain degree, part-time probation officers) may be misused by protagonists of a false economy in preventing the employment of qualified full-time probation officers where their services are vitally needed.

Second: The volunteer can render valuable service in supplementing (rather than substituting for) the work of the regular probation officer both in large and small communities. He may be assigned as an individual or as a member of an organization to maintain frequent contacts with a child on probation and to collaborate closely with the probation officer in charge. It is considered good policy to hold each volunteer responsible for only one or two youngsters, and the type of case must be carefully selected. Volunteer service of this type is also rendered by the person who acts as

---

[52] See Marjorie Bell, "The Volunteer Aids the Court," *Yearbook*, N.P.P.A., 1936, pp. 156–174 (quotation on p. 160); this article is based on replies to a questionnaire on the use of volunteers from sixty larger probation departments throughout the country. The questions concerned sources from which volunteers were recruited, methods of selection, the number of volunteers used, the kind of work assigned, the type of training and supervision given, and the success of the program.

[53] Barnes and Teeters, *op. cit.*, p. 387.

sponsor to a juvenile when he is released on parole from an institution.[54]

In various cities members of the Big Brother and Big Sister organizations and similar youth service agencies carry out such programs. A good example of this kind of service is provided by the Juvenile Delinquency Clinics in Fayette County, Pennsylvania. Here, in the county seat (Uniontown) and in several townships, businessmen, clergymen, and professional men have banded together for the purpose of giving supervision and counsel to boys assigned to them by the juvenile court upon the recommendation of the chief probation officer, to whom these lay workers are responsible and with whom they meet for frequent consultation.[55]

In addition to their actual service, these men and women provide a good channel to the public at large for an interpretation of the meaning of probation, the problems presented by delinquent conduct of children, and the need for community facilities for youth conservation and crime prevention.

3. PROBATION AS A TREATMENT PROCESS
a. Selection of Probationers

Probation, as we pointed out earlier, has been described as a system of treatment. It is a treatment form in its own right and, if properly administered, should not be applied as a substitute for any other kind of case disposition. Nor should it be misunderstood by the child and his parents, or by the judge and the public, as an act of leniency. Obviously the selection of children who will profit from this treatment process requires great care.

The juvenile court judge places a child on probation after having studied the social case history and the recommendations of the probation officer and, if available, the diagnosis and prognosis of the court psychiatrist. He further takes into consideration the facts dis-

---

[54] See Chapter XIII, pp. 473–474.

[55] For further details about this project, see Ruth W. Love, "Boys of Today —Citizens of Tomorrow," *Federal Probation,* October–December 1947, pp. 43–48. See also Burlyn Pike, "I Was in Prison, and Ye Came Unto Me," *Federal Probation,* June 1949, pp. 29–33, describing the work of the Louisville, Kentucky, Council of Churches in the field of crime and delinquency prevention, including volunteer probation service. The experiences of a volunteer Big Brother over a period of 24 years are described in Melbourne S. Applegate, *Helping Boys in Trouble,* Association Press, 1950.

closed and the impressions gained at the court hearing. In most instances he is likely to order probation as a kind of "middle of the road" disposition. There are cases in which the simple discharge of the child, even with a reprimand by the judge, does not seem sufficient; on the other hand, the situation in these cases does not warrant the removal of the child from his home and his commitment into the controlled environment of an institution. Within these limits lie the range of probation and its potentialities.

More positively expressed, probation should be ordered whenever these requirements are met: The home surroundings must appear sufficiently conducive to the proper upbringing of the child, and the adjustment of the boy or girl in an atmosphere of freedom as it exists in the ordinary life of the community must be feasible, with the help of the court's supervisory authority. It follows that probation should not be "handed out" automatically in all cases in which the child has committed his first serious offense or when he has been referred to the court because of delinquent acts for the second or third time. Any such mechanistic use of probation nullifies its fundamental purpose of serving as a specific form of treatment geared to the specific needs of the child under consideration. The decision should not be influenced by emotional appeals to the judge to give the child "another chance." Finally, probation should never be resorted to simply because proper institutional facilities are lacking; unfortunately this happens all too frequently, although with misgivings on the part of many judges. The selection of probation as a proper treatment must be governed solely by all factors of personality and environment that are apparent in an individual case. (See Appendix Case No. 15.)

Attempts have been made to establish prediction tables, based on these various factors, as a guide for probation and parole selection. But, as Sanford Bates says, "The prognostic tables should never be a substitute for executive or judicial judgment, but will be a logical means of applying the accumulated experience of the past to the important problems of the future." [56] Pauline Young adds to this that "each institution, department, and community needs to develop its own experience tables and not rely upon those of other groups,

---

[56] Sanford Bates, *Prisons and Beyond*, Macmillan, New York, 1936, p. 120.

which may strongly reflect unique elements in their peculiar situations." [57]

b. Supervision of Probationers

Since probation is a treatment process, it is important that the probation officer at the beginning formulate some kind of treatment plan. In many instances he already knows the child and his family from the investigation prior to court hearing. The probation officer should conceive his or her task of supervision as that of a counselor, a "Big Brother," or "Big Sister." He, therefore, will strive to win the confidence of the child. In order to be successful, he must be accepted by the parents and other members of the family. Sometimes he has to break down an attitude of resistance in the parents, who may consider the probation officer's interest and activity as an intrusion into their rights. He will have to interpret to them the real meaning of his assignment—namely, helping the child in his readjustment.

Probation is predicated upon certain conditions. These conditions may be general and applicable to all children placed on probation, or they may be especially determined by the court in the individual situation. The general conditions include obedience to the parents, regular school attendance, the keeping of early hours, the following of instructions by the probation officer, the staying away from undesirable companions and from disreputable places, and the notification to the court of any change of address. Many of these conditions, often enumerated in a form letter given or sent to the parents, are full of negatives. In order to interpret the meaning of probation as a positive constructive measure, it is desirable that such a communication include some kind of opening and closing statement, like the following sample:

What does probation mean?
Probation means that the court has confidence in the good character of your child. Probation means that your child will remain in your home; you will continue to be responsible for your child. The court through its probation officer will help you in supervising your child. . . .

---

[57] Pauline Young, *Social Treatment in Probation and Delinquency*, McGraw-Hill, New York, 1st ed., p. 621.

Remember—everything that has been mentioned here is necessary for the welfare of your child. We, the Court, and you, the parents, want to see your child grow up into a fine American citizen, healthy in body, mind and spirit.[58]

Special conditions may consist of payment of restitution for damages, living with a relative (because of inadequacy of the parental home), attendance at a special school, affiliation with an approved recreational agency, and carrying out of medical recommendations.

The probation officer must himself be convinced that his is a positive and constructive task. No conscientious probation officer will be satisfied with merely keeping the child under his supervision out of another conflict with the law. As Lou, in his previously cited work *Juvenile Courts in the United States*, points out, "To be really constructive, the plan must take into account not only the weak qualities of the probationer, but also his good qualities, upon which the desired superstructure of normal conduct and character may be built. It must be based upon an understanding of all the factors of the problem of the probationer, including his personality, his habits and reactions and the reasons for them, his mental life, his physical strength and weaknesses, the home influences, and the bearing of the school régime on the child's development." [59]

The contacts of the probation officer with a child can be established either through home visits or through the child's reporting at the office of the probation department; sometimes a specially assigned room in a neighborhood settlement house is used for this purpose. In the home, the probation officer sees the child as a part of the family; he wins an insight into the attitude of the parents toward the child, the child's relationship to his brothers and sisters, and the physical environment of home and neighborhood. The probation officer often finds himself in the position of undertaking reconstructive work with the whole family, since the child's behavior is frequently an outcome of unstabilized home conditions. The picture of family units seriously damaged by the death or desertion of one or both parents or by divorce, poverty, ill health, or alcoholism is familiar to most probation officers. But even if these adverse factors do not exist, the

---

[58] A form containing these statements is being used by the Municipal Court of Philadelphia.

[59] *Op. cit.*, p. 153.

home visit is still an indispensable tool, because, in addition to the previously mentioned advantages, it is the most readily available means to obtain the participation of the members of the family in the treatment process and to stimulate their responsibility for carrying it forward. The probation officer may find favoritism for another child, or an overly critical parent, or a nagging relative. It is the probation officer's job to reduce friction and to help to eliminate those factors that disturb the child emotionally and thus produce his

A Probation Officer Interviews a Girl (posed picture). *(Courtesy Probate Court, Juvenile Division, Muskegon County, Michigan)*

rebellious acts. Only frequent contacts in the home with the various members of the family will enable him to do so. The child's reporting to the probation department office or other designated place, at regular intervals, has value in that it affords the probation officer an opportunity to converse with the child alone, unhampered by the presence of other members of the family and by the frequently crowded conditions of the home. However, this form of reporting should be restricted to children over twelve years of age.

There is, of course, no general rule regarding the frequency of contacts. Each individual case demands a different method. Except in rare cases, the *Juvenile Court Standards* suggests that "home visits at least once every two weeks are essential to effective supervision, knowledge of the assets and liabilities of the family, and correction of unfavorable conditions." [60]

One of the most important prerequisites for constructive probation work is the probation officer's intimate knowledge of the community's resources. He will keep himself informed of the child's progress in school. Frequent conferences should be held with the principal or teacher. In an increasing number of instances and with gratifying results, conferences are also being held with the school counselor or school social worker. School authorities are usually quite willing to cooperate with the probation department.[61] Older children on probation should be assisted and guided by the probation officer in the choice of and preparation for a vocation. (See Appendix Case No. 1.) He must be familiar with existing health centers and family service agencies and collaborate with them. He must be fully acquainted with the various recreational and character-building groups to which he can refer his probationers. In certain cases of deep-rooted emotional disturbances, he should utilize the services of child-guidance clinics or similar facilities. (See Appendix Case No. 3.)

There has been considerable discussion regarding the use of case work principles within the authoritarian setting of a court—even such a non-criminal tribunal as the juvenile court—and, more particularly, within the authoritarian framework of probation. Thirty years ago, social case work consisted of individual social treatment directed largely toward the manipulation of environmental factors on the one hand and toward moral and intellectual persuasion on the other. But today's concept of case work is quite different. It is predicated upon the belief that "change enforced upon an individual from

---

[60] P. 8.

[61] Concerning cooperation between probation officer and school personnel, see J. O. Reinemann, "The Juvenile Court and the Schools," *Newsletter*, National League To Promote School Attendance, September 1949, pp. 40–43; and Robert C. Taber, "The Potential Role of the School Counsellor in Delinquency Prevention and Treatment," *Federal Probation*, September 1949, pp. 52–56. See also Appendix Case No. 7.

outside is, in all truth, no change at all," and that the social worker's job is to "help the individual make responsible voluntary choices of his own from among the alternatives open to him and accept the consequences of his own judgments and decisions." [62] These principles, based upon the findings of the advancing science of human behavior, were developed and found ready acceptance in the fields of child guidance, family welfare, school counseling, foster-home care and, with certain modifications, institutional placement. But within the orbit of the court and the probation department, the modern case work idea did not at first seem applicable. Several factors appeared to militate against it: The relationship among probation officer, child, and parent is not founded upon a voluntary desire for help on the part of the client (to use the social case work term), but is a direct result of the compulsion of the law or—in cases of juvenile incorrigibility, waywardness, and disobedience—of the generally accepted standards of behavior which the child has violated. The police officer, detention home superintendent, judge, and probation officer possess and use the power of enforcement. Another element is that of time. Private social agencies are fairly free in letting the client change himself and his attitudes without haste, but the machinery of a court is bound by specific time limits. A discrepancy between case work principles and court and probation practice seemed, therefore, quite obvious.

However, not only social case work has developed in recent years; the working methods of the juvenile court and probation also have undergone significant changes. They, too, have been strongly influenced by the discoveries of social and psychological scientists in the realm of human conduct and its motivations. As has been stated repeatedly in previous chapters, delinquent behavior quite frequently results from emotional disturbances. To relieve tensions within the individual, to help him find acceptable outlets for his drives, and to guide him in overcoming his frustrations are the functions of social case work. Probation, which aims to strike at the root causes of the individual's unlawful attitudes and acts, must therefore accept the

---

[62] Kenneth L. M. Pray, "The Principles of Social Case Work as Applied to Probation and Parole," *Federal Probation*, April–June 1945, pp. 14–18. For a historical evaluation of the development of case work, see Annette Garrett, "Historical Survey of the Evaluation of Casework," *Journal of Social Casework*, June 1949, pp. 219–229.

tools that case work supplies. Fundamentally, case work is founded upon the respect for the individual as a unique personality and the recognition of his worth; equally, probation is based upon the idea of the dignity of every human being. The relationship between probation officer and probationer should be one of mutual respect, understanding, sincerity, and confidence. The concept of authority inherent in probation does not stand in the way of achieving and maintaining such a relationship. The psychology behind the authoritarian approach in probation is not essentially different from the generally accepted principle which recognizes that in every group setting, such as family, school, club, office, and factory, any behavior of an individual that is harmful to the group calls for disciplining that individual. To teach respect for the rights of every person, for his well-being and for his property, has been one of the essential concepts of probationary treatment. The probation officer's misuse of authority in the form of threats, carping imperatives, bullying, shouting, and condemning will not achieve the desired ends. It is necessary to interpret to the juvenile on probation, in a way that he understands and accepts, the meaning of authority, the need for discipline, and the consequences of non-conforming behavior.

This aspect is well summarized in the report, "Case Work—Group Work," of the National Conference:

> During probation . . . case work has a contribution to make. In keeping with case work philosophy the delinquent and the probation officer must see probation as an experimental period of social adjustment. During the period, the individual must learn to live with authority. He must be helped to discover and develop his capacity to take responsibility for himself, as a member of the community, accepting its standards and rules of behavior.[63]

A practical example of the role of case work principles in probation work is presented in the following quotation:

> In working with the child on probation . . . the probation officer may find it necessary to be directive in his treatment, particularly in the early stages of his supervision. If Johnny's stealing has been diagnosed as stemming partly from Johnny's feeling of rejection by his mother, the probation officer may need to restrict Johnny's activities as a practical expedient while the mother is helped to understand her

---

[63] *Report No. 13*, p. 18.

son's need for affection and understanding. At the same time, of course, mutual bonds of understanding and respect are being constructed between the probation officer and Johnny, but until Johnny reaches a point at which he begins to understand himself and to desire to overcome his stealing, certain artificial restraints may be highly necessary. Johnny's understanding of himself and his mother, and her understanding of herself and Johnny, will come about only as the probation officer has time to devote to these troubled two.[64]

But case work is not the only tool with which probation can work. Another instrument is group work. It has been well stated that "social treatment of the group life of the maladjusted child or individualized case work therapy represents manipulation of the two forever interacting aspects of personality, and that treatment of social relationships by group work may affect emotional attitudes just as successfully as treatment of emotional attitudes by case work may affect social relationships." [65]

For the most part, the utilization of group work for children on probation has been through referral to existing recreational groups in the community. Although in a number of cases such referrals have proved of great assistance to the rehabilitative work of the probation officer, a group of problem children remains that does not fit into the framework of normal play groups. For this type of youngster a definite need for so-called "sheltered play groups" exists, where

---

[64] Ben Meeker, "Probation Is Casework," *Federal Probation*, June 1948, pp. 51–54 (quotation on p. 53). For further information on this subject, see John Slawson, "The Use of the Authoritative Approach in Social Case Work in the Field of Delinquency," *American Journal of Orthopsychiatry*, October 1938, pp. 673–678; Pauline Young, *Social Treatment in Probation and Delinquency*, McGraw-Hill, New York, 1st ed., Chapters XIV–XVII; Peter Geiser, "The Court as a Case Work Agency," *Yearbook*, N.P.P.A., 1942, pp. 102–108; Gladys E. Hall, "Social Case Work in Probation and Parole," *ibid.*, pp. 121–132; Robert C. Taber, "The Value of Case Work to the Probationer," *ibid.*, 1940, pp. 167–179. For an excellent discussion of the personality of the probation officer and the use of authority, see Nathaniel Cantor, "The Function of Probation," *ibid.*, 1941, pp. 277–297, especially pp. 292 and 296. See also Hyman S. Lippmann, "The Role of the Probation Officer in the Treatment of Delinquency in Children," *Federal Probation*, June 1948, pp. 36–39; David Crystal, "Family Casework in Probation," *Federal Probation*, December 1949, pp. 47–53.

[65] Harry Manuel Shulman, "Experimental Group Treatment of Maladjusted School Children," *Yearbook*, N.P.P.A., 1941, pp. 342–359 (quotation on pp. 345–346).

"they can have the experience of creative play without the pressure of unequal competition and particularly without the stimulation to defensive behavior that comes from directly competitive play." [66] In such a set-up, individual treatment within group activity is possible. It has been suggested that the field of probation should experiment in the use of such sheltered recreational activity groups under its own auspices as a treatment method on a par with the case method. It has been further suggested that probation should have "control of its sheltered recreational groups under its own leadership, but that they should be set up within existing community recreational facilities, not in competition with them. In this way the ends will be served both by taking advantage of the previous experience of recreational agencies and by setting up these sheltered programs within centers well known to children, and less likely to stigmatize the participants. Wherever possible, well-adjusted children ought to be mingled with problem children in such sheltered activity programs, to give the problem child the constructive experience of association with normal children." [67]

An interesting example of a program in which a juvenile court uses group activities as a tool of probation is the work of the Citizenship Training Department of the Boston Juvenile Court. There, a group setting exclusively for boys on probation is provided for a limited time, to be followed by the use of existing community resources that are open to all youngsters.

The Citizenship Training Department is an adjunct of the Juvenile Court and has been in operation since 1936. All boys between the ages of twelve and seventeen placed on probation by the Boston Juvenile Court are required to report to the Citizenship Training Department immediately following their appearance in court. Boys on probation to the district courts of Greater Boston are also admitted at the request of the judges of these courts. The boys are required to attend the program of this department for twelve weeks, five days a week, for two hours in the afternoon. The Department

[66] Harry Manuel Shulman, "Group Work—A New Program for Probation," *Yearbook*, N.P.P.A., 1939, pp. 116–129 (quotation on p. 123). The author formerly was director of the Hawthorne-Cedar Knolls School, New York, which received boys and girls from the ages of twelve to sixteen years on commitment from the Children's Court of New York City.

[67] *Ibid.*, p. 128.

is located at the Boston Young Men's Christian Union, where offices, classrooms, a gymnasium, and basketball courts are available. The staff consists of a director with extensive experience in the field of social work and in probation, a boys' worker, a part-time examining physician, a psychiatrist, a research worker, and a secretary. The purpose of this program is to study the nature and scope of the child's problem and to outline and initiate, in collaboration with the probation officer, a program of treatment for each boy. This treatment attempts to develop in the boy a healthy attitude toward the law, the family, and the institutions under which he must live. The boy's active participation and effort are necessary, even in deciding the most appropriate form of treatment. These are the ways of achieving the purpose of this program: The boy becomes a member of a group averaging about sixteen boys; the socializing influence of this group is a helpful medium through which the staff can work with the boy. Physical training in the form of systematic exercises and games is utilized. Classroom discussions are used for gaining insight, information, and discipline in clear thinking. Visual education is employed in the form of original drawings, moving pictures, and slides. The leaders hold frequent informal talks with individual boys. Membership in clubs, groups, settlement houses, and other community groups is encouraged by interpreting them to the boy so that he may understand their function and be attracted to their activities.

This program does not attempt to act as a substitute for the work of the probation officer with the individual boy; rather, it aims to supplement the probation officer's efforts by providing intensive group-work experience and making available to the boy on probation a number of activities of an educational and recreational nature. It affords a good opportunity to observe the boy as a participant in group activities and thus to win a better understanding of his personality. At the end of a twelve weeks' period, the boy is referred to a neighborhood club or settlement, through which contact with him is maintained. If necessary, medical treatment, particularly dental care, is provided. If psychiatric services are required, the proper referral is made. For special needs the department has made use of camps. The camps proved to be an opportunity for follow-up work with some of the boys who had been out of the department for two years and who were selected with the assistance of the probation officers for a six weeks' camp experience.

In a pamphlet describing this program, the reasons for the establishment of the Citizenship Training Department are explained as follows:

> As a result of day-to-day observations of boys passing through the Boston Juvenile Court, the conclusion was reached that it is unnecessary to send all of them to a psychiatric clinic for study, that the great majority are normal but badly trained. This led to the establishment of a department in the court which was organized to make a systematic, progressive study of each case, without any preconceived notions; to see whether the boy can be helped to develop self-discipline through educational or other methods, and where the need for psychiatric treatment exists, to make sure that it is provided. The program is based on the following principles: Many normal boys are delinquent because of a lack of training in the fundamental qualities of good citizenship and good manhood. They are often not vicious or pathological, but essentially untrained.[68]

Whether one agrees with this statement or not, it cannot be denied that the close integration of an intensive group-work program with the probation service is based on sound ideas.[69]

Another example of using group activities in probation work is reported from the Westchester, New York, County Juvenile Court. There, with seven boys on probation who came from particularly underprivileged environments, a club was organized by a probation officer. The group served as a nucleus, and membership was also

[68] *The Citizenship Training Department of the Juvenile Court*, Boston Juvenile Court, November 1941.

[69] For further details on the Citizenship Training Department program of the Boston Juvenile Court, see Kenneth I. Wollan, "The Use of Group Activity in Probation Work," *Yearbook*, N.P.P.A., 1938, pp. 240–255; "The Citizenship Training Program of the Boston Juvenile Court," *ibid.*, 1941, pp. 379–388; "A New Treatment Program for Juvenile Delinquents," *Journal of Criminal Law and Criminology*, March–April 1941, pp. 712–719. See also "Boston Training Project," *Probation*, October 1943, pp. 25–27; Judge John F. Perkins, *Common Sense and Bad Boys*, The Citizenship Training Department, Boston Juvenile Court, 1946; George H. Grosser, "An Internship for Probation Officers," *Focus*, May 1949, p. 76. *Note:* Presiding Judge John F. Perkins of the Boston Juvenile Court initiated the idea of the Citizenship Training Department; Mr. Wollan has for many years served as its director; Mr. Grosser was one of its instructors. A more recent publication concerning this program is a pamphlet, *The Citizenship Training Department of the Boston Juvenile Court*, prepared by John J. Connelly, presiding justice, Boston Juvenile Court, 1950.

opened to a few boys not on probation. This experiment developed into a club with many activities, such as camping, dramatics, and athletics, and finally a girls' club was also organized. This venture shows how successfully wards of the court can mingle with other children in a group setting and how the leadership of the probation department can serve simultaneously the recreational needs of both the probation and the non-probation group.[70]

An intensive group therapy program has been launched by the Treatment Clinic of the Children's Division of the Court of Domestic Relations of New York City. Both children and parents are being treated at the same time. The program is the result of an experimental project conducted with fifty children and twenty adults. According to Dr. Harris B. Peck, Senior Psychiatrist of the Clinic, the most promising area of research lies in the field of group therapy, through which a considerably larger number of patients can be reached than heretofore.[71]

c. Length and Termination of Probation

In accordance with its individualistic character, the length of probation is dependent upon the needs and requirements of every case and upon the progress made in each situation. The law usually gives the judge wide discretion in setting the duration of probation. It has become the custom in most juvenile courts not to limit the time of probation in advance. It is also recognized that, as a rule, short-term probation is of little value. Guidance and counseling require time before improvement in the child's behavior can be achieved; human conduct usually does not lend itself to rapid treatment and cure. On the other hand, probation should not be unnecessarily prolonged. Not only does unjustified extension of probation increase the probation officer's case load, it also tends to slacken his efforts to re-educate the child and destroys in the mind of the youngster the valuable incentive of a discharge from supervision within the foreseeable future. The *Juvenile Court Standards* recommends a general minimum probation period of from six months to one year.

---

[70] This experiment has been written up by its originator, Amedeo W. Taiano, in "Using the Group in Probation Work," *Yearbook*, N.P.P.A., 1941, pp. 360–378.

[71] See *The New York Times*, October 20, 1949, and January 15, 1950.

Probation can be terminated in various ways. In cases in which a definite time limit is set, the term of probation expires automatically; otherwise, it is left to the probation officer to determine when the objectives of probation have been met and consequently to ask the judge to discharge the boy or girl from probation. Violations of probation may also lead to its termination. The committing of a new offense is considered a violation of probation *per se*, and non-compliance with the general or specific conditions of probation is termed a technical violation. The probation officer has considerable discretion in determining whether the child and his parents are living up to the conditions imposed. If a violation of probation occurs, the child is returned to court for further planning and treatment. The probation officer should acquaint the probationer and his family with this decision and prepare them for the impending appearance before the judge. This appearance may lead to detention for further study and observation, to continuance of probation, to foster-home placement, or to commitment to a training school. In any event, the probation officer will endeavor to secure the cooperation of the child and his family by explaining in detail what any one of these steps means so that the probationer and his parents will have an unbiased knowledge of the purposes of these services.

As was mentioned in Chapter IX, probation of a juvenile may legally last until his twenty-first birthday. Most of the juvenile court laws of the various states, regardless of whether the upper juvenile court age limit is eighteen (as in most states) or lower or higher, contain provisions extending juvenile court jurisdiction to the age of majority, provided the individual case has come to the attention of the court before the young person has reached the upper juvenile court age limit.

d. Evaluation of the Effects of Probation

Has probation been successful as a device of modern correctional treatment, especially in juvenile cases? To measure success or failure of probation is difficult without undertaking very detailed studies of individual cases, with a follow-up over several years after termination of probation. A major obstacle to such surveys is that home visits and personal interviews of individuals who had been on probation as juveniles several years before are inadvisable, since they would often be deeply resented and might cause damage to the reputation of the individual and his family. On the other hand, the purely negative yardstick of recidivism during the period of probation and within a certain time afterward is not necessarily conclusive. Moreover, human behavior is difficult to classify and codify for statistical purposes.

No wonder, therefore, that wide discrepancies are recorded in all attempts to evaluate probation success statistically. The gap ranges from a failure rate of 84.6 per cent reported by the Gluecks,[72] to a success average of 75 per cent mentioned by Sutherland.[73] An analysis of case records of 500 children (400 boys and 100 girls) studied at the Judge Baker Guidance Clinic and placed on probation in the Juvenile Court of Boston revealed that among the boys permanent success was recorded in 43 per cent of the cases, temporary success in 34 per cent, and failure in 21 per cent of the cases. In 2 per cent the outcome was undetermined. The permanent success rate for the girls was 76 per cent; temporary success, 12 per cent; and failure, 12 per cent. The study was undertaken at a time when from five to seven years had elapsed after termination of probation.[74]

Austin H. MacCormick, Executive Director of the Osborne Association, states: [75] "Based on actual performances over a term of years, a good juvenile court and probation service, operating in a community with adequate social resources and utilizing them fully, can put as high as 90 per cent of its juvenile delinquents on probation the first time around and 50 to 75 per cent the second or third time around, and get as high as 75 to 80 per cent successes." Notice that MacCormick does not make a hypothetical statement—he bases his conclusion upon practical experiences and actual performances of various courts throughout the country. Moreover, he considers that good probation work is possible everywhere, provided these requisites are met: a good juvenile court with probation service, a community with adequate social resources, and an efficient co-ordination of both.[76]

---

[72] Sheldon and Eleanor Glueck, *One Thousand Juvenile Delinquents*, Harvard University Press, 1939, p. 173.

[73] *Op. cit.*, p. 402.

[74] See Belle Boone Beard, *Juvenile Probation*, American Book Company, 1934, pp. 147, 208–209.

[75] "The Community and the Correctional Process," *Focus*, May 1948, p. 88.

[76] See also Karl Holton, "A Yardstick for Measuring Probation," *Federal Probation*, January–March 1943, pp. 41–43; James N. York, "Evaluating the Everyday Work of a Probation Office," *ibid.*, September 1948, pp. 24–29; John Schapps, "Probation in California—Self-analysis," *Focus*, January 1950, pp. 1–6.

The extra-mural treatment of probation, then, is one of several dispositions that the juvenile court may consider and enforce. Another form of disposition, commitment, is the subject of the next two chapters.

Chapter XII

COMMITMENT

1. HISTORICAL TREATMENT OF INSTITUTIONAL CARE IN THE UNITED STATES

THE Quaker, John Griscom (1774–1852), of Burlington, New Jersey, deserves most of the credit for introducing into this country the latest concepts of child-saving from eighteenth- and early nineteenth-century Europe. Griscom, primarily an educator, had long been familiar with the work of Johann Heinrich Pestalozzi (1746–1827) in Switzerland and Jean Frederic Oberlin (1740–1828), who labored in the Vosges Mountains among the poverty-stricken peasants of Waldbach.

The great Pestalozzi had established a school for orphans at Neuhoff in 1775. It was in this school that he formulated his principles of education, which are still recognized in pedagogic circles. Although he and his equally famous successor, Philipp Emanuel von Fellenberg, were not concerned with delinquency, their philosophy of training children made a deep impression on such American pioneers as Griscom, Bronson Alcott, and John M. Keagy of Philadelphia. These educational leaders were also familiar with Oberlin's work. Pastor Oberlin, in addition to helping the people of his parish build roads, sponsored a public health program, encouraged agriculture and industry, and established "infant schools" similar to those of Froebel's kindergartens.

In 1818, Professor Griscom, who at the time was teaching school in New York City, made a tour of European children's schools and was favorably impressed by the fine work they were doing for abandoned and "depraved" children. His description of these schools may be found in his *Memoirs*. In the preceding year, he had been moved "by the condition of the poor and criminal classes in the city of New York and invited several of his friends into his parlor upon

429

William Street, to consider some practical measures for the cure of pauperism and the elimination of crime." [1] Out of this meeting developed the Society for the Prevention of Pauperism.

The care and treatment of the juvenile delinquent of New York City at the time were deplorable. In the 1819 report of the Society, for example, we read of the Bellevue prison: "Here is one great school of vice and desperation; with the confirmed and unrepentant criminals we place these novices in guilt,—these unfortunate children from ten to fourteen years of age, who from neglect of parents, from idleness or misfortune, have been doomed to the penitentiary by condemnation of law." [2]

John Griscom, 1774–1852.

Four years later, when Griscom had completed his tour of European schools for delinquent and dependent children, the Society apparently felt that the time was ripe for some social action. So in 1822

---

[1] B. K. Peirce, *A Half Century With Juvenile Delinquents: The New York House of Refuge and Its Times,* Appleton, New York, 1869, p. 33.

[2] Quoted by Homer Folks, *The Care of Destitute, Neglected and Delinquent Children,* 1902, p. 199. By permission of the Macmillan Company, Publishers.

777

this group of progressive humanitarians urged the establishment of a juvenile institution or reformatory to which children of tender years might be sent rather than to the county jails and state prison, as had been the practice up to that time. In the report of the Society for 1821 we find the following specification:

> These prisons should be schools of instruction rather than places of punishment, like our present State prisons. The youth confined there should be placed under a course of discipline severe and unchanging, but alike calculated to subdue and conciliate. . . . The end should be the youth's reformation and future usefulness.

The type of administration planned by these forward-looking men was as unusual as their philosophy of penal treatment. In 1823, the name of the Society was changed to the Society for Reformation of Juvenile Delinquents. The members threw their resources into the battle to secure an institution that would translate their objectives into active practice. The Society received authority from the state to manage the school—a revolutionary departure from traditional methods of control. With an initial subscription of $18,000 from private individuals, a Board of Managers was elected and the school was opened on January 1, 1825.

Each subscriber had a voice in the management. It was truly a community venture, divorced as far as possible from state control, and dedicated to the tutelage of children who were unfortunate enough to have inadequate home surroundings or indifferent parental care.

The New York City House of Refuge was opened on January 1, 1825, the first of its kind in the United States. With impressive services, the building, which was a bleak barrack leased from the government, was dedicated. It stood on the present Madison Square, which, at that time, was well uptown and away from business and city confusion. The first children to become inmates were six boys and three girls gathered from the streets. The founders envisaged this institution as a "prison, manufactory and school." In fact, the Reverend John Stanford, one of the founders, spoke thus to the nine children in his opening address:

> You are to look at these walls which surround the building, not so much as a prison, but as an hospitable dwelling, in which you enjoy comfort and safety from those who once led you astray. And, I may

venture to say, that in all probability, this is the best home many of you ever enjoyed. You have no need for me to tell you, that the consideration of all these favors should stimulate you to submission, industry, and gratitude. You are not placed here for punishment, as to produce your moral improvement.[3]

The First House of Refuge—1825. New York City.

In 1839 the House of Refuge gave up this makeshift set of buildings and moved to the site now occupied by Bellevue Hospital; in 1854 it moved to Randall's Island. In 1932, when the New York State Vocational Institution was established at West Coxsackie, the House of Refuge was merged with it and came under the jurisdiction of the State Department of Correction. To date, this establishment has cared for some 35,000 boys and 5,000 girls.

Before discussing the qualified success of the House of Refuge, we shall outline briefly the stories of the next two institutions that followed the New York experiment. Boston opened its institution in 1826 and Philadelphia in 1828.

The Boston institution, erected about two and a half miles from the city, near the House of Industry, was called the House of Reformation. Its first superintendent was Reverend E. M. P. Wells, a former Episcopal rector whose régime greatly impressed the French

---

[3] Peirce, *op. cit.*, p. 377.

Commissioners, de Beaumont and de Tocqueville, when they visited this country to make a survey of prisons and penal philosophy a few years later.

Apparently not satisfied with the work of the Boston House of Reformation, an "association of gentlemen of great respectability" purchased Thompson's Island, in Boston Harbor, in 1833, on which to erect a farm school for the "reformation of boys exposed to extraordinary temptations and who were in danger of becoming vicious and dangerous." In 1835 this new farm school merged with another private institution that had been previously organized under the name of Boston Asylum To Care for Indigent Orphans. To this institution were sent boys who were not yet considered delinquent. Ralph Waldo Emerson worked out a system of education for this school but it was not received with any enthusiasm. But because its "broader institutional conception and its support by private philanthropy" possessed more meaning for child development than did the House of Reformation, interest in the earlier school began to lag.

The Philadelphia House of Refuge grew out of the deep concern, expressed as early as 1823, of the members of the Philadelphia Prison Society for young vagrants. Conferences were held between the members and the guardians of the poor. Recommendations called for a "suitable place for the reception of all minors taken up by the watchmen . . . strolling the streets without homes, who are now committed to the common prisons." [4] Nothing resulted from these recommendations, but in 1826 the Society of Women Friends, which was engaged in visiting women in the Arch Street Prison, offered to "assist in the management of a House of Refuge for Juvenile Offenders should such an establishment be formed." This project was eventually carried through, and in 1828 the House of Refuge was established. Its first building, on Ridge Road and Coates Street (Fairmount Ave.), was little more than a prison.

In 1850, as a result of friction between the increasing numbers of colored children and white, new buildings for Negro children were erected at some distance from the center of the city (22nd and Poplar), and by 1872 separate schools for white boys and girls were erected on adjoining ground. At the turn of the century, the boys'

----

[4] See Negley K. Teeters, *They Were in Prison*, Winston, Philadelphia, 1937, Chapter V, for an account of the establishment of this institution.

department moved to the country and became known as the **Glen Mills School.** Later, through the efforts of Mrs. Martha Falconer, the girls' department established itself among the rolling hills of Dela-

A Study in Contrasts—The Philadelphia House of Refuge, 1828.

ware County, at Darlington, about two miles from the boys' school. Today it is known as Sleighton Farm and ranks among the best of its kind in the country.

These three Houses of Refuge and the Boston Asylum were the only institutions for juvenile delinquents until 1845, when a municipal boys' reformatory was established in New Orleans. Two years later, the first state reform school for boys was founded in Westboro, Massachusetts. This school became the Lyman School for Boys in 1884. Thus Massachusetts deserves credit for opening the first state reform school for delinquents.

2. PHILOSOPHY OF THE EARLY HOUSES OF REFUGE

Despite the glowing language used in the early reports of the three or four first Houses of Refuge, they were little better than prisons. In neither achitecture—there were walls around them—nor in personnel did they differ much from the conventional prison. Perhaps, however, the Boston House of Refuge could refute that charge. For in this institution was to be found a crude, but real, system of classification, promotion, and self-government. In 1831, about five years after the Boston school had opened, de Beaumont and de Tocqueville found many features of treatment which met with their approval.

The unusual conditions of the Boston House can be attributed to the first superintendent, Reverend E. M. P. Wells, who was one of those rare individuals who can inspire the young. He had been expelled from Brown University because he refused to "bear witness against his college mates" in a student prank. Thus one of the first rules of his Boston House of Refuge was that no boy or girl should be required to give information on the faults of another. As the well-known writer on early prison practices, Orlando F. Lewis, said: "Thus did one of the earliest reform schools go on record as intolerant of 'snitching' and of government through stool-pigeons." [5]

The French students of penology wrote glowingly of Reverend Wells' system of classification, which also embraced his system of punishments and rewards. As we look at it in retrospect, it stands out against the stern moralistic philosophy of the day; it was crude as judged by today's standards yet it was full of common sense.

The system called for what the superintendent labeled *Mal Grades* and *Bon Grades*, three in each category, described as follows:

---

[5] *The Development of American Prisons and Prison Customs, 1776–1845,* Albany, 1922, p. 303. Dr. Lewis' book discusses these early institutions at some length.

First Mal Grade: Those who are positively inclined to do wrong.
Privations:
1. Deprived of play and conversation, except with members of the same grade, or when necessary, with those with whom they work.
2. Not to go to superintendent's room.
3. Not to vote at elections.

Second Mal Grade: Those positively and regularly inclined to do wrong.
Privations:
1. Those of first Mal Grade.
2. Not to converse with any boys, except when necessary about their work.
3. Not to speak to superintendent except when permitted.
4. Deprived of regular seat, and kept constantly under an inmate sheriff, and never dismissed from such surveillance except in bedrooms.
5. Deprived of cake and other extra food.

Third Mal Grade: Positively, regularly, and continually inclined to do wrong.
Privations:
1. Those of First and Second Mal Grades.
2. Food: Bread and water. Must wear bracelets or a visor, and be kept in a solitary room.

Thus we see that punishments were varied for the first three grades; solitude and deprivation of food, except for the barest essentials, were the extreme penalty. There was no corporal punishment, for it had been outlawed by *vote of the children themselves,* and they agreed to give their own word of honor to behave. One does wonder, however, that bracelets (handcuffs) and the visor (hood) were tolerated in such a healthy atmosphere.

As Lewis explains: "The spirit of the place was based upon the knowledge and anticipation of the pleasures awaiting the one who maintained good conduct, privileges ever before the inmate of the so-called Bon Grades."

These gradations were as follows:

Third Bon Grade: Positively trying to do right.
Privileges:
1. Any that the Mal Grade offers.
2. To go to the city under a monitor, when twenty-five marks have been acquired.

3. To walk about grounds, under a monitor.
4. To go to Gymnasium and reading room.
5. To use the books and papers in the assembly room, by permission.
6. To hold office, by election.

Second Bon Grade: Positively and regularly trying to do right.
Privileges:
1. Privileges of all previous grades.
2. To go to the city, for twenty-five marks acquired, without a monitor, if it is the third time.
3. To be entrusted with keys of secondary importance.
4. Capable of holding office by appointment.
5. Permitted to take books from reading room.
6. Also to use papers in assembly room, without permission.
7. Other things being equal, to have preference before all inferior grades.

First Bon Grade: Positively, regularly, and continually trying to do right.
Privileges:
1. Those of all previous grades.
2. To walk about the stockade without a monitor; to sail and swim without a monitor.
3. To go to one's room without permission, and into dining room when necessary.
4. To leave one's seat in assembly room without permission.
5. Other things being equal, to have preference before all lower grades.
6. To have the use of recreation room.
7. To be entrusted, when necessary, with the most important keys.
8. To have one's word taken on all common occasions.
9. To have one's birthday celebrated.
10. To wear undress uniform.

These penalties and privileges show that a man of vision had given considerable thought to the problems of discipline, reformation, and classification in an age when such matters simply were not discussed. The child was able to work himself out of a situation in which he had little freedom to a situation in which he enjoyed respect, honor, and self-reliance.

But such a plan of rewards and privations must be accepted nowadays with some reservations. In the first place, we see it only on paper; and secondly, some of the features are no doubt open to criticism on the basis of good pedagogy. Such a system would undoubtedly develop some nasty little prigs and at the same time would engender considerable resentment among the more undisciplined and virile boys. Many different types of status and social approval are possible, especially in the world of young boys and girls, and all children do not want the same kind. Many of them will not accept the kind established by adults.

Nevertheless, Mr. Wells did know children, and from this distance we can safely say that he played square with his charges. Dr. Francis Lieber, noted contemporary student of penology and one who undoubtedly knew Wells personally, wrote: "We know of no instructor who has seen deeper into the human heart, and knows more thoroughly to what principles of the human soul he may apply." [6]

The New York City House of Refuge was under the direction of Joseph Curtis, an educator of children who (to quote Lewis) "would subordinate system to personality, as a method of education. He chose by far the harder method, but the one offering the possibility of rich rewards. He aimed to develop the individuality of the child, bring out his powers of self-expression. He believed in the development of character rather than routine." [7] Progressive though he was, Curtis was a stern disciplinarian. At the table, the children "must be silent, holding up a hand if they wanted water, a thumb for vinegar, three fingers for bread, and one finger for salt." Curtis remained only one year. The chief characteristic of his brief management was the tendency of the children to escape. Judged by modern standards of child care, this is no indictment of Curtis. He insisted before his managers that an educational institution could not be managed like a factory.

He was succeeded by N. C. Hart, a successful high-school teacher, who was amiable and a good organizer and administrator. Hart developed a code of rules and a system of grades and merit badges that afforded the children some incentive for diligence and good conduct. He made the establishment quite successful in child training, helped by the close interest of the board of managers and the special attention of the ladies' committee on the education of the girls. The new

---

[6] Quoted by Lewis, *op. cit.*, p. 307.
[7] *Ibid.*, p. 301.

régime devoted less time to school and more to work. The children
worked eight hours a day making brass nails, cane seats for chairs,
and whipstocks, weaving and willow working (covers for bottles
and demijohns), and shoemaking.[8]

A few years ago, an account of the first child to be indentured to
a "foster" home was discovered in the archives of the old New York
House of Refuge. It was the case of Diana Williams, Mulatto, aged
13, sent to the school for stealing, or what today is often referred to
as "jack rolling." She behaved well at the Refuge and was farmed
out to one Ebenezer Foote and his wife of Delhi, Delaware County.
See got along well there and the last report, in 1837, stated that she
had married and had gone west. The covenant Diana signed charged
her "her mistress to faithfully serve, her secrets keep, her lawful commands every where readily obey. . . . She shall not waste her
mistress's goods, nor lend unlawfully to any: she shall not commit
fornication, nor contract matrimony within the said term: At cards,
dice, or any other unlawful game she shall not play. . . . Nor haunt
Alehouses, Taverns, nor playhouses, but in all things behave herself
as a faithful Apprentice ought to do." The "said Mistress shall procure and provide her sufficient Meat, Drink, Apparel, Lodging, and
Washing, fitting for an Apprentice [and] give her one-quarter
schooling in each year . . . and a new suit of Apparel and a Bible
at the expiration." [9]

In addition to the indenture system, we noted in an earlier chapter
that the New York institution resorted to farming out children on
distant farms. In 1828 it is recorded that eight boys were sent to
Ohio.

We have little data on which to form an opinion concerning the
efficacy of these early Houses of Refuge. Few, if any, follow-up
studies were made of the children. The French commissioners, de
Beaumont and de Tocqueville, record the following statistics, which
account for all children who had left the institution from the date
of opening to 1833:

Of 427 male juvenile offenders sent back into society, 85 have conducted themselves well, and the conduct of 41 has been excellent; of

---

[8] For a comparison of the "honor" systems of the New York and Boston
schools, see the philosophy of the former as set down by B. K. Peirce, op. cit.,
pp. 365–367.

[9] "Diana Signs the Covenant," Probation, April 1942, pp. 105–106.

34 the information received has been bad, and of 24 very bad; of 37 among them the information is doubtful; of 24 rather good than otherwise, and of 14 rather bad than good.

Of 86 girls who have returned into society, 37 have conducted themselves well; 11 in an excellent manner; 22 bad, and 16 very bad; the information concerning 10 is doubtful; 3 seem to have conducted themselves rather well, and 3 rather bad than otherwise. Thus of 513 children who have returned from the house of refuge in New York into society more than 200 have been saved from infallible ruin.[10]

The first superintendent of the Philadelphia House of Refuge was Dr. John M. Keagy (1795–1837), a graduate of the medical school of the University of Pennsylvania and an ardent disciple of Pestalozzi. He remained there only a year and then became head of a Friends' school.[11] Keagy was succeeded by Edwin Young. De Beaumont and de Tocqueville, who visited the school, found nothing to indicate lack of vision or repressive measures, but they were not as impressed by the New York and Philadelphia schools as they had been in Boston. They said:

> The system of these establishments, founded upon a theory much more simple [than the Boston school], has the merit of being within reach of all the world. It is possible to find superintendents who are fit for the Philadelphia system: but we cannot hope to meet often with such men as Mr. Wells.[12]

The Philadelphia House of Refuge petitioned the Pennsylvania legislature to be attached to the public school system and, as such, to be under the jurisdiction of the state department of education. The managers of the school have always looked upon the institution as an educational rather than a penal one. Although they very early

---

[10] Quoted by Homer Folks, *op. cit.*, p. 204. By permission of the Macmillan Company, Publishers.

[11] We do not know why Keagy left, but judging from his interest in education, he probably could not subscribe to the policy of the Board of Managers which put labor ahead of academic instruction in the school. We know that Keagy, as early as 1826, had correspondence with Bronson Alcott, noted progressive pioneer in educational philosophy. At the time, Keagy was principal of a "Pestalozzian School" in Harrisburg, Pennsylvania. In 1827 he published the "Pestalozzian Primer."

[12] *On the Penitentiary System*, Philadelphia, 1833, p. 121. See also their conversation with the superintendent of the Philadelphia House of Refuge, pp. 230–231.

The Second Philadelphia House of Refuge, 1860–1870.

insisted that no stigma should be attached to their school, the fact remains that it does bear such stigma, just as any other reform school does. The Supreme Court of the state, in 1838, had this to say: "The House of Refuge is not a prison but a school; where reformation, and not punishment is the end. . . . The object of the charity is reformation by training the inmates to industry; by imbuing their minds with principles of morality and religion by means of furnishing them with means of earning a living and above all by separating them from the corrupting influence of improper associates." [13]

When these words were written, the Philadelphia House of Refuge was surrounded by a high wall, and within that wall the most repressive routine was the rule. Here is the order of the day in this so-called "educational" institution:

The rising bell sounded at a quarter to five o'clock in the morning. By seven o'clock the children were to have dressed and had morning worship. At that time breakfast was served. From seven-thirty until noon the children were at work. Their industries included, for boys: book-binding, shoe-making, winding bobbins, making brass nails, umbrellas, furniture, cane-seats and bonnet-reeds; for girls: sewing, knitting, cooking, and other domestic duties about the institution.

Dinner and lectures were between noon and one o'clock. From then until five o'clock, shop-work. Supper was at five, after which there was *one-half hour* devoted to play. School work engaged the children from that time until a quarter to eight. Evening prayers preceded the time for retiring which was scheduled for eight o'clock. Children were placed in their rooms and the doors locked. On Sundays religious exercises monopolized the entire day.[14]

It is recorded that the children sold flowers to passers by through enclosures in the wall. "A great throng would stop and watch these little ones, and sometimes give a few cents for the flowers. It was a sad sight—free children on the one side and the imprisoned ones, of the same age, in their coarse clothing, on the other." [15]

The first industrial school for girls in this country was established in 1854 in an old brick mansion at the edge of the town of Lancaster, Massachusetts. The institution had a farm for outdoor work for the

[13] Quoted by J. P. Shalloo, "The Rise of Juvenile Institutions in the United States," *Prison Journal*, July 1947, p. 295.

[14] Quoted by Teeters, *op. cit.*, p. 169.

[15] *Journal of Prison Discipline and Philanthropy*, Philadelphia, 1893, p. 10.

girls, a feature which at the time was quite new. The commissioners reported to the legislature as follows:

> The commissioners can entertain no doubt that the organization should be that of a family and the government, as nearly as practicable, that of a parent. They believe that great moral and religious power abides in the idea of parental government and family organization, which has not been developed in any public reformatory institution in this country, and that, if this legitimate power were wrought out into ultimate action, it would effect far more in the way of reforming juvenile delinquents than measures based upon any other idea.

The commissioners wanted cottages to house eight to twelve girls, but for practical reasons they settled on thirty. When the cottages were finally erected, they served from twenty-five to forty inmates each. There were no walls or fences around the school and even the windows were not barred. It was truly a "village of homes"—a great advance over the earlier Houses of Refuge with their cell-like dormitories, their walls, and their repressive programs.

3. THE EVOLUTION OF THE COTTAGE OR FAMILY-TYPE INSTITUTION

Earlier, we described the cottage or family-type school operated by Frédéric Auguste Demetz at Mettray, near Tours, France. Most of the credit for developing the family unit in reform schools has gone to this progressive jurist. We also pointed out that as early as 1788, the Philanthropic Society of London conceived child-saving in terms of small family units; that in 1830 Captain Edward Pelham Brenton, working with the Children's Friend Society, opened a small retreat for vagrant boys near London; and that in 1833 Dr. Johann Heinrich Wichern, with his "Inner Mission," established the justly famous Rauhe Haus at Horn, in Germany. All these establishments deserve credit for pioneering the cottage or family-type institution. In fact, Demetz received his ideas primarily from Wichern's Rauhe Haus.[16]

The cottage system spread to the United States and took root first at the institution for girls at Lancaster, Massachusetts, in 1854. Four years later, this same system was developed at the boys' school at Lancaster, Ohio.

---

[16] See Chapter II, pp. 57–60.

State Industrial School for Girls, Lancaster, Massachusetts, 1854—First Cottage-Type Reform School in this Country.

In the Lancaster, Ohio, school for boys, the first cottages were log cabins, each of which housed forty boys. The custodians were known as "Elder Brothers." Each cottage was named for a river. Every effort was made to eliminate the characteristics of a prison, although the régime, like that at Mettray, was severe. The boys worked eight and a half hours on the farm each day, except Sunday. On this day their time was taken up with many religious services, "moral review of the week," and "a walk on the farm." Attempts to escape subjected the guilty ones to "degradation and to confinement in a dark cell for two weeks, or to expulsion and transfer to the penitentiary." [17] We shall discuss this institution in some detail later, when we make an evaluation of institutions as places to "correct" juvenile delinquents.

As children's reform schools were authorized in the various states, they were built on the cottage basis. Most of them were and are attractively designed, but they all follow a traditional pattern. They are usually in isolated areas and make much of farming. Some of them rival college campuses with their groves of shade trees, brick or stone cottages, and tastefully arranged flower gardens. The layman visiting any of these institutions is struck with their apparent beauty and is often misled by the surroundings to label them as delightful places to send children. Few students of delinquency who are acquainted with these schools, however, can give a clean bill of health to any of them. Although the cottage type of school is far better than the older prison-like Houses of Refuge, criticism today questions the whole concept of institutional treatment of youthful offenders. More on this point will be said later.

From the beginning, children sentenced to the Houses of Refuge were under the indeterminate sentence—that is, the court set no time limit, leaving the release up to the management of the schools. The managers had jurisdiction and supervisory authority over the children until they reached their majority. A definite program, however, was installed in the school which, it was hoped, would result in "reformation." Many homeless children—not necessarily delinquent—were released from the schools as indentured servants or ap-

---

[17] For a contemporary account of this first boys' cottage institution, see the *Journal of Prison Discipline and Philanthropy*, Philadelphia, October 1858, pp. 153–168.

prentices; after their release, only a minimum of supervision was exercised over the foster home and the child. Since the House of Refuge had control over the child until he was of age, and since many youngsters sent to it were not delinquent, city magistrates often hesitated to send children to the institution for such a long period of close supervision. So they continued to send minors to the city jails as the lesser of two evils.

A Typical Cottage-Type Reform School—Glen Mills School, near Philadelphia, Pennsylvania.

Summarizing, the first stage of institutions for delinquent children was an era of prison-like structures and was characterized by an extremely repressive program; the institutions served as substitutes for the county jail and adult penitentiary. The second phase was characterized by cottage or family-type establishments erected in rural areas or on the outskirts of small towns. Also, during this second era a number of private enterprises were started whose aim was to rehabilitate unfortunate or abandoned children. In these institutions novel experiments in self-government and community living were

inaugurated. Perhaps the most famous of these was the George
Junior Republic at Freeville, New York, conceived and operated for
many years by William Reuben George.[18]

The early Houses of Refuge were co-educational, with separate
quarters for boys and girls. Later the sexes were separated in special
schools, although today a few states still maintain one institution for
both boys and girls. For example, the Pennsylvania Training School
at Morganza houses both sexes, although they are rigidly segregated;
other states that still combine the two sexes in one establishment are
Idaho, Kentucky, Mississippi, Nevada, New Hampshire, North
Dakota, South Dakota, Utah, and Vermont. Several states also maintain separate schools for colored children.

Even though co-education has apparently proved successful in a
few institutions, notably in the Louisville and Jefferson County home
at Anchorage, Kentucky, (Ormsby Village), in 1946 the National
Conference on the Prevention and Control of Juvenile Delinquency
expressed the belief that this practice is not to be encouraged.

List of Early Children's Reform Schools

1824   House of Refuge, New York City
1826   House of Reformation, Boston
1828   House of Refuge, Philadelphia
1845   Boys' House of Refuge, New Orleans
1847   Lyman School for Boys, Westboro, Massachusetts
1849   State Industrial School, Rochester, New York
1849   House of Refuge for Boys, Baltimore
1850   House of Refuge, Cincinnati
1851   House of Refuge, Morganza, Pennsylvania
1853   State Reform School, Portland, Maine
1854   State Reform School for Boys, West Meriden, Connecticut
1854   House of Refuge, St. Louis
1856   State Reform School, Lansing, Michigan
1856   Boys' Industrial School (formerly called "the reform farm") Lancaster,
           Ohio
1858   State Industrial School, Manchester, New Hampshire
1860   State Industrial School for Boys, Waukesha, Wisconsin

Notice that the manner of naming the institutions varied from year
to year. First they were called Houses of Refuge, and they were to
be just that—asylums for underprivileged children. Later the name
was changed to Reform School, to remove all doubt about what their

---

[18] See Chapter XIII, pp. 494–496.

purpose was. But in time children who had "served time" in a reform school were stigmatized. Since trade training was emphasized, the name Industrial School came into use. But even this name began to carry stigma and, conversely, it stigmatized boys and girls who attended training schools of their own volition. Nor does the name House of Correction help. In time, it was considered best to give the school the name of a person or of its location.

In 1946, there were approximately 166 schools under public auspices in this country serving delinquent children. Of these, 115 were state and national schools and 51 were county and municipal institutions. During 1946, the state and national institutions cared for an average of nearly 22,000 children, of whom approximately 16,000 were boys and 6,000 girls. Including the county and municipal institutions as well as the fairly large number of private or semiofficial schools, the total average population has been estimated to exceed 30,000.[19]

4. SPECIAL INSTITUTIONS FOR DELINQUENTS

a. Catholic Institutions

Before we make an evaluation of institutional treatment for delinquents, a word should be said about the special Catholic institutions for delinquent children. The Catholic church maintains child welfare agencies, to which juvenile judges often refer cases, especially if the children belong to this faith. Boys are sent to protectories and girls to institutions operated by the Order of the Good Shepherd. The treatment in both types of institutions maintained by the Catholic church is highly regimented and emphasis is placed on religious instruction.

The Order of the Good Shepherd owes its origin to a nun who, in 1818, entered a Catholic order under the name of Sister Mary of St. Euphrasia. A woman of remarkable ability, within a few years she was raised to the position of Mother Superior of the House. She was concerned over the lack of training of the nuns in various convents that dealt with depraved and fallen womanhood. So in 1831 she conceived the idea of setting up a home for training. In 1835, Pope Gregory XVI granted her establishment a Generalate. The new congregation was to be known as the Congregation of Our Lady of

---

[19] *Social Work Yearbook, 1949*, Russell Sage Foundation, p. 282.

Charity of the Good Shepherd, with headquarters at Angers in France. With approval of the bishops, she could found new houses, supervise them, admit novices, and make provision for training.

The growth of the Order was remarkable. During her lifetime, Mother Euphrasia established over 100 houses in as many countries, including several in South American countries and the Philippines. At this time there are sixty houses in the United States. The first one was established in Louisville, Kentucky.

Today the Order of the Good Shepherd deals with delinquent and problem girls. In the larger cities it maintains separate institutions for younger girls who are truant problems and others devoted largely to the treatment of venereal cases, including prostitutes. Admission is usually through the local juvenile or morals court or by the girl's own volition.

b. Schools for Truant Children

Special institutions for the correction of truant children have been in existence for some time. Sometimes known as "parental schools," they have almost always been a part of the regular public school system. The first parental schools were organized in Boston in 1896 and in Buffalo in 1897. The child is placed in such an institution only when his case of truancy is serious. Some of these schools have also been used for children who, in addition to truancy, have committed minor offenses. A good example of such an institution is the Shallcross School, a residential school for truant boys between the ages of 8 and 14½ years, operated by the Board of Public Education of Philadelphia. Since it has a capacity of not more than 96 boys, the personnel can give intensive individual attention to the pupils; also, a very close working relationship exists between the administration of this institution and the counseling service of the school system.[20]

5. CRITICISM OF INSTITUTIONAL TREATMENT FOR DELINQUENTS

a. General Criticism

The criticism hurled against institutional incarceration of children is not new. Many persons through the years have looked upon the

---

[20] For further details on parental schools, see Reckless and Smith, *Juvenile Delinquency*, McGraw-Hill, New York, 1932, pp. 178–180.

practice as one of despair which easily developed into a habit. "Out of sight, out of mind" is the thesis accompanying the concept of imprisonment.

William Tallack, for many years secretary of the Howard League of London, wrote of the "institution craze" that marked the thinking of many students of delinquency in mid-Victorian England. His objections, voiced in his book *Penological and Preventive Principles*, published in 1896, were as follows: First, institutional treatment shifts parental responsibility to the state; second, lack of classification produces a collection of tender youth and more calloused delinquents which makes possible the training of sly and hardened criminals; third, many children are sent back to depraved surroundings, including homes, where no interim preparation has been effected.[21] He speaks of the large training ships as "floating prisons" filled with all kinds of corruption; of reformatories where outbreaks, riots, and fire-setting were the rule. Tallack does make a distinction between reformatories wherein criminal youth are incarcerated, and industrial schools to which non-criminal children are sent for trade training.

Although the above criticism is none too logical, it demonstrates that the practice of institutional treatment was not considered a panacea even at that time.

It is difficult to be tolerant of institutional treatment either for juvenile delinquents or for adults. When imprisonment was first conceived, it was undoubtedly regarded as a gratifying step forward in coping with the offender. It mitigated the more barbaric practice of capital punishment and the brutal and diabolical forms of corporal punishment. But its long history of over a century has proved that it has not measured up to the high hopes set by its founders. It is the purpose of this section to show the evils of the conventional reform school and to demonstrate further that in the light of advances made in the social sciences, psychiatry, and adolescent psychology, the reform school is so outmoded that its use should be drastically curtailed.

The program and philosophy underlying these reform schools are fundamentally similar. Superintendent and staff officers are often

---

[21] William Tallack, *Penological and Preventive Principles*, Wertheimer, Lea & Co., 1896, pp. 342–348.

college graduates, with some training in psychology and sociology. The atmosphere seems wholesome to outsiders and to the uninitiated; the staff appears sympathetic, and it generally is, if the children conform. However, some of the more "progressive" schools show a tendency to gear the responsibilities of the young inmates higher than the inadequate training and the more or less inferior homes they came from before their incarceration warrant.

The problem manifests itself not only in the training itself, but in the after-care as well.[22] Generally a parole plan, handled in some cases by trained personnel, is set up to insure supervision, but once again the tendency is to expect too much from the released child. It is assumed that the training afforded in the cloistered atmosphere of the institution will carry over into the community experience of the child. But it seldom does. Reform schools rarely permit any objective studies to be made of their training programs or of their after-care. If such studies were made, honestly and courageously, the schools would not be under attack so frequently. In recent years the criticism has come from so many sources that administrators are beginning to chafe under it. Some refuse to accept it, complaining that the attacks are not constructive but altogether negative. Others, more tolerant see justification for the criticism and are engaged in self-appraisal. But appraisal can be honest only when it is performed by some capable outsider who can apply scientific and objective criteria to the administration, plant, and training program.

Another criticism may be made against even the best of the reform schools. Despite the wishful thinking of the administration that their particular school is an educational rather than a reform school, a definite stigma is attached to those who have been sent to or paroled from them. Such a school is still a prison in the eyes of the public, especially in the neighborhoods from which the children are sent. The children look well and are generally given adequate medical treatment. They have sports and amusements, often many more than the average child experiences in his own neighborhood. But the routine is monotonous and regimented; the daily life is abnormal and stultifying. The discipline, based on mid-Victorian concepts, tends to be severe. The punishments, especially in the boys' schools, are often downright brutal. Practically every school resorts to flogging,

[22] See pp. 471–474 regarding parole of juveniles from institutions.

and the most ingenious forms of physical sadism are the rule in many schools. Dire warnings are issued against such offenses as insubordination, irregular sexual practices, and, of course, running away. Running away is a most heinous offense; often the inmates of the entire cottage where the runaway child resides are severely disciplined as a penalty for "permitting" the inmate to abscond. But many a homesick boy or girl, tiring of the "beautiful" campus and benevolent despotism of the administration, takes French leave.[23]

The children sent to reform schools are sex-starved; the older adolescent girls suffer keenly in this isolation. Since most of the girls are put away by the court for sexual irregularity at this most critical age in their lives, it seems very short-sighted to deny them the wholesome companionship of the opposite sex. If sex is a problem, it will never be solved by locking girls up in a penal institution. In boys' institutions may be found many who are there only because they did not like school—but we can never solve truancy by locking up a boy in such a place. Truancy is symptomatic of something that needs to be investigated, sometimes by a psychiatrist. In short, it is possible that investigation at the time of arrest or detention and a sympathetic probation program might keep hundreds of these youngsters out of correctional institutions, some of which are nothing but crime-breeding factories. It is a truism in penology that many of our professional and highly processed criminals started to learn the intricacies of their craft in our reform schools. The criminal climate permeates these schools. The more repressive the régime—and administrators admit that repression is necessary to stifle criminal tendencies—the more persistent is this kind of atmosphere.

The above criticism, general in its nature, is made despite the good that prevails here and there in some of the more progressive schools. But just as the adult prison is an anachronism and a failure, so is the juvenile reform school. There may be some children who should be sent to these places; but as penal science expands, employing child-guidance clinics, psychiatric services, the technique of well-trained social workers, and the knowledge and application of medical

---

[23] The reader is referred to a revealing quasi-fictional book, one of the few dealing with children's institutions, which describes the conditions in a girls' reform school—Felice Swados, *House of Fury*, Doubleday, Doran, New York, 1941; see also Willard Motley, *Knock on Any Door*, Appleton-Century-Crofts, New York, 1947.

science, it will be difficult to find a child who will respond better in a reform school than he will in his own home or a foster home. Child care, whether of a dependent, neglected, or delinquent child, is a community problem and it must be faced by the resources of the community. If possible, the child must be treated where he is found. If his home is definitely undesirable, other homes are ready, or can be made ready, to receive him. If the child is merely practicing the *mores* of his neighborhood and of his parents, it is the duty of the trained worker to find some plan that is applicable to the situation rather than to pull him away from his family and send him to a school where he is not only stigmatized but is trained in antisocial practices. Many juvenile court judges refuse to send children to reform schools.

b. Specific Criticism

Up to this point we have been general in our criticism. We shall devote some space here to specific cases taken from various reliable sources. As stated above, few reform school administrators have the courage to initiate an objective evaluation of their schools or of their after-care programs by an impartial agency or group of investigators. The only sources available from which we may assemble evidence are the following: (1) Investigations made by some legal body usually after a scandal or serious irregularity has been brought to light, such as those in the Whittier, California, school in 1940; the Ferris School for Boys at Wilmington, Delaware, in 1944; the Eldora, Iowa, boys' school in August 1945; or the Morganza, Pennsylvania, school for boys and girls in 1948. (2) Investigations made by the Osborne Association of New York, a private body that has for one of its purposes the evaluation of institutions of a penal nature. Or (3) investigations made by private individuals, such as those made in 1948 by the journalist, Albert Deutsch. Periodically, of course, we read in the press of trouble in a school where resentment suddenly breaks out and attracts publicity. Such has been the case at the St. Charles, Illinois, school for delinquent boys, or, on occasion, at the Ohio Boys' School at Lancaster.

First let us take the Whittier, California, school, now known as the Fred C. Nelles School, conceded by many to be one of the most progressive in the country. The physical plant and the topographical setting of this school rivals most college campuses, seated as it is in the quiet little college town of Whittier, near Los Angeles. The per capita cost today exceeds two thousand dollars per year. Dr. Norman Fenton, writing of this school in 1935, said: "The architectural rebuilding and improvement of Whittier has been accompanied by the evolution of a newer philosophy of child guidance. The story of Whittier . . . offers a fine means of describing the evolutional treatment of delinquent children." [24] At the time Dr. Fenton wrote, the Whittier school did enjoy a deservedly good reputation, which was all too short-lived.

A report on this school made by the Osborne Association in 1940 commented favorably on the beautiful surroundings, but it added: "Yet it is sadly true that the school has made greater progress in the direction of building sufficiency than toward the development of a favorable psychological atmosphere required to carry on the work for which it was established." The report condemned the administration for failure to supply the boys with underwear and suggests that the school should release the boys "outfitted with at least a full suit of clothing"; that "marching of all boys from the cottages to the hospital daily for sick call is an unreasonable and unnecessary procedure"; and that "the honor clubs . . . are simply an instrument for the enforcement of rules and regulations."

But the Osborne Association also set down some of the school's good points. The housing was considered splendid; the provision of "cottage parents" made for a "warm atmosphere of friendliness." The library was considered well above the average. There was a classification clinic. Nevertheless, the report seemed to qualify practically every commendation awarded the school.

Before the Osborne Association made its visit, a Mexican boy had "committed suicide" in the Lost Privilege Cottage. An investigation had been made by the Director of Institutions and the administration was exonerated of any blame for this tragic death. But shortly after the visit a second boy committed suicide. Governor Olsen called for another investigation, with Judge Ben Lindsey, prominent jurist and authority on delinquency, heading the committee.

The Lindsey report, submitted December 6, 1940, indicted the school and its management, and scored the Director of Institutions

---

[24] *The Delinquent Boy and the Correctional School*, Claremont College Press, California, 1935, p. 15.

for "white-washing" the management in the earlier investigation of the alleged suicide of the two boys. The letter sent to the Governor with this report said:

> After duly considering all the data presented, it is the conviction of this committee that the costly program administered at Whittier is not truly correctional. It is further our conviction that gross inefficiency, mismanagement, and irresponsibility are the basic factors of the difficulty.

The letter continued by stating that the boys were badly in need of guidance; that the inmates were "subjected to brutality, abuse and intimidation such as the 'rabbit punch,' 'kidney punch,' 'duck-walk,' 'the squats' and other bizarre but painful methods." It stated that gross racial discrimination existed and, in addition, the school's cost was outrageously high.

Further, the letter stated that the investigation made by the Director of Institutions into the death of one of the boys "was based on inadequate information" which made it later impossible to ascertain definitely the true cause of the boy's death. One gets the suggestion as one reads the report, that this boy did not take his own life, but that he met death at the hands of another, probably a supervisor or guard. Gross brutalities were committed by the supervisors so frequently in the Lost Privilege Cottage that the boys lived in constant fear.

While this investigation was being carried on and during the interim when new administrative officers were being selected, *over two hundred* boys ran away. The school was completely demoralized. A new superintendent was appointed and many improvements were made. But he soon resigned. Here is a glaring example of a misguided and mistaken notion of penal philosophy, sugar-coated by the application of the word "educational" to a reform school.

A new dispensation was inaugurated in California in 1940 and subsequent years which finally took over the Whittier School. We refer to the Youth Correction Authority, which we have discussed elsewhere. Regardless of how effective this advanced concept may be, it is still shackled with all the evils of institutional practice and thus will have difficulty in maintaining a meaningful program for the rehabilitation of youthful offenders.

Let us continue with specific institutions. Take the example of the

Ohio Industrial School for Boys, located at Lancaster. The history of this school has always been dubious. It enjoyed some distinction for introducing progressive measures (it was the first cottage-type school for boys in the country), but it has long been considered a most repressive institution. The Osborne Association in 1935 criticized its buildings as fire hazards and the educational program as far from adequate. It added that the personnel "means well" and does not "willfully commit acts of cruelty." Flogging loomed large in its discipline.

This school was further, and searchingly, investigated in 1939. The report stated: "The philosophy of the School is based on two sets of facts . . . the first is that since the boy has sinned he owes a debt to society [and] must be punished in repayment of this debt . . . he is thought of as a criminal . . . as a problem boy rather than as a boy with problems. Suppression and repression are considered the only kinds of treatment to which the boy will respond. These notions are strongly impressed on new employees and on visitors. Second, emphasis is placed on the maintenance and operation of the institution to the disadvantage of the boy. Economy is the watchword. . . . There is a perfect cycle of rationalization: 'These are bad boys. They may have committed crimes. Most of the boys are dumb. By and large they are a poor lot. Very little can be done for them. It is a hopeless task, so why waste a lot of effort.' " [25] This survey was the fifth the school had experienced since 1919. Albert Deutsch, as recently as February–March, 1948, found conditions in this same school little better than they had been in 1940.

The Osborne Association of New York has surveyed many of the juvenile institutions of the country. It has already visited several states and has appraised their institutions. Here and there a few have merited some favorable comment, but the vast majority have been found mediocre, and many have been found downright repressive and inhumane in their program of treatment. Here we find political domination; there we find old firetraps used for buildings. In this school we see a lack of many of the comforts and ordinary decencies we might expect where the care of children is the main objective;

---

[25] T. C. Holy and G. B. Stahly, *Survey of the Boys' Industrial School, Lancaster, Ohio*, published by the State Department of Public Welfare in cooperation with the Bureau of Educational Research, Ohio State University, 1940, p. 30.

in that school we come upon untrained personnel with an attitude respecting their job bordering on that of the average prison guard. One cannot help feeling, after reading the reports of this fact-finding organization, that reform school treatment is futile for delinquent boys and girls.[26]

Let us sample a few of these reports on institutions scattered throughout the country, quoting or paraphrasing the *Handbooks*.

The Missouri Home for Girls, at Chillicothe, is characterized by "ill-defined administrative policies, shameful overcrowding, dissension among staff members . . . and the housing of girls in dilapidated fire-traps under physically and morally unhealthy conditions." The Kentucky House of Reform, Greendale, is described as "neither humane nor constructive and is a discredit to the state." The State Training and Agricultural School, Nashville, Tennessee, is "understaffed, overcrowded . . . with facilities as run down and antiquated as its system of child care." In an Arkansas institution for females, girls were beaten in the nude and then placed in solitary confinement for fifteen days on a diet of bread and water.

The State Training School for Boys at Chehalis, Washington, "has the negative distinction of being the only one visited on the Pacific Coast requiring strict silence among the inmates throughout the meal hour." The boys "actually lift their chairs in slow motion so that . . . hardly a sound can be heard in the diningroom." At the Iowa Training School for Boys, at Eldora, "boys committing sex offenses have their heads shaved, are whipped, and assigned to the Discipline Cottage for a period of ten to fifteen days." At Red Wing, Minnesota, in the school for boys, the investigators found "antiquated buildings, ill-adapted to the program, and the danger of continual overcrowding." In the Kansas Industrial School for Boys, at Topeka, they found "a lack of understanding which the majority of the officials displayed in discussing their work and the absence of purpose or direction in the functioning of the institution."

These samples of conditions may convince the reader that this mode of "reforming" boys and girls of teen-age is a national disgrace or, speaking conservatively, is of questionable value. The re-

---

[26] See the Association's *Handbooks of American Institutions for Delinquents,* First Edition, Vols. I, 1938; II, 1940; III, 1940; IV, 1943. This latest report sets up desirable standards for juvenile training schools.

ports reveal an utter bankruptcy of educational procedure and understanding in the treatment of delinquency. Although the Osborne Association studies were made several years ago, there is plenty of reason to believe that conditions at present are no better, although some institutions have doubtless profited by such indictment. For example, an editorial in the school paper of the Boys' Industrial School at Topeka, Kansas, on December 5, 1949, read as follows:

Ten or twelve years ago this school was being highly accepted nationally and even universally as "one of the worst institutions of its kind to be found anywhere. . . ." The dishonor was achieved after a survey made of all juvenile correctional schools.

That was years ago. Today BIS, as we know it, is one of the best, not only in the west but in the whole 48 states. Young men (boys ten years ago) who visit the school now after being away 10 or 12 years can hardly believe their eyes when they see the changes that have been made.

As one visitor put it: "When I was here we had to stay HERE. Now you guys get passes to go home and passes into town. You have a bus to take you into town for shows, picnics, and everything."

This boy listed only a few of the liberties the boys have now. He mentioned the family-style eating setup at the dining-room—when only the biggest boy at each table got all he wanted. He thought the new cafeteria style was much better. In other words, he said: "I was born ten years too soon."

In the same issue of the school paper the following also appeared:

Neatness—Whether in school, at work, or home, neatness which goes along with cleanliness is a good policy to follow. It is a valuable habit and will do nobody any harm.

When you come home from work you don't feel "just right" until you have cleaned up a bit.

Everyone admires and looks twice when a neatly dressed boy comes down or up the walk. It isn't the clothes you wear, it's the way you wear them; it isn't the hair you have, it's the way you comb it.

Even your shoes should be neat. Are your laces always tied? Did you shine your shoes? Look at 'em, everyone else does.

No more cruelty in the Kansas boys' school. But a barrage of subtle suggestions to be neat and polite.

As stated above, a more recent investigation of some ten of these reform schools was made by Albert Deutsch; his findings were published in the *Woman's Home Companion* for March, 1948 and later in book form. Prefacing his descriptions of these ten schools, Deutsch makes this statement:

> The facts as I found them, shock me profoundly. They add up to a black record of human tragedy, of social and economic waste, of gross brutality, crass stupidity, totalitarian regimentation and a corroding monotony even deadlier for children's personalities than physical violence.[27]

Allowing for a few notable exceptions where "staff members try to give kindly and intelligent guidance," he adds that "for the most part they are handicapped by public indifference, legislative penury and administrative inertia, or by the traditional view that juvenile offenders are miniature criminals and child reformatories are juvenile prisons."

Let us look at some of the criticisms made by Mr. Deutsch of specific schools in 1948. At the Illinois State Training School for Boys at St. Charles, where corporal punishment was officially prohibited, "many a boy has had his ear drums broken in beatings." The water cure, euphoniously referred to as "hydrotherapy," was a punishment meted out to trouble makers in the disciplinary cottage. The boy was stripped naked and subjected to a seventy-five-pound stream of water played on him from a fire hose. At the Indiana State Training School at Plainfield, boys were required to wax floors "moving backwards" as a punishment; they were also subjected to "duck walking," in which a boy is forced to grasp his ankles with his hands and waddle across the room. At the Ohio Industrial School for Boys at Lancaster, the inmates wore oversize shoes and worn-out prison-made clothing, and were fed unpalatable food, which they had to eat in silence. During the meal the boys undergoing punishment stood in the dining room with their faces to the wall. Whippings were one of the punishments at the Lancaster school and were officially sanctioned by the state authorities. At the Boonville, Missouri, reform school Deutsch found: (1) that it was a bad reform school and had been bad for many years; (2) that its youngest inmate was nine years old and its oldest was twenty-four; (3) that terror-stricken boys

---

[27] See also *PM* for February and March, 1948, and *Our Rejected Children*, Little, Brown, Boston, 1950.

had been escaping from this school for years—400 made off during the year of his investigation.[28]

In December 1949, the Colorado Industrial School at Golden was roundly criticized by Attorney General John W. Metzger. Appearing before the state planning commission, he listed his charges: (1) fire escapes locked; (2) the existence of a virtual dungeon where inmates were confined up to twenty-one days on a diet of bread and water; (3) a ward where boys had to sleep under bright lights throughout the night; (4) seven inmates in the school infirmary suffering from welts from whippings.[29]

All the features referred to in the preceding pages are inherent in the reform school concept. We can agree with Mr. Deutsch that some schools do have good intentions but, on the whole, they are struggling to do the impossible. The correctional school represents an outmoded philosophy in the light of newer concepts of behavior treatment.

Earlier, we made some negative comment regarding the Whittier, California, reform school, which was thoroughly investigated in 1940. This school is now under the California Youth Authority and, of course, should be freed from many of the earlier handicaps that marred its program. Let us see what Mr. Deutsch found in this school in 1948. Speaking of regimentation in reform schools, he writes:

> One of the shocking examples of regimentation I saw was the "toilet line" at the "lost privilege cottage" at the Whittier Boys Schools in California—ironically, it is named the Thomas Jefferson cottage. [Whittier] still retains many of the repressive features noted at the institution in 1941 when two boys committed suicide in the disciplinary cottage.
>
> Twenty-seven boys, arms folded, stood in three straight lines in the center of the cottage lavatory facing three open toilets. The boys followed one another in rotation, each rejoining the line when finished. After each had taken his turn, they marched out. There were seven "toilet lines" like this daily—before and after each meal and before bedtime. Individual visits to the toilet were rarely permitted and then only under a supervisor's guard.

[28] This material is digested from Albert Deutsch's investigations reported in *PM*, February–March 1948, and in the *Woman's Home Companion*, "Is This Reform?," March 1948.

[29] From a news dispatch from Denver, December 8, 1949.

In this same institution, as well as in the Preston School of Industry in the same state of California, Deutsch found a most bizarre habit among the inmates. It is known as "rag sniffing." The boys sink their nostrils in rags soaked with gasoline or furniture polish for no other purpose than to go on a perverted jag.

One wonders, in reading of the perennial investigations that are made of these reform schools, that any constructive rehabilitation can ever come from them.

As we have noted, in addition to flogging, which is practiced almost universally in these reform schools, other ingenious punishments are conceived. Many of these are diabolical and sadistic. Some, described by Deutsch, are worth setting down here.

Duck walking—The offending child must grasp his ankles and waddle about like a duck.

The squats or *bouncing*—Deep-knee bending for a specified period or number of times. Some children have been sentenced to 5,000 squats, worked out in intermittent sessions to prevent collapse.

Brick-counting—The child must stand erect with his nose touching the wall.

Star-gazing—The child must stand erect with his eyes turned up to the ceiling.

Standing in line (also *Toeing line*)—One of the most widespread forms of discipline encountered, especially popular where corporal punishment is forbidden. The boy (or girl) stands erect in absolute silence, sometimes for hours, often with hands upraised.

Rice polishing—Boys crawl on their knees across a floor strewn with rice grains until bleeding starts or until suffering is intense enough to satisfy disciplinarian that justice has been done.

The slicks—Shaving the heads of runaways or other offenders.

Burlap party—Rule offenders are made to push piles of burlap bags across floors flooded with water. When the bags are soaked through, they have to wring them and then resume sopping up water with burlap until floors are dry.

Walking posts—Marching between or around posts for a prescribed number of hours. In one institution, boys carry forty-pound packs on their backs while making the circuit of the "bull pen."

Runaway pills—Dosing captured runaways with laxatives to "help them run," a practice in at least one institution.

The cold tub—Disciplinary hydrotherapy wherein violators are thrown into tubs filled with ice water.

> *Fire-hose water cure*—Boy is stripped naked and a heavy jet of water is played on his back from fire hose.

The Attorney General's National Conference on Prevention and Control of Juvenile Delinquency (1946), in its *Report* on institutional treatment, makes this statement about cruel disciplinary techniques:

> Corporal punishment and other abuses, are still far too prevalent Among the disciplinary practices in training schools that have been reported by qualified and reliable observers in recent years are the following: whipping or spanking with sticks, wire coat hangers, paddles straps; striking about the face and head with fists and sticks; handcuffing to the bed at night; use of shackles and leg chains; shaving of the head; cold tubbings; "standing on the line" in a rigid position for hours at a time; confinement in dark cells and dungeonlike basement rooms; silence rules; knee bends; a modified lockstep in marching formations; permitting boy monitors to discipline other boys, including corporal punishment. Such disciplinary abuses are completely indefensible.[30]

Although most of the punishments herein described are employed primarily in boys' institutions, it must not be implied that girls are free from unique and fantastically cruel punishments. Girls with unusually beautiful hair sometimes have their tresses shorn by an irate matron if they dare to run away or engage in incipient homosexua relationships. The cold bath is often used to "subdue" emotionally unstrung girls. Some girls' schools use the "line toeing" method of subduing the recalcitrant inmates. Dark "thinking rooms" are frequently used for stubborn cases and, of course, many ordinary privileges are revoked when rules are broken.

The per capita cost of institutional treatment is worth mentioning In general, it is expensive to send a child away from his community If reformation resulted, of course, there would be no criticism of the financial outlay. The annual cost is from $300 to over $2,000 Probation costs much less.

In some states, it costs more to keep girls than boys; in other states boys are more expensive. For example, in New Jersey in 1945, the per capita cost at the girls' school at Trenton was $576.83; at the Boys' School at Jamesburg, $746.09. In Massachusetts, the boys also

---

[30] *Report No. 6*, pp. 36–37.

ost more than the girls—at the girls' school at Lancaster the per
apita cost was $582.49, whereas at the Lyman Boys' school at West-
oro the cost was $1,011.40 per inmate. In California (Ventura),
he girls cost more than the boys.[31]

One of the most unwholesome aspects of imprisonment is the
revalence of deviant forms of sexual behavior. Persons familiar
vith institutional life are aware of this phenomenon, but authorities
how little willingness to face it.

In boys' schools, the young boy, known in prison parlance as a
unk or by some other arresting name, is often the center of bitter
nmities and even feuds which frequently precipitate brawls. Inmates
vho go foraging for a "girl friend" usually have a knife on their
erson which is used on the slightest provocation. Clifford Shaw,
1 his *Jack Roller*, tells of this activity in a boys' reform school.[32]

The administration makes every effort to eliminate homosexual
ctivity, which is considered by most staff officers as the most repre-
ensible evil confronting them. Rarely does a boy have a room of
is own, since most boys' schools are shackled with the ubiquitous
ormitory housing plan. In many schools the sleeping rooms are kept
ghted all night long, and a guard allegedly keeps an eagle eye on
he sleeping boys. Staff officers attest to the fact that some boys
esort to the most ingenious devices to gravitate to their "friends"
uring the night hours. The younger boys are in great demand
mong the older and more highly processed delinquents. Shortly
fter their introduction into the school they find themselves catered
 by one or more "protectors," who agree to fight their battles for
em in return for sexual favors. Once in the clutches of one of these
wolves," the young boy is doomed.

However, a change in attitude toward this vexing problem may
evelop as a result of Dr. Kinsey's and his associates' startling find-
gs. A considerable and, possibly, major portion of the male
opulation, so they assert, has at least some homosexual experience
etween adolescence and old age. About 60 per cent of the pre-

---

[31] These figures are from "State and National Correctional Schools," *Ameri-
n Prison Association,* 1945. The latest bulletin, published in August 1949, does
ot include per capita costs. However, it would be safe to double those reported
r the year 1945.
[32] *The Jack Roller, A Delinquent Boy's Own Story,* University of Chicago
ress, 1930, pp. 106–107.

adolescent boys engage in homosexual activities. If, therefore, homo
sexual practices are found rampant in penal and correctional institu
tions, which, because of their all-male character, are much mor
conducive to these activities than the so-called normal free com
munity, this phenomenon takes on a somewhat different social an
psychological significance in the light of the findings regarding th
rest of the population.[33]

Homosexual behavior is not restricted to boys' institutions. It
likewise prevalent in girls' schools. Many girls sent to these place
are there on sex charges and find the situation almost unbearabl
They easily turn to various forms of erotic behavior and, as in boy
schools, debauch the more sensitive and feminine of their fellov
inmates. Girls' schools permit more freedom than their male counter
parts; thus sexual laxity is more easily indulged. Friendships easil
develop and soon evolve into "crushes." The same subtle, beneath
the-surface struggles found in the boys' schools are present in th
female establishments. The more feminine younger girls are in de
mand among the more masculine and older inmates. J. L. Moren
who has made a study of this behavior in a school for delinquer
girls, states:

> Among the normal and tolerated forms attraction takes between ade
> lescent girls there is one phase which has often allured the fantasy c
> poets. Soon after a first meeting they fall into feverish courtship c
> each other, vow that they will be friends forever, dream and plan tc
> gether, confide their deepest secrets. This is the "crush."
> In institutions for girls as no other outlets for the play of sexu
> energies are given, these "crushes" take on often a more active an
> exaggerated form. They are more active . . . because the homosexu
> current . . . dominates the community . . . [and because of] th
> greater rivalry displayed when the same girl is the object of sever
> girls' attention.[34]

Liaisons between white and colored girls are frequent where segre
gation is limited only to separate cottages in an institution. To quo
Moreno on this phenomenon:

---

[33] See Alfred C. Kinsey, Wardell B. Pomeroy, and Clyde E. Martin, *Sexu*
Behavior in the Human Male, Saunders, Philadelphia, 1948, pp. 168, 610, 66
[34] *Who Shall Survive?*, Nervous and Mental Disease Publishing Co., Wasl
ington, D.C., 1934, p. 229.

As long as crushes occur within the white population their effect upon conduct is similar to that outside in the open community. But it is different and without parallel in a normal environment when white girls have crushes on colored girls, not only as individuals, but *en masse*. This form of crush greatly outdoes in intensity, variability of attitudes, and effect upon conduct the fancy of a white girl for another white girl.

This bizarre form of behavior we have rarely found to be mutual. It is a one-sided attraction of the white girl for the colored. The white girl goes through all the gestures of courtship, sends notes, makes dates, and tries to keep the mysterious conduct secret. As long as it lasts, she is as if in a trance.[35]

Moreno says that the colored girl enters this relationship as if it were a game, whereas it is quite serious to the white girl. The blacker the skin of the Negro, the more she is pursued by the white girl and the more she despises the courtship; but the blonder the white girl, the more successful will be her campaign. Says Moreno: "The colored group as a race exults in being for once in a superior position toward the white race. It is a big show for them and inflates their ego. Often the colored girl reacts like a proud, rough fellow who accepts signs of affection but acts as if he doesn't care for them." He explains that the colored girl is accepted because she is "something utterly different. . . . The physical differences of the white and colored race, the 'strange' appearance of the colored girl compared to the white seems to provide the attribute of 'distance' and unapproachability. Further the Negro girl has in the imagination of the white, boldness and braveness, a spontaneity of conduct that she envies, as well as appearing more muscular and stronger than herself." [36]

The more progressive superintendents of female institutions accept these explosive situations and attempt to deal with them tactfully rather than punish the culprits, especially cases that have marked indications of being purely voluntary "crushes." Much of this type of tension could be avoided if the Negroes were permitted to mingle freely with the whites—go to class together, work together, and live in the same cottages.

---

[35] *Idem.*

[36] *Ibid.*, p. 231; the same problem is discussed by the author of a revealing book dealing with delinquency in reform schools, William Bernard, *Jailbait*, Greenberg, New York, 1949, pp. 166–167.

The sex problem is rarely mentioned, and almost never discussed in conferences of superintendents of boys' or girls' schools—at least in such a way that the public may read or hear about it. In the proceedings of such conferences one almost never sees an article written or hears a paper read on the subject. Yet it is a universal problem of the first magnitude.[37]

Observations in a variety of girls' reform schools disclose that there is no universal policy of dealing with the sex problem. Some administrators frown on crushes and make futile attempts to stamp them out, separating girls and scrutinizing their daily habits carefully. In other institutions flirtations are not repressed, but when behavior begins to be "serious," tasks are changed and obstructions are tactfully placed so that the participants find it difficult to carry on.

Some administrators foster the conviction that a rigorous program of work, physical education, and constant surveillance will stamp out this institutional curse. No doubt such a program does reduce it, but so long as boys and girls possessing plenty of animal activity are segregated according to sex, there will remain a fertile field for homosexual tendencies. The only solution is the abolition of the conditions that foster such behavior. Such a solution would unquestionably involve the practice of permitting inmates some opportunity for normal contact. Provisions for the entertainment of visitors of the opposite sex might be provided as a part of the school program. More frequent furloughs home would also be helpful. Society, through its penal program, deliberately discourages the traditionally normal mechanisms of sex and thus encourages various forms of sexual aberration. It is obvious that some bold plan of social action is needed. The need for study is also obvious. It seems odd that so few articles on the subject are available in the professional journals. Nor can we find any mentioned in the excellent Cabot bibliography which deals with books and articles written in the field of juvenile delinquency.

The problem of personnel in reform schools represents another

---

[37] Even in the clinical journals there is little to be reviewed. See Margaret A. Otis, "Perversions Not Commonly Noted," *Journal of Abnormal Psychology*, Vol. 81, 1913, pp. 113–116; also Charles A. Ford, "Homosexual Practices of Institutionalized Females," *Journal of Abnormal and Social Psychology*, Vol. 23, No. 4, January–March 1929, pp. 442–448.

erious difficulty. Although the staff officers in boys' schools may
lead a reasonably normal life and have their families living in the
vicinity of the institutions, unmarried women in the girls' schools are
not so fortunate. They usually live on the grounds, which, all too
frequently, are long distances from metropolitan areas with their
cultural advantages. Thus their lives tend to be stultifying. Young
college women who accept a post in a girls' school stay but a short
time. They marry or seek greener pastures in the fields of social work
or teaching.

If reform schools expect to attract capable personnel, they must
revise their salary scale and go to great lengths to permit staff members to get away at frequent intervals for relaxation and recuperation
in order to ward off the deadening institutionalization that develops
in even the most progressive institutions. Provisions for tenure, promotion, and pensioning should be made in the light of the best
modern institutional procedure and not at the caprice of an arrogant
or crotchety superintendent. Courses of study should be provided,
and periodical leaves of absence should be made mandatory; the
state should provide financial assistance in such ventures. In those
institutions that still attempt to provide "house parents"—that is,
married couples for the various cottages—some adjustment to the
modern philosophy of the forty-hour week must be made. In short,
every effort should be made to increase the morale of the staff members. The practice of permitting only the superintendent, for example, to attend conferences at state expense should be modified so that
an opportunity is given to other staff officers to share in the fruitful
discussion and "good times" of the traditional periodic conventions.
Let us close this analysis of reform schools by quoting again from
Albert Deutsch; these remarks were made before members of the
American Prison Association:

> Ugly practices are hidden behind slick modern phrases: I found cell-
> blocks referred to as "lost privilege cottages," caretakers and custodians
> called "cottage parents," a mass juvenile prison regimen referred to as
> "individualized treatment," isolation cells called "meditation rooms,"
> kitchen drudgery and other forms of industrial exploitation of child
> labor called "vocational rehabilitation" and whips and paddles as "tools
> of control." [38]

---

[38] Quoted in *Focus*, November 1948, p. 179.

Further, he lists the "Ten Deadly Sins of public institutional treatment of child delinquency:

1. Regimentation.
2. Institutional monotony, including work, food, recreation, etc
3. Mass treatment.
4. Political partisan influence.
5. Public penury.
6. Isolation—physical and spiritual.
7. Complacency.
8. Excess of physical and mental punishment.
9. Babelism—"the profusion of neologisms that sound impres sively modern while hiding an ugly reality."
10. Enforced idleness.[39]

If a public crusade of education were to be waged against such brutality administered in the name of rehabilitation, reform school might become, to quote a worker in the field of delinquency, "purifi cation centers rather than garbage incinerators." [40]

6. RUNAWAYS FROM REFORM SCHOOLS

One of the most important problems in reform schools is that of the runaway boy or girl. Traditional obligations make this offens perhaps the most serious that a child can commit. Flogging in man boys' schools and hair cutting in some girls' schools are administere as penalties for this "heinous" offense. The administration ver rightly consider it a cardinal responsibility to society and to th court to keep their charges secure. This is obviously quite difficul since there are usually no walls around the premises. Most school however, do use bars at the windows of rooms and dormitories an the doors are generally locked at night. Although these bars ar sometimes disguised as a sort of iron filigree or as artistic ironwor they are nevertheless designed to restrain. Much sophistry is em ployed by the superintendent of a school in giving the uninitiate public the impression that traditional restraints are not necessary keep their charges secure.

---

[39] *Proceedings*, American Prison Association, 1948, pp. 50–56.
[40] Robert E. Coulson, "Evaluation of Experience in Correctional Institutions *ibid.*, pp. 38–46.

Few studies of runaways have been made. But since the problem is a serious one, it should be recognized by administrators and public alike. Much of the energy and cunning of staff officers is employed in maintaining restraints and in keeping inmates secure within the grounds. Frequent countings of the children are one method; establishing an "honor" system is another. Delegating authority to older children to keep a watchful eye on newer arrivals is another.

One study of runaways was made some years ago by Dr. Zena A. O'Connor, who made an objective study of 119 runaway boys from Children's Village, a semi-public institution in New York State.[41] In addition to those who absconded, a controlled group of non-runaways was studied. Forty-five, or 37.8 per cent, of the runaways had a pre-institutional history of truancy; of the controlled group, 26, or 31 per cent, were truants before their incarceration. The study shows many interesting factors in the two groups which cannot be discussed here. The conclusions, however, are of interest: (1) The only difference established between the two groups was the difference of chronological age. (2) "Success on parole" is more frequent with the control group (non-runaways) than with the runaway group. (3) No reliable differences were established between the two groups in factors taken from case histories. (4) Certain cottages provide more runaways than do others. (5) Runaways were most numerous in July; least numerous in November. (6) Reasons for absconding were: lack of fair play; desire to get home to see what family changes had taken place; lack of satisfaction in school program; incompatible cottage masters and matrons and frequent upsetting changes in personnel; suggestibility when group runaways were planned; feeling there should be more "tryout" classes; and the merit system.

Recommendations suggested by this study are also of interest: (1) "Graduation" or release from the school should be scheduled for times least likely to disrupt the educational and other programs. (2) The newly committed boy should be adequately prepared in his home community for what he may expect at the reform school. (3) More individualized care should be given the new boy during the quarantine period. (4) Curricula to meet the specific needs of

---

[41] "The Runaway Boy in the Correctional School," Teachers College, Columbia University, No. 742, 1938.

each boy should replace the traditional educational system. (5) Cottage personnel should be well trained to meet their obligations to the boys. (6) Running away should be regarded by the inmates as failure rather than a feat of heroics—this means changing the point of view of the inmates, which is extremely difficult. (7) A specific penalty should be invoked for running away rather than some harsh treatment which will embitter the returned boy. (8) Some other type of treatment should be worked out for habitual runaways who have demonstrated that they cannot make an adjustment in a reform school.[42]

Another study of runaways was made by Mary Huff Diggs, this time of girls from a training school. The study showed that more than half of those who were habitually addicted to making off came from disorganized homes in which parents were either separated or divorced. It was noted, also, that these girls had physical defects or were shorter in height or lighter in weight, indicating a possible lack of early physical care.[43] However, since nothing in this study indicates the reasons why the girls left the institutions it has little bearing on the problem under discussion.

A constructive approach to the runaway problem is reported in an account of the Los Prietos Camp for Boys, conducted by the probation departments of Ventura and Santa Barbara counties in California.

> Naturally the question of running away comes up, for there are no fences around camp, no locks on the doors, and no corporal punishment. "Of course you could run away," the boys are told. "But what would you be running from? Only yourself and your problems. That is what you did before; now you will want to stay and lick them." Two boys did run away to go home. They were rounded up and brought into the probation office in Santa Barbara where they could hardly talk fast enough to express their remorse. It was all a mistake. "Could they please go back?" The probation officer considered. Finally he said, "I'm sick and tired of having to chase around after you two. If you want to go back you'll have to get there, somehow, yourselves. I won't take you. Maybe the supervisor will let you in and maybe he won't. I can't promise anything. Now get along." It took the boys six hours to get to Paradise, trudging over the state highway that climbs into San

---

[42] This paragraph is a summary of Chapter VII of the study.
[43] This study is reviewed in *Focus*, N.P.P.A., September 1949, p. 132.

Marcos Pass and down into the canyon. The supervisor who was expecting them took two very tired boys in. But for several days they worked alone and ate alone, shunned by the other campers.[44]

The foregoing material has not made pleasant reading. But most reform schools are not very pleasant places to visit or to live in. Just as the conventional prison for adults is a failure, so is the reform school. Some institutional administrators are bitter against those who expose the cruelty, inertia, and sterile drift all too frequently found in state-supported institutions for children. The only solution to this serious situation is for more honesty on the part of reform school personnel so that these conventional criticisms may no longer be valid.

We shall defer to our next chapter a discussion of what institution administrators can do to "clean house" so as to remove the stigma so indelibly attached to the reform school. Our conclusion is that the reform school stands condemned before those who have any sympathetic interest in the delinquent and maladjusted youth of our nation.

We now wish to turn to the problem of parole, or after-care, of children released from reform schools.

7. PAROLE OF JUVENILES FROM INSTITUTIONS

Juvenile parole, or, as it is preferably called, "after-care," has for many years constituted a neglected field in the child-welfare program. Little uniformity is to be found, partly because of the great differences in the state set-ups of institutions, and partly because many schools and institutions to which juvenile delinquents are committed are private or semi-private, and only to a certain extent subject to state regulations and state supervision. The trend in the field of adult parole toward greater centralization in the granting and supervising of parolees on the state level has not been followed in the juvenile field.

The history of juvenile parole goes back to the system of indenture, which originated in the early times of the Houses of Refuge. Releasing a child from institutional care and letting him return to the life of the free community after a period of well-regulated and,

---

[44] "Delinquents in Paradise," by Joyce Rockwood Muench, *Survey*, June 1949, pp. 310–311.

in general, strictly supervised intramural life of more or less long duration calls for a particular service of guidance and help toward adjustment. The child should, therefore, be prepared in the training school for this release, and an adequate investigation regarding the home and community conditions to which the child is destined to return should precede his actual release. One of the greatest difficulties in the whole correctional treatment of juveniles is encountered at this stage. As we have seen before, the home conditions from which the child has come to the institution have often contributed greatly to the child's maladjustment and his subsequent delinquent behavior. It is frequently asked whether the return of the child to this same environment is not bound to nullify any positive result of institutional training. This is one of the unsolved problems and no general advice can be given how to avoid the pitfalls connected with it. In many cases, the absence of the child from the home may have produced a change in attitude on the part of the parents toward the child and toward their own general responsibilities for family and home. Institutional placement may have been able to shape the child's habits of behavior; just as he was able to find his place as a member of the group in the institutional setting, he may now be better prepared to find his proper niche in the family circle. If parole of the youngster from the institution has not been a perfunctory administrative measure, but rather has been carried out by well-trained personnel, the adjustment of the child to life within his family and the adjustment of the members of the family to the child will be accelerated. On the other hand, in a considerable number of cases no change has taken place in the family set-up and the return of the youngster to his own home will seriously jeopardize his development. In those cases, the use of other family homes—the home of a relative or a friend of the family, or a working home—especially in the case of older girls, will be the proper solution.

In the administration of the granting and supervision of parole, three general systems can be discerned:

(1) Release on parole is granted by the board of managers of the institution; this still seems to be the prevalent custom, particularly in private institutions.

(2) The granting of parole and the supervision on parole are in the hands of the committing juvenile court; this system is often used

where institutions serve a rather large territory and cannot let their staff members travel to the various outlying counties for the purpose of investigation prior to release and supervision after release.

(3) A state agency—such as the Youth Authority in California, the Youth Service Commission in Wisconsin, the Youth Service Board in Massachusetts, and the Division of Juvenile Parole Services of the Illinois Department of Welfare—is charged with the preparation for, the granting of, and the supervision on parole of youngsters committed to institutions in those states. Such agencies usually function through regional offices for reasons of expediency, but the general administration is centralized in one state office, which sets standards and formulates rules for the carrying out of this assignment.

Where the matter of after-care is in the hands of the board of managers, the board frequently employs its own staff. A good example is the Sleighton Farm School for Girls in Pennsylvania, which has created for this purpose a so-called extension division, staffed with social case workers. A similar set-up is found at the State Agricultural and Industrial School, Industry, New York,[45] and at Long Lane Farm in Connecticut.

Committing juvenile courts usually carry out the granting and supervision of parole through their own probation officers. Sometimes, too, volunteers are called upon to perform the services of investigation prior to release and of supervision on parole.

Although administratively parole is quite different from probation, the principles of investigation and supervision are quite similar in both. No arguments will be offered here for any one of the three administrative schemes described, since the most important criterion is the quality of the service rendered. In general, however, the centralized agency has been found best equipped to achieve high standards of performance.[46]

The paroling authorities often require that the youngster to be released on parole must have a sponsor. This sponsor may be a

[45] For details, see Clinton W. Areson, "The Juvenile Delinquent Meets Case Work," *Yearbook*, N.P.P.A., 1944, pp. 84–98, especially pp. 94, 98.

[46] For further details on after-care, see Helen D. Pigeon, *Probation and Parole in Theory and Practice*, N.P.P.A., 1942, pp. 176–181; Emanuel Borenstein, "Release of the Child from the Institution," *Yearbook*, N.P.P.A., 1940, pp. 47–67; John B. Costello, "Institutions for Juvenile Delinquents," *The Annals*, January 1949, pp. 177–178.

friend of the family, a clergyman, or any other interested citizen, but he should be selected with utmost care by the paroling officials. The sponsor is no substitute for the person who officially supervises the youngster; rather, he cooperates with him and seeks his advice. Since a sponsor is responsible for only one individual, he can fully concentrate his efforts and available time on him. G. Howland Shaw has described the sponsoring of a juvenile delinquent as "simply the art by which an adult works out a constructive relationship with a youngster who has been or who is in trouble." To bridge the gap between the sponsor and the individual sponsored, however, is a difficult job, and Mr. Shaw emphasizes that "it is not a problem which can be easily solved by taking the boy to a baseball game . . . or having the boy to supper in one's home," [47] although these are, of course, ways of establishing a relationship with the youngster.

Persons belonging to civic organizations have in recent years volunteered to act as sponsors; in Philadelphia, for instance, members of the Junior Chamber of Commerce have successfully sponsored boys released from the Pennsylvania Industrial School. The National Exchange Club has embarked on a nation-wide program of supplying sponsors for boys returning to their homes from the National Training School.[48]

The most serious criticism made of paroling studies by correctional institutions is that they are not thorough. In addition, the institutions do not carry their cases long enough to see what happens to the children in later years. Apparent success is not enough. If institutional treatment is to continue, all the resources of treatment must be utilized and, in the evaluation of such treatment in after-care life, scientific techniques must be applied by objective investigators—methods that have not as yet been employed.

----

[47] G. Howland Shaw, "Sponsoring a Delinquent," *Federal Probation*, December 1948, pp. 13–15; see also *Federal Prisons 1948*, published by United States Department of Justice, pp. 17–18, regarding the sponsoring of boys released from the National Training School.

[48] See Harry E. Brager and Richard A. Chappell, "Jim, Mr. Brown and You," *Federal Probation*, June 1949, pp. 46–48. For a study of success and failure of parolees from correctional schools, see Robert E. Coulson, *op. cit.*, and a rejoinder by Eleanor Glueck, *ibid.*, pp. 47–49.

Chapter XIII

COMMITMENT (*Continued*)

1. SOME UNRESOLVED INSTITUTIONAL PROBLEMS

In the previous chapter we traced the development of the state reform school and showed how it is failing to meet the problem of reform. It is apparent that the treatment of the delinquent child cannot be solved by the kind of institutional programs being operated in our state schools. In justice, it should be mentioned that many states expect their correctional schools to take any delinquent child, regardless of his mental or emotional capacity and regardless of his previous delinquent record. The business of the administrators then becomes primarily one of custody rather than of correction. And they are expected to exercise that custody without benefit of walls or other obvious signs of restraint.

There seems little prospect that we can eliminate the reform school or destroy the philosophy of imprisonment for children. This concept is deeply imbedded in the thinking of legislators who hold the purse strings and who, in the last analysis, have the power to turn from outmoded systems of treatment. Much of the criticism of reform schools has to do with inadequate physical facilities such as decrepit buildings, worn-out heating systems, and general lack of repair. Certainly the administrations where inadequate plant facilities are the rule cannot be totally blamed or held responsible. Lack of funds for the attraction and holding of trained personnel is a legislative responsibility also. Many staffs are doing a tolerably good job with handicaps such as these.

Moreover, the general public frowns on any form of treatment that does not indicate obvious signs of punishment. The habitual reaction of most people is that a child or an older boy or girl who misbehaves or flouts the law should be restrained in a prison or a reform school. Thus institutions such as those discussed in the preceding chapter merely reflect the conventional thinking of the man on the street regarding delinquency control.

Nevertheless, many institutional administrators assume a haughty air concerning the criticism heaped upon their work. Yet they do little to refute such charges. They could suggest or even demand that their school be evaluated as an educational institution by some objective fact-finding group. Yet very few studies are made other than those previously mentioned—studies by the Osborne Association of New York or those initiated by a legislature after some scandal has been unearthed in its state.

Here and there some improvements are made either by administrators themselves or as a result of some investigation, but an over-all picture of the situation proves conclusively that conditions are substantially the same today as they were ten, twenty, or even thirty years ago, so far as apathy, cruelty and inadequate treatment are concerned. The National Probation and Parole Association, commenting on the Albert Deutsch study referred to in the previous chapter, says:

> Intended to arouse public concern, the article is shocking in its bare statement of facts. We need to be shocked—shocked into action in many, perhaps most of our states. . . . Public indifference and political patronage have combined to create child victims for whose mishandling the states will pay the price eventually in overcrowded adult prisons.[1]

Much of the criticism noted in the preceding chapter might be diminished if more adequate appropriations were forthcoming from penny-pinching legislatures and if the heavy hand of political patronage were lifted from the personnel, but the truth remains that the staffs themselves are responsible for much that ails the reform school. Institutionalization affects large numbers of the personnel, from superintendent down to the most inconspicuous staff member. It takes real courage to fight the insidious poison that permeates any facility dealing with the delinquent or the criminal.

Reform school administrators have attempted, futilely, to erase the stigma from their schools and their work by labeling their institutions "educational" rather than "reform" or "correctional." About

---

[1] *Focus*, N.P.P.A., July 1948, p. 127.

a decade ago reform school administrators began to identify themselves with the National Conference of Social Work, rather than
with the American Prison Association.[2] Their thesis was, and still is,
that their programs are more closely allied with agencies dealing
with the welfare of children than with those frankly working in the
penal and correctional field. Such an attitude may have some public
relations value, but it does not fool the children or their parents.

It is our purpose in this chapter to discuss some of the problems
that inhere in the institution and how they may be faced; to point
out some of the features that make up a progressive institution; and,
finally, to describe briefly a few schools in which reasonably good
treatment programs are in operation. The following discussion must
of necessity be brief.

Books and pamphlets dealing with standards for institutions responsible for the care and treatment of delinquent and dependent
children have been made available to the public for many years. Several years ago the late and distinguished Hastings Hart published a
work dealing with these aspects of the problem, and his book was
followed by many others.[3] Margaret Reeves described standards for
institutions for girls in her work of 1929;[4] Bowler and Bloodgood
described the plant and treatment programs in five state reform
schools for boys in 1935;[5] in 1944 Howard W. Hopkirk, director
of the Child Welfare League of America, published *Institutions
Serving Children*.[6] In 1946 the National Conference issued an excellent report on standards of treatment in and administration of children's correctional institutions.[7]

The early reports mentioned were excellent in their day. The more
recent surveys are thorough in their discussions of generalized treatment. But administrators are constantly frustrated by certain specific

---

[2] The National Conference of Juvenile Agencies is affiliated with the American Congress of Correction.

[3] *Preventive Treatment of Neglected Children*, in *Correction and Prevention*,
Russell Sage Foundation, New York, 1910.

[4] *Training Schools for Delinquent Girls*, Russell Sage Foundation.

[5] Alida C. Bowler and Ruth S. Bloodgood, *Institutional Treatment for Delinquent Boys*, Part I (1935) and Part II (1936), Children's Bureau Publication
Nos. 228 and 230, Washington, D.C.

[6] Russell Sage Foundation.

[7] *Report No. 6*, "Institutional Treatment of Delinquent Juveniles," Government Printing Office, Washington, D.C.

problems in their day-by-day relations with juveniles. It is our purpose here to dilate on a few of the more basic of these problems before we discuss the more conventional administrative and treatment phases.

As stated earlier, we must compromise with the reform school. The institution is with us and probably will be for many years to come. Millions of dollars are invested in expensive properties. Moreover, we are victims of the habit of committing children to institutions. Our first question is, then, if institutions are to be used in treating delinquents, which types of children are to be sent to them?

At present, we find most states permitting juvenile court jurists to send *any* child to an institution, regardless of the child's mentality, potentialities for therapy, emotional status, long record of offenses, or physical imbalance. However, most of the semi-public or private schools may refuse to receive certain types of children for whom they contend they have no facilities.

It is unfair to youngsters who have normal intelligence, or who are not psychotic, or who are first offenders, to be sent to an institution where all kinds of youthful derelicts are received. It would seem expedient, then, to use the institution either for children whose prognosis is good, or for those who need specialized professional therapy. No institution can take care of all types and do a good job. The state must set up adequate schools for defective delinquents—as in Massachusetts, New York, and Pennsylvania. It must set up other institutions for children who have serious emotional disorders —such as the school in New Jersey known as the Arthur Brisbane Child Treatment Center at Allaire, the only school, incidentally, in operation in this country which is not on grounds of a state hospital. This school was opened in 1946, with Dr. G. H. Lussier as its director. And the states must set up other schools for children who must be sent away because of poor home facilities or assets. Our states can no longer use their reform schools as catch-alls or dumping grounds for all types of delinquents. The insidious contagion of the reform school must be eliminated if genuine treatment is to result. As Sophia Robison points out, if the aim of the reform school is re-education for life, normal stimuli to ordinary wholesome living must be present in the treatment program.[8] Reform schools simply

[8] *Can Delinquency Be Measured*, Columbia University Press, 1936, p. 6. For a more detailed description of the purposes and the work of the Arthur

do not supply a wholesome environment for the development of normal children, and perhaps they never will.

Another persistent question posed by all administrators is: Should a reform school be surrounded by a wall or fence? This problem must be attacked with courage. There is altogether too much shilly-shallying and downright dishonest evasiveness among apologists of the reform school on this question. The older Houses of Refuge were surrounded by walls. When the move to take such schools to the country began in the middle and latter part of the nineteenth century, the cottage-type institution became quite popular. Usually there was not even a fence around the school. But as one administrator put it recently: "The staff became the wall." Responsibility for thwarting runaways was placed squarely upon the staff members. Consequently, repressions were introduced, including regimentation, marching, countings, hair-clippings, and other more ingenious restraints, such as spying on children by other children. Inmates continued to run away and punishments of the direst sort were inflicted when they were apprehended. Instead of a rational cooperation between staff and children we found—and still find—antagonisms that drag down the already unwholesome atmosphere of the school to new low levels. No lasting reform treatment can be accomplished in any school without a wall or a fence so long as absconding is looked upon as the worst offense a child can commit.

Some schools, notably girls' institutions, attempt to cope with this impossible situation by introducing what they please to call an "honor system." After a child passes a period of time in a reception cottage, she is removed to an "honor" cottage where she is under group controls. Many interesting experiments have been made with honor codes but, in general, they are doomed to failure. This failure is largely due to two factors: (1) Most youngsters sent to these institutions cannot absorb the type of honor superimposed from the top which calls for group restraint. There has been little, if anything, in their experience that will help them. As an example of what is expected, let us look at a practice that exists in many schools. If a child in an honor cottage runs away, all its residents are penalized, since it is considered their responsibility to keep each member in line

Brisbane Child Treatment Center, see Marion Robinson, "Mental Health for Child and Delinquent," *Survey*, June 1950, pp. 293–297.

with institutional controls. Such a responsibility calls for a very high degree of social insight that even children in the average schoolroom or Boy Scout troop would find difficult to accept. (2) Honor actually does not mean honor. It is usually diluted to such a degree and so patently false that the inmates have no difficulty in seeing through the ruse. Thus they resent it. The administrator of the reform school, for instance, who proudly boasts that the inmates are not locked in their rooms at night rarely shows visitors the metal enunciator placed in the jamb of each door which rings a bell in the matron's quarters if the occupant of the room leaves at any time; or the administrator who tells visitors that inmates are free to run errands between cottages usually fails to state that matrons and other staff members are alerted on each occasion. Such practices exist in many of the institutions that pose as "honor" schools. There can be no honor system unless the authorities are willing to accept the risks inherent in such a system. Self-government has a place in reform schools but a great deal of thought and experimentation are needed to work out a good system.[9]

The question, then, of whether or not a cyclone fence is to surround a reform school must be settled within the framework of the administration's philosophy on runaways. If custody is the prime responsibility of the administrator, it is futile to talk about wholesome training. Society must be willing to accept and support training schools that minimize the practice of absconding. True, everything must be done to inculcate principles of reliance and self-discipline into the inmates of these schools, but returned runaways must not be brutally punished. If a penalty is invoked, it must have some therapeutic value. Revocation of some privilege might have a wholesome effect. A reform school must be as normal as possible if worth-while treatment is to result. Many charming female administrators have contended that the wire fence (sometimes with barbed wire on the top) is there *not* to keep their charges from running away but to keep outsiders from coming in. This is pure casuistry and should be publicly branded as such. Running away can be reduced to a minimum if the child is properly and sympathetically briefed upon his arrival and is offered a program that will meet his needs while he is

---

[9] See Lorene Putsch, "Self-government in a Children's Institution," Child Welfare League of America, Inc., 1945.

in the school. Periodic visits home might also be permitted as well as frequent visits from parents and friends. The program is the thing that counts. If a rational program cannot be developed in an open institution, it is better that a wall be placed around the reservation and as normal a life as possible developed.

A third problem confronting administrators of reform schools is discipline. Everyone denounces cruelty in institutions, yet it is quite widespread. Regimentation of the most rigid sort is found in many schools administered by "experts" who, in conferences, read papers fairly dripping with institutional soothing syrup. These papers are for public consumption. Upon their return to the schools, they revert to the grim business of running them in a "workmanlike" manner. For example, it has been the practice of many boys' schools to discipline their charges with strict military drill. The top boys, known as cadet officers, control the other boys; "delegated authority" it is called. These cadet officers sometimes tend to become the meanest, toughest, and most sadistic inmates to be found in the school. Now this practice has been condoned in schools administered by well-known men who have made national reputations in the institutional field. Let us see what the report on institutional treatment of the National Conference has to say about such practices:

> Such disciplinary abuses are completely indefensible. Particularly vicious is the "monitor" system which permits older, more aggressive children to exert authority over the more timid and less mature. Not only does such a program fail to develop the positive value of leadership but it encourages those very anti-social tendencies which the training school is attempting to correct.[10]

Much has been written on discipline for children. Hundreds of conferences on children's problems have devoted a great deal of attention to this subject. It would seem necessary to ask the question: What kind of discipline do we want? Sheviakov and Redl, in an admirable little pamphlet, have answered this question as follows:

> 1. We want discipline based on devotion to humanitarian principles and ideals such as freedom, justice, and equality for all rather than discipline based on a narrower, more egotistic affiliation of "MY" group.
> 2. We want discipline which recognizes the *inherent dignity and*

---

[10] *Report No. 6*, p. 37.

rights of every human being, rather than discipline attained through humiliation of the undisciplined.

3. We want *self-direction, self-discipline* rather than discipline based on obedience to a Führer.

4. We want discipline based on understanding of the goal in view rather than discipline based on "taking someone else's word for it." [11]

Discipline should be a technique pointing toward the development of *self-discipline* rather than to regimentation. Authority must be *personal*, and its meaning in relation to society must be explained.[12]

The National Child Welfare Division of the American Legion also condemns repressive discipline: "Discipline should be firm but not tyrannical. Demerits should be given on the basis of punishment earned. The use of corporal punishment disregards the findings of scientific studies in the field of human endeavor, behavior and training. . . . Under no circumstances should such disciplinary methods as leg chains, irons, solitary confinement, stand-ups, lines, cells or bodily harm be used. Starvation, bread and water, etc., should be on the 'never used' list. . . . Runaways should be apprehended by duly constituted authorities only and no reward offered or paid to civilians for returning such children. The use of sirens, bells, whistles, bloodhounds and the like should be forbidden." [13]

A National Conference report dedicated to an analysis of the training school offers the following recommendations for discipline:

1. A positive attitude toward discipline should prevail in correctional schools based on the personality of the individual and the group in the school setting and the preparation of the individual for outside community living.

2. The discipline program must be fully integrated into the general treatment program. Discipline and morale cannot be considered as a separate unit of the school regime.

[11] George V. Sheviakov and Fritz Redl, "Discipline for Today's Children and Youth," Department of Supervision and Curriculum Development, National Education Association (Washington, D.C. 1201 Sixteenth St., N.W.), Fourth Printing, November 1945, p. 7.

[12] See Walter Bromberg and Terry C. Rodgers, "Authority in the Treatment of Delinquents," *American Journal of Orthopsychiatry*, October 1946, pp. 672–685.

[13] "Building Asset Citizens: Recommended Objectives for Juvenile Training Schools," Revised Edition, June 1941–3, National Headquarters, American Legion, Indianapolis, Indiana.

3. Regulations and restrictions must be fully compensated by positive rewards and goals which are realistic in terms of the child's daily life.

4. Because of the grave consequences attending corporal punishment, and its proven ineffectiveness, its use should be outlawed in every institution for juvenile delinquents.

5. There is no justification for physical abuse as a means of punishment. Not only are such methods harmful to the general health and development of the child but they engender feelings of resentment that will carry over into future antisocial reactions.

6. The indiscriminate use of disciplinary measures cannot be tolerated and they should be made the responsibility of a specified individual staff member or of a staff committee.

7. Suitable rewards must be maintained in order to insure the continuity of the program and the effectiveness of its application. All infractions requiring formal disciplinary action as well as special awards and recognition of merit should be made a matter of official record.[14]

It is difficult to do more than set forth the above principles, since disciplinary philosophy and method must of necessity grow out of the situation. Some students of the problem suggest books of rules for institutional management; others contend that the fewer the rules, the more fertile the field of growth in self-discipline.[15] Relationships among inmates of an institution and between inmates and staff members can develop in a healthy manner only if the staff accepts the concept of individual dignity and fosters the growth of self-respect and self-discipline. One thing is certain: Disciplinary matters should be handled by a committee of staff members rather than by only one person. The committee members should rotate so that fixed, rigid policies do not develop. No child coming before the disciplinary court should be allowed to "get away" with fabrications in his story. Before disciplinary action is meted out, the child's story must be squared against that of the reporting staff member. To realize a wholesome disciplinary atmosphere, a part of the in-service training for staff members should be to face up to the disciplinary problem. There is nothing more embarrassing in an institution than a situation in which a staff member "loses face" in the eyes of inmates. Such a humiliating experience need never happen if proper safeguards are developed in

---

[14] *Report No. 6*, pp. 39–40.
[15] See discussion of the British experiment at Q-Camp, pp. 508–512.

disciplinary policy. On the other hand, the inmate should be taught
to accept responsibility for his word as well as for his acts. He must
also be permitted either to tell his version of a situation without fear
of unfair discipline or, if he chooses, to remain silent rather than
report on another inmate. The code of a correctional institution, so
far as inmates are concerned, is relentless and strict. The administration and staff members must recognize this situation and develop
methods of dealing with inmates within this rigid framework. The
personality and dignity of the boy, or girl, must always be safe-
guarded.

Another problem constantly confronting administrators and staff
members of a reform school is the sex question. Every administrator
asks the theorist: What shall we do to control homosexual practices?
There is no constructive answer that is satisfying to the conventional
citizen. We have discussed these sexual practices in our previous
chapter and do not wish to repeat here what has been stated. Deviational behavior is traditional in all reform schools, both for boys or
for girls. Whatever control is suggested must be positive rather than
negative. The child must not be punished by shame or guilt feelings
or by corporal punishment. The solution must flow from a healthy
régime of treatment, understanding of adolescent problems by staff
members, and from progressive concepts of sex on the part of the administration.

Another problem of the reform school, much of which derives
from the homosexual complex, is the "ganging up" of older or
stronger boys against the new boy or the younger or smaller inmate.
This grim, relentless behavior persists in all schools. It is to cope with
this internecine warfare that many of the regimented punishments
have been inaugurated by superintendents. The whole process is insidious because a deadly climate soon develops which stamps the
institution for all time. This same tense atmosphere may be detected
easily in the juvenile detention quarters of our large cities as well as
in all conventional reform schools. The moment it becomes apparent
there is little hope for a healthy program to develop unless the administration has the courage to fight the tendency with daring and
with the latest scientific information regarding sex.

The following requirements are *musts* if the correctional institution is to be accepted as a dignified, integral part of the program of
training for delinquent children:

1. *Location of the institution.* The institution should be in the country rather than in a city. However, the site should be near a city of some size so that the following facilities may be utilized: psychiatric services, hospital and medical treatment, and recreational and cultural opportunities. The children should make periodic visits to the city. Extreme isolation may, to quote the pamphlet of the National Conference, "make it difficult to obtain and keep the services of good personnel, who will want to stay abreast of current developments in their field and take advantage of educational and cultural opportunities in nearby centers." [16] The advantages of a city, with its museums, art galleries, zoo, factories, and other such attractions, make it possible to develop an enriched program of activity for growing boys and girls.

2. *The type of plant for correctional schools.* The school should be of the cottage type, with provision for each child resident to have a room to himself. We have already discussed the dormitory curse in schools of this type and need not repeat our discussion here. Some dormitory provision might conceivably be made for certain situations in which closer supervision seems necessary. One of the most frequent charges made against correctional institutions is that they have become firetraps as a result of outmoded construction or of apathy in making needed repairs. All cottages should be fireproof and easily supervised. They should also be attractive, since they are literally the homes of children for relatively long periods of time. As the National Conference states: "Facilities provided in training centers for delinquents should include all the essential services of a well-organized small community. Ample light and ventilation should be provided for all offices, living and sleeping quarters, classrooms and shops. Ideally housing units should be sufficiently small to permit an approximation to the conditions of family life. Each cottage should have its own kitchen and diningroom. This may mean high costs for construction and personnel, but there are nevertheless great advantages in the use of these smaller residence units. . . . Units should permit the formation of homogeneous groups according to age, mental development and special need, and permit the growth of a healthy group spirit and atmosphere." [17]

---

[16] *Report No. 6*, p. 4.
[17] *Ibid.*, pp. 5–6.

There should be an administrative center, a receiving and orientation unit, housing units in which no more than 25 children should reside, adequate residential facilities for house matrons and staff officers who must reside on the grounds, school buildings, medical and mental hygiene centers, a chapel, shops for both maintenance and training (in a boys' school if that is a part of the program), and facilities for training in girls' schools. Farming should be made an interesting part of the program as well as a functional one. Adjuncts such as horticulture, animal husbandry, poultry, and bee-keeping should be included in the agricultural program.

The Federal Bureau of Prisons has published a *Handbook of Correctional Institution Design and Construction* (Washington, D.C., 1949). Chapter IX deals with the physical needs of a reform school. This is a valuable addition to the current literature of correctional schools and should have some effect on the future building programs of various states.

3. *Staff members.* Since successful child adjustment is possible only through the work of understanding personnel, it is essential that the best possible staff be assembled. In addition to adequate salaries, staff members should be provided with desirable working and living conditions, and with opportunities to get away from the institution periodically for relaxation and study. The state should make possible paid leaves of absence after relatively short periods of time. It goes without saying that politics should have nothing whatever to do with the selection of any member of the staff. Some sort of merit system should be employed in selecting those who work in correctional schools. Tenure on the job, opportunities for advancement, retirement pension, adequate provision for sick leave, and the like, should also be provided. In short, every inducement should be made to recruit professionally trained personnel and to keep them after they are selected. The trend toward a reduction in working hours should make itself felt in institutional work; the forty-hour week should be the goal toward which to strive.

4. *Classification procedure.* An initial diagnostic interval, perhaps of one month's duration, is important if progressive treatment is to be a part of the program. A special intake cottage should be provided. Facilities for diagnosis should be abundant and adequate, and should include tests of various types that will eventually show what each child needs. Psychological, psychiatric, medical, and social

examinations should be made. Educational and vocational tests should also be employed. Concerning classification by type, the National Conference makes these suggestions:

> Groupings within the institution should be the concern of the classification committee, which ought to include the cottage parents, counselors, and all others directly concerned with oversight and care. They will want to decide how to group the aggressive, antisocial leader; the submissive, easily led, easily dominated, suggestible, weak, inoffensive individual; the boy with neurotic symptoms, emotionally unstable, impulsive, and lacking in foresight; the child who becomes involved in difficulties because of an absence of acceptable patterns in his home and the presence of gang patterns on the street; the boy of superior or inferior intelligence, from a good home as well as from a slum area.[18]

As states develop systems of treatment centers—as, for example, California's Youth Authority—a centralized diagnostic center, set apart from any of the specialized units, should be provided. All children destined to be committed to an institution should be sent to this diagnostic center by the various county courts.

5. *Educational program.* Since we place great emphasis in this country on education and insist on compulsory attendance until adolescence, it is imperative that the program of the correctional school be largely dominated by a sound educational philosophy. We cannot improve on the recommendations set forth by the National Conference:

1. Every child in the institution should go to school a full day and full school term—at least up to the age of 14 and possibly 16.
2. The educational program should be flexible and it should include diagnostic and remedial services.
3. Well-planned and appropriate physical facilities should be provided.
4. A variety and abundance of objective teaching aids should be available, and modern teaching methods should be utilized.
5. The educational program should include experiences in the creative and home arts, in other manual activities and in human relationships.
6. Vocational education should be carried on under the guidance of well-qualified vocational teachers.

---

[18] *Report No. 6,* p. 13.

7. All members of the educational staff should be regularly licensed by State educational authorities.

8. The professional status of the educational staff should be comparable to that found in the best schools of the State.

9. There should be a competent director or supervisor for the entire educational program.

10. The educational program of the institution should be legally and in reality an integral part of the State's educational system.

6. *Group Therapy*. In recent years, group guidance or counseling has been introduced into some progressive institutions. Although group "therapy" is not new, its introduction into schools for delinquents is comparatively recent. This form of treatment gained considerable impetus during World War II, when it was used to treat soldiers who were suffering from emotional disturbances or who were under discipline. S. R. Slavson of the New York City Jewish Board of Guardians began to use this technique in 1934. A discussion of the meaning of group therapy will be found in Chapter XIV.[19] Its importance, however, as a part of the program of a progressive school for delinquents cannot be overlooked.

Space forbids an enumeration of the many phases of a well-rounded, progressive institutional program. We have already mentioned the importance of good diagnosis by the institutional staff or by the diagnostic center operated on a state-wide basis (as in California under the Youth Authority, at Elmira in New York state, and at Menlo Park, New Jersey), for young male offenders between sixteen and twenty-one years of age, or older.[20]

Equally good treatment, aside from the conventional education program discussed above, is highly important. Such treatment must always make provision for the individual and his basic needs. It is the atmosphere of the institution that counts most.

These recommendations are commendable but are extremely difficult of attainment.

Teachers in correctional schools should be adequately paid and

---

[19] See pp. 535–538.

[20] For more details on these diagnostic centers, see Chapter X, pp. 364–366, and Chapter XIV, pp. 530–531. For a detailed description of the set-up and the operation of the New Jersey State Diagnostic Center at Menlo Park, see Marion Robinson, "Mental Health for Child and Delinquent," *Survey*, June 1950, pp. 293–297.

should receive all the traditional emoluments that accrue to the profession. Tenure is highly desirable, but it is especially important that a progressive principal or supervisor set the tone of the school so that teachers with vision will not be discouraged in attempting to accomplish a good job. The writers of this book know how big an order it is to insist on a good school program for a correctional institution. The tendency is to use traditional methods of instruction and, worse, to fall back on a sterile discipline to coerce the children to learn. Rebellious children in many institutions are bowed down

Classroom in an Industrial School. (*Courtesy Pennsylvania Industrial School, White Hill*)

with futile punishments for not "showing the proper respect" for teachers or for schoolroom activities. In a good school system, conventional shibboleths and bromides are reduced to a minimum. Periodically, the teaching staff of the institution should make a list of these familiar bromides used to control children and should make a serious attempt not to employ them under any circumstance. The jargon of the reform school is painful to the visiting outsider; how much more nauseous it must be to child inmates who must submit to it every day. The child in the public school can escape this sort of patter by going home or by participating in normal activities of childhood, but the reform school inmate has no such escape.

Although we do not endorse trade training for boys, we do feel that vocational skills must be exploited by the training program so that those boys who wish to capitalize on their manual abilities may do so upon release. The facilities for training must be rich enough to present a challenge to as many children as possible. Such a program, of course, is expensive, and few single institutions can do an adequate job. What is needed is a system of small establishments within a state, patterned after the British Borstal system.[21] In that system a number of institutions or schools serve boys of different dispositions and personalities who have potential skills in various fields. Staff officers equipped to develop these specialized skills are sent to the schools where they are needed. It is too much to expect one institution in any of our average-sized states to operate an enriched vocational program. Yet such a program is necessary if we are to rehabilitate our potentially delinquent children.

Auto mechanics, foundry, sign-painting, and similar types of training for boys, and domestic science, household arts, and beauty culture for girls are important items in vocational programs. However, we must face the issue that boys, especially, who come from correctional schools may not engage in any type of work that is highly unionized. The situation is not so serious in some states, but in many states trade unions simply will not admit a boy to membership who has learned his trade (brick-laying, plumbing, sign-painting, and so forth) in a correctional school.

An interesting inquiry was made in 1947 to find out just what institutions were doing in "work-experience" training programs and what they recommended for inmates of correctional schools. It was found that many schools were engaged in production—that is, in making products to be sold to state agencies—or in maintenance work. The study indicated that the administrators of such institutions seemed to agree that there were desirable values to be obtained from productive work provided that adequate safeguards were maintained. It was further recommended that training in related subject matter should be provided. The inquiry showed that training was given in a wide variety of occupations. Factors limiting the variety of skills

---

[21] For details of the Borstal system, see pp. 539–543.

taught and the mastery of these skills were: length of stay of the individual in the school; usefulness to the institution of the products made; and usefulness of the training to the trainee when he leaves the school.[22]

Workshop in an Industrial School. (*Courtesy Pennsylvania Industrial School, White Hill*)

The development of hobbies is highly important and the institution should encourage this phase of the program. Keeping pets, making various types of gadgets by hand, knitting and weaving, ceramics, photography, painting and sculpturing, and a host of other latent interests and skills are important and valuable enough to be nourished. The possibilities for good in this field are enormous.

The religious life of the child should not be neglected. All creeds should be represented by ministers or chaplains who should be permitted to conduct services and to counsel with children of their

[22] Digest of *Bulletin No. 1,* New York State School of Industrial and Labor Relations, Cornell University, Ithaca, New York, March 1949. The survey was conducted by G. E. McGrew, State Department of Education, Camden, South Carolina.

denominations. However, proselyting should be discouraged if not totally forbidden. The outsider cannot realize the extent of this knotty problem to administrators. In one well-known institution the superintendent was persuaded by the representative of a religious sect to permit him to work among all children sent to the school whose records showed no church affiliation. Normally, this influence would do the child no special harm, but in this particular state several orthodox and fanatical sects are doing a land-office business. If the superintendent bars one such sect he finds himself in difficulty. He must, therefore, bar all but the generally accepted denominations.

Individual case work and group work activities should be encouraged and developed wherever possible.[23] And, of course, a well-rounded recreational program should be developed. Each child should be encouraged to participate, but he should not be forced into the program; nor should inmates be "recreated" to the point of exhaustion each day, as is so mistakenly done in some institutions administered by physical recreation "experts." Recreation should be a joyful experience for the child, not painful or obligatory. Hikes, swimming, athletics, trips to nearby cities—all should be a part of the program.

In a positive attempt to come to grips with the institutional problem, Professor Walter Reckless makes the following suggestions:

1. The creation and maintenance of a relaxed atmosphere in which the inmate person can defrost.

2. The curtailment of useless disciplinary rules and the placing of disciplinary action in the hands of professional staff who consider with the infracting inmate the reasons for his getting into difficulty and the need for disciplinary action.

3. Inmate participation on committees through the democratic process, so as to provide a two way flow (up from the bottom and down from the top), rather than a one way flow (imposition from the top).

4. Small operational units to do a specialized job with as homogeneous a group as possible.

5. In institutions for both juveniles and adults where the cottage plan can be used, the residence units should contain small homogeneous groups.[24]

---

[23] See *National Conference Report No. 6*, pp. 16–17, 30–35; also Clinton W. Areson, "Casework in the Training School," *Probation*, October 1947, pp. 10–14.

[24] "Trends in Treatment of Crime and Delinquency," *Yearbook*, N.P.P.A., 1948, pp. 1–14. See also John B. Costello, "Institutions for Juvenile Delinquents," *The Annals*, Vol. 261, January 1949, pp. 166–218.

One authority in the training school field, Richard Clendenen, has presented an interesting paper dealing with the synchronization of the school program with the latent assets of the outside community. He feels that many schools are already taking advantage of these facilities and are finding them of great benefit to the children —for example, encouraging volunteers who are interested in children to come to the schools to render whatever services they can; developing courses in sex education in conjunction with the local Parent-Teacher group; and mobilizing the library facilities of the school for wider use in the community.[25]

In the preceding pages we have sketched some of the salient points of good institutional philosophy and treatment. In the following pages we shall briefly describe some institutions, a few of which are privately operated, that are well known in the field of dependent and delinquent children. Naturally, all these institutions cannot be listed—there are dozens of them scattered throughout the country. The ones we have chosen are, for one reason or another, better known than most. Although these schools may not achieve the ideal in every phase of institutional procedure, they do represent a serious attempt to develop a constructive rehabilitative program.

Despite the good that may be accomplished in such schools, we must honestly face the situation and realize that even at best they are not normal places for children to grow in a healthy fashion. We must seek a final solution to delinquency treatment outside the correctional or reform school. Every conceivable effort must be made in the future to adjust the delinquent child by means of techniques and facilities already present or capable of being developed in the community where the child lives. The traditional reform school simply does not and cannot answer the challenge of delinquent youth.

It is quite possible that a new type of institution, based on a program similar to that operated by August Aichhorn near Vienna and described in his stimulating book *Wayward Youth*,[26] may be the answer. Very small groupings of children with intimate supervision (perhaps no more than ten children to a supervisor) by persons who understand the psychiatric approach and with a program adapted to

---

[25] "To Synchronize the Training School Program With Life in the Community," *The Child* (United States Children's Bureau), November 1949, p. 73.
[26] Viking Press, New York, 1925.

each child might be the answer to our training programs. Privacy and a maximum of individual freedom, and, conversely, a minimum of rules and authoritarian dicta, would be the chief characteristics of such a school.

Many students of the problem look to the development of camps as the answer to the problem. The *Handbook of Correctional Institution Design and Construction*, published by the Federal Bureau of Prisons, states: "One of the most interesting and promising developments in institutional experimentation for handling juvenile delinquents has been the building of camps. . . . There is little doubt that camps will be more widely utilized in the future for the custody and treatment of juveniles." [27] We have already discussed the Youth Authority camps in California. But, as we shall point out, since a need will always exist for some more restraining influence for certain types of delinquents, it is obvious that a small institution will be necessary in each state. But this institution need not be repressive or cruel.

Here is what the eminent Hastings H. Hart, who spent his entire professional career in child-saving work, had to say about institutions for children as early as 1910:

> The juvenile reformatory is not designed as a permanent institution in which to bring up children to manhood and womanhood. However good an institution may be, however kindly its spirit, however genial its atmosphere, however homelike its cottages, however fatherly and motherly its officers, however admirable its training, it is now generally agreed among those who are familiar with the needs of children of this class that institutional life is at best artificial and unnatural, and that the child should be returned at the earliest practicable moment to the more natural environment of the family home—his own home if it is a suitable one, and if not, then some other family home.[28]

2. PROGRAMS AND ACTIVITIES OF SOME INDIVIDUAL INSTITUTIONS

a. The George Junior Republic

The founding and development of the George Junior Republic at Freeville, New York, cannot be overlooked in any treatise of neg-

---

[27] Chapter IX of the *Handbook*.
[28] "The Juvenile Reformatory," in *Preventive Treatment of Neglected Children*, Charities Publication (Russell Sage Foundation, New York), 1910, p. 12.

lected and delinquent childhood. William Reuben George (1866–1936) was born near the village of Freeville; as a young man, he went to New York City. He became interested in the problem of delinquency when Theodore Roosevelt was police commissioner of that city and, as a special policeman, he carefully surveyed the conditions of the youth of the East Side during the early '90's. Shocked at the conditions he uncovered, he tried to improve them by organizing boys' clubs. These were not successful in the atmosphere of poverty and misery that marked the neighborhood.

George finally decided to take some of the youngsters to his farm upstate, where they would receive a taste of country life during the summers. He was aided by newspapers and various fresh air funds, but he found that the children did not appreciate benefits they did not have to work for. Therefore, in 1895, he took about 150 boys and girls from the slums to Freeville. He set up a summer school on an abandoned farm and some of his original group remained with him through the winter. In the summer of 1896, the George Junior Republic was born.

It was a *republic* because the children conducted their own government, electing a president and other officers. They even organized a prison. The "citizens" held a town meeting at regular intervals and decided their own program of community and civic action, with, of course, the skillful advice of Mr. George. His thesis was that people cannot prepare for citizenship without assuming its responsibilities. Hard work and dependability formed the basis of his community. Children over sixteen were allowed to vote on all projects.

The George Junior Republic grew impressively. Mr. George started this great experiment with literally ten cents in ready money. Today, the plant is worth half a million dollars. Approximately 3,000 children have been trained for citizenship in this institution. So famous was the work that a number of wealthy parents voluntarily sent their children to him rather than to privately endowed schools. When Baden-Powell was organizing his Boy Scouts in 1908, he made a prolonged visit to the George Junior Republic.

In 1908, the National Association of Junior Republics came into being. Other schools became identified with this association: the Carter Republic at Redington, Pennsylvania; the National Republic at Annapolis Junction, Maryland; the George Junior Republic at Litchfield, Connecticut; and schools at Chino, California, Grove

City, Pennsylvania, and Flemington Junction, New Jersey. Other institutions patterned along similar lines were established elsewhere.

In these miniature towns labor is voluntary, but the motto is "Nothing without labor"; food, clothing, and lodging must be paid for by the inmates. Schooling and labor for five hours per day are compulsory.[29]

A valid criticism of programs of the Junior Republics is that the boys are acting in an abnormal atmosphere. Boys of a similar age on the outside are not weighted down with the admonition to be "good citizens"; they can engage in normal boy pursuits. In limited doses, every growing boy should learn something of a citizen's responsibilities, but in such institutions the dosage is likely to go beyond the saturation point.

b. Children's Village—Dobbs Ferry, New York

Another example of a progressive school for delinquent and otherwise maladjusted boys is the well-known Children's Village at Dobbs Ferry, New York, established in 1851 and located on the Hudson River not far from New York City. Some 50,000 boys between the ages of eight and sixteen have received training in this institution. Boys come from the Children's Court of New York and twenty-seven other states; others come, without court commitment, from private homes.

Although this school has had many different types of management and philosophy, in recent years it envisages its objectives as follows: (1) the reclamation of the boys committed to it; (2) continuous experimentation in the field of juvenile maladjustment; and (3) placing at the disposal of schools and social agencies the results of studies made at the Village.[30]

Boys who are not mentally defective or physically abnormal are sent to the school when they have been adjudged delinquent by the

---

[29] See Donald T. Urquehart, "Crime Prevention Through Citizenship Training at the George Junior Republic," in Eleanor and Sheldon Glueck's *Preventing Crime,* McGraw-Hill, New York, 1936, pp. 305–330. See also Carol Hughes, "Turning Toughies into Citizens," *Coronet Magazine*, March 1949; and Henry LaCossitt, "Happy Land of Teen-Agers," *Collier's,* December 31, 1949.

[30] George C. Minard, "Educational Experimentation With Problem Boys at Children's Village," in Sheldon and Eleanor Glueck's *Preventing Crime,* McGraw-Hill, New York, 1936, pp. 291–304.

court. Other boys, who parents feel are beyond their control, are also sent. The population is about 450, most of whom are between the ages of ten and sixteen. The conventional tests—social, psychological and psychiatric—are made after the boy arrives and his program of treatment is set up on the basis of the findings.

Modeled on the form of government of a village in the State of New York, Youth Government is a general participation program in which every boy plays a part. The constitution, which the boys themselves assisted in writing, provides for a board of trustees. The elective officers are the mayor, judge, clerk, and treasurer. After thirty days, the new boy becomes a voting citizen. He may lose his citizenship privileges temporarily on infraction of the rules.

Small groups, well-trained personnel, a home-like atmosphere (but with the ubiquitous dormitory), and a meaningful program for each boy feature this establishment. Since the management has always welcomed outside appraisal of its work, this school is among the top-ranking private institutions of the country.

c. Wiltwyck School for Boys

Wiltwyck School, located near Esopus, New York (across the Hudson River from Hyde Park), is a private institution to which delinquent and emotionally disturbed boys, between the ages of eight and twelve, are sent from the Children's Court of New York City and the city's Welfare Department.

The school came into being in 1937, specifically for the care and treatment of delinquent Negro boys. When the race discrimination amendment was passed by the New York City Council, the Board of Directors of the School formally advised the Children's Court and the Department of Welfare that Wiltwyck would accept for treatment both Negro and white children. Today the Board consists of white and Negro members, including Protestants, Roman Catholics, and Jews. The same is true of the staff and of the children.

This institution has thus made a singular contribution to the ideas and practice of interracial living together. This achievement was possible because of the atmosphere of the school, which is characterized by freedom and warmth and the almost complete absense of emotional tension. In addition, the adult-staff response to the child is marked by genuine acceptance and real affection, rather than by indifference and neglect. The widely accepted motion picture, *The Quiet One*, was made with this school as a background. It portrays admirably the effect of lack of parental affection on a boy. Most of the eighty boys enrolled at Wiltwyck come from broken homes. Group therapy and counseling by trained personnel represent one of the main features of the school. One of the members of the Board is Mrs. Eleanor Roosevelt, who takes an active interest in this venture.[31]

d. Ormsby Village, Anchorage, Kentucky

This institution is officially called the Louisville and Jefferson County Children's Home, but it is better known as Ormsby Village. For many years it has been regarded as one of the most progressive institutions of its kind in the country. Actually, since it takes children from both city and county who are regarded as dependent, neglected, and delinquent, it is a child-caring organization in the broadest sense. The institution has an interesting history that goes back to the old Louisville House of Refuge, which was organized in 1854.

Ormsby Village is one of the few institutions in the country that champion coeducation. The management insists that this kind of régime is normal, although it recognizes the inherent hazards by maintaining a constant but intelligent vigilance over its administration. Girls and boys are separated in cottages, but on many occasions both sexes are brought together. The Osborne Association has this to say about this institution:

> Too much cannot be said of the wholesome tone of life that exists at Ormsby Village. It is a real community and a genuine spirit of community interests pervades the place. Despite the fact that long continued neglect tends to make such children problem children, constraint is notably absent here. The camaraderie of children and officers is inspiring to observe in cottages, classrooms, work and play. The spirit of mutual goodwill is even a feature in the dining room where boys and girls sit together in small groups with a staff member and where they apparently go not merely to eat but also to participate in one more cultural experience. This is as it should be because a great deal of what

---

[31] For further details, see Robert L. Cooper, "Racial Antagonism as a Factor in Delinquency," *Yearbook*, N.P.P.A., 1946, pp. 77–85. Mr. Cooper was former director of the school. See also *The New York Times*, Sunday, February 12, 1950, p. 58.

we call cultural improvement . . . has emanated from what has trans-
pired around the table.

Not only are Ormsby children not institutionalized but they do not
look so and their behavior on the campus is in no way different from
the normal reactions of children gathered together anywhere. They
wear their own clothes, which are individualized and varied in style
as those of a public school group. The advantages in the way of self-
esteem that accrue to the child from such a system of unregimented
dress are obvious.[32]

Mixed Dining Room, Ormsby Village, Anchorage, Kentucky. *(Courtesy
Superintendent H. V. Bastin)*

Despite the sympathetic management (Mr. and Mrs. H. V. Bastin)
and administrative personnel, vouched for by the Osborne Association, Ormsby Village is not without its problems. Obviously these
problems flow from the same old traditional policy of institutional
treatment. We must question the philosophy of caring for dependent, neglected, and delinquent children in one institution. Of
course, this program is heroic as an ideal but it is questionable so
far as therapy is concerned. Many delinquent children need more

---

[32] *Handbook of American Institutions for Delinquent Children,* First Edition, 1940, Vol. II, p. 132.

supervision, more specialized programs, and more skillful guidance than do other types of thwarted childhood.

The problem of discipline is another area in which a specialized philosophy calls for separation of types. Ormsby Village has its problem with runaways, although most of those who abscond are returned. The treatment of runaway children presents a serious challenge to even the most progressive institutions. Corporal punishment is no longer employed at Ormsby Village. Thus each case of discipline is handled by trained personnel, including the psychologist and social workers. Detention is resorted to and rebellious or recalcitrant children lose the status of citizenship.

Coeducation at Ormsby Village—A Saturday Night Dance. (*Courtesy Superintendent H. V. Bastin*)

Space forbids a more lengthy discussion of this institution. It is without doubt one of the few excellent establishments for delinquent children. It seems strange that the managements of hundreds of other similar institutions cannot take a cue from Ormsby Village and clean up their own establishments.

e. Hawthorne-Cedar Knolls School, New York

The Hawthorne school for boys was opened in 1906, and the Cedar Knolls school for girls in 1913, by the New York City Jewish Board of Guardians for the care and treatment of delinquent and troubled children of the Jewish faith. These schools have long been considered among the best of their kind in the country. Now known officially as the Hawthorne-Cedar Knolls School, it is situated in Westchester County and occupies 228 acres of farm land. There are at present eleven cottages, each housing from fifteen to twenty children. Normal family life and professional care are the features of this school. The children come to the school by way of the Children's Court of New York City.

The child-guidance clinic, which includes psychiatric social workers, psychologists, and psychiatrists, is responsible for the intensive study and the formulation of treatment for each child, and for the interpretation of the needs of the child to other staff members responsible for his education and day-by-day activity. Individual psychotherapy is available for those children who need it. Counseling with the child's family by the School's social workers is also a part of the program of adjustment. (See Appendix, Case No. 10, pp. 725–727.)

f. The Federal Government's Natural Bridge, Virginia, Camp

The National Training School for Boys, in Washington, D.C., has long been the Federal juvenile institution for boys convicted of Federal offenses. The Federal Bureau of Prisons operates other institutions for older youth, but the one in Washington is usually associated with juveniles. The establishment was opened in 1866, but it has been a unit of the Federal Bureau only since 1939. The history of this institution has been spotty so far as discipline, treatment, policy, and capable personnel are concerned. Since no studies have been made of the school, at least for public view, we must rely on observations from visitors. In general, the institution compares both favorably and unfavorably with many others of a similar type.

Since 1944, the Federal Bureau has maintained a camp for about seventy of the younger boys sent to the National Training School. After careful screening, this small group is sent to the camp, where it has the benefit of an open, minimum security régime. The experiment thus far seems to be quite successful.

The physical set-up is an abandoned CCC camp in the foothills of the Blue Ridge Mountains, some 200 miles from Washington. Many forestry projects, such as trail-building, roadside stabilization, telephone-line maintenance, and pulpwood production, are available. The boys may earn up to three dollars per month. After an initial quarantine or orientation period of two weeks, each boy is assigned to a team of ten. Each team is supervised by a senior and a junior counselor. Since the counselor is the keystone of the Natural Bridge program, it is essential that trained personnel be secured for this valuable and interesting experiment. The counselor's work with the boys includes not only day activity but evening discussion and hobby work as well. There are town meetings, vocational education, discussion groups, and recreational activities in addition to the forestry work.

This experiment has not been in operation long enough to evaluate its impact on those released. But the management is convinced that the operation of the camp through small groups with intimate counseling is both practical and sound. As H. G. Moeller, Supervisor of the Juvenile Section of the Federal Bureau of Prisons, states:

> Selective intake permits grouping in fairly homogeneous units. The relatively lower cost of construction and operation of plant permits a higher ratio of personnel to boys than is possible in the more formal institution. The setting contributes to the development of a relaxed, informal atmosphere and at the same time provides needed opportunities for blowing off steam. Camp projects lend themselves easily to programs which emphasize individual responsibility and recognition as well as a sense of personal accomplishment in work well done. Experience in treating the individual in such a setting indicates at least one direction in which we may move in providing more diversified services for the re-education and re-training of socially maladjusted youth.[33]

g. An Appraisal

Many private schools in this country enjoy excellent reputations among welfare workers and the public generally. They have the advantage of being able to screen types of boys who appear to be

---

[33] "The Natural Bridge Camp," *Yearbook*, N.P.P.A., 1948, pp. 162–173.

untrainable so far as their programs are concerned. Administrators of state schools complain that they must take all types—a situation that seriously handicaps them.

But we know of the private schools only through their reports and publicity brochures, or through some free-lance writer who has visited the schools and has written them up in the slick-paper magazines. Since we only see their good points, we find it difficult to appraise them objectively.

No institution in this country begins to approach the ideal training program. At least, the authors of this book do not know of any. The institutional stigma is always there. Children must conform to the traditional controls, and, at best, little therapy is administered in accordance with the professional standards we have suggested.

For example, let us comment on a few of the situations existing in one of the private schools we have described in this chapter:

1. Cottage life is supposed to afford the boys the home experience they have missed. Cottage parents are provided, yet the chores are regimented and the boys sleep in dormitories instead of in individual rooms.

2. Boys over fourteen may smoke if they have their parents' consent. Yet cigarettes are doled out—one after each meal and one before bedtime—and they must be smoked in the presence of the house mother.

3. No boy may leave the immediate premises around his cottage without a pass. A pass must be obtained to go from one cottage to another, to the recreation hall, to the administrative building, or to any other point. There are many roll calls, which, naturally, irritate the boys.

4. Discipline: first come deprivations; second, the "slipper"; and third, detention in a drab county detention building off the campus, which the boys fear.

3. FOSTER-HOME PLACEMENT FOR DELINQUENT CHILDREN

In an earlier chapter we discussed the development of foster-home placement for neglected and dependent children. Aside from indenture, a custom quite prevalent in colonial times, children were farmed out to families at an early date. For example, in 1869 a system of visitation of delinquent children in family homes was established by the state of Massachusetts. This system called for the appointment of a visitation committee for the oversight of indentured children, who at the time, numbered over 1,000 in that state alone. The ambitious program of placing out in foster homes, carried on by the Children's Aid Society of New York under the zealous direction of Charles Loring Brace, was described earlier.[34]

There are, according to Herbert D. Williams, four types of foster-home care: the adoption home, the boarding home, the wage home, and the free or work home.[35] Foster-home placement, regardless of the type, has a definite part to play in the treatment of children, whether dependent or delinquent, who are referred to the juvenile court. The dispute that has raged for many decades among practitioners in the fields of social work and education regarding the relative advantages of institutional placement or foster-home care can be considered as closed. Practically everyone now realizes how futile it is to play one type of child-care against the other. Despite what has been stated in our previous chapter, as well as in this one, on institutional care, it must be accepted that certain types of children will of necessity be placed in institutions for treatment. All are in agreement that the child needs some family life, but if such a situation cannot be furnished, the institution must be utilized.

The foster home offers to the child, as much as it is possible, a substitute for family life. The institution provides group living and, if it is small enough or organized in small family-like units, it can also provide a certain atmosphere of family life. (See Appendix, Case No. 8, pp. 721–723.)

What has been said applies to all children whose cases are heard by the juvenile court, including those brought before that tribunal for reasons of dependency, neglect, or delinquency. Regarding delinquent children, in particular, it is true that institutional placement is too easily resorted to in many instances. The reason for this tendency is partly that foster-home placement has been largely restricted to children who are dependent and neglected but who otherwise do not show any behavior difficulties. Many private child-placing agen-

---

[34] See Chapter II.
[35] "Foster Homes for Juvenile Delinquents," *Federal Probation*, September 1949, pp. 46–51.

cies are not willing to accept children who show emotional disturbances which manifest themselves in unlawful acts. Also, many couples who are able and equipped as foster parents to take care of "normal children" are not prepared or willing to take into their own home children who have shown delinquent traits.

However, juvenile court judges are often still motivated by the concept of blame, and feel that a delinquent child needs punishment rather than the kindly treatment he could receive in a foster home.

There are many notable examples of delinquent children, especially younger ones, who have been placed in foster homes with remarkable success. Mr. Williams, in the article alluded to above, cites what he calls "the most ambitious undertaking in this field," the work of the Children's Aid Society of Boston. A study was made of 501 problem and delinquent children placed in foster homes over a ten-year period. It was demonstrated that most of them made a better adjustment in carefully selected foster homes than in institutions; the reason given was that family life in a community setting offers more of what society demands of a child than does an institution.[36] On the basis of this study, the conclusion was reached "that approximately 85 per cent of normal children who have been labeled as delinquent, because they have committed delinquent acts . . . make a satisfactory adjustment in foster boarding homes and cease to be delinquents." [37]

It is stated, on the other hand, that the adolescent delinquent usually does not fit into a foster home because "the struggle to define himself as separate from and yet a part of his own family, he may find duplicated even more painfully in a foster home." [38]

Many juvenile courts use local departments of welfare or private child-placing agencies to carry out the foster-home program for the children referred to them. A few courts, notably the one in Allegheny County, Pittsburgh, Pennsylvania, and the juvenile court of San Joaquin County, California, have organized their own foster-

---

[36] William Healy, Augusta Bronner, Edith M. H. Baylor, and J. Prentice Murphy, *Reconstructing Behavior in Youth*, Knopf, New York, 1929, pp. 5, 12, 249, 253.

[37] *Loc. cit.*, p. 48.

[38] Ruth Gilpin, "Foster Home Care for Delinquent Children," *The Annals*, January 1949, pp. 120–127, especially p. 125.

home department, which directly selects the homes, places the children, and supervises them through its own staff of probation officers.[39]

Foster-home placement brings about a great number of problems, especially regarding the relationship between foster parents and natural parents. The scope of custody conferred by the court, either directly upon the foster parents or upon the child-placing agency, is seldom clearly defined; in any event, the natural parents retain a certain amount of custodial rights over their children, even after they are placed. They are also financially liable for the support of their children. Another problem is frequently created by the dual authority of the court and the child-placing agency, whether public or private, over the supervision of foster homes.

The type of child who may best adjust to foster-home placement can generally be determined through careful analysis by the court facilities—assuming that the court maintains testing and investigating personnel. As listed by Mr. Williams, the following types of children may benefit from foster-home placement:

> Foster homes work best for those who have a need for affection, individualized attention, who require close and more intimate relationships with adults and those whose personal habits and attitudes are not such as to make them too conspicuous in a community. Other factors which determine whether the delinquent child should be sent to the institution instead of a foster home are inherent in the community resources when contrasted with the institution. Some children are in need of special educational tutoring and remedial work which may not be available in the community where a suitable foster home is located, but the institution may have such specialized services. This is also true of the psychotherapy which may be needed in a particular case. . . . Some neurotic children do better in a foster home than in an institution if psychotherapy is also available. Children who do not respond to case work treatment are not ready for foster home placement, nor are those with strong aggressions against parent persons.[40]

It should also be emphasized that many children who find it difficult to adjust in one foster home may do exceedingly well in another.

---

[39] See Kay Kunkel, "Foster Placement as Court Function," *Focus*, N.P.P.A., September 1949, pp. 146-149.

[40] *Loc. cit.*, p. 49.

Just how many trials should be tendered the child is a debatable question. But if the testing and diagnostic services of the court or agency are adequate, several foster-home opportunities are more desirable than commitment to an institution.

A good example of placement in rural areas is reported from Michigan. There, the juvenile court of Pontiac places in farm homes children who cannot be returned to their own homes but who do not need strict institutional care. The court employs a full-time supervisor for this project. A total of 213 children have been placed since this program began in 1940. Since foster parents in farm areas are more willing to accept boys, 194 of the children were of the male sex; 75 per cent of these boys made satisfactory adjustments on the farm, with no known recurrence of misbehavior.[41]

A special type of home for delinquent children is the boarding home established and subsidized by a public or private agency for the specific purpose of caring for a small number of difficult court-committed cases. It is usually conducted as a private home by a husband and wife, and differs from an ordinary foster home in that the operation of the home is a full-time job for both the woman and the man. A good example of this arrangement is the Berks County Boys' Home of Reading, Pennsylvania. This home takes care of twenty-five boys under the supervision of a superintendent and his wife. In addition, a number of counselors are responsible for the boys in their leisure time. During the thirty-five years of its existence, 886 boys have resided in this home-like atmosphere. A close working relationship exists between the home and the juvenile court's probation staff and the local child-guidance clinic. Commitment to the home is through the juvenile court and the work is financed by the county authorities.[42]

It may be seen, then, that the foster home can make a definite contribution to the treatment of many types of juvenile delinquents. Naturally, abuses occur in some foster homes and children must be taken from those where cruelty or apathy is found. One further handicap in this type of service is that the financial remuneration is not high. In some places it is actually less than the cost of the food

---

[41] See *Focus*, N.P.P.A., January 1948, p. 32.
[42] For further details, see *The Quarterly*, official publication of the Pennsylvania Association on Probation and Parole, March 1949, pp. 10–13.

the child consumes. Many foster parents take children only because they are fond of them and find it a pleasing challenge to give them a home and to work with them. This attitude is, perhaps, the greatest asset in this mode of placing out problem children. Yet if an effective job is to be done in the over-all area of foster-home placement, adequate financial rewards must be available. Certainly foster-home placement is far less costly, both financially and psychologically, than is institutional commitment. It further eliminates the stigma that inevitably follows an institutional experience.

Playground at Boys' Home in Reading, Pennsylvania. *(Courtesy Pennsylvania Association on Probation and Parole)*

4. THE BRITISH EXPERIMENT AT Q CAMP

In treating delinquency experimentation is important and necessary. It is too much to expect new ideas in treatment to originate in institutions, although here and there some excellent departures from tradition do emanate from clinics within the walls of prisons or reform schools. Postulates enunciated by psychiatrists, social workers, and others trained in the intricacies of human behavior seldom receive a hearing in official circles. Thus it is important that private agencies and organizations blaze new trails.

One of the most interesting forms of democratic living among delinquent boys in recent times was undertaken in a pioneering venture from 1936 to 1940 in a camp near a village in Essex, not far from London. It was officially known as Q Camp, or the Hawkspur Experiment. What took place there should be recorded here, since nothing has ever been tried in this country that parallels it.

Here was centered a program characterized by the "shared responsibility" of a small number of staff officers and of a small workable group of "members" of the male sex between the ages of 16½ and 25 who had found it difficult to adjust to conventional society.

The Q Camp experiment was, in reality, a therapeutic institution rather than a model community, but its most significant feature was the partnership it emphasized. The members were sent there on their own volition and they remained on the same basis. Although those responsible for the experiment did not claim to have discovered any new principle in treatment, they did claim "to have achieved a real synthesis of sound theory with bold practice, of painstaking study of behavior with personal regard for those whose conduct" was studied.

Through its therapeutic program the camp attempted to study and treat antisocial behavior and maladjustment by environmental and educative means, with a scientific seriousness comparable to that used in individual methods of psychotherapy.

Each member of the camp participated in the government that was finally agreed upon. The attempt to achieve orderliness, without which no group of human beings can possibly live together, was subject to change when enough of the group felt it was necessary. Each member accepted voluntarily the amount of responsibility he felt inclined to accept. Public approval and disapproval were the most potent forces at work during the life of the experiment. Only on very rare occasions was authority from above invoked. In fact, during one brief period of the experiment pure anarchy was tried, but it was obvious even to those advocating it that it could not prove satisfactory if work was to be performed.

Members were accepted at their own evaluation. Each was ap-

praised by his work, or by his willingness to work, but he was not
punished in the traditional sense if he balked or refused to accept his
share of responsibilities. Group sanctions were sufficient to elicit
acceptable behavior from anyone not measuring up to the levels of
responsibility imposed by the entire membership.

Although Q Camp was engaged in the task of re-education, a
technique was evolved for developing human personality through
work training. The main points of this technique were:

1. Faith was shown in the judgment of each member.

2. The minimum of compulsion was used, and that only in the
initial stages (but not until after the first month).

3. Work was allocated according to ability and the results were
judged in terms of effort and will.

4. The contribution of each member was valued.

5. Work was arranged so that no one was placed on a job beyond
his powers (one group that was willing to work at anything, but
only for short periods, was known as the "General Muck Abouts").

6. Everyone felt personally responsible for the job as a whole and
each felt free to criticize and make suggestions.

Significant features of Q Camp fall under the following heads,
descriptions of which must be omitted because of lack of space:
the element of pioneering; employment, including hobbies; economics, including work to be done, wages, fines, and so forth;
affection (perhaps the most potent factor in emotional readjustment); absence of traditional punishment; use of the individual approach of therapy; value of the group; informal relations between
members and staff; shared responsibility between staff and members;
interstaff cooperation; cooperation of nonresident medical psychologists; formal therapy, such as visits to specialists; physical
health; training of student helpers; documentation and keeping of
records; and examination before admission.

The psychiatric approach was much in evidence at Q Camp. Careful analysis was carried on and much relief was noted in the development of the individual's adjustment to life.

The importance of the experiment at Q Camp can best be summarized by one of those most keenly interested in what was accomplished there from 1936 to 1940. He writes:

I think the most outstanding lesson of Q centers round the instinc-
tive craving of a gregarious creature to be accepted and valued by his

fellows. The men selected for admission were wanted by the Committee of Management; they were welcomed by the Camp Chief and his staff, who looked for and found likeable human qualities in them and looked forward to the pleasure of seeing them increase in sociability as many others had done. They were accepted by their fellow members with a measure of cordiality roughly corresponding with their social attractiveness. Most of them had been unwanted in a previous social environment, and many could not believe that the friendship now offered to them was sincere nor that the camp community had a real use for them. The extent to which a man came to be valued and to know that he was valued in the Camp became the measure of the success of his treatment there.[43]

All members who came to the camp might be labeled "behavior" problems, but none of them possessed any deep-seated psychotic or psychoneurotic traits, nor did any have a long history of incarceration. They were sent by various social agencies, physicians, probation officers, magistrates, parents, or friends, or they came of their own initiative. Since failures were surprisingly few among those who were expected by the staff to succeed, the committee was justified in believing in its form of therapy.

This camp was forced to close because of the war, but its results were widely debated among leaders in the field of correctional treatment. The camp's director, W. David Wills, is a follower of Homer Lane, an American who went to Britain in 1912 after a successful career as director of an institution for delinquent boys, the Ford Republic, located near Detroit, Michigan. Lane, born in Hudson, New Hampshire, in 1876, started his work with boys in Boston about 1902. Later he went to Detroit and founded his school, which was based on democratic principles, free expression, and self-government. He was a close friend of Thomas Mott Osborne, who was one of this country's outstanding penologists.

Lane was called to England to open a new school for delinquents, both boys and girls, located on a farm in Dorsetshire. He called his school the Little Commonwealth. Here again he brought into play the principles of democracy and self-expression. This remarkable educator of young children, until recently almost totally neglected in his native country, repudiated the conventional concepts of pun-

---

[43] For further details, see W. David Wills, *The Hawkspur Experiment*, Allen & Unwin, London, 1941. The above quotation is by a member of a committee that followed this interesting experiment.

ishment, restraint, and regimentation, and in their place established
and put into practice the following principles: (1) love, which to
Lane meant admiration for the personality without sentimental pity
(it was he who coined the happy phrase "being on the side of the
child"); (2) freedom from any authority of any one individual but
the acceptance of responsibility developed through group controls;
and (3) self-government, which meant no control by conventional
authority but only by that authority derived and evolved through
the group itself.

Homer Lane had great influence in Britain. Aside from David
Wills, mentioned above, one of his staunchest supporters is A. S.
Neill, headmaster of the famous Summerhill school, who has written
incisively on problems of children and parents. David Wills' experiment at Q Camp is an example of what we may eventually expect in
the future not only from Britain's educators but from experimenters
in some of our more progressive states—*e.g.* "Highfields," the Hopewell, New Jersey, project on the former estate of Charles Lindbergh.
This farm-school deals with certain types of delinquent boys who
voluntarily attend for from one to six months and participate in
group therapy and outdoor forestry work.[44]

5. THE BRITISH APPROVED SCHOOLS

There are no state-supported reform schools for younger children
in Britain. Rather, some 150 quasi-public or private schools of various
types exist to which young children are committed by the lay judges
of the juvenile courts. These schools, known as "approved schools"
merely because they have been given a stamp of approval by the
Home Secretary, have grown up during the past two hundred years,
and many of them are of recent origin. In an earlier chapter we
discussed child-saving in England. Some of the schools we mentioned
are still in operation and today are a part of the approved school
system.

Some of the schools are provided especially for Catholic or Jewish
children, but many take youngsters of any religious belief. There

---

[44] See pp. 531–532 for more details on the New Jersey experiment. For more
information regarding Homer Lane, see E. T. Bazeley, *Homer Lane and the
Little Commonwealth,* George Allen & Unwin, London, 1928 (second edition,
1948); also Homer Lane, *Talks to Parents and Teachers,* Hermitage House,
New York, 1949.

are also a few nautical schools for boys where seamanship is taught.

One feature of British child treatment is that their schools, by and large, take what is known as "care and protection" cases as well as delinquent children. In the United States we tend to separate these two groups, although many private schools take both.

It would not be quite accurate to make the assertion that in none of the approved schools do we find repression and regimentation, two of the salient characteristics of our public reform schools. Nevertheless, the great majority of the British schools are almost completely free of the features that we have criticized in our own schools. Only a few of the very old schools show outward signs of being schools for delinquent children. Most of them are in attractive settings, and few, if any, restraints are in evidence. For example, the children wear no uniform clothes; they are dressed exactly as are children in the free community. The schools are divided according to age groups: for boys, Junior Group schools are from ten years of age to just under thirteen; Intermediate Group, from thirteen to fifteen; and Senior Group, over fifteen. For girls: Junior Group, under fifteen; Senior Group, over fifteen.

Until recently, the lay juvenile court judges, upon advice of the trained probation staffs of their courts, sent children to those schools that seemed to have the most adequate facilities and programs for the specific needs of individual children. Now what are known as classifying centers for approved schools are being developed. At present there are three of these centers. Children are first sent to these allocation diagnostic depots, where their potentialities and needs are studied. From there they are sent to the approved school that seems best suited to their needs. This innovation is still in its initial stage, but, as it is patterned after the seemingly successful Borstal practice, this period of observation will probably be of great aid in allocating the child to the institution best suited to his needs.[45]

---

[45] This information is from *Penal Reform In England*, edited by Leon Radzinowicz and J. W. C. Turner, Macmillan, London, 1946, Chapter VIII. One of the writers of this book visited some approved schools in England during the summer of 1949 and found the information given above still valid at that time.

Chapter XIV

THE ADOLESCENT AND DELINQUENCY

1. THE YOUNG MALE DELINQUENT

TRUANCY and incipient delinquent behavior of young children present a serious problem to local communities. But the hue and cry from law-enforcement officers, juvenile court officials, and social workers concerning the violent crimes committed by older youth is especially loud.

Starting with the report of the Wickersham Commission, in 1931, which stated that of the prison population at that time, 54.8 per cent were under twenty-one when committed, statistics of crime and prison populations have emphasized with monotonous regularity the youth of our criminals. And these statistics do not include the 20,000 boys under eighteen years of age who are committed annually to our reform schools, whom we described in Chapter XII.

Here are some data for the year 1949 from the *Uniform Crime Reports* of the Federal Bureau of Investigation: Children under twenty-one years of age who were arrested and fingerprinted numbered 117,562, or 14.8 per cent, of the total number; added to this number were 129,509 (16.4 per cent) between the ages of twenty-one and twenty-four—a total of 247,071 persons under twenty-five years of age, or 31.2 per cent of the total. These youngsters and adolescent youth were charged with 54.1 per cent of the total cases of robberies, 59.5 per cent of the total of burglary, 44.8 per cent of the total of larceny, and 67.0 per cent of the total of auto theft. Approximately one-half of all crimes against property during 1949 were committed by youth under twenty-five years of age.

One need not resort to reading sensational books like those by the late Courtney Ryley Cooper to get a picture of the delinquency of the older youth. Even the more sober and restrained works give great cause for alarm. Aside from the traditional crimes, the country is periodically shocked by cold-blooded and often bizarre crimes committed by emotionally disturbed youngsters and youth. It is this type of crime that Cooper played up in his sensational work, *Designs in Scarlet*.[1] More recently, the Minneapolis *Tribune* presented a series of articles written by Victor Cohn, entitled "Who Are the Guilty?," which gives a gruesome picture of "young killers" in our midst.[2]

But it was an earlier work, *Youth in the Toils*, that focused the attention of authorities on the delinquency of the older boy. The authors of this book, Leonard V. Harrison and Pryor M. Grant, devoted a great deal of attention to the fact that boys between the ages of sixteen and twenty-one committed crimes out of all proportion to their number in the total population. This group committed serious crimes more frequently than it did minor offenses. For example, in New York City, of the lesser offenses for which persons were arrested in 1936, those under twenty-one committed only 4.5 per cent of the total; whereas of the more serious offenses, they were responsible for 9.3 per cent of the homicides, 8.1 per cent of the felonious assaults, 29.4 per cent of the rapes, 24.7 per cent of the robberies, 42 per cent of the burglaries, 39.2 per cent of the larcenies from highways and vehicles, 13.1 per cent of the larcenies from persons by stealth, 22.3 per cent of the sneak thievery, and 18.1 per cent of offenses involving the carrying of firearms.[3]

This book pointed out the demoralizing conditions that surround youthful offenders when they are thrown into jails, prisons, and courts of the metropolitan centers. Perhaps no other book has so dispassionately dramatized community responsibility toward American youth. It would be pleasant to record that the delinquency rate of this young group began to drop because of this deep concern; but this is not the case. The war years did show some drop, since millions of boys from this age group were in the armed services. But there was still considerable concern in the larger cities and in camp cities where service men fraternized with adolescent, thrill-seeking girls. Instead of the more serious offenses, this period was conspicuous for

---

[1] Little, Brown, Boston, 1939.

[2] December 7–29, 1948.

[3] Macmillan, New York, 1938, pp. 44–45. See our discussion of the development of the Youth Correction Authority by the American Law Institute, Chapter X, pp. 354–358.

sexual irregularity. Thousands of "victory girls" catered to the service men; the down-town areas of the large cities were filled with young couples "out on a spree." Instead of a high crime rate, a low moral tone was evidenced wherever service men and their girl friends were not supervised by canteens or the other community agencies that swung into action at the time.

Let us summarize some conclusions presented by Professor Thorsten Sellin to the American Law Institute in 1940 concerning youthful offenders:

1. In *all* violations of the law, without regard to the type of offense, the youth group does not show excessive participation. When one considers that some thirteen per cent of the population over fifteen years of age falls in the 16–20 year group, the participation of this group in the total offenses dealt with by police and judicial agents seems relatively small. This is due to the fact that the youth group has a very low rate of violations compared with older groups in offenses such as drunkenness, disorderly conduct, vagrancy and ordinary traffic violations, which together comprise four-fifths of the transgressions of the law.

2. In crimes against property the offense rates of youth are abnormally high, and since these offenses comprise the majority of serious crimes the rates for the latter as a whole are very unfavorable to the youth group, but crimes of violence against the person and crimes involving fraud or the violation of trust are more common in certain older age groups.

3. Within the 16–20 year group, the rates involving serious crimes tend to rise with increasing age. The 18–20 year olds are apparently more criminal than the 16–17 year olds. Our data indicate especially high total rates for the 19 year old group.

4. From the point of view of the absolute numbers of offenders, then, the youth group does not present an overwhelming problem, but its high crime rates in those very offenses most conducive to the development of a habit of law breaking and professional forms of criminality calls for the most intelligent approach possible to the problem of reducing and preventing the delinquency of youth.[4]

Before discussing measures of coping with the vast number of adolescents who commit various types of violent crimes, let us con-

---

[4] *The Criminality of Youth*, American Law Institute, Philadelphia, 1940, pp. 67–68.

sider for a moment the plight of millions of older boys and girls. True, the vast majority of children grow up to become tolerably good citizens without becoming neurotic or delinquent. It is only some two or even less per cent that become delinquent who cause us concern. Yet this small percentage is too large to ignore.

Yet we cannot generalize about causes. Each case of a delinquent boy or girl is different. Many may fit the pattern in which easy spending and a riotous time at late hours are the most conspicuous features, but thousands of delinquent acts perpetrated by older boys or girls do not develop from such causes. It is significant, however, to note that in a large proportion of these cases a good time is the ultimate goal. Boys sixteen and older are convinced they need a car and plenty of spending money to have and to hold the more glamorous girls. They lose their sense of perspective and go to extreme lengths to get a car even though they know they are in danger of arrest if they are apprehended.

Often the first borrowed or stolen car leads directly to membership in a gang specializing in the theft of automobiles. A respectable and reasonably well-intentioned boy becomes a criminal before he is aware of it. After they have been sent to prison, many of these youngsters manifest a hatred of society and develop not only a desire for revenge but a better technique for carrying on crime. A warden of one of our Federal prisons stated recently that most of his prisoners were young fellows who stole automobiles just for a good time and unwittingly drove them across state lines and thereby committed a Federal offense. He contended that most of them were not criminals in the accepted sense but merely thoughtless adolescents who might better be released and put to work under supervision.

In addition to these thousands of older boys who go criminal through circumstances we have hundreds who are inferior psychologically or emotionally. In recent years much attention has been focused on young psychopaths or, as many psychiatrists allude to them, the constitutionally psychopathic inferior or C.P.I. This group commits many crimes of violence: the fourteen-year-old New York boy who strangled the baby he agreed to watch as a "baby sitter"; the seventeen-year-old boy in Oklahoma who killed his girl because she refused to "go" with him; the Chicago boy of the same age who killed his young sweetheart while witnessing a gangster movie at a Loop theater and insisted that he did not know why he committed such an atrocious act; the two boys who murdered an eighty-two-year-old man in Ashby, Massachusetts, "by mistake"; the seventeen-year-old boy in Bedford Hills, New York, who murdered two sisters, aged seven and nine; and the two young thugs who ran amuck and killed six people in Ohio before one of them was shot and killed and the other captured. Most of such crimes lack any real motive and seldom bring their perpetrators any financial gain whatsoever.

The country was literally dumbfounded a short while ago when two zoot-suit youths, twenty-one and twenty-three years of age, held up a Baltimore and Ohio train, western fashion, near Martinsburg, West Virginia. At first it looked like the work of veteran criminals, but the subsequent bungling in attempting to escape showed that the crime was committed by amateurs. One of the boys was fatally shot in Washington, D.C., when he pulled a gun on a pursuing police officer in a pawn shop. The other was taken without any resistance. Both were ex-convicts from Ohio. In another case, the sports world was shocked by the shooting, apparently without a rational cause, of a Philadelphia ball-player by a nineteen-year-old Chicago girl. When asked why she had done such a deed, she is said to have replied, "Ask my psychiatrist." Still another case was that of the Roanoke, Virginia, choir boy, sixteen years of age, who killed his sweetheart and was sentenced to ninety-nine years.

Our cities, both large and small, supply a crop of these tragically maladjusted young people every month of the year—in New York City, Chicago, Philadelphia, Los Angeles—they are found everywhere. These young killers should have had psychiatric treatment when they were still in the pre-adolescent stage. If they had been critically observed while in school, there is no doubt that certain symptoms of abnormal behavior could have been detected. Follow-up treatment would have been of obvious social benefit.

Few objective studies have been made of young killers to determine why they kill or what manner of persons they are. However, Dr. Ralph Banay has made an intensive study of twenty cases of children, ranging in age from eleven to seventeen, who had committed murders. By a composite statistical picture, he shows a preponderance of unfavorable factors in the home life of these children as well as in personal and family relationships. In twelve cases out of the twenty, father-mother relationships were poor; in ten cases, the mother-child relationships were distressing. The mental condition of the children varied: three were definitely psychotic; four were border-line or defective; two were emotionally starved, neglected, or abused; and five were "model" children. Previous delinquencies had occurred in only five of the twenty cases.[5]

Another study of fifty-four cases of boy and girl homicides between the ages of nine and nineteen, covering the years 1921 to 1947 inclusive, was undertaken by Dr. C. H. Growden of the Ohio Bureau of Juvenile Research. Comparing these fifty-four cases with over 8,000 unclassified delinquents, the outstanding observation of the study was the great similarity between children involved in homicide and those involved in other types of delinquency. This similarity manifests itself in such items as intelligence, emotional instability or "normalcy," age, and physical condition. Aside from one lone case, none of the boys or girls premeditated their action for any length of time. Motive for these crimes were what the children considered "mistreatment, continued irritation or dictatorial interference in their personal liberties." The study's conclusion makes this interesting observation: "Only rarely do children who commit homicide show a tendency to manifest anti-social and non-cooperative attitudes, or a tendency to continue acts of violence. On the whole, it seems fairly safe to assume that, given the same degree of constructive attention as to other delinquents . . . they are as good a social risk as those who commit any other form of serious delinquency." [6]

These studies involve only small samples, but they indicate that "young killers" are not as vicious or potentially and consistently dangerous as much of the current literature has pictured. It is highly important, therefore, that more studies be made before we can do more than generalize why children commit such acts of violence.

The recklessness of youngsters with automobiles is another serious problem. It is alleged that some 7,500 persons are killed annually by automobiles operated by youths under twenty-five years of age. Insurance companies have increased premium rates on policies held by

---

[5] "Homicides Among Children," *Federal Probation*, March 1947, pp. 11–19. See also Lauretta Bender and Frank J. Curran, "Children and Adolescents Who Kill," *Journal of Psychopathology*, Vol. I, 1940, pp. 297–322.

[6] State Bureau of Juvenile Research, Department of Public Welfare, Columbus, Ohio, August 1949.

young adults. Attention has been focused recently on juvenile demons who play games with their speeding cars, often killing themselves or innocent bystanders. One writer, Ralph Wallace, calls this perverted form of play "teenicide." [7] The gruesome games played by these irresponsible juveniles are known by such names as "chicken," in which a car going some sixty miles per hour is permitted to guide itself with no one at the steering-wheel; "sport," in which the youngsters crouch on the floor of the car, each one operating the clutch, brake, and accelerator independently; and "dip-thrill," in which the car is run at terrific speed over depressions in a road. Certainly one cannot help wondering what is the matter with the young boys and girls who would dare participate in such obviously dangerous behavior.

An article in *Life* magazine, showing the various methods of self-destruction of youngsters, mentions the attempts made by citizens of Los Angeles and Dallas, Texas, to substitute traffic schools and simulated "hot-rod" games to offset the lurid dangers of these perverted games of adolescents.[8]

Aside from the large number of youthful delinquents who drift or jump into crime, there are, of course, many hardened young crooks and murderers who are "graduates" of gangs of juvenile criminals and who have engaged in various forms of criminality for years. Many have learned their "trade" in reform schools. They attach themselves to gangs of racketeers, gamblers, panderers, or "high jackers," and, playing the game according to the code, develop into highly processed professionals. But even these gangs are, in part, produced by the same general social and economic conditions that encourage youngsters to drift into a career of delinquency.

Nor can we overlook the hundreds of young adults—sixteen to twenty-one—who are in our Federal reformatories for violating the Dyer Act, which makes it a Federal offense to drive a stolen car over a state line. Although we are not condoning the theft of automobiles, something should be said about the carelessness of owners who actually, though unwittingly, aid and abet thieves. Citizens must realize that by placing temptation in the path of potential thieves

---

[7] See his article in *Collier's*, May 28, 1949; also "How 4 Teenagers Met Death," by George Mills, *Look*, February 14, 1950, pp. 52 ff.

[8] "The Hot Rod Problem," November 7, 1949, pp. 122 ff.

they become in a sense responsible for the commission of certain types of crimes.

The Special Crime Study Commission on Juvenile Justice in California has appropriately recommended that "it shall be a misdemeanor to leave an automobile unattended without locking the ignition." Justifying such a proposal, the Commission stated that about 85 to 90 per cent of all automobiles that are stolen have the ignition key left in them. Most of these thefts are of the "joy-ride" type, involving boys of juvenile court age. Any measure that will reduce the number of automobiles available with keys in them will reduce the opportunities for this kind of theft.[9]

The problem of the juvenile urban gang is another phase of the total picture of lawlessness among youth. We have referred to that before in our discussion of the gang. San Francisco, Los Angeles, and Brooklyn have been plagued by these warring juvenile gangs. In New York City the Central Harlem Street Clubs Projects, created in 1947, established a Commission on Street Clubs, to study this type of maladjustment among boys between the ages of eleven and twenty-three. They found three causes of antisocial club behavior: (1) the glorification of violence and "commando" tactics during the war years; (2) tension resulting from racial differences; and (3) deep-seated frustrations as the result of political, social, and economic discrimination on racial, religious, or nationality basis. They found that punitive and repressive methods cannot control the street gang; that such tactics by the police merely heighten antisocial antagonism. The answer seems to be one of introducing trained workers into the gang. The project has not been in operation long enough for its results to be appraised in a constructive manner.[10]

The problem of the young adult offender, then, is a grave one for society. What has been done to cope with this menace? Let us first examine the traditional reformatory to which convicted young offenders are generally sent.

2. THE REFORMATORY

It is a historical accident that the reformatory became an institution for youthful convicted offenders. The heroic efforts of prison

[9] *Report,* June 30, 1949, pp. 41–42.
[10] See James R. Dumpson, "An Approach to Antisocial Street Gangs," *Federal Probation,* December 1949, pp. 22–29.

reformers and administrators which brought the reformatory into being were really concentrated on a new type of prison for adults to supplant the penitentiary, which was considered a failure.

A few words of historical background will suffice to explain how and why the reformatory for older boys came into existence. The prison institution we know as a penitentiary was established during the early part of the nineteenth century, following the initial and earlier reforms of the Philadelphia Prison Society.[11] The development of this institution need not be summarized here, but it is important to state that some thirty years after it was conceived it was universally regarded as a failure.[12]

In 1870, some of the leaders in the prison world called a meeting at Cincinnati, Ohio, to discuss penal matters. As a result, the National Prison Association (now known as the American Prison Association) was formed. Most of the items on the agenda dealt with a system of penal treatment that was enjoying widespread approval in England and Ireland; it was known here as the Irish System, but in Britain it was called the Progressive Stages System, and in Ireland it was called the Intermediate Stages System. It had its origin in the "mark" system, introduced by Alexander Maconochie on Norfolk Island, off the coast of Australia, in 1840. The basis of this system was that prisoners were stimulated and encouraged to move to eventual freedom through stages by means of their own efforts in earning a prescribed number of credits or marks. Returning to England, Maconochie, one of the world's most advanced penologists, introduced his system in the Birmingham jail. Later it was modified somewhat by Sir Joshua Jebb, director of British prisons at the time, and introduced by him into Ireland. Here it was further adapted to local conditions by Sir Walter Crofton, who was in charge of the penal establishments in that country. Penologists from the United States witnessed the successes of this type of treatment and returned home singing the praises of Crofton and his Irish System.

---

[11] The Philadelphia Society for Alleviating the Miseries of Public Prisons, founded in 1787, and largely responsible for the movement to change the congregate jail of Philadelphia into a penitentiary in 1790. See Barnes and Teeters, *New Horizons in Criminology*, Prentice-Hall, New York, 1943, Chapters XXII and XXIII.

[12] For documentary evidence, see N. K. Teeters, "Tomorrow's Prison," *Social Service Review*, Vol. XX, No. 2, June, 1946, pp. 221–230.

Briefly, this system called for training of the inmates as well as an *indefinite* or *indeterminate* sentence. Neither feature was unique. In the Houses of Refuge established in New York, Boston, and Philadelphia during the 1820's, children were sentenced on an indeterminate basis rather than for a fixed term of imprisonment. But the fixed sentence for adults was the practice everywhere. It was Maconochie who denounced the system of fixed sentences. His reason was that the fixed sentence blasted all hope on the part of the convicted man of getting his release until he had served all his time. Thus he had no incentive for diligent work, good-habit formation, or good behavior. Also, trade training had been employed in prisons and children's Houses of Refuge.

Exponents of the Irish System from abroad came to the meeting at Cincinnati and spoke enthusiastically of the system. Sir Walter Crofton was there, and so was Miss Mary Carpenter, one of Britain's leaders in the field of juvenile delinquency. Penologists from the United States thought they saw a new era in the treatment of criminals. They urged the abolition of the penitentiary, or "congregate" prison, as it was known—a place characterized by "mass treatment," and, as a substitute, called for the establishment of a new type of institution to be known as a reformatory. The year before (1869) a law authorizing the creation of just such an institution at Elmira, New York, had been passed by that state's legislature, but financial difficulties delayed construction. The institution was finally opened in 1876, but only for the reception of young first offenders between the ages of sixteen and thirty. The veteran penologist, Zebulon R. Brockway, was appointed superintendent. Thus the reformatory became a training school for young convicted offenders rather than a substitute for the penitentiary as was originally hoped by the penal leaders of the day.

Despite their disappointment in not securing the type of institution they had hoped for, the reformatory idea proved so popular that by 1900 twelve states had created new ones either by renovating older buildings or by erecting new plants. At the present time, practically every state boasts a reformatory for the reception of young adult male offenders.

The Elmira reformatory served as a pattern for others. It was "stately and imposing," its buildings "ornate," with "their lofty spires and turrets taking on an added air of dignity because of the institution's elevated location." Here the boys were divided into three grades. At entry, the inmate was placed in the second grade. At the end of six months of good conduct, he could be promoted to the first grade, and with six more months of good conduct he could be paroled. Misbehavior was punished by demotion to third grade, where a month's good conduct was required for restoration to the second grade. Incorrigible inmates had to serve the maximum sentence provided by law for their offenses. There was a marking system by which achievements were measured. In this respect, the reformatory followed the practice of Maconochie and Crofton. The philosophy behind the institution was one of *reformation* or rehabilitation rather than one of expiation or penitence, as had been the philosophy of the early penitentiaries.

A Typical Old-Style Reformatory. Originally the New Jersey Reformatory, Rahway; now the State Prison Farm. (*Courtesy New Jersey State Department of Institutions and Agencies*)

Great enthusiasm, and some criticism, heralded the reformatory both in this country and abroad. For example, Sir Evelyn Ruggles-Brise, director of Britain's prisons, visited Elmira and returned home to found his famous Borstal system, which we shall briefly discuss below. Major Arthur Griffiths, inspector of British prisons, writing in 1894, described the régime at Elmira as one of mildness, "where most of the comforts of a first-class boarding house, ample diet, military music, the study of Plato, and instruction of interesting handicrafts are utilized in the process of amendment." [13]

In its early days, the reformatory had very definite defects, and many of these same defects are still present in the reformatories to which the older boy is sent today. Although the institution was established primarily to reform delinquents, it did not provide the right psychological surroundings to expedite this brave aim. The system of discipline was repressive, varying from benevolent despotism to tyrannical cruelty. Floggings were frequent, and even the great Brockway did not spare the rod. Little, if anything, was done to give the boy any sense of collective responsibility for the conduct of the prison community and no significant attempt was made to provide any social or political education.

In addition, and perhaps more important, there was no wide acceptance of the notion generally held today that delinquents cannot be treated as a single, unified group, but must be dealt with as individuals or classes of individuals of different psychological and biological types, and that these types must be scientifically differentiated through a careful psychiatric study and a detailed sociological study of environment.

It did not take long for critics of repressive punishment for the offender to denounce the reformatory. Instead of becoming a real instrument for treatment, it merely became a junior prison. As had the earlier House of Refuge, the reformatory started out with glowing words and well-meant action, but it could scarcely avoid the same kind of sterile thought that had permeated the junior institution. Since boys sent to it were considered "bad," they needed, above all else, a rigid discipline in addition to trade training. This attitude, of course, is still prevalent. Trade training, the *modus vivendi* of the establishment, was and still is attacked. Thousands of young delinquents are not capable of learning a trade; nor can they fit into a routine of training that requires manual skill or aptitude. Commenting on the reformatory as a means of actually meeting the specific

---

[13] *Secrets of the Prison House*, Chapman & Hall, London, 1894, Vol. I, p. 6.

purpose for which it was originally intended, the Osborne Association wrote in 1929:

> The history of Elmira raises the question, significant for every state, of how successful a reformatory program is likely to be which stresses regimentation, even though the routine is in worthwhile pursuits. At Elmira, as in many other American reformatories, the inmates are walking a chalk-line as surely as though they were in a prison. The chalk-line is broader than in some prisons, and it leads along more interesting paths: academic instruction, trade school, gymnasium work, etc. It is nevertheless the chalk-line of routine with all the old-time stress on regimentation, which so easily becomes stereotyped and futile and which is doubly monotonous for the young.[14]

The best the Elmira system could do was to attempt to teach the inmates good habits of industry. Its grading system broke down: "The tendency was to put everyone who behaved himself into the first grade, leaving only a few in the second grade and those actually under punishment in the lowest grade. The old prison discipline which placed emphasis on being a good prisoner regardless of anything more fundamental, such as achievement in school or shop or character, was dominant still." [15]

Criticism of the reformatory has been widespread. Reports and surveys are full of caustic condemnation of plant, program, personnel, release methods, and basic philosophy. In short, the reformatory is just another prison. But it made one contribution to the science of penology. It projected the idea of the indeterminate sentence, which had been introduced earlier in the children's House of Refuge.

Improvements have come slowly. For example, practically all the early establishments followed the old penitentiary cell-block type of construction, with bars, bolts, narrow cells, little sunlight or fresh air, and high walls. The "lock psychosis" was everywhere apparent. Guards were drawn from the poorly educated classes and were chosen more for their brawn than for their intellectual capacity. The boys were numbers rather than persons. Mass order formation was the rule, and great emphasis was placed on military drill. The motto

---

[14] *Handbook*, 1929, "American Prisons and Reformatories," p. 692.
[15] From the Attorney General's *Survey of Release Procedures*, 1940, Vol. V "Prisons," p. 25.

seems to have been "Wear the boy out with a rigid daily routine so that he will be ready for bed early."

In more recent years, some states have built new institutions on the cottage plan, eliminating the stone wall and substituting cyclone fences. Some have added watch-towers, manned by sharpshooting guards. The Federal reformatories, for example, are in this class. Escape is just as difficult under such conditions as it is from the older walled institutions. The Annandale, New Jersey, institution for boys is an example of the cottage-type reformatory. Here the buildings are attractive and, to the outsider at least, tranquillity seems to be the dominant note.

But the cell-block idea for the incarceration of the older boy will not down. For instance, Pennsylvania, as recently as 1941, equipped its new reformatory at White Hill, near Harrisburg, with cell-blocks. It does not help matters much to name the blocks after Indian tribes, as was done there; they are still cell-blocks and evidence the old mass-treatment technique.

In the preceding chapter, we called attention to the *Handbook on Correctional Institution Design and Construction* (1949), which will unquestionably serve as a useful guide to state commissions contemplating new plants for housing and treating persons convicted of crimes and sentenced to imprisonment. A great deal of thought and expert planning went into this manual. The Federal Bureau of Prisons deserves great credit for meeting this long-felt need.

A boy sent to a reformatory by the court is received in what is usually referred to as "quarantine" block. His stay in this segregated unit is from thirty to sixty days, during which time he is interviewed and tested by various members of what is known as the classification clinic—sometimes referred to as the diagnostic clinic. This group is composed of professional members of the institution's staff, notably the medical officer, psychologist, director of the school, supervisor of trade training or industry, and, if the establishment is more progressive, the social worker and psychiatrist. The chaplain also interviews the boy.

The institution, of course, already has the commitment papers and the boy's record, which have been supplied by the court. His record, together with the information elicited by the initial interviews during the quarantine period, gives a reasonably clear picture of the new inmate's potentialities, attitudes, and physical, emotional, and

New Jersey Reformatory at Annandale—A Fine Example of a Cottage-Type Reformatory. (*Courtesy New Jersey Department of Institutions and Agencies*)

intellectual handicaps, so that a treatment program can be formulated for him. After all information has been assembled, the classification clinic meets and discusses every angle of the case. The boy's desires are, theoretically, considered insofar as they fit into the industrial and educational facilities of the institution. If formal schooling is needed or desired, the boy's time is largely taken up with an educational program. If he is capable of learning a trade, suitable facilities are provided. Many institutions have farms, and boys showing aptitudes in agriculture are given farm training.

Part of the program of a progressive reformatory is to clear up any physical or emotional handicaps the boy may have. In short, every effort is made to adapt the program as well as the facilities to the individual boy. Periodic interviews follow throughout the length of incarceration which afford the boy an opportunity to discuss his institutional attitudes with members of the clinic. If reassignment seems expedient, the clinic considers it and acts accordingly.

This is the theory of classification or diagnosis and treatment in a reformatory. The effectiveness of the program depends on the integrity of the trained personnel, the physical facilities of the institution, and the atmosphere or climate of the establishment. If repression and the "lock psychosis" dominate the reformatory, little lasting value can emerge. In some reformatories, an honest attempt is made to carry on a meaningful program as free as possible from regimentation.

Perhaps the greatest responsibility of the classification clinic is preparation for parole or final release. Thus a parole plan for each boy is eventually prepared. Contacts with social agencies, members of the boy's family, or members in his community who know or will vouch for him are initiated either through personal interview or correspondence. On the basis of information received from such sources, together with the boy's record of achievement during his incarceration, the clinic formulates a post-institutional plan. Final date for his release is eventually set and his parole officer is notified. The boy is then released to the supervision of the paroling authority of the state and his readjustment in the community is negotiated.

Here, then, very briefly, is the procedure of a reformatory in its attempt to formulate a treatment program for those committed to its program. The procedure, which follows along the lines developed by the older penitentiary during the years, is known best by the term classification. A sustained movement has developed to staff prisons with professionally trained personnel. Although many reformatories have adopted such a staff in the treatment area, many still carry on with untrained political appointees who do little more than keep their inmates secure and engaged in a routine program of mass treatment.

Here is a picture of the diagnostic center for the state of New York, located at Elmira. During the fiscal year from April 1, 1946, to March 31, 1947, 1,320 inmates were received at the center. This is an average of 110 prisoners per month. Here are some interesting data for that period: [16]

1. All the counties of New York committed inmates to the Reception Center. The five counties comprising New York City contributed about 60 per cent of the intake.

2. All types of offenses were represented, from wayward minors to those convicted of first degree murder but not sentenced to death. Of the 1,320 commitments, 771, or 58 per cent, were convicted of felonies.

3. Indeterminate sentences, with definite minimums and maximums, were fixed by the court in 165 cases, or 21 per cent of the 771 felony cases received.

4. The average time spent at the Center was 75 days.

5. During the year, 1,250 inmates have been transferred. These have been distributed as follows:

Institutions	Number Transferred	Per Cent
New York State Vocational Institution	544	43.4
Elmira Reformatory	427	34.2
Wallkill	33	2.6
State Prisons	129	10.3
Mental Hospitals	4	.3
Institutions for Defectives	113	9.2
	1,250	100.0

The diagnostic center maintained by the state of New Jersey is unique in that it is set distinctly apart from any other type of institution and is housed in its own building. This center, located at Menlo Park, was opened in November 1949, and ultimately is to

[16] This information is taken from "The New York State Reception Center," by Glenn M. Kendall, *Federal Probation*, September 1948, pp. 42–47.

serve both juveniles and adults. The facilities in operation can accommodate sixty inmates or patients, but when finally completed they will have a capacity three times this number.

At present, the diagnostic center is concerned only with juvenile cases referred to it not only by the courts throughout the state but by other institutions, private and public welfare agencies, and by private individuals. The new procedure does not take any powers from the courts; its role is purely advisory. It merely places at the disposal of the judge an analysis of the defendant's personality, significant facts about his life history and environmental conditions, potentialities, liabilities, and assets. The final disposition of the case is left solely with the judge. The director of this new clinic is Dr. Ralph Brancale.

New Jersey is in the process of establishing a form of "short-term" treatment for certain types of youthful offenders who, in the judgment of the classification and diagnosing authorities, do not need conventional reformatory restraints. It is the assumption that many young offenders can be "processed" for community supervision, on a type of probation, by adopting new techniques outside the traditional prison but within the framework of an informal group experience.

A group-centered project without any restraints whatsoever is to be set up in a farmhouse situation at "Highfields," on the former estate of Charles Lindbergh, near Hopewell. As the preliminary report states:

> Every activity will be carefully oriented to emphasize the interdependence of individuals and to point up the necessity for accepting mutual responsibility. Every device will be used to build up a valid self-confidence as the only possible basis for a sound confidence in other people.

Admissions to this type of treatment center will be voluntary. When the court is confronted by a youthful offender deemed suitable for this short-term specialized treatment, execution of sentence will be suspended on condition that he agree to attend this farm home for a period ranging from one to six months. Persons expected to submit to this treatment are generally those who are not good probation risks but who are not necessarily repeaters. The program will consist of the following:

1. Group interaction sessions; in other words, a form of group therapy.

2. Individual counseling.

3. Self-government.

4. Individualized projects such as building a radio, writing a short story, overhauling a gas engine, etc. Each boy is expected to select and carry through to completion some such project.

5. A well-rounded program of work, recreation, and specially directed educational activities.

The youth who will be "invited" to attend this farm establishment are those who find it difficult to settle down in their environment without getting into such trouble as "borrowing" automobiles, going on all-night joyrides, or engaging in sexual brawls. There is no doubt that the New Jersey authorities are counting heavily on "guided group interaction," which is the term used in that state for group therapy.

This is frankly an experiment. In many ways it is similar to the California Youth Authority camps, although it does not emphasize productive labor to a large degree. There is a plan, however, to use those young adults sent to the training center in such work projects as truck gardening, reforestation, and soil conservation. But the main objective of the plan is the attempt to develop some degree of insight into the boys' own problems. In short, the New Jersey authorities are counting heavily on the benefits of guided group interaction. This clear break from traditional penology will be watched with great interest by all penologists who feel that little is now accomplished by the conventional and traditional forms of imprisonment.

Testing an institution's effectiveness calls for trained and objective investigators, plenty of time and money, and a general knowledge of the efficacy of the various types of institutional therapy. For these reasons, we find few capable studies of the effects of life within a reformatory or of post-institutional reform. Perhaps the most thorough and objective studies of this type are those conducted by Drs Sheldon and Eleanor Glueck of Massachusetts.[17]

---

[17] *Five Hundred Criminal Careers*, Knopf, New York, 1930; *One Thousand Juvenile Delinquents*, Harvard University Press, 1934; *Later Criminal Careers* Commonwealth Fund, New York, 1937; and *Juvenile Delinquents Grown Up* Commonwealth Fund, New York, 1940.

The data offered in these studies do not make one enthusiastic over the effectiveness of American reformatories. The original study dealt with 510 men (these are older boys) released on parole from the Massachusetts Reformatory at West Concord between 1911 and 1922. Of the 510, the criminal records of 422 were traceable. It was found that of this total, 89, or 21.1 per cent, had made a reasonably adequate adjustment; 307, or 72.7 per cent, had committed recorded crimes during the parole period; and 26, or 6.2 per cent, had committed crimes for which they were not arrested. In short, 80 per cent of the cases were failures. One must, of course, qualify this failure by stating that had these same men been placed on probation rather than sent to the reformatory, there is a good chance that they would have continued a life of crime. In other words, we have no way of knowing just how much these boys were influenced in their later criminal careers because of their incarceration. But it is obvious that the institution did not *reform* the boys.

In their follow-up study of these paroled men, the Gluecks report this finding: "There is an appreciable decrease in the proportion of delinquents and criminals during the second five years as compared with the first. That the trend away from criminality is definitely upwards is indicated by the fact that by the fifth year of the second period 42.7 per cent of 321 men then involved had become nondelinquent." [18]

These authors analyzed 63 different factors in the lives of the offenders to determine what led the men away from crime. Their conclusion was that it was *aging* or maturation, which reached its peak after the age of thirty-five. If the individual has not settled down by that time, he is not likely to do so later. What is needed above all else, certainly in the opinion of the Gluecks, is more and more careful, objective follow-up studies of children, older youth, and adults after they have left the institution and even after they have left supervision of parole officers.[19]

The future of the reformatory is uncertain. It has definitely become a sort of training establishment to teach habits of industry

---

[18] *Later Criminal Careers*, Commonwealth Fund, New York, 1937, pp. 75–76.
[19] For a penetrating article on follow-up needs, see Sheldon and Eleanor Glueck, "Follow-up Studies: Their Nature and Value," in *Encyclopedia of Criminology*, edited by Vernon C. Branham and Samuel B. Kutash, Philosophical Library, New York, 1949, pp. 167–173.

rather than the responsibilities of citizenship. Dr. William Healy refers to the psychic contagion of incarceration that is found in any institution.[20] Paraphrasing Healy, the Wickersham Commission further indicts the penal establishment as follows:

> The gathering of a group of offenders under one roof . . . creates a milieu through the common unit of selection—the commission of a crime. Naturally, then, crime will be the principal interest of the members of this milieu, their common tie, their first and chief topic of conversation. Here is an atmosphere in which crime is something to be admired. Such a milieu will go far toward solidifying delinquent behavior patterns already acquired.[21]

This criticism applies not only to the reformatory but to juvenile reform schools as well. It is just this practice of collecting into one institution many, often hundreds, of children or youth who have the commission of crime as their one common interest that is so sterile from the standpoint of good penology. Obviously, some radically different concept of treatment will have to be devised if delinquents are to be regenerated for social living.

In closing this section on the reformatory, we shall quote from a report sent to the New York legislature by the Prison Association of New York on February 2, 1942:

> The Elmira Reformatory was established by law largely through the efforts of the Prison Association seventy-two years ago. The intent and expressed purpose of this institution was the housing of the youthful first offender. The intervening time, however, has witnessed a wide and marked departure from the original thought, and recent studies, made at the institution, indicate that only approximately one-fourth of the inmates are first offenders, and over half are of low average intelligence. Other factors have been brought out, but suffice it to state at this time that the entire plan and program of the institution is retarded by virtue of the character of the prisoners sentenced. It stands to reason that the better interests of society will be served if the proper type of inmate is given the opportunity to benefit through the facilities offered by this institution.

The place of the reformatory in the penal program for older youth may gradually be worked out so that it will approach what its

---

[20] *The Individual Delinquent*, Little, Brown, Boston, 1915, p. 312.
[21] Vol. I, "Causes of Crime," p. 87.

original advocates intended it to be—a truly rehabilitative institution. Some treatment for young offenders will then be part of a well-rounded, integrated state program. Perhaps the solution lies in establishing several small units throughout a state, each housing a small group of boys possessing the same type of personalities, as in the British Borstal system.

Possibly the most hopeful innovation is the technique of group therapy. We mentioned this technique earlier in connection with progressive children's institutions. A few words about this process are also of importance here, since, in the opinion of the writers, it is certain to be adopted in more penal establishments, whether for the treatment of juveniles or of adults.

3. THE PLACE OF PSYCHOTHERAPY IN THE CORRECTIONAL INSTITUTION

Individual psychotherapy by the psychiatrist or the psychiatric social worker has long been considered a valuable tool in dealing with maladjusted children and adults. And group therapy itself is not new in certain areas. But, aside from the work of S. R. Slavson at the New York Jewish Board of Guardians since 1934, group dynamics is relatively new in the juvenile field. A few words concerning group therapy as it is beginning to be applied to the correctional field in New Jersey and California, for example, are necessary.

Group therapy had its beginnings many years ago, when it was utilized in dealing with sick people—the tubercular, in particular. But it gained widespread use during World War II when the armed forces had only a few trained personnel to meet the serious problem of maladjusted soldiers. Forms of mass treatment had to be adopted, especially in processing certain men for combat duty, and group therapy was applied to those who found it difficult to conform to discipline. After the war, it was but natural that the technique should be accepted in connection with inmates of penal institutions. Although this movement has not been widespread, it will undoubtedly prove to be one of the most fruitful innovations in the correctional field since the war.

In discussing group therapy, one is likely to think of a wide variety of techniques, ranging all the way from Alcoholics Anonymous, testimonial meetings, and Couéism to the highly analytical varieties employing the dynamics of Freud or Adler. Regardless of philosophy

or technique, all types fall into two categories, according to Dr. Gile
Thomas of Columbia University's Department of Psychiatry and
Medicine.[22] These are: (a) the repressive-inspirational (Christian
Science, Couéism, Alcoholic Anonymous) and (b) the analytic
(orthodox Freudian analysis). In the former type the patient is urged
to control himself and to suppress his worries or frustrating desire
with the suggestion that he find a satisfying outlet in his work, community activity, or religion. The latter type calls for release o
catharsis, so that the individual may become free to follow his own
social objectives. As Dr. Thomas puts it, "Analytic therapy urges the
loosening of repression, the conscious recognition and analysis o
unconscious wishes; it aims to free energy bound in needless repression . . . so that the individual will himself find suitable social out
lets."[23]

That both methods are scientifically sound and have worked re
markably well is attested to in the literature. The inspirational type
was employed as early as 1905 by Dr. J. H. Pratt in Boston, when
he developed a group method of dealing with tubercular patients. In
his original efforts, he brought the patients together to explain their
disease to them, since his time was so limited that he could not give
them individual attention. He found this group experience to be salu-
tary to all the patients, who received a "lift" from talking over their
ailment with others similarly afflicted. The individual patient found
he was able to bear up under his physical disease and thus develop a
healthy attitude. This type of therapy spread in medical circles; in
time it was applied to neurotics, psychotics, psychopaths, and others
who were mentally disturbed.

The analytic approach is, of course, quite different. As Dr. Paul
Schilder points out, human life centers about a limited number of
basic problems which must be mastered not only emotionally, but
intellectually. These problems must be liberated from merely verbal
involvements and become concrete.[24] This technique is vastly more
analytical than the inspirational type. But both types of therapy make
it possible for the patients to speak openly of their problems before
others; through emotional stress and through verbalizing their ag-

---

[22] See the cogent article by Dr. Thomas on group therapy in *Psychosomatic
Medicine*, Vol. V, 1943, pp. 166–180.

[23] *Ibid.*, p. 167.

[24] *Ibid.*, p. 175.

gressions, they may clarify their actions and gain some degree of insight into their repressions and hatreds.

Another type of psychotherapy that has gained wide approval was originated and developed by Dr. J. L. Moreno at Beacon, New York. Known as psychodrama, it is a procedure in which the individual acts out a given role in the presence of co-actors, thus revealing the deeper levels of his personality.

Experimentation with group therapy in the armed forces was found to be highly successful. Although it is often assumed that the therapist or group leader or integrator must have psychiatric training, this is not necessarily the case. It is essential, however, that the leader be skilled in integration. Whether he guides the verbalization of group members or chooses the non-directive technique, he must have the ability to synthesize. Potential group therapists may be drawn from psychiatry, psychology, sociology, social case work, counseling, or guidance.[25]

In New Jersey, where this technique is referred to as "guided group interaction," the leader is a sociologist. In the Youth Authority Camps of California, the leaders are known as counselors, and most of them have social work background. The idea of group therapy is spreading to reform schools and reformatories for older boys. The literature is also growing, and in-service training courses are being set up in various jurisdictions. The National Training School for Boys at Washington, D.C., operated by the Federal Bureau of Prisons, is also experimenting with group therapy.[26]

---

[25] See Robert M. Lindner's article on therapy in *Encyclopedia of Criminology*, Philosophical Library, 1949, pp. 490–497.

[26] For a bibliography on group therapy, see S. R. Slavson, *An Introduction to Group Therapy*, Commonwealth Fund, New York, 1943, and *The Practice of Group Therapy*, International Universities Press, New York, 1947; and S. H. Foulkes, *Introduction to Group-Analytic Psychotherapy*, Grune & Stratton, New York, 1949. See also Joseph Abrahams and Lloyd McCorkle, "Group Psychotherapy of Military Offenders," *American Journal of Sociology*, March 1946, Vol. 51; S. R. Slavson, "Mileau and Group Therapy," *Yearbook*, N.P.P.A., 1948, pp. 119–130; Samuel B. Hadden, "Group Therapy in Prisons," *Prison World*, September–October 1948, pp. 17 ff.; James J. Thorpe, "Group Therapy," *Proceedings*, American Prison Association, 1948, pp. 184–189; Marshall H. Clinard, "The Group Approach to Social Reintegration," *American Sociological Review*, April 1949, pp. 257–262; and F. Lovell Bixby and Lloyd W. McCorkle, "Applying the Principles of Group Therapy in Correctional Institutions," *Federal Probation*, March 1950, pp. 36–40.

In discussing the results of the group therapy program at the National Training School for Boys, Director James V. Bennett of the Federal Bureau of Prisons had the following to say in his 1948 report:

Some significant results have already been noted. For instance, during the early stage of the program the sessions were stormy, and the members of the group showed resentment toward this form of treatment by hostile and aggressive behavior. Next came an attempt to use the psychiatrist or psychologist as an errand boy, or an intermediary or magic helper, between the group and the institution. This was followed by period during which certain members of the group indicated that they were willing to discuss their problems, but hesitated to do so because they feared that group reaction would be shown by ridicule, or by resentment or reprisal for the co-operation they were showing. Soon however, the entire group turned to the therapist for advice and information and began to accept itself as a group. Then the boys began to relate pertinent aspects of their own experiences, with every member participating and giving well-meaning advice. When the patterns of one boy's behavior became evident, the group informed him of what he was doing to himself, tried to help him with advice, and then left responsibility to correct himself up to the boy.[27]

S. R. Slavson, whose work is well known to students of children's problems, contends that it is the group situation itself, not so much the program of activity, that brings about such amazing improvements in so many emotionally disturbed children. He adds that it is the make-up of the group that promises success in such therapy—differences of age and sex as well as types of behavior. And, of course, at the center must be a trained therapist. He suggests the following preventive program to combat the trend of emotional disturbances in children, which he regards as a threat to the national welfare:

1. Required courses on the meaning of children's behavior and their emotional needs at the high-school level.

2. Federal, state, and local funds to be allocated for setting up similar courses for adults, with a publicity campaign to make such courses attractive.

3. Courses in the meaning of child behavior and in the dynamics of group situations as an essential part of teacher training.[28]

---

[27] *Federal Prisons 1948*, p. 39.
[28] Alexander Klein, "He Lets Them Grow," *Survey*, February 1949, pp. 75–80.

4. THE ENGLISH BORSTAL SYSTEM

In 1897, Sir Evelyn Ruggles-Brise, director of British prisons, came to the United States to study the reformatory system. After visiting the institutions at Elmira, New York, and Concord, Massachusetts, he returned to his home country and immediately set apart a specialized institution at Borstal, near Rochester, in Kent. He planned to deal with young offenders between the ages of sixteen and twenty-one. Ruggles-Brise was particularly impressed with the enthusiasm of the reformatory program, which included trade training and vocational guidance. He also liked the elaborate planning for the parole period or after-care.[29]

The first Borstal was launched in one wing of a prison. Younger men were segregated from the older and were offered a special program of trade training, instruction, and drill work. A system of rewards for diligence and good behavior was set up—the hallmark of a reform discipline. The program proved so successful that other prisons were used for the same purpose.

In 1910, the specialized prison wings were abandoned and an industrial institution was taken over at Feltham, near London. By 1923, the conviction had evolved that the many features of the conventional prison had to be abandoned in favor of unique, specially designed structures. By 1930, several unwalled Borstals had been developed and an elaborate system of specialized institutions had been created. A classification center was first established at Wormwood Scrubs (at present at Latchmere House, just outside London), to which boys sentenced by the court are sent for preliminary examination and diagnosis. The age limit was raised to twenty-three, and the Borstals began to function as an integrated system.[30]

Among the many features of the modern Borstals that offset, to some degree at least, the prison atmosphere of the American reformatory, are the installation of the so-called "house plan," patterned after that of the preparatory school and university, from which many of the personnel were originally drawn; the substitution by the staff

---

[29] See his book, *The English Prison System*, Macmillan, London, 1921, p. 91.
[30] For an excellent analysis of the Borstals, see William Healy and Benedict Alper, *Criminal Youth and the Borstal System*, The Commonwealth Fund, New York, 1941.

members of "civies" for the ubiquitous uniform; and the development of intimate personal relationships between the boys and the administrative officers. The unwalled Borstals are most progressive in administration and treatment, employing some of the best techniques in therapy known to penal science.

Each of the Borstal institutions, whether it is a walled or unwalled establishment, is used for a specific type of boy or young adult—called "lads" in the British setup. If, in the judgment of the local judge, a boy is not suitable for some type of Borstal training, he may be sent to jail or prison. In such cases a representative of the Prison Commission attempts to persuade the judge to reverse his decision.

Every boy under the Borstal system must stay in a quarantine center for thirty days. Here he is subjected to a battery of tests, and subsequently a diagnosis is made of his case. Women known as "lady visitors"—voluntary untrained social workers—interpret the training program to the families of the boys.

The problem of allocation is admittedly serious. To find the best possible Borstal for the specific needs of each boy is a difficult task. The process of differentiating the boys into types is one that taxes the best thought. Each boy is assigned to his Borstal training for a period of four years. The first six to thirty-six months are spent in actual training; the remainder of the time is spent under supervision outside the institution on what is known as *license*, similar to our parole. The after-care service is conducted by the Borstal Association.

Certainly one of the unconventional features of the over-all Borstal philosophy is this after-care treatment. We in the United States have nothing to match it. Ruggles-Brise had stated at the outset that his hope for the success of the system rested upon the sympathy of interested people in the free community. Thus he enlisted the cooperation of those who had a deep concern for boys. At first, the association was purely private, but funds were gradually allocated to employ a paid staff. On this staff are both full-time and part-time personnel who are concerned with the rehabilitation and adjustment of the released boy in his community. Among the part-time workers are ministers, school teachers, and other trained workers in allied fields.

Still another set of workers who handle the after-care of Borstal lads are Borstal Voluntary Associates who serve in a friendly and sympathetic role and thus augment the personal service to the boy and his family. These volunteers are drawn from religious and charitable organizations, which represent the intelligent and understanding group of the community. Thus the Borstal parolee finds two persons interested in his welfare—the official parole officer and his *sponsor*. Both make visits to the boy's home and report their findings to the central office. Revocation of license may result as in our system of parole.

In evaluating the Borstal system, we must keep in mind that such a system would be difficult to develop in the United States. England is compact enough for any form of national service to be easily administered from a central office. Here we have forty-eight states, each with its own institutions, separate governments, and distinct penal codes. Even if the Federal government should take over prisons and reformatories, distances are so great that specialized institutions for different types of offenders would make the allocation process expensive and unwieldy.

Nevertheless, some of our larger states could develop a system of such specialized units with a central diagnostic center. Even in our larger states there would be no need for more than one maximum security reformatory in which to house and train the poorer risks. Other units could be small, open establishments or barrack-camps, each with a particular type of training program adapted to the various needs of the boys. Agriculture, horticulture, reforestation, soil conservation, animal husbandry, and other highly important phases of our economy could be developed and taught in such schools or camps. Boys from the industrial areas could be sent to trade-training institutions if they were interested and potentially equipped for such training. The California Youth Authority has made an excellent beginning along these lines. The Federal government might well abandon its Training School in Washington, D.C., and set up a system of this type, with scattered units all over the country where boys and young men who have been convicted of Federal offenses could be afforded training. At present, one camp is being maintained at Natural Bridge, Virginia. We described this camp in Chapter XIII.

Many features of the Borstal system have meaning for us in the United States. Aside from the small, specialized units, perhaps the greatest feature worth emulating is the personal relationship between staff and inmates. This relationship makes possible the complete elimination of regimentation and repression, both of which are an integral part of our reformatory system. The practice of having the staff officers wear civilian clothes is healthful from a psychological point of view. And again, the work of diagnosis in the central allocation center is significant. Lastly, the intimate relationship between members of the after-care Borstal Association and the license or parole staff, both working conscientiously in the interest of the boy, is extremely valuable in the work of rehabilitation.

Since the war several new establishments have been opened in England for both boys and girls. Several manor houses have been acquired and adapted to the specific functions of a training program. The Borstal at Hewell Grange for boys and the one near Maidstone, known as East Sutton Park, for girls, are quite progressive. The buildings and grounds are stately and beautiful and completely open. Of course, the better risks are sent to these units.

The system, however, is not perfect. Students from abroad contend that there is still too much repression and rigidity in the program. Securing and retaining understanding personnel is a constant problem. Salaries are none too high and working conditions make an independent home life precarious for staff officers. Young, virile men, the kind who make the most fruitful contributions to Borstal or reformatory life, become discouraged because of these and other professional reasons and withdraw to other careers. In the last analysis, high-caliber personnel is obviously one of the cardinal requisites for penal work. But the story is the same throughout the world; it is difficult to secure and to hold such personnel.

Two other criticisms have been offered by Healy and Alper, who have made an analysis of the Borstal system. The first of these is the lack of psychiatric treatment:

It is true, as the Borstal people say, that we in America have concerned ourselves with psychiatric classification of offenders and with statistical researches, while the Borstal System has been devoted to experiments in treatment. But the two approaches are by no means incompatible; indeed, in a scientifically well-oriented program both are indispensable. Treatment not based on diagnosis or etiology is not in line with the effective development of therapy in medicine or any of the biological sciences. Psychiatry as applied to the study of offenders has advanced far beyond the explanation of criminality in terms of mental abnormality. Together with psychiatric social work it has revealed many of the traumatic life experiences and emotional attitudes, the feeling of being thwarted or deprived, which lead to the acceptance of ideas of criminality as being for the particular individual a suitable form of behavior.

To be sure . . . no small part of the work done with Borstal lads partakes of the nature of psychotherapy; yet it is equally true that the fine endeavor to utilize personal influence is based very largely on the subjective impressions of the individual members of the staffs. Their knowledge of the causations of human behavior is not that of the psychiatrist who patiently unearths a life story and has the opportunity of fitting it together with what a psychiatric social worker has learned with equal patience from the stories of the families. In spite of the splendid chances offered by the Borstal setting for such expert work, psychiatrists are not at hand to undertake it.[31]

The other criticism is the definite limit of the sentence to four years. In this country, the exponents of the indeterminate sentence point to the fact that no one knows at the outset just how long it will take to reform or adjust a delinquent to the accepted rules of social living. Since each individual is different, different cases take longer or shorter periods. However, one progressive feature of the Borstal system is that the offense is not the determining factor in considering the amount of time to be spent in duress. More important are the background of the offender, his record, potentialities, interests, and capacities.[32]

One of the writers of this book visited several Borstals during the summer of 1949, and was, on the whole, much impressed with the work being done. However, two points should at least be mentioned. First, the authorities rely too much on trade training; it is admitted that only about one in four of the boys thus trained actually pursues skilled work upon release. Second, too much paternalism exists in the system, mainly as a result of the earlier idea of democratizing culture by enlisting university men to come to the Borstals to serve as "house masters." A trend away from this idea has developed in recent times and more adequately trained personnel are enlisted.

---

[31] *Op. cit.*, pp. 227–228.
[32] For later details on the Borstal system, see Molly Mellanby and R. L. Bradley, "The English Borstal System after the War," *Federal Probation*, December 1948, pp. 19–22.

5. THE YOUNG SEX DELINQUENT

a. The Male Sex Delinquent

In a discussion of the sex delinquent, various phases of the problem call for review. It is our purpose in this section to deal first with boys and young males and then with girls and young females. It is well known that most delinquencies committed by girls are sexual, whereas most delinquencies committed by boys and young men are non-sexual.

The sex act committed by the young male adult is usually violent and commands great attention in the press. These offenses are distressing and many end in murder. We read so often of such brutal murders in the scare-heads of the country's newspapers that we feel they are actually more prevalent than they are. Each generation sees itself as the worst so far as sex crimes are concerned. As early as 1893 even the eminent Krafft-Ebing deplored the increasing number of sex crimes.[33] It is probable, however, no more such cases occur today than occurred formerly, in proportion to the population. We are just more efficient in getting the facts assembled and circulated.

Perhaps the most notorious case involving the sex angle occurred in Boston in 1874. It has become a classic. This was the case of Jesse Pomeroy, a fourteen-year-old boy who murdered a four-year-old child in a most revolting manner. Pomeroy was sent to the Charlestown, Massachusetts, prison for life, in solitary confinement. He remained in his solitary cell for almost forty years (perhaps the longest interval on record), seeing no one but his keepers and his mother, infrequently. He was subsequently transferred to the Bridgewater State Farm, where he died, an old man, in 1932. Another equally sensational case in which sexual deviation was a part was the famous Loeb-Leopold affair of 1924. This involved two brilliant and wealthy but morally perverted young students of the University of Chicago. These young adolescents, seventeen years old, brutally murdered a younger boy, their purported motive being to prove they could commit a "perfect crime." Psychiatry was brought into this case by the famous defense lawyer, Clarence Darrow, but the state was not prepared to accept its scientific implications; thus these abnormal

---

[33] *Psychopathia Sexualis*, F. A. Davis Co., Philadelphia, 1893, p. 378.

boys were sent to the Illinois state prison for "life and ninety-nine years." [34]

A discussion of certain types of sexual offenses is necessary for an understanding of what controls and preventive treatment we need in our society. First we may dispose of the young boy who becomes a companion of the homosexual who depends to large degree upon juveniles for his gratification. More often than not this abnormal relationship is congenial, since the older man uses rewards to keep the youngster under his control. Aside from the debauchery of the child, the legal problem in these situations is "contributing to the delinquency of a minor." It is not our purpose here to go into detail concerning the pathology of the homosexual, which is a subject that only indirectly affects the juvenile. Of course, the invert adult was once a child and was thus a deviate from birth or from an early age. He may be doomed to play the role of the homosexual for physiological or psychological reasons. Some inborn glandular anomalies may be responsible for the former, whereas the latter may be explained by mistakes and exaggerations in family relations, faulty sex education, accidental sex experiences at an early age, or to a denial of normal sexual outlet.

It is important here, however, to point out that the true homosexual is a pathetic person indeed and is much misunderstood both by the layman and police officer alike. The public assumes that he is a degenerate rather than a person suffering from an affliction contracted through no fault of his own. Though many homosexuals are fine and sensitive, they are anathema to society; thus we have no qualms in persecuting them. Many outstanding persons in the realms of art, music, and other cultural fields have been thus afflicted. Many homoseuxals manage to work out a satisfactory adjustment with their own kind. All our large cities have a *demi-monde* of such persons who enjoy a sort of free-masonry among themselves. Those whose deviation does not grow out of physiological causes can get relief through psychiatry if they are so motivated. Glandular therapy has

---

[34] For details concerning these two famous historical cases, see A. Warren Stearns, "The Life and Crimes of Jesse Harding Pomeroy," *Journal of the Maine Medical Association*, Vol. 39, April 1948, pp. 79 ff.; and, for the latter case, Irving Stone, *Clarence Darrow for the Defense*, Doubleday-Doran, New York, 1941, Chapter XI.

been helpful to those whose affliction rests on some biological foundation.[35]

What we are interested in at this point is the practice of some homosexuals to use young boys as a means of getting sexual relief. Here we find a problem that cannot be handled by psychiatrists, but rather by law enforcement agencies. The child must be rescued from the clutches of older men or boys and restored to his home. The disposition of the man is, of course, outside the purport of this section. We can not overlook the fact, however, that some young boys aid and abet—even seek out—older males who need their cooperation. They do this because of the rewards that are bestowed on them. Thus these children show signs of maladjustment because of their willingness to aid the homosexual.

There is also the problem of females who use young boys for normal as well as deviational sexual gratification, a practice that is well known to the police of our larger cities. Again, the legal problem is "contributing to the delinquency of a minor."

Although what we have described above is not too prevalent, certainly the extent of socially disapproved sexual practices among young boys is widespread. It must be frankly stated that most of this behavior is quite normal in our culture, for whatever reason. Teachers, law enforcement officers, and parents who are enlightened in the slightest degree will admit this phenomenon of our civilization. We are referring especially to masturbation, exhibitionism, childish lewdness, the tormenting of young girls by young boys, and the like. Scarcely a public-school toilet or playground fence is free for long of some lewd picture or word scrawled there by school boys. The same is true of public rest rooms. If this thesis is correct—that is, that considerable sexual lewdness is normal in our juvenile population, just as there is a certain normality in masturbation—our discussion of sexual delinquency among the young must deal only with persistent behavior of this type.

Dr. Kinsey and his associates' study reveals that ultimately about 92 per cent of the total male population are involved in masturbation leading to orgasm. Regarding heterosexual petting, these researchers found that between 18 and 32 per cent of the younger population

---

[35] See Martha W. MacDonald, "Criminally Aggressive Behavior in Passive Effeminate Boys," *American Journal of Orthopsychiatry*, Vol. 8, 1938, pp. 70 ff.

indulge in petting leading to climax in each age period prior to marriage.[36]

A study that has bearing on this problem was made some years ago by Lewis J. Doshay, M.D. In examining and treating thousands of boys in the clinics of the Children's Court of New York City, Dr. Doshay was surprised to find that few male sex delinquents ever returned to the clinic because of another sex offense. In attempting to secure data on this situation, he was even more surprised to find so little literature dealing with the subject. His work, *The Boy Sex Offender and His Later Career*, is the result of his concern.[37]

A follow-up study, covering six to twelve years, of a group of 256 juvenile, but not feebleminded, young male sex offenders is reported in Dr. Doshay's book. The delinquents were divided into two groups: 108 with a record of sex offenses only, and 148 with a record of other types of delinquency. The main sex offenses for which the 108 youngsters were brought into the court clinic were: excessive masturbation; self-exposure (exhibitionism); pronounced obscenity either spoken or written; touching girls' privates; heterosexual experiences; fellatio; sodomy; and sex attempts on small girls. Although 47 cases in the group committing sex offenses were in the 7-to-14-year age group, 83.4 per cent of all this group were past puberty. In the mixed group of 148 cases, sexual behavior was only incidental to the general pattern of delinquency, which included such offenses as stealing, desertion from home, truancy, and ungovernableness.

The records of these boys were checked six years after their last contact with the court clinic. During this interval only 2.8 per cent of the sex group (the 108 cases) became involved in any further delinquency, sexual or otherwise, whereas 27.1 per cent of the over-all delinquent group (the 148 cases) were returned to court for delinquent or criminal behavior. The author found that the former group, by and large, came from homes possessing more preventive checks than did the latter group. Although it is quite possible that this situation may have existed, his statement regarding one phase of the treatment imposed by the court which seemed to have a healthy

---

[36] See Alfred C. Kinsey, *et al.*, *Sexual Behavior in the Human Male*, Saunders, Philadelphia, 1948, pp. 499, 533. Also see the Kinsey study regarding incidence of homosexuality, pp. 168, 610, 663.

[37] Grune & Stratton, New York, 1943.

effect on the subsequent lives of the sexual group is open to considerable question. He contends, on the basis of his study, "That male juvenile sex delinquency is self curing, provided the latent forces of shame and guilt, inherent in the moral-cultural pattern, are properly stimulated into action."

Imparting the knowledge of the boy's sex offense "to his family in the open process of a juvenile court and clinic" shakes "the boy's mental faculties . . . to their very foundation. . . . Strong reservoirs of shame [are dislodged] from attachment to the inactive memories of infantile rectal and bladder control days and powerful self-generating barriers against recidivism are laid down in the personality which effectively and lastingly resist a return to sexual offense." [38]

Such a technique seems contrary to all we have learned about the behavior of children and adolescents. Shaming a person is in the same category as the "ordering-forbidding" method of control; we may get immediate conformity but not often conversion. What is needed to bring about a conformity to socially acceptable behavior is an understanding of the atypical behavior pattern, without the slightest onus of blame. From that point on the therapist must use dignified and professional techniques, not shame or punishment.

We may now turn to the more spectacular and pathological types of offenses—many of which are committed by the adolescent or post-adolescent male. There are many shocking cases in this category, and a large percentage end in rape and even brutal murder. In considering cases of rape we must distinguish between "rape with consent" or statutory rape, and forced rape. The laws of the several states decide the legal age of the girl below which sexual intercourse is considered statutory rape. It is usually sixteen years.

Most boys and young men convicted of rape are normal in their sexual desires. Occasionally an individual cannot control his appetite for sexual satisfaction and proceeds to violate all norms of decency in his unbridled lust. He may go to shocking extremes—perhaps he specializes in young girls or even elderly women. Such persons have obviously passed the borderline of normality and have entered the realm of the pathological. They are either definitely psychotic or

[38] Quotes from p. 168.

belong to that group which we have discussed elsewhere—the C.P.I. or constitutional psychopathic inferior.[39]

It is needless to describe here any of the revolting cases that are luridly reported in the daily press. They all take the familiar pattern of unbridled lust leading to a shocking attack on some hapless female victim. Instead of being chastised with relentless frenzy by society and law enforcing agencies, the sick individuals who commit these offenses should be given psychiatric treatment and, if necessary, segregated in a non-punitive institution until they are cured of their pathology. More to the point, young children manifesting diagnostic symptoms of sexual aberration should be treated psychiatrically before they reach the dangerous age of adolescence.

Dr. Clarence A. Bonner, superintendent of the Danvers State Hospital of Massachusetts, in calling for research on the subject of sexual pathology as well as for early diagnosis, makes the following summary:

1. The sexual psychopath seems to be of constitutional origin, but environment plays an important part in the development of these tendencies.

2. The sexual psychopath strikes without warning and takes advantage of the helpless, in a strategic location where quick escape is possible.

3. Persons showing these tendencies should be identified and files on a national scale should be kept.

4. Differentiation between the psychotic and the true sexual psychopath should be determined by psychiatric observation.

5. Once identified, the sexual psychopath should be placed in indefinite custody, as he represents a constant and continued menace in any community.

6. Early recognition and treatment are essential in dealing with this condition. Control and modification are theoretically possible in the early years.[40]

---

[39] For descriptions of sex offenders, see Bertram Pollens, *The Sex Criminal*, Emerson Books, Inc., 1938, especially Chapter VII, "Infantile Sexuality." Also, Friedrich Leppmann, "Essential Differences Between Sex Offenders," *Journal of Criminal Law and Criminology*, September–October 1941, pp. 366–380.

[40] "Who and What Are Sexual Psychopaths?," *Focus*, N.P.P.A., July 1948, pp. 103–105. For suggestions concerning control of dangerous sex offenders, see also Morris Ploscowe, "The Sexual Psychopath: Some Suggestions for Control," *Prison World*, July–August 1947, pp. 18 ff.

Many sex murders are the result of *fetishism* which was so aptly described years ago by the great sexologist, Krafft-Ebing. Persons thus afflicted have an insatiable urge to satisfy their erotic sexual appetite by having an experience with some part of the body or with an article of clothing of some member of the opposite sex. It may be hair, eyes, shoulders, feet, or any portion of the body; or underthings, stockings, gloves, or hat. If they are frustrated or detected in seeking this satisfaction their escapade may end in violence or even murder. The case of William Heirens, the 17-year-old Chicago youth, attracted national attention back in 1945 and 1946. His case illustrates this point. In his early youth he had been taught to look upon sex as wicked but had developed a lust for female underclothing. His career of ruthless violence, including three murders, is apparent from the following court sentence, which committed him to a *prison* in Illinois, *not* a hospital for persons suffering from psychological anomalies:

> He pled guilty to 30 charges and received sentences on 24 burglaries of one year to life, to run concurrently; on three murders, Natural Life, to run consecutively; one robbery, one year to twenty to run consecutively; one burglary, one year to life, to run consecutively; one assault to commit murder, one year to fourteen, to run consecutively.[41]

Cases of this type demonstrate that society cannot afford to wait until the crime is committed to protect potential victims from sexually diseased individuals. On the other hand, it is not scientific to send them to the electric chair or to a prison of the conventional type for long terms, as is so frequently done. In fact, practically no provision exists for handling cases such as Heirens'.

New Jersey's Commission on the Habitual Sex Offender points out that the average citizen knows very little about the scope and nature of sex crimes but, as a result of headlines in the nation's press, he is oversupplied with misinformation on the subject. Some of the popular fallacies the Commission would like to correct are:

1. *That the sex offender progresses to more serious crimes:* Statistics clearly show that progression from minor to major sex crimes is exceptional rather than the rule.

---

[41] For a psychiatric analysis of this astonishing case, see *Journal of Criminal Law and Criminology*, Vol. 38, No. 4, November–December 1947, pp. 311–341.

2. *That dangerous sex criminals are usually repeaters:* Actually, of all serious crimes, only homicide shows a lower record of recidivism.

3. *That sex offenders are oversexed:* Most of those treated have turned out to be physically undersexed.

4. *That there are "tens of thousands" of homicidal sex fiends abroad in the land:* Only an estimated five per cent of convicted sex offenders have committed crimes of violence.

The Commission concludes by stating that there is more danger of being murdered by a relative or other intimate associate than by some unknown sex criminal.

A two-year study of 102 sex offenders in Sing Sing prison was made by Dr. David Abrahamsen, carrying out the directive of the Governor's Commission on the Problems of the Sex Offenders of New York State. The study revealed that those studied suffered from some form of mental or emotional disorder—a real or near psychosis or extreme neurosis; that every offender had experienced some severe emotional deprivation in childhood from such causes as brutal, neglectful, or over-indulgent parents; and that there was little evidence of "oversexed" behavior. There was little correlation to intelligence, since the majority of the offenders compared favorably with the general population. The report concluded that many sex offenders should be incarcerated in prison so long as they continued to be considered dangerous. The report also warned against using the term "sexual psychopath" loosely.[42]

A sane approach to the problem is advanced in an article by Dr. Frederic Wertham, entitled "Psychiatry and the Prevention of Sex Crimes." [43] Wertham points out that there are two extreme points of view about repressing sex crime. There is the purely legal point of view, which calls for permanent police supervision, stern punishment, denial of parole from prison, and complete ostracism from society. The other approach is purely medical or psychiatric: the psychiatrist should be the ultimate authority to sit in judgment.

Neither view is wholly defensible. One New York sheriff once

---

[42] For details of the New Jersey study, see *The Welfare Reporter,* New Jersey Department of Institutions and Agencies, Trenton, March 1950, pp. 10 ff. For summary of the New York study, see *Survey,* April 1950, p. 200.

[43] *Journal of Criminal Law and Criminology,* Vol. 28, No. 6, March–April 1938, pp. 847–853.

recommended shooting every "child-attacker" on the spot, without going to the trouble of a trial. The philosophy of savage punishment has been tried for centuries and has failed miserably. Sexually diseased persons are impervious to the conventional sanctions set up by society. It would be just as logical to warn a person suffering from a bad cold that he would be sent to the electric chair if he coughed. On the other hand, we have never yet experimented with handing over sex criminals to psychiatrists, and there are reasons for believing that this practice would be of little avail. A psychiatrist could not very well assume the roles of prosecutor and judge without fatally sacrificing his function as a professional therapist. The psychiatrist depends for his success upon his ability to gain the confidence of his patient. If the patient were aware that giving his confidence might lead to a sentence in a penal institution, he would become suspicious and would withdraw from questioning.

The solution seems to lie in proper cooperation among judges, psychiatrists, and social workers. We must rely on the psychiatrist to get the relevant facts, but these will be of little value unless prosecutors and judges are willing to be guided by them. In most states, the present use of psychiatrists is a travesty of both medical science and justice. The prosecutor or counsel for the defense usually fights against the facts rather than accepts them as a basis for a scientific disposition of the case.[44]

Of course, psychiatrists seldom agree completely in diagnosis. This lack of agreement, however, is no reflection on the profession. The core of psychiatry and mental hygiene is certainly sound and is something of which medicine and social science may alike be proud. No other socio-medical movement of our times holds so much promise for the relief of human suffering and for the curative control of social ills.

The partial disrepute into which psychiatry has fallen in connection with criminology has been due exclusively to the handicaps imposed on it by courtroom procedure and rules of evidence. Science can function respectably only when it is devoted to the cause of establishing truth, whereas criminal lawyers in the courtroom are frequently unable to win their case unless they obscure the truth.

---

[44] See Frederic Wertham, *The Show of Violence*, Doubleday, New York, 1949.

Psychiatrists can present their material in the courtroom only in answers to questions put to them by the attorneys, which often means that they cannot present their reports completely or coherently.

As Judge Gerald F. Flood, of Philadelphia, former president of the Pennsylvania Prison Society, aptly points out in *The Prison Journal* (January 1950), "We shall be better off when the psychiatrist is never called by the Commonwealth or the defense as a witness, and when he is considered as an assistant to the judge, or the sentencing authority—, when his diagnosis is based always upon thorough examination, when it is treated frankly as tentative, and when he will follow the convict through his entire period of imprisonment, probation and parole."

In the state of Massachusetts the psychiatrist need not debase himself or his profession. There his profession has been dignified in criminal cases through the Briggs Law, passed in 1921. This law provides that when a person is indicted for a capital offense, or is known to have been indicted for any other offense more than once in the past, or to have been previously convicted of a felony, notice shall be given to the Department of Mental Diseases, which shall then be called upon to examine the person to determine his mental status. The person's mental status, of course, may affect his criminal responsibility. The Department then files a report to the clerk of court in which the trial is to be held. The examination must be made by two psychiatrists appointed for the purpose by the Department of Mental Diseases. If the defendant is found to be suffering from some mental disorder or pathological mental state, the report is read to court and jury and the court merely orders a verdict of "not guilty by reason of insanity." Then, instead of a prison term, the defendant is sent to a mental hospital for treatment. Few states match the Massachusetts law. California and Indiana make it mandatory for the court to appoint experts in all cases where the issue of insanity is pleaded. Similar laws have been found to be unconstitutional in other states. We are thus a long way in this country from a practical and scientific disposition of delinquents who manifest pathological mental conditions.

But, to quote Dr. Wertham, if we wish to prevent sex crimes we must do more than improve our criminal procedure against those who have already become confirmed sex criminals, important as this is. We must "first correct and improve the circumstances under which they grow up." [45] We shall have more to say on this point in our discussion of the constitutionally inferior psychopath.[46]

b. The Female Sex Offender

In approaching the problem of sexual delinquency among girls and young women, it is imperative that we attempt to be objective. Our purpose in this book is not to moralize on delinquent behavior but rather to try to understand it. Only by understanding can an honest program of treatment be developed. We must state at the outset that sexual conflict is experienced by practically every human being at one time or another. On the one hand, he, or she, feels at an early age, and certainly at puberty, the paradoxical joys and frustrations of the sexual hunger; on the other, the restraints and taboos of the mores of a particular culture. Steering a middle course so that a rich, normal, and satisfying sexual unfolding may result without violating the mores is indeed a difficult task. Since the female is the passive member of the species, she is constantly aware of the aggressiveness of her male opposite. She learns that despite her passivity she must develop techniques of coquetry in order to play the part nature intended for her with as much adroitness as she is capable of. It is obvious that the girl who learns to develop and exploit her feminine charms to the fullest within the framework of a sensible interpretation of the mores will probably be successful sexually, at least until marriage. Those girls who, for one reason or another, exercise a degree of sexual laxity may find themselves in trouble, which, however, may be offset by a chance happy marriage. But thousands of girls, either through pregnancy or venereal infection, may run afoul of the law. It is this group that we are considering in this section.

Most of the girls apprehended by police officers on the streets of our large cities, and those who appear before juvenile and adolescent courts, and also those who end up in our reform schools are sexual problems. Consequently, the female sexual delinquent has been the object of much study by authorities of delinquent behavior.

Starting with the classic work of W. I. Thomas, *The Unadjusted Girl*,[47] we find that most of the books and articles dealing with the

---

[45] *Ibid.*, p. 853.
[46] See pp. 563–565.
[47] Little, Brown, Boston, 1923.

delinquent girl emphasize the sexual aspect. It is from this group of maladjusted girls that most of our prostitutes, whether they ply their trade in brothels or belong to the upper class of "kept women," are drawn. We shall defer our discussion of prostitution until later. Here we are interested in the problem of the sexual laxity of young girls and its relationship to delinquency.

One of the most interesting studies of sexual female delinquents is that by the Goldbergs,[48] which dealt with a group of 1,400 girls who had experienced some serious difficulty in their sexual life. The girls ranged in age from four to sixteen; 516, the largest number of any one age, were fifteen years old. Most of the girls were somewhat retarded mentally, although the vast majority of them had passed or were in the sixth grade. Sixteen of the 1,400 girls had had their first sex experience as early as the sixth year; 332, or 29.4 per cent, were fifteen before their first experience. A wide variety of males had been responsible for the first experiences; "stranger pickups" accounted for 290, or 26.3 per cent, of the cases, whereas "friend acquaintances" accounted for 484, or 43.8 per cent. Other males involved in illicit relationships were neighbors, 59; boarders, 42; fathers, 36; stepfathers, 26; peddlers, 14; mother's friends, 13; janitors, 10.

Places where clandestine sexual acts took place are listed as follows: furnished rooms, 256, or 24.2 per cent; men's homes, 213, or 20.1 per cent; girls' homes, 194, or 18.3 per cent; hotels, 23; motion picture theaters, 15; back roads and alleys, 9; and houses of prostitution, 4.

Certainly no one cause can be attributed to the sexual delinquency of the young girl. Unwholesome home life with apathetic parents may account for much of it. Faulty sex education may also be a primary cause. The eternal pursuit of sexual gratification, with an attendant lack of moral control resulting from faulty development of inhibitions, is certainly at the basis of most sexual laxity. This is particularly true of girls with retarded mentality who find school boring and frustrating.

A study made by Mary Louise Webb [49] showed that the sexual

---

[48] Jacob A. and Rosamond W. Goldberg, *Girls on City Streets*, Foundation Books, New York, 1940.

[49] "Delinquency in the Making: Patterns in the Development of Girl Sex Delinquency in the City of Seattle," *Journal of Social Hygiene*, 1943, pp. 502–510.

delinquent pattern started with feelings of shame or dissatisfaction about the home which led to open rebellion or chronic truancy. The author further showed that delinquent habits often began during periods of truancy; first by harmless trips downtown, always with some other maladjusted girl; later, by attending movies or all-night lunchrooms and dance halls; and finally by frequenting taprooms and cheap hotels. This is probably the conventional pattern. Street-walking, easy pick-ups with strange boys or men, and a strong desire for excitement or petting thrills complete the picture of wayward adolescent girls.

The policewomen in our larger cities spend much of their time checking the activities of minor girls and their male companions. Their task is often difficult, since so many of the girls, despite their youthful appearances, are no longer minors. Little can be done if the girls involved are over twenty-one. But many young girls are accompanied to the movies by older boys or men so that the police-woman finds plenty to do to check possible sexual exploitation.

Aside from the supervision of movies, taprooms, and soft-drink hangouts, and the prevention of exploitation of young girls by older men, the detection and apprehension of runaway girls present another problem that calls for a high degree of alertness on the part of the policewoman. Many of these runaway girls picked up on the city's streets are infected and thus a prophylaxis is an immediate necessity.

The adolescent female sexual offender presents a real challenge to the resources of the community. A more meaningful school curriculum for the intellectually dull girl who develops physically more quickly than her male contemporary would obviously be helpful. The fourteen-to-sixteen-year-old girl has little interests in the fourteen-to-sixteen-year-old boy who attends classes with her. If she is retarded mentally, her mind wanders to thoughts of taprooms, dance halls, and company with older men, so that her studies have little meaning for her.

The young pregnant girl is another serious problem. Many of these girls are sent to reform schools. Regardless of what is done in solving the problems of the unmarried mother and illegitimacy, it becomes increasingly serious when the girl is sentenced to a correctional institution. Hundreds of girls and women enter girls' reform schools and reformatories each year and have their babies while under institutional sentence. There are mothers with their babies in jails and detention quarters in many towns and cities of this country.

Little publicity is given to this problem, but it is obvious that the situation is shocking. In one of the very few studies of this question, by Eugene Zemans and Robert J. Cole, we find the following facts: In 1947 there were 364 babies born in 37 institutions, 15 girls' reform schools, 14 women's reformatories, and 8 prisons. It was found that in some states laws do not permit their institutions to take pregnant girls, and other institutions do not have facilities to care for prenatal and postnatal mothers. Of the total of the 364 babies, 148 were born in hospitals of eight correctional schools and the remainder in county, state, or municipal hospitals outside the institution. The term "illegitimate" is stamped on the birth certificates of such babies in Iowa, Minnesota, New Jersey, Ohio, and West Virginia if the mother is not married. Twelve other states reported that the word is not stamped on the certificate. In Illinois, Montana, and New Mexico the words "father's name unknown" are written on the certificate, and in Wisconsin the answer to the question "Is mother married?" is entered.

The newborn babies are "disposed of" in a variety of ways. Relatives are permitted first claim if they wish the babies. If not, state and county welfare departments, orphanages, or other agencies or institutions are pressed into service to handle the problem. Zemans and Cole asked the superintendents of the female institutions two significant questions: "Should every prospective inmate mother be given the right to bear her child outside the institution?" and "Should the baby be separated from its mother at birth, remain with the mother only during her stay in the hospital, or remain with the mother in the institution up to two years, assuming the mother is competent and the institution has proper facilities?"

There was unanimous agreement that girls should have the right to bear their children outside the institution. There was little agreement regarding the second question. Some thought the child should be separated from the mother after the period of hospitalization; others felt provision should be made for the child to remain with the mother indefinitely or to be returned to her upon release.

This study points up several phases of the problem of the female sexual offender who is sent to the reform school or prison. The stigma of being born in a prison is tragic and to have "illegitimate"

Mothers, with their children, exercising at Tothill Fields Prison, England (from an old print).

placed on the birth certificate is adding insult to injury. The study makes the following recommendation: "This entire matter should be examined on a state-wide basis in order to determine whether or not this problem, particularly as it relates to female juvenile delinquents, is concerned, is adequately and humanely met on a case to case basis." [50]

c. Prostitution as a Social Problem

We are concerned here with prostitution only because its members are recruited from the ranks of adolescent girls—the juvenile female sex offender. Since prostitution, like poverty, is one of our oldest problems and one that baffles solution, no discussion of juvenile delinquency can avoid the subject. Moreover, much misinformation is abroad concerning this profession.

The moral crusade that swept the country after 1912 attempted to stamp out the licensed houses of ill-fame, as they were so frequently called. As a result, the entire institution became clandestine. Few cities today tolerate licensed, segregated districts. Since the proprietors and "madames" who operate houses must move in a shady realm, they tend to be controlled by syndicates of racketeers who are affiliated with the political organization in power in our various municipalities.

Students of the problem are authority for stating that the old house of ill-fame operated by a "madame" is rapidly passing from the American scene. The problem of prostitution nowadays involves street-walkers, female "lone wolves," and the more sophisticated "call girls."

Some observers believe that the frenzied crusade to stamp out licensed districts did far more harm than good and actually increased the social dangers of prostitution. In the early days there may have been only sporadic medical supervision, but today there is practically none. We find scattered houses all over a city or single women plying their trade. The increase in the congestion of cities made prostitution easier to hide and the growing popularity of the automobile and the easy accessibility of the public taxi put sexual vice on wheels.

---

[50] Eugene Zemans and Robert J. Cole, "Prison Babies," in *The Mother*, American Committee on Maternal Welfare, Vol. X, No. 1, October 1948 (quotation on p. 5).

The attempt to put down interstate traffic in prostitutes through the Mann Act of 1910—frequently called the white-slave act—accomplished little in controlling the evil. In fact, it turned out to be one of the largest assets of the modern blackmail racket. This Federal act was passed in an attempt to stamp out the ruthless activities of procurers or "pimps" who, in the words of the moralist, "sell a girl into a life of shame." During the lush days of immigration from Europe, many girls were enticed and even kidnaped into prostitution and held without a knowledge of English, but relatively few girls enter prostitution under duress.[51]

The reasons why girls enter the profession are numerous, but the economic motive leads. However, in most cases economic pressure does not take the form of necessity. Many prostitutes, not of the "kept woman" variety, come from the domestic servant class. They become bored with the drab life they lead and with the low wages and lack of economic security. Girls employed in the cheaper stores also feel the attraction of easy money in prostitution.

There are also many "call girls" who cater to hotel guests but who, for regular employment, work in many of the swankier women's shops of our large cities. These girls are sophisticated and alluring and sell their services high.

A considerable number of girls become prostitutes as a result of their inability to resolve infantile sexual urges. This point of view has been admirably developed by the British psychiatrist, Dr. Edward Glover.[52] It is his contention that many prostitutes are psychologically and sexually insecure—that is, insecure in love—and possess an unconscious urge to obtain revenge for neglect, and thus turn to prostitution to find what to them is the best method of meeting their personal desires. They voluntarily choose this life and rarely leave it.

Many young girls, raised in slum areas or even in fashionable apartment houses where an informal prostitution is frequently practiced before their eyes at an early age, naturally turn to the profession through pathological imitation. Generalizing, we may say that van-

---

[51] It is of interest to note that as early as 1882, Charles Loring Brace scotched this contention by stating: "Public women of this kind are not generally, as is supposed, the victims of deception and wrong by men." *Gesta Christi*, 1882, p. 317.

[52] "The Psycho-Pathology of Prostitution," *Institute for the Scientific Treatment of Delinquency*, London, 1945.

ity, moral or sexual weakness, adversity, and, to a degree, romance, together with some sexual perversity, are the main reasons for prostitution.

But how can young girls be discouraged from entering this sordid profession? Certainly sex education in the schools would be helpful.[53] Knowledge concerning syphilis and gonorrhea as well as pregnancy should be widely diffused, without moralizing. Counseling services in the schools should be expanded and guidance programs for marginal girls should be strengthened. Sympathetic and understanding policewomen in the larger cities should give this phase of their program high priority.

But what we need most is a reorientation of attitudes concerning prostitution. In many states today it is considered a crime rather than a social problem. It is absurd to round up street-walkers or raid houses of assignation, arrest the girls, and send them away for treatment unless there is some object other than to penalize them.

A superintendent of a reformatory for women, to which most of the inmates had been sent because of prostitution, told one of the writers a few years ago that the program he had been pursuing in his institution merely "cleaned up the prostitutes, taught them how to make up and fix their hair in the latest style, and thus prepared them for a higher class clientele upon release." Cynical though this attitude may be, it is probably fairly common. What does the prostitute who has been sent to a reformatory for plying her trade have to look forward to upon release? She is taught housework, sewing or needlework, laundering, or some other such activity. She receives medical treatment if she needs it. Then she is paroled, returned to the city she came from, and is expected to be contented with a housemaid's job, where she usually receives in a week what she formerly received in one night's work at her trade.

We do not intend here to offer a solution to the institution of prostitution. We are convinced, however, that prostitution should not be considered a penal problem. Girls arrested should be given medical treatment if they are infected; then they should be thor-

---

[53] In an article urging sex education, Ray H. Everett, secretary of the Social Hygiene Society of the District of Columbia, reviews the failure throughout the world to regulate prostitution. "Can We Regulate Prostitution?," *Federal Probation*, Vol. XI, October–December 1947, pp. 39 ff.

oughly questioned and investigated by psychiatrists and social case workers. Most of these girls, if apprehended early enough, may be saved from the worst ravages of the profession. Since the prognosis in most cases is none too bright, it is particularly important to develop preventive programs in the schools and also to appoint trained women with police powers to cope with the wide sexual irregularity current in every community.

Most of the younger girls who are sent to our state reform schools are there for sexual indiscretions, but these cases could be treated much more effectively in the homes and neighborhoods. Few, if any, girls' schools of this type do more than segregate the girls during the most explosive period of their lives and teach them domestic arts. Practically no psychiatric therapy or social case work is provided as an integral part of the program, except in extreme cases. The money spent by the state in keeping up reformatories and reform schools for prostitutes and sexually irregular girls might well be spent on better counseling services in schools and on diagnostic depots with psychiatrists and social workers. Through such a program girls could be given individualized guidance and treatment.

A daring experimental approach to the problem of prostitution has been made in Baltimore, Maryland, by the Protective Service Division of the city's Department of Welfare and by the Rapid Treatment Center. Although these two agencies use fundamentally the same case-work approach, they differ widely in other respects. At the Protective Service Division, case work is supported by the authority of court action in the form of probation for one year, whereas at the Rapid Treatment Center the authority resides only in the worker herself, who has but two interviews in nine days in which to stimulate and lay a foundation for change in the client's behavior and attitudes. The main function of the Rapid Treatment Center is to give medical treatment for syphilis.

Results have proved that many prostitutes actually want to change and can change their life patterns when they are offered understanding help in a setting in which they are treated like human beings and are shown some trust. In such a setting some girls are able to nurture the positive self that has been denied them in all their thoughts and actions.[54]

[54] For an analysis of this approach, see Rosa Wessel, editor, *A Case Work Approach to Sex Delinquents,* Pennsylvania School of Social Work, Philadel-

6. THE PSYCHOPATHIC PERSONALITY

Current literature is full of descriptions of a type of behavior, primarily among young people, that cannot be explained along conventional lines. We have already alluded to the *constitutionally psychopathic inferior* type, labeled C.P.I. for short. Reports of this criminal behavior are appearing in the newspapers and popular journals as well as in the professional journals. Whenever a particularly brutal murder is committed, especially by a juvenile or young adult, popular discussion reverts to the C.P.I. or criminal psychopath.

Heated discussion and conflicting opinions have revolved about this peculiar breed for some time. Psychiatrists are, as a rule, cautious men, and many refuse to acknowledge the C.P.I. or the psychotic personality as a distinct clinical type. Yet this entity has been identified for a long time by different scientific names. The type was identified as early as 1835 by J. C. Prichard, who called it *moral insanity*. By 1891, J. A. L. Koch, a German psychiatrist, gave this type the name *psychopathic personality*.[55] Adolf Meyer and Emil Kraepelin both considered persons manifesting certain behavior patterns as belonging to a specific group apart from those suffering from mental disturbances then known to the psychiatrist.

In the recent past, considerable research has been conducted on the psychopathic personality. However, it is not our purpose here to review the results of this research or to enter into the conflict that persists even at present among psychiatrists concerning this dangerous type of personality. The many articles and books on the subject may prove valuable to the reader.[56] A perusal of these works shows

---

phia, 1947. See also Florine J. Ellis, "Social Treatment of the Sex Delinquent," *Yearbook*, N.P.P.A., 1946, pp. 139–153. Additional articles are Mazie F. Rappaport, "A Social Agency Helps the Prostitute on Probation," *Yearbook*, N.P.P.A., 1945, pp. 124–135; and Evelyn C. Hyman, "Holding the Promiscuous Girl Accountable for Her Behavior," *ibid.*, 1948, pp. 190–201.

[55] See Hervey Cleckley, *The Mask of Sanity*, C. N. Mosby Co., St. Louis, 1941, p. 176.

[56] A symposium, "The Psychopathic Individual" (1924), presents the views of such authorities as William A. White, Loren B. T. Johnson, S. A. Silk, Lucile Dooley, and Ben Karpman. Other early works are Ben Karpman, *The Problem of Psychopathies*, State Hospital Quarterly, 1929; Eugen Kahn, *Psychopathic Personalities*, Yale University Press, New Haven, 1931; Arthur P. Noyes, *Modern Clinical Psychiatry*, Saunders, Philadelphia, 1935; and D. K. Henderson, *Psychopathic States*, Norton, New York, 1939.

the state of confusion and caution existing in the psychiatric world regarding the psychopathic personality.

Dr. Ben Karpman is particularly vocal in cautioning against glibness, not only by laymen but by psychiatrists as well, in labeling various types of emotional behavior psychopathic. He maintains that in some 25,000 consecutive cases he studied at St. Elizabeth's Hospital in Washington, only 250 to 275 could be diagnosed as psychopathic personality without psychosis; and of this group, he contends, eighty-five to ninety per cent were of the "spurious or psychopathoid" type. Here is what Dr. Karpman says about the confused situation regarding this clinical entity: "It is perhaps more likely that in studying 100 consecutive cases diagnosed psychopathic personality, what we get is not an understanding of the patient, but a study of the mind of a psychiatrist, that is, what he means when he makes a diagnosis. . . . In his view, if he [the patient] doesn't quite play ball with others . . . if he spends money too freely, borrowing from others without repaying, indulges in behavior that runs counter to the accepted social code, then he is promptly labeled psychopathic." [57]

Although we may be accused of oversimplification, we wish to set down a few statements concerning this potentially dangerous type of personality. The term psychopath has been glibly used both by experts and laymen alike. Although it has been used in the past as a catch-all for persons suffering from emotional states that at first glance baffle specific classification, certain symptomatic patterns of behavior seem to be emerging.

First, considerable agreement exists among authorities that many psychopaths are better than average in intelligence and in some instances superior. There is agreement, also, that psychopaths are almost completely amoral, impulsive, and with few if any inhibitions.

Second, the psychopathic personality may be found in every walk of life, especially in the professions: in business, in academic positions, in medicine, in politics, and even in psychiatry itself.[58] These, of course, represent adult cases, although they were obviously undetected as possessing dangerous potentialities in childhood.

[57] "Psychopathy as a Form of Social Parasitism—A Comparative Biological Study," *Journal of Clinical Psychopathology*, Vol. X, No. 2, April 1949, pp. 171–172.

[58] Cleckley, *op. cit.*, Chapter XIX, "The Psychopath as Psychiatrist."

Third, thousands of these persons are given free rein in society either because they have not been detected or because our laws make no provision for their commitment or segregation by psychiatrists, hospitals, or courts. Moreover, many show no signs of psychosis and are thus regarded as sane.

Fourth, the psychopath is not always psychotic, nor does he ordinarily suffer from any distortion of reality—no hallucinations, for example—nor is he necessarily neurotic, although he may manifest neurotic or hysterical symptoms. As a rule he "acts out" rather than forms neurotic symptoms; such acting out usually causes unhappiness for those about him, but this unhappiness causes him little or no guilt feelings or remorse. His behavior usually leaves a pathetic trail of misery, unhappiness, and concern among his closest friends and acquaintances, but he remains blithely oblivious.

The question of what causes persons to be afflicted with this emotional pattern is debatable. Some, but not all, psychiatrists are certain that there are accompanying physical anomalies or stigmata in their makeup. Nor is there agreement concerning the parts played by heredity and environment. The literature is full of claims and counterclaims on these two points and need not concern us here. (See Appendix, Case No. 4, pp. 714–716.)

These persons usually manifest their asocial and egocentric tendencies in childhood or early youth, and, although they develop physically or intellectually, a specific form of emotional immaturity persists. Dr. M. J. Pescor, former warden and chief medical officer at the Medical Center for Federal Prisoners, Springfield, Missouri, has the following to say about causation:

> At one time [psychopathic behavior] was considered a hereditary or constitutional condition representing a type of inferiority; hence the name "constitutional psychopathic inferior" was adopted. At the present time the most popular theory is that the psychopath is the product of a poor home environment in which parental rejection plays a major role. . . . However, there is an accumulation of evidence showing that some psychopathic behavior, at least, can be explained on the basis of brain injury, infection, and other organic factors.[59]

In a review of Robert Lindner's *Rebel Without a Cause*,[60] in which the author tells the story of a psychopath and his subsequent

---

[59] "Abnormal Personality Types among Offenders," *Federal Probation*, Vol. XII, June 1948, pp. 3–8.
[60] Grune & Stratton, New York, 1944.

"cure" by a technique involving hypnosis, we find these words regarding causation: "It has been known for a long time that the development of criminal psychopathy is based on important fundamental early defects in identification and early faulty conditioning to authority, and to unresolved oedipus situations." [61]

Many classifications of the psychopathic personality have been made on the basis of symptomatic behavior. Some of these classifications cross over into other clinical entities, such as the psychoses and the psychoneuroses. Some eminent students of the type list ten or more classes; others narrow them down to three. Dr. Pescor lists three: (1) those with pathologic sexuality, a group including various sexual perverts and homosexuals; (2) those with pathologic emotionality, a motley assortment of abnormal individuals who do not fall conveniently into the psychotic or psychoneurotic classification; and (3) those with asocial or amoral trends, who are the "psychopaths proper" and may be found in our prisons and correctional institutions.[62]

Regardless of whether heredity or environment plays the more important role in the etiology of criminal psychopathy, or whether three or more types are distinguishable, we are concerned here with the fact that many of these persons commit vicious crimes while they are still children.

Some young killers may be definitely psychopathic. But we must be careful not to generalize. Merely because they cannot be adjudged insane does not mean that they should be executed or imprisoned. Many psychopathic personalities are in our prisons and reform schools, simply because our legal machinery has thus far done nothing to identify this group. Courts can do nothing more than send them to prison for long terms.

This type presents two serious problems to society. The first is the problem of early detection. Even if a child-guidance clinic diagnoses a child or adolescent as a psychopathic personality, no provision is made for his segregation from society. Nor is the clinic compelled to advise school authorities of the diagnosis. In our great desire to protect the child as well as his distraught parents, society

---

[61] S. Bernard Wortis, in *Journal of American Psychiatry*, Vol. 101, 1944–1945, p. 841. Dr. Wortis is connected with Bellevue Hospital in New York City.

[62] *Op. cit.*, p. 7.

is left vulnerable against a potential danger at any time during the natural life of such a person. A physician who examines a client and finds him suffering from leprosy or from some other highly contagious (dangerous) disease must notify the authorities, who will promptly isolate and segregate the menace. But the social or moral "leper" is diagnosed by a psychiatrist or a clinic with no police power to demand that he be segregated.

The other problem concerns what is to be done after the psychopath has committed a violent crime—or any crime, for that matter. Again no specialized institution or treatment is available. As we stated above, upon conviction the culprit is sent to prison or is executed. Yet he is not responsible for his behavior or his affliction.

Our laws must be tightened in order to cope with this situation. Juvenile courts should be given authority to handle all cases of children and youth up to some specific age, either eighteen or twenty-one. Thus these young killers, regardless of their symptoms, would be taken from the criminal court and disposed of in the more humane and protective atmosphere we have provided for juveniles.[63] Our smaller counties should be provided with adequate funds to develop an efficient juvenile court with all the services necessary for adequate diagnosis. And, without further delay, specialized institutions should be created to deal with psychopaths. Whether these persons are curable or not need not concern us here.[64] So long as there is hope, society must try to effect a cure. But no person thus diagnosed should ever be permitted to return to a normal or free society until a cure is effected.

Whether the psychopath can be cured or not, segregation in some type of institution where he can be studied over a long period of time would permit those in the fields of research and treatment to learn more about this ailment. Some work along this line has been done by the Federal prisons through the United States Public Health

---

[63] See Chapter IX, pp. 304–305.

[64] It is agreed that the psychopath presents a poor prognosis. Dr. Pescor states, however, on the basis of F.B.I. reports, that 63 per cent of those who had been out of the Medical Center at Springfield, Missouri, for three to five years were still out of trouble. See Hulsey Cason and M. J. Pescor, "A Statistical Study of 500 Psychopathic Prisoners," Public Health Reports Vol. 61, No. 16, April 19, 1946, pp. 557–574. Pescor thinks the aging process has much to do with rehabilitation.

Service. At the Northeastern Penitentiary at Lewisburg, Pennsylvania, work was carried on for a short duration, although the psychopaths mingled with the general prison population. At the Chillicothe, Ohio, Reformatory a form of treatment was given to a small group of habitual offenders who were taken from the general prison population and subjected to an exaggerated form of regimentation for a prolonged period of time. It was assumed that this form of "over-discipline" would develop a capacity to adjust to the less regimented free society.[65]

Various forms of group therapy with self-analysis have been sponsored by psychiatrists in penitentiaries and reformatories. Thus far no final answers have been developed concerning this breed of sick personality. But society must be protected in some way. Careful early diagnosis is important, but more significant is an attempt to make such information available to all who should be permitted to know. Certainly some answer must be found that will aid in cutting off at the source potentially dangerous individuals who may kill violently and without warning.

7. THE DEFECTIVE DELINQUENT

The defective delinquent has long been recognized by penologists and administrators, but only within recent years have special institutions been set apart for their reception and possible treatment. Even now only a few states have specialized establishments to care for troublesome mentally retarded delinquents: New York, at Napanoch and Woodbourne; Pennsylvania, at Huntingdon; and Massachusetts, at the Bridgewater State Farm. In all other states, and even in those mentioned above, many defective delinquents and criminals may be found in reform schools and adult prisons.

No definition of a defective delinquent will satisfy everyone who works with this group. For instance, a mentally retarded young offender who, by accident or peculiar force of circumstances, gets

---

[65] For a description of this form of therapy, see Edward M. Glaser and Daniel D. Chiles, "An Experiment in the Treatment of Youthful Habitual Offenders at the Federal Reformatory, Chillicothe, Ohio," *Journal of Clinical Psychopathology*, Vol. 9, No. 3, July 1948, pp. 376–425. This article is significant and is well worth serious study. For a review of the various therapies that have been applied to psychopaths, see Robert M. Lindner, "Therapy," in *Encyclopedia of Criminology*, Philosophical Library, New York, 1949, pp. 490–497.

into trouble with the law may not be labeled a defective delinquent. On the other hand, there are those who may not commit a serious offense, but who possess all the attributes of a potentially dangerous criminal. Dr. Karl Birnbaum defines the defective delinquent as an individual "who, due to inherent (innate, constitutional) defects of the psychic functions shows criminal tendencies requiring special training in special institutions." [66]

Since institutions for this type of offender are so few, we shall describe the work being done in the Pennsylvania Institution for Defective Delinquents at Huntingdon. The program of this institution stems from a resolution adopted by the American Prison Association and an act passed by the Legislature of Pennsylvania. The resolution reads as follows:

> The defective delinquent is an offender, who, because of mental subnormality at times coupled with mental instability, is not amenable to the ordinary custody and training of the average correctional institution and whose presence therein is detrimental to both the type of individual herein described and to the proper development of the methods of rehabilitation of other groups of delinquents. Further, the defective delinquent because of his limited intelligence and suggestibility requires prolonged and careful training, preferably in a special institution to develop habits of industry and obedience.[67]

The basic assumption of the philosophy of the Huntingdon institution is that this type of offender is "capable of profiting from a rehabilitative program aimed at the development of habits of industry and obedience" provided enough time is afforded and the program is geared to the individual. The process is painfully slow but not hopeless. Each inmate is subjected to planned progression from closely supervised activity wherein little self-responsibility and direction are entailed, to activity with a minimum of supervision and direction wherein all objectives are capable of expression. The inmate moves along this program in accordance with demonstrated proficiency and readiness for increased responsibility. Traditional objectives are stressed, because the inmates have never learned them in free society. These objectives include formation of regular habits

---

[66] *Thirty-second Annual Report of the Municipal Court of Philadelphia,* 1945, p. 405.

[67] *Fifty-sixth Annual Congress of the American Prison Association,* 1926.

of work, creation of a spirit of cooperation in work and play, and training in specific situations in habits of self-reliance, dependability, honesty, and trustworthiness.

When the inmate is received from the courts he passes through the diagnostic clinic and is given the usual tests. After a thirty-day interval, during which the inmate is in quarantine, he is absorbed into the population and begins the program developed through the clinic's findings and recommendations. At intervals thereafter he is reclassified by the clinic staff, which is guided by reports on the inmate's progress.

Classification includes the following aspects: custody, guidance, housing, school and work assignments, discipline, physical and mental health, the determination of date for parole, and planning for adjustment.

The time element in an institution for defective delinquents is naturally very important. All inmates are sent by the court on an indeterminate basis. The establishment therefore has the grave responsibility of preparing the inmate for release to society. Since the defective delinquent learns slowly, the time spent in the institution varies with the capacity to learn and absorb the various elements and phases of the program. Length of time spent by inmates at Huntingdon ranges from 20 to 120 months. In one year the average was 51 months.

The average intelligence of the inmates for the biennium, June 1, 1946 to May 31, 1948, based on the Wechsler-Bellevue Test, was 66 (Standard Deviation, 11.7); the chronological age at admission was 18.8. The I.Q. range was 16 to 110, and the chronological age range was from 15 to 49. Of the 367 delinquents received at Huntingdon during this period, 78.7 per cent ranged between 15 and 20 years of age upon admission.

It may be seen from the above data that the institution does not have a very hopeful group with which to work. Of 184 cases entering the institution and analyzed by the classification clinic between June 1, 1947, and May 31, 1948, we find 15 inmates amenable to training with sufficient capacity; 132 amenable but below average competency; 16 resistant to program; 18 "too overly dependent" to use training helpfully; 3 physically handicapped.

In addition to trade training, the following phases of the program are vitally important in this type of institution: 1. Personal hygiene and grooming. (It is apparent that most boys are badly in need of instruction in proper methods of bathing and general principles of personal cleanliness, such as care of hair, teeth, hands, and so forth.) 2. Proper methods of eating. (Quite frequently a defective will devour food in a slovenly, crude manner.) 3. Improved appearance through care of clothing and proper methods of dressing. (A majority of defectives are totally unaware of the importance of personal appearance. Sewing on buttons, making slight mends, handling clothing properly, shining shoes, and so forth, are important.) 4. Methods of keeping clean and tidy quarters. 5. Attempts to improve posture through military drill and exercise. 6. General rules of deportment, good manners, and interpretation of institution rules.

Instruction is given in the traditional trades. Some of the brighter boys can profit by skilled trade training, but most of them must be taught maintenance tasks and semi-skilled activities.

Release from an institution for defective delinquents sounds incongruous, yet society has not yet been ready to adopt a policy of segregating for life those persons who, by reason of defective mentality or other incapacity, cannot live in a free society without getting into trouble. Until the time comes when an indeterminate sentence is actually indeterminate, institutional administrators must release those who demonstrate good work habits and progress in their training program and who can submit a post-institutional plan that has meaning. Here is the procedure followed at Huntingdon incidental to release:

> The training program aims to return those individuals to their homes who can and do learn enough to behave properly and work regularly under continuing supervision in free society.
>
> Readiness for parole is determined by careful study and observation of the progress shown by each individual member of the population. The individual has this review of his institutional record at stated intervals. The classification clinic, acting for the Board of Trustees, conducts these personal interviews and evaluates the progress made.
>
> When the parole factors . . . so warrant, the Board initiates parole planning (job, sponsor, and home). Such planning is carried on in co-operation with the Court probation officers. When a satisfactory plan is evolved, the Board originates specific recommendations for release, forwarding such recommendations (*via* the Department of Welfare) to the Court of original commitment for final disposition. The

final decision to release for another community test is always the exclusive authority of the Court of proper jurisdiction.[68]

It may be seen from the above that the administration of the school does not pass on release or parole unaided. The committing court shares in this responsibility. The Huntingdon institution reports that there are few escapes or attempted escapes from the school. Custody is, of course, important. Many boys are capable of accepting minimum custody but others must be under strict surveillance at all times.

No institution of this type can ever hope to improve the mentality of the defective delinquent. But much improvement in developing good work and personal habits can be made with most of those sent to this type of school. One advantage of a specialized institution is that there are few of the disrupting influences that constantly occur in a prison or reform school that is obliged to mix normally intelligent boys with the defective types. Another advantage is that the program can be geared to low intelligence. Patience, understanding, and time seem to be the salient features of a program for defective delinquents. We mentioned earlier that older defective types should not be mingled with the younger boys. Yet this anomalous situation exists at the Huntingdon school. Some inmates there, for instance, are close to fifty years of age. Many of these men are unimprovable and tend to disrupt the smooth operation of the program for the boys. They should be removed and sent elsewhere—but where, no one seems to know.

The proof of the efficacy of treatment is adjustment to society upon release. Can defective delinquents keep out of trouble if they are paroled from an institution?

The staff at Huntingdon has prepared a study of releases and recidivism covering the three-year interval from June 1, 1945, to May 31, 1948. Of the 398 individuals released (paroled) from the institution, 72, or 18.1 per cent, were repeaters, judged by offenses reported either by the Pennsylvania State Police Bureau of Criminal Identification or by the Federal Bureau of Investigation. These sources were used because the Huntingdon staff is not always advised by the county courts' supervisory agencies of successful termination of paroles or of further involvements of parolees. A recidivist in this

---

[68] Mimeographed material supplied by Superintendent John D. Pennington and chief psychologist, Leonard John Mack, February 1949.

study is defined as a person sentenced to any penal institution or jail for a period in excess of three months. Over the three-year period of the study, the average length of time out of the institution was 8.3 months before the repeater committed his first new offense.

What was the intelligence of those who relapsed to crime? Of the 398 inmates released on parole, 106 had an I.Q. of less than 60. Of this number, 12, or 11.3 per cent, were recidivists, as compared with the average over-all rate of 18.1 per cent. Below an I.Q. of 70 were 238 individuals, of whom 32, or 13.4 per cent, were recidivists. Of an I.Q. of 70 or better, 160 were released. Of this upper intelligence group, 40, or 25 per cent, were repeaters. In other words, the higher the intelligence rate the higher the rate of recidivism, or conversely, the lower the I.Q. the better the adjustment to community living seems to be. The following table shows these data.

Recidivism by Intelligence Groupings

	30–39	40–49	50–59	60–69	70–79	80+	Total	Average
Releases by I.Q.	1	28	77	132	145	15	398	
Recidivists by I.Q.	0	4	8	20	35	5	72	
Percentage of Recidivists by I.Q. in relation to Releases by I.Q.	0	14.3	10.4	15.2	24.1	33.3		18.1

On the basis of this short-term study, the management of the Huntingdon institution has come to the conclusion "that the very defective, after long and intensive disciplinary and vocational training, and with very careful screening, can be safely and successfully returned to the community." [69]

Lack of adequate data and shortness of elapsed time make impossible any conclusions on the training of defective delinquents or on their ability to adjust to a free society upon release. Since so few states have specialized institutions for this type of delinquent, we can only wait for more studies to see what intensive training furnished in these establishments can do for society. If those who fail to respond to close supervision and training can be segregated for life, society will be less alarmed by the delinquency of this troublesome group.[70]

---

[69] *Ibid.*

[70] See the article on the defective delinquent by Samuel B. Kutash in *Encyclopedia of Criminology*, Philosophical Library, New York, 1949, pp. 124–127.

Part III

COMMUNITY RESPONSIBILITY

Chapter XV

PREVENTIVE SERVICES

1. INTRODUCTORY STATEMENT

A DISCUSSION of preventive services must be somewhat selective, since so many agencies, movements, and concepts of social action are doing yeoman service in the field. We have mentioned the need of "all out" action on all fronts. We cannot hope to prevent delinquency or to cope with its inevitable merging into serious crime unless community action is thoroughgoing and courageous. Frequent appraisal of all phases of preventive work is necessary in order to stave off the dry rot of inertia and complacency. Every type of sustained social action dedicated to preventing delinquency should be examined periodically in an objective way by a board of experts, and reports on these examinations should be publicly distributed. Only in this way can we know what is being done and what progress is being made.

In this chapter we wish to assay some preventive aspects of the problem and some treatment programs. Both prevention and treatment have their functions in the total picture and each deserves careful evaluation. First we shall deal with the work of the police; second, with the work of recreational and character-building agencies; third, with school curriculum and counseling; fourth, with the child-guidance and habit clinics; and fifth, with social case work and social group work. We shall defer until the next chapter the work of community co-ordinating councils and of governmental action.

2. THE WORK OF THE REGULAR POLICE FORCE

a. Safeguarding the Minor Delinquent

Regardless of how much we may wish our American youth to keep out of the clutches of the law, we must resort to our regular

578 *PREVENTIVE SERVICES*

police force to apprehend any individuals who commit overt acts against society. Moreover, we must rely on the police to do all within their constituted power to prevent delinquency. An efficient, well-paid, sympathetic, and alert police force is the first bulwark against juvenile delinquency. Guidance centers, school counseling, and character-building agencies may come first in prevention, but it is the police officer to whom we must turn for protection of life and property against the predatory behavior of maladjusted persons, juvenile and adult alike.

The question of police power is a difficult one. We must guard against overzealous law-enforcing agents who too often place the individual's rights in jeopardy, but at the same time we must also assist these agents of society in doing the duty with which we have charged them.[1]

The National Conference has examined this perplexing question in its report on the role of police. Starting with the cardinal principle that "the first duty of law enforcement is the protection of society," the report states the "needs and privileges of the individual" should be given "secondary but very important consideration." [2] It then proceeds to examine controversial procedures and police problems in handling juvenile delinquents. Let us take arrest procedure. The report points out that while legislation does not specifically prohibit arrest by law-enforcing officers, "other provisions make arrest of juveniles meaningless." It further states that "there should not be any attempt to curb the arresting power of police with respect to any person who has violated the law." Nor should the police officer be prohibited from questioning juveniles when he is in uniform. The report goes on to state that many arrests of juveniles are not made under ideal conditions, since it would be impractical for most towns and cities to safeguard the rights of children to a nicety. A sensible compromise would naturally be highly desirable, but in most of our cities law-enforcement standards are shoddy. The rights of children must be scrupulously safeguarded at the same time that society is protected against delinquents.[3]

---

[1] Lawrence D. Morrison, "The Police and the Delinquent Child," *Yearbook,* N.P.P.A., 1947, pp. 117–137.

[2] *Report No.* 7, Government Printing Office, Washington, D.C., 1947, p. 1.

[3] See Chapter VIII for details on arrest.

Now let us look at the dilemma of detention. We have discussed detention in another chapter but here we are appraising it against the backdrop of the rights of childhood. The Conference report says:

> Certain recommendations provide that no child (a person under either 16 or 18 depending on State law) should ever be held in a jail or lock-up. There are almost a thousand communities in this country with more than 10,000 population. There are slightly more than 200 juvenile courts. There are only 145 detention homes. Where are dangerous juveniles to be held? In a town in a Western state a dangerous juvenile delinquent, who had committed an armed robbery and had shot a police officer, was released after arrest because the nearest detention home was 165 miles away. The State law prohibited detaining any juvenile under 17 in the police lock-up. Sufficient police were not available to transport this juvenile to the detention home. After release the juvenile stole an automobile, and escaped from the custody of his parents.[4]

The report answers this problem by stating that "the solution lies in the direction of more and better detention facilities, which should be the concern of every community." It should be noted that the report, though deploring that the youth in question was obviously dangerous and finally got away, did not recommend his *detention in a jail or police lock-up*. Yet it is a sad commentary on this country that thousands of children are held in jails for long periods of time without any segregation whatever from adults. One of the first things our police authorities could do would be to demand detention quarters for juveniles instead of complaining that they must avoid arresting and detaining children. Yet this poses the question of how decent are detention quarters? We have heard police officers, especially policewomen, state on occasion that juveniles are better off in precinct station houses, for example, than in juvenile detention houses. Since most children are detained only long enough for the arresting officer to contact the parents, they are safeguarded against the contaminating influences of the larger detention house.

Another question posed by the Conference report deals with interrogating juveniles. The question is asked: "Why should juveniles not be questioned by an officer in uniform?" The report also discusses the length of questioning by the arresting officer. "What objection can there be to an extended interview of a seventeen year

---

[4] *Loc. cit*, p. 4.

old boy or a fifteen year old boy involved in a long series of felonies when justice to society requires that the case be cleared?" We have already pointed out that children should be detained in special detention homes with adequate facilities. The report concludes along this line by adding that "while in custody delinquents should be handled with the highest ethical practices." [5] Protracted questioning of a minor should scrupulously be avoided and forbidden.

A great discrepancy exists between what we want and ought to do in arresting, detaining, and questioning juveniles and what actually takes place as a result of public inertia or slipshod police methods. We cannot expect the police to do the impossible, but they are in a position to initiate important reforms. For instance, they could demand that they be divested of the onus that is heaped upon them as a result of present practice.

b. Crime-Prevention Units of Police Departments

As early as 1929 the police commissioner of New York City appointed an Advisory Committee on Crime Prevention for the purpose of studying ways and means to establish some plan to cope with the problem of delinquency. The following year the Crime Prevention Unit was set up within the police department. In due time, twenty-five experienced social workers were appointed as crime-prevention officers. The director of the Unit was made deputy police commissioner and a program of activities was drawn up. In the manual of police procedure, the purposes of the crime-prevention unit were set forth: (a) to carry on a broad program for the reduction of delinquency in New York City; and (b) to help put into operation measures for the rehabilitation of juvenile delinquents and wayward minors. To carry out these objectives the Unit was charged with supervision of dance halls, cabarets and nightclubs, pool and billiard parlors, gambling centers, places displaying and selling obscene literature, and any other place where the morals of minors might conceivably be corrupted. It was further charged to patrol the areas where the delinquency rate was high. The regular police were charged to bring to the attention of the Crime Prevention Unit all cases of wayward minors and delinquent children. The Unit, better known as the Juvenile Aid Bureau, was primarily con-

---

[5] *Ibid.*, p. 5.

cerned in (1) helping to secure more adequate social treatment for individual juvenile delinquents; (2) finding and removing community conditions that make for crime; (3) building up constructive forces for the prevention of crime; and (4) developing a different attitude on the part of youth toward the law and law-enforcing agencies.[6]

A number of the larger cities have established crime-prevention bureaus as adjuncts of the regular police departments. An important offshoot of this work in many cities is the recreation feature. Boys' clubs are established in the congested neighborhoods or in areas of high delinquency. Sports of all kinds are provided for in these clubs. Boys apprehended by the police often find themselves enrolling as members rather than going to jail. In New York City, the Police Athletic League (meaningly abbreviated PAL), sponsored by the Police Department and supported by the public, has gone into the recreation field on a grand scale. While operating on a city-wide basis, PAL directs its energies to those youngsters who live in neighborhoods where adequate recreational facilities are lacking. In 1948, on a budget of almost $950,000, it operated more than one hundred recreation centers and employed 300 professional recreation directors; it maintained a summer camp for 600 boys and conducted sports tournaments for thousands of children in baseball, softball, basketball, soccer, track and field, and boxing, and supervised one hundred playstreets and playgrounds. Other features of its program are musical activities, crafts, excursions and outings, teen-age dances, and visits to sports events. It also conducts radio programs over two local broadcasting stations. In Washington, D.C., a "Junior Police and Citizens' Corps" was organized in 1942 by a police officer, Oliver A. Cowan, along similar lines.

This is one of the contributions the police are making to crime prevention. In some quarters this activity is considered laudable. However, critics maintain that recreational activities should be set up and administered through regular channels—notably municipal recreation commissions or settlement houses—and that the police are not

[6] See Henrietta Additon's article, "The Crime Prevention Bureau of the New York City Police Department," in Sheldon and Eleanor Glueck's *Preventing Crime*, McGraw-Hill, New York, 1936, pp. 215–236. See also James B. Nolan, "The Crime Prevention Work of New York City," *Federal Probation*, April–June, 1947, pp. 18 ff.

employed to fraternize with delinquents or potential delinquents. For example, a survey of the Philadelphia police department in 1948 by a trained police investigator from another city recommended that the police leave recreation work to those specifically trained for it.

Without disparaging the police officer who feels he can be a "pal" to the children on his beat by taking off his coat and playing ball with them, we must remember that both in theory and in practice the primary function of the police is the apprehension of criminals. A policeman cannot be a "good sport" and a crime detector. This does not mean that he cannot be civil to children and adults on his beat. Dignity and honesty are important in performing his main task— law enforcement. The reason why police officers are so generally feared by children is that ignorant adults, mostly parents, frighten children into being good with the threat of "calling the police."

c. *The Place of the Policewoman in Delinquency Control*

The introduction of women into the metropolitan police force was an important step toward socializing the arrest as well as the treatment process. Obviously, many functions of police work can be delegated to women.

As early as 1921 the National Probation Association suggested among other functions: (1) detective work on special cases involving women and children; (2) locating missing women and children; (3) maintaining a bureau of information for women desiring help from the police; (4) patrol work, including general supervision and inspection of amusement parks, dance halls, cabarets, cafes, motion picture theaters, skating rinks, and other public amusement places; scouting and patrol work on the streets, in public parks, and around railroad stations.[7] These are the essential duties of most policewomen today.

The idea of policewomen grew out of the older movement of supplying matrons in city jails and lock-ups. This practice goes back as far as 1845 in New York City.[8] The first known appointment of

---

[7] Quoted by Henrietta Additon, *Proceedings of the 10th Annual Conference of the International Association of Police Women*, 1924, p. 52.

[8] Katherine Bement Davis, "The Police Woman," *The Woman Citizen*, May 30, 1925.

a woman to do preventive-protective work with children and young girls was in 1905, in Portland, Oregon. During the celebration of the Lewis and Clark Exposition in that city, Mrs. Lola Baldwin, secretary of the Travelers' Aid Society, was empowered to protect women and girls from the advances of male transients. So fine a job was done by Mrs. Baldwin and her corps of volunteers that Portland organized the "Department of Public Safety for Protection of Young Girls and Women." The workers were known as operators rather than as policewomen.

In May 1910, the city council of Grand Forks, North Dakota, passed an ordinance creating the position of police matron, who was also to assume duties that today are recognized as those of policewomen. However, the first real policewoman in the United States was Mrs. Alice Stebbins Wells, who was appointed in September 1910, in Los Angeles, California. She was specifically asked to assist in investigations involving women and children.[9]

During the period between 1910 and 1915, about sixteen cities added women officers to their police departments, and, as a result of World War I, several other cities followed suit.

In 1949, there were 894 policewomen employed full-time in 129 cities, an increase of over sixty per cent over 1940. It is estimated that approximately 1,000 women are employed in this profession throughout the country.[10] There are 175 in New York City, 79 in Chicago and 60 in Detroit.

In some cities policewomen are merely an adjunct to the regular police force, but in others they are under special crime-prevention units and are supervised by women. About forty cities—San Francisco and New York, for example—equip their policewomen with motorcycles and guns. In San Francisco, policewomen are dressed in simulated male attire. In a few of the cities women are expected to be college graduates, although most accept candidates with only a high-school education. Some units boast several officers who hold master's degrees.

Aside from a few limited duties such as traffic control (San Francisco) and prevention of shop-lifting in downtown department stores

---

[9] Chloe Owings, *Women Police*, Frederick H. Hitchcock, New York, 1925, pp. 10, 102.
[10] "The Outlook for Women in Police Work," *Bulletin No. 231*, United States Department of Labor, Women's Bureau, 1949, p. 7.

(Miami, Florida) the functions of the policewomen are essentially the same throughout the country. They patrol public amusement parks, bus and railway terminals, and any other places where youngsters congregate. They are particularly effective in detecting runaway girls or male adults who make a practice of exploiting female minors.[11] Since contributing to the delinquency of adolescent girls is a common practice in all cities, the problem is obviously serious in the larger metropolitan centers. In addition, the policewoman is closely affiliated with the counseling services of the public schools, and a large share of her work is identified with high-school girls. Many of the women pursue their duties along case-work lines, employing the newer philosophy of adjustment and treatment in counseling and guidance services rather than resorting to penalties. In other words, the trend is away from the use of arrest and punitive methods and toward guidance. It is for this reason that policewomen should have adequate training in personality and adolescent psychology. Much of this training can be absorbed in an in-service training program. Many incipient cases of delinquency are thwarted by good work done by policewomen.

Let us look at a typical day in the headquarters of the policewomen of a large city. The following is taken from a report by the supervisor of a policewomen's unit: [12]

10:35 a.m. Senior Police Woman received call from Counselor in one of the public schools. A mother and her young daughter are on the way to the office. Child is a truant and incorrigible. She stays out late at night, disregards parental authority and refuses to conform in school. After an interview of over an hour girl is placed under supervision. Mother wants girl arrested but it seems wiser to give child a chance to adjust. In the meantime additional information about the home and the girl has been acquired. Girl is told when to report for second interview and it is made clear to her that if she fails to obey rules laid down her mother is to report and she will be sent to House of Detention to be disposed of by juvenile court procedure.

---

[11] A manual for the use of policewomen has been published by the Federal Security Agency, Social Protection Division, under the title "Techniques of Law Enforcement in the Use of Policewomen with Special Reference to Social Protection," Government Printing Office, 1945.

[12] Courtesy of Mrs. Norma Carson, Senior Police Woman, Policewomen's Unit, Crime Prevention Division, Bureau of Police, Philadelphia, Pennsylvania.

10:45 a.m. Police bring in runaway girl. Mother is sent for and girl held pending arrival of parent. Meanwhile complete history of girl is taken down. Mother wants supervision rather than arrest and arrangements are made accordingly.

9:05 to 12 noon. Thirteen telephone calls are received. Eight of these are complaints—two from neighbors, four from parents and two from schools. One of the schools has a situation that involves girls fighting after school and two police women are requested for 2:30 p.m. Two police women who have been in court during morning are assigned to school. The other five calls include a request for the Senior Police Woman to speak on the work of the Unit to a group of church women; two agencies who desire information on certain clients being handled by members of the Unit, and two police women who are working on home calls and complaints report in concerning their activities.

Luncheon is managed between these numerous calls. The afternoon starts with an interview with a man involved in a complaint concerning four young girls who are spending much time in his home. After interviewing two of these girls and their parents, it seemed advisable to talk with the man. No evidence of immorality is found but the situation is considered too dangerous for the girls who are all under age. The man is warned that his actions will be watched and if the girls are found in his home he will be dealt with severely.

2:00 p.m. A mother comes in from the Municipal Court to make a complaint about an 18 year old daughter who refuses to live at home. The case is thoroughly investigated and arrangements are made to handle the matter.

2:30 p.m. Call from an employment agency which is having trouble with a woman who insists on "parking herself in the office" and can be persuaded to leave only after she is given money. Two police women are sent to the agency where they question the woman and place her under arrest.

From 1:30 to 4:30 p.m. seven telephone calls are made by the police women to various agencies and schools. The afternoon calls include a report from one member of the Unit working on the streets, calls from school Counselors and complaints from parents regarding their youngsters.

The number of police women on duty on this day was 13 and the Senior Officer. Of these 13 members of the Unit, two were scheduled to be on street duty from 4:00 p.m. until midnight; four from midnight until 8:00 a.m.; two were on duty in office; two were in Court and later in office and three were working on cases and complaints.

The 4:00 p.m. until midnight officers made two arrests, visited train and bus terminals, taprooms, luncheonettes and amusement places and checked on all-night theatres.

The midnight to 8:00 a.m. officers made three arrests and patroled a portion of the central city. They questioned nine girls on the streets and in amusement places, taking two to City Hall for questioning after which they were sent home.

Obviously, the duties of the policewoman are diverse. Cooperation from school administrators is of great importance, as is an efficient integration of all social agencies, such as the Social Service Exchange, Travelers' Aid, and Family Society. The policewoman should be intelligent and should have enough training in the meaning of social work to understand the functions of the various community resources serving problem children and adults as well.

Few of the smaller cities have policewomen. This situation is unfortunate, since there is a real need for alert, understanding women in small towns where so little, other than parental supervision, is achieved in supervising young girls. The snares that attract adolescents are present in small towns as well as in big cities, and it is far better for efficient and tolerant female officers to exercise supervision and control than for the casual male policeman on his beat.

The writers of this book endorse the activity of policewomen in crime-prevention work. But they wish to warn that it is just as important to have sympathetic and trained personnel in this work as in reform schools or in any agency that deals with children or youth of tender years. Brazen, hard-boiled tactics—all too frequent even with policewomen—have no place in a female police unit.

3. THE SCHOOL'S RESPONSIBILITY FOR THE PREVENTION OF DELINQUENCY

a. Curriculum Adjustment

One of the most hopeful signs of the times was the publication in 1948 of a symposium entitled "Juvenile Delinquency and the Schools" by the National Society for the Study of Education.[13] Its purpose was to focus the attention of teachers and school administrators upon their responsibility for preventing delinquency. In its introduction this publication maintains that of all the various com-

---

[13] *Forty-seventh Yearbook*, Part I, University of Chicago Press, 1948.

munity agencies serving youth the school must carry the heaviest responsibility in conditioning childhood.

> . . . [the school] must have a program that is broad and rich and stimulating; a place that is safe and comfortable and conducive to varied learning activities; a staff that is professionally prepared, interested and wise in the ways of dealing with children, personally well adjusted, and professionally secure. Such a school will have as its goal the best possible development of all boys and girls.
>
> Along the way it will have to stop now and then to concentrate on the problems of those children who have failed, but the school will think of *their* failure as *its* failure. . . . The schools should be better able, not only to help redirect the delinquent behavior, but to see how to avoid its continued and needless repetition so that the way of all children will have been made safer.[14]

The symposium points out the fundamental truth that it is not just enough to see that *most* children are equipped for life through the school's curricula, but that *all* children of the entire nation must be served; that teachers should be carefully briefed in their training so that they may better understand the signposts that point the way to delinquency. This symposium should be required reading for all active teachers as well as for those now in training.

The school must share with church and home the responsibility of supplying our youth with the tools necessary to meet life, whether these tools be morals, democratic ideals, or individual restraints. In addition, and more specifically, the school is charged with the task of equipping the child with knowledge to assist him in the competitive struggle he must inevitably face. Yet the school is constantly blamed for failure to measure up to such grave responsibilities. The symposium admits this failure. Part of the criticism is justified, although much of the failure is due to a penurious financial policy in many local communities. Teachers' salaries are notoriously low. Many services that are considered as essential in child development are still regarded by many school boards as frills and thus are not adopted or are the first to be eliminated in a policy of retrenchment.

The public school does a fair job with the pupil of average intelligence, a poor job with superior children, and practically no job with the dull group. Subjecting a group of retarded children to a curricu-

---

[14] *Ibid.*, p. 8.

lum far above their ability to understand is cruel in its effects on the group, and it is financially wasteful. There should be special classes in which special skills adapted to the potentialities of the child are taught. Truancy and incipient incorrigibility in the school-room are frequently a challenge to the school to supply a régime where such behavior will not manifest itself.

Thousands of boys and girls drop out of school because they are offered no opportunity to learn anything that their limited mentality can grasp. Relatively few teachers are equipped by training to cope with this group. Since teachers are overworked and underpaid, as a rule, such a condition puts a premium on meeting the situation on a low level of adjustment—stern disciplinary measures in the school-room or a command to go to the principal's office. The principal rarely has the insight to deal effectively with the problem, so he holds the boy in an outer office with some silly multiplication or long-division problem to solve, hoping that this kind of penalty will do the trick. Either the school muddles through until the boy is old enough to go to work or else it badgers him into submission. Of course, counseling services can be helpful but if the diagnosis calls for a change in curriculum in order that the child's needs will be met, and there is no such curriculum, it is obvious that the school has failed.

Vocational guidance should be an integral part of every public school, especially of every secondary school, and for all types of pupils. In addition, an honest vocational program should be provided to meet the needs of the average pupil at the time he finishes school. Too many children who drop out of school merely stumble into jobs for which they are not vocationally prepared and for which they develop indifference and even hatred. Many children with ability get into blind-alley jobs which it is difficult to leave. In numerous cases vocational unfitness builds up deep resentments that may ultimately lead to crime or to some psychosis or other patho-logical behavior.

Boys and girls leave school to look for work—any work that will relieve them of the utter boredom that permeates the average school curriculum without vocational guidance. Children who contemplate leaving such schools give little thought to occupational adjustment. A serious problem confronting educators is that the group from which most delinquents emerge—judged by police records, correctional institutions, and crime-prevention organizations—cannot take advantage of skilled jobs in industries, nor can they be trained for such jobs, because they do not possess the necessary special aptitudes or the intelligence.

This marginal group of young people possesses few assets that will enable them to carry through without leaning toward a delinquent career. What can be done with these boys and girls in the public school?

Because modern production methods are so elaborate and the machines so expensive, few school systems have the funds to enter the field of vocational training on a wide scale. Most authorities agree that the school cannot be expected to teach trades, but that certain fundamentals can be taught to boys and girls that will be of service to them—and to society—in later life. As one vocational expert states it, such "values lie in the fields of home maintenance, automobile operation and care, consumer education, and hobby work. . . . As far as exploratory values are concerned, latent interests are much more likely to be discovered through free activity on a voluntary basis than through prescribed, formal exploratory courses on a compulsory basis." [15]

Guidance personnel is probably much more practical and economical than expensive machinery, which will be outmoded after a few years and which may be used to teach many who will never take advantage of the training. Preparing for life the large number of marginal boys and girls who leave school before the completion of traditional courses, in most cases, involves expert counseling. Although faulty vocational training is not directly responsible for the majority of adolescent delinquency, much frustration and muddling through could be eliminated by proper guidance and vocational education. Few marginal children are capable of great self-motivation.

We cannot expect the school to assume the responsibility of training the boy or girl specifically to go out and land a job. Courses in typing, shorthand, commercial work, and similar subjects do definitely prepare for a specific field of work. But there is a limit to such skills. Manual training for boys, with a knowledge of the use of tools and the properties of metals, woods, and plastics, and home

---

[15] Walter H. Magill, *Administering Vocational Education*, Guide to Action Series, Educational Publishers, Inc., Philadelphia, 1941, p. 6.

economics and beauty culture for girls are valuable, but in most instances they do not prepare for specific jobs. Schools should continue these subjects and enrich their curricula as new demands arise for the semi-skilled. Expensive trade training for the marginal youth of a community is not the answer to this serious problem.

One other field can be dealt with courageously by the school. This is preparation for marriage. Judge Jacob Panken of the Domestic Relations Court of New York City, in an article, "The Real Delinquent—The Parent," lays particular stress on the need for such instruction; he feels that "we should require all high school pupils to take courses in parent responsibility and child guidance." [16]

Dr. Evelyn Millis Duvall, in a discussion of the Town Meeting of the Air on "What Is Wrong with American Marriages?," stressed "high schools, colleges, churches, Y.M.'s and Y.W.'s, and similar agencies must be encouraged to increase their courses in preparation for marriage and family relations." [17] Comprehensive and dignified courses in sex education should, therefore, be an integral part of the school program. These courses should be handled by trained personnel, aided by physicians and psychiatrists as well as by experts in budgeting, home economics, and child care. The school, largely because of the mid-Victorian codes of morality, has not done its part in grappling with this most fundamental of all problems. Fortunately, these codes are being drastically modified.

It is the thesis of many well-meaning people that the home and the church are the centers of sex education and preparation for family life. Both institutions could obviously do a great deal, but the fact is that they have both failed miserably. So far as the home is concerned, most parents are steeped in the traditional inhibitions of sex and are ill-prepared by experience to unfold gradually the fundamentals of the sex drive. Intelligent parents, emancipated from religious dogma and Victorian prudery, welcome such training from schools prepared to accept this responsibility. The school cannot shirk this duty any longer. Already some of our western states, notably Oregon, are dealing with this problem in a workmanlike manner.

The Toms River, New Jersey, High School has made a notable

---

[16] *The New York Times Magazine*, December 22, 1946.
[17] *Bulletin of American Town Meeting of the Air*, February 13, 1947.

contribution in this respect. Its courses on family relationships and related topics have attracted nation-wide attention. It has published carefully organized outlines of these courses, which cover the social background, the structure of the family and society, adjustment before and after marriage, the functions of the family, and community relationships. Similar courses are given in a great number of high schools and in more and more colleges and universities.[18]

b. Counseling—The Visiting Teacher

The National Conference, in its report on school and teacher responsibilities (*Report No. 15*), asks whether the "teachers . . . are alert to telltale signs of potential delinquent behavior." This is probably a fair question to ask, yet we cannot expect the overworked and underpaid teacher to be a master craftsman in all fields of child development. We shall discuss the place of the school counselor in the school system below. But here we may list the telltale signs of incipient trouble as given in the report:

Is the child unfriendly or seclusive?
Is he failing in his school work?
Does he play truant?
Is he in good physical condition?
Does he show many fears?
Is he rejected or unwanted at home, on the playground, or in the school?
Does he run with a gang?
Does he have any contact with a supervised recreational program in the community?
Does he have a church or Sunday school affiliation?
Does he plan to leave school?
Does he live in a high delinquency neighborhood?
Does the child show marks of poverty?
Does he live in a crowded and unattractive home?
Does he have academic limitations or special disabilities that interfere with his learning?
Does he come from a broken or deserted home?
Does his mother work outside the home?

---

[18] See Lester A. Kirkendall, "Education for Marriage and Family Life in the Schools," *Marriage and Family Living*, Spring 1948, pp. 31–32; also Henry Bowman, "The Teacher as Counselor in Marriage Education," *ibid.*, pp. 1–7.

The report continues by stating that a poorly trained teacher will not detect many of these danger signals. Teachers must possess insight to identify such limitations to a well-rounded child life. Every effort should be made by school boards to see that properly trained teachers are employed and that a system of counseling be inaugurated to cope with children thus handicapped.[19]

An important adjunct of the modern school in dealing with behavior problems is the counseling service. In many schools this service is handled by the visiting teacher although it is often called guidance or counseling service.

The visiting teacher movement has its roots in the fields of education and social work. In 1906 and 1907, New York City, Boston, and Hartford, Connecticut, "developed simultaneously but independently a similar type of work to meet a common need." [20] In New York the movement originated in two settlement houses, Hartley House and Greenwich House, where settlement workers felt the need for getting acquainted with the teachers of the children who frequented the settlements. Two visitors were assigned to the schools and homes of three districts in order to learn more about the children in whom they all had a common interest. In January, 1907, a committee was formed to develop this work; the Public Education Association took the lead. In 1913, the New York Board of Education took over this pioneering work.

In Boston, in 1907, the Woman's Education Association established a home and school visitor in the Winthrop School to "bring about a greater harmony between the two and to make more effective the education of the child." [21] By 1923, seven visiting teachers had been

---

[19] The reader is referred to the several excellent articles in the *Yearbook, op. cit., supra,* which deal with the problem of detecting incipient delinquency in the schoolroom: "Prevention of Delinquency Through Guided Group Experience," by Ruth Strang; "The Delinquent in the Classroom," by Norman Fenton; "How School Services Help To Prevent Delinquency," by Bess Goodykoontz; "The Role of the Administrator in Relation to Juvenile Delinquency," by William C. Kvaraceus.

[20] *The Visiting Teacher in the United States,* The Public Education Association of New York City, 1921.

[21] J. J. Oppenheimer, *The Visiting Teacher Movement,* New York, Joint Committee on Methods of Preventing Delinquency, 1925, p. 3. Quotation from *Report of the Home and School Visitor,* Winthrop School District, Boston, 1908.

provided for the elementary schools of Boston and two for high schools.

In Hartford, the work was pioneered in the Barnard School in 1907 upon the suggestion of the director of the Psychological Clinic. The visiting teacher assisted the psychologist in securing the history of the children and in carrying out the recommendations of the Clinic in regard to social service, physical treatment, or school adjustment.

Other pioneer movements began in Philadelphia in 1909; Worcester, Massachusetts, in 1910; Rochester, New York, in 1913; [22] Kansas City, in 1915; Minneapolis, in 1916; Chicago, in 1919; and during the period from 1913 to 1921 in Newton, Massachusetts; Mt. Vernon, New York; Utica, New York; Mason City, Iowa; and Fargo, North Dakota. Today organized services falling within the purview of the visiting teacher service exist in over 266 cities. [23]

No history of this significant movement would be complete without a word concerning the White-Williams Foundation of Philadelphia. In another connection we commented on the Magdalen Society, established in Philadelphia in 1800. It had for its original purpose the care of wayward or sexually delinquent girls. [24] After carrying on this work for over a hundred years, the Society succumbed to newer concepts; in 1916, it scrapped its quaint name and became known as the White-Williams Foundation.

The board of this organization decided, with approval of the superintendent of schools, to take up the study of delinquency in the public schools. The work was begun in the Bureau of Compulsory Education when girls came to procure working certificates. From this beginning, vocational guidance was developed. The service naturally led into educational guidance prior to vocational selection. Eventually, counseling and certain visiting teacher functions evolved. Today, Philadelphia maintains 225 full-time school counselors and

---

[22] Rochester has the distinction of being the first city to support and direct visiting teacher services without outside funds.

[23] These figures, together with much of this material, are from a pamphlet issued in 1945 by the Federal Security Agency, United States Office of Education, entitled "The Place of the Visiting Teacher Services in the School Program." See also "School Social Services," in *Social Work Yearbook*, 1949, pp. 457–462.

[24] See p. 74.

103 full-time attendance officers, by far the greatest number of any city in the United States.[25]

In essence, the visiting teacher or guidance service of the public schools is concerned with the problem child—or perhaps it should be stated "with children with problems." For example, in earlier days, in Rochester, New York, work began with a study of the causes of truancy and non-attendance in school. This later evolved into the study of many kinds of behavior difficulty, with an emphasis on prevention.

In 1921, the National Committee on Visiting Teachers was formed. Financial backing was granted by the Commonwealth Fund of New York for a country-wide demonstration service. At the time, the Committee stated its purpose was to help the "child who was tending toward delinquency, who fails to 'get along' in his school, home or neighborhood environment, who is troublesome, or 'difficult,' or maladjusted." [26] The Committee maintained that the school is in a strategic position to undertake child welfare work and that "sound social case work is valuable in making the work of the school more effective." [27]

The Committee placed thirty visiting teachers in as many different communities for a demonstration period. Cooperation with boards of education was guaranteed; in fact, the local school board paid one-third of the salary and the Committee guaranteed the rest. From this pioneer experiment the best material on the work of the visiting teacher has been collected.[28]

---

[25] See Robert C. Taber, "The Potential Role of the School Counselor in Delinquency Prevention and Treatment," *Federal Probation*, September 1949, pp. 52–56; also Frank J. O'Brien, "The Role of Social Services in Education," *ibid.*, pp. 120–133. The Division of Pupil Personnel and Counseling of the Philadelphia Board of Public Education published a most informative five-year report on school counseling in September 1947. See also Rachel Dunaway Cox, "The School Counsellor's Contribution to the Prevention of Delinquency," *Federal Probation*, March 1950, pp. 23–28.

[26] Oppenheimer, *op. cit.*, p. 10.

[27] *Ibid.*, p. 11.

[28] Among the publications resulting from this experiment are J. J. Oppenheimer, *The Visiting Teacher Movement*, 1925; Mabel Brown Ellis, *Visiting Teacher in Rochester*, 1925; Mary B. Sayles, *The Problem Child in School*, 1929; and Jane Culbert, *The Visiting Teacher at Work*, 1930. These are the four basic books dealing with the movement prior to 1930.

Although the services performed by the visiting teacher vary in different school systems, various phases of child welfare may conceivably fall within an over-all functional philosophy. These are: (a) acting as attendance officers; (b) working out problems causing non-attendance; (c) working out adjustment of behavior problems; (d) investigating home-school relationships; (e) referring problems to outside social agencies; (f) treating children's difficulties directly. In a report of some 250 cities, it was found that services (b), (c), (d), and (e) are most frequent.[29]

Visiting teachers should obviously be trained for their exacting duties. However, qualifications vary in great degree. One city reported: "Normally we require a state teacher's certificate, 3 years' experience, an A.B. degree, 1 year professional training in social work, or 12 weeks' summer school in social work." Another city reports: "A married woman gives one-third of her time to this work. She has no degree, but considerable experience in social work."[30] In any event, the visiting teacher should be trained to speak the language of the teacher. She should understand child psychology and have a good knowledge of social work and the findings of psychiatry. In general, the training for such positions should be along the lines of psychiatric social work, but with real understanding of the art of school teaching. Assuming that visiting teachers are well trained, it follows that school boards should not burden them with routine administrative duties that can be handled equally well by clerks. This tendency exists in too many school systems today.

It is not to be implied that everything is rosy in every school where counseling exists. The counseling atmosphere is prepared and nurtured primarily by the principal of the school. If he or she has little insight into counseling philosophy, even a good worker can be of little service to the problem child. It is not enough for a city to boast that it employs a hundred counselors or a counselor in every school. Counseling services must be dignified and professional. The counselor cannot be asked to do trivial administrative tasks. Nor can a counselor, on the other hand, permit herself to become institutionalized or routinized by her job. She must accept her responsibility by

---

[29] "The Place of Visiting Teacher Services in the School Program," *Federal Security Bulletin*, 1945, p. 25.
[30] *Ibid.*, p. 27.

viewing each child as a personality with potentialities for good rather than as a little scourge to society. She must possess insight and a capacity to work with the agencies in the community with no feeling of authoritarianism which, unfortunately, begins to grip many persons who deal with children in trouble.

The school, then, can be of great service in preventing delinquency as well as in dealing with incipient delinquency. A complete reorientation of types of curricula is of first importance. Courses of study are still far too traditionally imposed. An example of the concern that many secondary school educators are experiencing is in the field of mathematics. It has been frequently stated that high-school mathematics is too complex for most children who will not go on to college. Why, then, should they be burdened with mathematics which they cannot grasp or ever use in life? One could apply the same logic to foreign languages, grammar, and the natural sciences.[31]

Aside from curricular changes, which, incidentally, have come altogether too slowly, the school must see that its teachers are alert to frustration and maladjustment among their children so that they will know where they may turn for help. Of course, an adequate counseling service must be prepared to cope with atypical children in a professional manner.[32] But money is needed for such a program, and communities must see that well-informed citizens are elected to boards of education who see this responsibility and who are willing to act.

4. THE CHILD-GUIDANCE CLINIC

a. Origin and Early Days

Aside from the juvenile court and the concept of probation, the child-guidance clinic is considered the most important advance made in this century toward the understanding and treatment of the emotional problems of the child. Although the court broke down the

---

[31] The reader is referred to an excellent analysis of what can be done in gearing curricula to various types of children, Helen E. Weston, "The Role of the School in Crime Prevention," *Yearbook*, N.P.P.A., 1939, pp. 28–42.

[32] For practical suggestions on cooperation between school and juvenile court, see John Otto Reinemann, "The Truant Before the Court," *Federal Probation*, September 1948, pp. 6–12.

raditions surrounding criminal procedure, it was soon found neces-
ary to seek out scientific techniques in dealing with problem chil-
ren. Probation, of course, was already available. But diagnostic tools
vere practically nonexistent. At this point the child-guidance clinic
resented itself.

The judge of the Chicago Juvenile Court, Merritt W. Pinckney,
ound in his city a clinic known as the Juvenile Psychopathic Insti-
ute, organized in 1909 under the sponsorship of Mrs. W. F. Dummer
nd headed by Dr. William Healy. (It is interesting to recall that a
ioneer in this field was Dr. Lightner Witmer of the department of
sychology at the University of Pennsylvania, who had established
psychological clinic as early as 1896, primarily for service to col-
ge students.) The clinic headed by Dr. Healy in Chicago embraced
oth medical and psychological techniques. When Judge Pinckney
sked for help, Dr. Healy enthusiastically tendered his knowledge
nd facilities to the examination of the juvenile wards of the court
oth in diagnostic summaries and prognoses.[33]

In 1920, the Chicago clinic was renamed the Institute for Juvenile
esearch. Its reputation spread throughout the country. A few years
arlier, Judge Harvey Humphrey Baker, first judge of the Juvenile
ourt of Boston, had been impressed by this new adjunct of the
venile court and urged that one be established in his city. After
udge Baker died, such a clinic was established, bearing his name, in
917. Dr. Healy and his assistant, Dr. Augusta Bronner, were called
rom Chicago to direct its activities. This establishment, the Judge
aker Foundation, is known today as the Judge Baker Guidance
enter. Only recently has Dr. Healy retired from active work in this
linic.

Movements as important as the child-guidance clinic do not de-
elop independently. In the case of the clinic, two social movements
ombined to focus attention on the emotional problems of the indi-
idual. The first was the establishment of the National Committee
or Mental Hygiene through the efforts of the late Clifford Beers and
is supporters. Beers had been institutionalized after a complete

---

[33] For an analysis of the child-guidance clinic and a historical treatment of
s origin, see "Orthopsychiatry, 1923–1948: Retrospect and Prospect," Ameri-
an Orthopsychiatric Association, Inc., 1948. This book is a veritable gold mine
f material dealing with the treatment of problem children.

mental breakdown. Upon his release, he organized the mental hy
giene movement and later wrote of his experiences in his famou
book, *A Mind That Found Itself*.[34] The movement grew as the year
passed and subsequently widened its scope to include studies in men
tal deficiency and problems of delinquency.

A second movement that made itself felt in the field of treatmen
was the refinement of the social work profession. Social worker
were beginning to find employment in mental hospitals as well as i
clinics in New York and Massachusetts and in the Phipps Psychiatri
Clinic of Johns Hopkins Hospital in Baltimore. Through the syn
thesis of professional techniques in the analysis of children's an
adults' behavior problems, social workers, psychologists, and psychi
atrists became indispensable in clinical work. Dr. Herman Adler in
troduced a type of social work in his Chicago clinic—he had suc
ceeded Dr. Healy—and the Judge Baker Clinic in Boston added
social worker to its staff, although in its early years it gave primaril
a diagnostic, prognostic, and advisory service only. Social worker
in various cooperative agencies were called upon to assist in the treat
ment of individual cases.

At Smith College and at the New York School of Social Work
formal training in psychiatric social work was introduced, and othe
schools followed this trend. The Pennsylvania School of Social Worl
in Philadelphia set up a program of psychiatric work which is wel
known in this field today. All accredited schools are on the graduat
level.

In 1920, Henry W. Thurston, associated with the New Yorl
School of Social Work and an early authority in the field of chil
care, was asked by the Commonwealth Fund of New York to formu
late a plan for work in child welfare. After considerable analysis o
the problem, it was proposed to carry on a five-year plan with th
following purposes:

1. To develop the psychiatric study of difficult, predelinquent, an
delinquent children in schools and juvenile courts and to develop soun
methods of treatment based on such study.

2. To develop the work of the visiting-teacher whereby the invalu
able early contacts which our school systems make possible with every
child may be utilized for the understanding and development of th
child.

---

[34] Doubleday-Doran, New York, 1923.

3. To provide courses of training along sound lines for those qualified and desiring to work in this field.

4. To extend by various educational efforts the knowledge and use
of these methods.[35]

These aims were realized through the cooperative efforts of sev-
ral agencies and organizations interested in the problems of child-
ood. Among these were the New York School of Social Work, the
ureau of Children's Guidance, the National Committee on Mental
Hygiene, and the Public Education Association of New York. The
ist-named organization established the National Committee on Visit-
ng Teachers to carry on demonstrations of visiting-teacher work in
arious towns and cities.

This exploratory work began in 1922. Two hundred and twenty-
ve juvenile courts throughout the country were apprised of the
rogram and many jurists gave a most enthusiastic response to the
ims of the work. However, it should be recorded that some judges
nsisted that such a service was not needed. The most promising solic-
ation came from the juvenile court of St. Louis, which had already
arried on volunteer psychiatric work in the treatment of juvenile
ases.

The Commonwealth Fund carried on a number of demonstrations
n the field of diagnosis and treatment. Among the progressive cities
nat took advantage of this service and later integrated the results of
ne demonstrations with the facilities already at their disposal were—
n addition to St. Louis—Norfolk, Dallas, Monmouth County (New
ersey), St. Paul and Minneapolis, Los Angeles, Cleveland, and Phila-
elphia.

Thus the philosophy of the child-guidance clinic became firmly
stablished as one of the most fruitful methods of dealing with the
elinquent and problem child. Its extreme value lies in its practice
f enlisting all that is known to science in dealing with the behavior
f the human being: the psychological, sociological, psychiatric, and
ne functions of social work. Starting in those pioneer days with
nly a few clinics, usually in the larger cities, they are now spread
ll over the country. They are supported privately, through com-

---

[35] This and the other material set down here is taken from George S. Steven-
on, M.D., and Geddes Smith, *Child Guidance Clinics: A Quarter Century of
Development*, Commonwealth Fund, New York, 1934, p. 21.

munity chests; publicly, through taxes; and by various colleges an
universities. The oldest tax-supported clinic is connected with th
Essex County Juvenile Court, Newark, New Jersey. It was founde
and directed by the late Dr. James S. Plant, long an authority i
the field of child care.

Here are the results of the five-year program requested by th
Commonwealth Fund:

> In the eight clinics permanently established as the direct result of th
> demonstrations, the pattern of child guidance has been clarified. Th
> focus of professional attention had shifted from delinquency and th
> court to the more subtle evidences of non-adjustment in the home an
> school. Much had been learned as to the means of linking the clini
> with the community. The mutual responsibility of clinic and soci:
> agencies, in particular, had gradually been revealed, and concrete meth
> ods had been worked out to give it effect. Financial policies had bee
> shaped and tempered by failures and successes. Channels through whic
> the clinic might realize its educational opportunities had been traced.³

b. The Child-Guidance Clinic in Action

A child-guidance clinic is defined by Dr. Pauline Young as "
co-ordinated attempt in the study and treatment of personality an
conduct disorders of children and youth, using the arts of the psy
chiatrist, psychologist, or psychometrist, and the social worker." ³
The average clinic functions in the following manner:

> (a) The case comes to the clinic with a statement of the problem
> presented as seen by the referring agency or person; (b) which is fol
> lowed by the collection of data by the investigators of the clinic; (c
> there follows discussion among the specialists for the purpose of arriv
> ing at the facts; (d) which are then analyzed with a view of agreein;
> on a diagnosis; (e) to be followed by the formulation of a program o
> treatment; (f) whereupon attempts are made to carry out the program
> (g) accompanied by reexamination and evaluations of the progran
> adopted, and the diagnosis upon which it was based; (k) with th
> further effort of arriving at valid generalizations of principles and a
> improvement of techniques.³⁸

---

³⁶ Stevenson and Smith, *op. cit.*, p. 47.

³⁷ *Social Treatment in Probation and Delinquency*, McGraw-Hill, New Yorl
1st ed., p. 599.

³⁸ Louis Wirth, "Clinical Sociology," *American Journal of Sociology*, Vo
27, July 1931, p. 51.

It may be seen from this picture that the total child must be scrunized in the clinic, not only in diagnosis, but in prognosis and treatment as well. Close teamwork among all personnel engaged in the work is necessary for best results. Most clinic cases come from the public school, the home, or social agencies, rather than from the juvenile court. Most cases deal with types of maladjustment rather than with overt delinquency.[39]

There are two types of child-guidance clinics. The first type includes both diagnosis and treatment. In these clinics, social workers are usually called upon to carry out the treatment recommended, especially if it calls for home visitation, the securing of a job, replacement in a foster home, the development of a hobby, joining a club, or furnishing something the lack of which is presumed to be the predisposing cause of the child's difficulty. The second type is merely diagnostic. In this capacity, the clinic may also serve as a consulting agency to the school or the juvenile court.[40] It studies cases referred to it, makes diagnosis, and offers recommendations. Often clinics are accused of failure because the court or school ignores its recommendations or carries them through without much conviction.

Upon being referred to a clinic, the child is given a thorough examination in a sympathetic and informal manner. The medical physician makes his routine examination and notes any evidences of malfunctioning of organs or glands and lack of proper nourishment. The psychologist administers the usual tests to measure potentialities. Starting with the early Binet-Simon intelligence tests, psychological research has evolved and refined many excellent criteria for measuring various types of intelligence. It is needless here to name or describe the many now in use in the various clinics.[41] The social worker

---

[39] Some excellent cases for examination purposes were prepared by the Commonwealth Fund in 1932 and edited by Mary B. Sayles. See also the first set of Judge Baker Foundation Studies, which were the first of their kind; also Mary Augusta Clark, *Recording and Reporting for Child-Guidance Clinics*, Commonwealth Fund, New York, 1930; and Healy and Bronner, *Treatment and What Happened Afterward*, Judge Baker Guidance Center, Boston, 1939.

[40] For a discussion of the cooperation between guidance clinic, school, and juvenile court, see Daniel O'Keefe, "Mental Hygiene Facilities for the Juvenile Delinquent," *Federal Probation*, June 1948, pp. 31–35; Samuel W. Hartwell, "The Guidance Clinic and the Court," *ibid.*, September 1948, pp. 3–7.

[41] See Ralph Banay, *Youth in Despair*, Coward-McCann, New York, 1948, pp. 134–135 for a short description of the most frequently used intelligence tests. See also Chapter VIII, pp. 269–273.

makes a study of the child's environment, including family, neigh
borhood, work habits, recreation, and religious practices. The psy
chiatrist also holds one or more interviews with the youngster a
well as with one or both parents. In many cases, especially wit
young children referred to the clinic by the family or by the schoo
the examinations are made very subtly, so that the child's behavic
runs along its usual daily pattern. After the data have been collecte
and the examinations completed, the staff meets in consultation an
agrees on an analysis of the case. A program of readjustment or trea'
ment is then formulated.[42]

The work of Healy and Bronner at the Judge Baker Guidanc
Center in Boston has long been recognized as outstanding. Here is a
analysis of one set of 400 cases studied. Two hundred and seven c
the total were classed as *personality and behavior problems*, and wer
distributed as follows:

(a) Severe personality problems 4
    Besides 20 of the abnormal and psychotic personalities, this
group includes those, for example, exhibiting extremely rebellious,
headstrong, irritable, impulsive, oversensitive, obstinate, eccentric,
reckless types of behavior. Combinations of these and of other
manifestations often led us to consider the case as a severe problem.

(b) Milder personality problems 4
    In addition to less serious forms of the above we placed in this
category milder and simpler patterns of high-strung, distractible,
"sissified," cowardly, immature, demanding, domineering, ambi-
tionless, and other undesirable behavior.

(c) Definite neurotic manifestations 4
    Besides 9 extremely neurotic cases listed in another [category]
here we have included those showing neurotic habits, fears, tantrums, physical symptoms, self-starvation, etc.

(d) Undesirable behavior in direct reaction to life situations 5
    Without specifying the life situations it may be stated that
under this head clearly belong certain problems of defiance, tem-

---

[42] Recently, there has been a trend among social workers to make a large
and more significant contribution to guidance than a mere compounding o
social history. The psychiatric social worker is playing a more important rol
in treatment. See *The Case Worker in Psychotherapy*, Jewish Board of Guard
ians, New York, 1947; also Ethel L. Ginsburg, "Psychiatric Social Work," i
Orthopsychiatry, 1923–1948, American Psychiatric Association, Inc., 1948, pp
470–483.

per tantrums, special hatreds, compensatory excessive daydreaming or fabricating, various inferiority reactions, asocial tendencies, quarreling, "spoiled child" wilfulness and irresponsibility, mild depressions, etc.

(e) Conduct expressing exaggerated sexual interests 6

Non-delinquent unwholesome sexually based infatuation, sexual obsessions, fetichism, homosexual tendencies, etc.

(f) Educational maladjustments 10

Reading disabilities, school failure in spite of high I.Q., dissatisfaction with academic course, etc.

Several of the cases also displayed habits such as enuresis, thumbsucking, stammering, food dislikes, masturbatory practices, many of which are found in combinations.[43]

In the 207 cases thus represented, 151 were referred to the clinic directly from the family, 40 from the social agencies, and 13 from schools, and 3 came voluntarily. None was sent from the court. Here we get a picture of the work of a child-guidance clinic which truly serves the community.

There were 280 boys and 120 girls in this group of 400 cases. Of the personality behavior cases (207), 136 were boys and 71 were girls. In addition, 137 were labeled *noncourt delinquents*, 101 of whom were boys and 36 girls; of the 56 in the court group, 43 were boys and 13 were girls. Age distribution: 76 under 10; 157 between 10 and 13; 156 between 15 and 17; and 11 over 17.

Before commenting on the prognosis and treatment of this group of 400, it should be called to the attention of the reader that previous work of this clinic had been criticized by Drs. Sheldon and Eleanor Glueck in their definitive study, *One Thousand Juvenile Delinquents*.[44] The Gluecks have long been considered as careful research investigators in the field of delinquency and crime. Their opinions, backed by the findings of their studies, have been recognized for many years by both professional workers and by the many laymen interested in the delinquency field.

The Gluecks found that of approximately one thousand cases (actually 905) handled by the Judge Baker Clinic and the Boston

---

[43] William Healy and Augusta Bronner, *Treatment and What Happened Afterward*, 1939, p. 17. For an analysis of the mental age of these children see p. 93 of this book, where we discuss the role of feeblemindedness and delinquency.

[44] Harvard University Press, 1934.

Juvenile Court, 798 (88.2 per cent) had committed additional delinquencies during the five-year period following diagnosis by the clinic. Two-thirds of the 905 boys were arrested for serious offenses. The average number of arrests for each of the group who repeated (recidivated) was 3.6. The conclusion reached by the authors was that "the treatment carried on by the Clinic, Court, and associated community facilities had very little effect in preventing recidivism." [45]

This statement, coming from careful investigators, gave the critics of child-guidance clinics the opportunity to bolster up their prejudice against such agencies and to state that delinquent children were being coddled by advocates of these scientific techniques. The wave of vociferous discussion that was stimulated by the publication of the Gluecks' study eventually simmered down so that definite conclusions could be drawn.[46] It has been pointed out in defense of the court and clinic that the Judge Baker Foundation was at that time only a diagnostic center and had not yet embarked on a treatment program; that in only 21 per cent of the cases were all the recommendations made by the clinic for the treatment of the boys carried out,[47] and that what would have happened to these boys had they been sent to a reform school or prison might have been far worse.

The results of this study stimulated the friends of both court and clinic to check on their methods and to integrate the work of both more closely. The Gluecks themselves come to the conclusion that both the court and the clinic must be retained, since these agencies provide much more satisfactory treatment than did the old criminal court procedure of an earlier period. Moreover, they decided that the clinic "furnishes not only a scientifically valid attitude and a source of needed adult education, but very tangible immediate assistance to the Court." [48] Officials of both the Boston Juvenile Court

[45] *Ibid.*, p. 233.

[46] See *Yearbook*, N.P.P.A., 1934, pp. 63–103; see also Healy, Bronner, and Shimberg, "The Close of Another Chapter in Criminology," *Mental Hygiene* April 1935, pp. 208–282.

[47] See Benedict Alper, "Forty Years of the Juvenile Court," *American Sociological Review*, April 1941, pp. 235–236.

[48] *Ibid.*, p. 239. See Chapter XIII of their work for recommendations.

and the Judge Baker Clinic cooperated wholeheartedly with the Gluecks in their study.

Although a later follow-up study by the Gluecks of their one thousand delinquent boys, *Juvenile Delinquents Grown Up*,[49] has no bearing on the controversy, it is of interest that the investigators found that both recidivism and the number of the more serious offenses tended to decrease as the boys grew into manhood. The maturation process, in which the young adults accept responsibilities such as a family, or the commonplace *aging* process seems to slow down many juvenile delinquents. The Gluecks also made an analysis of various types of peno-correctional treatment inflicted on their cases and worked out prediction tables based upon each type of treatment.

To return to Dr. Healy's *Treatment and What Happened Afterward*, this 1939 study of 400 delinquent cases shows that 323, or 81 per cent, established favorable careers after treatment by court and clinic. Dr. Healy comments on the study made in 1934 by the Gluecks:

> On account of the well-merited wide reading that Gluecks' "One Thousand Juvenile Delinquents" has received, a statement is warranted concerning the treatment aspects of the cases they analyzed and followed—especially since the original source of their facts was our own clinical records of certain cases studied by us for diagnosis and advice during the years 1917 to 1922. With all the splendid values that this work presents, its picturing of treatment is necessarily very inadequate, since so little thorough-going and well-oriented treatment of these delinquents was carried out by anyone. It is unfortunate that the title page implies that these 1,000 delinquents received clinical treatment—even though the text indicates the opposite—because this has led to misunderstandings and erroneous statements.[50]

At the time of Dr. Healy's study, the clinic was undertaking treatment as well as diagnosis. Of the 400 cases, treatment by the clinic's facilities was carried on for two years and nine months. The following table shows the response and lack of response to recommended treatment.

---

[49] Commonwealth Fund, New York, 1940.
[50] *Op. cit.*, p. 11.

Graded Evaluations of Careers

Favorable	Totals	Personality or Behavior Problems	Noncourt Delinquents	Court Delinquents
Unexpectedly rapid or unexpectedly good response and continued success	39	19	10	10
Problems solved, less rapidly but with steady improvement	174	111	54	9
Problems solved, but some adjustments limited by intellectual handicaps or unmodifiable life situations	22	17	2	3
Main problem solved, but some undesirable personality traits persisting	30	11	12	7
Problem successfully solved, although in early stages individual occasionally influenced by bad environment	16	2	7	7
Much improvement in most particulars but not all	24	16	7	1
Much improvement, but limited by intellectual handicaps or unmodifiable life situations.	16	13	2	1
Great success for over 5 years following early period of great failure	2	0	1	1
Total favorable	323	189	95	39
	(81%)	(91%)	(70%)	(70%)

Unfavorable				
Mild personality problems, for which referred, largely unresolved	3	3	0	0
Failure through new delinquency after 2½ to 5 years of much improvement or even great success	9	0	8	1
Largely failure	30	10	15	5
Great failure	35	5	19	11
Total unfavorable	77	18	42	17
	(19%)	(9%)	(30%)	(30%)
Grand Total	400	207	137	56

The work done by the various types of behavior or child-guidance clinics is convincing evidence that scientific knowledge of the various ramifications of the etiology of maladjustment in children is essential. Diagnosis by specialists in the various fields and the subsequent treatment of maladjusted children and of children who commit overt delinquent acts are extremely important. The work being accomplished in the hundreds of clinics that are adjuncts of the court or serve them as community agencies is recognized as extremely valuable by all specialists in the problems of children and adolescents. These clinics are a welcome substitute for the hit-and-miss methods used by the older courts and for the slipshod methods even now employed by backward juvenile courts in many jurisdictions.[51]

The setting up of school counselors also helps feed the clinics and saves hundreds of children from unhappy experiences with the law. Although some elements of the public may resent scientific analysis and treatment of the young child, the tendency fortunately is in the direction of an ever-widening expansion of scientific treatment for children who obviously manifest incipient behavior difficulty.

Obviously, we cannot expect too much of the child-guidance clinic. The terms "success" or "cure," especially so far as behavior is concerned, are relative. Such intangibles as "keeping out of trouble" and "behaving himself" need not be criteria of success when behavior maladjustment is concerned. If a child who has had clinic experience avoids arrest as a delinquent, a police officer might look upon treatment as successful. Yet that same child may continue to be a problem to himself, and years later he may have serious difficulty of a mental nature.

Interesting statements regarding the success of clinics are made by Hartwell when he sums up the results of the clinic in Worcester, Massachusetts.[52] He contends that the children themselves con-

---

[51] For excellent discussions of modern methods in this field, see Helen L. Witmer, *Psychiatric Clinics for Children*, and Lois M. French, *Psychiatric Social Work*, Commonwealth Fund, New York, 1940; Frederick H. Allen, *Psychotherapy With Children*, Norton, New York, 1942; Helen L. Witmer, *Psychiatric Interviews With Children*, Commonwealth Fund, 1946; and Eugene Davidoff and Elinor Noetzel, *Child Guidance Approach to Juvenile Delinquency*, Child Care Publication, New York, 1949.

[52] Samuel W. Hartwell, Chapter XVIII in Sheldon and Eleanor Glueck's work, *Preventing Crime*, McGraw-Hill, New York, 1936.

PREVENTIVE SERVICES

sidered their treatment successful in a larger percentage of the cases than did any other group of evaluators. Next in order were the police officers—no doubt because the children were "keeping out of trouble." Parents were third in order; they would probably have been pleased at any slight indication of recovery. Teachers of the children were fourth in order, "because," as Hartwell explains, "of the educational approach which the teacher must make no matter how thoroughly she may understand the child's emotional problem." [53] Last in order were the foster parents, "explained by the fact that, no matter how intelligent or well trained they are, they feel the clinic to be, in a certain degree, in competition with them." [54]

If the reader is further interested in the functioning of child-guidance clinics, he may read what has been done in Cleveland and Philadelphia in excellent articles by Drs. Henry C. Schumacher and Frederick H. Allen, respectively, in *Orthopsychiatry, 1923–1948.*[55] A Study of the work of the Essex County, New Jersey, clinic, which was for many years under the direction of the late Dr. James S. Plant, will also be rewarding. In *Personality and the Cultural Pattern* (1937), Dr. Plant pointed out that maladjustments of environment or personality must be balanced through treatment in which emphasis is made on changing the environment rather than on modifying the personality.

c. Habit Clinics

Similar to the child-guidance clinic is the habit clinic, which usually serves pre-school children. The habit clinic grew out of the earlier well baby clinics of hospitals. Physicians attending youngsters brought to these baby clinics by their mothers were aware of the many bad habits evidenced at a very early age. The Habit Clinic of Boston was started in November 1921, in connection with the Community Health Association of that city. Dr. Douglas A. Thom has been in charge of this clinic for many years.

The name habit clinic was adopted because it was acceptable to general medical practitioners, pediatricians, social workers and psychiatrists. Since the philosophy of the habit clinic is preventive, it

---

[53] *Ibid.,* p. 376.
[54] *Idem.*
[55] American Psychiatric Association, Inc., 1948, pp. 377–393, 394–413.

deals with early symptoms of behavior problems, such as feeding, enuresis, sex, temper tantrums, pugnacity, shyness, destructiveness, convulsions, and mental retardation. The procedure adopted by the habit clinic is similar to that of all clinics dealing with problem children. In addition to careful investigation of the child, the family situation is appraised and follow-up work is carried on by social workers. The habit clinic encourages mothers who bring their children to hospitals for medical check-ups to have their youngsters examined for latent behavior problems. In this way, preventive work can begin at the earliest possible date.[56]

d. *The Guidance Center in London*

A movement similar to our child-guidance approach to the problem of personal maladjustment has been pursued in London by the Institute for the Scientific Treatment of Delinquency. Begun in 1932, it had for its chief aim the provision of facilities for examination and, where possible, treatment of cases of "anti-social" conduct, especially of young persons. By 1937 it had become a well-established clinic boasting of adequate equipment and personnel for examination, diagnosis, and treatment of delinquent "out-patients." The I.S.T.D. deals primarily with the older and more serious *pubertal* youth, since most younger children's cases are disposed of by probation officers or in the local guidance clinics. A report on the work of the Institute, covering the years 1937 to 1941, has been prepared by Dr. Edward Glover, chairman of the scientific committee and co-director of the psychopathic clinic. The following tables, taken from this report, will show the type of work being done by this distinguished clinic.

---

[56] For further details of the habit clinic, see D. A. Thom, "Habit Clinics for the Child of Pre-school Age," United States Children's Bureau, *Publication No. 135;* also by the same author, "The Importance of Recognizing Delinquent Trends During Childhood," *Federal Probation*, March 1948, pp. 29–32. The concluding statement of the latter article is worth mentioning: "There is reason to believe that much would be gained if our present-day concepts of the psychological principles underlying asocial behavior could be utilized by parents, teachers, nurses, general practitioners, and others who come in daily contact with the child, and whose influence is exerted upon the maturing child at a time when it will be most effective." Dr. Thom also wrote the excellent pamphlet *Guiding the Adolescent*, United States Children's Bureau Publication No. 225, Government Printing Office, 1933 (revised 1946).

Offenses

	Under 11 '38	Under 11 '41	11–14 '38	11–14 '41	14–17 '38	14–17 '41	Totals '38	Totals '41
Theft	1	4	4	7	20	22	25	33
Behavior Problems	–	5	–	2	–	4	–	11
Beyond Control	1	0	0	1	10	5	11	6
Sex Cases	0	1	0	0	10	5	10	6
Receiving	–	0	–	0	–	1	–	1
Breaking and Entering	0	1	1	0	0	3	1	4
Being on Enclosed Premises	0	–	1	–	0	–	1	–
In Need of Care and Protection	–	1	–	0	–	0	–	1
Truancy	–	0	–	0	–	1	–	1
Falsely Giving a Fire Alarm and Damaging Public Property	0	–	0	–	1	–	1	–
	2	12	6	10	41	41	49	63

Diagnosis

	Under 11 '38	Under 11 '41	11–14 '38	11–14 '41	14–17 '38	14–17 '41	Totals '38	Totals '41
Mentally Defective	–	1	–	0	–	2	–	3
Borderline Defective	0	2	2	1	5	2	7	5
Borderline Psychotic	0	1	0	0	2	0	2	1
Psychoneurotic	0	5	2	7	13	15	15	27
Character Case	0	1	1	1	15	7	16	9
Psychopathic Personality	0	1	0	1	1	12	1	14
Sex Pervert	0	–	0	1	1	–	1	–
Normal	1	0	1	0	1	2	3	2
Organic	0	–	0	–	1	–	1	–
Non-delinquent	1	1	–	0	–	0	–	1
Failed Appointment	1	0	0	0	2	1	3	1
	2	12	6	10	41	41	49	63

One note of explanation is pertinent. The report states that in arriving at the diagnosis of "psychoneurotic" delinquency, two standards are adopted: either the patient has suffered or is still suffering from a simple psychoneurosis (*e.g.*, anxiety states, conversion hysteria, or obsessional neurosis) to which the delinquent act, however important socially, is psychologically regarded as a secondary reaction; or the delinquent act itself is hysterical (or obsessional) in character—in other words, it is a "social symptom" or "character reaction" identical in nature with a private psychoneurotic symptom. Dr. Glover cites as an example of this latter type a genuine kleptomania, in which the delinquent act is identical with an obsessional act in all but two respects—*viz.*, that society is attacked in some manner and that the punishment courted is not, as in the true neurotic case, an "unconscious self-punishment," but a real punishment inflicted by society.

The "psychopathic" group includes persons whose faulty emotional development has given rise to various forms of unstable and abnormal behavior, some of which are legally considered delinquent. In this category are to be found some cases of sexual abnormality (or, as they are now coming to be called, *deviational*), but Dr. Glover admits the difficulty of classifying persons *conveniently* in this group.

When the complete examination of the child is finished, the results are taken to the director by the psychiatric social worker. In his report the director "indicates the relative importance of the environmental, psychological and organic factors relevant in the case and gives his provisional diagnosis in terms that will be clear to the court or other persons referring. A recommendation as to disposal follows and reasons." Included in the methods of treatment to be followed are "psychotherapy," "psychological observation," "institutional treatment" (such as home for inebriates, Borstal, mental hospital, and so forth), and "environmental changes" in home, school, work, and so on.

One further note is of interest: The actual disposition of the case does not often follow the clinic's recommendation. Dr. Glover points out that in 1940, of the 55 per cent of the cases needing it, only 32.46 per cent received treatment; in 1941, of 63.5 per cent needing it, only 38 per cent received it. But he notes that a larger percentage is getting the kind of treatment needed as the years progress.[57] The I.S.T.D., which has been subsidized by the government, has been experimenting recently with aggression among children. It has inaugurated a sort of rumpus room, under supervision, where

---

[57] The above material is taken from Edward Glover, M.D., "The Diagnosis and Treatment of Delinquency," published by I.S.T.D., London, undated (*c.* 1944). For further details of this clinic as well as of another British clinic, The Tavistock Clinic, see Kate Friedlander, *The Psychoanalytic Approach to Juvenile Delinquency*, International Universities Press, 1947, pp. 219–225; also, John Bowlby, *Forty-Four Juvenile Thieves: Their Characters and Home Life*, Baillière, Tindall and Cox, London, 1947.

children are permitted to drain off aggressive tendencies among themselves. When they have had enough of this boisterous play, they pass on to the usual conferences, which are similar to those described in our section on the child-guidance clinic.

5. THE SOCIAL CASE WORKER AND DELINQUENCY CONTROL

We have discussed the contribution of the schools of social work in setting up school counseling and have pointed out their interest in the child-guidance clinic movement. Social work is as much dedicated to delinquency prevention as to any other field of maladjustment and should be appraised objectively.

In our chapter dealing with the early historical movements concerned with child-saving, we noted that the social workers made a distinct and notable contribution. In those early days the philosophy of social work sprang largely from humanitarian motives. Placing-out in foster homes as well as in institutions was largely in the hands of social workers. Many of the early institutions dedicated to childhood employed social workers. In time, several schools of social work were organized and the profession was developed along case work lines. Today there are some basic differences in the philosophies of these schools, but they all emphasize professional training on the graduate level.

Modern social work places the emphasis of treatment on a level above that of the bare necessities of physical life. Treatment is expressed in terms of the client's emotional problems as well as his relationship and trust in the worker. To be successful, this relationship must be acceptable and satisfying to the client. This new concept pushes the older philosophy of temporary material relief and the mere accumulation of social data into the background and places the relationship between worker and client on a dignified basis.

Although the social worker may still be concerned with social history, including family, schooling, interests, and other potentialities of the client—adult or child—it is to the more latent attitudes of the client that the case worker turns. The social worker is as much concerned with the emotional life of the child as is the psychiatrist. In fact, the psychiatrist leans more heavily upon the social worker (the psychiatric social worker) in furnishing motives for a child's behavior. It is not to be implied that the social worker attempts psychiatric treatment; rather he translates the results of the psychiatric consultation into social work concepts and uses his own modes of therapy. As Hartwell states: "The psychiatrist, the psychologist and the social worker are so closely associated in their attempts to alter undesirable behavior and personality traits of children, that it is not easy to separate the functions of each." [58] Charlotte Towle points out that the social worker needs *rapport* not only with the child patient but also with the family. Close identification with the child, perhaps necessitating identification by means of a mother or father relationship, is highly important in the social worker's therapy.[59]

Writing on this use of transference in case-work treatment, Mary Secrest Odmark says:

> Every human being needs someone to believe in him to build up his conscious ego. Without a close personal relationship with someone, the individual is helpless and alone. It is my conviction that the feeling of acceptance which the client gains from the worker is so important that the kind of intellectual interpretation he receives is secondary by comparison. The emotional relief the client receives from catharsis is the important element in his cure.[60]

We need not get into the controversy regarding when a social worker becomes a psychiatric social worker. But when the professionally trained case worker finds himself associated with clinics or treatment centers and works side by side with the psychiatrist, he may label himself a psychiatric social worker. Ethel L. Ginsburg makes this distinction on the basis of clinical experience in understanding behavior and in using knowledge to help troubled people.[61]

Thus the social case worker can be of marked assistance in treating the delinquent. We shall now turn to the social group worker to see what his essential role is in prevention of delinquency.

6. SOCIAL GROUP WORK AND DELINQUENCY CONTROL

The development of the social group work philosophy in recent years has been of interest to persons engaged in the prevention of

---

[58] Samuel W. Hartwell, "The Psychiatrist," in *Orthopsychiatry, Retrospect and Prospect, 1948*, American Orthopsychiatric Association, 1948, p. 575.

[59] "The Social Worker," *ibid.*, p. 586.

[60] *American Journal of Orthopsychiatry*, Vol. 16, 1946, p. 296.

[61] "Psychiatric Social Work," *ibid.*, pp. 470–483.

delinquency, not because it focuses its attention primarily on disorganization but because it has introduced a new technique in understanding all types of social interaction. In a brief statement, social group work envisages planned and orderly ways of working with various persons in groups. The group worker is not concerned specifically with delinquency or with any other type of maladjustment; his concern is centered on developing dignified and meaningful supervision and guidance for individuals participating in group activities.[62]

Social group work attempts to supply trained leadership for the various community agencies that are dealing with leisure-time pursuits, club work, hobbies, and other such activities. It is not a new approach, but rather a new method. Those who have developed this new technique are convinced that activities furnished by community agencies such as settlements, clubs, neighborhood centers, and similar institutions are merely the means of furthering other socially desirable and perhaps even more significant ends. Group work is an educational process emphasizing the personality development and social adjustment of the participant.

When it is evident that a certain individual who is a member of group work activities—club, ball team, sewing class—has limited social capacity or possesses unusual emotional needs, the social group worker, trained in his craft, will recognize the need for sharing the responsibility with a psychiatrist, a psychologist, or psychiatric social worker. It is in this area that the social group worker makes one of his greatest contributions—in dealing with maladjusted persons. He singles them out of the crowd and turns them over to the proper specialists if he finds he does not possess the training to handle them himself. Group work can divert certain pre-delinquent tendencies into socially approved avenues by skillfully directing the wishes and desires of individuals into activities where certain satisfactions accrue or where status of the individual is heightened.

Social group work is not essentially a preventive to delinquent behavior and should not be so considered. A study of the type of clientele served by group work agencies revealed that this type of

---

[62] Grace L. Coyle, *Group Work with American Youth*, Harper, New York, 1948; and Harleigh B. Trecker, *Social Group Work: Principles and Practices*, Woman's Press, New York, 1948.

community activity is "not in general identified closely with the underprivileged and insecure elements in our population, nor with the age groups among which delinquency is most prevalent." [63] The question is, then, whether some agencies, by the nature of their programs, attitudes, and methods, do screen out the boys and girls who are handicapped physically, mentally, economically, or racially; or who are emotionally maladjusted; or who have an unfortunate and unhappy family background. The advocates of group work will certainly shun any discriminatory tactics but will continue to make the claim that they are designing their programs to help everyone who takes advantage of their offerings.

Evidence indicates that more purposeful work with social groups at play (recreational agencies), in club work (settlements), at summer camps (Y.M. and Y.W.C.A.), and in counseling (Big Brother and Big Sister) leads many persons away from frustration and insecurity into more meaningful and socially approved ways of living.

In other words, group work agencies can be expected to take responsibility for both the prevention and treatment of delinquency, but usually only as a part of their present service to individuals and to the community. To the extent that the guidance service is provided and the group work process is effectively utilized, the potentialities for prevention and treatment of delinquency are enhanced.

Group work enters the field of "character building" with a much more professional attitude than do most of the traditional organizations. Trained personnel is, of course, the most conspicuous feature of social group work. Standards have been increased in the recent past and many schools of social work offer a course of training in the field on the graduate level.

Closely associated with the philosophy of social group work is Fritz Redl, of the Department of Social Work of Wayne University. Dr. Redl has written on such subjects as guidance and counseling and has, in fact, carried on pioneer work in delinquency control in the Detroit group project at Pioneer House. This project served as a clinic for other case working agencies.[64] Dr. Redl, who is a psy-

---

[63] Ellery F. Reed, "How Effective Are Group Work Agencies in Preventing Delinquency?," *Focus*, N.P.P.A., November 1949, pp. 170 ff.

[64] For details concerning this project, see Fritz Redl, "Clinical Group Work," *American Association of Group Work Proceedings*, 1943, also "Diagnostic Group Work," *American Journal of Orthopsychiatry*, January 1944.

chiatrist rather than a social worker, has two convictions concerning treatment which are sound enough to be considered favorably in many treatment centers. They are: (1) Guidance or group counseling is ineffective in groups of more than eight or ten. (2) For every hour spent on actual group work activity, the group leader should spend five hours in record-writing and case work contacts. Such high standards dignify the profession as well as the treatment program. In older methods of guidance or supervision, workers were obliged to assume back-breaking case loads and thus spread their skill superficially over wide areas. Group work can also be of service in probation and parole work with young offenders.[65]

7. THE ROLE OF THE CHURCH IN THE PROGRAM OF DELINQUENCY TREATMENT AND PREVENTION

Throughout this book we have implied that the responsibility for inculcating the cultural aspects of life into the fabric of American youth rests in the last analysis with the home, school, and church. We have discussed at some length the role played by family and home. Here we wish to make a few remarks concerning the role of the church.

Aside from attendance at church services, including the conventional Sunday School, the religious institution has many other means of preparing the child to accept the mysteries of life and his responsibilities toward his fellow man. Participation of the church in community life is, obviously, of tremendous importance. When we make this statement we are conscious of the fact that most people think of the church merely as a physical building presided over by a minister. Yet we all know that it is people who make a church. It is the members who must help bear the responsibility of safeguarding the good name of the community and of protecting its children from baneful influences. Thus, although we may discuss the church as a mechanical institution, we must not lose sight of the fact that it is a living institution and must be kept alive through the efforts of its membership as well as its pastor.

Before discussing some of the areas in which the church may be of value in the field of delinquency prevention, it is important to

---

[65] See Harry M. Shulman, "Group Work—A New Program for Probation," *Yearbook*, N.P.P.A., 1939, pp. 116–129. See also Chapter XI, pp. 419–425.

point out the basic fact that the church varies in time and place regardless of its thesis that it stands for the immutables of life. For example, attitudes concerning human pastimes such as dancing, attendance at Sunday movies or athletic events, and the liberal observance of the Sabbath generally, vary as to time and geography. Then, too, the church is divided into various philosophic shades, running the gamut of unbending orthodoxy to humanism.

It may be assumed that the church, regardless of its point of view regarding theology, supernaturalism, Sunday observance, or the baptismal rite, is deeply concerned with the well-being of the youth of the community. With this premise assumed, we may now explore the possibilities whereby the organized church may be of service in dealing with the prevention and control of delinquency.

In preceding chapters, several references were made to the role that the church and its representatives can play in the treatment of delinquency. The following instances were mentioned in particular:

(1) The clergyman is often consulted by the probation officer before a treatment plan is formulated. His knowledge of the home situation and his position as spiritual adviser to the members of the family frequently enable him to render valuable help to the probation officer who is investigating the background of a child.[66]

(2) Among the possible court dispositions is the commitment of a child to a foster home or a private institution, or his placement under the guardianship or custody of an individual. In accordance with the Standard Juvenile Court Act, the laws of many states contain a provision that the court shall, whenever practicable, select a person or an agency or institution governed by persons of the same religious faith as that of the parents of such a child.[67]

(3) A number of churches maintain denominational institutions providing care for young delinquents. The Panel Report on Church Responsibilities of the National Conference makes some very valuable recommendations for this service:

> Church leaders, rabbis, priests and ministers should see that religious institutions operated by their respective groups lead the way in programs for the treatment of delinquency. Their programs should be frequently analyzed. They should be willing to try bold experiments.

---

[66] See Chapter VIII, p. 268.
[67] See Chapter IX, pp. 329–330.

They should make the best use that science and human experience have made available in this important field of religious ministry.[68]

(4) In the field of probation and parole, clergymen have served as volunteer probation officers or as sponsors.[69] But even if they are not connected in any such formal way with probation and parole supervision, they have frequently been called upon by probation and parole officers for consultation and help in rehabilitating youngsters who were under court surveillance. Along this line, Judge Ray G. Cowan, of the juvenile court of Kansas City, Missouri, calls a conference of the city's ministers each year to discuss and explore the possibilities of enlisting the interest of children who have come before him in church activity.[70]

In the preventive field, many churches and synagogues have in recent years included various forms of recreation in their activities' program. This has been done not only in order to attract young people to the church but also because many clergymen consider it an important part of the church's responsibility to provide healthful, supervised, leisure-time programs in the form of discussion groups, dramatic presentations, motion pictures, athletic leagues, social dances, and glee clubs. They also sponsor Boy Scout and Girl Scout troops. Opposition, particularly on the part of older church members, to such a "worldly" program is waning, especially if the ministers make a real effort to point out to the members of their congregations the natural interest of young people in such character-building recreational activities. However, it should not be overlooked that in certain more fundamentalist denominations opposition still prevails.

Frequently the church buildings where these activities take place are open not only to the young members of the congregation but have become community centers and welcome youngsters irrespective of their religious affiliation. These programs thereby contribute to a removal or at least a lowering of barriers, especially in smaller communities, between members of different religious denominations. In many communities throughout the country certain ministers,

---

[68] *Report No. 14*, p. 21. For a discussion of institutional programs see Chapter XIII, pp. 475–494.

[69] See Chapter XII, p. 474.

[70] See *Focus*, N.P.P.A., July 1949.

priests, or rabbis have, through their dynamic leadership and enthu-siasm, developed programs of wholesome recreation and character training that have attracted nation-wide attention.[71]

Expansion of church-sponsored programs in character training also points in the direction of the greater responsibility of the church and its leaders within the whole community. In recent years an in-creasing number of churches, in many cities and towns, have taken a really active part in community organization. The neighborhood council movement [72] is a good example for such active participation of clergymen and lay representatives of different faiths in com-munity affairs. In order to promote youth leadership, it has been suggested that young people who are active in church work be dele-gated to youth councils and youth commissions.

There are a number of fields in which churches and synagogues can collaborate on the local level in combating conditions that undermine family life and are dangerous to the morals of children and adults alike. For instance, they might take united action to secure proper law enforcement, especially regarding gambling, prostitution, the sale of obscene literature, and similar vices. They might jointly impress upon the local authorities the necessity for strict control of the various places of commercial recreation. One of the most impor-tant areas where church participation can be of greatest value is in the promotion of good housing. Churches and synagogues should feel called upon to assume leadership in the movement to eradicate blighted areas in our cities and rural districts.[73]

A good example of active church participation in delinquency prevention is reported from Philadelphia, where in one part of the city the Catholic as well as the Protestant churches have been actively engaged in the Referral Program of the Crime Prevention Associa-tion. The Protestant Committee, under the leadership of the Women's Department of the Philadelphia Council of Churches, has formed an organization consisting of both clergy and laymen living and working in that particular area. Similarly, monthly meetings of the various conferences of the St. Vincent DePaul Society in the

---

[71] As one example we mention Dallas, Texas. See Vern Swartsfager, *The Bell Ringers,* Macmillan, New York, 1948.

[72] See Chapter XVI, pp. 655–659.

[73] For the particular responsibilities of the rural church, see *Report No. 17* of the National Conference, pp. 28–32.

same neighborhood have resulted in improved techniques in reaching the boys referred to them.[74]

Several churches have established youth and family consultation services offering free advice by trained experts. A good example is the Episcopal Service for Youth (formerly called Church Mission of Help), which has established youth consultation services in many sections of the country. Equally well known is the work of the Salvation Army for the care of unmarried mothers and their babies. Practically all church denominations have organized some form of social service.[75]

Although not affiliated with any particular religious body, but rather functioning as nation-wide independent agencies, the Young Men's Christian Association, the Young Women's Christian Association, and the Young Men's and Young Women's Hebrew Association deserve mention in this connection.

The Quakers (The Religious Society of Friends) have done outstanding work in many fields of human relationships through their social service organization, the American Friends Service Committee. From the large list of their activities, the following should be mentioned in a text on delinquency prevention and treatment. Recognizing the evils connected with substandard housing, the American Friends Service Committee has been instrumental in promoting urban and rural redevelopment on a self-help basis in a number of communities. Their leaders have initiated many projects designed to overcome tensions between groups of different nationalities, creeds, and races. Carrying their centuries-old concern for the criminal and for the mentally sick into present-day fields of endeavor, they have taken an active part in movements on the local or state level aimed at the improvement of services and programs in penal, correctional, and mental institutions. They were stimulated by the experience of a number of conscientious objectors of World War II, some of whom were prisoners in Federal institutions themselves, while others did volunteer work in penal and mental institutions as

---

[74] For further details, see *Annual Report of the Crime Prevention Association of Philadelphia 1949*, p. 5; for a description of the Philadelphia Referral Plan, see, *infra*, Chapter XVI, pp. 661–662.

[75] For a detailed description, see *Social Work Yearbook 1949*, Russell Sage Foundation, New York, "Catholic Social Work," pp. 85–92, "Jewish Social Work," pp. 260–269, "Protestant Social Work," pp. 358–366.

a substitute for military service. They have recently set up a program of assigning units of young people from twenty-one to thirty-five years of age to serve as internes over a period of several months in various institutions for juvenile and adult offenders and in mental hospitals. Members of the units work as assistant cottage fathers or mothers and as instructors in handicrafts or academic courses. It is hoped that these experiences will prompt the participants to retain an alert interest in the problems of treatment of offenders and to participate actively as citizens in the promotion of desirable standards in this field.[76]

The foregoing is a testimony to the fact that many religious leaders and their congregations have come to realize the impelling need to gear the application of their religious tenets to the social exigencies of every-day life. Such a conviction calls for an active role of churches and synagogues, and their spiritual leaders as well as their lay members, in combating juvenile delinquency through preventive-treatment measures.

---

[76] For further details on this project, see Phoebe Bailey, "An Experiment in Institutional Service," *Prison World*, September–October 1949, pp. 29–30.

Chapter XVI

SOCIAL ACTION

1. INTRODUCTION

WE HAVE SEEN that the handling of individual cases of juvenile delinquency combines aspects of treatment as well as prevention. The work of the juvenile court and the child-guidance clinic and the use of probation and institutional placement are, of course, primarily devoted to treatment; but all these instruments also serve the purpose of prevention, inasmuch as they attempt, in the individual case situations, to keep delinquent behavior from developing into more serious criminal attitudes and acts.

Social action in the field of juvenile delinquency, too, embraces features of treatment as well as prevention. For instance, the provision of treatment facilities in a given community where such facilities are either inadequate or entirely lacking, may rightfully be the avowed aim of social action. This possibility will be discussed later in this chapter in more detail. Usually, however, social action in the field of juvenile delinquency centers around the preventive aspects of the problem.

A parallel might be found in the realm of medicine, where the treatment of a patient is focused chiefly upon his cure but also upon his immunization against the recurrence of the sickness. On the other hand, public health has developed mainly along lines of prevention, although it is "not limited to prevention, should public action be necessary to provide curative service." [1]

Let us for a moment pursue further the analogy with public health philosophy and practice. Prevention of juvenile delinquency, seen as an objective of social action, should be so broad in its approach

---

[1] Harry S. Mustard, "Public Health," *Social Work Yearbook*, Russell Sage Foundation, New York, 1945, p. 328.

as to include a comprehensive interest in the problems of youth in general. In the field of public health we have more and more come to realize that its purpose and aim are not exclusively or primarily the absence of sickness and infirmities, but rather the guarantee of physical, emotional, and social well-being for all. In the same way must an intelligent and constructive delinquency prevention program envision the conservation of our entire youth rather than just the protection of individual children or groups of children from becoming delinquent.

The present chapter deals with social action in the field of juvenile delinquency as carried out by government agencies on the Federal. state, and local levels, and with unofficial and voluntary social action as expressed through citizen participation in the attack upon juvenile delinquency as a community problem.

2. GOVERNMENTAL AGENCIES

a. On the Federal Level

Federal agencies operating in the fields of social security (in the rather broad connotation of this term), public health, and justice are concerned with the problems of youth in general, and of delinquency control, treatment, and prevention in particular.

The United States Children's Bureau was established by act of Congress in 1912, as part of the Department of Commerce and Labor.[2] When in 1913 a separate Department of Labor was created, the Children's Bureau was placed in the new department. Since 1946, it has been a unit of the Social Security Administration of the Federal Security Agency. The United States Children's Bureau's purpose is to "investigate and report upon all matters pertaining to the welfare of children and child life among all classes of the people," especially, *inter alia,* on orphanages, juvenile courts, desertion, employment of children, and legislation affecting children. Special activities of the Bureau include planning, in cooperation with other Federal and with state and local agencies, national organizations, and citizens' groups, for the prevention and control of juvenile delinquency, the development of group work, services to unmarried mothers and children

---

[2] For origin and development of the United States Children's Bureau, see Emma Octavia Lundberg, *Unto the Least of These,* Appleton-Century, New York, 1947, pp. 144–153.

born out of wedlock, and safeguards for adoption and foster care.

The great contribution which the United States Children's Bureau, in cooperation with the National Probation and Parole Association, made toward the development of juvenile court standards, ultimately resulting in the drafting of the *Standard Juvenile Court Act*, was described before.[3] Since 1927, the Bureau has rendered invaluable service through the compilation and publication of juvenile court statistics from hundreds of courts throughout the country; it has hereby provided the only available statistical source material for evaluation of the problem of juvenile delinquency on a nation-wide basis. The reports contain such items as sex, age, race of children involved, reasons for reference to court, sources of referral to court, places of detention care, and case disposition. The new method of collecting these statistical data, in use since 1946, through state departments rather than from local juvenile courts directly, was described in an earlier context.[4] Since 1945, the Bureau, in cooperation with state departments of welfare and institutions, has also published annual reports on children in public institutions, including institutions for the delinquent.[5]

The Social Security Act of 1935 provided for annual Federal grants to the states to enable them to establish, extend, and strengthen, especially in predominantly rural areas, welfare services for the protection and care of homeless, dependent, and neglected children and children in danger of becoming delinquent. These funds, amounting to $3,500,000 annually, are administered through the United States Children's Bureau.[6]

Although the Bureau's activities have been widespread and quite effective, both in their administrative and advisory aspects, they have been hampered by insufficient appropriation. The 81st Congress, therefore, was urged by the National Probation and Parole Association to increase the Bureau's budget in order to strengthen its educational and consultative services. Other recommendations included legislation to authorize the use of Aid to Dependent Children funds

---

[3] See Chapter IX, pp. 291–292.

[4] See Chapter IX, p. 337.

[5] Reference to this publication was made in Chapter XI, p. 390.

[6] For a detailed description of the United States Children's Bureau's functions and operation, see Katherine F. Lenroot (Chief of United States Children's Bureau), "The Government and Child Welfare," *Yearbook*, N.P.P.A., 1948, pp. 80–95.

to transport runaway children back to their homes and to provide grants-in-aid to states for the development of modern facilities and programs for the treatment of crime and delinquency.[7]

The original impetus for the creation of the United States Children's Bureau came from the first White House Conference on Child Welfare, held in 1909 at the call of President Theodore Roosevelt. Since then, the Bureau has been the chief promoter of the White House Conferences, which convene approximately every ten years. In 1919, designated as "Children's Year," the Conference adopted a set of standards for child care which have had wide influence. The 1930 Conference resulted in the adoption of a "Children's Charter," embodying basic goals for the welfare of children.[8] The fourth White House Conference, on "Children in a Democracy," was called at the suggestion of President Franklin Delano Roosevelt and had its first meeting in January 1940. The keynote of the Conference was "Our Concern—Every Child," and the recommendations touched upon all aspects of child life.[9] The Midcentury White House Conference on Children and Youth in December 1950, was convoked in order to evaluate progress made since previous conferences, to assess the status of services and opportunities provided children and youth in the United States and the problems affecting their welfare, and to point out the advances that can and should be made during the next decade.[10]

---

[7] See Barbara Bent Bates, "Attention, 81st Congress," *Survey Midmonthly*, December 1948, p. 369. The need for Federal funds for the transportation of runaway children was strongly advocated in an article in the *Chicago Daily News*, reprinted under the title "Runaway Children's Problem" in *Juvenile Court Judges Journal*, April 1950, p. 25.

[8] See *The Delinquent Child*, Report of the Committee on Socially Handicapped, The White House Conference on Child Health and Protection, edited by Frederick P. Cabot, chairman, Century, 1932.

[9] See *Social Work Yearbook*, Russell Sage Foundation, 1945, p. 104; *ibid.*, 1947, pp. 93–94; *ibid.*, 1949, p. 103; also, "Children in a Democracy," General Report Adopted by the White House Conference on Children in a Democracy, January 1940, Government Printing Office, Washington, D.C.; and Elsa Castendyck, "Juvenile Courts in the Light of the White House Conference," *Yearbook*, N.P.P.A., 1940, pp. 34–46; Katherine F. Lenroot, "Summing Up the Previous White House Conferences," *The Child*, October 1949, pp. 52–54.

[10] For details, see Katherine Lenroot, "The Midcentury White House Conference and Social Workers," *Social Work Journal*, July 1949, pp. 135–137; Melvin A. Glasser, "To Focus on Child's Mental, Emotional and Spiritual Growth and Development," *The Child*, October 1949, pp. 54–55, 61.

THE CHILDREN'S CHARTER

WHITE HOUSE CONFERENCES ON CHILD HEALTH AND PROTECTION HAVE RECOGNIZED THE RIGHTS OF THE CHILD AS THE FIRST RIGHTS OF CITIZEN· SHIP AND ARE PLEDGED TO THESE AIMS FOR THE CHILDREN OF AMERICA

REAFFIRM "CHILDREN'S CHARTER" OF THE 1930 WHITE HOUSE CONFERENCE ON CHILD HEALTH AND PROTECTION

Resolution No. 809, Twenty-Eighth Annual National Convention, The American Legion, San Francisco, California, September 30, October 1, 2, 3 and 4, 1946.

WHEREAS, The American Legion has, through the past 21 years, followed the principles of child welfare which are set out in the "Children's Charter" adopted by the White House Conference in 1930; and

WHEREAS, Those principles should now be newly called to the attention of the people of the United States; therefore, be it

RESOLVED, That we do now reaffirm the principles set forth in the Children's Charter and pledge ourselves to strive earnestly toward a full accomplishment of its objectives, which are as well the objectives of The American Legion.

I For every child spiritual and moral training to help him to stand firm under the pressure of life

II For every child understanding and the guarding of his personality as his most precious right

III For every child a home and that love and security which a home provides; and for that child who must receive foster care, the nearest substitute for his own home

IV For every child full preparation for his birth, his mother receiving prenatal, natal, and postnatal care; and the establishment of such protective measures as will make childbearing safer

V For every child health protection from birth through adolescence, including: periodical health examinations and, where needed, care of specialists and hospital treatment; regular dental examinations and care of the teeth; protective and preventive measures against communicable diseases; the insuring of pure food, pure milk, and pure water

VI For every child from birth through adolescence, promotion of health, including health instruction and a health program, wholesome physical and mental recreation, with teachers and leaders adequately trained

VII For every child a dwelling place safe, sanitary, and wholesome, with reasonable provisions for privacy, free from conditions which tend to thwart his development; and a home environment harmonious and enriching

VIII For every child a school which is safe from hazards, sanitary, properly equipped, lighted, and ventilated. For younger children nursery schools and kindergartens to supplement home care

IX For every child a community which recognizes and plans for his needs, protects him against physical dangers, moral hazards, and disease; provides him with safe and wholesome places for play and recreation; and makes provision for his cultural and social needs

X For every child an education which, through the discovery and development of his individual abilities, prepares him for life; and through training and vocational guidance prepares him for a· living which will yield him the maximum of satisfaction

XI For every child such teaching and training as will prepare him for successful parenthood, home-making, and the rights of citizenship; and, for parents, supplementary training to fit them to deal wisely with the problems of parenthood

XII For every child education for safety and protection against accidents to which modern conditions subject him —those to which he is directly exposed and those which, through loss or maiming of his parents, affect him indirectly

XIII For every child who is blind, deaf, crippled, or otherwise physically handicapped, and for the child who is mentally handicapped, such measures as will early discover and diagnose his handicap, provide care and treatment, and so train him that he may become an asset to society rather than a liability. Expenses of these services should be borne publicly where they cannot be privately met

XIV For every child who is in conflict with society the right to be dealt with intelligently as society's charge, not society's outcast; with the home, the school, the church, the court, and the institution, when needed, shaped to return him whenever possible to the normal stream of life

XV For every child the right to grow up in a family with an adequate standard of living and the security of a stable income as the surest safeguard against social handicaps

XVI For every child protection against labor that stunts growth, either physical or mental, that limits education, that deprives children of the right of comradeship, of play, and of joy

XVII For every rural child as satisfactory schooling and health services as for the city child, and an extension to rural families of social, recreational, and cultural facilities

XVIII To supplement the home and the school in, the training of youth, and to return to them those interests of which modern life tends to cheat children; every stimulation and encouragement should be given to the extension and development of the voluntary youth organizations

XIX To make everywhere available these minimum protections of the health and welfare of children, there should be a district, county, or community organization for health, education, and welfare, with full-time officials, coordinating with a state-wide program which will be responsive to a nation-wide service of general information, statistics, and scientific research. This should include:

(a) Trained, full-time public health officials with public health nurses, sanitary inspection, and laboratory workers

(b) Available hospital beds

(c) Full-time public welfare service for the relief, aid, and guidance of children in special need due to poverty, misfortune, or behavior difficulties, and for the protection of children from abuse, neglect, exploitation, or moral hazard

★

For EVERY child these rights, regardless of race, or color. or situation, wherever he may live under the protection of the American flag

Courtesy National Child Welfare Division, THE AMERICAN LEGION, Indianapolis, Indiana

In 1946, Congress enacted the National Mental Health Act to provide for a nation-wide program to cope with mental iilness, including those manifestations of social and mental ills that are called delinquent behavior. Responsibility for the carrying out of the provisions of this law was given to the Mental Hygiene Division of the United States Public Health Service, which—like the United States Children's Bureau—is a part of the Federal Security Agency. The main features of the program as developed under this act are: (1) to foster and expand research on the problems of mental health; (2) to promote training of personnel in the various mental health specialty fields; (3) to support and stimulate the efforts of the states to develop adequate mental health programs, particularly the preventive phases of the work. What this federal service offers to those who on the local level are dealing with the treatment and the prevention of delinquency is outlined by Dr. R. H. Felix, Chief of the Mental Hygiene Division, United States Public Health Service:

> The ultimate goal of the Public Health Service in the grants-to-states program is the establishment by the states of one mental out-patient clinic for each 100,000 of population, a figure recommended by the National Committee for Mental Hygiene. It is hoped that eventually every community will be served by a general, all-purpose mental hygiene clinic which would accept for consideration all persons presumed by the referring agent to be in need of psychiatric help. Aside from its value in furnishing psychiatric help to patients suffering from mental or emotional disturbances, the clinic can be an important educative force in the community. By interpreting the meaning of a delinquent's behavior and suggesting methods of helping him make a satisfactory social and emotional adjustment, it can spread knowledge of mental hygiene to parents, teachers, probation officers, and others dealing with delinquents. It also can offer consultative services to courts, probation departments, and other agencies on persons about whom the referring agency is concerned.[11]

The Bureau of Prisons within the Department of Justice was established in 1930. Its functions are to supervise the administration of the Federal penal and correctional institutions, to oversee the development of a system of classification of prisoners and individualization of treatment, and to make provisions for the care and custody

---

[11] Robert H. Felix, M.D., "The National Mental Health Act and Juvenile Delinquency," *Federal Probation*, April–June 1947, pp. 9–13.

of Federal prisoners committed to jails and other local institutions. Institutional facilities for Federal juvenile offenders include the National Training School for Boys, Washington, D.C., the Federal Correctional Institution at Englewood, Colorado, for younger improvable male offenders, and the Natural Bridge Camp in Virginia.[12] As of June 30, 1948, 619 juveniles were under sentence in these Federal institutions.[13]

The United States Probation System, within the Administrative Office of the United States Courts, is charged with the investigation of the social backgrounds of offenders appearing before the Federal courts, the supervision of offenders selected for probation treatment [14] and of those persons released from Federal correctional institutions on parole or conditional release, and, in the field of juvenile delinquency particularly, with the diversion of juvenile offenders to local juvenile courts capable of handling juvenile problems.[15] It publishes the excellent quarterly, *Federal Probation*, which contains not only articles pertaining to Federal judicial and correctional problems but material dealing with the entire field of probation, parole, and institutional treatment for the juvenile and the adult offender, as well as with prevention of crime and delinquency. Frequent reference to this publication has been made in our discussion.

The Judicial Conference of Senior Circuit Judges of the United States, at their conference in October 1946, asked the Chief Justice of the United States to appoint a committee to study and make recommendations with reference to the general operation of Federal probation and to the specific problems of juvenile delinquency. This committee, composed of six United States District Judges, submitted a report which dealt with such subjects as the purpose of juvenile delinquency laws, the functions and qualifications of the probation officer, chamber hearings for youthful offenders, the length of probation periods, local responsibilities for prevention and control of delinquency, and the need for adequate detention and foster-home facilities. The report contained many progressive recommendations,

---

[12] For a description of this camp, see Chapter XIII, pp. 501–502.
[13] *Federal Prisons 1948*, published by United States Bureau of Prisons, p. 7.
[14] See Chapter XI, pp. 396–397.
[15] See Chapter IX, p. 291.

and, in view of the fact that the Judicial Conference of 1947 directed its circulation among the judiciary as information and for the purpose of discussion at the judicial conferences of the various circuits, it should bring about fruitful results.[16]

The Federal Bureau of Investigation, within the United States Department of Justice, deserves mention here in connection with its semi-annual publication of the Uniform Crime Reports, based on reports received since 1930 from local and state police departments. Statistical information contained in these reports regarding age, sex, race, and type of offense is based on fingerprint records. They can well serve as a basis for an evaluation of offenses committed by the youthful offender (above juvenile court age), but they are unreliable in respect to arrests of juveniles, because in many localities children are not fingerprinted.[17] A new report form as basis for the collection of Uniform Crime Reports is being developed which will not depend upon the taking of fingerprints. This method should, therefore, "result in greater coverage of statistics on arrests and particularly on arrests of children." [18]

Although not a governmental agency *per se*, and only of a temporary character, the National Commission on Law Observance and Enforcement should be mentioned here. Appointed by President Herbert Hoover in 1929, it consisted of ten lawyers and a woman college president, who were charged with the task of studying "the entire question of law enforcement and organization of justice." It came to be known as the Wickersham Commission because its chairman was George W. Wickersham, a former Attorney General of the United States. Although this commission owed its origin primarily to the controversy over the prohibition amendment, its reports, of which fourteen were published, covered a much more comprehensive field, and its findings, based upon the research of many practitioners and theorists in the criminological field, are still of considerable value.[19] In the field of juvenile delinquency in par-

---

[16] For details, see "Reports of the Committee on Probation with Special Reference to Juvenile Delinquency," *Federal Probation*, March 1948, pp. 3–9.

[17] For a discussion of fingerprinting, see Chapter VIII, pp. 224–226.

[18] Edward E. Schwartz, "Statistics of Juvenile Delinquency in the United States," *The Annals*, January 1949, p. 19; see also I. Richard Perlman, "The Meaning of Juvenile Delinquency Statistics," *Federal Probation*, September 1949, pp. 63–67, especially p. 66.

[19] Government Printing Office, Washington, D.C., 1931.

ticular, the "Report on the Child Offender in the Federal System of Justice (Report No. 6)," and the "Report on the Causes of Crime (Report No. 13)," deserve special mention. Volume II of the "Report on the Causes of Crime" is entirely devoted to the "Social Factors in Juvenile Delinquency—A Study of the Community, the Family and the Gang in Relation to Delinquent Behavior"; its authors are Clifford R. Shaw and Henry D. McKay.

Through the initiative of Attorney General Tom C. Clark, the National Conference for the Prevention and Control of Juvenile Delinquency was held in Washington, D.C., on November 20–22, 1946. Thirteen Federal agencies and departments collaborated with the Department of Justice in the preparation of this meeting. Over 800 representatives of Federal agencies, state and local governments, and private groups national either in scope or influence, in the fields of welfare, education, recreation, and religion, attended the sessions. The work of the Conference was accomplished through individual panels meeting simultaneously throughout the first two days of the Conference and reporting their recommendations to the whole Conference on the third day. The final reports, as presented to the plenary session and approved after full discussion, covered the following: (1) Community Co-ordination, (2) General Recommendations for State and Community Action, (3) Juvenile Court Laws, (4) Juvenile Court Administration, (5) Juvenile Detention, (6) Institutional Treatment of Delinquent Juveniles, (7) Rôle of the Police in Juvenile Delinquency, (8) Housing, Community Development, and Juvenile Delinquency, (9) Recreation for Youth, (10) Mental Health and Child Guidance Clinics, (11) Youth Participation, (12) Citizen Participation, (13) Case Work—Group Work, (14) Church Responsibilities, (15) School and Teacher Responsibilities, (16) Home Responsibility, (17) Rural Aspects of Juvenile Delinquency, (18) Statistics.[20]

We have made frequent reference to the contents of these reports.

---

[20] All eighteen panel reports were published by the Government Printing Office, 1947. See also "National Conference for the Prevention and Control of Juvenile Delinquency" (containing the message from the President of the United States and a statement by Supreme Court Justice Harold H. Burton), *Federal Probation*, October–December 1946, pp. 3–4; and "Prevention and Control of Juvenile Delinquency" (Address by United States Attorney General Tom C. Clark), *ibid.*, pp. 4–8.

Although their quality varies a great deal and a number of statements are overlapping and repetitious, the reports are extremely valuable; they present and attack the problem of juvenile delinquency realistically. This overlapping was bound to produce contradictory statements in some instances; for example, in the matter of fingerprinting of juveniles the members of the panel on the Rôle of the Police clashed with the group studying Juvenile Court Administration. The great publicity given to the Conference itself and the subsequent widespread distribution of the panel reports, of which over 60,000 copies were sold during a two-year period, have undoubtedly stimulated thought and action on the community level.[21]

The Office of Education, also a part of the Federal Security Agency, has, among many other assignments, the responsibility of advising state and local authorities about school problems, including clinical procedure for the handling of child behavior problems and methods of instruction for people with special needs. The Federal program of vocational education is administered by this office under provisions of the Smith-Hughes and George-Dean Acts, later superseded by the George-Barden Act (1946). Funds available under this program have been used to assist states in providing pre-service and in-service training for police officers and other correctional personnel. This agency also collects information on public and private residential schools for delinquent children and publishes it in its "Statistics of Children in Special Schools and Classes for Exceptional Children."

As a means of coordination, the Inter-Departmental Committee for Children and Youth, composed of representatives of the various branches of the Federal Government concerned with the well-being of children and youth, was established in May 1948 by the Federal Security Administrator at the request of the President of the United States.

b. On the State Level

The functions of state governmental agencies in the administrative program dealing with juvenile delinquency were described in several

---

[21] According to the Continuing Committee of the National Conference, which suspended operation in February 1949, several hundred local conferences were held, patterned after the National Conference (see *Focus*, May 1949, p. 86; see also Chapter I, pp. 10–11, and Chapter XVI, p. 662).

earlier contexts. Reference was made to the few existing state juvenile courts and to the supervisory and advisory services rendered by state departments to local juvenile courts.[22] State participation in the administration of probation in several states was also mentioned.[23] The new approach in handling adolescent and juvenile delinquents on the state level, as exemplified by the Youth Authority in California and similar agencies in Minnesota, Wisconsin, Massachusetts and Texas, has also been described.[24]

Although the picture of state participation in juvenile court and probation administration is still more or less sporadic, the responsibility of state agencies regarding the establishment and management of institutions for delinquents has become quite generally accepted. There are still numerous private institutions for delinquent children with their own boards of managers, though subject to general state control and inspection. Many of them, however, have for years received considerable financial aid from the state because they could not otherwise continue to function. A goodly number of them would be ready and willing to be taken over entirely by state authorities, but the state might not be prepared to do so, either because no adequate machinery has been established in the state government for the management of such institutions or because the particular institution might not fit into a planned institutional program of the state.

It should be remembered that many of the private institutions owe their origin not to any planful response to existing needs ascertained by objective and scientific surveys, but rather to the best though whimsical intentions of individuals endowing good causes with their wealth, or to narrow sectarian aspirations of religious bodies. Tradition and personal vested interests have often played an important role in the perpetuation of private institutions that should either be closed or incorporated into a well-planned state institutional program. Depression and inflation have been instrumental in accelerating the latter process.

In spite of the general trend toward state responsibility for institutions, there is still room for the establishment of special institutions on the local level, as for instance, the so-called "parental schools,"

---

[22] See Chapter IX, pp. 336–338.
[23] See Chapter XI, pp. 395–396.
[24] See Chapter X, pp. 354–371.

i.e., 24-hour-a-day schools for truants which are administered by the local school boards—and for small institutions provided by city or county governments for short-term care.

To say that the state is the proper governmental unit for providing and managing institutions for delinquents is not enough. The question arises as to which state department is best qualified for this function. The answer is complicated by the extreme lack of uniformity in the structure of our state governments. Most states have welfare departments or boards or similarly named agencies, but the scope of their functions differs, particularly in respect to the administration of institutions. Several states have separate departments of correction in charge of penal and correctional institutions for adults as well as for juveniles. Some institutions for the mentally defective delinquent or the psychopathic offender are found under the administration of departments of health. The National Conference, after enumerating the various types of administrative control of institutions for juvenile delinquents which are at present in existence in the various parts of the country, proposed the following:

> It is generally accepted that state institutions for juvenile delinquents should not be administered by a department which is chiefly concerned with the correction of adults. In view of the case-work functions involved, most experts in the field believe that juvenile training schools should be the administrative responsibility of the State public welfare agency. However, in view of the function of the training school as an educational center, there is an appreciable body of opinion favoring administration of the institution by State educational authorities or through a cooperative relationship between the State departments of education and welfare.[25]

The proper assignment of institutional administration to the state department that is best fitted for this job is by itself not yet a guarantee for the success of the program. In an earlier connection,[26] several prerequisites for adequate intramural treatment were described in detail. These prerequisites should be studied and put into practice by the officials on the upper level of government. Persons of the highest caliber should be appointed for the actual manage-

---

[25] "Institutional Treatment of Delinquent Juveniles," *Report No. 6*, pp. 2–3.
[26] See Chapter XIII, pp. 475–494.

ment of the institutions and for the administrative control of the
entire institutional program within the state.

Assuming responsibility for the prevention and treatment of juvenile delinquency on a more comprehensive scale than institutional
placement alone, some state departments and agencies have organized
special divisions or bureaus devoted to this task. Their services are
mostly advisory to local agencies dealing with the delinquency
problem. They can perform a much needed job by arousing local
communities to the need for programs of delinquency prevention
and control.

Illinois, for instance, has organized a special division on delinquency prevention, now called "Division of Youth and Community
Service," within the state Department of Public Welfare. This division has for many years promoted annual state-wide conferences on
delinquency prevention and through a staff of experts seeks to stimulate local action for youth programs, primarily through the establishment of community councils. Among the other points of its ambitious program are the publication of several manuals in the field of
delinquency prevention, e.g., "A Study of Youth Centers," "Police
Manual," "Manual for Probation Officers," "Recreation Manual";
the organization of Big Brother and Big Sister Committees, and of
community centers, Teen Towns, and Youth Centers; and assistance
in the formation of "Juvenile Police Divisions" within local police
departments and assistance upon request in the training of probation
officers.

One of the outstanding examples of state-local collaboration in
delinquency prevention is the work of the Division of Community
Services for Delinquency Prevention of the New Jersey Department
of Institutions and Agencies. The activities of this bureau consist of
the following: to render advisory and consultation service to local
communities in all matters pertaining to juvenile welfare services;
to raise the level of county juvenile court services and to compile an
annual census of children dealt with by juvenile courts; to further a
closer relationship between schools and social agencies and to develop
a greater awareness on the part of teachers of the mental hygiene
aspects of the educational process; and to engage in research
projects.[27] Legislation sponsored by the Division of Community

---

[27] Details of this program are described by the Director of this Division,
Douglas H. MacNeil, "Two and One-half Years of State-Local Collaboration

Services and passed in 1947 authorized municipalities to creat agencies called "Municipal Youth Guidance Councils" for the purpose of co-ordinating local child and youth welfare services. Some thirty municipalities have created such councils.[28]

In some states, mobile mental hygiene clinics, organized on a state-wide basis and staffed with psychologists and social workers, have traveled through all parts of the state and have provided preventive services, especially in rural areas not otherwise reached by such facilities.[29]

As a necessary basis for concerted state action in the field of juvenile delinquency control, information must be made available on the extent of the problem and the existing preventive and treatment facilities. The development and improvement of uniform statistics is definitely a state function, especially in view of the collection of nation-wide statistical reports by the United States Children's Bureau on the basis of figures from states rather than from local authorities.[30] In addition to the figures which are required by the United States Children's Bureau and which contain only the most rudimentary data, more detailed statistics should be collected by the state authorities so that a reliable evaluation of existing services and an appraisal of gaps in the state correctional program can be facilitated.

Since legislation in the field of crime and delinquency is centered in the states, it is natural that many state legislatures, prompted by the great amount of publicity on child delinquency or prodded by

---

in Delinquency Prevention," *Yearbook*, N.P.P.A., 1948, pp. 252–262; see also the very good brochure, "Delinquency Can Be Prevented," by Sanford Bates, Commissioner, New Jersey Department of Institutions and Agencies (published by its Division of Community Services for Delinquency Prevention in June 1946), which contains many valuable suggestions for state-local cooperation in delinquency prevention, including a guide for appraisal of community progress in delinquency control in the form of a rating scale.

[28] See Douglas H. MacNeil, "The State and Delinquency Prevention," *Newsletter*, National League To Promote School Attendance, September 1949, pp. 43–46. For a critical appraisal of the Municipal Youth Guidance Council Act, see Paul G. Cressey, "Delinquency Prevention Begins at Home," *Focus*, May 1949, p. 78–82.

[29] A service of this kind was offered in Michigan; see Lowell J. Carr, "State Plan for Delinquency Prevention," *Yearbook*, N.P.P.A., 1942, pp. 36–45; see also National Conference *Panel Report No. 17*, "Rural Aspects of Juvenile Delinquency," p. 49.

[30] See Chapter IX, p. 337.

concerned citizens' groups, have created special committees devoted to the problems of juvenile delinquency. These committees sometimes consist of members of the legislature only, or they are augmented by practitioners in the field and by interested lay citizens. Their objective usually is the preparation of needed legislation, including the appropriation of funds for state services in this field. Detailed state-wide surveys have been undertaken by some of these committees to serve as a basis for legislative and budgetary proposals.

Similar committees, with the same objective, have been appointed by the governors of states; they frequently cover the whole field of youth guidance and conservation. During World War II, such groups were formed in many states in connection with the Federal and state offices of Civilian Defense.[31]

Whereas commissions of this type have concerned themselves with the juvenile delinquency problem as part of the larger program of youth conservation in general, other bodies, such as the State Crime Commissions, which became active at about the same time as the National Commission on Law Observance and Enforcement, have approached the problem as one of several aspects of the total phenomenon of criminality.[32]

Dr. Lowell Juilliard Carr, in his article "Organization for Delinquency Control," which is based on a comprehensive survey of state participation in this field up to the year 1948, describes the scope of the most spectacular state program of this kind, the one in New York State:

> Governor Dewey appointed a study committee in 1943, and on the basis of this committee's report in 1945 approved the creation of a "temporary" State Youth Commission to expire July 1, 1950. This commission, with very explicit powers of spending state money to release local money for preventive purposes, has proceeded to develop what is perhaps the most comprehensive plan for the control of juvenile delinquency yet proposed in the United States.
>
> Standing, of course, on the technical services provided by the public and private social agencies and law enforcement bodies of the richest

---

[31] See Katherine F. Lenroot, "Federal and State Action," in the "Juvenile Delinquency" issue of the *Survey Mid-Monthly*, March 1944, pp. 93–95, 105–106.

[32] There are also some local crime commissions, as, for instance, the one in Chicago, which has been in existence for over thirty years.

state in the Union, this plan is aimed at stimulating local communities to help themselves. During its first year the New York commission expended more than $300,000 of state money which in turn released more than $500,000 from local municipalities outside of New York City, a grand total of more than $800,000. For what? Mainly the three things: (1) the establishment of local Youth Bureaus for young people; (2) recreation projects; and (3) educational projects which include guidance clinics. In 1948 this program was working through eleven Youth Bureaus and three new traveling child guidance clinics added to the state's previous eight. There were also 520 recreation projects under way.

Such a statement, however, conveys no idea of the comprehensive scope of the Youth Commission's approach. In "Prevention in Action," published in July 1946, the commission sketched a program which, pivoting on the Youth Bureaus and the special projects, is designed to articulate and co-ordinate the entire educational, clinical, law enforcement, and public relations agencies in the state. One of its most significant lines of attack is the early discovery of maladjusted children in the schools.[33]

Summarizing the whole picture of state activities in this field, Carr states:

Out of 39 states on which data were available, 23 had set up special bodies of some kind: 5 central planning bodies; 6 co-ordinating and educational bodies; and 12 commissions whose functions ranged from advice to the drafting of new children's codes. This seemed to indicate a widespread feeling that something needed to be done either to strengthen the juvenile court or to supplement it with additional services. Organizations carrying on social action in the delinquency field were reported from twelve states. The 1946 National Conference for the Prevention and Control of Juvenile Delinquency has had lasting effects in seven out of the twelve states reporting active organizations.[34]

---

[33] *The Annals*, January 1949, pp. 64–76 (quotation on p. 66). According to Governor Dewey, the State Youth Commission provided state aid to 700 local youth projects throughout the state; see *The New York Times*, October 9, 1949. The life of the State Youth Commission later was extended to July 1, 1953; in April 1950, over two million dollars were appropriated to the Commission. Most of this money was earmarked for state aid to localities for the establishment and operation of youth centers (see *The New York Times*, April 2, 1950).

[34] *Ibid.*, pp. 75–76. See also the same author's article, "Most Courts Have To Be Substandard," *Federal Probation*, September 1949, p. 33.

In preparation for the 1950 White House Conference on Children and Youth, practically all states organized planning committees or councils, some officially established, others on a voluntary basis.[35]

c. On the Local Level

If juvenile delinquency control and prevention are viewed as part of a broad program of youth conservation, the local governmental agencies in county, city, borough and school district, which are concerned (or should be concerned) with this problem, amount to a goodly number.

It has been stressed again and again that the real focus of the attack upon juvenile delinquency and its contributing factors should be in the local community, and that without concerted action on the local level, state and Federal programs cannot succeed.

The responsibilities and the scope of work of those local public agencies which are dealing with a child manifesting delinquent behavior were presented in previous chapters. The function of the municipal police as a law-enforcing agency and their activities in the field of crime prevention were enumerated before,[36] and the jurisdiction and operation of the juvenile courts and their probation departments, overwhelmingly local in character, were described in detail.[37] Reference was also made to the existence of institutional placement facilities on the local level, although the number of such facilities is gradually diminishing.

Other local public functions that are directly related to the physical and mental well-being of our youth in general, and to the prevention of delinquency in particular, are centered in the city and county departments, boards, or commissions charged with the administration of public welfare or assistance, public health, sanitation and housing inspection, and recreation.

Concerning recreation, the National Conference reports, "It is in the community that recreation as a function of government takes its roots, and it is in the town, city or county that recreation becomes wedded to the people." [38] In spite of this general trend, however,

---

[35] See Katherine Lenroot, "This Is Your Conference," *The Child*, September 1949, p. 48.

[36] See Chapter XV, pp. 577–586.

[37] See Chapters IX and XI.

[38] "Recreation for Youth," *Panel Report No. 9*, National Conference, p. 82; see also text of a suggested local recreation ordinance, *ibid.*, pp. 91–92.

public recreation in the various communities is quite sporadic. In many municipalities public recreation is administered as a part, and often a very minor and neglected part, of the numerous functions of a city department. Frequently the funds allotted for recreational purposes are pitifully small and inadequate. A great deal remains to be done to make the public realize that recreation is not one of those "new-fangled frills" invented by the government and somewhat akin to the *panem et circenses* of the Roman emperors; but rather that it is a medium through which the physical and mental energies of youth as well as of adults are exercised in a wholesome way. There are signs of much progress. The number of playgrounds, playfields, and community centers all over the country is continuously increasing. In 1946, more than $54,000,000 were expended for municipal recreation projects by 1,488 communities. As the *Social Work Yearbook* points out:

> No standard pattern of organization or program is desirable or practicable in municipal recreation, but several factors are considered essential to successful recreation service. They are (a) a full-time, trained recreation executive; (b) a year-round program serving all the recreation interests of the people without restriction as to race, religion, age, or sex; (c) availability and use for recreation of all suitable city-owned property; (d) a segregated recreation budget; and (e) a governing board or commission of responsible citizens.[39]

The role of the school in a program of delinquency control has been discussed in this text from various angles. The problem of the truant child, the inadequacies of the school curriculum, the parental schools, and the school guidance services were commented upon in previous chapters. Within the large scope of delinquency prevention, the school has an additional role to play. The Panel Report on School and Teacher Responsibilities of the National Conference advised city, county, or district boards of education to employ school staffs qualified to understand child behavior and to work with pupil problems; to provide specialized services for the schools, including those of visiting teachers, guidance counselors,[40] attendance workers,

---

[39] Howard Braucher, "Recreation," *Social Work Yearbook*, Russell Sage Foundation, 1947, p. 432; see also *ibid.*, 1949, pp. 427–429.

[40] See Robert C. Taber, "The Potential Role of the School Counsellor in Delinquency Prevention and Treatment," *Federal Probation*, September 1949, pp. 52–56.

and remedial specialists; to establish a child guidance clinic in co-operation with other community agencies; to provide adequate health services, with regular physical examinations, and with attention to both mental and physical health; and to make school facilities available for youth and adults through a program of community activities that utilizes the plant to the maximum.

Special emphasis is laid upon the provision for an adult education program, including parent education courses which will provide an opportunity for parents to study child development and family relations under the leadership of specialists in this field. As the Panel Report points out:

> The most effective parent education is attained when the school invites fathers and mothers to participate in the planning, development, and evaluation of an adequate school program. Frequent conferences between school staff and parents, as well as the utilization of the special abilities and skills of certain parents in the everyday program, will help combine the home and school into a single effective force. Encouragement should be given to the development of good home-school relationships. The organization of parent-teacher groups should be encouraged and professional leadership should be provided to guide them.[41]

Many parents who are badly in need of the help and advice which are offered in adult education courses or through programs of parent-teacher associations show their lack of interest by staying away from all such activities; often they are not at all aware of being in need of such help. Significantly, the approach in these cases which the National Conference recommends is based on the idea of establishing relationships between home and school through individual contacts. "Social forces or individuals in the community outside the schools that already have strong rapport with the parents can often help to bring this about. Such persons may include the family doctor, the welfare worker, the county agent, the public-health nurse, the parish priest, minister, or rabbi, a labor leader, or the official of a neighborhood club to which the parent belongs." [42]

A quite different approach, using compulsory methods, was used in the San Francisco experiment, which, after its beginnings in 1943,

---

[41] "School and Teacher Responsibilities," *Panel Report No. 15*, p. 7.
[42] *Ibid.*, pp. 7–8.

received nation-wide publicity and was copied in several other communities. This was the so-called "Parental School," [43] later known as the San Francisco Parent Guidance Center. Its program consisted of an experimental night-school class, conducted by the Board of Education, to which parents were referred from the juvenile court, chiefly its Boys' Division, with instructions to attend for eight consecutive Monday evenings. The number of referrals of parents amounted to 53 families in 1943, 64 in 1944, 117 in 1945. Since these were war years, more mothers than fathers were enrolled; only in 52 instances were fathers (either singly or with the mothers) required to take the course. Attendance was carefully recorded; the parents were reminded of their obligation to complete the course and were given to understand that lack of cooperation on their part would have to be reported to the court, and that this would be taken into consideration in connection with later decisions concerning the cases of their children. The topics discussed at these sessions by specialists in the various fields included education, law, play, work, health, religion, social relationships, and personal development, as they relate to proper parenthood.

In view of the wide public interest in this project, the National Probation and Parole Association undertook a study of its scope, method of operation, and results. These are some of the conclusions of the four months' survey:

The parents of delinquent or neglected children may or may not be themselves delinquent, inadequate or ignorant. Whether to punish, to aid, or educate them is a grave question frequently involving complex situations and obscure personality factors. Hence any course of action, any form of treatment, should be based on a knowledge of individual needs. There was too little evidence that this was the case in San Francisco. While group instruction cannot be a substitute for personal counselling or case work, there is, nevertheless, a real and valid place for it in a comprehensive educational health and welfare program in most communities.

But special schools for parents of delinquent children can be dangerous liabilities unless certain hazards are successfully avoided; the mere form of parental education can easily be mistaken for the substance of what the better school departments are offering today for all youth

---

[43] Not to be confused with the term "parental school" as applied to boarding schools for truant children.

and for all mothers and fathers. The extravagant claims which so commonly attach to novel and popular undertakings can be misleading and ultimately disillusioning; urgently needed professional services such as intensive family case work can be impaired or even omitted in favor of a superficial program.

The argument that mandatory segregated school attendance for certain parents is as beneficial as compulsory education is for children overlooks the fact that to most boys and girls school is a common part of normal living, while for adults it can easily become a humiliating experience associated with failure. This was borne out in a number of interviews with both parents and probation officers in San Francisco. It is safe to say that an "invitation" by a judge (no matter how tactfully given) will be interpreted as compulsive and in the presence of children at court may easily result in mothers and fathers being conditioned to reject the services offered. This was brought out by the parents interviewed in this study.[44]

Heeding this criticism, the San Francisco authorities have modified the referral system decisively in recent years; the compulsory aspects were all but dropped. Now the court referee familiarizes the parents of children in trouble with the program of the Guidance Center and suggests that they voluntarily take advantage of what it has to offer. As the *Annual Report* of the San Francisco Juvenile Court Department for 1948 points out, referrals continue to be screened to admit those parents most likely to benefit from the program. Discussion leaders have now become quite proficient in the presentation of their subjects, and interest in the program is relied upon to maintain attendance. There have been a few withdrawals because of lack of interest, change in working hours, change of residence, and health reasons. The number of individuals referred in 1946 was 202; in 1947 it was 260; and in 1948 it amounted to 183. The decrease in 1948 is explained by two factors, namely the general improvement in the total delinquency situation and a further refinement in methods of referral.[45]

---

[44] John Schapps, *A Study of the San Francisco Parent Guidance Center,* N.P.P.A., 1946 (mimeographed), p. 17.

[45] For more details, see "Youth Services Unlimited," *Annual Report of the San Francisco Juvenile Court Department 1948,* p. 64; see also Howard Whitman, "Let's Stop Blaming the Parents," *Woman's Home Companion,* September 1949, p. 159. For a discussion of the problem of "punishing parents" for the delinquent acts of their children, see Chapter IX, pp. 300–304.

An earlier experiment of conducting a parent school for fathers and mothers of children referred to the court for delinquent behavior was undertaken in 1931 by the Domestic Relations Court of Columbus, Ohio, in cooperation with the Ohio State University. Parents were invited through a formal letter signed by the judge to attend "a parents' meeting conducted by the Court as one of the conditions of the child's probation." Before the invitations were sent out, probation officers had personally talked to those parents who were expected to derive some benefit from a lecture course on child care and training and had stimulated their interest.[46] In Baltimore, Maryland, the probation department of the juvenile court, in cooperation with the board of education, worked out a program in parent education with classes meeting once weekly for eight weeks. These sessions are brought to the attention of the parents by the judge so that they may enroll voluntarily. Particular emphasis is laid upon the value that parents whose children were committed to training schools may receive from this instruction. Such subjects as proper time and frequency of visits to the institution and the adjustment of the child after his discharge from institutional care are part of these courses. One of the results of this program was an increase in visits to the training schools by parents who attended these classes.[47] In more recent years, several communities inaugurated voluntary parent education courses open to all interested parents; it was not considered wise to single out parents of delinquent children and to organize courses exclusively for them.

In a growing number of cities, a new public agency has been established in recent years in the form of a board, commission, or department devoted to city planning. The unplanned and often haphazard development of many of our large population centers during the past fifty years has produced difficult problems of traffic congestion, deterioration of center city blocks, and lack of community facilities in urban areas of highest population density. We have at last come to realize that we must avoid the disastrous continuance of such planless and uncontrolled development, with its attendant thwarting of the physical and mental growth of the next generation.

[46] For more information on the Columbus project, see Sheldon and Eleanor Glueck (edd.), *Preventing Crime*, McGraw-Hill, New York, 1936, pp. 413–427.

[47] For more details on this program, see E. Preston Sharp, "Teamwork in Maryland," *Juvenile Court Judges Journal*, January 1950, pp. 9–10, 26.

Although city planning and urban redevelopment authorities have concentrated primarily on the aspects of traffic engineering and housing, they have not neglected to include in their scope of operation the planning of basic community facilities and services in the field of education, including adult education, health (physical and mental), sports, and recreation. The important role that intelligent and comprehensive city planning has to play in the prevention of delinquency and in the larger program of youth conservation and reclamation has been well described by the Panel Report on "Housing and Juvenile Delinquency" of the National Conference:

> The provision of certain community facilities such as sewers, water, paving, power, and schools, is unquestioned, and the responsibility for their planning and installation is definitely established by local customs, procedures, and regulations.
>
> But the responsibility of planning and providing for the other community facilities is not as well defined either by regulations or custom. These other facilities, often considered secondary, but which have a definite relation to juvenile behavior, are: outdoor play areas adjacent to dwellings for the use of small children; neighborhood playgrounds for the use of both children and adults; meeting rooms or halls for clubs, classes, and special interest groups; indoor areas for group care and activities for small children.
>
> The community has the sole responsibility for the provision of the following: large parks, swimming pools, and athletic fields; hospitals and branch health clinics, including prenatal, well-baby, and immunization clinics; branch libraries; community houses with playfields, gymnasiums, and auditoriums.
>
> In addition to planning for all community services and facilities the local government must program, budget, and finance these things if they are to be made available when needed. Without doing this, the best of plans are meaningless and the community may very likely fail in providing services and facilities where and when required without delay. And so it is that, as a means of forestalling conditions that are favorable towards juvenile delinquency, the local community has the responsibility and the means of seeing that its present and future housing has the necessary community services and facilities that will make it a healthy addition to the community.[48]

---

[48] "Housing and Juvenile Delinquency," *Report No. 8*, pp. 27–28.

3. CITIZEN PARTICIPATION

a. Delinquency as a Community Problem

In a democracy, all governmental actions on the federal, state and local level, as described so far, must not only be based on "the *consent* of the governed"; in order to become truly successful, they must also be supported and supplemented by the active and continuous interest of all citizens.

The publicity accompanying the spectacular numerical increase of juvenile delinquency cases during World War II, though often using sensational and unscientific means of presentation and frequently indulging in exaggerations and generalizations, produced at least one good result: It made the individual citizen and many citi-

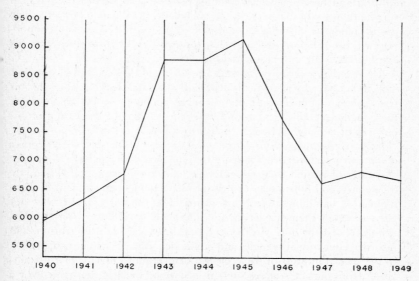

Juvenile delinquency cases disposed of in Municipal Court (Juvenile Court) of Philadelphia during calendar years 1940–1949. (The trend of the Philadelphia figures is quite similar to the general trend throughout the United States.)

zens' groups "delinquency conscious." It thus provided fertile ground in which to sow the seeds of a positive and constructive approach to the youth problem. Those persons who were attracted merely by a sense of morbid curiosity or who "talked juvenile delinquency" and showed seeming concern about it only because it had become some kind of a fad soon fell by the wayside. But a strong nucleus of serious-minded individuals went on to study the facts and to initiate actions along the lines of treatment and prevention.

Before we discuss the various forms that citizen participation can take, let us cite some of the answers which the Panel Report on "Community Co-ordination" of the National Conference has given to the question: "Why is delinquency a problem for the whole community?"

Because it is a composite problem: Human behavior is the result of many types of influences on the individual. A child's character, personality and ability to grow up without seriously deviating from the rules of society, are determined by such things as his home life, his cultural and hereditary background, his economic status, his physical surroundings, what he sees, hears, and reads, his companions and their group standards, his physical and mental health, his educational opportunities, his religious training, his recreational opportunities and his community's law enforcement program.

Because many organized groups are involved: When a child does get into difficulty, the way he is handled, the facilities available for his treatment and guidance, and the timing and manner in which all of these facilities go into action on his behalf have a definite bearing on his chances of becoming a stable, useful member of society.

Because the program of services has usually "just grown": Whether community services are adequate or poor, the basic pattern is usually the result of many years of spasmodic, and, too often, stunted growth. The courts and police may or may not have developed specialized techniques for handling juvenile problems. The schools may or may not have adjusted their service in consideration of children with special problems of behavior. Most of the health, welfare and recreation, and informal educational agencies and public departments can be traced back to the special interest of some citizen or group of citizens, or to stimulation from outside sources such as a State or Federal department or a State or National voluntary agency operating in a specialized field. The resulting pattern of services is, therefore, understandingly complex and not uniformly developed.

Because it affects all citizens: No intelligent approach to doing something about juvenile delinquency can be limited to services for children and youth who have become involved in the law. The needs of every young person in the community must be taken into consideration. In turn the cost of delinquency in money, property damage, unhappiness, personal insecurity, etc., is borne by every citizen.

Because specialized services are necessary: Quite properly experience has resulted in the development of specialized agencies and specialized workers to meet the various problems of children and youth. There exists a need for the co-ordination of the functions and programs of specialized agencies dealing with the problems of youth, including those causative factors leading to juvenile antisocial behavior.

Because the problem is rooted in the basic strains of our culture: Since the problem of delinquency has its roots deep in the conflicts, uncertainties and confusions that characterize America, the most fundamental approach to the problem is in terms of the values, habits, and structure of the total community. The attack on delinquency cannot be merely piecemeal, nor limited to formal agencies and institutions; it involves the attitudes and behavior of the entire citizenry.[49]

In answer to the question "What can the community as a whole do about delinquency?" the report points out the following objectives:

Getting the facts about and studying the total picture of community needs and resources as related to the problem.

Promoting public understanding and the ways in which it should be or is being handled in the community.

Promoting a balanced growth and maximum quality of community services in this field.

Relating the problem of delinquency to other social problems so that it is seen and handled with the proper perspective.

Co-ordinating the service programs of all agencies dealing with children and youth.

Taking action to correct community conditions which contribute to delinquency.[50]

b. Citizens' Councils

Numerous citizens' groups have been organized on the state and, in particular, on the local level, devoted either to the problem of juvenile delinquency or to the larger matter of youth welfare in

---

[49] "Community Co-ordination," *Report No. 1*, pp. 1-3.

[50] *Ibid.*, pp. 3-4; the same idea is well expressed in Lester D. Crow and Alice Crow, *Our Teen Age Boys and Girls*, McGraw-Hill, New York, 1945, pp. 336-337.

general, of which the delinquency problem constitutes an important part. The immediate impetus to the formation of such groups might be found in the impact of a particularly heinous crime committed by a youngster, or in the discovery of some shocking conditions in the community producing antisocial behavior among youth, or in the awareness of a general rise of unlawful acts by children and adolescents as dramatized by the large number of police arrests and referrals to the juvenile court.

The composition of these citizens' committees, often called "citizens' councils," varies from locality to locality. Sometimes a number of individual citizens, genuinely concerned about the problem and anxious to be of help in its solution, have banded together for this purpose. More often, already existing organizations such as civic groups, fraternal and service organizations, women's clubs, and church groups have joined forces for a concerted attack upon delinquency. Some committees are composed entirely of lay citizens; in others, practitioners in the field of education, child care, and related areas meet with lay people for common deliberation and action. In some communities the initiative originated with alert public officials who realized the importance of citizen participation in this matter and who, therefore, appointed committees composed of representative citizens as fact-finding and advisory groups.

Somewhat related to this type of citizens' groups are the several boards and commissions created by law for a definite purpose. They are composed of citizens who are selected for this appointment by local or state officials in view of their particular knowledge or their representative position in the community, political or otherwise. The function of these commissions ranges all the way from purely advisory service to policy-making power. They are established, for instance, in connection with the maintenance of a house of detention for children, with the operation of the juvenile court and its probation department, with the administration of local and state welfare departments, with the management of institutions, guidance centers, and classification clinics.

Special "probation committees" are in operation in California. According to the juvenile court law of that state, the judge of the superior court in each county (or, in those counties that have more than one judge, the judge who has been designated to sit in juvenile court) appoints a committee of citizens of good moral character to function as a probation committee. The number of the members of this committee is nine in all counties having a population of over 600,000; in the other counties it is seven. These probation committees have a general supervisory and advisory function regarding the work of the county juvenile courts and their probation departments. Upon request of the court or the county board of supervisors, the probation committee may be asked to examine the qualifications and the management of any agency or institution to which wards of the juvenile court are committed. If the court requires it, the probation committee may also exercise friendly supervision over the wards of the juvenile court, and the members of the committee may be called upon to make investigations and recommendations to the court. In conjunction with the juvenile court, the probation committee can establish special committees and councils with delinquency prevention as their object, and can cooperate with or participate in the work of any such existing councils devoted to the improvement of recreational, health, and other conditions in the community that affect juvenile welfare. Finally, the probation committees are empowered to nominate probation officers and assistant probation officers for the juvenile courts; the judge will then appoint probation officers from such a list. In Los Angeles County, the probation committee is the administrative body of the detention home, called Juvenile Hall, while, as has been mentioned elsewhere, the probation department there is an independent agency under the direct control of the county board of supervisors.

Returning now to the more spontaneously created and less circumscribed citizens' groups who really represent the "grass roots" movement of a democratic citizenry, we find that not only their composition but also their objectives vary a great deal from one state, city, or town to another. The aims and purposes of these groups, often formulated only after a long, drawn-out process of discussions, consultations, and surveys, depend on such local circumstances as the existence and efficiency of public and private youth-service agencies, the amount of real interest and readiness on the part of the whole community, and the extent of cooperation and encouragement from public officials. The scope of interest and activities of these citizens' groups is necessarily influenced by the representativeness of their constituent members or affiliated organizations, the availability of funds, and the strength of leadership. Consequently, their attack

might be centered upon the creation or the improvement of one particular service in the treatment or preventive program; or their target
might be a much broader one, such as cleaning up unhealthy community conditions and sponsoring local and state legislation.

Several samples of activities of this kind on a *state-wide* basis are
recorded by the Panel Report on "Citizenship Participation" of the
National Conference:

> In the Far West, a women's organization in one of the leading cities
> became conscious of the needs of mentally defective children, and
> worked until the State Legislature passed the "Children's Colony Bill."
>
> The youth conservation committee of one of the largest women's
> organizations in one state assumed leadership in promoting passage of
> a health and physical education law, which defines the goals of physical
> education, the area of health instruction and provides for a program of
> school health examinations, from the first through the twelfth grades.
> Another has established youth centers, helped create and supervise
> playgrounds, opened, equipped, and staffed libraries. In cooperation
> with the state youth authority and other groups, the organization in
> that state sponsored seven youth workshops during the summer.
>
> In one state the members of several state organizations stumped the
> state and secured 111,000 signatures petitioning a place on the ballot for
> an amendment to the constitution increasing state school aid.
>
> The citizens of five communities in one state are cooperating with
> the community school service program of the state department of pub-
> lic instruction to discover the best ways to improve all areas of rural
> living, including schools, libraries, recreation, health, home and family
> living, and economic welfare.[51]

A notable example of a citizens' council on a state-wide level is
the Georgia Citizens' Council, which was created by act of legislature of that state in 1945. Its objectives are to enlist and co-ordinate
the volunteer efforts of all state-wide civic, business, religious, labor,
fraternal, and other organizations in programs to improve the human
resources of the state and to provide specific recommendations and
suggestions for more effective volunteer citizen action in such programs. The Council consists of twenty-one members, including
manufacturers, ministers, college presidents, attorneys, businessmen,
a representative of the press, and civic and lay religious leaders; six
members are women. They are appointed by the governor and serve

---

[51] *Report No. 12*, p. 8.

SOCIAL ACTION

with the special needs in the various fields of human activities. This

Council has since its inception paid particular attention to the prob-

Georgia's 159 counties have any type of juvenile court; 10 per cent

of the prison population is twelve to eighteen years of age; two-

thirds of Georgia's boys and girls, seven to seventeen years of age,

are not reached by any of the programs of youth-serving organiza-

tions; 656 children of fifteen years and under were in jails in eighty-

eight counties during 1947. One of the Council's many services is to

make available on request a staff of three field representatives, trained

citizen groups in any community to find and meet community needs.

The Council holds an annual citizens' conference, conducts an an-

"Georgia's Community Resources," is sent to more than 2,000 com-

In 1943, the New York State Citizens' Council was formed. Its

tion, and direct field service to individual communities in the state.[53]

Numerous examples of citizens' group activities on a *local* basis are

[52] For further information, see "United Citizens' Action to Improve Georgia's
Resources," prepared by Georgia's Citizens' Council, Atlanta, Georgia, 1946;
see also "Georgia's Citizens' Council—Another Thing We Like About the
South," *Saturday Evening Post*, December 28, 1946; "Fifth Annual Citizens'
Conference Proceedings' Issue," Georgia's Human Resources, December 1948;
see also brief Report of the Fourth Annual Conference of the Georgia's
Citizens' Council, *Focus*, January 1948, p. 19.

[53] For more information on the program and the results of the activities of
this council, see Edward G. Olsen, "Co-ordinating Community Educational
Services," *The Annals*, September 1949, pp. 130–135, especially pp. 133–134.

The development of a boys' camp was the goal of a service club in one southwestern city.

In a large eastern city, a service club co-operates with the school system in making available to any student needing it, full and adequate eye care.

In a far-western city, a women's organization has established a creative activities program in housing projects throughout the city.

In still another city, a women's organization sponsored a meeting of persons in a position to develop an over-all plan for recreation and entertainment of young people. The dean of the school of drama and the superintendent of schools met together with the arts and radio chairmen of the interested women's organization to discuss ways of extending wholesome recreation for children.

Several years ago, four members of a women's organization in a western capital made a survey of juvenile delinquency in their city and gave a report to the organization. Out of this grew an interest in establishing a youth council. It is administered by a board which is composed of interested lay people and executives of social agencies. Volunteers serve as hostesses in the youth canteen, and for the dances.

In one small city, a free class for young cabinetmakers is conducted by a men's organization. Boys bring their own material—old cracker boxes, barrel staves, packing cases—any kind of waste lumber, and make anything they desire. The class meets each Saturday morning, from 9 until 12, in the shop room of the high school.

In another small city in the West, a business association has taken over the civic center and the promotion of all activities in the building. This led to a recognition of the dire need of an organized youth program in the community. The youth program was developed under a committee on youth welfare, and a director was hired. After four months, there was so much interest in it that three of the leading fraternal organizations of the city offered to assist by appropriating $100 a month. Most of this money was used to hire an additional staff member, and the balance financed additional equipment needed for the program. Representatives of the three lodges were added to the civic center committee, thus broadening the community participation in the program.

Citizens in a rural county formed a recreation committee to attempt to provide additional opportunities in leisure-time activities for their young people.[54]

---

[54] It should be mentioned in this connection that several farmers' organizations, the 4-H Clubs, and other rural groups have been active in providing leisure-time activities for farm children and thus have contributed considerably to preventive work in delinquency.

In one county at a special ceremony in the spring, young people who have reached 21, assume formally the right to vote. All organizations and groups in the community take part in the program. In preparation for the ceremony, the young people hold at least nine voter meetings.

In a rural community of 300 families, the pastor and parents became concerned about the increasing problems of young people. Discussion groups of parents were formed and met monthly in the homes of the members. These small groups of both parents discussed the various problems facing their children, studied how they might meet them, and planned broader action where indicated.[55]

Citizen participation also manifests itself in various forms of direct services to institutions for juvenile delinquents. Veterans' organizations, fraternal groups, and professional associations have been sponsoring specific programs and activities in training schools, have donated equipment for sports and athletics, or have been organizing special recreational events. The American Legion, for instance, is responsible for an annual outing of the boys at Glen Mills School, Pennsylvania, on Memorial Day. Many similar forms of sponsorship by citizens' groups are reported from all parts of the country. A good example is the La Tuna Boys Camp of the Los Angeles County Probation Department. A group of press photographers who had heard about this camp not only donated the equipment for a modern dark room but for a number of years have volunteered their services as instructors, in teams of two each week, to teach the boys methods of photography.

At El Retiro School for Girls, also operated by the Los Angeles County Probation Department, five girls received scholarships in 1948 to schools of higher learning. These awards were sponsored by several women's organizations interested in the institution. At Chabot Ranch, a boy's camp administered by the Alameda County, California, Probation Department, an elaborate arrangement of electric toy railroads, complete with stations, signal towers, and tunnels, was donated by the local Association of Model Railroaders. Once a week a member of this group comes to the school to work with the boys on this model and to instruct them in methods of modern railroading.

In Cincinnati a group of women organized themselves with the purpose of sponsoring girls in state and county correctional institutions. Each sponsor volunteers to write to a girl, send her small presents, visit her, and help her find employment when she returns

---

[55] These examples are listed in *Report No. 12*, National Conference, pp. 3–7.

to the community. In order to be well prepared for such an under
taking, the sponsors attended lectures given by psychiatrists, socia
workers, and community leaders.

Many other training schools report the use of volunteers who a
coaches, group leaders, and handicraft teachers contribute to th
recreational program. In a number of schools these citizen volunteer
play vital roles in religious programs, and in still others they act a
big brothers or big sisters to individual children in the institutions
Such utilization of volunteers is considered a good means for syn
chronizing the training school program with life in the community.[56]
Citizen participation in the form of volunteer work as probatior
officers and of sponsorship of children to be released on parole from
institutions is described elsewhere in this text.[57]

Still another form of civic activity in this field is reported from
academic institutions. American colleges and universities have in re
cent years shown a distinct trend toward supplementing classroom
study with field work. Some colleges, such as Temple, Smith, and
Lafayette, offer outside laboratory work to expand the scope of cer
tain courses, particularly those dealing with the social sciences
Antioch and Bennington place their students in outside jobs for par
of the year so that they can acquire practical experience. A numbe
of colleges have assigned their students to field work in preventior
and control of juvenile delinquency.

The City College of New York is engaged in a program devotee
to improving certain conditions in the local community. Thi
program, administered by the Community Service Division of th
College, pools the resources of students who are taking education
sociology, physical education, and psychology courses and applie
them to various welfare projects. Students work with youth and
adult groups in an effort to combat juvenile delinquency and racia
tension in the Hamilton Grange neighborhood around the College
According to a report in *The New York Times* of May 15, 1949, th
director of the division, Professor Harry N. Shulman, stated tha
since the work began delinquency rates in that neighborhood de

---

[56] See the thought-provoking paper by Richard Clendenen, "To Synchroniz
the Training-School Program with Life in the Community," *The Child*, No
vember 1949, pp. 73–77.

[57] See Chapter XI, pp. 411–413, and Chapter XII, pp. 473–474.

creased 73 per cent as compared to a 20 per cent decline for Manhattan as a whole. He also observed that racial amity in the neighborhood has substantially improved. One of the most interesting aspects of this project is the work with street gangs. Two-men student teams work with juvenile gang members in an effort to guide their normal competitive spirit into healthy channels.

A somewhat similar program is reported from another section of New York City. Columbia University, the Jewish and Union Theological Seminaries, and other institutions in the neighborhood have joined in sponsoring the Manhattanville Neighborhood Center, which serves a large, densely populated, and racially mixed neighborhood immediately north of Morningside Heights, where some of the previously mentioned institutions are located. Here, too, a "Street Club Project" is in operation which attempts to use the nucleus of gangs as a means of guiding gang members into healthy activities.[58]

During the Spring of 1949, a group of twelve students at Lafayette College set out on a program of contributing their efforts to the curbing of juvenile delinquency. They became "big brothers" to twelve boys ranging in age from eight to fourteen years, who had had difficulties with the law. Several times each week and on Sundays the students entertain the youngsters at fraternity houses, join them in recreation, and take them on hikes. It is planned to expand the program in the future so that each boy who has been before the local juvenile court will have a "big brother" at the College. This experiment also stimulated a number of civic and fraternal organizations at Easton, Pennsylvania, where the College is located, to organize a boys' club for underprivileged youth.

c. Neighborhood and Community Councils and Other Area Projects

In the years before World War II, a movement that attempted to give some direction to citizen participation in delinquency control and prevention gained nation-wide attention. Again its cradle was in California. It became known as the "Co-ordinating or Community Council Movement." In the larger cities the term "neighborhood council" is used, indicating that the geographical area of operation of such a council is only a part of the whole urban community.

All three terms denote an important characteristic of this move-

---

[58] See *The New York Times*, May 8, 1949.

ment; it is not directed from above, either from the governmental level or by some national or state organization, but rather it is the outgrowth of community responsibility felt by individuals and groups. It receives its impetus from citizens bound together by a common interest in the welfare of their immediate neighborhood. It aims at co-ordination of all the existing and potential assets and services of the community toward a common objective.

Kenneth S. Beam, who from 1935 to 1937 made a special study of this movement on behalf of the National Probation and Parole Association, and who is now director of Coordinating Councils, Inc., San Diego, California, listed the following five features as common characteristics of community councils:

1. They are organized on a community basis in towns and small cities, and on a neighborhood basis in large cities.

2. They bring together city and county officials, representatives of private agencies and civic organizations interested in the welfare of children, youth, the family, and the community.

3. They emphasize the importance of citizen or lay participation.

4. They do not act as agencies but as counseling or coordinating bodies.

5. They are interested in the prevention of delinquency. Some make this their major objective while others consider it secondary.[59]

The community council, then, is a community attempt to co-ordinate agencies and facts—agencies that have an immediate or remote bearing on the child and his problems, and facts that lend themselves to an analysis of causes of unrest, disorganization, and confusion of children and older youth. Within the community lie many valuable resources that, when mobilized in a realistic manner, can do much to further the understanding and serving of youth. The effort takes hard-headed thinking and action; it also takes sustained interest. Trained personnel is needed for guidance but the backbone of any council must be the volunteer citizen. Only if and when he accepts this responsibility can satisfactory results accrue from the community council.

The observation that these councils are not directed by a governmental agency is not at variance with the fact that in many instances

---

[59] Kenneth S. Beam, "Community Coordination" (Report of a National Survey of Coordinating and Neighborhood Councils), *Yearbook*, N.P.P.A., 1937, pp. 47–76, especially p. 48.

the initiative for the organization of such councils came from interested and wide-awake public officials. As a matter of fact, according to Kenyon J. Scudder, one time chief probation officer of Los Angeles County, California, and at present superintendent of the California Institution for Men at Chino, California, the idea of the co-ordinating council was originated in Berkeley, California, as early as 1919 by Chief of Police August Vollmer. The first actual council in Los Angeles County was launched April 4, 1932, when juvenile court judge Samuel Blake, together with the probation department, "called together seven hundred officials, police officers, social workers and representatives of organizations interested in the reduction of delinquency." [60]

Assuming that the delinquency rate is the responsibility of the whole community, the leaders in the movement insisted that all agencies and individuals dealing with the problems of youth should be asked to cooperate in studying delinquency and working out solutions to the problem. As Kenyon J. Scudder says:

> The Plan offers one means of frequent contact. By bringing together in round table groups the leaders of each community with representatives of the law enforcing agencies, they can better understand and deal with local problems. Before gathering in a group they do not know each other. After the first or second meeting an entirely different attitude develops between agencies, resulting in a spirit of confidence and cooperation and understanding. Petty jealousies and criticisms are supplanted by a cordial desire to work together. Each agency sees help in the picture. The community forces are at last arrayed for combined action.[61]

A co-ordinating council is usually composed of law enforcement officials; teachers or school counselors; workers in family welfare,

---

[60] See speech by Kenyon J. Scudder in the *Proceedings*, Attorney General's Conference on Crime, Washington, D.C., December 10-14, 1934, pp. 413-424. See also Sheldon and Eleanor Glueck (edd.), *Preventing Crime*, McGraw-Hill, 1936, pp. 25-45. The Berkeley, California, Council is described by Nathaniel Cantor in *The Annals*, September 1941, p. 155.

[61] *Proceedings*, Attorney General's Conference on Crime, Washington, D.C., *op. cit.*, p. 417. For a description of the work of the Los Angeles Coordinating Council Movement in the field of delinquency prevention under the sponsorship of the County Probation Department, see John M. Zuck, "The Probation Officer Participates in Delinquency Prevention," *Yearbook*, N.P.P.A., 1948, pp. 282-286; see also Chapter XI, pp. 402-404.

child care, and health agencies; leaders in character-building organ
izations and civic groups such as service clubs (Rotary, Lions
Kiwanis, and so forth), parent-teacher associations and women'
clubs; and church representatives. In the neighborhood council spe
cial efforts are being made to have lay citizens take an active par
in the work.

The idea spread throughout the country following the initia
movement in Berkeley and Los Angeles. But California, the cradle o
the movement, today still maintains more local groups than an
other state. Fully 300 councils are functioning in that state; abou
100 of them are in the Los Angeles area alone. San Francisco an
Sacramento are also well organized. The California Youth Authorit
has given great impetus to the councils, since part of its philosophy
perhaps the major part, is pointed toward delinquency control.[6]
In addition to the excellent work of the probation department of Lo
Angeles County in guiding and stimulating local groups in copin
with problems of youth, the accomplishments of the San Dieg
County councils are also worthy of mention. It is perhaps the bes
established council of its kind in the whole country, both in solidit
of structure and in financial security. Although the initial interes
goes back to 1920, this council was organized in 1942 as a public
supported agency and is financed by the County of San Diego. A
already mentioned, it has at its helm the pioneer, Kenneth S. Beam
who for many years directed the councils of Los Angeles County
The program of the council is county-wide and emphasizes co-ordi
nation of all existing agencies for the welfare of youth. Althoug
control of delinquency is of paramount importance, the activities o
the council are manifold. The central office provides guidance an
advice to newly organized community movements as well as to thos
that are firmly established. City-wide and county-wide conference
are held periodically, at which times speakers of national importanc
are engaged to discuss youth problems and community needs. Hand
books on a variety of subjects dealing with the home, the neighbor
hood, and the community are published when the need is presented
Among the activities of the council, in addition to delinquency stud
and control, the following should be mentioned: publication of Th
Family Log, an illustrated booklet published by the council, whicl

---

[6] See Chapter X, pp. 366–367.

timulates families to keep a record of the activities of each member
n order to sustain the interest of the home; publication of *A Hand-
ook of Answers for Parents*, which attempts to develop home activities along the lines of recreation and family life; the unique de-
elopment of a day-school camp in the near-by mountains where
very school child within the county may spend a week during the
chool year without interruption of school work. The council also
ublishes an excellent magazine, *The Coordinator*.

California has been fortunate in its experience with co-ordinating
ouncils, since it has available the interest and financial help of the
osenberg Foundation of San Francisco as well as trained guidance
nd assistance from the Youth Authority. But above all, the coun-
ils have become an integral part of community life and are en-
usiastically accepted by parents, public officials and private
gencies.[63]

Chicago, where in the stockyard district a community council was
rganized as far back as World War I (the "Back of the Yards"
Jeighborhood Council), has more recently developed the so-called
Chicago Area Project" in various parts of the city. Guided by so-
iologists of the Institute for Juvenile Research under the leadership
f Clifford R. Shaw, it is based upon the active participation of citi-
ens of the area organized in neighborhood committees. At the
econd National Conference of Coordinating Councils in 1937, the
roject, then five years old, was described as follows:

> The Chicago Area Project is a program which seeks to discover by
> actual demonstration and measurement a procedure for the treatment
> of delinquents and the prevention of delinquency in those neighbor-
> hoods of the city which have for more than thirty-five years produced
> a disproportionately large number of delinquent boys and girls in the
> Cook County Juvenile Court. The program is in operation in three
> such neighborhoods. Its primary feature is the emphasis which it places
> upon the participation of the residents of the neighborhood in planning
> and operating the program. The Project seeks to determine to what ex-
> tent constructive changes can be effected in the social environment of
> the neighborhood with consequent reduction in the volume of delin-
> quency, by providing to the residents facilities and professional guid-

---

[63] See Lowell J. Carr, *Delinquency Control*, Harper, New York, 1940, Parts
 and V, for further details on community councils.

ance for the development of their own program for the welfare of their children.[64]

This, then, is the method of the "autonomous neighborhood" approach to the delinquency problem as demonstrated by the Chicago Area Project: It does not try to impose from the outside any social organization upon the neighborhood, rather does it accept and encourage the natural local groupings, such as churches, nationality clubs, lodges and societies, play groups of children, youths, and adults, and gangs. Since juvenile delinquency, especially in deteriorated areas, has been recognized as a characteristic manifestation of the social life of these neighborhoods, a feasible approach to the solution of the problem is to bring about constructive changes in the attitudes, moral codes, and standards of the neighborhood as a whole. The natural leaders in these areas, therefore, are being induced to form organizations or to use existing organizations for the purpose of reducing the delinquency rates in their own areas of residence. Thus in a neighborhood predominantly populated by Americans of Polish background, a Polish Catholic Church or organization would serve; in a sector where a great many Italo-Americans live, an Italian athletic club or church might become the focal point of activities.

The operating bodies of the Chicago Area Project are the neighborhood committees. Its active members may be local merchants, physicians, lawyers, members of the clergy, truck drivers, barbers, factory workers, or housewives. Former leaders of delinquent gangs may also be found among them. Contributing members run into hundreds, and a large proportion of the local population participates in the committee's annual fund-raising festival and contributes to the

---

[64] Ernest W. Burgess, Joseph D. Lohman, and Clifford R. Shaw, "The Chicago Area Project," *Yearbook*, N.P.P.A., 1937, pp. 8–28; see also Fred A. Romano, "Organizing a Community for Delinquency Prevention," *Yearbook*, N.P.P.A., 1940, pp. 1–12, and Edward Haydon, "Community Organization and Crime Prevention," *ibid.*, 1942, pp. 23–33. A somewhat similar project, though on a much more limited scale geographically and of only temporary duration, was the "Neighborhood Center for Block Organization," under the auspices of the Union Settlement Association in New York City; for details, see Rudolph M. Wittenberg, "Personality Adjustment Through Social Action," *American Journal of Orthopsychiatry*, April 1948, pp. 207–221. For a description of a delinquency prevention project of the Lower West Side Health Committee, New York City, see Elizabeth Fajen, "Curing Delinquency at the Source," *Survey Midmonthly*, October 1946, pp. 261–262.

expense of the program. The committee enjoys the cooperation of public and private agencies in the field of education, health, and recreation. It makes effective use of trained case workers and group workers but only on the basis of equality and cooperation with the local lay committee members. In order to function effectively, it must have a permanent paid staff, and it is desirable that more and more local residents be gradually trained for this work. The authorities have recognized the value of the neighborhood approach by appointing, so far as practicable, qualified local residents as probation, parole, and truant officers.

Summarizing the various activities of the neighborhood committees, both regarding their general work of neighborhood improvement and their special treatment program for the individual delinquent, John R. Ellingston, in his book *Protecting Our Children from Criminal Careers*, gives the following account:

Neighborhood Committees of the Chicago Area Project sponsor community centers, summer camps, children's nurseries, mothers' clubs, sports and tournaments, playgrounds, co-operation with the schools, adult education, community forums, community newspapers, housing improvement, employment centers, and rehabilitation programs for delinquents, probationers, and parolees of all ages. These last seem to offer the most practical means of effectively cutting down recidivism among residents of delinquency areas. Instead of cold-shouldering the youngster or adult returned from the courts, the reformatory, or the prison and driving him back to the companionship of delinquents and criminals, the neighborhood committee smooths his return to full participation in its affairs. The committee members are not outsiders, offering him a pseudo-fellowship as charity, but responsible citizens of his own neighborhood, speaking his own language, and whom he knows.[65]

A similar approach to the handling of young delinquents through citizens living in the neighborhood was launched in 1942 by the Crime Prevention Association of Philadelphia. It became known as the "Referral Plan" or the "Philadelphia Plan." This project concerned itself with boys who were arrested but whose delinquency was not considered serious enough to call for probation or commitment, and also with boys against whom some informal complaint was filed by parents, neighbors, schools, or crime-prevention officers.

---

[65] Prentice-Hall, New York, 1948, pp. 333, 334.

These cases are referred to a neighborhood committee composed of volunteers living in the respective areas; the boy is assigned to a member of the committee, who visits him in his home in order to determine what his problem is. If recreation seems to be the need, the boy is introduced into some recreational program near his home. If, on the other hand, the problem involves a question of health, school, family, or some condition in the community contributing to the delinquency of minors, such problems are referred to the proper agencies. Once a month each organization or group participating in the plan makes a brief report to the Association concerning each boy seen, action taken, and recommendations for further referral if necessary. Many of the neighborhood committees—there were 77 active groups in 1949—are special subdivisions of existing organizations such as church groups, parent-teacher associations, and particularly community councils. The community council movement in this city showed renewed vigor after it was coordinated in the Federation of Community Councils of Philadelphia, which acts as an advisory and stimulating agent to local neighborhood councils. Here, too, a local conference for the Prevention and Control of Juvenile Delinquency, patterned after the National Conference, was organized and made wide use of citizen participation in the deliberations of its various panels.[66]

True to the character of neighborhood councils as a "grass roots' movement, and in view of the great variety of their organizational structure and purposes, no attempt has been made to form a national organization or federation. The San Diego group, however, under the name of Coordinating Councils, Inc., serves as a reference bureau and clearing house for the interchange of ideas, information, and data having to do with the general field of community coordination. It provides consultant service for communities desiring to organize or to improve the services of various types of councils, and for communities endeavoring to prevent delinquency and crime through the elimination or control of the basic conditioning factors. The kind of

---

[66] For details, see J. Francis Finnegan, "The Philadelphia Conference on the Prevention and Control of Juvenile Delinquency," *Yearbook*, N.P.P.A., 1948, pp. 263–273; see also *Annual Reports*, Crime Prevention Association of Philadelphia, 1948, pp. 6–7, and 1949, pp. 5–6, for details on the Referral Plan. A similar project in the Bronx, sponsored by the New York City Youth Board, is described in "Piloting Youth," *Focus*, May 1950, pp. 71–72.

advice and stimulation emanating from such an information center is indeed needed. For although the council idea is a good one, the mortality rate has been high; initial enthusiasm often wanes and becomes desultory. Finances are precarious and many dynamic professional workers look for greener pastures. Volunteer support lags just as it does in any community venture. As Ben Solomon says in his work *Juvenile Delinquency: Practical Prevention*, "If we cannot create and maintain a public, tax-supported professionally staffed bureau to do this local job,—which we strongly advocate and which eventually must come—then this type of citizen council is next best." [67] Thus, as the San Diego experience, the Chicago Area Project, and a few other local examples show, it is extremely important to provide the community councils with trained, paid personnel.[68]

Somewhat akin to this proposition is a suggestion made by Edwin J. Lukas, executive director of the Society for the Prevention of Crime, New York City. After criticizing the lack of coordination of the various departments and agencies, public and private, which are related to the delinquency and crime problem, he proposes to inaugurate a "single, over-all community co-ordinating bureau." Likening it to the War Industries' Mobilization Board, which proved eminently efficient, he feels that such a bureau should be charged with "the mandatory mission to allocate the activities of police, schools, civic organizations, health and leisure-time organizations, family service agencies, guidance clinics, and all the others whose potentialities are related to the presently known attacks on the behavior problem." [69]

Lack of coordination of existing services on all governmental levels and within the sphere of private social work, as well as between public and voluntary agencies, is indeed one of the most crucial problems. This lack of coordination has produced on the one hand the overlapping of some services; on the other hand, it has left wide gaps of unmet needs, either in certain geographical

---

[67] Youth Service, Inc., Peekskill, N. Y., 1947, p. 10.

[68] The findings of a survey on coordinating councils are included in an article by Lowell J. Carr, "Organization for Delinquency Control," *The Annals*, January 1949, pp. 74, 75.

[69] Edwin J. Lukas, "Crime Prevention: Who Prevents What?," *Federal Probation*, June 1948, pp. 19–23.

areas or regarding particular categories of social problems. Fortu
nately, it is being realized more and more that the coordination o
welfare services is just as necessary and just as attainable as th
efficient organization of business and industry for which this country
has achieved world-wide recognition. Several pilot projects hav
been undertaken to demonstrate the possibility and the value o
real coordination in the child care field.

A practical project of this nature was carried out several years ag
in St. Paul, Minnesota. There the United States Children's Bureau, i
cooperation with local, public, and private agencies, established
special child welfare service to study the prevention and treatmen
of behavior problems in children. Over a period of five years, fron
1937 to 1942, this "Community Service for Children," as the projec
was locally called, was active in an area of St. Paul covering one an
a half square miles and extending from a central business district to
predominantly residential section. The population of the project are
was approximately 20,000. The study was not limited to incipien
delinquency but included other types of minor maladjustment. Th
emphasis of the project was on early identification of children witl
behavior problems. The purpose of the experiment was interpretec
to the community through churches, schools, neighborhood organ
izations, playground associations, P.T.A.'s, and city-wide case work
group work, and health agencies. From these organizations, as wel
as by parents and other interested individuals, children were referrec
to the Community Service for study. With each child referred, th
staff accepted two responsibilities, namely, to work out the bes
possible treatment program for the child himself, and second, to
interpret to all persons interested in the child the reasons for hi
difficulty, the progress or lack of progress being made in his treat
ment, and the need for early identification of the child's problems
During the whole period of the project, 1,466 children were regis
tered for service. Of these, 739 were registered only for group ac
tivities; the remainder, 727 children, coming from 535 families
required and received one or more of the individualized types o
diagnostic and treatment service from the Community Service Staff

Thus not only was needed service rendered to individual childrer
but valuable research information regarding the causation of malad
justments of children was gathered and gaps in the general child wel
fare program of the area and the city as a whole were pointed out

One of the main achievements of the "St. Paul Experiment in Child Welfare," as it became known nationally, was the co-ordination of basic community services for children, namely, the schools, the law enforcement agencies (police, juvenile court), and the public and private social agencies. A co-ordination center for community services for children was established, providing liaison service between all agencies dealing with children. This co-ordination center continued to operate even after the project itself had come to a close, and functions now as an important part of the total community child welfare program.

Beyond the immediate area in which the project was carried out, its implications for other communities became apparent. As the official report stated,

> The project accepted the philosophy that each child must be treated as a whole and his problems as a unit regardless of the number of problems or the areas of his life affected. The experience of the project shows that minor and incipient problem behavior in children can be identified by the community and that if adequate community services are effectively coordinated much of this problem behavior can be corrected and modified or, if not susceptible to correction, prevented from developing into more serious forms. Its experience further emphasizes the fact that the community services called upon to work in a coordinated program must include not only the social agencies, which are primarily concerned with the neglected, dependent, and delinquent child or the child in need of special care, but also the health and law enforcing agencies and the agencies established to serve all children, such as the group-work agencies, the recreational agencies, and the schools.[70]

---

[70] *Children in the Community* (The St. Paul Experiment in Child Welfare), United States Children's Bureau Publication No. 317, Government Printing Office, 1946, p. 158. A condensed summary of the findings is contained in *Helping Children in Trouble*, United States Children's Bureau Publication No. 320, Government Printing Office, 1947. For another area project sponsored by the United States Children's Bureau—in cooperation with the School of Social Service Administration of the University of Chicago, and other local agencies— see Henry W. Waltz, Jr., "A Community Experiment," *Yearbook*, N.P.P.A., 1936, pp. 60–66, describing the Chicago Probation Project. Still another project undertaken on the local level by the United States Children's Bureau—in cooperation with state and municipal agencies—is described in "A Community Plans For Its Children: Final Report of the Newport News, Virginia, Project," Children's Bureau Publication No. 321, Government Printing Office, Washington, D.C., 1947.

d. Youth Participation

The principles of modern education call for the active participation of students in the school programs. The idea that the pupil shall unquestioningly absorb what the teacher brings before him belongs to the past; initiative and constructive participation in curricular and extra-curricular activities is encouraged. Similarly, it is today widely recognized that youth itself has a very vital part to play in community affairs in general and in the delinquency prevention program in particular. It seems significant that the National Conference considered the matter of youth participation so important that one of its eighteen panels was assigned exclusively to the study of this topic.

Such participation of young people can take various forms: (1) Youth is often represented on the previously described citizens' councils or neighborhood and community councils. "Their point of view and their direct testimony regarding conditions and attitudes should be sought whenever it is pertinent to matters with which a council is dealing." [71] (2) Youth has been given a certain amount of representation on the programming bodies of youth-serving organizations, but as the panel report on youth participation of the National Conference points out, "Adults generally keep this field of policy-making for themselves. They decide what is right or wrong, what is safe or dangerous, what is good or bad for the reputation of the organization. Yet it is precisely these decisions in which young people want to have a voice." [72] (3) A most promising movement is apparent in the growing number of youth councils which are usually composed of delegates of existing youth organizations and which seek to bring together these local groups in some form of federation so that it may serve as a sounding board for the voice of youth in the affairs of the community.[73] Here youth itself constitutes the active membership and elects its own officers.

There may be some adult sponsorship in the form of advisory

---

[71] "Community Co-ordination," *Report No. 1*, National Conference, p. 24.

[72] *Report No. 11*, p. 8; see also Lester D. Crow and Alice Crow, *Our Teen-Age Boys and Girls*, McGraw-Hill, New York, 1945, p. 316.

[73] The existence of inter-organization youth councils is reported from at least twenty-seven communities in various parts of the country; see pamphlets of the Youth Division of the National Social Welfare Assembly, New York, "Youth United for a Better Home Town" and "Underlining Youth Councils."

committees, but adult control must be avoided if the real character of the youth council is to be preserved. A good example of real participation of such a council in the tackling of the delinquency problem is reported from San Francisco:

A Session of "Youth Builders," New York. *(From the "March of Time" release, "Youth in Crisis." Courtesy "The March of Time," produced by TIME Inc.)*

The Delinquency Prevention Committee was activated when the chairman of the Governor's Committee on Juvenile Justice requested the opinion of the San Francisco Youth Association on the cause and cure of juvenile delinquency. This committee has been most diligent in its work, exploring the project through group discussions, calling in experts in the field and visiting Juvenile Halls, Juvenile Courts, and the areas of the city with the highest index of juvenile delinquency. The committee's report, when finished, will be the result of the best thinking that its members are able to bring to bear on the problem. The report will be taken by the delegates to their respective groups for consideration and possible change before being submitted to the Governor's Committee.[74]

Many problems are involved in this particular aspect of youth participation. Research has shown that not more than one out of four young persons have an active and effective connection with any of the major voluntary youth-service agencies.[75] Youngsters who are in danger of becoming delinquent are seldom members of established youth-serving organizations; either they are actually excluded because they do not live up to the standards of membership eligibility, or they suspect that they would not be welcome in view of their home background, or they may dislike any organization that is under adult sponsorship or direction. They form their own gang or unaffiliated street clubs, and wherever a local youth council is in existence, the problem develops as to whether or not such groups should be invited into the council.

Other difficulties are found in the natural conflict between adults and youth. The report of the National Conference on youth participation dissects some of the barriers resulting from attitudes on either side; it seeks to explore why adults are so reluctant to share the responsibility with youth, and lists first, "lack of understanding of how growth takes place."

Adults find the facts of "growing up" during adolescence harder to take. They are impatient with what seems to them irresponsible antics. They forget that any new skill can be learned only through a period of awkward trial-and-error experimentation. Since most youngsters who constitute later "delinquency risks" have been exposed to thoughtless handling by adults and have been pushed around a lot in their community, this source of "opposition to adults" is especially strong in them.[76]

There is a curious twist in many an adult's mind regarding adolescents. He expects too much and too little at the same time. "They are

---

[74] Thomas A. Rowe, "A Youth Council in Action," *Survey Midmonthly*, December 1948, p. 361. For a description of the early stages of a similar youth council organization in New York, see Morris L. Eisenstein, "The Youth Council: A Challenge," *Survey Midmonthly*, November 1948, pp. 332–335.

[75] "Youth and the Future—Report of the American Youth Commission," quoted in *Report on Youth Participation*, National Conference, p. 3.

[76] *Op. cit.*, p. 8.

impatient with youngsters who cannot function adequately as soon as they are given a chance to try out their first steps in self-determination and democratic responsibility." [77] On the other hand, adults underestimate the potentialities of youth because "shocked by the occasional misbehavior of youngsters they know, and even more appalled by newspaper reports of extreme behavior of irresponsibles here and there, adults get used to the idea that young people can't do anything and aren't much good, on the whole." [78] Barriers on the side of youth are naturally the result of the adults' way of rearing their children. Consequently, young people are "deeply suspicious of being treated like children, of being assigned safe tasks rather than the privilege of participation in more glorious enterprises, of being expected to fit obediently into a preorganized pattern rather than of being allowed to help design their own." [79]

These barriers are not insurmountable. In order to facilitate and stimulate constructive youth participation, the National Conference has formulated a number of principles:

It is the responsibility of civic groups and public-spirited individuals to see to it that the greatest possible number of young people have an opportunity for participation in constructive youth programs.

The adults of any community should cooperate with its young people in developing a variety of voluntary associations such as clubs, youth organizations, and recreational centers suited to their needs and interests. In the preparation of programs, young people should play a decisive part. These programs should be sufficiently flexible to allow for individual growth and initiative.

It is important for group leaders to recognize that young people secure satisfaction by forming "natural" groups of congenial associates, to accept these groups as they are, to recognize the natural leaders in all such groups, and to work with them on this basis for the benefit of all members. A constant objective in working with young people should be to participate with them in experiences through which all come to understand, to accept, and to learn to live cooperatively with people different from themselves.

It is recommended that civic-minded adult organizations, individual citizens, youth-serving organizations, schools, churches, and others cooperate with each other: to provide opportunity for young people

---

[77] *Ibid.*, p. 9.
[78] *Ibid.*, p. 9.
[79] *Ibid.*, p. 11.

to participate in the affairs of the community; to enlist young people in projects designed to improve community life; to encourage young people to get the facts, to share the facts, and to act on the facts; to support young people's action when it is based on facts and thoughtful judgment even though some adult groups may try to curb or to obstruct the action.

Programs in order to be constructive substitutes for undesirable, destructive, or antisocial activities, must offer an equal degree of interest and satisfaction of basic needs, new experience, and real adventure and must have a purpose understandable by young people if their interest is to be enlisted and maintained.[80]

There are many good examples of active youth participation in programs devoted to the prevention of delinquency. A group of adults and adolescents have been working together in the Metropolitan Youth Conference of Greater New York under the leadership of Professor Frederic Thrasher. This council is sponsoring teenage canteen activities, and youth forums in local centers and on the radio. In California, 3,000 teen-age youths have met in conference in various parts of the state where boys and girls themselves have an opportunity to discuss the problems and programs of their youth organizations and youth councils. The young people publish their own magazine *Teen News*. The California Youth Authority has been much interested in this movement and has given advice and assistance.[81]

A very promising experiment is reported from Bergen County, New Jersey. There the YMCA inaugurated a "Parent-Youth Clinic," which has by now been conducted in about 50 communities of the county through locally organized community groups and is designed to reach more than 10,000 parents and children. The idea is to have the problems that confront parents and children alike discussed by parents and children in an open forum. The meetings are well prepared. In order to give the discussion a practical give-and-take value, parents and their own children are put on the panel together and the audience is invited to take part. It is recommended

[80] *Ibid.*, pp. 4, 6.

[81] See Karl Holton, "The California Youth Authority," *Yearbook*, N.P.P.A., 1946, pp. 124–125; also Duane Robinson, *Chance to Belong*, Woman's Press, New York, 1949, the story of the Los Angeles Youth Project, 1943–1949.

that the groups should include both boys and girls, because they have common problems. The panel is put primarily in the hands of youngsters by having a high-school boy or girl serve as moderator. Such questions as the use of the family car, dating, late hours, weekly allowances, and payment for work around the house are aired. This venture, although still in the early stages of development, has attracted nation-wide attention. The fact that it does not involve any expense and does not require "imported" experts makes it adaptable to small and large communities.[82]

In Ferndale, Michigan, a few years ago, young people and their parents cooperated in developing a "code of behavior" which later was published in a leaflet entitled "The Code of Parents and Youth." Although it is impossible to state that such an undertaking actually has resulted in a decrease of juvenile delinquency, it seems an excellent means of finding out just what young people expect of themselves in the way of standards of conduct, as against the standards imposed by their elders.

A youth panel of three boys and three girls was part of a Delinquency Prevention Conference held under the sponsorship of the Division for Youth and Community Services of the Illinois Department of Welfare in cooperation with the Big Brothers and Sisters Association. Among the recommendations of the panel were the following: "Close family ties should be fostered; communities should place more emphasis on activities bringing youth and adults together; parents should give more parties at home and get better acquainted with their children's friends; more specific instruction about marriage and family life should be given in high school." [83]

Teen-agers in the Seattle, Washington, public schools, in response to the question "What kind of parents do boys and girls want?," prepared a statement entitled "When Parents Fill These Basic Needs, Delinquency Hasn't a Chance." Under the subheadings of "love, understanding, trust, joint planning, respect, privacy, responsibility, friendships, religion," the ideas contained in this statement hold suggestions not only for parents, but for all people working in the field

---

[82] For further details, see Karl Kohrs, "Parent-Youth Clinic in Action," *Parade* (syndicated Sunday newspaper supplement), December 12, 1948, pp. 5–7.

[83] Reported in *Federal Probation*, September 1948, p. 65.

of child welfare and education who need to gain and hold the respect and confidence of youngsters.[84]

A survey was made in 1947 among over 5,000 teen-age youngsters in Florida, upon the suggestion of a juvenile court judge, G. Bowden Hunt, who believes that young people should have a chance to express their own thinking. Questionnaires submitted to the youngsters dealt mainly with the influence of the home, the school, the church, the radio, and the motion pictures on young people. In answer to the question about what they considered the main causes for juvenile delinquency, the youngsters listed alcohol, divorce, both parents working, juke boxes, and lack of religious training, as the five major reasons.[85]

Reference was made in an earlier chapter to an interesting and novel project in Muskegon, Michigan, where—with adult guidance— a juvenile jury, consisting of high school students, hears and disposes of traffic offenses involving drivers under seventeen years of age. This plan has its particular value in that it gives the young offender the benefit of judgment by people of his own age group who know driving conditions and temptations. Another important result is that "the juror gets an opportunity to know of traffic hazards and of laws . . . and that he has an opportunity to take part in a civic duty that should make him a better citizen."[86]

The value of youth's own contribution toward the solution of youth problems found signal recognition in the fact that young people were invited to participate in the various phases of the Mid-Century White House Conference on Children and Youth in 1950.

e. Welfare Councils, Community Chests, and Social Work Conferences

Between the two world wars, a growing specialization in the field of social welfare became apparent, especially in urban areas. This development called for the creation, on the community level, of co-ordinating and planning bodies which, on the one hand, would

---

[84] The statement was published under the heading "Teen-Agers State Their Case," in The Child, August 1949, p. 30, and was reprinted in Federal Probation, September 1949, p. 86.

[85] See "Out of the Mouths of—," Focus, May 1948, pp. 75–76.

[86] Ralph W. Daniel, "A Juvenile Jury for Young Traffic Offenders," Focus, January 1950, pp. 23–26.

work for the elimination of overlapping and duplicating services and, on the other, would ascertain gaps in the entire welfare program and strive for improvement of existing services and for the provision of new ones which were needed. Such local community welfare councils became known as councils of social agencies, social planning councils, or health and welfare councils. In 1949, approximately 400 cities in the United States had such councils. As a rule, they are composed of delegates from public and private agencies and departments operating in the fields of health, welfare, and recreation. The delegates usually consist of professional workers as well as board members from the constituent groups; often other civic-minded individuals attend as delegates-at-large or ex-officio members, such as the mayor of the city and representatives of organizations and governmental departments that are performing duties in fields related to social welfare and public health. Notwithstanding great varieties in the different communities, the program of community welfare councils in general includes the following common features:

1. *Co-ordinating activities.* Councils provide means for representatives of operating agencies to come together, share their experiences, develop mutual understanding, and arrive at effective working relationships. . . .

2. *Fact finding.* A basic function which underlies almost every council activity is the continuous and systematic gathering of facts about the community—its health and welfare needs and the agencies which exist to meet them. . . .

3. *Joint action.* The facts are considered and a logical course of action agreed upon by the interested parties. Decisions are reached by group-thinking through the committee process. The council then takes steps to see that agreed-upon improvements in the community program are put into effect. This action is also a joint effort by interested citizens and organizations. . . .

4. *Improving the quality of service.* Many of the council activities are aimed at improving the quality of existing health and welfare services. . . .

5. *Common services.* Although councils seldom operate direct services for individuals, except possibly on a demonstration basis, they commonly conduct activities to assist operating agencies in carrying on programs. . . .

6. *Developing public understanding.* A principal function of a coun-

cil is to quicken public awareness of community problems and develop an understanding of how agencies are dealing with them. . . .[87]

The community chest is a local cooperative organization of private welfare and health agencies principally devoted to the raising of funds through annual campaigns or otherwise for the support of its member agencies. Such a program eliminates the need for separate fund-raising drives by individual agencies. These drives proved to be costly and often only moderately successful to the soliciting groups and quite annoying to the public, which was solicited in an endless succession of appeals. The particular value of community chests is that they disburse the collected funds in accordance with ascertained and budgeted needs. Although it dates back to 1913, the community chest movement received particular impetus during World War I, at the outset of the Depression, and in World War II. In 1947, 841 campaigns using the Community Chest method were recorded.[88]

Both movements—the local welfare council and the community chest—covering, as they do, the total area of social welfare and health, naturally include in their scope of interest and activities services devoted to the treatment and prevention of juvenile delinquency. They are, therefore, important media for citizen participation in this field of endeavor.

Finally, another channel of high-lighting social needs and of promoting social action in the welfare field must be mentioned. Conferences, usually held once a year, and local, regional, state-wide, or nation-wide in scope, serve as opportunities for social workers and laymen interested in social welfare to "share experiences, consider and discuss current problems, report the results of studies and research, raise questions and offer ideas, suggestions, and recommendations, and sometimes to formulate platforms, endorse specific proposals, and engage in more or less vigorous social action." [89]

On a national scale, the National Conference of Social Work is regarded as one of the most important forces in American social

---

[87] Merrill F. Krughoff, "Councils in Social Work," *Social Work Yearbook*, Russell Sage Foundation, 1949, pp. 151–152.

[88] Fred K. Hoehler, "Community Chests," *Social Work Yearbook*, Russell Sage Foundation, 1949, p. 126.

[89] Jane Chandler, "Conferences of Social Work," *Social Work Yearbook*, 1949, p. 135.

work. Its origins go back to 1874, when the first conference of this kind (then called "National Conference of Charities and Correction") was held in New York City. At recent conferences the attendance has fluctuated between 3,000 and 7,600. In addition to the general sessions of the Conference, its program is composed of twelve special sections, one of which is devoted entirely to delinquency. Another important national conference is the Annual Congress of Correction held under the auspices of the American Prison Association. A great number of organizations devoted to specialized fields of interest in the whole orbit of correctional work are affiliated with one or both of these large conferences and hold joint as well as separate meetings. Among such organizations are the National Probation and Parole Association, the National Council of Juvenile Court Judges, the National Conference of Juvenile Agencies, and the National Association of Training Schools.

State and regional conferences are held in many parts of the country, either devoted to the entire field of social service or to the specific area of correctional work. The previously mentioned state associations of probation and parole officers also convene in annual or more frequent meetings for common deliberations. In numerous instances, progressive legislation in the welfare field in general, or in the correctional field specifically, has been enacted as a result of the expressed wishes of these gatherings. Spearheading demands for social action in the form of needed legislation, but also in the formulation of program and the raising of standards in the public welfare field, are such organizations as the State Charities Aid Association in New York and the Public Charities Association of Pennsylvania, recently named the Pennsylvania Citizens' Association for Health and Welfare. The latter has been especially active in the correctional field through one of its divisions, the Pennsylvania Committee on Penal Affairs, which for many years has been headed by the nationally known protagonist of modern correctional services, Leon T. Stern.

Social action in the field of delinquency control, treatment, and prevention, as described in this chapter, depends for its success upon an intelligent interpretation of the problems involved to the public. The need for such interpretation and the various media available will be presented in the following chapter.

Chapter XVII

INTERPRETATION

1. THE NEED FOR INTERPRETATION

WHY is it necessary to interpret the problem of juvenile delinquency, its causation, treatment, and prevention, to the public?

First, there is a general reason. The growing complexity of our social and economic life has necessitated an expanding governmental machinery on the Federal, state, and municipal levels. This machinery is the result of the steady population increase, the industrialization of large segments of our country, the formation of centers of high population density, the hazards connected with the ebbs and peaks of the economic curve and the ensuing demands for social security, the recognition of public health needs, and the growing awareness of the responsible role that the United States has to play in world affairs. Government, which was simple and easily comprehended in the eighteenth and nineteenth centuries, has become an intricate mechanism. Government in a democracy must always be understood by the people. It therefore behooves the agencies on the various levels of government to keep the public informed of their functions and to interpret their activities in a manner that can be perceived by the ordinary citizen. Private firms and corporations, well versed in employing the means of advertising, have always realized the importance of public relations. Governmental administrators, however, have too long remained unmindful of the fact that theirs, too, is a "selling" job. Gone forever are the times of *laissez faire*, the days when that government was considered best that governed least and that was in the news as little as possible. More and more in recent years this attitude has changed; and although the Federal government probably has done most in the field of public relations, state and local authorities have also embarked upon this new activity with great vigor. At a time when steadily increasing public

676

expenditures on all levels of government place a heavy tax burden upon the individual citizen, the need for rendering an account of the stewardship of public agencies becomes quite apparent. Private social welfare agencies, depending in large measure upon contributions of the citizenry through community chest channels, are in exactly the same position. They, too—sometimes even more than governmental agencies—consider the interpretation of their work to the public at large as one of their important tasks.[1]

Secondly, in the specific field of juvenile delinquency control and prevention there are additional compelling reasons for the need of interpretation. The reaction of the general public toward crime has always been so strongly laden with emotion and often with hysteria that the modern objective and scientific approaches to its causation and treatment have encountered formidable misunderstanding, if not hostility, on the part of the "man on the street." Whenever public opinion polls are conducted, especially after a particularly heinous crime has shocked the community or after some startling reports of crime waves or juvenile delinquency increases have been published, the responses are quite revealing. They indicate that—to cite just a few examples—probation and parole are among the most misunderstood governmental activities,[2] that juvenile courts are accused of coddling prospective gangsters, and that the establishment of psychiatric clinics in penal institutions is considered a sign of weakness. Frequently, too, the various media of communication (the press, the radio, and so forth) create in the public mind a distorted picture of the phenomenon of crime and the persons and agencies charged with law enforcement and crime control. The public, therefore, must be educated so that it is able to appraise unemotionally that group of antisocial individuals whom we call lawbreakers and offenders. Once convinced that the application of methods of revenge and retribution

---

[1] See Mary Swain Routzahn, "Public Relations in Social Work," *Social Work Yearbook*, Russell Sage Foundation, 1949, pp. 397–402; Helen Cody Baker and Mary Swain Routzahn, *How To Interpret Social Welfare*, Russell Sage Foundation, 1947; Viola Paradise, *Toward Public Understanding of Case Work*, Russell Sage Foundation, 1948.

[2] The lack of public understanding of juvenile court functioning was pointed out in two articles in *Federal Probation*, September 1949: Judge Gustav L. Schramm, "The Juvenile Court Idea," p. 22, and Harrison Allen Dobbs, "In Defense of Juvenile Courts," p. 24.

has failed to produce results benefiting the community, the public mind must be prepared to see in the treatment approach to delinquency and crime the more effectual method of dealing with the age-old problem. To achieve this goal of general understanding is indeed the prerequisite for the advancement and improvement of curative services in the correctional field. Modern programs of dealing with the offender require money, and although the sums needed constitute only a minimal fraction of the total public expenditures, they are more likely to be criticized than the levies for many more expensive budgetary items. The desirable aim of interpretation is to create not only a willingness to pay for such services through local, state, and Federal taxes or community chest contributions, but also to alert the community into demanding an effective and progressive program of combatting crime and delinquency and their causes through public as well as private agencies. Along the same line, Edwin J. Lukas, executive director of the Society for the Prevention of Crime, New York City, suggests that the community should be informed of what those dealing with crime and delinquency control know about the causes of crime. Every community, he states, has its roster of famous offenders whose external behavior is quite well known, but whose internal drives and other surrounding circumstances are literally unknown to the average citizen. He therefore proposes that

> . . . We should examine painstakingly and publicize the personal, social and family histories of a sizeable sampling of the more recent crop of the community's juvenile and adult offenders. The public's awareness of the specific social and psychological circumstances which contributed to the antisocial behavior of locally notorious offenders would be helpful in securing its co-operation for creating some of the basic tools with which to prevent a repetition of that behavior among others.[3]

The following outline deals with the various media of interpretation. It attempts to appraise the use made of them at present, whether good or bad, and it tries to evaluate the potentialities which these media offer for a really intelligent job of public education in this field.[4]

---

[3] Edwin J. Lukas, "Crime Prevention; Who Prevents What?," *Federal Probation*, June 1948, p. 21.

[4] See J. O. Reinemann, "Developing Community Understanding of Probation and Parole Work," *Journal of Criminal Law and Criminology*, May–June

2. THE PRESS

In spite of the expanding development of radio, motion pictures, and television, the press remains the most important and accessible medium for channeling information to a large number of people.

The question as to whether the influence of the newspapers, particularly through their reporting of individual crime stories, is one of aiding or preventing antisocial behavior has been discussed elsewhere in this text.[5] Two other questions concerning the press may be asked: How do newspapers present such matter as probation, institutions, and parole? And how can newspapers be used for interpreting to the public the more scientific approach to the offender and particularly to the juvenile delinquent?

Let us preface the answer to these questions with a brief appraisal of the functions of the newspaper. Joseph J. Canavan, former chairman of the New York State Board of Parole, in "Newspapers and Crime" states that "a good newspaper is devoted to the presentation of facts which would interest the reader. The better the paper, the less it is affected by the influence that can be exerted by any pressure group, whether the group is fundamentally selfish or unselfish in its aims." News is the "unusual act, either because it is more important or contrary to the ordinary run of happenings." [6] A conflict situation is always news, and crime—the epitome of conflict—is news of the first magnitude.

Applying this principle to the reporting of matters in the correctional field, it is natural that the well-behaved probationer and the conforming parolee are not news; nor are the 98 per cent of children of juvenile court age who never run afoul of the law. But succumbing to the tendency of easy generalizations, which is so widespread among the general public and which in its ugly forms of bigotry and prejudice is gnawing on the fundamentals of our democratic life, the press often uses a single occurrence to condemn an entire group of individuals or a whole system. Through headline emphasis for the general reader and editorials for the more discriminating subscriber,

---

1942, pp. 23–31; see also Judge Patrick T. Stone, "The Public Is Very Much in the Dark About Probation and Parole," *Federal Probation*, December 1948, pp. 7–9.

[5] See Chapter VI, pp. 172–177.

[6] *Yearbook*, N.P.P.A., 1939, pp. 293–303 (quotations on p. 295).

the philosophy and practice of probation and parole are being attacked whenever a probationer or parolee commits a serious offense. During World War II, some newspaper stories on the juvenile delinquency situation made it appear as if the whole American youth were running riot. Actually, despite the considerable increase in juvenile offenses, the total percentage of children referred to juvenile courts never amounted to much more than 2 per cent of the entire child population of the respective age groups.

Newspaper reporting in generalizing terms is not only unfair to sincere and able administrators in charge of law enforcement and correction, it also tends to jeopardize the chances of the persons on probation and parole who earnestly try to lead law-abiding lives. They are thwarted in their endeavor by rebuffs from members of the community who as a result of newspaper stories have formed in their minds the stereotyped picture of an ex-convict as being always a potential recidivist. Similarly, the youngster who has been involved in delinquencies and has been placed on probation or sent to an institution will face difficulties of readjustment in a community whose attitude of suspicion against anybody who has had a "brush with the law" may be the result of generalizing newspaper articles.

Nobody will deny the press the right to criticize; and there is indeed much in society's approach to the crime and delinquency problem that can well stand constructive criticism based on established facts, objective surveys, and responsible reporting. If corrupt practices occur in the administration of parole, if scandalous conditions exist in penal and correctional institutions, if incompetence or political interference characterize probation administration, if juvenile courts, detention quarters for children, and diagnostic and treatment clinics are poorly equipped and inadequately staffed, then it is the duty of the journalist to bring these conditions to the attention of the citizenry in the most impressive manner his newspaper can employ.

Practitioners in the field of crime and delinquency control have often pondered the question of how to utilize the press most efficiently for the furthering of modern approaches to this problem; how through the use of the daily paper to enlist the necessary community backing, both moral and financial, for scientific treatment facilities for offenders; how to combat the still all too prevalent notion that the solution of the crime and delinquency problem lies in larger sentences, less probation and parole, the use of the whipping post, the curtailment of juvenile court jurisdiction, and the handling of children's cases along lines of criminal procedure.

Gilbert Cosulich, formerly director of publicity of the National Probation and Parole Association, in an article "Probation and Parole Publicity in the Press," stresses the importance of the "human interest" angle in the news story. "The trick is," he states, "to relate a specialized subject (probation or parole) to a general reader interest." [7] He suggests the following types of newspaper publicity:

(a) Interviews, statements made at public meetings or professional conferences ("information which can be constructive without being dull").

(b) The editorial ("many of the smaller dailies and most of the rural weeklies will use a well written non-controversial comment prepared by outsiders").

(c) The "human interest" or feature story ("success stories about unnamed probationers or parolees might well be used").

(d) The straight news story ("this includes information regarding annual reports, case loads, new appointments, distinguished visitors to the probation and parole offices, field trips, in-service training institutes, city, county, state and national conferences").

F. Perry Olds, of the editorial staff of the Milwaukee *Journal*, addressing probation and parole officers at the 40th Annual Conference of the National Probation and Parole Association in San Francisco in April 1947, discussed ways and means of approaching the press:

Through a council of social agencies if there is one, through some designated representative if there is no council, newspapers should be approached whenever an important misrepresentation of fact or a backward editorial appears. Most of you have good newspaper contacts;—develop them. If you have none, create them.

You are believers in the casework method. You should apply that method in your newspaper relations. Surely making a social asset of a newspaper is worth at least as much as making a social asset of some single unfortunate lawbreaker. Your newspaper case may be a tough one and it may be a long time before you feel safe in closing it, but once you have won, such a case will pay you and your successors dividends for many years.

---

[7] *Yearbook*, N.P.P.A., 1940, pp. 271–281 (quotation on p. 273). What is said in this paper regarding probation and parole is equally true for the problem of juvenile delinquency and all its ramifications.

Another thing you can do—, individually, in your local councils, in your state and national associations,—you can start a movement to establish in every school of journalism an orientation course in social values and social problems, to the end that graduates of these schools may have a better comprehension of social needs than many who now report the news and edit the papers.

Finally you can try to get participation by newspaper people in your lay and mixed committees. There should be a newspaperman or two on every council of social agencies and on the board of every private social agency. It is only when newspapermen get out of their offices and themselves and into nonpartisan public affairs that they acquire new and better backgrounds, new and better ideas.[8]

3. THE PERIODICALS

A great number of scientific journals are being used to interpret the problems of juvenile delinquency to the academic reader. Articles dealing with the subject have appeared in periodicals in the fields of criminology, sociology, law, education, psychology, psychiatry, mental hygiene, social hygiene, anthropology, social work, recreation, and public administration. Magazines serving specifically the practitioner in the field of delinquency control and treatment are *Focus* (formerly *Probation*) of the National Probation and Parole Association, and *Federal Probation*, published by the Administrative Office of the United States Courts.[9]

In recent years a flood of articles has appeared on the various aspects of juvenile delinquency in many of the popular journals,

---

[8] F. Perry Olds, "The Place of the Press in Crime Control," *Yearbook*, N.P.P.A., 1947, pp. 245–259 (quotation on p. 257). Other articles dealing with this subject are Frank Luther Mott, "Public Relations of Probation and Parole," *Yearbook*, N.P.P.A., 1943, pp. 12–17; Roy Hofheinz, "Telling the Public," *Probation*, February 1940, pp. 74 and 91; "Make the Newspapers Work for You," *Probation*, October 1945, pp. 13–18; Leopold Lippman, "Probation and Parole Are News," *Probation*, February 1944, pp. 71–79; Donald E. Long, "Developing Public Support for Juvenile Courts," *Yearbook*, N.P.P.A., 1947, pp. 260–272 (esp. 268–269); Irving Halpern, "Probation and the Press," *Probation*, December 1939, pp. 49–54; see also Gertrude W. Simpson, *Working with Newspapers*, National Publicity Council for Health and Welfare Services, New York, 1945. Examples of good newspaper articles on juvenile delinquency are mentioned in Lester D. Crow and Alice Crow, *Our Teen-Age Boys and Girls*, McGraw-Hill, New York, 1945, p. 318.

[9] Frequent references have been made to articles in these two publications.

especially in women's magazines. Some of them have served the very practical purpose of arousing the reader to an awareness of gaps in the existing services. For instance, the national disgrace of keeping children awaiting court hearing in jails and their commingling with adults accused of crime has been the subject of widespread publicity and has actually startled a number of communities into action. Other topics that are part of the general picture of juvenile delinquency, such as alcoholism, venereal disease, illegitimacy, broken homes, and mental illness, have been aired with a healthy frankness. Such discussions have contributed to a much broader and deeper understanding of human problems which only a few years ago could not have been publicly discussed in deference to old-fashioned and ill-placed prudery.

4. THE RADIO

There are approximately sixty million radio receiving sets in the United States. The size of its audience is radio's greatest advantage. Dr. Lowell Juilliard Carr, in his paper "Interpreting Probation and Parole through the Radio," listed as radio's other assets "the emotional values of the living human voice, the person-to-person relationship of speaker to listener, and the facility of contact, that is to say, the ease with which the listener can establish contact." On the other hand, Dr. Carr pointed out such limitations of broadcasting as 'the one-way character of the communicative contact, the lack of immediate reaction from the listener, the utter dependence on voice, the transient impression of the moment, the brevity of the contact which ordinarily lasts from ten to thirty minutes, the superficial nature of the contact because of the ease with which the listener can tune out, and finally the completeness of listener control, that is to say, the continuing necessity of continuity of interest." [10]

Everyone who wants to use the radio as a tool of interpretation has to be aware of these advantages and limitations. In the presentation of the juvenile delinquency problem through radio channels it was found that case histories, because of their human interest value, are almost always more interesting than any other type of material. Necessarily, the identity of the persons involved must be carefully disguised. Case stories may be narrated by one person or, preferably,

---

[10] *Yearbook*, N.P.P.A., 1940, pp. 282–287 (quotation on p. 282).

dramatized. If the latter form is chosen, explanatory remarks by the announcer should be brief and should serve as leads to the following action scenes rather than be self-sufficient. Statistical data should be most sparingly quoted, and then only in round figures. The series "Youth in the Toils," presented in Spring of 1940 by the American Law Institute, successfully employed these techniques. The purpose of these broadcasts was to draw attention to the problem of the adolescent offender and to win support for the idea of the Youth Correction Authority.[11] Professional radio actors were used in the dramatic episodes and on each program one leading expert in the correctional field—a judge, sociologist, criminologist, or psychiatrist—participated as commenting speaker. A good radio play, *A Friend in Deed*, was presented by the National Probation and Parole Association in April 1941, commemorating the centennial of probation through a dramatization of the story of John Augustus and the first probation case. The radio script shows that only slightly over 25 per cent of the spoken words were assigned to the announcer, all the rest being dedicated to dramatic action.

In a radio drama, so Dr. Carr advises, "A dialogue should snap, the situation should move rapidly, the characters should be well distinguished by differences in voice. Ordinarily these are matters which the average radio station will perhaps insist on handling through their respective script writers and radio actors." [12]

Another, though less effective, form of presentation is that of the dialogue or interview. The Juvenile Court of Allegheny County, Pittsburgh, Pennsylvania, used this method in a radio discussion of such subjects as the new juvenile court building and detention home, medical care of the children coming into court, and psychological and psychiatric examinations.[13]

The panel discussion or radio forum, with or without participation of the studio audience, has become a popular form of presenting problems of social significance, including juvenile delinquency. Good examples of this type of program on a nation-wide scale were "The Town Meeting of the Air" broadcasts: "Are Parents or Society Responsible for Juvenile Crime?" and "What's Wrong with the Com-

---

11 See Chapter X, pp. 355–358.
12 *Ibid.*, p. 286.
13 See "Listening in to The Juvenile Court," *Probation*, June 1938, pp. 73–75.

ics? [14] Many such round-table programs on juvenile delinquency and related subjects have been broadcast over local stations and national networks.

In an article "How To Use the Radio," Gertrude Binder, formerly public relations director of the National Probation and Parole Association, gives several hints on how to use current radio programs as vehicles for the interpretation of juvenile delinquency problems. She says, for instance, "Many newscasters like to conclude their programs with amusing anecdotes gleaned from the day's news and have difficulty in finding a sufficient number of such items. Any organization that works with human beings has stories of this sort to release from time to time, provided someone with a news sense is on the lookout for them." Another channel is the women's programs. "The various women broadcasters have large and faithful followings interested in the kind of material about human beings and work with them that is done by probation and parole departments." [15] Finally, the handling of juvenile delinquency cases could be presented as one of many social services in a community and, therefore, could be included in any regular weekly programs sponsored by local community councils and chests, chambers of commerce, parent-teacher associations, or service clubs.[16]

In 1940, the Bureau for the Prevention of Juvenile Delinquency, within the Probation Department of the Domestic Relations Court of New York City, inaugurated a series of dramatized broadcasts over station WNYC, entitled "Why Children Come to Court." Mayor F. H. LaGuardia wrote the script for the first broadcast, directed the program, and appeared in the leading role. In subsequent programs several of the serious contributing causes of delinquency were dramatized in the form of a typical case, followed by an analysis of the case through a child welfare expert.[17]

---

[14] See *Town Meeting Bulletin*, Vol. 11, No. 43, February 21, 1946, and Vol. 13, No. 45, March 2, 1948.

[15] *Probation*, February 1946, pp. 82–86.

[16] For more details, see Beatrice K. Tolleris, *Radio, How, When and Why To Use It*, National Publicity Council for Health and Welfare Services, New York, 1946.

[17] For further information, see "For Tomorrow: A Court Defends the Child and Family Today," *Annual Report of the Domestic Relations Court of the City of New York*, 1940, pp. 70–71.

Because of the growing public interest in juvenile delinquency, the initiative for the presentation of this problem on the air has recently come from the radio stations themselves. From Savannah, Georgia, it is reported that as a result of the publication of the Juvenile Court's report on its activities from 1944 to 1947, the local station WDAR invited the judge and the chief probation officer to present a series of weekly radio programs entitled "You and Youth." For this program the radio station received the George Foster Peabody award in recognition of meritorious public service. The citation emphasized that the station "not only contributed wisely and helpfully to problems of juvenile delinquency, but provided a program pattern which has attracted much favorable notice over a wide area, and which can, with profit, be studied and adapted by other broadcasters." [18]

The contents and the form of such programs depend necessarily on the purpose of the broadcast. It might be the aim to spread general information on the scope and character of the situation regarding child offenders in a given community; or the intention might be to awaken interest in a special project under discussion which would serve the prevention and treatment of juvenile delinquency. An interesting example of broadcasts with a special purpose is cited by Judge Donald E. Long of the Domestic Relations Court, Portland, Oregon, in an article "Developing Public Support for Juvenile Courts." A tax measure providing for a new juvenile home and court building was to be on the ballot. According to Judge Long, the radio was used to explain to the voters the significance of this tax measure. There were some panel discussions, some straight factual talks, some question and answer series, and some human interest scripts.[19]

Television has been used occasionally for the interpretation of the phenomenon of juvenile delinquency. Even more than the radio, television calls for dramatization in order to hold not only the auditory but also the visual interest of the audience. Using television as a direct means of juvenile delinquency prevention, the popular bandmaster, Paul Whiteman, has organized "TV-Teen Clubs" all over the country. This program is a combination of Saturday-night enter-

---

[18] For details, see *Focus*, November 1948, pp. 185–186, and September 1949, p. 155.

[19] See *Yearbook*, N.P.P.A., 1947, pp. 260–272 (especially p. 270).

tainment for "teen-agers" and a talent show, and has become known as the "Lambertville, New Jersey, Story" because it originated in that town near Mr. Whiteman's home. Chief probation officer Charles T. G. Rogers of the San Diego Juvenile Court originated a weekly television program, "Seen and Heard Too," on which teen-agers discuss their problems with guest experts; the first topic was the curfew ordinance.

5. THE MOTION PICTURE AND THE THEATER

Two types of motion pictures may convey to the public the scope and implications of juvenile delinquency, its causes and its treatment —the documentary film and the fictional (or feature) film.

Early examples of documentary films were "Youth and Crime," a 1936 *March of Time* release, and "Boy in Court," produced by the National Probation and Parole Association in 1940, depicting the story of juvenile courts and probation through the case history of a boy who, as a result of neglect at home, joins a gang that specializes in automobile stealing. This film has been shown to hundreds of audiences throughout the country and has proved particularly helpful as a visual supplement to lectures before citizens' groups. More recent *March of Time* releases were "Juvenile Delinquents" and "Youth in Crisis." The latter, produced during World War II, dealt with the problems of youth as a result of the war, and the work done by intelligent communities to meet these problems.

The documentary film series "This Is America" contains at least three documentary films dealing with the problem under discussion: "Children of Mars," built around the story of an American family where the mother is working in a war factory; "Children's Village," showing the well-known boys' school of that name in Dobbs Ferry, New York; and "Who's Delinquent?," the story of two boys jailed for stealing a car and running down a policeman, an incident which, because of increasing teen-age crime, inspires a crusading editor to inquire into the causes and treatment of delinquency. His reporters find children in jail, an inefficient court, no social treatment; in the community they stumble upon bad homes, crowded schools, flourishing ginmills, and apathetic or ineffective social and recreational agencies. He enlists the churches and civic and business leaders to attack these conditions. The National Conference and the National

Probation and Parole Association contributed ideas to this film.[20]

Another picture, "Report for Action," is a dramatization of the "Handbook on First Steps in Organizing State and Local Conferences on Prevention and Control of Juvenile Delinquency," prepared by the Continuing Committee of the National Conference. This film was widely shown in September 1948, designated as "National Youth Month," in order to promote a series of youth conferences. The Theater Owners of America, under Charles P. Skouras, gave valuable help and made their theaters available without cost for private showings of the film to community groups.[21]

"Make Way for Youth," produced for the Youth Division of the National Social Welfare Assembly, shows dramatically the tragic result of racial tension and ensuing gang fights and the subsequent formation of a youth council whose activities result in real community understanding and the establishment of a recreation center through youth's own efforts. The film's actors are high-school boys and girls and adults from a typical American community; Melvyn Douglas is the narrator.[22]

On the local level, there are pictures like "Forestry Camps," produced by the Los Angeles Probation Department, and "Challenge to Crime," a Y.M.C.A. film showing how some juvenile delinquency problems were solved in Moline, Illinois. The Juvenile Court of Kansas City some years ago released a picture showing the operation of the court and of four children's institutions caring for delinquent and dependent children.[23]

A color film short is "Playtown USA." It shows how a typical American community—Decatur, Illinois—realized the need for expanded public recreation facilities and how it stimulated individual families to participate in leisure-time activities. The dangers of juvenile delinquency are pointed out in this film (produced by the Chicago Film Studios) as one of the reasons for an over-all recreation program.

[20] For a rather complete listing of documentary films of this nature, see "Selected Motion Pictures 1949–1950," published by Association Films, Inc. (formerly Y.M.C.A. Motion Picture Bureau), New York, pp. 29–30.

[21] See *Survey Mid-Monthly*, July 1948, pp. 235–236; also "Accent on Youth," Bulletin of the National Conference on the Prevention and Control of Juvenile Delinquency, May 1948.

[22] See *Survey Mid-Monthly*, March 1948, p. 69.

[23] See *Probation*, December 1942, p. 58.

The American Legion has produced a set of sound slide films on the subject of "Child Welfare and Parenthood Training"; one of them is entitled "The Juvenile Delinquent in Court."

From Great Britain came "Children of the City," showing how a Scottish town handled the delinquency problem, and "Children on Trial," a part fictional, part factual film, using the "approved schools" for delinquent juveniles as a background.

The beginnings of fictional films with juvenile delinquency as their theme go back to 1937, when "Dead End" was adapted for the screen by Lillian Hellman from Sidney Kingsley's drama. Since that time a veritable avalanche of fictional motion pictures depicting juvenile crime has descended upon the American public. Unfortunately, many of them have been primarily devoted to the emotional appeal and to cheap sensationalism and excitement, and often portrayed law-enforcement officials, judges, probation officers, wardens, and superintendents of institutions in a distorted and frequently unfair light. These pictures, too numerous to mention, only occasionally conveyed the real problems inherent in juvenile misconduct. A notable exception was "Boys' Town," with its true background of Father Flanagan's Home for wayward boys in Omaha.

More recently, the motion picture industry has become aware of the great possibilities of the screen to present the many social problems of our times in an earnest and thought-provoking way. "Snake Pit" (dealing with the treatment of mental ills), "The Lost Weekend" (portraying alcoholism as a sickness), "Not Wanted" (having as its subject the fate of unmarried mothers), "Gentleman's Agreement," "Home of the Brave," "Lost Boundaries," and "Pinky" (tackling the race problem) are excellent examples. In order to produce serious films with educational as well as entertainment value, the motion picture producers have called upon experts in their respective fields for advice. "Knock on Any Door," based on the popular novel of the same name by Willard Motley, was produced by Columbia Pictures with the advice of the National Probation and Parole Association; its high point is a forceful and moving challenge to the public conscience by the defense attorney (played by Humphrey Bogart) for Pretty Boy Romano, who is a product of Chicago's worst slums. The locale of "Bad Boy," an Allied Artists' Production, is the Boys' Ranch at Copperas Cove, Texas, sponsored by the Variety Club International, which has won the praise of former

Attorney General Tom C. Clark for its efforts in rehabilitating boy offenders released to the ranch by the courts. "City Across the River," a Universal-International Picture, is adapted from Irving Shulman's book "The Amboy Dukes," a story of boys' gangs in Brooklyn. Its narrator is the newspaper columnist Drew Pearson, who states in the beginning of the picture, "To most of us the city where juvenile crime flourishes always seems to be the city across the river. But don't kid yourself. It could be your city, your street, your house." [24] In "The Kid from Cleveland," a Republic picture released in September 1949, the interest of members of the Cleveland Indians baseball team in redeeming a boy who runs to them for protection is the central theme. It shows the possibility of using a boy's hero worship and love of the game in helping him to readjust. The friendly interest and understanding of juvenile court officials for the boy whose delinquent behavior is rooted in the home and its surroundings are effectively interpreted. [25]

"The Quiet One," one of the best pictures in this field, was produced on a shoestring as a documentary film by Film Documents, Inc., was "discovered" at the Edinburgh Film Festival, and was then shown in commercial theaters to capacity audiences. Its central character is a ten-year-old Negro boy from Harlem, who is unwanted, unloved, and uncared for. He gets into trouble and is sent to Wiltwyck School, an inter-racial school for maladjusted boys, near Esopus, New York, where many of the film's scenes are taken. Here at first he makes no friends and rebuffs all treatment attempts until one of the counselors slowly wins his confidence. *The New York Times* praised the film with these words: "Not since that classic, 'The River,' caught the terror and tragedy of the Mississippi's wastage, have we had such eloquence in an American documentary film." [26]

"The Quiet One" compares favorably with such outstanding foreign films as the Russian "Road to Life" (shown in this country for the first time in 1932), which introduced the audience to the life of the "Besprizorni," the large number of children who, after World War I, the Revolution, and the Civil War, were roaming through

---

[24] See *Focus*, July 1949, p. 123.

[25] See *Focus*, January 1950, pp. 19–20.

[26] February 20, 1949, Section 2; see also *Harper's Magazine*, February 1949, pp. 99–100. The Wiltwyck School is described in Chapter XIII, pp. 497–498.

the vast areas of the Soviet Union; [27] and with the Italian master-piece, "Shoeshine," which told the story of two boys made homeless and parentless by World War II, and which pointed up problems very similar to those presented by the Russian waifs thirty years earlier.

Scene from "The Quiet One" *(Courtesy of Film Documents, Inc., New York)*

A later Italian film dealing with the unbridled youth of that country in the postwar period is "Under the Sun of Rome." A French picture,

[27] See J. O. Reinemann, "Films of Social Significance," *Prison Journal*, July–October 1938, pp. 476–480.

"The Cage of the Nightingales," has as its background a reform school where an oppressive spirit prevails and where disobedience and revolt are frequent occurrences. Into this institution a young instructor comes with a belief that even the worst offenders are redeemable. After many set-backs he succeeds in winning over the boys placed in his charge, although he is continuously hampered and distrusted by the oldfashioned and cruel superintendent. The instructor uses music as a means of gaining the youngsters' cooperation and particularly for giving the worst ring-leader (who has an exquisite singing voice) a sense of achievement. The waywardness of children, caused by the misery and desolation of life in a war-ravaged city—Berlin in the days following Germany's defeat in 1945 —has been masterfully depicted in "Germany Year Zero," a film directed by the well-known Italian creator of "Open City" and "Paisan," Roberto Rossellini.

The United Nations has produced two films, "Children of Darkness" (in Spanish) and "Cross-Roads of Life" (in French). The first deals with basic fundamentals of good juvenile delinquency treatment, and the second with more advanced theory and practice, including psychoanalytical concepts employed within the institutional setting.

The legitimate theater has only occasionally been employed as a vehicle for the portrayal of juvenile delinquency problems. The very successful "Dead End" by Sidney Kingsley has already been mentioned. In 1944, Elsa Shelley's "Pick-Up Girl" was produced on Broadway and ran for six months; the entire play takes place in a courtroom. The "heroine," a fifteen-year-old girl, is the victim of a poverty-stricken home, an indigent father, a harassed and bewildered mother, and her own lack of direction.[28]

Several local and state agencies dealing with delinquency control have chosen the form of amateur dramas to interpret their activities to the public. The play "As the Twig Is Bent" was produced by the Juvenile Court of Lucas County, Toledo, Ohio, in 1940; Judge Paul W. Alexander himself appeared in the cast.[29] "Passing the Buck" presents a courtroom scene with youth on trial, and deals with such other subjects as the use of leisure time, problems of the adolescent

---

[28] See *Probation*, June 1944, pp. 134–135.
[29] See *Probation*, June 1940, p. 149.

girl, institutional needs, and delinquency prevention councils. It was produced by the Division for Delinquency Prevention of the Illinois Department of Public Welfare, in cooperation with the Big Brother and Sister Association of Illinois.[30] The Catholic Big Brothers of Cincinnati used the dramatic form of a juvenile court mock trial, entitled "From the Shadows of Dead End," as a means of educating the public in their work and the philosophy behind the juvenile court.

6. OTHER METHODS OF INTERPRETATION

Among the more conventional means of reaching the public are lectures, exhibits, pamphlets, and reports.

The publicity given to the juvenile delinquency phenomenon has prompted many organizations, especially civic groups, parent-teacher associations, women's clubs, veterans and service organizations, and church groups, to include this topic in their lecture programs. Usually an individual speaker is called upon to address a group. Recently panel discussions have won increasing favor because a variety of speakers not only adds to the liveliness of the presentation but also brings out a diversity of viewpoints. In order to enliven a talk, documentary films, picture slides, or charts have been successfully used as a visual auxiliary.

Youth itself has become immensely interested in the problem of juvenile delinquency.[31] Many high-school classes have included it in their curriculum of social studies. Panels of youngsters have very frankly discussed this topic in high-school assemblies or community meetings.[32]

Exhibits interpreting juvenile court work, probation, and delinquency prevention are used either in connection with general state or local exhibitions and fairs, in which the agencies having jurisdiction over correctional matters participate, or as a part of specific exhibits relating only to welfare work and affiliated topics, or at

---

[30] See *Probation*, June 1940, p. 145; April 1942, p. 123.

[31] See Chapter XVI, pp. 666–672.

[32] An interesting educational program is reported from Buffalo, New York, where representatives of the probation department of the juvenile court regularly address pupils of the elementary and high schools on the prevention of crime; see Bernard J. Bird, "Telling Youth About Crime," *Yearbook*, N.P.P.A., 1940, pp. 13–23.

special occasion such as professional conferences, anniversary cele-
brations, and "juvenile court weeks." [33] Whoever plans and prepares
such an exhibit has to keep in mind that his purpose is "to catch the
eye" of the visitor. Which modern techniques of visualization are
available? Photography, including the special form of photomontage;
movable lantern slides, if possible in technicolor; silent or sound motion picture reels; and panoramas and cycloramas are now most frequently employed. Statistical curves should be used sparingly and
preferably in connection with photographs or other visual aids. The
new isotype method has developed a comprehensive but easily in-
telligible picture language based on a system of symbols of various
colors, sizes, and forms. Catchy slogans are another requirement for
efficient exhibits. They may be used in connection with statistical,
photographic, or other pictorial illustrations, as shown in the exhibits
of the Department of Correction, the Domestic Relations and Family
Courts, the Courts of Special Sessions, and the Juvenile Aid Bureau
of the Police, at the City of New York Pavilion of the "New York
World's Fair" in 1939–40.[34]

Various public and private agencies dealing with delinquents have
distributed leaflets or bulletins describing their function either to the
public at large or specifically to their clients. Case histories are frequently included in these circulars. Reprints of newspaper editorials
often serve as pamphlets.[35]

The periodic—mostly annual—reports of public departments dealing with the delinquency problem are another useful vehicle of interpretation. In order to win the public's attention, these reports should
be written in a concise form and in a style as free from technical

---

[33] Phoenix, Arizona, has held such "Juvenile Court Weeks" annually since
1938. The "Family Fair," sponsored by the San Diego Coordinating Councils,
in which about 60 child and family welfare agencies participated and which
attracted about 10,000 persons, featured exhibits of family welfare, group work,
educational, religious, and other agencies working in the field. This "Family
Fair," which was held in May 1949, is described in the special issue of *The
Coordinator*, published by the San Diego County Coordinating Councils.

[34] For technical details, see Janet Lane and Beatrice K. Tolleris, *Planning
Your Exhibit*, National Publicity Council for Health and Welfare Services,
New York, 1949.

[35] Good examples are "Problem Children—The Job," a leaflet issued by the
Community Chest of Akron, Ohio, and the "Delinquency News Letter" of the
Michigan Child Guidance Institute; a series of pamphlets by the Los Angeles

verbiage as possible; they should be liberally illustrated with photographs. Charts and graphs are much more impressive than statistical tables. Statistics, in any events, should always be accompanied by textual explanations.[36]

7. RESEARCH

Although the publication of research material is likely to reach only a limited sector of the population, it must be considered a peculiar part of community interpretation.

An increasing amount of fact-finding statistical material is being

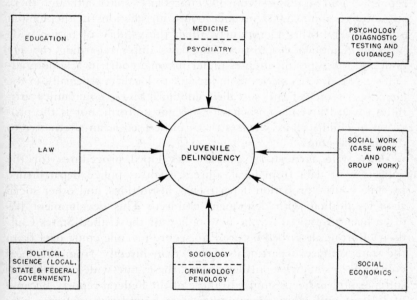

The Juvenile Delinquency Problem—Target of Many Sciences

Probation Department was described in detail in *Probation*, December 1938, pp. 24–26. See also Alexander Crosby, *Pamphlets That Pull*, National Publicity Council for Health and Welfare Services, New York, 1948.

[36] Good examples are "Focus the Child," Report of the Juvenile Court of Allegheny County, Pennsylvania, 1947; "Youth Services Unlimited," Report of the San Francisco, California, Juvenile Court Department for 1948; "Report from Your Juvenile Court," Report of Jackson County, Kansas City, Missouri, Juvenile Court for 1948. See also Beatrice K. Tolleris, *Annual Reports: How To Plan and Write Them*, National Publicity Council for Health and Welfare

published. On the national level the previously mentioned Uniform Crime Reports of the Federal Bureau of Investigation and the Juvenile Court Statistics of the United States Children's Bureau are the most important sources of information, in spite of the fact that they are necessarily incomplete and thus do not give an accurate picture of the extent of the juvenile delinquency problem. The Federal Bureau of Investigation reports are based on fingerprint data, and only a limited number of jurisdictions allow children of juvenile court age to be fingerprinted. The reports of the United States Children's Bureau do not cover the whole country; for instance, the 1948 report is based on reports from 399 courts in 17 states, although there are actually about 3,000 juvenile court jurisdictions in the United States. Several other factors may affect the validity of nation-wide juvenile delinquency statistics; state laws differ regarding the age limit and the types of offenses under juvenile court jurisdiction; administrative practice varies from locality to locality, especially in the handling of official and so-called unofficial cases; community attitudes toward juvenile misbehavior are not uniform, nor is the provision of child welfare services that can be used as an alternative to the juvenile court.

Many state agencies have lately developed procedures for the collection of data from local sources, such as police departments, juvenile courts, probation departments, institutions, and other social agencies dealing with delinquent children. This development has often been prompted by the new policy of the United States Children's Bureau, described before,[37] to secure juvenile court data from the state welfare departments rather than directly from the local courts. To a somewhat smaller degree, these state-wide compilations suffer from handicaps similar to those of the Federal reports, because of lack of uniformity even within state boundaries, except where state juvenile courts or centrally organized probation departments are in existence.

Consequently, the smaller the geographical unit the more reliable the collection of juvenile delinquency statistics; but the lack of uni-

---

Services, New York, 1946. A rather unusual annual report was published by the York County, Pennsylvania, Juvenile Court in 1946; its chief probation officer, Henry Lenz, wrote it in the form of a "personal letter directed particularly to the young people of York County."

[37] See Chapter IX, p. 337.

form definitions and procedures imposes a definite limit upon the comparability of local studies with those of other cities or counties.

Within these limitations, however, much profitable use can be made of national, state-wide, and local statistics in the form of research studies. Local studies have been undertaken by some councils of social agencies viewing the juvenile delinquency picture in relation to general community problems and services; a record is kept for each family in which a serious social breakdown has occurred (juvenile delinquency, adult crime, child neglect, divorce, illegitimacy, mental disease, mental deficiency), and the history of the family's contacts with various welfare and health agencies is recorded. Such a study points up the interdependency of the various problems within the same family during a given time and the need for coordination of services provided by social agencies.

Another group of local delinquency studies deals with sociological and ecological factors. Conditions in the neighborhood in which delinquents live are the subject of these research projects. Based on the smallest geographical unit for which population and housing figures are available—usually the census tracts [38]—many surveys of areas of high delinquency have been made. They often relate the delinquency incidence rates to such other information as density of population, proportion of owner-occupied dwelling units, sub-standard housing, average monthly rental, chief occupational groupings of the population, racial and nationality background of the inhabitants,

---

[38] *The Reports on Population and Housing of the 16th Census of the United States: 1940* (United States Government Printing Office, Washington, 1942) gives the following definition of a census tract: "Census tracts are small areas, having a population usually between 3,000 and 6,000, into which certain large cities (and sometimes their adjacent areas) have been subdivided for statistical and local administrative purposes, through co-operation with a local committee in each case. While this subdivsion into tracts has been more or less arbitrary, several principles have been followed in general in laying out the tracts for each city. The tract areas are established with a view to approximate uniformity in population, with some consideration of uniformity in size, and with due regard for natural barriers. The tracts are intended to remain unchanged from census to census and thus to make possible studies of changes in social and economic characteristics of the population within small sections of the city." The disadvantage of using figures based upon the census is caused by the fact that it is undertaken only decennially; thus accurate, up-to-date information is seldom available in view of the many changes in the composition of a neighborhood and the movement of the population during a ten-year period.

number of gainfully employed women, number of illegitimate births, number of tuberculosis or infant deaths, and number of persons receiving public assistance. Social base maps have been produced showing delinquency rates in their relationship to prevalent unwholesome influences in neighborhoods such as taverns, poolrooms, gambling establishments, and places of cheap entertainment, and to existing social and recreational services such as settlement houses, neighborhood centers, Y.M.C.A.'s and Y.W.C.A.'s, health centers, and similar agencies.

Juvenile courts and probation departments have mostly been satisfied with the collection of rudimentary statistical data regarding their case load and have published them in their annual reports in a more or less elaborate form. Research studies that go beyond such compilations have been undertaken in only a small number of jurisdictions. The reason for this situation is primarily lack of money and personnel, but also responsible is a certain misconception of the need for and the value of research on the part of the "practical-minded" administrators.[39] There are notable exceptions. A questionnaire was sent by the Research Committee of the National Probation and Parole Association to local and state probation departments in 1948, asking if they published any research material and also whether or not they considered research on the local and state level as being of value to their own department as well as to the profession of correctional work. Seven out of twenty-five state departments answered in the affirmative regarding published research material; among local departments fifteen out of thirty-nine answered positively. Regarding the desirability of research, twenty state departments and thirty-four local departments gave affirmative responses. The Municipal Court of Philadelphia, for instance, has over the years encouraged research studies by staff members in its probation and medical departments and has published them in its comprehensive annual reports. The Essex County, Newark, New Jersey, Probation Department, in cooperation with Rutgers University, has launched a formidable research project on probation outcomes covering 1,000 cases.

On the state level, the Ohio Bureau of Juvenile Research and the

---

[39] See John Otto Reinemann, "Research Activities in the Probation Department," *Yearbook*, N.P.P.A., 1946, pp. 196–217.

Illinois Institute for Juvenile Research have rendered outstanding services. The New York State Youth Commission initiated surveys of problem children.[40]

A notable example of a research study of this kind is the report on "Needs of Neglected and Delinquent Children," which was presented to the General Assembly of Connecticut by this state's Public Welfare Council in 1947 and which was undertaken by Community Surveys, Inc., as authorized by the General Assembly. Its purpose was to discover the underlying causes of delinquency and neglect, and, if possible, to formulate a program of prevention that would supplement the existing program of care and treatment. The study was based upon available data on 4,538 delinquent children and 898 neglected children who during the fiscal year 1945–46 had come to the attention of the Connecticut authorities. The study covered such items as place of residence, age, sex, race, intelligence, and type of offenses of the children, birthplace and age of the parents, and the family structure and the number of children in the family. However, although some useful information could be gained from these findings, they revealed only little about the underlying causes.

Therefore, a special, more detailed study, using a ten per cent sample of the cases, was undertaken which concerned itself with the investigation of the total family picture. The inquiry was directed at finding other types of breakdown in the family unit besides the delinquent behavior of the child in question. The following types of breakdown of a serious nature were studied: delinquency of other members of the family, neglect, crime, mental disease, mental deficiency, illegitimacy, economic need, and major illness. In addition to these easily ascertainable factors of major family breakdowns, the survey also included such symptoms of family disorganization as emotional instability on the part of one or more members of the family, disinterestedness of parents, and the effect of family disorganization on the children. The latter item included such aspects as deprivation of affectional needs, deprivation of physical needs, deprivation of social needs, deprivation of family security, overindulgence, and overprotection.

The conclusions reached were summarized as follows: (a) the

[40] For details, see Lowell Juilliard Carr, "Organization for Delinquency Control," *The Annals*, January 1949, pp. 64–76 (especially pp. 67 and 72).

central causal factor behind most child neglect and juvenile delinquency lies in family disorganization; (b) the causal factor in family
disorganization most frequently found is emotional instability of
the parent; (c) a disorganized family life sets in motion processes
harmful to children who may react to them by becoming delinquent
or by developing traits that lead to breakdown later on; (d) from
disorganized families come other serious and costly social break-
downs—mental disease, mental deficiency, crime, and divorce.

The study also suggested a practical program of early diagnosis
and of treatment service in order to deal effectively with the problem of family disorganization.[41]

The New Jersey State Department of Institutions and Agencies
undertook a study of community vulnerability to social breakdown.
Other agencies engaged in some kind of delinquency research, in
cooperation with universities, are the Ohio Welfare Council, collab-
orating with Ohio State University, and the California Youth
Authority, which for several years allocated money for research
workers at the University of Southern California. A number of
states reported that special studies serving as basis for administrative
and legislative action were under way or had been completed.[42]

In general, criminological research has been seriously hampered by
lack of funds. Juvenile delinquency studies have, therefore, been conducted sporadically and without relationship to one another. As
Walter C. Reckless emphasizes, "The field of criminology needs
well-planned basic studies with adequate finances." [43] Those research
works, he continues, which, according to responses to a questionnaire sent to psychiatrists, psychologists, sociologists, and others active in research in delinquency and crime, have contributed most to
the increase of our knowledge of delinquent and criminal behavior
enjoyed some degree of financial support. They were: Sheldon and
Eleanor T. Glueck, *One Thousand Juvenile Delinquents, Juvenile*

---

[41] For details regarding this project, see *Needs of Neglected and Delinquent
Children* (A Report to the 1947 Connecticut General Assembly by the Public
Welfare Council), Hartford, Connecticut, 1946; for a summary of the findings,
see Reginald Robinson (director of the study), "Beneath the Surface of Juvenile
Delinquency and Child Neglect," *Survey Midmonthly*, February 1947, pp. 41–52.
[42] See Carr, *op. cit.*
[43] Walter C. Reckless, *The Etiology of Delinquency and Criminal Behavior*,
Social Science Research Council, New York, Bulletin 50, 1943, p. 159.

Delinquents Grown Up, and *500 Criminal Careers;* William Healy and Augusta F. Bronner, *New Light on Delinquency and Its Treatment;* Clifford R. Shaw, *Delinquency Areas;* Clifford R. Shaw and Henry D. McKay, *Social Factors in Juvenile Delinquency;* Franz Alexander and William Healy, *Roots of Crime;* Frederic M. Thrasher, *The Gang;* Thorsten Sellin, *Culture Conflict and Crime;* and Ernest H. Sutherland's articles on the "White Collar Criminal." These are the classics in the field, and nobody can doubt their long-term value. But development in the scientific techniques and the continuous societal changes call for a permanent research program in the criminological field.

Reckless puts first on his list of recommendations the establishment of a "small compact Academy of Research in Delinquent and Criminal Behavior." It should be composed of "persons actively engaged in criminological research from the several contributing scientific disciplines." He points out that "adult and juvenile courts, police departments, parole and probation agencies, correctional institutions, constitute the best and most available research laboratories in criminology." [44]

Good use has already been made of case material of juvenile courts in several instances. The standard work, *Social Treatment in Probation and Delinquency*, by Pauline V. Young of the University of Southern California,[45] is based mainly on the contents of case records of the Juvenile Court and Probation Department of Los Angeles County. Among the more recent studies, William C. Kvaraceus' book, *Juvenile Delinquency and the School*,[46] makes extensive use

---

[44] *Ibid.*, pp. 157–160. Several studies undertaken or at least co-sponsored by these agencies are listed as being in progress in *Research Relating to Children* (An Inventory of Studies in Progress; Reported December 1, 1948–June 30, 1949, to the Clearinghouse for Research in Child Life), United States Children's Bureau, Government Printing Office, 1950). It is highly commendable that the Children's Bureau considers it as one of its functions to act as clearing and information center for such research studies. Every state should designate one central agency (a state welfare department, a research institute, or the like) to act in this capacity. Such an agency would avoid duplication of efforts, and would facilitate information concerning the scope of research studies in progress, and their completion and availability in printed or mimeographed form.

[45] McGraw-Hill, New York, 1st ed.

[46] World, New York, 1945.

of material from the juvenile court and the children's bureau (a unit of the public school system) in Passaic, New Jersey. Maud A. Merrill's *Problems of Child Delinquency* [47] utilizes social histories and statistics of 300 cases referred to the juvenile court of a rural county in California. In her book *Child Offenders*,[48] Harriet L. Goldberg draws extensively from her assignment as assistant corporation counsel to the "School Part" of the Children's Court of New York City, which handles cases of truancy, unlawful detention of children from school by parents, and misconduct within the school. Paul W. Tappan's *Delinquent Girls in Court* [49] is largely based upon experiences and case material of the Magistrates' Courts of New York City, especially the Wayward Minor Court.

The Cambridge-Somerville (Massachusetts) Youth Study is also worthy of comment, for it represents a long-range analysis of delinquency and community treatment. Perhaps for the first time in history a carefully constructed control group was employed, in the belief that a study using the best methods of medical science would be helpful in arriving at conclusions. The over-all study was carried on from 1935 to 1945 and dealt with two groups of young boys who, in time, entered adolescence.

The children to be studied were carefully selected from the schools of the two Boston suburbs, Cambridge and Somerville. After the period of selection was passed, the two groups consisted of 325 boys each. Meticulous matching of the boys into pairs was then carried out. This was based on more than one hundred relevant variables, with a clinical interpretation of the personality of each boy. The group to be studied was referred to as the T group; the control group was called the C group. Every conceivable type of treatment was afforded the treatment group—medical examination and treatment, counseling, psychiatric analysis, recreational opportunities, and school program. The control group received no help whatsoever.

In looking at the results of this long-range study, we find some interesting data. Of the boys past the age of seventeen, we find 27, or 39.7 per cent of the C group, and 23, or 32.9 per cent of the T

[47] Houghton Mifflin, Boston, 1947.
[48] Grune & Stratton, New York, 1948.
[49] Columbia University Press, New York, 1947.

group, who became "more or less serious delinquents." Of the entire group of treatment boys, we find 76 listed as having had a court appearance on a serious delinquent charge, and 67 of the control group boys. Including minor offenses, 90 treatment boys and 85 control boys showed evidences of delinquency. Here is what the director of the study, Edwin Powers, has to say regarding the somewhat doubtful effects of treatment:

> Though the counselors were unable to stop the rapid advance of young boys into delinquency with any greater success than the usual deterrent forces in the community, some of the boys were evidently deflected from delinquent careers which, without the counselors' help, might have resulted in continued or more serious violations. Thus, the evidence seems to point to the fact that though the first stages of delinquency are not wholly averted when starting treatment at the 8-to-11-year level, the later and more serious stages are to some degree curtailed.[50]

Although delinquency was apparently not checked by the various treatment devices traditionally employed by the community, the study indicated that many of the boys who had counseling services felt that they had been materially helped in analyzing their own emotional problems. The Ella Lyman Cabot Foundation, under which this significant research was financed, plans to continue its study and in the future will publish a series of pamphlets indicating some of the results of its experience.

The recent ten-year study on delinquency, made by Drs. Eleanor and Sheldon Glueck, is also most significant. It embraced two groups of boys: 500 delinquent and 500 non-delinquent. Their findings point up the fact that if a child's family life is adequate, the chances are only three in a hundred that he will turn out to be a delinquent. On the other hand, if his family relationships are strained, the chances are ninety-eight in a hundred that he will succumb to a delinquent career.

These authors found from their studies of family life that little progress can be made in delinquency control until the home relation-

---

[50] "An Experiment in Prevention of Delinquency," *The Annals*, January 1949, pp. 77–88 (quotation on p. 87).

ships between parents and children can be strengthened "by a large-scale, continuous, pervasive program designed to bring to bear all the resources of mental hygiene, social work, education, and religious and ethical instruction upon the central issue."

Summarizing their findings into what they call a dynamic causal pattern, the Gluecks held that delinquents as a group are distinguishable from non-delinquents in the following manner:

1. Physically: in being solid, closely knit, muscular in constitution;
2. Temperamentally: in being restlessly energetic, impulsive, extroverted, aggressive, destructive, often sadistic;
3. In attitude: by being hostile, defiant, resentful, suspicious, stubborn, socially assertive, adventurous, unconventional, non-submissive to authority;
4. Intellectually: in tending to direct and concrete, rather than symbolic, intellectual expression; and in being less methodical in their approach to problems;
5. Socio-culturally; in having been reared to a far greater extent than the non-delinquent boys in homes in which the "under the roof culture" was "bad," that is, homes of little understanding, affection, stability or moral fiber.[51]

8. CONCLUSION

This book itself is an attempt at interpretation. The interpretation does not include any ready-made explanation of the causes or any sure-fire prescription for the cure and prevention of delinquency. The *challenge* of the problem remains. But in the history of mankind forces have always risen to meet a challenge. The authors have desired to be constructive and encouraging in their presentation of all endeavors that have been undertaken for the purpose of resolving the problem. If they have written critically, they have done so in order to spur advance and progress.

The danger exists of exaggerating or minimizing the extent and import of child delinquency. The pitfalls of either extreme may be avoided if the problem is seen as part of the total picture of our children's growth in the midst of the frustrations and the achievements, the conflicts and the blessings, of present-day society.

---

[51] Digest from *The New York Times*, October 21, 1950. See their work. *Unraveling Juvenile Delinquency*, Commonwealth Fund, New York, 1950

Appendix

CASE HISTORIES

CASE HISTORIES

The following case histories are chosen to illustrate the statements made in the various chapters of this book regarding causation and treatment of delinquency. All are taken from actual case records, but they are presented in a summarizing narrative form and do not constitute copies of detailed case-record entries.

The selection of the material was made in an attempt to include cases of boys and girls of various age groups showing different degrees of misconduct as well as different types of factors contributing to the delinquent behavior. The choice of cases also was governed by the wish to include a variety of angles or viewpoints from which cases are seen and written up. Thus cases handled by the detention home worker, the juvenile court probation officer, the family agency case worker, the school counselor, and the institutional staff member are included.

Several reports were especially prepared for this text from the files of the Municipal Court of Philadelphia and Youth House—Girls' Camp, New York City. The others were contained in articles and conference papers of practitioners in the correctional field and are quoted here with the permission of the publishers. All identifying data in the cases are disguised.

CASE 1

PHYSICAL HANDICAP AS ONE OF SEVERAL FACTORS CONTRIBUTING TO DELINQUENT BEHAVIOR

Kenneth was fourteen years old when he was first referred to the Juvenile Court. He is the oldest of six children. The family live in a fairly good neighborhood in an eight-room, poorly furnished home. The father works as a machinist. The immediate reason for the boy's apprehension by the police was a number of burglaries, in the immediate vicinity of his parental home, in which he and another boy were involved.

An investigation of this case revealed an unfortunate physical condition from which the boy had suffered since birth. It is a serious organic nervous disease affecting his spine, resulting in incontinence. He also had bilateral club feet. He has spent many years in hospitals and, therefore, his intellectual development has been retarded. Since his ninth year he has attended special schools of the public school system. He has continually received medical attention and has to wear a special contraption for his bladder control. Although a fairly good student in school, where for the past two years he has been assigned to the workshop class, he was unable to make friends in his own neighborhood. Because of his physical condition, which also causes a peculiar odor, he is shunned by boys of his own age.

An older boy befriended him but unfortunately his interest in Kenneth was only motivated by a desire to use Kenneth for his antisocial acts. The older boy picked out certain apartments and showed Kenneth how to enter the buildings and to steal valuable objects. Kenneth, who obviously for the first time in his life had found some "recognition," all too willingly followed the older boy's suggestions.

The psychiatric examination pointed up his mental retardation as a result of irregular and poor school attendance and the long hospital treatments. "He appears socially immature, has a childish outlook, is over-suggestible and lacking in proper sense of social obligation and responsibility. He is frank about his offense, but shows no real repentance."

The boy was placed on probation. Medical supervision was also ordered by the court. An operation for his club feet was performed and he continued to receive treatment for his kidneys.

There seems to be no doubt that the physical deficiency of this boy produced a social inferiority feeling which contributed to his delinquent behavior. It should be pointed out, however, that other circumstances must be considered as possible additional factors contributing to Kenneth's misconduct. For many years there had been a great deal of quarreling between the parents. The mother particularly was found to be unstable and difficult to live with. Little if any training was given to the children, as became apparent when one of Kenneth's sisters was referred to the court for sex delinquency.

After Kenneth was placed on probation, the probation officer maintained frequent contacts with the home, the school, and the hospital to which the boy had to go for weekly treatments. No further delinquencies were recorded over a period of two years since the boy's court appearance until the time of this writing. At present, the boy is anxious to find a job, but further training seems to be required. He is very much interested in electrical work, in which he received some initial instruction in school. In spite of the handicap of Kenneth's home conditions, the probation officer was able to establish a moderately good relationship with the family and the boy. The probation officer at present is engaged in finding some suitable trade school for the boy's vocational ambitions.*

CASE 2

FAMILY DISSENSION AS A FACTOR IN DELINQUENCY

The Harpers have two boys—Arthur, eleven, and Richard, ten. The boys are healthy and have high average intelligence; their delinquencies have not yet assumed serious dimensions, although they have persisted over a period of six years. The parents are attractive and fairly intelligent. Mrs. Harper is a bit of a reader. She has read some books on the care and training of children.

The police referred this case to the juvenile court when Arthur, age five, was wandering the streets at midnight while his parents were out at a party. At the time of this early contact with the family, Mrs. Harper charged her husband with infidelity (nothing definite, just suspicion); he charged her with drinking and with keeping late hours in homes of friends. During the six years of their marriage, he had left home four times. His work record was poor. He had lost a good position because of negligence, and the family was on relief.

The problems of the Harpers have some of their roots in two other families—those from which the parents came. Mr. Harper's family was socially inferior to that of his wife. His mother, a poor widow, reared her children by supplementing scrubbing with relief. Mrs. Harper's father worked at a skilled trade, saved, bought well-selected property. His three older children entered professions. Marian, the youngest, was ready for college when he died. Her mother was left financially able to send her away to a small college.

---

* From the files of the Municipal Court of Philadelphia. The name of the boy is fictitious.

At the end of her sophomore year, she returned home and secured
work in an office. She renewed friendships with a group of her old
high-school friends, among them Charles Harper, who had left high
school at the end of his second year. They fell in love. Marian's
mother disapproved of the marriage but consented when she discovered that the girl was pregnant. Arthur was born six months after
the marriage.

Charles Harper's mother also disapproved of the marriage. She
regarded Marian as a spoilt, extravagant girl who looked down upon
the Harpers because her family had more money and education.
Soon after the wedding she realized that the ceremony had been too
long delayed, and from that time on she regarded Marian as "bad."

So in spite of youth and genuine love for each other, the Harper
marriage began under the cloud of a deep sense of guilt, feelings of
inferiority in regard to both their families, and Charles' feeling of
social and intellectual inferiority to Marian. Both were far from
ready for the responsibilities of parenthood when these responsibilities descended upon them.

It is not surprising that Arthur is a rejected child; perhaps more
so than the three children who followed him at rather brief intervals.
The mother (having read books) informs us that her husband rejects
Arthur. At the age of nine, the boy, already a chronic runaway with
a very bad record at school, was referred to a psychiatrist, who reported that the boy was consciously aware of his mother's rejecting
attitude and was trying all kinds of techniques, including aggressive
destructiveness as well as infantile regressive behavior, to get emotional response from his parents. Obviously both parents rejected
the boy. Later Richard was diagnosed by a psychiatrist as suffering
from "complete rejection due to parental discord." It was felt that
the mother identified the boys with her feeling toward her husband.

I would remind you that the attitudes of Marian and Charles
Harper were in conflict. They did not hate each other; they loved
and hated, admired and disapproved. If they were vaguely conscious
of their rejection of the children, they felt guilty about it and tried
to compensate, an effort that resulted in utter inconsistency in treatment of the children. How could these children feel secure?

It is doubtful that Charles Harper's accusation that his wife drank was true. She did, however, escape from home by spending much time visiting with friends. Mr. Harper's drinking seems to be on the way toward becoming a serious problem.

The wife's mother has urged separation, although she has stood sturdily by the family with personal and financial assistance. The need of accepting this assistance is the basis for increased feelings of inferiority and guilt on the part of both the Harpers.

Arthur and Richard are in constant conflict with parents and teachers. It is said that at the age of three Arthur remarked as his father reeled into the home, "Oh! drunk again"; at which his father threw him against the wall. Both boys are at present robust and good-looking. Arthur has enuresis, and it is reported that at one time Richard had chorea and suffered from night terrors. Richard at six began to run away and once started a fire. He told his mother that he wanted to leave home because of noise and arguing between his parents. But when both boys were placed in an institution for dependents, they ran away three times and came home. Then the parents, yielding to parental love and their feeling of guilt, asked permission to keep them at home. Their request was granted; necessarily, since the institution refused to readmit them.

Things came to a climax while Mr. Harper was in the army. The boys left home and not only burglarized a food shop but damaged the shop to the extent of several hundred dollars. Being on their own, it was natural for them to steal food. The vandalism can be explained only as catharsis for pent-up frustrations. Both, especially Richard, were very defiant when brought in by the police. When questioned as to why they left home, Richard blurted out, "Our Mother is worried and she takes it out on us."

Mrs. Harper, through the Red Cross, secured the release of her husband from the army that he might assume responsibility for the discipline of his boys. There was a conference at the juvenile court, which ended with assurances all around: "Daddy's home now and there will be no more trouble."

Several months later, the mother brought Arthur to the court for emergency placement. He was insolent and disobedient at home and refused to attend school. Arrangements were made for placement in the only institution available at the time. After these arrangements were completed, Mrs. Harper proceeded to discuss her own problems. Her husband was working but spending money on liquor. Two weeks before, they had separated; but the night before, he had begged for reconciliation and had been readmitted to the home. It seemed to the caseworker (but she did not reveal her thoughts) that Arthur was being shoved aside so that his problems should not intrude upon the reconciliation of his parents.

Mrs. Harper expressed grave doubt about prospects for her marriage. She said, "My mother thinks I should separate. Most of my friends think he won't reform and I should leave him. Only one friend thinks I should stay with him. She says I love him." At that she paused and looked at the worker with a question in her eyes. She was silently asking the worker, "Do you think I love him?"

The immaturity of this young woman is appalling. She is a mere adolescent, reveling in a hectic romance which she mulls over with her friends. But she is the mother of four children, two of them requiring the utmost in consistent discipline and understanding.

At present Arthur is receiving psychotherapy. Clinic appointments are at nine each Monday morning. Sunday afternoon his father calls for him at the institution and brings him home. Monday his mother takes him to the clinic and back to the institution. Aside from whatever value the treatment may have, this arrangement is helpful to Arthur and his parents. He is away from the strain and strife in the home but keeps contact through the weekly visit. These few hours and this attention from his parents relieve his feeling that he is rejected. Efforts the parents put forth alleviate their own sense of guilt and stimulate them to undertake parental responsibility.

Arthur cannot remain long in the institution where he is at present. Both Arthur and Richard should be removed from home for one or two years. They need a fairly small institutional setup, a place that will accept them back if they run away a dozen times. Frequent visits from parents and to their homes would make running away unnecessary. Case work with boys and parents during their institutionalization would prepare both for the happy return of the boys to their home. Psychiatric treatment for parents and children would be available.

Such an institution is not at hand. We can only hope to help through such case work service as is available. A probation officer handling this case would need keen understanding and great skill in establishing effective rapport as well as time to give intensive service. The situation is moving rapidly and odds are against us.*

CASE 3

POST-TRAUMATIC BEHAVIOR DISORDER

Harold, eleven years and nine months of age, got into an argument with several school pals over some candy. First there were only words, but suddenly Harold pulled a penknife out of his pocket and stabbed one of his companions in the right shoulder. Fortunately the knife had a short blade and no serious injury was inflicted upon the victim, who was discharged after emergency treatment at the hospital.

This was not the first time that Harold had shown a "hot temper." He had a school record of being impulsive, and about two years prior to this incident he had struck two teachers in school.

He had, however, not been known to the Court except for trespassing two and a half years before this referral, and at that time no further action was considered necessary.

Harold is the only child of parents who separated, after a seven-year marriage, at the time when Harold was three and a half years of age. The whereabouts of his father is unknown. His mother now lives with another man whom Harold calls his stepfather. Both the mother and the "stepfather" are genuinely interested in the boy's welfare. They live in a two-room apartment, which is fairly well furnished and very clean. The neighborhood is poor. Both the "stepfather" and the mother are working. The mother, when questioned about the boy's behavior, related that about two years prior to the stabbing affair, Harold was hit by a truck and suffered a fractured skull and brain concussion.

The psychological examination of the boy showed that he has normal-dull mental ability, that he has fair verbal facility, but that his memory span for digits is inadequate and he has difficulty in visual discrimination. His judgment is poor and he is lacking in plan-

---

* From Irene Kawin (Deputy Chief Probation Officer, Cook County Juvenile Court, Chicago), "Family Dissension as a Factor in Delinquency," *Yearbook*, N.P.P.A., 1946, pp. 69–73.

fulness. There are indications of possible organic involvement. His intelligence quotient is 87.

The psychiatrist referred to the serious head injury the boy had received, and observed that since that time he has manifested personality changes; "he has become aggressive, impulsive, irascible and undisciplined." Referral to a neuropsychiatric clinic for study and treatment was recommended and the judge followed that recommendation, placing Harold on probation at the same time. Three months after the court hearing, Harold was involved in a stealing episode in school but the school authorities, after investigation of the case, felt that Harold was innocent in the matter.

At the time of this writing, almost a year after the stabbing affair, Harold has received regular psychiatric treatment at a hospital clinic and also has been supervised by a probation officer. He has responded favorably to both social and medical treatment. His school report shows perfect attendance. He has a fair scholastic standing and has recently been made a member of the school safety patrol.*

CASE 4

A PSYCHOPATHIC ADOLESCENT OFFENDER

In 1938, a 16-year-old youth was received at the National Training School for Boys. With no show of emotion or remorse, he admitted stealing 48 cars and talked casually of a series of 15 arrests which began when he was 11. He had stolen from his teachers and his neighbors. He had broken into stores and public buildings, stolen chickens, pigeons, mules, and even a race horse. During a prior commitment to a municipal training school for truancy, he had run away four times.

At the National Training School for Boys he was described as "sulky, pugnacious, untruthful and self-centered." A year after his commitment he ran away. He obtained a gun from his father's home and early in the evening hailed a taxicab with the intention of robbing the driver and stealing the car. At a lonely spot on the highway he shot the driver in the head and tried to drive away. The cab stalled;

---

* From the files of the Municipal Court of Philadelphia. The name of the boy is fictitious.

he took the driver's wallet and fled through the woods. Fortunately, the victim, though critically injured, recovered.

While he was awaiting trial, the young man laughed and wise-cracked about his offense. His attitude was one of complete indifference. Committed to a Federal reformatory on an 8-year sentence, he was placed under a special program of treatment. Reports indicated normal intelligence and no evidence of insanity, but he was described as "markedly emotionally unstable," and one who "loses complete control of himself when angry."

After four months he was placed in the general population of the institution, but within a few weeks, following displays of temper and threats to escape, it became necessary to return him to the special program. During the next several months his adjustment was erratic and highlighted by increasingly serious disciplinary difficulties. He intimidated and assaulted other youths and was abusive, insolent, and disrespectful toward staff members. He finally took part in a gang attack upon an officer and incited a riot.

Diagnosed an aggressive psychopath, he was transferred to the Medical Center for Federal Prisoners, where he was confined for four years as a prisoner-patient. Initially, he made a good superficial adjustment and talked repeatedly of his intention of settling down. But gradually his behavior deteriorated, and he found himself again in difficulties. He assaulted another patient without provocation and at another time he was discovered to have a dangerous weapon in his possession. Also he was found to be continuing his former practice of abusing and trying to intimidate other inmates. Finally, it was decided to move him to a penitentiary, since it was believed that he had received the maximum benefits from the hospital program.

Within a month of his transfer he had been reported for striking another prisoner, for using abusive language to a staff member, and for destruction of government property. And so the pattern continued—assaultiveness, high temper, lack of control, hostility toward authority, and a callous disregard for the rights and feelings of others.

When, after nearly eight years, he was released and returned to his home community, relatives and former friends tried to assist him. He requested a job that would involve hard physical labor and a minimum of contact with others. One which met these specifications was found, but he left after working only a few hours. He worked briefly on a lunch counter, but his repeated arguments and disputes with customers led to his dismissal. Finally, he accepted a job selling magazine subscriptions with a traveling crew. In the first town at which the team stopped, he entered a private home and was discovered by the owner rummaging through her possessions in search of valuables. He is now serving a sentence in a state prison.*

CASE 5

GUIDANCE DURING THE DETENTION PERIOD

Jean, age 15, is one of the eight children of Puerto Rican parents: she is somewhere in the middle of the siblings row. She was sent to the Detention Home by Children's Court for truancy. She had been warned twice and therefore actually knew that the next time it would mean being "sent away." She dreaded this but still could not change the pattern.

When Jean first came to the Detention Home she seemed anxious, bewildered about what had happened to her. In her talks with the social worker, she spoke vaguely about her family situation, mentioned that her parents were separated, and gave a vague picture of an underprivileged family with many children, without bringing out any negative feelings toward any member of the family. Her truancy problem was not understood at this point: all that Jean could bring out about it was that she had been bored in school.

During her stay at the Detention Home, Jean did not present any difficulties in the group situation. The cottage supervisors described her as withdrawn, reading and drawing by herself most of the time. After a few weeks stay though, Jean became increasingly more interested in her art work: she seemed to be strikingly talented for drawing and painting. Simultanously, the supervisors reported how much more outgoing and cheerful Jean had become in the group situation. She became increasingly more productive in her art work and was stimulated in this by the interest of some staff members and the recognition she got from the other children for her achievements. She did large colored plates for decoration of the Recreational Hall and became the artist of the newspaper of Girls' Camp, "Camp Echo."

---

* From *Federal Prisons 1947*, United States Department of Justice, pp. 5–7.

During this time, Jean also became more productive in her talks with the social worker: she brought out some meaningful material which could be utilized in helping her toward a beginning insight in her truancy problem: she could see it mainly in her deep conflict about her parent's separation and a recent disappointment which she had experienced in her friendship with a young woman in whose home she had felt the happiness of an only child and which she had lost.

As far as we can see it, Jean's home situation is realistically quite unfavorable, but seeing the unusual inner resources of this child, her obvious capacity for sublimation and also judging from the excellent adjustment she made to a satisfying environment during her short period of detention, we think that her prognosis for the future is good if she can be helped further in her development.*

CASE 6

A PRE-ADOLESCENT GIRL IN DETENTION

Katherine is an 11-year-old only child whose mother had a mental breakdown right after the child's birth. She was committed to a State Hospital and for the first five or six years of Katherine's life, Mrs. L. was discharged and re-committed several times. The commitments were usually made by her husband, who after a few months or a year would feel guilty and at his wife's request have her again discharged to his custody. Those periods when her mother was hospitalized, Katherine spent in various foster homes. As soon as her mother was released from the hospital, Mr. and Mrs. L. would again take the child to live with them. Mrs. L. was extremely disturbed and her behavior during these intervals was no doubt frightening and destructive to the child. When Katherine was about 7 years of age, she was placed in an institution where she was unhappy. Meanwhile, her parents had been divorced and her father remarried and took her back into his new home. Katherine was terribly unhappy

---

* Published by courtesy of Youth House—Girls' Camp, Welfare Island, New York (Miss Alice Overton, director), the temporary detention facility for girls up to age sixteen found delinquent by the Children's Courts of New York City. The name of the girl is fictitious. The work at Youth House, New York City, including Girls' Camp, is described in Chapter VIII, pp. 249–252.

because she felt that her father and stepmother took her stepsister's side against her. She feels responsible for the break-up of this second marriage of her father. Subsequent to this she was again placed in an institution but ran away and her father had to take her into his home. The two lived alone and she resented his strictness, and more than that, the way he constantly talked against her mother. Katherine had had permission from the Court to see her mother at intervals in the past few years. Perhaps because she never knew her mother well she idealized her and resented the father's attacks. While she was living at her father's, Mrs. L. would secretly send money and presents to her daughter and whenever she saw her she in turn would talk against her husband to the child.

Katherine came to Court because she had taken some money from her father and had left home. When we first got to know Katherine she appeared very quiet, poised, an intelligent child, wise beyond her 11 years. She showed little emotional response and seemed wary of adults in general. She was withdrawn in the group setting, very neat about her personal appearance and conforming to authority. She did not seek out relationships with adults. As time went on she appeared less wooden in facial expression and behavior. She appeared to gain security from acceptance by older girls and particularly from attention by supervisory and case work staff. She sought out the case worker repeatedly for interviews and talked freely about her life, whereas previously she had been too fearful to express her real feelings about her parents. We felt that she gained a little insight and could better evaluate what she could expect from her parents. Simultaneously, Katherine appeared to be reaching out for signs of affection and acceptance from her cottage supervisors. She became less rigid in her personal habits.

Katherine's petition was changed from delinquency to neglect and at present a foster home is being sought for her. The strain of not knowing where she will eventually land is telling on Katherine, and she does become anxious and depressed at times. However she talks of this readily and is thinking constructively in terms of life in a foster home. She raises relevant questions and is accepting of the visiting limitations and other factors she will have to adjust to.

Because Katherine is pre-adolescent, it is difficult to evaluate whether her personality will be able to weather the storms which are bound to come in the next few years, and whether her ability to

elate to people will continue to improve. We do feel that she has
gained security in this setting where she has felt freer to show her
personality as a whole and not only those facets which in the past
have gained her the approval of adults in general and her parents in
particular.*

CASE 7

A BOY ON PROBATION

George was 15 years and 5 months old when he was brought to
the court's attention for the first time. He is the only child of foreign-
born parents who married six years after their immigration to U.S.A.
The father who is a musician and works wherever he can find a job,
is a good provider and is greatly interested in his family and home.
So is the mother who is a good housekeeper. They live in a rented
house in a rather undesirable neighborhood.

Almost simultaneously two different charges were brought against
the boy. A neighbor complained about a broken window pane, the
result of a ball game on the street with two other boys. The boy at
first denied being on the street at the time of the accident, but later
admitted it. The second charge was that of a sex offense committed
with a girl who was only a few months younger than George.
George was not the only boy with whom this girl had relations.
Both offenses when investigated were not found to be the outlet of
any deep emotional disturbance. Despite the seriousness of the second
charge it proved to be rather incidental. During the interviews with
the probation officer who investigated the case the boy seemed to
be rather diffident, he "appeared to be a day dreamer." He said
that he was interested in sports and outdoor life. The school report
showed from 2 to 7 absences during each of the previous five months.
His academic work was poor. At the time of the investigation he repeated the 9A grade. The physical examination revealed nothing
extraordinary. The mental examination disclosed an intelligence
quotient of 108.4. The psychologist suggested that "he should con-

---

* Published by courtesy of Youth House—Girls' Camp, Welfare Island, New
York (Miss Alice Overton, director), the temporary detention facility for girls
up to age sixteen found delinquent by the Children's Courts of New York City.
The name of the girl is fictitious.

centrate on mechanical subjects, as he is more apt to fail with abstract material." The psychiatrist found him to be "quiet, uncom-
municative, and extremely diffident" and recommended probation
The probation officer concurred in this recommendation.

The boy was placed on probation by the judge and also referred
to an agency which has as its objective the establishing of contacts
between individual boys and settlements, boys' clubs, recreation
centers, etc. This agency reported soon after the court hearing that
George joined the Y.M.C.A. where he was attending regularly.

The probation officer during the 17 months of probation had more
than 50 contacts with the boy, his parents, and the school. The
parents from the very beginning had been very co-operative. On one
occasion when George was troublesome in school, the mother herself
brought him to the courthouse stating that although he had been
behaving well at home, she and her husband would not tolerate any
misconduct of the boy in school, and requested the probation officer's advice. The father took a special interest in his son by teaching
him to play the cornet. The boy's attitude toward the probation
officer developed from diffidence, which he had shown so markedly
during the investigation, into confidence and frankness. This change
did not come overnight, however. It was primarily brought about by
the probation officer's continuous interest in George's school difficulties. The probation officer was startled by the fact that George
although a mentally normal boy, played truant in more or less regular
intervals for a certain number of days, not only before and during
the investigation, but also in the month following the court hearing
When he was attending school, the reports were intermittently
good and poor. The teachers reported that he was "indolent in the
classrooms, seemed to have no interest, and simply idled his time
away." During the absences, of which the parents were not aware
unless notified by the school, he was found to spend his time in cheap
movie theaters. There was no misconduct in the home, according to
the parents, who would not have shielded their boy in case of misbehavior. It was clearly felt that the main difficulty was George's
lacking adjustment in the school. The probation officer had frequent
contacts with the school counselor and also discussed this matter
with the parents. He suggested that a transfer of George from high
school to a vocational school should be tried, and he got in touch
with the principal of the vocational school, explaining the case to

him in full. The transfer was arranged on a trial basis and worked out very well.

At the first home visit after the transfer—that was about 3½ months after the boy was placed on probation—the father showed the probation officer several metal trinkets which George had made, and stated that his son was very much interested in his work and had expressed his desire to attend school after his sixteenth birthday which then was only two months off. At the next visit George greeted the probation officer by showing him some kitchen utensils he had made out of metal. He continued going to school after the summer vacation and after he had passed his sixteenth birthday. Still, there were ups and downs in George's school life. There were reports of occasional absences, and once a complaint of misconduct and insolence in the classroom was made. On the whole, however, the boy continued his good behavior both in home and in school. His academic work in school was fair. A few weeks before his seventeenth birthday George informed the probation officer that with the consent of his parents he had obtained work in a printing shop and was learning the trade. He seemed to be very enthusiastic about his work. As his probation had proven satisfactory he was then discharged from the court's supervision.

A check-up about eight months after probation had ended revealed that George continued his good conduct. Besides his regular work in the shop he was attending an evening class where he gained supplementary instruction in the printing trade. In his spare time he played cornet as the pupil of his father.[*]

CASE 8

FOSTER HOME PLACEMENT OF AN "INCORRIGIBLE" GIRL

Betty at the age of seventeen was referred to the juvenile court by her mother for stealing. This was about ten months ago. Since leaving school at the age of sixteen, she had been employed as a maid in three different households. Each time she lost her job because of stealing. In the last place she had taken her employer's watch and

---

[*] From the files of the Municipal Court of Philadelphia. The name of the boy is fictitious.

other articles. His first impulse was to notify the police but upon second thought he took her home.

Exploration revealed that Betty had been examined three years ago in a child guidance clinic because of lying at home, inability to get along with other children and other problems. She had been adopted at the age of two and one-half by her present parents who had delayed in informing her of the adoption. She was an illegitimate child who had been placed with her adoptive parents. She got along all right until when she was five years old she was discovered in sex play with little boys. Following this episode the mother supervised her very closely and would not permit her to play with other children. Her mother said she could not manage the child although she had tried all methods of discipline including whipping her and placing her in a dark closet for several hours. There was also a history of lying and day dreaming. The mother regretted she had adopted Betty while the father blamed her misbehavior on poor heredity.

Three years ago the parents had a child of their own. Betty's behavior grew progressively worse. She began truanting from school, stayed out late at night, and was disobedient. The mother expressed a desire to have her removed from the home but added, "I don't need to tell you how dearly we love Betty because after all she did fill our empty arms for a while." The psychiatrist felt there was little hope of Betty's adjustment in her own home because of the maternal rejection which increased after the birth of her younger brother. Placement either in a foster home or an institution was recommended in April of 1941, but this recommendation was not carried out until in November 1943, she was referred to the juvenile court and a petition of incorrigibility was filed.

Interviews with the parents substantiated the previous history of rejection. They wanted Betty placed in an institution, at least until she became of age. The worker interviewed Betty, discussed with her the petition and the court hearing. She was willing to leave her parents and to accept boarding home placement. At the hearing the judge decided to take her out of her home. On the same day Betty was introduced to a foster mother who was able to give her warmth and understanding. She has remained in this home for ten months. There were frequent interviews with the foster parents and with Betty. She was introduced to young people in the community. The foster mother arranged parties and permitted Betty to invite her

:iends to the home. There has been no recurrence of her former
ehavior of lying and stealing. However, whenever she went home
) visit her mother, some of her former symptoms reappeared. Once
ie returned from a week-end at home, heart-broken and crying.
'he foster mother called the worker to say that Betty had had a
:rrible experience. While at home she had invited her best girl
iend to go bowling with her. As the girl friend was on her way to
leet Betty, she was struck by an automobile and killed. For about a
eek Betty cried considerably and spent much time in bed. The
)ster mother did not realize that this was fantasy to cover up some
nbearable experience with her mother. It was necessary to see both
)ster mother and child to work this through. The visits home are
iminishing as Betty feels more secure. She is becoming more inde-
:ndent and mature emotionally.*

Case 9

SOCIAL TREATMENT OF THE SEX DELINQUENT

Jane, a seventeen year old, was referred to a family agency for
ıse work service by the Juvenile court. Jane's parents died when she
as seven. Afterwards she lived with an older married sister, who was
:lected as guardian for her, her two sisters and brother. Jane has
ways been a difficult child; and several times the sister has turned
› the juvenile court for help. Since Jane seemed unable to get along
ith her family, plans were made to send her to a vocational school,
here she could learn dressmaking and acquire a high school di-
oma. Although Jane says she enjoyed this school, she did not return
› school for her last year and it was at this point that she became
ore difficult. She was very insolent and disobedient and unwilling
› assume any of the household duties.

About seven months before the agency's first contact with Jane,
ıe left home and went to another city to live with relatives. Dis-
tisfied because things were not as she had anticipated, after a very
iort period of time she returned home. Several weeks later she
:gan remaining away from home at night and when questioned

---

* From Mary B. Mulvey (Children's Worker, Juvenile Court, Pontiac, Michi-
n), "The Child and the Case Worker," *Probation*, February 1945, pp. 84–85.

about her activities, assumed a very antagonistic attitude. Any at
tempt to enforce discipline was met with complete defiance. He
hours, companions, attitude and activities became increasingly un
bearable to her sister. However she did not seek help until she wa
positive Jane had a venereal disease. Since Jane refused to go to th
doctor regularly her sister asked the juvenile court to pick her up
as an incorrigible child, roaming the streets and refusing to work
Jane was taken to the detention home where a physical examinatior
revealed gonorrhea and syphilis. She was kept in the detention hom
until she was cured of gonorrhea and the syphilis was no longe
contagious provided she continued her treatments when released. I
was at this point that the juvenile court asked the Family Society
to work with Jane. The sister was willing to have her return home

Jane is a rather nice looking girl of medium size and height bu
with a generally sullen expression. The first time Jane came in to se
the caseworker she was shy and said little. She was protective o
herself and family, almost everything she said about her family wa
good. In later interviews she was able to express her feelings towar
the family.

She was unwilling to admit that she had contracted venereal dis
ease through sexual relations. She seemed to have a deep feeling o
guilt and repeatedly told the caseworker she had contracted it eithe
through kissing or drinking after someone who had it. It was foun
necessary to give Jane a great deal of reassurance to relieve her guil
about being infected. Jane seemed to feel that everyone she met or
the street knew about it. She said once, "You may think I'm crazy
but nobody speaks to me when I go down the street any more. Evei
my younger sister doesn't want to be seen with me." Again anc
again she was assured that no one could tell by looking at he
whether or not she had a venereal disease. She felt so guilty abou
having syphilis that she often told people and when she was ques
tioned as to why she did so she said, "I may as well tell them becaus
they can tell by looking at me."

Jane made a poor adjustment at home after her release from th
detention home. She was sensitive and felt that the family was con
tinually reminding her that she had syphilis. She remained awaу
several nights and was insolent toward the sister and other member
of the household. The sister finally asked her to move.

The agency found a room for her at the YWCA. Jane obtained

job and things ran along smoothly for several weeks. Then Jane began telling the other girls that she had to go to the doctor quite often which aroused their suspicions. The caseworker discussed with Jane the reasons why she should not tell people this since she appeared to be in good health.

She did not remain long at the Y and moved numerous times over a period of weeks, each time locating the room on her own. Every time she made a change or got into some difficulty or needed help financially, she would come to see the caseworker. Often she did things which she knew were wrong but the caseworker never expressed disapproval. She was Jane's friend and accepted her. The caseworker did very tangible things for Jane such as paying the rent, giving her money for food or a pair of shoes, even though the girl was sometimes vague as to how she spent her salary.

Although she often went away from the office angry and irritated, Jane always returned to the caseworker when she got in a jam. There were many ups and downs in the treatment of Jane. She evidenced extreme mood swings of adolescence. Sometimes she was very cheerful and then again she was sullen and hostile. Even though Jane did not work for several months, the caseworker kept before her the idea that she would have to get a job to support herself. The caseworker now says: "Jane is working and still coming in to see us each week. We hope that she will continue to gain enough strength and satisfaction from our interviews with her to obtain more satisfaction from her work and to establish a closer tie with her family." *

Case 10

INSTITUTIONAL TREATMENT OF A BOY WHO CAME FROM A MOTHER-DOMINATED FAMILY

Nathan, aged fifteen, of normal intelligence, was committed for truancy. His family was financially comfortable and of good social standing in their community. Closer study however revealed unwholesome intrafamilial relationships. The father and two sisters as well as the boy were completely dominated by the mother.

* From Florine J. Ellis (Social Treatment Specialist, Social Protection Division, Federal Security Agency), "Social Treatment of the Sex Delinquent," *Yearbook*, N.P.P.A., 1946, pp. 145–147.

In his earlier years the boy by aggressiveness had attempted to achieve some individuality. With the onset of adolescence he showed the same submissive traits as did the father. The truancy remained as the only expression of his former aggressiveness.

He presented many unwholesome personality traits. He was markedly ingratiating, a trait highly acceptable to the mother. He was a snob and a dandy, extremely lazy, and he expected everything to revolve around his desires. No matter how inadequately he functioned, he always expected much praise and great rewards for his slight efforts. He soon earned the dislike of boys and staff. The mother found as much fault with us as she had with the schools Nathan had attended in the past. She considered that her family had been degraded by the court's action. She wanted us to give her boy special indulgences since he came from so good a family. The mother was helped to see that her attitude was hindering the boy who would have to conform to routine and achieve status on his own merits. She was then able to permit the institutional program to be effective.

The treatment program outlined was that all institutional personnel would insist on his meeting standards or accepting the consequences in deprivations and punishments. The social worker was the only one willing to listen sympathetically to his complaints and dissatisfactions. After six months of such a program, during which time the boy went through cycles of good and bad behavior, the relationship with the social worker became close enough so that it was possible to point out to the boy that he made himself seem unreasonable and objectionable both to staff and boys. He was able to accept this fact. It was also pointed out that he had many talents which he was not using to his own advantage.

Soon it became possible to uncover some of the origins of these traits, and as he reviewed his own life the boy expressed much bitterness and hostility against the mother because she had never considered his wishes and had forcibly dominated him. He reoriented himself in terms of understanding what he wants of life and how to fulfil these needs. This meant putting his mother's wish second to his own. He found it much easier then to relate himself to people and was quite happy as his new attitude earned him friends and gained him recognition.

The new traits of which we approved were vigorously disapproved by the mother. Soon mother and son were in considerable conflict as the boy was no longer willing to submit to her control. At one point she became so obstreperous that she threatened to sue the institution for alienation of her son's affections. She insisted he had come to us a good boy but we were making him bad. Finally the boy himself realized the mother's limitations and was not disturbed by her extravagant declarations. He had found real security in his relationships with the social worker, the cottage father, and with two male teachers who were all aware of his needs and gave him much positive encouragement to make his own plans. His relationship with girls improved and he was able to establish several lasting friendships.

He was paroled to his home with much misgiving after a year and a half of substantial growth in the institution. These misgivings were shared with the boy as he was now well aware of his weaknesses and strengths. For the first four months there was some doubt as to what direction his adjustment at home would take. We felt that he should have the experience of returning home as a test for himself. If it seemed that he would be unable to withstand the mother's domination, we planned to gain his cooperation in living elsewhere. Fortunately he did not yield. With encouragement from his social worker who continued to supervise him, he was able to establish himself at home and command respect for his wishes from his mother. This was finally rendered easier when he left high school and found a job. He has been working regularly and has maintained a normal adjustment in all areas.*

---

* From Abraham J. Simon (Acting Director of Case Work, Hawthorne-Cedar Knolls School, Hawthorne, New York) and Dorothy Dunaeff (Senior Psychiatric Case Worker, Hawthorne-Cedar Knolls School, Hawthorne, New York), "Differential Levels in the Institutional Treatment of the Juvenile Delinquent," *Yearbook,* N.P.P.A., 1942, pp. 158–160. The Hawthorne-Cedar Knolls School is described in Chapter XIII, p. 501. For a good popular description of the work at this school, see Gertrude Samuels, "A New Road for the Juvenile Delinquent," *The New York Times,* Magazine Section, April 23, 1950.

CASE 11

INSTITUTIONAL TREATMENT OF A REJECTED CHILD WHO PRESENTED SERIOUS BEHAVIOR DISORDERS

Isaac, a boy of fourteen and one-half, with high intelligence, was committed for stealing, truancy, vandalism, sexual perversions, and general incorrigibility. He was a handsome boy who always made a good impression until people got to know him; an only child whose mother died and whose father abandoned him when he was two years old. Reluctantly cared for by relatives, he was passed from one branch of the family to another, and finally to an orphans' home. From his very infancy he presented serious behavior disorders.

In the institution he had no regard for routine or discipline; he made the most unreasonable demands. He was bitter and antagonistic, even to two people whom he professed to like, the farmer and his social worker. His pleasure in farm work was encouraged even at the expense of formal school work in which he had no interest. Both these people spent a great deal of time with him, remained consistently patient and sympathetic, and made no comment on his general misbehavior. His poor behavior was discussed with him when it was directed against these two people. They would stress their desire to continue to be his friends, but pointed out that behavior such as this provoked others into disliking him. Continuous exposure to this kind of handling brought out a good deal of self blame on his part, and some expression of doubts as to his worthwhileness. He clung to these two contacts and made conscious efforts to seek their advice and follow their guidance. As he was able to achieve some success in adjusting, higher and higher standards were presented and he was stimulated to meet them. The farmer and the social worker frequently shared experiences and ideas about him. These people became not only his ideals, but his conscience.

By the end of the second year he was able to do well, but his past reputation appeared to be held against him. He was tried in a new cottage and told exactly why the change was made. Progress was then more rapid, the new cottage parents supplementing his two meaningful friendships.

The social worker then helped the boy reorient himself to his own past. By eliciting memories and piecing them together, the

worker was able to help the boy understand that his misconduct was
a consequence of his deprivations. He was told that while these explained his bad behavior, society did not excuse it on that account.

He then became concerned about planning for his future. Farming
was his vocational choice. In order to earn admission to a farm school
he turned to academic school work with a new interest. He went to
a farm school after three years in the institution and prepared himself there for a job.

He experienced some difficulties on parole but continued to maintain his friendship with the same social worker who helped stabilize
him. He succeeded in being reasonably happy and self-supporting.
At the age of twenty-one, he felt impelled to enlist in the United
States Air Corps, three and one-half years after leaving the institution.*

Case 12

THE VALUE OF GROUP LIVING IN INSTITUTION TREATMENT

The problems of Perry at fifteen were many and complicated.
He had been stealing from stores and from his home. He was reported as brutal to other children at school to the point where
teachers feared he might inflict serious injury. He was out of hand
at home, he was untruthful and was generally considered a misfit in
the community. The social worker commented in the original letter
of referral that Perry needed protection, security and peace. The
boy had a rejecting and unstable family background. His mother
and father had been divorced and both had remarried, leaving Perry
without acceptance in either home. He had tried living with each
without success or happiness.

The boy was ugly in appearance due to a serious sinus operation
which had necessitated the removal of a large part of the nose
cartilage. He had a chronic sinus infection which made him breathe

* From Abraham J. Simon (Acting Director of Case Work, Hawthorne-
Cedar Knolls School, Hawthorne, New York) and Dorothy Dunaeff (Senior
Psychiatric Case Worker, Hawthorne-Cedar Knolls School, Hawthorne, New
York), "Differential Levels in the Institutional Treatment of the Juvenile De-
linquent," *Yearbook*, N.P.P.A., 1942, pp. 154–155.

through his mouth. Also, to complicate the picture, he had a bad case of pyorrhea which made his breath offensive. He was confused and generally presented a most pathetic picture of dejection and rejection. In spite of all this, he had a warm, friendly side which revealed his great desire to be with other human beings who would accept and appreciate him.

At the Junior Republic he was considered a pest. One could hardly speak to him without finding oneself the object of his full attention. To add to his problems, during the first weeks at the school he made homosexual advances to other boys in the cottage. It was discovered that he had had a rather prolonged period of homosexual activity with other boys some years before he came to us. The stimulation of seeing boys in a nude state around the cottage and in the shower room reactivated this interest.

At this point the cottage group was called into consultation. In Perry's absence his situation was talked over with the boys with care to point out that other boys facing similar problems had grown up to be normal, healthy adults. The boys' cooperation was asked in giving Perry some kind of acceptance in his cottage, and protection against further homosexual activity. Several of the older boys promised leadership in the plan and the rest agreed to help. No further trouble occurred in the cottage. His position on the campus improved somewhat and interestingly enough his original misdeeds were forgotten.

Some months after Perry's arrival, the boxing coach saw him looking longingly into the ring as two boys fought. At the end of the bout the coach called him into the ring to spar with one of the boys. Perry's natural skill as a boxer was immediately apparent. His prestige developed immensely and continued to grow in subsequent months as he appeared with the boxing team throughout the state in exhibition bouts.

After two years he stands in one of our highest forms in citizenship. He is head waiter in the school dining-room. He has his own set of friends. It was natural that he did not always know how to handle his new found laurels and that at times he became overly aggressive; however, his desire to do the right thing brought him over these periods. It was also necessary to resolve his feelings of guilt over his early homosexual experiences through personal interviews. Plastic surgery is being arranged for him.

The improvement in this boy is due to many things; however, highlighted in his therapy, are two areas of social experience which met certain urgent emotional needs in his personality. He needed protection, he needed support, he needed acceptance from his fellowmen, and he needed to build up his own feelings of worthiness. The group experiences reported above seem to have provided these essentials. There has been a reinforcement and build-up of the total personality. The boy has more self-acceptance and self-esteem. Certain basic emotional satisfactions completely absent in his rejecting home have been met in a setting where friendliness and approval characterize his social relationships.*

CASE 13

THE VALUE OF GROUP LIVING IN INSTITUTION TREATMENT

Silas was thirteen and a half at the time of referral. He had been seriously handicapped by an asthmatic condition which was considered partly psychogenic. In a foster home at which he had been living, he began to steal and run away. Silas was an illegitimate child. His mother had eventually married, and had two daughters by her husband. The mother was seemingly a well-meaning person but ineffectual and at times rejecting. The stepfather was an irritable man who had originally been quite fond of Silas, but upon the birth of his own two children had become cruel and rejecting. The stepfather had epileptic attacks about once a month.

Silas was a very large fat boy with a troubled face, likeable, congenial, and friendly. He was rather passive, quiet, and not outspoken. He had good average intelligence. Silas had had the benefit of psychiatric care but he had not responded favorably as he would not talk about himself or his problems and the psychiatrist had consequently terminated treatment. At the Junior Republic he had many problems of adjustment. He ran away a number of times. Once he stole a car and smashed it up. He had frequent attacks of asthma.

---

* From Kenneth I. Wollan (Director, Connecticut Junior Republic, Litchfield, Connecticut), "The Value of Group Living in Institution Treatment," *Yearbook*, N.P.P.A., 1948, pp. 134–136. The work of the George Junior Republics is described in Chapter XIII, pp. 494–496.

However, he was generally liked and trusted in many areas in his social intercourse with other boys.

Midway in his two years with us came an experience which proved crucial in the stabilizing of the boy. In one of my discussion courses we had been reviewing the life of a famous author who had been an illegitimate child. We had been discussing the fact that the author had eventually been able to look upon his heritage without embarrassment or pain. For some weeks we had been discussing the kinds of feelings that develop out of our family background. After this particular discussion, Silas followed me to the office and asked to speak to me privately. After some hesitation he blurted out that he wanted to know about his father. This occasion proved to be the beginning of many interviews which eventually led to a planned meeting with the mother at which time the boy and his mother talked for many hours about the circumstances of his birth. This was the core of his problem, and not until he had found such topics treated freely and objectively in group discussion could he openly face this highly painful area of his feelings. I wish I could report that his asthma cleared up, but this was not the case. I can report, however, that a great stabilization took place in the entire personality of the boy and that he left the school with an excellent record which he has maintained outside.*

CASE 14

DELINQUENCY PREVENTION THROUGH THE EFFORTS OF A SCHOOL COUNSELOR

Andrew, a 13-year-old, was referred to the counselor in a junior high school by the attendance officer who was concerned about his home conditions. His mother had died suddenly 7 months before, and Andrew was living with his stepfather, Mr. S., in a well-kept three-story house. Mr. S. concerned himself very little with the care or supervision of Andrew, who was still grieving over his mother's death and apparently craved attention and affection. The counselor made

---

* From Kenneth I. Wollan (Director, Connecticut Junior Republic, Litchfield, Connecticut), "The Value of Group Living in Institution Treatment," *Yearbook*, N.P.P.A., 1948, pp. 140–141.

arrangements for a weekly interview, and established phone contact with Mr. S. who felt that provision of food, clothing, and shelter was the limit of his responsibility toward Andrew, and that Andrew was old enough to take care of himself.

The counselor's contacts with Andrew became daily occurrences due to his lack of lunch money, inadequate clothing, minor ailments, and lack of body cleanliness. He frequently called Mr. S. who, though polite and agreeable, seemed annoyed. He sent him summer camp information, urging him to provide summer supervision, but he refused to consider camp. Andrew insisted, however, that his stepfather appreciated his concern.

Early in the fall term Andrew became involved in numerous conflicts with boys in school and in the neighborhood. Investigation disclosed the boys were making Andrew unhappy because of his shabby clothes and lack of material things, including money. Their taunts had so upset Andrew that he had displayed his stepfather's revolver, threatening to use it if they didn't "lay off." The counselor wrote Mr. S., urging him to come to school to see him. When Andrew was questioned regarding the failure of Mr. S. to acknowledge the letter, he broke down and wept. He said his stepfather was drinking heavily, and that he had to go to taprooms frequently to bring him home; and that when he was intoxicated, he frequently tried to beat Andrew. The counselor then referred the case to the Society to Protect Children from Cruelty.

Suddenly Andrew showed signs of care and supervision. When the counselor congratulated him on his appearance, he said his father's "girl friend" had moved in and was taking care of him. In a few days the "girl friend" called the counselor, soliciting his help. She said Andrew was "incorrigible," that he stole money from his stepfather and the boarders, and that he appropriated money given him to pay bills. Andrew admitted these thefts to get money for candy and the movies, and to buy radio equipment for a set he was building. When questioned about the possibility of thefts outside the home, he replied: "I can't help taking money when I want things, but I'd never take anything except at home, for I might get caught and be put away. But my family would be ashamed to send me to jail."

The conflicts between Andrew and Mr. S. became more frequent and more serious. Mr. S. destroyed the radio set Andrew had worked on for three months, and Andrew stayed out of the home as much as possible. He spent considerable time with an uncle (his mother's brother) who, he said, wished to come to the school to see the counselor. Arrangements were made. The uncle was a fine looking man, kindly, sympathetic, and intelligent. He said the family had never interfered so long as Mr. S. had provided for Andrew, but they were now anxious to do something. Mr. S. resented the interference of both the school and the Society to Protect Children from Cruelty, and had refused to discuss the situation with relatives.

Arrangements were made for Andrew to bring his radio equipment to school and keep it in the electric shop. The shop teacher reported that Andrew was doing electrical work and reading books on electronics at college level, in spite of his mediocre school work.

As the tension at home between Andrew, his stepfather, and the "girl friend" increased, Andrew stayed away from home more and more. Fortunately, a cousin of his father's became interested in him and allowed him to spend much time at her home. While hitching a ride on a truck in order to get to his cousin's, Andrew fell and broke his clavicle. Mr. S. refused to go to the hospital or to assume any responsibility. The cousin called the counselor, asking for financial help in getting clothes for Andrew, and was referred to the Union Benevolent Society which bought him trousers and underwear. A member of the faculty provided a heavy coat.

The Society to Protect Children from Cruelty reported that they had located Andrew's father, who was willing to provide financial assistance; and that they had referred Andrew's case to the Legal Aid Society in order to protect his property rights inasmuch as the house supposedly had belonged to his mother. His stepfather had allegedly taken possession of it and was renting rooms as well as living there.

When Andrew's case was taken into court by the Legal Aid Society, The House of the Holy Child (a child-placing agency) accepted the legal guardianship of Andrew. The cousins with whom Andrew had been living were appointed foster parents. The Legal Aid Society is continuing the case in court until settlement of Andrew's property rights is completed.

The Society to Protect Children from Cruelty referred Andrew to Temple Hospital because of deformity of both feet. The diagnosis was congenital deformity, and surgery was performed during the summer vacation. Andrew had both feet in casts from July 15 to November 15, and received Home Teaching Service provided by the Board of Education. His cousin reports that Andrew has built up quite an extensive electrical repair service in the neighborhood.*

CASE 15

A STEALING EPISODE OF A GROUP OF BOYS

Before the Juvenile Court there stood seven boys, ranging in age from 13 years and 3 months to 17 years and 8 months. They had broken into a candy factory and a biscuit factory and had stolen several boxes of candy and biscuits, which they distributed among their friends in junior high school. Some of the boys also admitted having entered another factory where ten automobile tires and four tubes were stolen. There was also $15 taken from the cash box in one factory and $25 from the safe in the other factory. This money was shared by the boys and some of the tires were allegedly sold to an adult person who, however, could not be located. All boys admitted that they had participated in one or several of these stealing escapades. The investigation of the social background of the boys revealed the following:

ALBERT, 14 years of age, is the oldest of 7 children. The father is employed as a weaver earning approximately $60.00 a week. The family occupies a 7 room house, which is fairly well furnished and is located in a moderately good neighborhood. Although he had never been officially referred to the Court before, his parents reported that he was recently brought home by railroad detectives for having trespassed on railroad property and for throwing stones. He also had been playing truant. The supervision in the home is by far not as strict as it should be and according to the parents' statements, Albert is increasingly getting out of control. He is of dull-normal intelligence. He was placed on probation.

BRUCE, 13 years and 3 months of age, is the oldest of four children. Both parents are working and the family live in a fairly good neighborhood, in a well furnished house. The mother's employment is

---

* From Robert C. Taber (Director, Division of Pupil Personnel and Counseling, Philadelphia Public Schools), "The Potential Role of the School Counselor in Delinquency Prevention and Treatment, *Federal Probation*, September 1949, p. 53.

motivated by the fact that the father only works part-time. According to the school report, Bruce displays mediocre ability. His entire performance and response are affected by a lack of stability, lack of motivation and lack of effort. He gives up very easily. There is no doubt that this boy is pampered at home, and that particularly due to the employment of both parents there is little supervision. His intelligence is normal. He, too, was placed on probation.

CHARLES, 13 years and 11 months, obviously was led into this trouble by the influence of his other companions. He is the oldest of three children and his father receives $25 a month unemployment compensation, which is supplemented by a public assistance grant. The family live in a fairly well furnished home in the same neighborhood as the two previously mentioned boys. His parents are interested in the education of their children. No complaints regarding his behavior in school have been received. However, his progress in school is slow, due to his mental retardation. He has an intelligence quotient of 74 and, according to the psychiatric report, has inferior judgment and reasoning ability, and therefore is easily influenced. Charles was placed on probation.

DAVID, 15 years and 3 months, is the second of a group of six children. He acted as a look-out at the time when the boys broke into the factories. His father is unemployed and the family must subsist from the wages earned by an older brother, who works as a baker's helper, and supplementary public assistance. They live in a poorly furnished but rather well kept home in the same neighborhood as the other boys. David's school report is poor in all subjects as well as cooperation and attendance. He is repeating the 9th grade. This is due to the boy's low intelligence. He has an intelligence quotient of 69. The psychological report emphasizes that he has inadequate comprehension of every day problems and that his reasoning is poor, but he can be trained to work with his hands. He attends a boys' club and has indicated an interest in workshop activity. He was placed on probation.

ELMER, 15 years and 6 months of age, is the youngest of four children. His parents separated when he was 8 years of age. The mother is employed and earns $38 a week. The maternal grandmother also lives in the home and assists with the supervision of the children. The house is fairly well furnished and is located in a moderately good neighborhood. According to his mother, Elmer was born three weeks prematurely, had pneumonia nine times, and at the age of 7 suffered a severe fall resulting in concussion of the head. His left ear is defective. He is a low-grade moron, as his intelligence quotient of 58 indicates, and he has been classified by the psychiatrist as a defective delinquent. He attends the sixth grade of elementary school, where his conduct and attendance have improved after previous failures. His scholastic standing is as good as can be expected from a boy of his limited intelligence. Shortly before this stealing episode, the boy barely escaped being electrocuted by a live wire, when he was playing on railroad property, and had to spend some time in a hospital for the treatment of his burns. Elmer was placed on probation.

FRANCIS, 16 years and 5 months, is the 6th of 9 children. The parents separated at the time when Francis was 11 years of age. The mother is working in order to keep the family together, with financial assistance from an older son. Consequently, there is little supervision over Francis; he had, however, never been in any previous trouble. As a matter of fact, he is quite willing to do his share in helping around the house. Three other siblings had been previously referred to the Juvenile Court for minor offenses. One of the sisters had been placed on probation for incorrigibility. Prior to that, the record of the Probation Department showed that a protective agency had recommended placement of the three younger children in view of the undesirable home conditions caused by the parents' separation and the father's abuse of the family. However, placement was not considered necessary by the Court and the mother was assisted in her efforts to keep the family together by a probation officer who supervised the family for more than a year. The family lives in a partly residential and partly industrial neighborhood. The boy attends junior high school, after having graduated from a parochial elementary school. He, too, was almost electrocuted by a live wire when playing with Elmer around box cars on the railroad tracks. He still suffers from severe burns. He is a mentally normal boy, frank in his manner but easily influenced. He was placed on probation.

GRIFFITH, 17 years and 8 months, is the 7th of 13 children, of whom 8 are still living with the parents, while the older brothers and sisters are married. The father has been out of work for some time and the family has to live on a public assistance grant. An older and a younger brother had been known to the Court for having thrown plaster into a moving street car and having injured a passenger. Both had been on probation for several months. The family lives in a mixed residential, business, and industrial neighborhood. The home is poorly furnished and very untidy. Griffith has left school in order to get employment but has no steady job. Investigation has shown that he has been the ringleader in this stealing affair. The psychiatric examination revealed that he has subnormal intelligence, that he is self-centered and defiant of authority. The Court considered institutional training necessary and, therefore, committed Griffith to a correctional institution with the possibility of parole after six months.

This case history was written up immediately after the juvenile court hearing. Therefore, no further report regarding the adjustment of these boys subsequent to the court disposition was yet available.*

---

* From the files of the Municipal Court of Philadelphia. The names of the boys are fictitious.

BIBLIOGRAPHY

BIBLIOGRAPHY

CHAPTER I

Delinquency as a National Problem

Allen, Robert S., *Our Fair City*, Vanguard, 1947.

————, *Our Sovereign States*, Vanguard, 1949.

Banay, Ralph S., *Youth in Despair*, Coward-McCann, 1948.

Barnes, Harry Elmer, and Negley K. Teeters, *New Horizons in Criminology*, Prentice-Hall, 1943.

Bernard, William, *Jailbait (The Story of Juvenile Delinquency)*, Greenberg, 1949.

Binford, Jessie F., "Post-War Problems of Youth," *Federal Probation*, October–December 1947, pp. 7–11.

Bossard, James H. S., *The Sociology of Child Development*, Harper, 1948.

Bowlby, John, *Forty-four Juvenile Thieves: Their Characters and Home Life*, Baillière, Tindall & Cox, London, 1947.

Branham, Vernon C., and Samuel B. Kutash (edd.), *Encyclopedia of Criminology*, Philosophical Library, New York, 1949.

Burroughs, Harry E., *Boys in Men's Shoes*, Macmillan, 1944.

Burt, Cyril Lodowic, *The Young Delinquent*, University of London Press, 1938.

Cabot, P. S. de Q., *Juvenile Delinquency: A Critical Annotated Bibliography*, Wilson, 1946.

Carr, Lowell J., *Delinquency Control*, Harper, 1940.

Catton, Bruce, *The War Lords of Washington*, Harcourt, Brace, 1948.

Cooper, Courtney Ryley, *Designs in Scarlet*, Little, Brown, 1939.

Crow, Lester D. and Alice, *Our Teen Age Boys and Girls*, McGraw-Hill, 1945.

Drucker, Saul, and Maurice B. Hexter, *Children Astray*, Harvard University Press, 1923.

Ellingston, John R., *Protecting Our Children from Criminal Careers,* Prentice-Hall, 1948.

Faris, Robert E. L., *Social Disorganization,* Ronald Press, 1948.

Folks, Homer, "Four Milestones of Progress," *The Annals of the American Academy of Social and Political Science* (later referred to as *The Annals*), November 1940.

Frank, Lawrence K., *Society as The Patient,* Rutgers University Press, 1948.

Goldberg, Harriet, *Child Offenders,* Grune & Stratton, 1948.

Healy, William, "A New Program for the Treatment of Youthful Offenders," *American Sociological Review,* August 1940.

————, *The Individual Delinquent,* Little, Brown, 1915.

Hirsch, N. D. M., *Dynamic Causes of Juvenile Crimes,* Sci-Art Publishers, 1937.

Hollingshead, A. B., *Elmtown's Youth,* Wiley, 1949.

Hush, Howard, *Eastwick, U.S.A.,* Dutton, 1948.

Irey, Elmer L., and William J. Slocum, *The Tax Dodgers,* Greenberg, 1948.

Johnson, Arthur C., "Our Schools Make Criminals," *Journal of Criminal Law and Criminology,* November–December 1942.

Juvenile Delinquency and the Schools, Forty-Seventh Yearbook, Part I, National Society for the Study of Education, University of Chicago Press, 1948.

Lindsey, Benjamin, and Wainwright Evans, *Revolt of Modern Youth,* Boni & Liveright, 1925.

Lowrey, Lawson G., "Delinquent and Criminal Careers," Chapter XXV in Vol. II of *Personality and Behavior Disorders,* edited by J. McV. Hunt, Ronald Press, 1944.

Lunden, Walter A., *Systematic Source Book in Juvenile Delinquency,* University of Pittsburgh Press, 1938.

Merrill, Maud A., *Problems of Child Delinquency,* Houghton Mifflin, 1947.

Minehan, Thomas, *Boy and Girl Tramps in America,* Farrar & Rinehart, 1934.

Motley, Willard, *Knock On Any Door,* Appleton-Century-Crofts, 1947.

Mowrer, Ernest R., *Disorganization: Personal and Social,* Lippincott, 1942.

National Commission on Law Observance and Enforcement (Wickersham Commission), Vol. I, "Causes of Crime," 1931.

National Conference on Prevention and Control of Juvenile Delinquency, *Summaries of Recommendations for Action,* Government Printing Office, 1947.

Nebraska Law Review (Symposium on Young Offenders), Vol. 29, No. 4, May 1950.

Neumeyer, Martin H., *Juvenile Delinquency in Modern Society,* Van Nostrand, 1949.

Panken, Jacob, *The Child Speaks,* Holt, 1941.

Plant, James, *Personality and the Cultural Pattern,* Commonwealth Fund, 1937.

Polier, Justine Wise, *Everyone's Children, Nobody's Child,* Scribner, 1941.

Porterfield, A. L., "Delinquency and Its Outcome in Court and College," *American Journal of Sociology,* Vol. XLIX, 1943.

Reckless, Walter C., and Mapheus Smith, *Juvenile Delinquency,* McGraw-Hill, 1932.

Richmond, Winifred, *The Adolescent Girl,* Macmillan, 1925.

———, *The Delinquent Boy,* Farrar & Rinehart, 1933.

Robison, Sophia, *Can Delinquency Be Measured?,* Columbia University Press, 1936.

———, "Wanted—An Index of Crime and Delinquency," *Proceedings,* American Prison Association, 1945.

Schwartz, Edward E., "A Community Experiment in the Measurement of Delinquency," *Yearbook,* N.P.P.A., 1945, pp. 157–181.

Slawson, John, *The Delinquent Boy: A Socio-Psychological Study,* Badger, 1926.

Solomon, Ben, *Juvenile Delinquency—Practical Prevention,* Youth Service, Inc., Peekskill, N. Y., 1947.

Steffens, Lincoln, *The Shame of the Cities,* McClure, Phillips, 1904.

Sutherland, E. H., *White Collar Crime,* Dryden Press, 1949.

Tappan, Paul, *Juvenile Delinquency,* McGraw-Hill, 1949.

———, "Unofficial Delinquency," *Nebraska Law Review,* Vol. 29, No. 4, May 1950, pp. 547–558.

Thurston, Henry W., *Concerning Juvenile Delinquency,* Columbia University Press, 1942.

Understanding Juvenile Delinquency, United States Children's Bureau, Publication 300, Government Printing Office, 1943.

Van Waters, Miriam, *Youth in Conflict,* Republic Printing Co., 1925.

Warner, W. Lloyd, and Paul S. Lunt, *The Social Life of a Modern Community*, Vol. I of Yankee City Series, Yale University Press, 1941.

Whyte, William Foote, *Street Corner Society*, University of Chicago Press, 1943.

CHAPTER II

*Historical Development of the Concept of Delinquency
and Child Care*

Batt, J. H., *Dr. Barnardo, the Foster Father of Nobody's Children*, Partridge & Co., London, 1904.

Baylor, Edith M., and Elio D. Monachesi, *Rehabilitation of Children*, Harper, 1939.

Brace, Charles Loring, *The Dangerous Classes of New York and Twenty Years Work Among Them*, Wynkoop and Hallenbeck, N. Y., 1872.

————, *Gesta Christi: A History of Humane Progress Under Christianity*, Armstrong & Son, New York, 1882.

Bready, J. Wesley, *Dr. Barnardo*, Allen & Unwin, London, 1930.

Caldwell, Robert G., *Red Hannah*, University of Pennsylvania Press, 1947.

Carpenter, Mary, *Reformatory Schools for the Children of the Perishing and Dangerous Classes*, C. Gilpin, London, 1851.

Clay, Walter L., *The Prison Chaplain: A Memoir of the Rev. John Clay*, Macmillan, London, 1861.

Du Cane, Edmund F., *The Punishment and Prevention of Crime*, Macmillan, London, 1885.

Earle, Alice Morse, *Child Life in Colonial Days*, Macmillan, 1899.

————, *Curious Punishments of Bygone Days*, Stone, Chicago, 1896.

Folks, Homer, *The Care of Destitute, Neglected and Delinquent Children*, Macmillan, 1902.

Fredericksen, Hazel, *The Child and His Welfare*, W. H. Freeman, San Francisco, 1948.

Griffiths, Arthur, *Secrets of the Prison House*, Vol. II, London, 1894.

Hart, Hastings, *Preventive Treatment of Neglected Children*, Charities Publication, New York, 1910.

Ludwig, Frederick J., "Rationale of Responsibility for Young Offenders," *Nebraska Law Review*, Vol. 29, No. 4, May 1950, pp. 521–546.

Lukas, Edwin J., "Fashions in Crime Prevention," *Yearbook*, N.P.P.A., 1946, pp. 19–39.

Lundberg, Emma O., *Unto the Least of These*, Appleton-Century-Crofts, 1947.

Mayes, Herbert R., *Horatio Alger, A Biography Without a Hero*, Macy-Macious, 1928.

O'Donoghue, Edward Geoffrey, *Bridewell Hospital, Palace, Prison, Schools from the Death of Elizabeth to Modern Times*, John Lane, Ltd., London, Vol. II, 1929.

Peirce, B. K., *A Half Century with Juvenile Delinquents*, D. Appleton & Co., 1869.

Pike, Owen, *History of Crime in England*, Smith, Elder & Co., London, 1873–6.

Powell, J. C., *The American Siberia*, H. J. Smith & Co., Chicago, 1891.

Sanders, Wiley B., "Some Early Beginnings of the Children's Court Movement in England," *Yearbook*, N.P.P.A., 1945, pp. 58–70.

Starkey, Marion L., *The Devil in Massachusetts*, Knopf, 1949.

Teeters, Negley K., *They Were in Prison*, Winston, 1937.

Thurston, Henry W., *Concerning Juvenile Delinquency*, Columbia University Press, 1942.

————, *The Dependent Child*, Columbia University Press, 1930.

Whitney, Janet, *Elizabeth Fry, Quaker Heroine*, Little, Brown, 1936.

Williams, A. E., *Barnardo of Stepney*, Allen & Unwin, 1943.

Wines, Enoch Cobb, *State of Prisons*, Cambridge, Mass., 1880.

CHAPTER III

Biological Factors

Baker, Harry J., and Virginia Traphagen, *The Diagnosis and Treatment of Behavior Problem Children*, Macmillan, 1935.

Cantor, Nathaniel, "Recent Trends in Criminological Research in Germany," *American Sociological Review*, June 1936.

Christie, Amos, "Physical Defects in Delinquent Boys," *Journal of Juvenile Research*, Vol. 8, 1939, pp. 13–22.

Doll, Edgar A., "The Comparative Intelligence of Prisoners," *Journal of Criminal Law and Criminology*, August 1920.

Dugdale, Richard, *The Jukes*, Putnam, 1877.

Fink, Arthur E., *Causes of Crime*, University of Pennsylvania Press, 1938.

Grimberg, L. H., *Emotion and Delinquency*, Bretano, 1928.

Goddard, H. H., *The Kallikaks*, Macmillan, 1912.

————, *Feeblemindedness: Its Causes and Consequences*, Macmillan, 1914.

————, *The Criminal Imbecile*, Macmillan, 1915.

Healy, William, and Augusta Bronner, *Treatment and What Happened Afterward*, Judge Baker Guidance Center, 1939.

Holmes, Samuel J., *The Trend of the Race*, Harcourt, Brace, 1921.

Holzinger, Karl J., *Twins: A Study of Heredity and Environment*, University of Chicago Press, 1937.

Hoskins, R. G., *The Tides of Life*, Norton, 1933.

Karpman, Benjamin, "Milestones in the Advancement of Knowledge of the Psychopathology of Delinquency and Crime," in *Orthopsychiatry: Retrospect and Prospect*, American Orthopsychiatric Association, 1948.

Mihanovich, Clement S., "Who Is the Juvenile Delinquent?," *Social Science*, Vol. 22, No. 2, April 1947.

Montagu, M. F. Ashley, "The Biologist Looks at Crime," *The Annals*, September 1941.

Murchison, Carl, "American White Criminal Intelligence," *Journal of Criminal Law and Criminology*, August–November 1924.

Myerson, Abraham, *The Inheritance of Mental Diseases*, Williams & Wilkins, 1925.

Newman, H. H., *Multiple Human Births*, Doubleday, Doran, 1940.

Parmelee, Maurice, *Criminology*, Macmillan, 1918.

Reckless, Walter C., *Criminal Behavior*, McGraw-Hill, 1940.

Schlapp, M. G., "Behavior and Gland Disease," *Journal of Heredity*, Vol. XV, 1924.

————, and E. H. Smith, *The New Criminology*, Liveright, 1928.

Sheldon, W. H., *et al.*, *The Varieties of Human Physique*, Harper, 1940.

————, *et al.*, *Varieties of Delinquent Youth*, Harper, 1949.

Tredgold, A. F., *Mental Deficiency*, William Wood & Co., 1914.

Tucker, William B., "Is There Evidence of a Physical Basis for Criminal Behavior?," *Journal of Criminal Law and Criminology*, November–December 1940.

Tulchin, Simon H., *Intelligence and Crime*, University of Chicago Press, 1939.

Wallace, E. W., "Physical Defects and Juvenile Delinquency," *New York State Journal of Medicine*, Vol. 40, 1940.

Westlund, Norman, and Adelaide Palumbo, "Parental Rejection of Crippled Children," *American Journal of Orthopsychiatry*, Vol. 16, 1946.

CHAPTER IV

Nationality, Race, and Delinquency

Brown, F. J., and J. S. Roucek, *Our Racial and National Minorities*, Prentice-Hall, 1937.

Brown, G. Gordon, *Law Administration and Negro-White Relations in Philadelphia*, Bureau of Municipal Research, Philadelphia, 1947.

Diggs, Mary Huff, "The Negro Child and the Law," *Focus*, N.P.P.A., January 1948, pp. 7–12.

Dollard, John, *Caste and Class in a Southern Town*, Yale University Press, 1937.

Frazier, E. Franklin, *The Negro in the United States*, Macmillan, 1949.

Glueck, Eleanor, "Culture Conflict and Delinquency," *Mental Hygiene*, Vol. 21, January 1937.

Griffith, Beatrice, *American Me*, Houghton Mifflin, 1948.

Hayner, Norman S., and Charles N. Reynolds, "Delinquency Areas in the Puget Sound Region," *American Journal of Sociology*, Vol. 39, 1933.

Johnson, Charles S., *The Negro in American Civilization*, Holt, 1930.

Kiser, Clyde Vernon, *Sea Island City*, Columbia University Press, 1932.

Lind, Andrew W., "The Ghetto and the Slum," *Social Forces*, December 1930.

Lohman, Joseph D., *The Police and Minority Groups*, Chicago Park District Police Training School, 1946.

McEntire, Davis, and Robert B. Powers, *A Guide to Race Relations for Police Officers*, Department of Justice, California, 1946.

McWilliams, Cary, *Brothers Under the Skin*, Little, Brown, 1948.

————, *North From Mexico*, Lippincott, 1948.

Myrdal, Gunnar, *An American Dilemma*, Harper, 1944.

National Commission on Law Observance and Enforcement (Wicker-sham Commission), Vol. I, "Causes of Crime," 1931.

Reuter, Edward B., *The American Race Problem*, Crowell, 1938.

Sellin, Thorsten, *Crime and the Second Generation of Immigrant Stock*, Foreign Language Information Service, Series C, No. 7, May 23, 1936.

Smith, William Carlson, *Americans in the Making*, Appleton-Century, 1939.

Spirer, Jess, *Negro Crime* (monograph), Johns Hopkins Press, 1940.

Taft, Donald, "Nationality and Crime," *American Sociological Review*, October 1936.

Tuck, Ruth, *Not With the Fist, Mexican-Americans in a Southwest City*, Harcourt, Brace, 1946.

Yen, Ching-Yueh, "Crime in Relation to Social Change in China," *American Journal of Sociology*, November 1934.

CHAPTER V

Socio-economic Factors

Alexander, Franz, and William Healy, *The Roots of Crime*, Knopf, 1935.

Barnes, Harry Elmer, and Negley K. Teeters, *New Horizons in Criminology*, Prentice-Hall, 1943.

Bogen, David, "Juvenile Delinquency and Economic Trends," *American Sociological Review*, Vol. 9 (1940), pp. 178–184.

Bonger, W. A., *Criminality and Economic Conditions*, Little, Brown, 1916.

Boorman, William R., "Delinquency Area: Another Viewpoint," *Religious Education*, Vol. 26 (1931), pp. 858–863.

Breckinridge, Sophonisba, and Edith Abbott, *The Delinquent Child and the Home*, Russell Sage Foundation, 1912.

Burt, Cyril, *The Young Delinquent*, University of London Press, 1938.

Caldwell, M. G., "The Extent of Juvenile Delinquency in Wisconsin," *Journal of Criminal Law and Criminology*, Vol. 32 (1941), pp. 148–157.

Cantor, Nathaniel, *Crime and Society*, Holt, 1939.

Carpenter, Mary, *Juvenile Delinquents*, Cash, London, 1853.

Carr-Saunders, A. M., and A. Netal, *Young Offenders*, Macmillan, 1942.

————, Hermann Mannheim, and E. C. Rhodes, *Young Offenders: An Inquiry into Juvenile Delinquency*, Macmillan, 1944.

Carr, Lowell J., *Delinquency Control*, Harper, 1940.

Elmer, Manuel C., "Maladjustment of Youth in Relation to Density of Population," Publication of the American Sociological Society, Vol. 20, pp. 138–140.

Fast, Howard, *The Children*, Duell, Sloan & Pearce, 1947.

Furfey, Paul H., *The Gang Age: A Study of the Pre-adolescent Boy and His Recreational Needs*, Macmillan, 1926.

Glueck, Sheldon and Eleanor, *One Thousand Juvenile Delinquents*, Harvard University Press, 1934.

Healy, William, *The Individual Delinquent*, Little, Brown, 1915.

————, and Augusta Bronner, *Delinquents and Criminals*, Macmillan, 1926.

————, and Augusta Bronner, *New Light on Delinquency*, Yale University Press, 1936.

Karpman, Benjamin, "Milestones in the Advancement of Knowledge of the Psychopathology of Delinquency and Crime," *Orthopsychiatry: Retrospect and Prospect*, American Orthopsychiatric Association, 1948.

Kawin, Irene, "Family Dissension as a Factor in Delinquency," *Yearbook*, N.P.P.A., 1946, pp. 60–76.

Longmoor, Elsa A., and Erle F. Young, "Ecological Interpretations of Juvenile Delinquency, Dependency and Population Mobility," *American Journal of Sociology*, Vol. 41, pp. 598–610.

Motley, Willard, *Knock On Any Door*, Appleton-Century-Crofts, 1947.

Murdock, George P., *Studies in the Science of Society*, Yale University Press, 1937.

National Commission on Law Observance and Enforcement (Wickersham Commission), Vol. I, "Causes of Crime," 1931.

Panken, Jacob, *The Child Speaks*, Holt, 1941.

Puffer, J. A., *The Boy and His Gang*, Badger, 1921.

Reckless, Walter C., and Mapheus Smith, *Juvenile Delinquency*, McGraw-Hill, 1932.

Richmond, Winifred, *The Delinquent Boy*, Farrar & Rinehart, 1933.

Robison, Sophia M., *Can Delinquency Be Measured?*, Columbia University Press, 1936.

Shaw, Clifford, *Delinquency Areas*, University of Chicago Press, 1929.

————, *The Jack Roller*, University of Chicago Press, 1929.

————, *Brothers in Crime*, University of Chicago Press, 1938.

————, and Henry D. McKay, *Juvenile Delinquency and Urban Areas*, University of Chicago Press, 1942.

Shideler, E. H., "Family Disintegration and the Delinquent Boy in the U.S.," *Journal of Criminal Law and Criminology*, January 1918, pp. 709–732.

Shulman, Harry M., "The Family and Juvenile Delinquency," *The Annals*, January 1949, pp. 21–31.

Slawson, John, *The Delinquent Boy: A Socio-Psychological Study*, Badger, 1926.

Smith, Mapheus, "Tier Counties and Delinquency in Kansas," *Rural Sociology*, Vol. 2 (1937), pp. 310–322.

Sullenger, T. Earl, *Social Determinants in Juvenile Delinquency*, Wiley, 1936.

Sutherland, E. H., *Principles of Criminology*, Lippincott, 1947.

Thrasher, Frederic M., *The Gang*, University of Chicago Press, 1927, 1936.

Van Waters, Miriam, *Youth in Conflict*, Republic Printing Co., 1925.

Vold, George, "Crime in Rural and City Areas," *The Annals*, September 1941, pp. 38–45.

Weeks, H. Ashley, "Male and Female Broken Home Rates by Types of Delinquency," *American Sociological Review*, August 1940, pp. 601–609.

West, James, *Plainville, U.S.A.*, Columbia University Press, 1944.

White, R. Clyde, "The Relation of Felonies to Environmental Factors in Indianapolis," *Social Forces*, Vol X (May 1932), pp. 498–513.

Whyte, William Foote, *Street Corner Society*, University of Chicago Press, 1943.

Wiers, Paul, *Economic Factors in Michigan Delinquency*, Columbia University Press, 1944.

————, "Juvenile Delinquency in Rural Michigan," *Journal of Criminal Law*, Vol. 30 (1939), pp. 211–222.

Wood, Arthur L., "Social Organization and Crime in Small Wisconsin Communities," *American Sociological Review*, Vol. 7 (1942), pp. 40–46.

CHAPTER VI

Cultural Phases of the Problem

Banay, Ralph S., *Youth in Despair*, Coward-McCann, 1948.

Blumer, Herbert S., and Philip M. Hauser, *Movies, Delinquency and Crime*, Payne Foundation Studies, Macmillan, 1933.

Cavanagh, John R., "The Comics War," *Journal of Criminal Law and Criminology*, May–June 1949, pp. 28–35.

Clinard, Marshall B., "Secondary Community Influences and Juvenile Delinquency," *The Annals* (Vol. 261), January 1949, pp. 420–454.

Cooley, E. J., *Probation and Delinquency*, Nelson, New York, 1927.

Cooper, Courtney Ryley, *Designs in Scarlet*, Little, Brown, 1939.

Crist, Judith, "Horror in the Nursery," *Colliers'*, March 27, 1948.

Deland, Paul, "Crime News Encourages Delinquency and Crime," *Federal Probation*, April–June 1947, pp. 3–6.

Dunn, C. V., "The Church and Crime in the United States," *The Annals* (Vol. 125), May 1926, pp. 200–228.

Eisenberg, A. L., *Children and Radio Programs*, Columbia University Press, 1936.

Ernst, Morris L., and Alexander Lindey, *The Censor Marches On*, Doubleday, Doran, 1939.

Forman, Henry James, *Our Movie Made Children*, Macmillan, 1933.

Frank, Josette, "Looking at the Comics," Child Study Association of America, New York, 1943.

Gruenberg, Sidonie M., "Comics as a Social Force," *Journal of Educational Sociology*, December 1944, pp. 204–213.

Hartshorne, Hugh, and Mark May, *Studies in the Nature of Character*, 3 vols., Macmillan, 1928–30.

Heininger, Robert, "Group Work as an Aid to the Treatment of Juvenile Delinquency," *Proceedings*, American Prison Association, 1937.

Kvaraceus, W. C., *Juvenile Delinquency and the School*, World Book Co., 1945.

Lindeman, Eduard C., "Underlying Social Causes of Crime," *Yearbook*, N.P.P.A., 1941, pp. 109–117.

MacDougall, Ernest D., ed., *Crime for Profit*, Stratford Press, 1933.

Merrill, Maud A., *Problems of Child Delinquency*, Houghton Mifflin, 1947.

Middleton, W. C., and Paul J. Fay, "Attitudes of Delinquent and Non-Delinquent Girls Toward Sunday Observance, the Bible, and War," *Journal of Educational Psychology*, Vol. 32 (1941), pp. 555–558.

Miner, John R., "Church Membership and Commitment to Prisons," Vol. 3 (1931), *Human Biology*, pp. 429–436.

Moley, Raymond, *Our Criminal Courts*, Putnam's, 1930.

————, *Are We Movie Made?*, Macy-Macius, 1938.

Shanas, Ethel, and Catherine E. Dunning, *Recreation and Delinquency*, Chicago Recreation Commission, 1942.

Slavson, S. R., "The Harlem Project," *Survey Midmonthly*, May 1948, pp. 167 ff.

Smith, Sampson G., "The Schools and Delinquency," *Yearbook*, N.P.P.A., 1948, pp. 274–279.

Solomon, Ben, *Juvenile Delinquency—Practical Prevention*, Youth Service, Inc., Peekskill, N. Y., 1947.

————, "Recreation and Delinquency," *Journal of Educational Psychology*, January 1948, pp. 284–290.

Thomas, Dorothy S. and W. I., *The Child in America*, Knopf, 1928.

Thrasher, Frederic M., "The Boys' Clubs and Juvenile Delinquency," *American Journal of Sociology*, July 1936, pp. 66–80.

Walton, Robert P., *Marihuana, America's New Drug Problem*, Lippincott, 1938.

Waugh, Coulton, *The Comics*, Macmillan, 1947.

Wertham, Frederic, "The Comics—Very Funny," *Saturday Review of Literature*, May 29, 1948.

Winters, S. R., "Marihuana," *Hygeia*, October 1940.

CHAPTER VII

The Orthopsychiatric Approach to Delinquency

Ackerson, Luton, *Children's Behavior Problems*, Vol. I (1931), Vol. II (1942), University of Chicago Press.

Aichhorn, August, *Wayward Youth*, Viking Press, 1935.

Aldrich, Charles A., *Babies Are Human Beings: An Interpretation of Growth*, Macmillan, 1938.

Alexander, Franz, and William Healy, *The Roots of Crime*, Knopf, 1935.

Alexander, Paul W., "Some Tested Techniques in Teaching Delinquency," *Educational Forum*, Vol. 8 (1943), pp. 1–7.

Anderson, John E., *Happy Childhood*, Appleton, 1933.

Bazeley, E. T., *Homer Lane and the Little Commonwealth*, Allen & Unwin, London, 1948.

Bowlby, John, *Forty-four Juvenile Thieves*, Baillière, Tindall & Cox, London, 1947.

Bowman, Karl M., "The Psychiatrist Looks at the Child Psychiatrist," *American Journal of Psychiatry*, Vol. 101 (1944), pp. 23–29.

Burt, Cyril, *The Young Delinquent*, University of London Press, 1938.

Clark, L. P., *A Psychological Study of Stealing in Juvenile Delinquency*, Nervous and Mental Disease Publishing Co., Washington, D.C., 1925.

Davis, W. Alison, and Robert J. Havighurst, *Father of the Man*, Houghton Mifflin, 1947.

Dollard, John, *et al.*, *Frustration and Aggression*, Yale University Press, 1939.

Dreikurs, Rudolph, *The Challenge of Parenthood*, Duell, Sloan and Pearce, 1949.

Eissler, K. R., ed., *Searchlights on Delinquency*, International Universities Press, 1949.

English, O. Spurgeon, and Gerald H. J. Pearson, *Common Neuroses of Children and Adults*, Norton, 1937.

————, *Emotional Problems of Living*, Norton, 1945.

Fodor, Nandor, *The Search for the Beloved*, Hermitage Press, New York, 1949.

Freud, Anna, and Dorothy T. Burlingham, *War and Children*, International University Press, 1944.

Friedlander, Kate, *The Psycho-Analytical Approach to Juvenile Delinquency*, International Universities Press, 1947.

Gesell, Arnold, and Frances L. Ilg, *Infant and Child in the Culture of Today*, Harper, 1943.

Hamilton, Gordon, *Psychotherapy in Child Guidance*, Columbia University Press, 1948.

Harms, Ernest, ed., *Handbook of Child Guidance*, Child Care Publications, New York, 1947.

Hartwell, Samuel W., *Fifty-Five "Bad Boys,"* Knopf, 1932.

Healy, William, *The Individual Delinquent,* Little, Brown, 1915.

————, *Mental Conflicts and Misconduct,* Little, Brown, 1917.

Keliher, Alice V., "Juvenile Delinquency: A Family Affair," *Federal Probation,* December 1948, pp. 26–29.

Lane, Homer, *Talks to Parents and Teachers,* Hermitage House, New York, 1949.

Levy, David M., "On the Problem of Delinquency," *American Journal of Orthopsychiatry,* Vol. 2 (1932).

————, *Maternal Overprotection,* Columbia University Press, 1943.

Lewin, Kurt, *et al., Authority and Frustration,* University of Iowa Studies in Child Welfare, 1944.

Maier, Norman R. F., *Frustration: The Study of Behavior Without a Goal,* McGraw-Hill, 1949.

Mowrer, Ernest R., *Disorganization: Personal and Social,* Lippincott, 1942.

Orthopsychiatry: Retrospect and Prospect, American Orthopsychiatric Association, 1948.

Peller, Lili E., "Character Development in Nursery School," *Mental Hygiene,* April 1948.

Rambert, Madeleine L., *Children In Conflict,* International Universities Press, 1949.

Reckless, Walter C., *The Crime Problem,* Appleton-Century-Crofts, 1950.

Ribble, Margaretha A., *The Rights of Infants: Early Psychological Needs and Their Satisfaction,* Columbia University Press, 1943.

Saul, Leon J., *Emotional Maturity,* Lippincott, 1947.

Slavson, S. R., *Introduction to Group Therapy,* Commonwealth Fund, 1943.

————, ed., *The Practice of Group Therapy,* International Universities Press, 1947.

Spock, Benjamin M., *The Common Sense Book of Baby and Child Care,* Duell, Sloan and Pearce, 1946.

Ziman, Edmund, *Jealousy in Children,* A. A. Wyn, New York, 1949.

CHAPTER VIII

Apprehension, Detention, and Investigation

Allaman, Richard, "True or False? Some Questions About Your Detention Home," *Focus*, May 1948, pp. 69–75.

Barnes, Harry Elmer, and Negley K. Teeters, *New Horizons in Criminology*, Prentice-Hall, 1943, Chap. XXXV.

Bates, Jerome E., "Notes on Recording," *Focus*, March 1950, pp. 56–57.

Bell, Marjorie, *Children Under Lock and Key*, N.P.P.A., 1944.

Bernard, William, *Jailbait (The Story of Juvenile Delinquency)*, Greenberg, New York, 1949, Chap. 10.

Bogen, David, "Large Scale Detention," *Probation*, February 1945, pp. 65–68, 86–90.

Casey, Roy, "Children in Jail," *Yearbook*, N.P.P.A., 1943, pp. 175–182.

Chornyak, John, "The Child in Detention as Seen by the Psychiatrist," *Yearbook*, N.P.P.A., 1939, pp. 151–156.

Close, Kathryn, "Jail Is No Place for a Child," *The Survey*, March 1950, pp. 138–143.

Cohen, Frank J., "The Child in the Detention Home Program," *Federal Probation*, January–March 1946, pp. 36–41.

Connolly, Vera, "No Straps, No Paddles," *Woman's Home Companion*, December 1947.

————, "Get the Children Out of Jails," *Woman's Home Companion*, November 1944.

Conover, Merrill, "Children in Jail," *The Child*, April 1943, pp. 143–147.

Cosulich, Gilbert, *Juvenile Court Laws of the United States*, N.P.P.A., 1939.

Delinquency Control Institute Progress Report, University of Southern California Press, 1949.

Freeman, Frank S., *Theory and Practice of Psychological Testing*, Holt, 1950.

Garrett, Annette, *Interviewing, Its Principles and Methods*, New York, Family Welfare Association, 1942.

Giardini, G. I., "Interviewing—A Two Way Process," *Yearbook*, N.P.P.A., 1948, pp. 177–189.

Hamilton, Gordon, *Principles of Social Case Recording,* New York, Columbia University Press, 1946.

Handbook of Correctional Institution Design and Construction, Federal Bureau of Prisons, 1949.

Hochreiter, Franklin C., "Streamlining Case Recording," *Federal Probation,* October–December 1943, pp. 16–18.

Houser, Arden, "The Juvenile Hall as a Treatment Facility," *California's Challenge in Corrections,* California Probation and Parole Association, Los Angeles, 1949, pp. 27–29.

Imler, Donald, "Training Peace Officers To Understand and To Work with Youth," *Federal Probation,* March 1949, pp. 42–44.

Joyce, John W., "The Social Service Exchange and Probation," *Federal Probation,* January–March 1943, pp. 34–37.

Kehoe, Harold B., "The Juvenile Hall as an Observation and Study Facility," *California's Challenge in Corrections,* California Probation and Parole Association, Los Angeles, 1949, pp. 23–26.

Lee, Rosalind, "Children at the Crossroads," *Hygeia,* December 1947.

Lenz, Henry, "Juvenile Detention: Ten Years' Use of Boarding Homes," *Yearbook,* N.P.P.A., 1942, pp. 133–148.

Lenz, Marjorie Wallace, "The Use of Boarding Homes for Detention," *Yearbook,* N.P.P.A., 1939, pp. 130–150.

————, "A Yardstick for Measuring Detention Homes," *Federal Probation,* April–June 1942, pp. 20–23.

Lott, George M., "The Juvenile Detention Home," *Federal Probation,* January–March 1942, pp. 35–39.

Lou, Herbert H., *Juvenile Courts in the United States,* University of North Carolina Press, 1927, Chap. VI.

MacCormick, Austin H., "The Community and the Correctional Process," *Focus,* May 1948, pp. 65–68, 86–89.

————, "Children in Our Jails," *The Annals,* January 1949, pp. 150–157.

————, and James H. Dooling, "Keeping Children out of Jails: It Can Be Done," *Federal Probation,* September 1949, pp. 40–45.

Maisel, Albert Q., "America's Forgotten Children," *Woman's Home Companion,* January 1947.

Marshall, Sarah E., "Social Service Exchanges," *Social Work Year Book, 1945,* Russell Sage Foundation, pp. 441–445.

National Conference on Prevention and Control of Juvenile Delinquency, Report No. 5, "Juvenile Detention," Government Printing Office, 1947.

Neumeyer, Martin H., *Juvenile Delinquency in Modern Society*, Van Nostrand, 1949, Chap. XII.

Norman, Sherwood, *The Design and Construction of Detention Homes for the Juvenile Court (A Preliminary Draft)*, N.P.P.A., 1947.

————, "Detention Facilities for Children," *Yearbook*, N.P.P.A., 1946, p. 87.

————, "The Detention Home," *The Annals*, January 1949, pp. 158–165.

————, "New Goals for Juvenile Detention," *Federal Probation*, December 1949, pp. 29–35.

Norman, Sherwood and Helen, *Detention for the Juvenile Court (A Discussion of Principles and Practices)*, N.P.P.A., 1946.

O'Shea, Vincent J., "Jersey City Prevents Delinquency," reprinted from *The Welfare Reporter*, official publication of the New Jersey State Department of Institutions and Agencies, September 1947.

Outlook for Women in Police Work, Bulletin No. 231, Women's Bureau, United States Department of Labor, Government Printing Office, 1949.

Pigeon, Helen D., *Probation and Parole in Theory and Practice*, N.P.P.A., 1942.

Robinson, Louis N., *Jails (Care and Treatment of Misdemeanant Prisoners in the United States)*, Winston, 1944.

Schilder, L. Clark, "Juvenile Offenders Should Be Fingerprinted," *Federal Probation*, January–March 1947, pp. 44–48.

Schmidl, Fritz, "Use of the Rorschach Personality Test," *Focus*, September 1948, pp. 133–136.

————, "The Rorschach Test in Juvenile Delinquency Research," *American Journal of Orthopsychiatry*, January 1947, pp. 151–161.

Simcox, Beatrice R., "Social Service Exchanges," *Social Work Year Book, 1949*, Russell Sage Foundation, pp. 494–497.

Standard Juvenile Court Act, Revised Edition, N.P.P.A., 1949.

Stern, Leon T., "In the Shadow of the Jails," *The Proceedings of the National Conference of Juvenile Agencies*, March 1946.

Studt, Ray N., "Detention as a Helping Experience," *Probation*, April 1944, pp. 101–106.

Sullivan, Agnes C., "Principles and Values in Case Recording," *Yearbook*, N.P.P.A., 1936, pp. 240–252.

Tappan, Paul W., *Juvenile Delinquency*, McGraw-Hill, 1949, Chap. XV.

Techniques of Law Enforcement in the Treatment of Juveniles and the Prevention of Juvenile Delinquency (Manual for the Guidance of En-

forcement Officers in Dealing with Juvenile Offenders), National Advisory Police Committee to the Federal Security Administrator, Government Printing Office, 1944.

Toland, Ruth S., and Ralph G. Wales, *Juvenile Detention in California* (*Current Practices and Recommended Principles*), Advisory Committee on Detention Home Problems, Los Angeles, California, 1946.

Warner, Florence M., *Juvenile Detention in the United States*, University of Chicago Press, 1933.

Whitaker, Carl A., "The Delinquent's First Interview," *Probation*, October 1944, pp. 15–20.

Wickes, Richard W., "There Are Children in Our Jails," *Probation*, December 1943, pp. 43–47.

Williams, Herbert D., "Foster Homes for Juvenile Delinquents," *Federal Probation*, September 1949, pp. 46–51.

Wright, Roberts J., "What! The County Jail Again?," *Federal Probation*, July–September 1944, pp. 17–20.

Wylegala, Victor B., "Juvenile Offenders Should Not Be Fingerprinted," *Federal Probation*, January–March 1947, pp. 44–48.

Young, Pauline, *Interviewing in Social Work*, McGraw-Hill, 1st ed.

————, *Social Treatment in Probation and Delinquency*, McGraw-Hill, 1937.

Youth House, New York City, *Fourth Annual Report 1947–1948; Fifth Annual Report 1948–1949* (mimeographed).

CHAPTER IX

The Juvenile Court

Abbott, Grace, *The Child and the State*, Vol. II, University of Chicago Press, 1938.

Alexander, Paul W., "Of Juvenile Court Justice and Judges," *Yearbook*, N.P.P.A., 1947, pp. 187–205.

————, "Punishing Parents," *Probation*, June 1944, pp. 154–156.

————, "What's This About Punishing Parents?," *Federal Probation*, March 1948, pp. 23–29.

Barnes, Harry Elmer, and Negley K. Teeters, *New Horizons in Criminology*, Prentice-Hall, 1943.

Beckham, Walter H., "Helpful Practices in Juvenile Court Hearings," *Federal Probation*, June 1949, pp. 10–14.

Bruno, Frank J., *Trends in Social Work (As Reflected in the Proceedings of the National Conference of Social Work, 1874–1946)*, Columbia University Press, 1948.

California, Final Report of the Special Crime Study Commission on Juvenile Justice of the State of–, Sacramento, 1949.

Canty, Alan, "The Youthful Problem Driver," *Yearbook*, N.P.P.A., 1942, pp. 210–223.

Carr, Lowell Juilliard, "Most Courts Have To Be Substandard," *Federal Probation*, September 1949, pp. 29–33.

Castendyck, Elsa, "Juvenile Courts in the Light of the White House Conference," *Yearbook*, N.P.P.A., 1940, pp. 34–46.

Chute, Charles L., "The Juvenile Court in Retrospect," *Federal Probation*, September 1949, pp. 3–8.

Controlling Juvenile Delinquency, United States Children's Bureau Publication 301, Government Printing Office, 1943.

Cosulich, Gilbert, *Juvenile Court Laws of the United States*, N.P.P.A., 1939.

Daniel, Ralph W., "A Juvenile Jury for Young Traffic Offenders," *Focus*, January 1950, pp. 23–26.

Dobbs, Harrison Allen, "In Defense of Juvenile Courts," *Federal Probation*, September 1949, pp. 24–29.

Ellingston, John R., *Protecting Our Children from Criminal Careers*, Prentice-Hall, 1948.

Friedlander, W., and Earl D. Myers, *Child Welfare in Germany—Before and After Nazism*, University of Chicago Press, 1940.

Goldberg, Harriet L., *Child Offenders (A Study in Diagnosis and Treatment)*, Grune & Stratton, 1948.

Harris, William B., "Struggle To Fix Liability in Juvenile Delinquency Cases," *Temple Law Quarterly*, January 1946, pp. 325–329.

Healy, William, "Thoughts About Juvenile Courts," *Federal Probation*, September 1949, pp. 16–19.

Juvenile Court Standards, United States Children's Bureau Publication No. 121, Government Printing Office, 1947.

Juvenile Court Statistics 1944–1945, Supplement to *The Child*, monthly publication of the United States Children's Bureau, November 1946.

Killian, Frederick W., "The Juvenile Court as an Institution," *The Annals*, January 1949, pp. 89–100.

Kvaraceus, William C., *Juvenile Delinquency and the School*, World Book Company, 1945.

Larson, John Farr, "Utah's State-wide Juvenile Court Plan," *Federal Probation,* June 1949, pp. 15–17.

Lenroot, Katharine F., "The Juvenile Court Today," *Federal Probation,* September 1949, pp. 9–15.

Loevinger, Gustavus, "The Court and the Child," *Focus,* May 1949, pp. 65–69, 89–91.

Long, Donald E., "A Yardstick for Measuring Juvenile Courts," *Federal Probation,* October–December 1942, pp. 34–36.

Lou, Herbert H., *Juvenile Courts in the United States,* University of North Carolina Press, 1927.

Lundberg, Emma Octavia, *Unto the Least of These,* Appleton-Century-Crofts, 1947.

MacNeil, Douglas H., "Judicial Treatment of the Juvenile Traffic Offender," *Focus,* November 1948, pp. 166–170, 182–184.

National Conference on Prevention and Control of Juvenile Delinquency, Reports No. 3, "Juvenile Court Laws," and No. 4, "Juvenile Court Administration," Government Printing Office, 1947.

Neumeyer, Martin H., *Juvenile Delinquency in Modern Society,* Van Nostrand, 1949, Chap. XIII.

Nutt, Alice Scott, "Juvenile and Domestic Relations Courts," *Social Work Year Book, 1949,* Russell Sage Foundation, pp. 270–276.

————, "Juvenile Court Function," *Yearbook,* N.P.P.A., 1942, pp. 94–101.

————, "The Responsibility of the Juvenile Court and the Public Welfare Agency," *Yearbook,* N.P.P.A., 1947, pp. 206–223.

Pigeon, Helen D., *Probation and Parole in Theory and Practice,* N.P.P.A., 1942.

Polier, Justine Wise, *Everyone's Children, Nobody's Child,* Scribner, 1941.

Pound, Roscoe, "The Juvenile Court and the Law," *Yearbook,* N.P.P.A., 1944, pp. 1–22.

————, "The Rise of Socialized Criminal Justice," *Yearbook,* N.P.P.A., 1942, pp. 1–22.

Radzinowicz, L., and J. W. C. Turner, ed., *Penal Reform in England,* Macmillan, London, 1946.

Reckless, Walter C., and Mapheus Smith, *Juvenile Delinquency,* McGraw-Hill, 1932.

Reinemann, John Otto, "Fiftieth Anniversary of the Juvenile Court Movement in the United States," *The Quarterly,* Pennsylvania Association on Probation and Parole, June 1949, pp. 8–9, 31–32.

————, "Forty Years of the Juvenile Court Movement in the United States," *Mental Hygiene*, April 1941, pp. 256–268.

————, "The Youth Criminal Law in Germany," *The Prison Journal*, January–April 1935, pp. 150–152.

Rubin, Sol, "The Legal Character of Juvenile Delinquency," *The Annals*, January 1949, pp. 1–8.

Sanders, Wiley B., *Juvenile Courts in North Carolina*, University of North Carolina Press, 1948.

————, "Some Early Beginnings of the Children's Court Movement in England," *Yearbook*, N.P.P.A., 1945, pp. 58–70.

Schramm, Gustav L., "A Juvenile Court Is a Court of Equity," *Federal Probation*, January–March 1947, pp. 35–37.

————, "Philosophy of the Juvenile Court," *The Annals*, January 1949, pp. 101–108.

————, "The Judge Meets the Boy and His Family," *Yearbook*, N.P.P.A., 1945, pp. 182–194.

Smith, Anna Kalet, *Juvenile Court Laws in Foreign Countries*, United States Children's Bureau Publication No. 328, Government Printing Office, 1949.

Smyth, George W., "Our Juvenile Courts," *Probation*, June 1946, pp. 142–143.

————, "Parents in Court," *Focus*, September 1949, pp. 135–140.

————, "The Juvenile Court and Delinquent Parents," *Federal Probation*, March 1949, pp. 12–17.

Standard Juvenile Court Act, Revised Edition, N.P.P.A., 1949.

Stern, Leon and Elizabeth Gertrude, *A Friend at Court*, Macmillan, 1923.

Stokes, Warrington, "Social Worker Plays Part in Court Process," *The Child*, December 1947, pp. 89–92.

Sullenger, T. Earl, *Social Determinants in Juvenile Delinquency*, Wiley, 1936.

Sutherland, Edwin H., *Principles of Criminology*, Lippincott, 1947.

Tappan, Paul W., "Children and Youth in the Criminal Court," *The Annals*, January 1949, pp. 128–136.

————, *Juvenile Delinquency*, McGraw-Hill, 1949, Chaps. VIII–XI.

Teeters, N. K., *Penology from Panama to Cape Horn*, University of Pennsylvania Press, 1946.

————, *World Penal Systems*, Pennsylvania Prison Society, 1944.

The Child, the Clinic, and the Court, New Republic Inc., New York, 1927.

The Child, the Family, and the Court, United States Children's Bureau Publication No. 193, Government Printing Office, Washington, 1939.

Thurston, Henry W., *Concerning Juvenile Delinquency*, Columbia University Press, 1942.

"Town Meeting: Are Parents or Society Responsible for Juvenile Crime?," *Bulletin of America's Town Meeting of the Air*, New York, February 21, 1946.

Understanding Juvenile Delinquency, United States Children's Bureau Publication No. 300, Government Printing Office, 1943.

Vaughan, Daniel J., "Should Parents Be Punished for the Delinquency of Their Children?," *Intramural Law Review of New York University School of Law*, May 1949, pp. 230–245.

Westwick, Atwell, "Wider Jurisdiction for the Juvenile Court," *Yearbook*, N.P.P.A., 1939, pp. 184–202.

Whitman, Howard, "Let's Stop Blaming the Parents," *Woman's Home Companion*, September 1949, pp. 4, 159–160.

Whitman, Samuel, "Stop Sniping at Parents," *The Child*, May 1947, pp. 184–189.

Winnet, Nochem S., "Is a Juvenile Court a Court?," *The Shingle* (Philadelphia Bar Association), June 1947, pp. 131–133.

Young, Pauline V., *Social Treatment in Probation and Delinquency*, McGraw-Hill, 1st ed.

Zuck, John M., "The Probation Officer Participates in Delinquency Prevention," *Yearbook*, N.P.P.A., 1948, pp. 280–295.

CHAPTER X

Expansion of the Juvenile Court Idea

Adolescents' Court Problem, The, Society for the Prevention of Crime, New York, 1941.

Attorney General's Survey of Release Procedures, Vol. II, "Probation," Government Printing Office, 1939.

Barnes, Harry Elmer, and Negley K. Teeters, *New Horizons in Criminology*, Prentice-Hall, 1943.

Beckham, Walter H., "One Court for Family Problems," *Yearbook*, N.P.P.A., 1942, pp. 80–93.

Blanshard, Paul, and Edwin J. Lukas, *Probation and Psychiatric Care for Adolescent Offenders,* Society for the Prevention of Crime, New York, 1942.

Bok, Curtis, *Backbone of the Herring,* Knopf, 1941.

————, *I, Too, Nicodemus,* Knopf, 1946.

Braude, J. M., "Boys' Court: Individualized Justice for the Youthful Offender," *Federal Probation,* June 1948, pp. 9–14.

Brill, Jeanette G., and E. George Payne, *The Adolescent Court and Crime Prevention,* Pitman, New York, 1938.

California Youth Authority; Report of Program and Progress, 1943–1948, Sacramento, California, 1949.

Cochran, William D., "Children of Divorce," *The Child,* September 1947, pp. 38–41.

"Design for Family Living," *Survey Midmonthly,* June 1948, pp. 206–207.

Dobbs, Harrison Allen, "Social Service for Probationers and Parolees," *Focus,* January 1949, pp. 7–12.

Duffy, F. Ryan, "The Value of Pre-sentence Reports to the Court," *Federal Probation,* July–September 1941, pp. 3–5.

Ellingston, John R., *Protecting Our Children from Criminal Careers,* Prentice-Hall, 1948.

Fiedler, William L., "Social Services in a Divorce Court," *Yearbook,* N.P.P.A., 1948, pp. 96–106.

Frank, Jerome, *Courts on Trial,* Princeton University Press, 1949.

Freeman, Dorothy, "The California Youth Authority," *Social Service Review,* June 1948, pp. 211–233.

Hamren, Vandyce, *California Youth Authority: Organization of the Youth Authority and Outline of its Program,* Sacramento, California, May 1949 (mimeographed).

Harrison, Leonard B., and Pryor McNeill Grant, *Youth in the Toils,* Macmillan, 1938.

Holton, Karl, "The California Youth Authority," *Yearbook,* N.P.P.A., 1946, pp. 116–126.

Kendall, Glenn M., "The New York State Reception Center," *Federal Probation,* September 1948, pp. 42–47.

Kennedy, T. Blake, "The Pre-sentence Investigation Report Is Indispensable to the Court," *Federal Probation,* April–June 1941, pp. 3–5.

Killian, F. W., "Pre-sentence Reports," *Probation,* October 1945, pp. 25–26.

Lewis, William Draper, "Treatment of Youth Convicted of Crime," *Federal Probation*, May 1940, pp. 20–23.

"Marriage and the Court," *Focus*, July 1949, p. 107.

McCormick, Paul J., "A Judge Discusses the Proposed Federal Corrections Act," *Federal Probation*, January–March 1944, pp. 3–13.

McLaughlin, Roy L., "Is Youth Authority a Design for Children?," *The Prison World*, September–December 1948, p. 8.

Nutt, Alice Scott, "Juvenile and Domestic Relations Courts," *Social Work Year Book, 1949*, Russell Sage Foundation, pp. 270–276.

Reeves, Elmer W., "Youthful Offender Law in New York Shows Positive Results in Operation," *The Welfare Reporter* (New Jersey Department of Institutions and Agencies), June 1949, pp. 16–18.

Reinemann, John Otto, "The Expansion of the Juvenile Court Idea," *Federal Probation*, September 1949, pp. 34–40.

————, "Wanted in Pennsylvania: Forestry Camps for the Rehabilitation of Delinquents," *Prison Journal*, April 1948, pp. 401–404.

Rubin, Sol, "Probation in the Divorce Court," *Probation*, April 1947, pp. 102–104.

————, "Changing Youth Correction Authority Concepts," *Focus*, May 1950, pp. 77–82.

Schwellenbach, Lewis B., "Information versus Intuition in the Imposition of Sentence," *Federal Probation*, January–March 1943, pp. 3–6.

Scudder, Kenyon J., "Progress in Handling the Adult Offender," *Yearbook*, N.P.P.A., 1947, pp. 13–26.

Sellin, Thorsten, "The Youthful Offender," *Federal Probation*, April–June 1942, pp. 14–17.

Smyth, George W., "Analyzing the Y.C.A. Act," *Yearbook*, N.P.P.A., 1941, pp. 241–246.

Socio-Legal Treatment of the Youthful Offender (A Statistical and Factual Analysis of the Work of the Adolescents' Court, Brooklyn), Probation Bureau, Magistrates' Court, New York City, 1939 (mimeographed).

Tappan, Paul W., *Delinquent Girls in Court*, Columbia University Press, 1947.

————, *Juvenile Delinquency*, McGraw-Hill, 1949.

The Child, the Family, and the Court, United States Children's Bureau Publication No. 193, Government Printing Office, 1939.

Ulman, Joseph N., "The Youth Correction Authority Act," *Yearbook*, N.P.P.A., 1941, pp. 227–240.

Wayward Minor's Court, The, Probation Bureau, Magistrates' Courts, New York City, 1939 (mimeographed).

Weiffenbach, Milton, "An Approach to Pre-sentence Investigation," *Yearbook*, N.P.P.A., 1942, pp. 165–176.

Westwick, Atwell, "Wider Jurisdiction for the Juvenile Court," *Yearbook*, N.P.P.A., 1939, pp. 184–202.

York, James N., "Evaluating the Everyday Work of a Probation Office," *Federal Probation*, September 1948, pp. 24–29.

Young People in the Courts of New York State, Legislative Document No. 55, Albany, New York, 1942.

Youth Correction Authority Act, Official Draft, The American Law Institute, Philadelphia, 1940.

Youth Court Act, Proposed Final Draft, The American Law Institute, Philadelphia, 1940.

Zeigler, Edwin B., "Pre-sentence and Pre-parole Investigation," *Yearbook*, N.P.P.A., 1946, pp. 154–162.

CHAPTER XI

Probation

Applegate, Melbourne S., *Helping Boys in Trouble*, Association Press, 1950.

Attorney General's Survey of Release Procedures, Vol. II, "Probation," Government Printing Office, 1939.

Barnes, Harry Elmer, and Negley K. Teeters, *New Horizons in Criminology*, Prentice-Hall, 1943, Chap. XXXV.

Bates, Sanford, *Prisons and Beyond*, Macmillan, 1936.

Beard, Belle Boone, *Juvenile Probation*, American Book Company, 1934.

Bell, Marjorie, "The Volunteer Aids the Court," *Yearbook*, N.P.P.A., 1936, pp. 156–174.

Cantor, Nathaniel, "The Function of Probation," *Yearbook*, N.P.P.A., 1941, pp. 277–297.

Chappell, Richard A., "Federal Probation Service: Its Growth and Progress," *Federal Probation*, October–December 1947, pp. 29–34.

Children Served by Public Welfare Agencies and Institutions 1945, United States Children's Bureau Statistical Series No. 3, Government Printing Office, 1947.

Cosulich, Gilbert, *Juvenile Court Laws of the United States*, N.P.P.A., 1939.

Coyle, Grace Longwell, *Group Work with American Youth* (*A Guide to the Practice of Leadership*), Harper, 1948.

Crystal, David, "Family Casework in Probation," *Federal Probation*, December 1949, pp. 47–53.

Fink, Arthur E., *The Field of Social Work*, Holt, 1949.

Flexner, Bernard, and Roger N. Baldwin, *Juvenile Courts and Probation*, Century, 1914.

Garrett, Annette, "Historical Survey of the Evaluation of Casework," *Journal of Social Casework*, June 1949, pp. 219–229.

Geiser, Peter, "The Court as a Case Work Agency," *Yearbook*, N.P.P.A., 1942, pp. 102–108.

Gittelson, George, "Racial Factors in Staff Selection," *Focus*, July 1949, pp. 97–102.

Glueck, Sheldon and Eleanor, *One Thousand Juvenile Delinquents*, Harvard University Press, 1939.

Glueck, Sheldon, ed., *Probation and Criminal Justice*, Macmillan, 1933.

Grosser, George H., "An Internship for Probation Officers," *Focus*, May 1949, pp. 75–77.

Hall, Gladys E., "Social Case Work in Probation and Parole," *Yearbook*, N.P.P.A., 1942, pp. 121–132.

Hamilton, Gordon, *Theory and Practice of Social Case Work*, Columbia University Press, 1940.

Holton, Karl, "A Yardstick for Measuring Probation," *Federal Probation*, January–March 1943, pp. 41–43.

"John Augustus—First Probation Officer," N.P.P.A., 1939.

Juvenile Court Standards, United States Children's Bureau Publication No. 121, Government Printing Office, 1947.

Kunkel, Kay, "Foster Placement as Court Function," *Focus*, 1949, pp. 146–149.

Lippmann, Hyman S., "The Role of the Probation Officer in the Treatment of Delinquency in Children," *Federal Probation*, June 1948, pp. 36–39.

Lou, Herbert H., *Juvenile Courts in the United States*, University of North Carolina Press, 1927.

Love, Ruth W., "Boys of Today—Citizens of Tomorrow," *Federal Probation*, October–December 1947, pp. 43–48.

MacCormick, Austin H., "The Community and the Correctional Process," *Focus*, May 1948, pp. 65–68, 86–89.

Manual for Probation Officers, Illinois Department of Public Welfare, Division for Youth and Community Service, 1949.

McNutt, Paul V., "Probation and Parole—Good Public Business," *Focus*, November 1948, pp. 161–165.

Meeker, Ben, "Probation Is Casework," *Federal Probation*, June 1948, pp. 51–54.

Moreland, Donald W., "John Augustus and His Successors," *Yearbook*, N.P.P.A., 1941, pp. 1–22.

National Conference on Prevention and Control of Juvenile Delinquency, Report No. 3, "Juvenile Court Laws," and Report No. 13, "Case Work —Group Work," Government Printing Office, 1947.

National Commission on Law Observance and Enforcement, Report No. 9, "Penal Institutions, Probation and Parole," Government Printing Office, 1931.

Neumeyer, Martin H., *Juvenile Delinquency in Modern Society*, Van Nostrand, 1949.

Nicholson, Marian B., "Juvenile Behavior Problems," *Social Work Year Book, 1949*, Russell Sage Foundation, pp. 276–283.

Perkins, John F., *Common Sense and Bad Boys*, The Citizenship Training Department, Boston Juvenile Court, 1946.

Pigeon, Helen D., "In-Service Training for Probation and Parole Officers," *Federal Probation*, July–September 1941, pp. 8–14.

————, *Probation and Parole in Theory and Practice*, N.P.P.A., 1942.

Pray, Kenneth L. M., *Social Work in a Revolutionary Age and Other Papers*, University of Pennsylvania Press, 1950.

————, "The Principles of Social Case Work as Applied to Probation and Parole," *Federal Probation*, April–June 1945, pp. 14–18.

Printzlien, Conrad P., "Deferred Prosecution for Juvenile Offenders," *Federal Probation*, March 1948, pp. 17–22; also, "Prosecution Deferred for Young Offenders," *Probation*, October 1946, pp. 1–8.

Reckless, Walter C., "Significant Trends in the Treatment of Crime and Delinquency," *Federal Probation*, March 1949, pp. 6–11, and in *Yearbook*, N.P.P.A., 1948, pp. 1–14.

————, "The Controversy about Training," *Focus*, January 1949, pp. 23–25.

————, "Training Probation and Parole Personnel," *Focus*, March 1948, pp. 44–48 (and comments on this article: "Training Reconsidered," *Focus*, November 1948, pp. 180–182).

Reinemann, John Otto, "Pennsylvania Experiments with Public-Service Training," *National Municipal Review*, October 1940, pp. 672–674.

————, "Probation and the Juvenile Delinquent," *The Annals*, January 1949, pp. 109–119.

————, "Probation Studied by the United Nations," *The Quarterly*, Pennsylvania Association on Probation and Parole, Autumn 1948, pp. 8–9.

————, "The Juvenile Court and the Schools," *Newsletter*, National League To Promote School Attendance, September 1949, pp. 40–43.

Shulman, Harry Manuel, "Experimental Group Treatment of Maladjusted School Children," *Yearbook*, N.P.P.A., 1941, pp. 342–359.

————, "Group Work—A New Program for Probation," *Yearbook*, N.P.P.A., 1939, pp. 116–129.

Slawson, John, "The Use of the Authoritative Approach in Social Case Work in the Field of Delinquency," *American Journal of Orthopsychiatry*, October 1938, pp. 673–678.

Standard Juvenile Court Act, Revised Edition, N.P.P.A., 1949.

Standards for Selection of Probation and Parole Officers, N.P.P.A., 1945.

Stern, Leon Thomas, "Adult Offenders," *Social Work Year Book, 1949*, Russell Sage Foundation, pp. 33–43.

————, "Probation Service in Pennsylvania," *The Quarterly*, Pennsylvania Association on Probation and Parole, November 1948, pp. 1–27.

Strode, Josephine, *Introduction to Social Case Work*, Harper, 1940.

Sullivan, Dorothea, ed., *The Practice of Group Work*, Association Press, 1941.

Susselman, Samuel, "The Role of the Psychiatrist in a Probation Agency," *Focus*, 1950, pp. 33–37, 50–52.

Sutherland, Edwin H., *Principles of Criminology*, Lippincott, 1947.

Taber, Robert C., "The Potential Role of the School Counselor in Delinquency Prevention and Treatment," *Federal Probation*, September 1949, pp. 52–56.

————, "The Value of Case Work to the Probationer," *Yearbook*, N.P.P.A., 1940, pp. 167–179.

Taiano, Amedeo W., "Using the Group in Probation Work," *Yearbook*, N.P.P.A., 1941, pp. 360–378.

Thurston, Henry W., *Concerning Juvenile Delinquency*, Columbia University Press, 1942.

Timasheff, N. S., *One Hundred Years of Probation*, New York, Fordham University Press, Part 1, 1941; Part 2, 1943.

Van Waters, Miriam, *Parents on Probation*, New Republic, 1927.

Wilson, Gertrude, and Gladys Ryland, *Social Group Work Practice (The Creative Use of the Social Process)*, Houghton Mifflin, 1949.

Wollan, Kenneth I., "A New Treatment Program for Juvenile Delinquents," *Journal of Criminal Law and Criminology*, March–April 1941, pp. 712–719.

————, "The Citizenship Training Program of the Boston Juvenile Court," *Yearbook*, N.P.P.A., 1941, pp. 379–388.

————, "The Use of Group Activity in Probation Work," *Yearbook*, N.P.P.A., 1938, pp. 240–255.

York, James N., "Evaluating the Everyday Work of a Probation Office," *Federal Probation*, September 1948, pp. 24–29.

Young, Pauline V., *Social Treatment in Probation and Delinquency*, McGraw-Hill, 1st ed., Chaps. XIV to XVII.

Zuck, John M., "A Probation Department's Role in Delinquency Prevention," *Federal Probation*, December 1948, pp. 16–19.

————, "The Probation Officer's Participation in Delinquency Prevention," *Yearbook*, N.P.P.A., 1948, pp. 280–295.

CHAPTER XII

Commitment

Aichhorn, August, *Wayward Youth*, Viking Press, 1935.

Armstrong, Clairette P., *660 Runaway Boys*, Graham Press, 1933.

Barnes, Harry Elmer, and Negley K. Teeters, *New Horizons in Criminology*, Chap. 37, Prentice-Hall, 1943.

Beaumont, Gustave de, and Alexis de Tocqueville, *On the Penitentiary Systems of the United States*, translated by Francis Lieber, Philadelphia, 1833.

Bixby, F. Lovell, "Juvenile Institutions," *Proceedings*, American Prison Association, 1941, pp. 85–90.

Carpenter, Mary, *Reformatory Schools for the Children of the Perishing and Dangerous Classes*, London, C. Gilpin, 1851.

Derby, Mary M., "The Values of Normalcy in an Institutional Environment—The Positive Aspect," *Proceedings*, American Prison Association, 1941, pp. 221–232.

Deutsch, Albert, "Is *This* Reform?," *Woman's Home Companion*, March 1948.

————, *Our Rejected Children*, Little, Brown, Boston, 1950.

Ellingston, John R., *Protecting Our Children from Criminal Careers*, Prentice-Hall, 1949.

Elliott, Mabel A., *Correctional Education and the Delinquent Girl*, Pennsylvania Department of Welfare, Harrisburg, Pa., 1939.

Fenton, Norman, *The Delinquent Boy and the Correctional School*, Claremont College Press, 1935.

Folks, Homer, *The Care of Destitute, Neglected, and Delinquent Children*, Macmillan, 1902.

Ford, Charles A., "Homosexual Practices of Institutionalized Females," *Journal of Abnormal and Social Psychology*, Vol. 23, No. 4, January–March 1929, pp. 442–448.

Griscom, John, *Year in Europe*, Collins & Co., New York, 1823.

Holy, T. C., and G. B. Stahly, *Survey of the Industrial School, Lancaster, Ohio*, Bureau of Educational Research Monograph, Ohio State University, Columbus, Ohio, 1940.

Houtchens, Max H., "The Values of Normalcy in an Institutional Environment—The Negative Aspect," *Proceedings*, American Prison Association, 1941, pp. 233–244.

Institutional Treatment for Delinquent Boys, United States Children's Bureau Publication No. 228 (Vol. I), 1935; No. 230 (Vol. II), 1936, Government Printing Office.

Lewis, Orlando F., *The Development of American Prisons and Prison Customs*, Albany, N. Y., 1922.

Moreno, J. L., *Who Shall Survive?* Nervous and Mental Diseases Publishing Co., Washington, D.C., 1934.

Motley, Willard, *Knock On Any Door*, Appleton-Century-Crofts, 1947.

National Conference on the Prevention and Control of Juvenile Delinquency, Report No. 6, "Institutional Treatment of Delinquent Juveniles," Government Printing Office, 1947.

O'Connor, Zena A., "The Runaway Boy in the Correctional School," Columbia University Ph.D. Dissertation, No. 742, 1938.

Osborne Association, New York, *Handbooks of American Institutions for Delinquents*, Vol. I, 1938; Vol. II, 1940; Vol. III, 1940; Vol. IV, 1943.

Otis, Margaret A., "Perversions Not Commonly Noted," *Journal of Abnormal Psychology*, Vol. 81, 1913, pp. 113–116.

Reckless, W. C., *Criminal Behavior*, McGraw-Hill, 1940.

Shalloo, J. P., "The Rise of Juvenile Institutions in the United States," *Prison Journal*, July 1947, pp. 293–298.

Shaw, Clifford, *The Jack Roller*, University of Chicago Press, 1930.

Swados, Felice, *House of Fury*, Doubleday, Doran, 1941.

Tallack, William, *Penological and Preventive Principles*, Wertheimer, Lea, London, 1896.

Wines, Enoch, *State of Prisons*, Cambridge, Massachusetts, 1880.

CHAPTER XIII

Commitment (Continued)

Areson, Clinton W., "Casework in the Training School," *Probation*, October 1947, pp. 10–14.

Bazeley, E. T., *Homer Lane and the Little Commonwealth*, Allen & Unwin, London, 1948.

Bromberg, Walter, and Terry C. Rodgers, "Authority in the Treatment of Delinquency," *American Journal of Orthopsychiatry*, October 1946, pp. 672–685.

Costello, John B., "Institutions for Juvenile Delinquents," *The Annals*, January 1949, pp. 166–218.

Hart, Hastings, *Preventive Treatment of Neglected Children*, Charities Publication, New York, 1910.

Hopkirk, Howard W., *Institutions Serving Children*, Russell Sage Foundation, 1944.

Lindeman, Harry W., "The Place of the Training School," *Yearbook*, N.P.P.A., 1948, pp. 143–152.

Minard, George C., "Educational Experimentation With Problem Boys at Children's Village," in Sheldon and Eleanor Glueck, *Preventing Crime*, McGraw-Hill, 1936, pp. 291–304.

Minor, Carroll R., "The Institution Looks Ahead," *Yearbook*, N.P.P.A., 1948, pp. 153–161.

Moeller, H. G., "The Natural Bridge Camp," *Yearbook*, N.P.P.A., 1948, pp. 162–173.

Oursler, Fulton and Will, *Father Flanagan of Boys' Town*, Doubleday, 1949.

Putsch, Lorene, "Self-Government in a Children's Institution," Child Welfare League of America, Inc., New York, 1940.

Reckless, W. C., "Significant Trends in the Treatment of Crime and Delinquency," *Yearbook*, N.P.P.A., 1948, pp. 1–14.

Reeves, Margaret, *Training Schools for Delinquent Girls*, Russell Sage Foundation, 1929.

Robison, Sophia M., *Can Delinquency Be Measured?*, Columbia University Press, 1936.

Sheviakov, George V., and Fritz Redl, "Discipline for Today's Children and Youth," Department of Supervision and Curriculum Development, National Education Association, Washington, D.C., 1945.

Urquhart, Donald T., "Crime Prevention Through Citizenship Training at the George Junior Republic," in Sheldon and Eleanor Glueck, *Preventing Crime*, McGraw-Hill, 1936, pp. 305–330.

Wills, David, *The Hawkspur Experiment*, Allen & Unwin, London, 1941.

Wollan, Kenneth I., "The Value of Group Living in Institution Treatment," *Yearbook*, N.P.P.A., 1948, pp. 131–142.

Young, Leontine R., "The Treatment of Adolescent Girls in an Institution," *Child Welfare League of America*, New York, 1945.

CHAPTER XIV

The Adolescent Offender

Attorney General's Survey of Release Procedures, Vol. V, "Prisons," Government Printing Office, 1940.

Barnes, Harry Elmer, and Negley K. Teeters, *New Horizons in Criminology*, Prentice-Hall, 1943.

Bixby, F. Lovell, "Highfields" (A plan for short-term treatment of youthful offenders), *The Welfare Reporter*, New Jersey Department of Institutions and Agencies, June 1950, pp. 3 ff.

————, and Lloyd W. McCorkle, "Applying the Principles of Group Therapy in Correctional Institutions," *Federal Probation*, March 1950, pp. 36–40.

Bowlby, John, *Forty-four Juvenile Thieves: Their Characters and Home-life*, Baillière, Tindall & Cox, London, 1947.

Bromberg, Walter, *Crime and the Mind*, Lippincott, 1948.

Clinard, Marshall W., "The Group Approach to Social Reintegration," *American Sociological Review*, April 1949, pp. 257–262.

Cohn, Victor, "Who Are the Guilty?," a series of articles in the *Minneapolis Star and Tribune*, December 7–29, 1948.

Cooper, Courtney Ryley, *Designs in Scarlet*, Little, Brown, 1939.

Doshay, Lewis J., *The Boy Sex Offender and His Later Career*, Grune & Stratton, 1943.

East, Norwood, Percy Stocks, and H. T. P. Young, *The Adolescent Criminal: A Medico-Sociological Study of 4000 Male Adolescents*, Churchill, London, 1942.

Eisner, E. A., "Relationship Formed by a Sexually Delinquent Adolescent Girl," *American Journal of Orthopsychiatry*, Vol. XV (1945), pp. 301–308.

Flexner, Abraham, *Prostitution in Europe*, Appleton-Century, 1941.

Foulkes, S. H., *Introduction to Group-Analytic Psychotherapy*, Grune & Stratton, 1949.

Glueck, Sheldon and Eleanor, *Five Hundred Criminal Careers*, Knopf, 1930.

————, *Five Hundred Delinquent Women*, Knopf, 1934.

————, *One Thousand Juvenile Delinquents*, Harvard University Press, 1934.

————, *Later Criminal Careers*, Commonwealth Fund, 1937.

————, *Juvenile Delinquents Grown Up*, Commonwealth Fund, 1940.

————, *Criminal Careers in Retrospect*, Commonwealth Fund, 1943.

Goldberg, Jacob A. and Rosamond W., *Girls On City Streets*, Foundation Books, New York, 1940.

Griffiths, Arthur, *Secrets of the Prison House*, Vol. II, Chapman and Hall, London, 1894.

Grünhut, Max, *Penal Reform*, Oxford Press, London, 1948.

Hall, Gladys Mary, *Prostitution in the Modern World*, Emerson Books, 1936.

Harrison, Leonard V., and Pryor M. Grant, *Youth in the Toils*, Macmillan, 1938.

Healy, William, *The Individual Delinquent*, Little, Brown, 1915.

————, and Benedict Alper, *Criminal Youth and the Borstal System*, Commonwealth Fund, 1941.

Henry, George W., and Alfred A. Gross, "The Sex Offender: A Consideration of Therapeutics," *Yearbook*, N.P.P.A., 1940, pp. 114–137.

Krafft-Ebing, Robert von, *Psychopathia Sexualis*, F. A. Davis Co., Philadelphia, 1893.

League of Nations Advisory Committee on Social Questions, Columbia University Press, "Prostitutes: Their Early Lives," 1938; "Social Service and Venereal Disease," 1938; and "Methods of Rehabilitation of Adult Prostitutes," 1939.

Leppmann, Friedrich, "Essential Differences Between Sex Offenders," *Journal of Criminal Law and Criminology*, September–October 1941, pp. 366–380.

MacDonald, Martha A., "Criminally Aggressive Behavior in Passive Effeminate Boys," *American Journal of Orthopsychiatry*, Vol. 8 (1938) pp. 70 ff.

McKelvey, Blake, *American Prisons*, University of Chicago Press, 1936.

Mellanby, Molly, and R. L. Bradley, "The English Borstal System After the War," *Federal Probation*, December 1948, pp. 19–22.

Osborne Association, New York, *Handbook*, "American Prisons and Reformatories," 1929.

Pollens, Bertram, *The Sex Criminal*, Emerson Books, 1938.

Reitman, Ben, *The Second Oldest Profession*, Vanguard Press, 1931.

Ruggles-Brise, Evelyn, *The English Prison System*, Macmillan, 1921.

Sellin, Thorsten, *The Criminality of Youth*, American Law Institute, Philadelphia, 1940.

Slavson, S. R., "Milieu and Group Therapy for Delinquents," *Yearbook*, N.P.P.A., 1948, pp. 119–130.

————, *An Introduction to Group Therapy*, The Commonwealth Fund, 1943.

———— (ed.), *The Practice of Group Therapy*, International Universities Press, 1947.

Tappan, Paul, *Delinquent Girls in Court*, Columbia University Press, 1947.

Teeters, Negley K., "Tomorrow's Prison," *Social Service Review*, Vol. XX, No. 2 (June 1946), pp. 221–230.

Thomas, Giles W., "Group Therapy," *Psychosomatic Medicine*, Vol. V (1943), pp. 166–180.

Thomas, W. I., *The Unadjusted Girl*, Little, Brown, 1923.

Webb, Mary Louise, "Delinquency in the Making: Patterns in the Development of Girl Sex Delinquency in the City of Seattle," *Journal of Social Hygiene*, Vol. 29 (1943), pp. 502–510.

Wertham, Frederic, "Psychiatry and the Prevention of Sex Crimes," *Journal of Criminal Law and Criminology*, Vol. 28 (March–April 1938), pp. 847–853.

————, *The Show of Violence*, Doubleday, 1949.

Wessel, Rosa (ed.), *A Case Work Approach to Sex Delinquents*, Pennsylvania School of Social Work, Philadelphia, 1947.

Zemans, Eugene, and Robert J. Cole, "Prison Babies," *The Mother*,

American Committee on Maternal Welfare, Vol. X, No. 1 (October 1948).

CHAPTER XV

Preventive Services

Additon, Henrietta, "The Crime Prevention Bureau of New York City Police Department," in Sheldon and Eleanor Glueck, *Preventing Crime,* McGraw-Hill, 1936, pp. 215–236.

Allen, Frederick H., *Psychotherapy With Children,* Norton, 1942.

Alper, Benedict, "Forty Years of the Juvenile Court," *American Sociological Review,* April 1941, pp. 230–240.

Banay, Ralph S., *Youth in Despair,* Coward-McCann, 1948.

Beers, Clifford, *A Mind That Found Itself,* Doubleday, Doran, 1923.

Carr, Lowell J., *Delinquency Control,* Harper, 1940.

Children Absent from School, Citizens' Committee on Children in New York City, 1950.

Clark, Mary Augusta, *Recording and Reporting for Child-Guidance Clinics,* Commonwealth Fund, 1930.

Coyle, Grace L., *Group Work With American Youth,* Harper, 1948.

Culbert, Jane F., *The Visiting Teacher At Work,* Commonwealth Fund, 1929.

Davidoff, Eugene, and Elinor Noetzel, *Child-Guidance Approach to Juvenile Delinquency,* Child Care Publication, New York, 1949.

Davis, Katherine Bement, "The Police Woman," *The Woman Citizen,* May 30, 1925.

Davis, W. Alison, and Robert J. Havighurst, *Father of the Man,* Houghton Mifflin, 1947.

French, Lois H., *Psychiatric Social Work,* Commonwealth Fund, 1940.

Friedlander, Kate, *The Psycho-Analytical Approach to Juvenile Delinquency,* International Universities Press, London, 1947.

Ginsburg, Ethel L., "Psychiatric Social Work," *Orthopsychiatry: Retrospect and Prospect, 1923–1948,* American Orthopsychiatric Association, 1948, pp. 470–483.

Glover, Edward, "The Diagnosis and Treatment of Delinquency," Institute for the Scientific Treatment of Delinquency, London, 1944.

Glueck, Sheldon and Eleanor, *One Thousand Juvenile Delinquents*, Harvard University Press, 1934.

————, *Juvenile Delinquents Grown Up*, Commonwealth Fund, 1940.

Hartwell, Samuel W., "The Worcester, Mass., Child-Guidance Clinic," in Sheldon and Eleanor Glueck, *Preventing Crime*, McGraw-Hill, 1936, pp. 357–377.

Healy, William, and Augusta Bronner, *Treatment and What Happened Afterward*, Judge Baker Guidance Center, Boston, 1939.

————, and Myra Shimberg, "The Close of Another Chapter in Criminology," *Mental Hygiene*, April 1935, pp. 208–222.

Juvenile Delinquency and the Schools, Forty-Seventh Yearbook, Part I, National Society for the Study of Education, University of Chicago Press, 1948.

Magill, Walter H., *Administering Vocational Education*, Educational Publishers, Inc., Philadelphia, 1941.

Morrison, Lawrence D., "The Police and the Delinquent Child," *Yearbook*, N.P.P.A., 1947, pp. 117–137.

Murphy, Fred J., "Delinquency Off the Record," *Yearbook*, N.P.P.A., 1946, pp. 179–195.

National Conference on Prevention and Control of Juvenile Delinquency, Report No. 7, "Role of the Police in Juvenile Delinquency," Government Printing Office, 1947.

Nolan, James B., "The Crime Prevention Work of New York City," *Federal Probation*, April–June 1947, pp. 18–21.

Orthopsychiatry: Retrospect and Prospect, 1923–1948, American Orthopsychiatric Association, 1948, pp. 377–393, 394–413.

Redl, Fritz, "Clinical Group Work," *Proceedings*, American Association of Group Work, 1932.

————, "Diagnostic Group Work," *American Journal of Orthopsychiatry*, January 1944.

Saul, Leon J., *Emotional Maturity*, Lippincott, 1947.

Shulman, Harry M., "Group Work—A New Program for Probation," *Yearbook*, N.P.P.A., 1939, pp. 116–129.

Stevenson, George S., and Geddes Smith, *Child Guidance Clinics: A Quarter Century of Development*, Commonwealth Fund, 1934.

Swartsfager, Vern, *The Bell Ringers*, Macmillan, 1948.

Thom, Douglas A., "Habit Clinics for the Child of Pre-School Age," Children's Bureau Publication No. 135, Government Printing Office, 1924.

————, "The Importance of Recognizing Delinquent Trends During Childhood," *Federal Probation*, March 1948, pp. 29–32.

Trecker, Harleigh B., *Social Group Work: Principles and Practice*, Woman's Press, 1948.

Vollmer, August, *The Criminal*, The Foundation Press, Inc., Brooklyn, 1949.

Weston, Helen E., "The Role of the School in Crime Prevention," *Yearbook*, N.P.P.A., 1939, pp. 28–42.

Williamson, Margaretta, *The Social Worker in the Prevention and Treatment of Delinquency*, Columbia University Press, 1936.

Wirth, Louis, "Clinical Sociology," *American Journal of Sociology*, Vol. 27 (July 1931).

Witmer, Helen L., *Psychiatric Clinics for Children*, Commonwealth Fund, 1940.

————, *Psychiatric Interviews With Children*, Commonwealth Fund, 1946.

Young, Pauline, *Social Treatment in Probation and Delinquency*, McGraw-Hill, 1st ed.

CHAPTER XVI

Social Action

Bates, Sanford, *Delinquency Can Be Prevented*, Division of Community Services for Delinquency Prevention, New Jersey State Department of Institutions and Agencies, 1946.

Beam, Kenneth S., "Community Coordination for Prevention of Delinquency," *Yearbook*, N.P.P.A., 1936, pp. 89–115.

————, "Community Coordination" (Report of a National Survey of Coordinating and Neighborhood Councils), *Yearbook*, N.P.P.A., 1937, pp. 47–76.

Braucher, Howard, "Recreation," *Social Work Year Book*, *1949*, Russell Sage Foundation, pp. 424–435.

Buell, Bradley, "How To Begin," *Survey Midmonthly*, March 1944 (Juvenile Delinquency issue), pp. 72–76.

Burgess, Ernest W., Joseph D. Lohman, and Clifford R. Shaw, "The Chicago Area Project," *Yearbook*, N.P.P.A., 1937, pp. 8–28.

Carr, Lowell Juilliard, *Delinquency Control*, Harper, 1940, Parts IV and V.

————, "State Plan for Delinquency Prevention," *Yearbook*, N.P.P.A., 1942, pp. 36–45.

————, "Organization for Delinquency Control," *The Annals*, January 1949, pp. 64–76.

Castendyck, Elsa, "Juvenile Courts in the Light of the White House Conference," *Yearbook*, N.P.P.A., 1940, pp. 34–46.

Chandler, Jane, "Conferences of Social Work," *Social Work Year Book, 1949*, Russell Sage Foundation, pp. 135–142.

Child Welfare at the Crossroads, United States Children's Bureau Publication No. 327, Government Printing Office, 1949.

Children in the Community (The St. Paul Experiment in Child Welfare), United States Children's Bureau Publication No. 317, Government Printing Office, 1946.

Clendenen, Richard, "To Synchronize the Training-School Program with Life in the Community," *The Child*, November 1949, pp. 73–77.

Close, Kathryn, "Four Grown-Ups and a Child," *Survey Midmonthly*, March 1944 (Juvenile Delinquency issue), pp. 79–83, 102–103.

Controlling Juvenile Delinquency, United States Children's Bureau Publication No. 301, Government Printing Office, 1943.

Cressey, Paul G., "Delinquency Prevention Begins at Home," *Focus*, May 1949, pp. 78–82.

Crow, Lester D. and Alice, *Our Teen Age Boys and Girls*, McGraw-Hill, 1945.

Daniel, Ralph W., "A Juvenile Jury for Young Traffic Offenders," *Focus*, January 1950, pp. 23–26.

Eisenstein, Morris L., "The Youth Council: A Challenge," *Survey Midmonthly*, November 1948, pp. 332–335.

Ellingston, John R., *Protecting Our Children from Criminal Careers*, Prentice-Hall, 1948.

Fajen, Elizabeth, "Curing Delinquency at the Source," *Survey Midmonthly*, October 1946, pp. 261–262.

Felix, Robert H., "The National Mental Health Act and Juvenile Delinquency," *Federal Probation*, April–June 1947, pp. 9–13.

Finnegan, J. Francis, "The Philadelphia Conference on the Prevention and Control of Juvenile Delinquency," *Yearbook*, N.P.P.A., 1948, pp. 263–273.

Gabower, Genevieve, "A Look at Ten Communities," *Survey Midmonthly*, March 1944 (Juvenile Delinquency issue), pp. 86–90, 104.

Glasser, Melvin A., "To Focus on Child's Mental, Emotional and Spiritual Growth and Development," *The Child*, October 1949, pp. 54–55, 61.

Glueck, Sheldon and Eleanor (edd.), *Preventing Crime*, McGraw-Hill, 1936.

"Good Ideas at Work" (Neighborhood Approach, Youth Participation, Referral Services), *Survey Midmonthly*, March 1944 (Juvenile Delinquency issue), pp. 84–85.

Guild, Arthur Alden, "The Organization of Social Work by Neighborhoods," *Yearbook*, N.P.P.A., 1936, pp. 37–45.

Haydon, Edward, "Community Organization and Crime Prevention," *Yearbook*, N.P.P.A., 1942, pp. 23–35.

Helping Children in Trouble, United States Children's Bureau Publication No. 320, Government Printing Office, 1947.

Krughoff, Merrill F., "Councils in Social Work," *Social Work Year Book, 1949*, Russell Sage Foundation, pp. 150–158.

Kurtz, Russell H., "Community Organization for Social Welfare," *Social Work Year Book, 1949*, Russell Sage Foundation, pp. 129–135.

Lenroot, Katherine F., "Federal and State Action," *Survey Midmonthly*, March 1944 (Juvenile Delinquency issue), pp. 93–95, 105–106.

———, "Summing Up the Previous White House Conferences," *The Child*, October 1949, pp. 52–54.

———, "The Government and Child Welfare," *Yearbook*, N.P.P.A., 1948, pp. 80–95.

———, "The Midcentury White House Conference and Social Workers," *Social Work Journal*, July 1949, pp. 135–137.

Lindeman, Edward C., "New Patterns of Community Organization," *Yearbook*, N.P.P.A., 1937, pp. 1–7.

Lukas, Edwin J., "Crime Prevention: Who Prevents What?," *Federal Probation*, June 1948, pp. 19–23.

———, "Fashions in Crime Prevention," *Yearbook*, N.P.P.A., 1946, pp. 19–39.

Lundberg, Emma Octavia, *Unto the Least of These*, Appleton-Century-Crofts, 1947.

MacCormick, Austin H., "The Community and the Correctional Process," *Focus*, May 1948, pp. 65–68, 86–89.

MacNeil, Douglas H., "The State and Delinquency Prevention," *Newsletter*, National League to Promote School Attendance, September 1949, pp. 43–46.

———, "Two and One-half Years of State-Local Collaboration in Delinquency Prevention," *Yearbook*, N.P.P.A., 1948, pp. 252–262.

Mayo, Leonard W., "Town and Village Councils," *Yearbook*, N.P.P.A., 1936, pp. 78–88.

Moving Ahead for Children and Youth (Program of the National Commission on Children and Youth), United States Children's Bureau Publication No. 329, Government Printing Office, 1949.

National Commission on Law Observance and Enforcement (Wickersham Commission), Report No. 13, "Causes of Crime," Government Printing Office, 1931.

National Conference on Prevention and Control of Juvenile Delinquency, Reports No. 1, "Community Coordination"; No. 2, "General Recommendations for State and Community Action"; No. 8, "Housing, Community Development, and Juvenile Delinquency"; No. 9, "Recreation for Youth"; No. 11, "Youth Participation"; No. 12, "Citizen Participation." Government Printing Office, 1947.

Newport News (Va.) Project: A Community Plans for Its Children, United States Children's Bureau Publication No. 321, Government Printing Office, 1947.

Olsen, Edward G., "Co-ordinating Community Educational Services," *The Annals,* September 1949, pp. 130–135.

"Reports of the Committee on Probation with Special Reference to Juvenile Delinquency," *Federal Probation,* March 1948, pp. 3–9.

Robinson, Duane, *Chance to Belong* (Story of the Los Angeles Youth Project, 1943–1949), The Woman's Press, New York, 1949.

Romano, Fred A., "Organizing a Community for Delinquency Prevention," *Yearbook,* N.P.P.A., 1940, pp. 1–12.

Rowe, Thomas A., "A Youth Council in Action," *Survey Midmonthly,* December 1948, pp. 360–362.

Schapps, John, *A Study of the San Francisco Parent Guidance Center,* N.P.P.A., 1946 (mimeographed).

Schwartz, Edward E., "Statistics of Juvenile Delinquency in the U.S.," *The Annals,* January 1949, pp. 9–20.

Scudder, Kenyon J., "The Coordinating Council at Work," *Yearbook,* N.P.P.A., 1936, pp. 67–77.

Sharp, E. Preston, "Teamwork in Maryland," *Juvenile Court Judges Journal,* January 1950, pp. 9–10, 26.

"Teen-Agers State Their Case," *The Child,* August 1949, p. 30.

Thrasher, Frederic M., "Reaching Crime Causes by Coordinated Action," *Yearbook,* N.P.P.A., 1936, pp. 1–23.

Waltz, Henry W., "A Community Experiment," *Yearbook,* N.P.P.A., 1936, pp. 60–66.

Wann, Harry A., "Community Coordination, Its Philosophy, Principles and Trends," *Yearbook,* N.P.P.A., 1938, pp. 296–307.

Ward, Frederick, "Probation Officer as a Leader in Community Organization," *Federal Probation*, July–September 1946, pp. 30–34.

White House Conference on Child Health and Protection: The Delinquent Child, 1932. *Dependent and Neglected Children*, 1933. Century, New York.

White House Conference on Children in a Democracy, Government Printing Office, 1942.

Wittenberg, Rudolph M., "Personality Adjustment through Social Action," *American Journal of Orthopsychiatry*, April 1948, pp. 207–221.

Your Town Against Delinquency, Publication of the Canadian Welfare Council, Ottawa, 1948.

Youth and the Future, American Youth Commission, American Council on Education, Washington, D.C., 1942.

CHAPTER XVII

Interpretation

Baker, Helen Cody and Mary Swain Routzahn, *How To Interpret Social Welfare*, Russell Sage Foundation, 1947.

Binder, Gertrude, "How To Use the Radio," *Probation*, February 1946, pp. 82–86.

Bird, Bernard J., "Telling Youth About Crime," *Yearbook*, N.P.P.A., 1940, pp. 13–23.

Cabot, P. S. deQ., "A Long-Term Study of Children: The Cambridge-Somerville Youth Study," *Child Development*, Vol. 11 (1940), pp. 143–151.

Canavan, Joseph J., "Newspapers and Crime," *Yearbook*, N.P.P.A., 1939, pp. 293–303.

Carr, Lowell Juilliard, "Interpreting Probation and Parole through the Radio," *Yearbook*, N.P.P.A., 1940, pp. 282–287.

Cosulich, Gilbert, "Probation and Parole Publicity in the Press," *Yearbook*, N.P.P.A., 1940, pp. 271–281.

Crosby, Alexander, *Pamphlets That Pull*, National Publicity Council for Health and Welfare Services, New York, 1948.

Halpern, Irving, "Probation and the Press," *Probation*, December 1939, pp. 49–54.

Hofheinz, Roy, "Telling the Public," *Probation*, February 1940, pp. 74–91.

Lane, Janet, and Beatrice K. Tolleris, *Planning Your Exhibit*, National Publicity Council for Health and Welfare Services, New York, 1949.

Lippman, Leopold, "Probation and Parole Are News," *Probation*, February 1944, pp. 71–79.

Long, Donald E., "Developing Public Support for Juvenile Courts," *Yearbook*, N.P.P.A., 1947, pp. 260–272.

Lukas, Edwin J., "Crime Prevention; Who Prevents What?," *Federal Probation*, June 1948, p. 21.

MacCormick, Austin H., "The Community and the Correctional Process," *Focus*, May 1948, pp. 65–68, 86–89.

"Make the Newspapers Work For You," *Probation*, October 1945, pp. 13–18.

Mott, Frank Luther, "Public Relations of Probation and Parole," *Yearbook*, N.P.P.A., 1943, pp. 12–17.

Needs of Neglected and Delinquent Children, Report to the 1947 Connecticut General Assembly, Hartford, 1946.

Olds, F. Perry, "The Place of the Press in Crime Control," *Yearbook*, N.P.P.A., 1947, pp. 245–259.

Paradise, Viola, *Toward Public Understanding of Case Work*, Russell Sage Foundation, 1948.

Powers, Edwin, "An Experiment in Prevention of Delinquency," *The Annals*, January 1949, pp. 77–88.

Reckless, Walter C., *The Etiology of Delinquent and Criminal Behavior*, Social Science Research Council, New York, Bulletin 50, 1943.

Reinemann, John Otto, "Films of Social Significance," *Prison Journal*, July–October 1938, pp. 476–480.

————, "Developing Community Understanding of Probation and Parole Work," *Journal of Criminal Law and Criminology*, May–June, 1942, pp. 23–31.

————, "Research Activities in the Probation Department," *Yearbook*, N.P.P.A., 1946, pp. 196–217.

Research Relating to Children (An Inventory of Studies in Progress), United States Children's Bureau, Government Printing Office, 1950.

Robinson, Reginald, "Beneath the Surface of Juvenile Delinquency and Child Neglect," *Survey Midmonthly*, February 1947, pp. 41–52.

Routzahn, Mary Swain, "Public Relations in Social Work," *Social Work Year Book, 1949*, Russell Sage Foundation, pp. 397–402.

Simpson, Gertrude W., *Working with Newspapers*, National Publicity Council for Health and Welfare Services, New York, 1945.

Stone, Patrick T., "The Public Is Very Much in the Dark About Probation and Parole," *Federal Probation,* December 1948, pp. 7–9.

Tolleris, Beatrice K., *Radio, How, When and Why To Use It,* National Publicity Council for Health and Welfare Services, New York, 1946.

————, *Annual Reports: How To Plan and Write Them,* National Publicity for Health and Welfare Services, New York, 1946.

Wachtel, Lillian, "Films About Facts," *Survey,* May 1950, pp. 240–242.

Waldron, Gloria, *The Information Film,* Columbia University Press, 1949.

NAME INDEX

SUBJECT INDEX

A

Abandoned child, 41

Adjustment of juvenile delinquency cases: without formal procedure, 319–321; by the probation officer, 398; through court hearing, 330

Adolescent: and delinquency, 3, 6, 34, 514–573; delinquency and crime rate, 14, 353, 514; Dr. Healy's statement on, 21–22; female, 23–24, *see also* Sex delinquency; snares for, 191–196, case history, 723–725

Adolescents' court, 344–354; in Brooklyn, 346–347; in Chicago, 350–351; in Manhattan, 347–349; in Philadelphia, 351; in Queens (New York City), 347–348

Adoption: as part of family court jurisdiction, 376–377, 379; as part of juvenile court jurisdiction, 299, 400

Adoption home (as one type of foster home), 504

Adult Authority in California, 375

Adult criminal cases, the influence of the juvenile court upon the handling of, 371–376

Adult education courses for parents, 640

Adult jurisdiction of juvenile courts, 299–304

Advertising (as responsible for the craving for the "good life"), 29, 36–37

Advisory Citizens' Committees (of juvenile courts and probation departments), 294, 648–649

After-care (following release from institution), 451, 471–474; *see also* Parole

Age limits in juvenile court jurisdiction, 14, 310–313; chart, 312

Agencies, *see* Child-guidance clinics; Child placing agencies; Governmental agencies; Juvenile court; Social agencies

Aggressiveness: in children in general, 27, 201–202; in delinquents, 25; as delinquency symptom in case histories, 709–713, 713–714; as experimented with at Guidance Center in London, 611–612

Agricultural colony at Mettray (France) (one of the earliest children's institutions), 61–64; picture, 63

Aid to Dependent Children, 289, 624–625

Alameda County (California), Chabot Ranch, citizen participation in program of, 653

Alcoholic, interest of John Augustus in problem, 386

Alcoholism (as a problem related to delinquency), 12, 129; case history, 709–713

Almshouses, 66, 68

Ambivalence, 204

American Bar Association: plan for family court, 378; plan for selection of judges, 314

American Friends Service Committee, 620–621

American Law Institute: promoting the Youth Correction Authority idea, 355–356, 371, 684; report by Dr. Sellin on *Criminality of Youth,* 516

American Legion: motion picture on child delinquency produced by, 689; sponsorship of Memorial Day services at Glen Mills School, 653; statement against repressive discipline in institutions, 482

American Orthopsychiatric Association (and its publication, *American Journal of Orthopsychiatry*), 197

American Prison Association, 477, 522, 569, 675

Analytical type of group therapy, 536

Ancient concept of delinquent child, 41–43

Angers (France) (location of early foundling home), 43

Annual reports of courts and probation departments, 694–695

Appeal against juvenile court decision, 333–334

Appointment of judges, 313–315; of probation officers, 395, 405–407

Apprehension, 217–226; for details *see* Arrests of children by police

Apprentice system, *see* Indenture of children

"Approved Schools" (England), 55–56, 512–513; motion picture on, 689

Area projects, 659–665

Arrests of children by police, 218–221, 577–578

Assignment of cases to probation officers, 400–401

Associations, *see* National, State associations

797

T